Critical Essays on "Causation and Responsibility"

Edited by
Benedikt Kahmen and Markus Stepanians

DE GRUYTER

ISBN 978-3-11-030212-7
e-ISBN 978-3-11-030229-5

Library of Congress Cataloging-in-Publication Data
A CIP catalog record for this book has been applied for at the Library of Congress.

Bibliographic information published by the Deutsche Nationalbibliothek
The Deutsche Nationalbibliothek lists this publication in the Deutsche Nationalbibliografie; detailed bibliographic data are available in the Internet at http://dnb.dnb.de.

Printing: Hubert & Co. GmbH & Co. KG, Göttingen
♾ Printed on acid-free paper.
Printed in Germany

www.degruyter.com

Contents

Benedikt Kahmen and Markus Stepanians

Introduction

This volume is a collection of essays probing, scrutinizing and sometimes rejecting the arguments and conclusions of Michael S. Moore's magisterial *Causation and Responsibility – An Essay in Law, Morals, and Metaphysics* (Oxford University Press 2009). A short introduction of the main theses and far-reaching aims of Moore's rich and ambitious book for those not (yet) acquainted with his work will help to put the essays of the present volume in their context.

Causation and Responsibility is the culmination of Moore's long-standing occupation with the role of causation in the attribution of both moral and legal responsibility. As its subtitle *An Essay in Law, Morals, and Metaphysics* suggests, it is a comprehensive and far-reaching attempt to lay bare and make explicit the normative and metaphysical foundations of central areas of the law, including, though not confined to, tort and criminal law. One of Moore's main theses is factual and metaphysical, the other is normative and moral. The main factual thesis defended in the book is that the concept of causation used in the law's tests for determining legal liability is an adaptation of the very notion of causation as it is used in ordinary and scientific explanation. Moore's main normative thesis is that the factual causal framework used by the law is normatively adequate because it is based on, and is a refinement of, the very framework we use in our everyday moral assessments of culpability and blame.

It follows from Moore's factual thesis that there is no such thing as a special and technical legal notion of causation peculiar to the legal purpose of ascertaining liability and distinct from the notion of causation as it is used in answering why-questions in everyday life and science. More precisely, *Causation and Responsibility* argues that the notion of causation implicitly involved in ascriptions of legal responsibility and in scientific explanations refers to a mind-independent natural relation between two instances of a certain type of complex spatio-temporal entities: 'states of affairs'. This causal relation is 'natural' in the sense that it is not a human construct; and it is 'mind-independent' in the sense that it holds, when it holds, independently of our thinking and talking about it. The metaphysical part of *Causation and Responsibility* is concerned with elaborating and defending this realist metaphysics of causation. Moore believes that this framework forms an essential part of the implicit understanding of legal liability as it manifests itself in the 'causation-drenched' language especially of tort and criminal law.

In the normative part of *Causation and Responsibility*, Moore argues that the realist understanding of causation implicit in central areas of the law is a good thing, too: that it forms a normatively adequate framework for ascribing legal liability which leads to morally plausible results when correctly applied. According to Moore, the normative adequacy of the realist causal framework is due to the fact that it forms the factual basis of our everyday moral assessments of culpability and blame as well. As Moore has argued in previous writings (collected in *Placing Blame: A General Theory of the Criminal Law*, Oxford University Press 1997), the relevant standard of adequacy for central areas of the law is morality in general and justice in particular. Like many other contemporary philosophers of law, Moore believes that the guiding function and purpose of the criminal law (and to a lesser extend of tort law as well) is the achievement of retributive and corrective justice. However, if justice is done only if the morally responsible are held legally responsible, then legal liability necessarily tracks moral responsibility. It follows that, according to Moore, there is an important necessary conceptual link between legal and moral responsibility, and thus between morality and law. This is what makes Moore a quite unusual specimen of a natural lawyer, and *Causality and Responsibility* a significant contribution to the contemporary revival of natural law thinking.

The emerging picture is that of a concept of legal liability as a refined and substantiated notion of moral responsibility, which presupposes and supervenes on causation as a natural relation between states of affairs. Moore is a realist tout court: He is a natural law theorist, a moral objectivist, and a metaphysical realist in science.

Due to its scope, depth, and meticulous arguments, Moore's *Causation and Responsibility* is likely to become the most important publication in the philosophy of law since the publication of Hart's and Honoré's *Causation in the Law* in 1959. Moreover, Moore's scholarship is breath-taking. One would be hard pressed to find another contemporary thinker with a comparable grasp of the problems and an equally sovereign command of the relevant literature in jurisprudence, action theory, moral theory, philosophy of language, ontology and metaphysics. In the course of developing a highly original view of its own, *Causation and Responsibility* discusses virtually all major theories and concepts surrounding the problem of causation in the law, including the 'but-for' counterfactual analysis, the harm-within-the-risk test, issues of foreseeability, accomplice liability, intervening causes, causal overdetermination, the question of the causal powers of omissions and absences in general, and so on.

In short, Moore's book is a comprehensive attempt to rethink, revise and reframe the conceptual scheme implicit in our legal and moral practice of assigning responsibility and blame. As such *Causation and Responsibility* is a godsend for anyone struggling to get a grasp on the intricate problems and issues it discusses. For all these reasons, those of us in the Law & Technology research group of RWTH Aachen's Human Technology Centre who had followed Moore's work over the last years welcomed its publication in the spring of 2009 as an excellent opportunity to perhaps reignite the lingering and increasingly provincial discussion among German lawyers and German legal philosophers concerning causation in the law. The research group quickly decided to invite Michael Moore to Aachen for an international and interdisciplinary conference of the author-meets-critics type. Our plan was to ask Michael to defend his views against the criticisms of readers specializing in the disciplines mentioned in the books subtitle, i.e. law, morality, and metaphysics. Michael immediately agreed to come, and the event took place from March 15th to 17th, 2010. At the risk of sounding immodest, everyone we talked to agreed that the conference was a resounding success both intellectually and socially. Indeed, it was so much fun that we decided to repeat it in very much the same format but a somewhat different mix of invitees a year later, from May 30th to June 1st at RWTH Aachen. Happily, the story repeated itself: A group of highly distinguished scholars from Europe and the US did their best to find gaps, holes and oversights in Michael's arguments, Michael once more commented extensively and off the cuff on each and every presentation, and the whole event found much acclaim. The articles collected in this book are the results of these two conferences.

For all that, in one respect our expectations were not fulfilled. As already mentioned, we had hoped that these conferences would be welcomed by German legal theorists as an opportunity to reconnect to the international debate. Unfortunately, this did not happen.

Our collection starts with a debate between Michael Moore, Richard Wright and Ingeborg Puppe concerning the most convincing account of causation in the law. One of the interesting discoveries at our conferences was the parallel between Wright's and Puppe's independently developed criticisms of the type of view advanced by Moore. Both Wright's and Puppe's arguments frequently draw on issues surrounding causal overdetermination and negative causality, which therefore call for separate discussion. The contributions from Friedrich Toepel as well as from Dieter Birnbacher and David Hommen scrutinise these cases. These contributions raise the more general question whether a counterfactual theory of causation can accommodate the demands for a singularist metaphysics of causation of the kind put forward by Moore in *Causation and Responsibility.* The essays by Geert Keil and Philipp Hübl make a suggestion about how this might be done. In between, Markus Stepanians challenges Moore's conclusions about "the true causal relata". The contributions from Stephen Mumford and Rani Anjum and Alex Broadbent focus on the relation between causation and responsibility. The subsequent essays by Benedikt Kahmen and Erasmus Mayr examine the ramifications of Moore's account for an account of rational agency. Finally, Thomas Schmidt and Alexander Aichele try to clarify the normative significance of causal relations in moral judgments from a systematic respectively a historical perspective, and challenge Moore on this issue. All contributions appear in this volume for the first time, with the exception of Richard Wright's "The NESS Account of Natural Causation", which was previously published as chapter 14 in *Perspectives on Causation* (Richard Goldberg ed., Hart Publishing 2011).

We would like to thank all participants for making both events such an intellectually and socially rewarding experience. Most of the credit, however, goes to Michael Moore for writing this wonderful book in the first place, for being such an impressive commentator and engaging debater, and for putting his rebuttals and comments in writing for inclusion into the present volume. Finally, we would like to thank the major financial sponsors for both conferences. The March 2010 event was funded by RWTH Aachen's *Human Technology Centre* (HumTec). The Friends of the RWTH Aachen supplied additional financial support. The members of HumTec's "Law and Technology" research group, in particular Magda Zietek and Daniel Gruschke, were in charge of the organizational details and made sure that everything went smoothly. The second conference 2011 was financed and organized by the DFG research group *Causation, Laws, Dispositions and Explanation at the Intersection of Science and Metaphysics.* Thanks for making this possible, we are truly grateful.

The NESS Account of Natural Causation: A Response to Criticisms

Richard W. Wright

The NESS (necessary element of a sufficient set) account of natural (scientific, 'actual', 'factual') causation is usually acknowledged to be a more satisfactory and comprehensive account than the traditional sine qua non (necessary condition) account. However, objections have been raised to the claim that the NESS account fully captures the concept of natural causation and properly handles all types of situations. Various types of counter-examples have been proposed. More fundamentally, it is argued that the NESS account is viciously circular, since causal terminology often is used in its elaboration and it relies upon the concept of causal laws.

Many of the objections raised against the NESS account assume that it is essentially the same as Herbert Hart's and Tony Honoré's 'causally relevant factor' account and John Mackie's INUS account. In this chapter Richard Wright distinguishes these three accounts, which differ in important ways that make the latter two accounts vulnerable to objections to which the NESS account is immune, and he offers an account of causal laws that he believes rebuts the claim that the NESS account is viciously circular. In the major section of this contribution, Wright argues that the NESS account handles properly the various types of situations that have been raised as alleged counter-examples to its comprehensive validity.

The Concept of Causation in the Law

Ingeborg Puppe

In the last decades, philosophical discussion of causality has seen a turnaround. After centuries of a nearly unchallenged generalist notion of causality, according which causality consists in the sequence of cause and effect being subsumable under a general law, philosophers and philosophically-minded jurists have recently turned to the notion of a causa efficiens, in particular to a physicalist notion of causality, that depicts the cause as a transfer of energy.

According to Ingeborg Puppe, the jurist can concur with such pluralism only in the sense that there are different attributive practices according to different areas of attribution. But the jurist cannot accept that for one and the same case, the judge can choose between different notions of causality. So Puppe seeks a single, philosophically justified notion of causality, that works across the board for at least one area, that of natural physical events. She does this by drawing attention to the various shortcomings of the traditional but-for test for causation and the notion of a causa efficiens. She argues that only the conception of a cause as a sufficient and minimal condition for the occurrance or endurance of the effect can yield the unified notion of causality the jurist needs. For the purpose of attribution it is necessary to accept every fact as cause, which we take as a reason for making a person responsible for a result, not only acts as a whole but also properties of acts and omissions.

Causal Overdetermination

Friedrich Toepel

This chapter attempts to outline a consistent account of John L. Mackie's concept of causation which avoids crushing arguments from Michael S. Moore's *Causa-*

tion and Responsibility. Friedrich Toepel comes to the conclusion that the concept of causes as necessary conditions is appropriate for singular causal statements while Mackie's INUS conditions (insufficient but non-redundant parts of an unnecessary sufficient condition) are only suitable criteria for regularity statements.

The main part of the chapter concentrates on a discussion of the symmetrically overdetermined concurrent-cause cases because they present the most significant problem for necessity accounts of causation. Symmetrically overdetermined concurrent-cause cases are characterized by situations like the following: A and B shoot C in the head. Each shot would by itself have caused death at the exact moment at which it happened in reality even if the respective other shot would never have been fired.

Toepel endorses the solution of the late Mackie of *The Cement of the Universe* who takes the view that the question asking for a discrimination between the alternative cause candidates has no answer here and therefore causation of each cause candidate cannot be assumed. Toepel tries to show that our intuitions which reject this solution are deceptive.

Toepel also examines the viability of fine-grained individuations as criteria for a distinction between symmetrically overdetermined concurrent cause-cases and pre-emptive overdetermination. Toepel comes to the conclusion that time differences are always relevant individuations, and differences of location also may become relevant for the solution of causal problems with some reservations. Finally, Toepel explains the appropriateness of a sufficiency account for regularity statements by outlining the characteristics of a typical laboratory situation, and I show where the different criteria for singular causal statements and regularity statements may be located in Toulmin's argumentation scheme.

Omissions as Causes – Genuine, Quasi, or not at All?

Dieter Birnbacher and David Hommen

Moore is one of the many law theorists who doubt that omissions can operate as factors in the causation of events and that in cases in which potential agents remain passive in spite of an obligation to intervene ascriptions of responsibility are justified exclusively by non-causal factors. Dieter Birnbacher's and David Hommen's chapter argues that this is an uneasy and essentially unstable position. It also shows that Moore himself, in *Causation and Responsibility,* does not consistently follow his exclusion of a causal role of omission in the context of casuistic analysis. Though Moore is to be praised for the clear stance he takes on the issue of negative causality, an analysis of the reasons given for the negation of causality by omission shows that these do not carry enough weight to compensate the sacrifice in theoretical coherence made by the special treatment of negative responsibility in cases of special obligations. It is proposed, instead, that the fact that responsibility for omissions is, as a rule, weaker than that for positive acts is better explained by non-causal factors such as the significant, though incomplete, correlation of the active-passive distinction with a number of normatively relevant factors and the greater social significance of moral and legal rules against active over against passive forms of wrongdoing.

Making Causal Counterfactuals More Singular, and More Appropriate for Use in Law

Geert Keil

Geert Keil's chapter deals with the metaphysics of the causal relation and with the analysis of singular causal statements. Keil takes issue with Moore's criticism of the counterfactual theory of causation and defends an amended, unambiguously singularist version of this theory. Contrary to Moore's demand that the commonplaces about causation must follow from the counterfactual analysis, Keil proposes to reverse the order of explanation, i. e., to start with bedrock intuitions about the nature of causality rather than with a general possible world semantics, and then to turn these intuitions into constraints for the class of counterfactuals that the counterfactual analysis has to consider.

On a number of counts, Keil simply defends Lewis' theory against Moore's objections. In other respects, he parts company with Lewis. He suggests to perform the counterfactual analysis with Davidsonian rather than with Lewisian events, to downgrade the role of causal laws, to dismiss misleading talk of singular events as "necessary conditions", to take seriously the ex post-character of singular causal statements, to make explicit the indexical character of the ceteris paribus clause that fixes the actual circumstances of the causing event, and to account for the "petering out" of causal chains by abandoning the alleged transitivity of causation. Keil argues that such a revised, unambiguously singularist counterfactual theory best captures our pretheoretical intuitions about causation, and that it is the most suitable theory for use in law.

Moore on "the true metaphysics of causation"

Markus Stepanians

What kind of entities can play the role of causes and effects? Moore argues in chapter 15 of *Causation and Responsibility* that plausible candidates for the role of causal relata have to meet two conditions of adequacy: They must have causation-dependent as well as causation-independent credentials. He goes on to suggest that spatio-temporal states of affairs fit both of these criteria best. The principal causation-independent reason for believing in states of affairs, says Moore, is provided by a truth-theoretic consideration advanced by Frank Ramsey: that spatio-temporal states of affairs are needed to play the role of truth-makers. Against Moore it is argued in Markus Stepanians's chapter that Ramsey's argument is not plausible and thus fails to provide causation-independent reasons for acknowledging states of affairs in our ontology. It is concluded that spatio-temporal states of affairs do not meet at least one of Moore's two conditions of adequacy for the role of "the true relata of the causal relation".

Events over Facts. Why Metaphysics Matters for Law

Philipp Hübl

Moore argues, among other things, that concrete states of affairs are the primary causal relata and that the counterfactual theory of causation is flawed for many reasons. As a counter strategy, Philipp Hübl make a case for Davidsonian events understood as changes of objects. The deep structure of causal explanations provides two slots, one for events as causes, and another for the circumstances relative to which we pick out single events using indexicals. The counterfactual theory of causation can be improved by limiting it to singular cases about token events. Nomological intuitions stem from our knowledge of the dispositions of those objects that undergo the changes. Moore's arguments for states of affairs as causal relata and his objections from cases of overdetermination seem to either confound types with tokens of events, or causation with causal explanation respectively. A similar problem appears with regard to omissions. Both problematic cases have the same spring: intuitions about moral and legal practice typically override our basic metaphysical intuitions.

With Great Power Comes Great Responsibility

Stephen Mumford and Rani Lill Anjum

Omissions are sometimes linked to responsibility. A harm can counterfactually depend on an omission to prevent it. If someone had the ability to prevent a harm but didn't, this could suffice to ground their responsibility for the harm. Stephen Mumford and Rani Lill Anjum present an argument for this based on the WGPCGR-thesis: With Great Power Comes Great Responsibility.

Mumford and Anjum argue, with reference to Moore's account in *Causation and Responsibility*, that moral and legal responsibility is based on the power we have as causal agents, but not on causation as such. Specifically, they contend that an agent can be held responsible for an act only under certain modal conditions: if it was within their power to act but also not to act. This is a modality that is less than necessity but also more than pure contingency. It allows agents to be responsible causally for some effect when it was their action that produced it, and that agents might be responsible for something non-causally when they had the power to prevent it and failed to do so. Mumford and Anjum also maintain that agents could be non-causally responsible for something if their action was a *sine qua non* for something else. They conclude that allocation of moral and legal responsibility is governed by three principles:

a. Without the ability to do *x*, but also to prevent *x*, one cannot be responsible for doing *x*.
b. With the ability to do *x*, one can (but need not necessarily) have a responsibility to do *x*.
c. The more able one is to do *x*, if one should do *x*, then the greater the responsibility to do *x*.

Explanation and Responsibility

Alex Broadbent

This chapter contends that Michael Moore is right to suppose that there is an intimate relation between causal, moral and legal responsibility, but that he fails to recognise what this implies for the theory of causation he must endorse. Commonplace causal judgements are selective, picking out only some of the many events that are, in some unselective sense, causally or nomically related to a given effect. Moore joins the majority of philosophers in supposing that selectivity is not part of the fundamental concept of causation, nor of the causal relation itself. This chapter argues that only a theory of causation on which causation is selective can play the role Moore hopes it can play in determining moral and legal responsibility. Moore's own conception of causation is shown to fall short of playing this role. Instead the essay advertises a contrastive conception of causation as more suited to Moore's goals.

Intentions, Intentional Actions and Practical Knowledge

Benedikt Kahmen

Does the law require a specific philosophy of action? Michael Moore prominently argues that it does and that it demands a volitional causal theory of action. This conception of agency lies at the bottom of attributions of moral and legal responsibility in his *Causation and Responsibility.*

However, when this theory is tested against a legal requirement for intentional actions, this theory turns out to be inadequate. This requirement is that agents have to know their intentional actions. The reason why the volitional causal theory does not meet this requirement is that agents of intentional actions must acquire this knowledge from a specifically agential stance that connects their knowledge of what they are doing with what they think are reasons for doing it. In short, this knowledge must be practical knowledge in Anscombe's sense. It turns out that the volitional causal action theory underlying Moore's account in *Causation and Responsibility* can neither satisfactorily explain how agents know their intentions, nor how they know their intentonal actions. Therefore, Benedikt Kahmen concludes, Moore's action theory must be supplemented with a theory of practical knowledge in order to meet the legal requirement to know one's intentional action. He outlines such a theory and contends, in effect, that the legally required practical knowledge is acquired by intending. Finally, he spells out the consequences of this approach for a causal action theory like Moore's in general, and concludes that an exclusively causal action theory is implausible in the law.

The Problem of Consequential Waywardness: Between Internalism and Externalism about Intentional Agency

Erasmus Mayr

In his contribution, Erasmus Mayr addresses one well-known problem in philosophy of action which raises difficulties for the standard naturalist picture of human agency, to one version of which Michael Moore, too, subscribes. The problem arises in cases where an agent intends to bring about an effect and does something which causes the effect, but the causal chain between what he does and the effect is too 'freaky' for the agent to have brought about the effect intentionally. As Mayr argues, these cases raise fundamental problems for any attempt to analyse intentional agency in merely causal and 'internalist' terms (i.e. in terms of the agent's mental states, their causal efficacy and 'fit' between what is happening and the agent's intention). Instead, Mayr claims, any satisfactory account of these cases which explains why the bringing about of the effect is not intentional must be, to a substantial degree, normative and externalist, since it must go beyond non-normative facts about what is happening locally at the time of the action and refer to the normative background within which the action is taking place. Mayr defends this externalist-normative alternative to the standard causalist analyses of consequential waywardness against the charge of being explanatorily empty and shows that it can deal with some problems that its rivals cannot deal with.

How to Understand the Problem of Moral Luck

Thomas Schmidt

In this chapter, Thomas Schmidt takes issue with Moore's claim that the phenomena typically associated with the notion of moral luck do not give rise to issues beyond those related to the problem of freedom of the will. In his attempt to establish this view, Moore pursues a line of reasoning which has already been proposed by Thomas Nagel. Against Moore and Nagel, Schmidt argues that identifying the problem of moral luck with the problem of freedom of the will is based on conceptually distorted views about control. According to Schmidt, Moore fails to see that he himself implicitly relies on a distinction between two sorts of control (which Schmidt labels 'control' and 'partial control'), which distinction, as Schmidt argues, has to be part of any appropriate conception of control for very basic conceptual reasons. Only when this distinction is made explicit, says Schmidt, does the nature of the problem of moral luck come to light. Solving this problem, then, requires, other than Moore believes, that one brings into play both considerations about control as well as an account of the normative grounds of blameworthiness. In view of this, as Schmidt goes on to argue, Moore's view that results of actions influence the degree of moral blameworthiness of the agent is much less plausible than it might otherwise seem.

Causation to Culpability: Why Imputation Matters

Alexander Aichele

This chapter raises some doubts on Moore's belief in the necessity of a metaphysical theory of singular causation to blame and punish a person for her wrongdoing. This the chapter does by defending the concept of imputation used in German philosophy of law since early enlightenment. After a critical survey of its use in present German law theory the concept is analyzed along the lines of Immanuel Kants *Metaphysics of Morals*. There, imputation denotes a moral judgment which implies but is not reducible to causation being no moral but a theoretical judgment about physical objects. Therefore, imputation involves two different judgments, a universal one about causality and a singular one about guilt. Since Moore grounds responsibility solely on causation his theory is unable to attain its object.

Further Thoughts on Causation (and Related Topics) Prompted By Fifteen Critics

Michael S. Moore

In his contribution, Michael Moore discusses each of the critical essays in this volume in detail. He locates his and his critics' arguments in the broader framework of his *Causation and Responsibility* and his numerous other works. He ultimately defends his account against the objections levelled by the other contributors.

Richard W. Wright*

The NESS Account of Natural Causation: A Response to Criticisms

1 Introduction

The NESS (necessary element of a sufficient set) account of natural (scientific, 'actual', 'factual') causation is usually acknowledged to be a more satisfactory and comprehensive account than the traditional *sine qua non* ('but for') account.[1] However, objections have been raised to the claim that the NESS account fully captures the concept of natural causation (hereafter "causation") and properly handles all types of situations. Various types of counter-examples have been proposed. More fundamentally, it is argued that the NESS account is viciously circular, since causal terminology often is used in its elaboration and it relies upon the concept of causal laws.[2]

---

* I am grateful to my critics for raising issues that forced me to develop further my elaborations of the NESS account, to Horacio Spector for helpful discussions during the early stages of preparation of this chapter, and to David Cheifetz and Tony Dillof for helpful comments during the final stage.

1 For example American Law Institute, *Restatement of the Law, Third, Torts: Liability for Physical and Emotional Harm* [Restatement Third] (St. Paul, Minnesota, American Law Institute, 2010) s. 26 comment c, s. 27 comments a, f–i and reporters' notes; A. Beever, *Rediscovering the Law of Negligence* (Oxford, Hart Publishing, 2009) 417–21, 426; D.A. Fischer, 'Insufficient Causes' (2006) 94 *University of Kentucky Law Review* 277, 281–84, 317; R. Fumerton and K. Kress, 'Causation and the Law: Preemption, Lawful Sufficiency, and Causal Sufficiency' (2001) 64:4 *Law and Contemporary Problems* 83, 83–84, 95–97; T. Honoré, 'Necessary and Sufficient Conditions in Tort Law' in D.G. Owen (ed.), *Philosophical Foundations of Tort Law* (Oxford, Oxford University Press, 1990) 363, 363–64, 366, 367, 374–77, 381–85; M. Kelman, 'The Necessary Myth of Objective Causation Judgments in Liberal Political Theory' (1987) 63 *Chicago-Kent Law Review* 579, 601–03; W. Lucy, *Philosophy of Private Law* (Oxford, Oxford University Press, 2007) 170–76; M.S. Moore, *Causation and Responsibility* (Oxford, Oxford University Press, 2009) 473–74, 486–90, 493; S.R. Perry, 'The Impossibility of General Strict Liability' (1988) 1 *Canadian Journal of Law and Jurisprudence* 147, 157; J. Stapleton, 'Choosing What We Mean by "Causation" in the Law' (2008) 73 *Missouri Law Review* 433, 443–44, 471–72, 474; J.J. Thomson, 'Some Reflections on Hart and Honoré, Causation in the Law' in M. Kramer et al (eds), *The Legacy of H.L.A. Hart: Legal, Political and Moral Philosophy* (Oxford, Oxford University Press, 2008) 143, 144, 148–50, 157, 163–64.

2 Beever (n.1) 422–25; Fischer (n.1); Fumerton and Kress (n.1) 84, 97–104; Kelman (n.1) 603–08; Moore (n.1) 477, 484, 494–95; Stapleton (n.1) 472–79; Thomson (n.1) 147–54.

Many of the objections raised against the NESS account assume that it is essentially the same as Herbert Hart's and Tony Honoré's 'causally relevant factor' account and John Mackie's INUS account. In section 2 of this chapter I distinguish these three accounts, which differ in important ways that make the latter two accounts vulnerable to objections to which the NESS account is immune, and I offer an account of causal laws that I believe rebuts the claim that the NESS account is viciously circular. In section 3 I argue that the NESS account handles properly the various types of situations that have been raised as alleged counter-examples to its comprehensive validity. In both parts, the most significant criticisms are addressed in the text, while other criticisms are discussed in the footnotes.

2 Distinguishing the NESS Account from Hart and Honoré's and Mackie's Accounts

The NESS account often is erroneously equated with Hart and Honoré's account of a 'causally relevant factor' and John Mackie's account of an INUS condition. This is understandable, since, although I have often noted the significant differences between the NESS account and the other two accounts, I drew on both of the other accounts in developing and elaborating the NESS account, credited Hart and Honoré with the initial elaboration of the weak sense of necessity that underlies each of the three accounts and distinguishes them from the traditional *sine qua non* account, and loosely used the NESS acronym to refer to Hart and Honoré's account as well as my own account.[3] However, the criticisms directed indiscriminately against all three accounts do not apply to the NESS account, owing to the significant differences between it and the other two accounts.

The weak sense of necessity that underlies all three accounts was initially elaborated in 1959 in Hart and Honoré's seminal treatise, *Causation in the Law.*[4] Contrary to the traditional insistence in law, and by many philosophers, that a cause be a condition that 'made a difference' by being strongly necessary for the occurrence of the consequence, in the sense that without it the consequence would not have occurred on the particular occasion, Hart and Honoré employed John Stuart Mill's scientific-method based account of causal laws

3 R.W. Wright, 'Causation, Responsibility, Risk, Probability, Naked Statistics, and Proof: Pruning the Bramble Bush by Clarifying the Concepts' (1988) 73 *Iowa Law Review* 1001, 1018–34.
4 H.L.A. Hart and A.M. Honoré, *Causation in the Law* (Oxford, Oxford University Press, 1959)

and singular instances of causation[5] to explain that a "causally relevant factor" need merely be "necessary just in the sense that it is one of the set of conditions jointly sufficient for the production of the consequence: it is necessary because it is required to complete this set".[6] Under this weak sense of necessity, which is also referred to as strong sufficiency, necessity is subordinated to sufficiency: a causally relevant factor need merely be necessary for the sufficiency of a set of conditions sufficient for the occurrence of the consequence, rather than being necessary for the consequence itself as in the *sine qua non* account.[7]

Hart and Honoré demonstrated the superiority of their weak-necessity account of a causally relevant factor to the *sine qua non* account in a variety of situations.[8] They also correctly emphasised that causation is an empirical rather than a merely analytical, logical or identity relation.[9] However, their account had some significant deficiencies, all of which are remedied in the NESS account. They apparently required that a causally relevant factor be either strongly

---

5 H.L.A. Hart and T. Honoré, *Causation in the Law*, 2nd edn (Oxford, Oxford University Press, 1985) 13–22, 111–13; see J.S. Mill, *A System of Logic* bk III ch. IV s. 1, ch. V ss 2–3, ch. VIII ss 1–4, ch. X ss 1–3; R.W. Wright, 'Causation in Tort Law' (1985) 73 *California Law Review* 1735, 1788–91.

6 Hart and Honoré (n.5) 112.

7 See Wright (n.3) 1020–21 for discussion of the different senses of necessity and sufficiency.

8 Hart and Honoré (n.5) 122–28, 206–07, 235–53.

9 Hart and Honoré (n.5) 114–15; see Fumerton and Kress (n.1) 90–93; Thomson (n.1) 148 fn. 7. Also to be ruled out are mere mereological relations—the relation between some entity and its constituent parts. See J. Collins, N. Hall and L.A. Paul, 'Counterfactuals and Causation: History, Problems, and Prospects' [Collins, Hall and Paul, Introduction] in J. Collins, N. Hall and L.A. Paul (eds), *Causation and Counterfactuals* (Cambridge, MIT Press, 1994) 1, 21–22, 44. Causation is an empirical relationship between concrete properties of distinct events or states of affairs. T.L. Beauchamp and A. Rosenberg, *Hume and the Problem of Causation* (New York, Oxford University Press, 1981) 251–52, 255–56, 281–82; J.L. Mackie, *The Cement of the Universe: A Study of Causation* (Oxford, Clarendon Press, 1974) 32–33, 256–58, 260–63, 266–67; R. Fumerton, 'Moore, Causation, Counterfactuals, and Responsibility' (2003) 40 *San Diego Law Review* 1273, 1278; L.A. Paul, 'Aspect Causation' in Collins, Hall and Paul (n.9) 205; Wright (n.3) 1033–34 and fn. 171. After long arguing otherwise, Moore now acknowledges this. Moore (n.1) 361–65, 368 fn. 61. Yet he persists in wanting to refer to whole events, rather than their causally relevant instantiated properties, as causes. See Moore (n.1) 366–68, 395–96. He apparently is driven to this position by his rejection of the 'harm within the risk' (HWR) limitation on attributable responsibility and his erroneous belief that the law's tortious-aspect-causation requirement is functionally equivalent to that limitation, which erroneous belief further leads him to claim that I support the HWR limitation. See Moore (n.1) 104, 166–67 and fn. 50. Contrary to Moore's claims, n.1 329–31, the law is not ambivalent between event-causation and aspect-causation, but rather clearly requires the latter, as I have shown while distinguishing, criticising and rejecting the HWR limitation. See Wright (n.5) 1759–74; R.W. Wright, 'The Grounds and Extent of Legal Responsibility' [Legal Responsibility] (2003) 40 *San Diego Law Review* 1425, 1479–1528.

necessary or independently strongly sufficient (sufficient for the occurrence of the consequence disregarding competing or duplicative conditions, but combined with the other weakly necessary conditions).[10] This requirement results in erroneous denials of causal contribution in the frequently occurring situations in which numerous conditions combine to cause the consequence, but none of them individually were (or could be proven to be) strongly necessary or independently strongly sufficient.[11] Hart and Honoré also submerged and sometimes confused the critical distinction between duplicative and pre-emptive causation by constructing an overlapping typology of overdetermined causation cases,[12] often emphasised 'making a difference' rather than sufficiency and thus sometimes erroneously employed strong-necessity rather than weak-necessity analysis in overdetermined causation situations,[13] interpreted the analysis of necessity as a hypothetical counterfactual analysis rather than a real world factual analysis,[14]

---

10 Hart and Honoré (n.5) 123–25, 206–07, 235–39, 245, 249. Hart and Honoré did not discuss situations involving conditions that were neither strongly necessary nor independently strongly sufficient. Writing separately, Honoré noted, without elaboration, that such conditions could be causes. A.M. Honoré, 'Causation and Remoteness of Damage' in A. Tunc (ed.), *International Encyclopedia of Comparative Law*, vol 11: *Torts* pt 1 (Tübingen, JCB Mohr, 1983) 7–107, 7–108, 7–115, 7–121. He apparently accepts the NESS account's extension of the weak-necessity analysis to encompass such situations. See text to n.147 below.

11 See section 3.5 below.

12 Hart and Honoré (n.5) xl, 122–25, 206–07, 235–53; see Honoré (n.10) 7–126 to 7–140; Wright (n.5) 1796–97.

13 Hart and Honoré (n.5) 29, 34–37, 239–41, 246–48, 250–51; Honoré (n.1) 368–69, 371–73, 379–80; Honoré (n.10) 7–109 to 7–111(1), 7–126; see Thomson (n.1) 156–57; Wright (n.5) 1797–1801. As Hart and Honoré generally understood, 'making a difference' should be understood in the sense of weak necessity rather than strong necessity. See M. Strevens, 'Mackie Remixed' in J. Keim, M. O'Rourke and D. Shier (eds), *Causation and Explanation* (Cambridge, MIT Press, 2007) 93, 97–98, 111–12; R.W. Wright, 'Acts and Omissions as Positive and Negative Causes' in J.W. Neyers et al. (eds), *Emerging Issues in Tort Law* (Oxford, Hart Publishing, 2007) 287, 294 fn. 20.

14 Hart and Honoré (n.5) lviii–lxi; Honoré (n.1) 370–72. But see Honoré (n.1) 376–79 (engaging in causal sufficiency analysis by matching actual concrete conditions against the abstract conditions in the antecedent of a causal law). For discussion of the many defects of the counterfactual-dependency analysis of causation, see Moore (n.1) 382–90, 392–425; Collins, Hall and Paul, Introduction (n.9) 2–12, 15–29; N. Hall, 'Two Concepts of Causation' in Collins, Hall and Paul (n.9) 225, 225–26, 232–48; J. Schaffer, 'Trumping Preemption' in Collins, Hall and Paul (n.9) 59, 67–71. Although I initially referred to the analysis of necessity in both the NESS account and the *sine qua non* account as a counterfactual analysis, see Wright (n.5) 1803–07, I have always insisted that the analysis is (or should be) a real-world 'covering law' matching of actual conditions against the required elements of the relevant causal generalisations rather than a counterfactual 'possible worlds' exploration of what might have occurred in the absence of the condition at issue. ibid; Wright (n.13) 296–97; Wright, Legal Responsibility (n.9) 1444–45 and interpreted sufficiency in terms of abstract, incomplete causal generalisations rather than complete instantiation of the causal laws underlying the causal generalisations,[15] and denied that human decisions and actions are governed by causal laws.[16]

Nevertheless, Hart and Honoré's account of a causally relevant factor was a major advance in the analysis of causation in both law and philosophy. Unfortunately, however, their account was overshadowed and distorted by their primary emphasis on elaborating supposedly factual 'common sense' principles for treating only some causally relevant factors as causes,[17] so that, initially, it received minimal attention in the legal literature.[18]

Hart and Honoré's account had a significant impact on non-legal philosophers, a number of whom subsequently published analyses of causation similar to Hart and Honoré's account, although generally without citing Hart and Honoré. The best known analysis was published in 1965 by a fellow professor at Oxford, John Mackie, who employed an acronym, INUS (for "insufficient but necessary part of an unnecessary but sufficient condition"), to facilitate reference to his analysis.[19] However, these philosophers only used the weak-necessity analysis to describe causal laws. For singular instances of causation they required that the condition at issue be necessary for the occurrence of the consequence in the particular circumstances, thereby converting their accounts into the *sine qua non*

---

fn.67; R.W. Wright, 'Once More Into the Bramble Bush: Duty, Causal Contribution, and the Extent of Legal Responsibility' [Once More] (2001) 54 *Vanderbilt Law Review* 1071, 1106–07; Wright (n.3) 1035–37, 1039–42; see n.119 and text to nn 118–19 below. The existence of these two very different methods of analysing necessity is noted by Moore, who however incorrectly describes both methods as 'counterfactual' and focuses on the second approach. Moore (n.1) 372–82, 390.

15 Hart and Honoré (n.5) 15, 22, 32, 44–45, 111–12, 124–25, 207, 237; Honoré (n.10) 7–53.

16 See section 3.6 below.

17 See R.W. Wright, 'The Nightmare and the Noble Dream: Hart and Honoré on Causation and Responsibility' in M. Kramer et al (eds), *The Legacy of H.L.A. Hart: Legal, Political and Moral Philosophy* (Oxford, Oxford University Press, 2008) 165. The introduction to *Causation in the Law* focuses entirely on this issue; it does not mention the distinction between natural causation and attributions of responsibility or their account of causally relevant factors. See Hart and Honoré (n.5) 1–7; *cf.* Hart and Honoré (n.5) 8–12.

18 See Wright (n.5) 1788 fn 227.

19 J.L. Mackie, 'Causes and Conditions' in E. Sosa and M. Tooley (eds), *Causation* (Oxford, Oxford University Press, 1993) 33, 34–37, originally published in (1965) 2 *American Philosophical Quarterly* 245 and revised and reprinted as chapter three of Mackie (n.9). Honoré states that Mackie "applied our idea" in developing his INUS account, Honoré (n.1) 365. However, unlike Hart and Honoré's account or the NESS account, Mackie literally requires that an INUS condition be insufficient by itself for the consequence and that the sufficient condition of which it is a part be unnecessary. Both restrictions are too strict.

account.[20] Mackie went further: he denied that identification of singular instances of causation requires any (even implicit) reference to causal laws or generalisations.[21] Mackie's arguments on these two issues do not withstand analysis and are contradicted by other arguments that he himself makes.[22] Yet, due perhaps to the handy INUS acronym, philosophers have generally referred to Mackie's INUS account of weak necessity rather than Hart and Honoré's earlier account.[23]

In 1985, I substantially revised and extended Hart and Honoré's account of a causally relevant factor and created the NESS acronym to refer to this revised and extended account.[24] According to the NESS account as initially elaborated, a condition *c* was a cause of a consequence *e* if and only if it was necessary for the sufficiency of a set of existing antecedent conditions that was sufficient for the occurrence of *e*.[25] The required sense of sufficiency, which (following a suggestion by Fumerton and Kress)[26] I call "causal sufficiency" to distinguish it from mere lawful strong sufficiency, is the instantiation of all the conditions in the antecedent ('if' part) of a causal law, the consequent ('then' part) of which is instan-

---

20 E.g. Mackie (n.9) 38–48, 62, 76–77, 126–27; see Wright (n.3) 1023 fn 113.

21 Mackie (n.9) 40–58, 76–78, 120–22. Fumerton, Kress and Moore seem to agree with Mackie. See Fumerton and Kress (n.1) 97. Despite Moore's insistence that singular instances of causation must always be "accompanied by" causal laws, Moore (n.1) 361–64, 472, 496–97, 506, and his declaration that the notion that one can directly observe singular causal relations is a "hog-choker of a premise", Moore (n.1) 363, he asserts that singular causal relations are basic and prior to causal laws, which are mere inductively derived generalisations from already identified (in some unexplained manner) true singular instances of causation. Moore (n.1) 361, 472–73, 497–99, 506. In the end Moore seems to abandon even this apparently superfluous role for causal laws and instead to opt for being a "reluctant primitivist". See Moore (n.1) xii, 505–12.

22 See Hart and Honoré (n.5) xxxix–xlii; Wright (n.3) 1023–34; text to nn 42–64, 156–59 below.

23 See Wright (n.3) 1023 fn 113.

24 Wright (n.5) 1788–1803.

25 See text to n.40 below for my current definition of a concrete NESS condition. The definition in the text here is itself a clarification of my initial definition, which literally merely required that a NESS condition be a necessary *member* of a sufficient set and thus failed to expressly incorporate the requirement, which has always been stated in my elaborations of the NESS account, that a NESS condition be necessary *for the sufficiency* of a sufficient set. E.g. Wright (n.5) 1790; Wright (n.3) 1019, 1021, 1041. Richard Fumerton and Ken Kress drew my attention to the ambiguity in my initial definition. See Fumerton and Kress (n.1) 94; Wright, Once More (n.14) 1103 fn 112.

26 Fumerton and Kress (n.1) 93, 101–02; see Wright, Once More (n.14) 1103 fn 113. Michael Strevens employs the term "causal sufficiency" for a similar, if not identical, concept of sufficiency. See text to n.73 below.

tiated by the consequence at issue.[27] A causal law is an empirically derived statement that describes a successional relation between a set of abstract conditions (properties or features of possible events and states of affairs in our real world) that constitute the antecedent and one or more specified conditions of a distinct[28] abstract event or state of affairs that constitute the consequent such that, regardless of the state of any other conditions, the instantiation of all the conditions in the antecedent entails the immediate instantiation of the consequent, which would not be entailed if less than all of the conditions in the antecedent were instantiated.

It is critically important when analysing singular instances of causation to distinguish causal relations from mere lawful relations. To do so one must include in the causal analysis the entire causal process up to the time of the occurrence of the consequence.[29] The definition of a causal law in the immediately preceding paragraph assures this by requiring that the instantiation of the consequent of the causal law occur immediately when all of the conditions in the antecedent of the causal law have been instantiated. A causal process consists of the instantiation of one or more simultaneously or successively operative causal laws.

Another critical feature of causal laws – and the related concept of causal sufficiency as distinct from mere lawful sufficiency – is their successional or directional nature, according to which the instantiation of the conditions in the antecedent of the causal law causes the instantiation of the consequent, but not vice versa.[30] Our knowledge of the required conditions in the antecedent of a causal law – and thus of the direction of causation – is based on experience and empirical investigation, by ourselves or others. Scientists employ Mill's Difference Method in carefully designed experiments to see if the non-instantiation of a supposed antecedent condition makes a difference in the occurrence of the consequence.[31] For example, we determine by observation or experimentation that eliminating a flagpole or changing its height eliminates or changes the length of the flagpole's shadow, but not vice versa.[32] In the causal law that is

27 I have always insisted on this. E.g. Wright (n.5) 1789, 1795–98, 1803–04, 1808–09, 1823; Wright (n.3) 1031, 1033, 1041–42, 1045–46, 1049–53.

28 See n.9 above.

29 See Fumerton and Kress (n.1) 103–04; Hall (n.14) 238–40; Honoré (n.10) 7–53, 7–107, 7–110; Schaffer (n.14) 67–71; Strevens (n.13) 113–16; Thomson (n.1) 153–54, 164; text to n.73 below.

30 Fumerton and Kress (n.1) 93; see sections 3.2 and 3.3 below.

31 See Mill (n.5) bk III ch. VII ss 2–4, ch. VIII s. 2.

32 However, as Hart and Honoré note, one should be careful not to treat human manipulability as a requirement for being a cause. Hart and Honoré (n.5) 36.

thereby derived, the successionally antecedent NESS conditions are grouped together in the 'if' part of the causal law and the consequent is stated separately in the 'then' part. The successional nature of causation is incorporated in the concept of causal sufficiency, which is defined as the complete instantiation of all the conditions in the antecedent of the relevant causal law.[33]

While the NESS account's definition of causal sufficiency relies upon the concept of a causal law, the concept of a causal law is defined above without any use of causal language. There is no conceptual circularity here, vicious or otherwise. Even if some circularity should be found to exist in these definitions, it would not be 'vicious'. The NESS account provides a description of the structure of causal laws and their instantiation that is acknowledged, even by its critics, to be illuminating and very useful for proper identification of singular instances of causation.[34]

Our knowledge of causal laws generally is incomplete, and even when it is complete we rarely refer to completely specified causal laws, since such complete specification would be extremely burdensome and unnecessarily detailed and lengthy.

We rather employ causal generalisations, which refer to only some of the antecedent conditions in the relevant causal laws and have only as much specificity as is possible and needed in the particular situation. For example, we usually refer to the causal generalisation that specifies that bringing a flame into contact with combustible material causes that material to burn, without referring to other necessary antecedent conditions such as the presence of oxygen or the absence of a soaking rain – unless the latter expected conditions did not exist in the particular situation or, conversely, existed but were not expected. Moreover, the generalisations that we employ usually refer elliptically to a large number of simultaneously or successively operative causal laws.[35]

---

33 See text to n.27 above. Interpreted in the usual manner, causal succession precludes temporally backward causation, through which events today change events in the past. However, the definition of causal succession in the text does not preclude such backward causation, which would occur if the present instantiation of the antecedent results in the immediately following instantiation of the consequent (paradoxically) in the past.

34 E.g. Beever (n.1) 426; Fischer (n.1) 277, 281–84, 302, 317; Fumerton and Kress (n.1) 83–84, 95–97, 102–04; Moore (n.1) 361–62, 368 and fns 59 and 61, 473–74, 486–90, 493; Stapleton (n.1) 443–44, 471–72, 474; Thomson (n.1) 144, 148–50, 163–64.

35 Hart and Honoré (n.5) xxxvii, 11–13, 31–32, 45–49; Honoré (n.10) 7–53; Mackie (n.9) 35–38, 66–76; Mill (n.5) bk III ch.IV s.1, ch.V ss 2–3; Moore (n.1) 477–78, 485; Strevens (n.13) 111–12; Wright (n.5) 1823–24; Wright (n.3) 1031–34, 1045–46. Hart and Honoré erroneously claim that Mill insisted that all of the conditions in the antecedent of the relevant causal law must be

However, when we make an assertion regarding a singular instance of causation, we are implicitly asserting that all the unstated as well as the stated conditions in the relevant causal generalisations and all the unknown as well as known conditions in the causal laws underlying the causal generalisations were instantiated on the particular occasion. Contrary to Hart and Honoré's account,[36] the NESS account insists that singular instances of causation always consist of the complete instantiation on a particular occasion of one or more causal laws, and that identification of a singular instance of causation always implies that such complete instantiation has occurred.[37] The implication may be based on direct particularistic evidence of the existence of one or more of the required conditions, or, as is always true for the unknown conditions in the causal laws and generally true for many (sometimes all) of the known conditions, is inferred from particularistic evidence of the network of causal relationships that encompasses the particular occasion.[38]

Even when the inference of an applicable causal generalisation (and the underlying causal laws) is based on a single observation of a singular instance of causation, the inference of causation in the singular instance comes after and depends upon the inference of the applicable causal generalisation. In such instances the order is (1) observation of the occurrence, (2) inference of the causal generalisation based on the observation, and (3) assertion of causation through enunciation of the singular causal statement, which implicitly invokes the causal generalisation.[39]

My initial elaborations of the NESS account were overly demanding. I incorporated the weak-necessity requirement in the definition of singular instances of causation. As I have previously stated, this is too restrictive. The weak-necessity requirement is sufficiently incorporated in a properly formulated causal law, which contains in its antecedent only those abstract conditions the instantiation of which is necessary for the sufficiency of the set of conditions that is sufficient for the immediate instantiation of its consequent. When analysing singular instances of causation, an actual condition *c* was a cause of an actual condition *e* if and only if *c* was a part of (rather than being necessary for) the instantiation of one of the abstract conditions in the completely instantiated antecedent of a

---

known before selecting only one or a few for explicit reference in a singular causal statement. Hart and Honoré (n.5) 15, 21, 22, 31, 44–47; Honoré (n.10) 7–53.

36 See text to n.15 above. But see Honoré (n.1) 367, 376, 385 (apparently accepting the NESS account's conception of causal generalisations and singular instances of causation).

37 See text to nn 25–27 above.

38 Wright (n.3) 1045–46, 1049–52.

39 Wright (n.3) 1031–34; see Mill (n.5) bk III ch.III.

causal law, the consequent of which was instantiated by *e* immediately after the complete instantiation of its antecedent, or (as is more often the case) if *c* is connected to *e* through a sequence of such instantiations of causal laws.[40] This formulation of the requirement for a NESS condition is more straightforward and simpler to apply than my initial formulation, which requires 'at least so much' descriptions of actual conditions in some situations in order to (validly) treat other conditions as NESS conditions.[41] However, care must be taken to make sure that the antecedents of the relevant causal laws include only abstract NESS conditions in the strict sense – that is, those abstract conditions the instantiation of which is necessary for the sufficiency of the set of conditions that is sufficient for the instantiation of the consequent.

The *sine qua non* account's strong-necessity analysis, properly applied,[42] is a corollary of the NESS analysis that gives the correct answer when there was only one set of conditions that was actually or potentially sufficient for the consequence on the particular occasion.[43] Contrary to what many assume,[44] the *sine qua non* analysis relies on an embedded analysis of (lawful rather than causal) sufficiency. To determine if some condition was strongly necessary for the occurrence of some consequence that actually occurred, one must 'rope off' the condition at issue and then, using the relevant causal generalisations, determine whether the remaining existing conditions were lawfully sufficient for the occurrence of the consequence – that is, whether the relevant causal laws would have been fully instantiated in the absence of the condition at issue. If they would have been, the condition at issue was not strongly necessary for the occurrence of the consequence.[45]

---

40 Wright (n.13) 297–98; Wright (n.3) 1045; see text to nn 27–29 above. Allan Beever fails to note my recent confinement of the weak-necessity requirement to the abstract conditions in causal laws. He rejects any necessity restriction in causal analysis and instead merely requires that a condition be a member of a sufficient set. This 'weak sufficiency' analysis opens the door to treating every condition as a cause. See Beever (n.1) 425–26; Wright (n.3) 1020–21.

41 Wright (n.5) 1793–94; Wright, Legal Responsibility (n.9) 1444–45; Wright, Once More (n.14) 1106–07; Wright (n.3) 1035–37; see text to nn 117–20 below.

42 See n.14 above.

43 Hart and Honoré (n.5) 112–13; Wright (n.3) 1021.

44 E.g. D.W. Robertson, 'Causation in the *Restatement Third of Torts:* Three Arguable Mistakes' (2009) 44 *Wake Forest Law Review* 1007, 1010 ("[W]hen we make causation-attribution decisions, necessity vel non is the heart of the inquiry.... In torts cases, the cause-in-fact inquiry is always an attribution question, never a predictive one, so sufficiency issues are not in play").

45 Wright (n.13) 296–97; see D.Lewis, 'Void and Object' in Collins, Hall and Paul (n.9) 277, 279, 288–89; n.119 and text to nn 118–19 below.

In overdetermined causation situations,[46] in which there were two or more (usually overlapping) sets of conditions that were each actually or potentially sufficient – for example, two fires each sufficient to destroy a house if the fire reaches the house while it is still standing, which merge and destroy the house (*duplicative causation*), or one of which reaches the house and destroys it before the other arrives (*pre-emptive causation*) – the NESS analysis reaches the proper conclusions regarding causation, while the *sine qua non* ('but for', 'made a difference') analysis as usually described and applied does not.[47]

The *sine qua non* analysis is able to reach the proper conclusion in many overdetermined causation situations if the consequence is qualified by the time at which it occurred,[48] and in a few more such situations if it is further qualified by the location at which it occurred.[49] However, employing such qualifications will greatly expand the proliferation of causes, especially if trivial differences in the time or location of a specific event – for example, due to gravitational forces exerted by nearby objects – are taken into account, rather than differences in the time or location of distinct events.[50] More significantly, in many situations it will be impossible to determine whether the condition at issue had any effect on the timing or location of the consequence, and a condition can be a cause even if it had no effect on the timing or location, or not be a cause even though (if not pre-empted) it would have caused the consequence at the same time and location.[51] The NESS analysis will properly resolve the causal issue in such situations; the *sine qua non* analysis will not.[52]

---

46 Contrary to the usual practice, Stapleton and Michael Strevens apply the term 'overdetermination' only to duplicative causation situations. Stapleton (n.1) 442 fn.19; Strevens (n.13) 104–05.

47 Wright (n.5) 1775–76, 1791–98; Wright (n.3) 1018–28.

48 Wright, Once More (n.14) 1112–14; Wright (n.13) 292 fn.14. Stapleton ignores these sources and my unsuccessful attempts to have the American Law Institute add a time-of-occurrence qualifier to the *sine qua non* test in s.26 of the Restatement Third of Torts when she implies that I do not recognise that the *sine qua non* account can be modified in this manner to resolve the causal issue in many cases. See Stapleton (n.1) 452 and fn.42; American Law Institute, *79th Annual Meeting, Proceedings 2002* (Philadelphia, American Law Institute, 2003) 273–76; American Law Institute, *82nd Annual Meeting, Proceedings 2005* (Philadelphia, American Law Institute, 2006) 81–84. The major defects in the Restatement Third's treatment of 'factual causation' are discussed in n.125 below.

49 F.Stella, 'The Vitality of the Covering Law Model: Considerations on Wright and Mackie' http://works.bepress.com/richard_wright/34/, accessed on 17/10/12, at 34–37.

50 Collins, Hall and Paul, Introduction (n.9) 46; Hall (n.14) 237, 239; Moore (n.1) 477–78; see text to nn 53–56 below.

51 Collins, Hall and Paul, Introduction (n.9) 23–24; Hall (n.14) 235–38; Schaffer (n.14) 70–71; Wright, Once More (n.14) 1112–14.

Some, including Hart and Honoré, Mackie, Michael Moore, Jane Stapleton and Robert Stevens, have stated that the *sine qua non* analysis can be further sharpened to reach the proper conclusion in overdetermined causation situations by specifying minute details of the consequence or qualifying it by the manner of its occurrence, 'as and how it came about'.[53] Both approaches are defective and extremely promiscuous.[54] The first approach will merely establish causation of some irrelevant detail of the consequence, rather than the consequence itself.[55] This objection applies as well to minute differences in the time or location of a specific event.[56] The second approach is viciously circular,[57] as Honoré and Moore now acknowledge.[58] Although Honoré notes that the law requires that a plaintiff identify the specific event for which she seeks redress, including the time, place and persons involved, he now rejects, as part of the causal analysis, qualifying the consequence by time, location or manner of occurrence.[59] Instead, he relies upon the NESS account's causal sufficiency analysis.[60]

---

52 Wright, Once More (n.14) 1112–14; see text to nn 83–88 and 96 below; see Stapleton (n.1) 452–53 and fn.45 (employing the NESS account's causal sufficiency analysis rather than her "duplicate necessity" analysis of "involvement", which is described in n.125 below, to avoid treating a pre-empted condition as a cause). Federico Stella acknowledged the need to turn to the NESS account to handle these types of situations. Stella (n.49) 38. Yet he otherwise preferred the time-and-location-qualified *sine qua non* account, in part because he erroneously assumed that the NESS analysis as applied in the law is not framed by a focus on the legally relevant conditions, Stella (n.49) 23, 39, but primarily (I believe) because he was concerned that "in Italy to abandon [the *sine qua non* test] would lead to real disasters. Our judges ... are very far from having a sound culture of proofs". Federico Stella, email to Richard Wright, 25 January 2005.
53 A. Becht and F. Miller, *The Test of Factual Causation in Negligence and Strict Liability Cases* (St. Louis, Washington University Press, 1961) 15–19; D. Coady, 'Preemptive Preemption' in Collins, Hall and Paul (n.9) 325, 327–33; Hart and Honoré (n.4) 118; Hart and Honoré (n.5) xli–xlii; Honoré (n.10) 7–111(2), 7–126; Mackie (n.9) 45–46; N.J. McBride and R. Bagshaw, *Tort Law*, 3rd edn (Harlow, Pearson Education Ltd, 2008) 535 fn.16; M.Moore, 'Thomson's Preliminaries About Causation and Rights' (1987) 63 *Chicago-Kent Law Review* 497, 510–11; R. Stevens, *Torts and Rights* (Oxford, Oxford University Press, 2007) 131, 133–34 and n. 12, 135; Stapleton (n.1) 442 fn. 19 ('death by two bullets'), 452 ('death by electrocution', 'death by explosion'). For hair-splitting semantic variations on this approach, see D. Lewis, 'Causation as Influence' in Collins, Hall and Paul (n.9) 75, 85–90.
54 Collins, Hall and Paul, Introduction (n.9) 46; Hall (n.14) 237–38, 239; Strevens (n.13) 96–97, 98–99, 111–12.
55 Fumerton and Kress (n.1) 96–97; Wright (n.5) 1778–80.
56 See text to n.50 above.
57 Wright (n.5) 1777–78; Wright (n.3) 1025.
58 Honoré (n.1) 378–79; Moore (n.1) 87 fn 16.
59 Honoré (n.1) 378–79; see Honoré (n.1) 368.
60 See Honoré (n.1) 377–79.

It therefore is puzzling that he states, without elaboration, that the *sine qua non* account will "point to the same causal conclusion" as the NESS account when "the [competing] causal processes are different" or "one culminates in harm before the other".[61]

Even initially, although stating that "[s]uch solutions are perfectly sound logically and legally", Hart and Honoré correctly noted that the second approach requires "first deploying the more fundamental notion of sufficient conditions and so identifying the causal process which culminated in the harm".[62] Similarly, Mackie notes that this approach relies upon determining which of the competing causal stories was completed in the particular situation.[63] Although Mackie does not acknowledge it, this is a causal sufficiency analysis rather than a strong necessity analysis. When even detailing the manner of occurrence will not distinguish the competing conditions using the *sine qua non* analysis, Mackie paradoxically asserts that none of the conditions individually were causes but all of them in the aggregate were.[64]

---

61 Honoré (n.1) 374.

62 Hart and Honoré (n.4) 118; see Hart and Honoré (n.4) 119; cf. Hart and Honoré (n.5) xli–xlii, 124–25 (no longer asserting that this approach is "sound logically and legally"). Although apparently not recognising what he is doing, Robert Stevens, in his attempt to defend the 'but for' test as the sole test of causation, employs causal sufficiency analysis rather than 'but for' analysis to reach the proper conclusion in several much-discussed overdetermined causation situations. He also resurrects the discredited privity of contract limitation on tort liability in order to explain the mechanic's lack of liability in the unused defective brakes case. See Stevens (n.53) 135–37; text to nn 83–94, 116–23 and 179–95 below.

63 Mackie (n.9) 45–46.

64 Mackie (n.9) 47, criticised in Moore (n.1) 354–56; Wright (n.3) 1026–27. Stevens claims to reject Mackie's aggregative move, not because it is illogical but rather because the law focuses on individual rather than aggregative responsibility. Stevens (n.53) 131. However, he implicitly employs it when assessing "substitutive" and consequential damages for infringement of a right. For example, if a plaintiff's dog was killed by two stab wounds inflicted by different defendants, each of which would have been sufficient by itself to cause the death of the dog, Stevens asserts that the two defendants are each liable for "the value of the dog" as "substitutive" damages for their respective infringements of the plaintiff's right to the dog, and also for any consequential damages that are a 'but for' result of the dog's death, but that double recovery is not permitted since "he only had one right to the dog". Stevens (n.53) 134. Yet the 'but for' test can only establish each defendant's causation of a distinct stab wound, not the death of the dog, and thus it cannot support holding either defendant liable for "substitutive" damages for the full "value of the dog" or for consequential damages caused by the dog's death. Rather, under the individually applied 'but for' test that Stevens claims to be applying, each defendant can only be held liable for the "substitutive" value of the rights infringement that is constituted by his or her stabbing of the dog, however that might be valued, and any consequential damages (of which there likely will be none) that are a 'but for' result of his or her distinct rights infringement.

The courts and the secondary literature generally do not qualify the consequence by specifying its non-salient details or the time, location or manner of its occurrence when describing or applying the *sine qua non* analysis.[65] Instead, in overdetermined causation situations they either reach incorrect conclusions on natural causation by using an unqualified *sine qua non* analysis[66] or employ question-begging, conclusory phrases – for example, "substantial factor", "material contribution" or "common sense causation"[67] – that confusingly merge the scientific issue of causal contribution with the normative issue of the appropriate extent of legal responsibility for the consequences of one's (legally relevant) conduct while failing to provide any test or guidance for resolving either issue.[68]

Philosophers have attempted to defend the *sine qua non* account and the usual employment of counterfactual analysis in that account by shifting the focus of the analysis from the occurrence of the consequence at issue to the occurrence of each step in the competing causal sequences. This attempt abandons (without acknowledgement) strong necessity in favour of a deficient version of weak necessity. Moreover, it works only in 'early pre-emption' situations, in which the pre-emption of the pre-empted causal sequence occurs before the completion of the completed causal sequence. It does not work in 'late pre-emption' situations, in which the pre-emption of the pre-empted causal sequence occurs at the same time as (or after) the completion of the completed causal sequence, nor in any duplicative causation situation.[69] In the duplicative causation

---

Moreover, although there is "only one right to the dog", it is a right that each defendant has separately and distinctly infringed, and thus, under Stevens' odd damages theory, each defendant should be fully but separately, rather than concurrently, liable for "substitutive" damages for his or her distinct rights infringement, regardless of any resulting "double recovery".

65 See e.g., Restatement Third (n.1) § 26; *Restatement (Second) of Torts* § 432(1) (1965); Hart and Honoré (n.5) xlii; Honoré (n.1) 378–79; n.48 above. Stapleton, rather than I, "falls into manifest error" when she asserts otherwise. See Stapleton (n.1) 452 and fn.42.

66 See Wright, Legal Responsibility (n.9) 1438–40; R.W. Wright, 'Liability for Possible Wrongs: Causation, Statistical Probability, and the Burden of Proof' (2008) 31 *Loyola Los Angeles Law Review* 1295, 1321–24.

67 E.g. *March v E & MH Stramare Pty Ltd* (1991) 99 ALR 423 (High Court of Australia) ('material contribution' and 'common sense'); *Athey v Leonati* (1996) 3 SCR 458 (Supreme Court of Canada) ('materially contributed'); *Sew Hoy & Sons Ltd v Coopers & Lybrand* (1996) 1 NZLR 392 (New Zealand Court of Appeal) ('material contribution'); *Fairchild v Glenhaven Funeral Services Ltd* [2002] UKHL 22, [2003] 1 AC 32 ('material contribution'); *Kingston v Chicago & Northwestern Ry Co* (1927) 211 NW 913 (Supreme Court of Wisconsin) ('substantial factor'); *Mitchell v Gonzales* (1991) 819 P 2d 872 (Supreme Court of California) ('substantial factor').

68 Wright (n.5) 1742–50, 1781–88; Wright, Once More (n.14) 1073–80; Wright (n.3) 1012–14.

69 See J. Collins, 'Preemptive Preemption' in Collins, Hall and Paul (n.9) 107, 109–10; Collins, Hall and Paul, Introduction (n.9) 18, 22–24, 32–33; Schaffer (n.14) 67–70. Philosophers tend to

situations, some *sine qua non* advocates hold fast. They assert that neither of the duplicative conditions was a cause and that the alleged consequence is either an uncaused miracle or was caused by the conjunction of the duplicative conditions although neither by itself was a cause.[70]

3 Alleged Deficiencies of the NESS Account

3.1 Spurious Weak Necessity

A common counter-example to the NESS account is the alleged conversion of a causally irrelevant condition *c* into a NESS condition by replacing a causally relevant condition *b* with two conditions, one of which is *c* and the other of which is a disjunction of *b* with the negation of *c*.[71] For example, if D's cutting off C's head was a necessary condition for C's death (or for the sufficiency of a set S of conditions sufficient for C's death), D's beheading C is replaced with the following two conditions:

1. Napoleon married Josephine.
2. Either Napoleon did not marry Josephine or D beheaded C.

Given the disjunction in condition 2, the set S is not sufficient for C's death unless we also include condition 1, so, apparently, Napoleon's marrying of Josephine is (erroneously) treated as a cause of C's death under the NESS account.

To counter this logical manoeuvre, Fumerton and Kress propose excluding from the set S of sufficient conditions any condition (such as condition 2 above) that contains a truth-functional constituent part (such as "D beheaded C") that by itself is lawfully sufficient for the consequence.[72] Without condition 2, S is no longer a sufficient set, so condition 1 is not a NESS condition. To be generally effective, this analytic counter needs to be broadened to exclude as a constituent part of any disjunctive condition in S a condition that is sufficient when conjoined with all the other conditions in S other than the condition with

focus on overdetermined causation situations involving pre-emptive rather than duplicative causation. E.g. Collins, Hall and Paul, Introduction (n.9); Hall (n.14); Schaffer (n.14); Lewis (n.53) 80–82; Thomson (n.1) 144, 150–51, 152–59.

70 See Collins, Hall and Paul, Introduction (n.9) 32–33; Lewis (n.53) 80; Mackie (n.9) 47. David Coady adopts the latter position for pre-empted conditions as well as duplicative causes. Coady (n.53) 326–28.

71 E.g. Thomson (n.1) 151; *cf.* Lewis (n.53) 77.

72 Fumerton and Kress (n.1) 95; Moore (n.1) 487–88.

which it is disjoined. However, such appended analytic restrictions not only seem ad hoc, they also are unnecessary given restrictions that are already embedded in the NESS account.

The requirement that a NESS condition be an actually existing condition rules out as a constituent part of any NESS condition the negation of any actually existing condition. Napoleon's marrying Josephine can be tentatively included in S as condition 1 only if it was an actually existing condition, but if it was then Napoleon's not marrying Josephine in condition 2 cannot be true, so condition 2 collapses down to the actual condition of D's beheading C, thereby making condition 1 not necessary for the sufficiency of S.

The logical manoeuvre that creates the spurious weak necessity is similarly precluded by the NESS account's requirement that each condition in S be part of the instantiation of a condition in a fully instantiated causal law. As Michael Strevens states in his revision of Mackie's INUS account in a way that makes it similar to the NESS account,

> it is not enough that a set of conditions be sufficient for the occurrence of *e*; it must be *causally sufficient* for *e*. .... Causal sufficiency ought to be defined, then, so that a set of conditions is causally sufficient for an event *e* only if the conditions represent a causal process that produces *e*. A set of conditions entailing *e* represents a causal process producing *e*, I propose, just in case each step in the entailment corresponds to a strand in the relevant causal web. ....
>
> [T]he step from the [statement of the causally irrelevant condition] and the disjunction [of the causally relevant condition and the negation of the causally irrelevant condition] to the [consequent] .... is not a causal entailment, as it does not correspond to a causal process recognized by the laws of physics. Indeed, it is hard to imagine a physics in which something in the world captured by the description $\neg r$ [or] *c* could be part of any story about causal influence. .... [W]hen what we regard as an intuitively irrelevant factor *r* is made essential to the entailment of an event *e*, it is always by way of disjunction or other logical construction that links *r* and *e* truth-functionally but not causally.
>
> The approach to causal claims taken by my revision of Mackie's account puts a considerable burden on the physical laws; they must determine what primitive causal connections there are in the world, hence determine the structure of the causal web. I think that they are quite capable of bearing that load, and that we do indeed look to the laws as the final arbiters on any question of causal connection.[73]

This third counter to the logical manoeuvre that creates spurious weak necessity has been criticised as being circular, since it assumes the prior specification of a

73 Strevens (n.13) 113–14; see Collins, Hall and Paul, Introduction (n.9) 22 ('we should say that the disjunctive event is not an event at all, hence not apt to cause (or be caused)'); Moore (n.1) 355–56 (same).

"relevant *causal* web", the structure of which is determined by reference to the "physical laws".[74] However, the NESS account does not refer circularly to causally relevant conditions or causal laws. It specifies the method for identifying causally relevant conditions – they must be instantiations of abstract conditions listed in the antecedent of an empirically derived causal law – and its definition of a 'causal law' does not employ causal terminology.[75]

3.2 Causal Directionality (No 'Backtracking')

When the sun is at a 45 degree angle to an upright flagpole and the shadow of the flagpole on the ground is 5 feet long, the laws of geometry and nature entail that the flagpole is 5 feet tall. However, as Fumerton and Kress state, "it would surely be mistaken to claim that the shadow causes the flagpole to be [5] feet tall. If anything, the direction of causation is from the flagpole's height to the length of the shadow".[76] Although Fumerton and Kress and others assume otherwise, this conclusion is correctly reached under the NESS account, which insists that singular instances of causation always involve the complete instantiation of an empirically derived causal law and that causal laws state a direction of causation, whereby the complete instantiation of the conditions in the antecedent of the causal law cause the instantiation of the consequent of the causal law, not vice versa.[77] Fumerton and Kress and others claim that the reference to causal laws and their inherent directionality is viciously circular.[78] However, as I have discussed above, this is not true.[79]

---

74 Thomson (n.1) 152–53.

75 See text to nn 25–29 above.

76 Fumerton and Kress (n.1) 102. Fumerton, Kress and Moore have the geometry wrong; they state that the flagpole must be 10 feet tall. Fumerton and Kress (n.1) 93, 101–02; Moore (n.1) 476–77, 483.

77 See text to nn 25–33 above.

78 See n.2 above; *cf.* Lewis (n.53) 77. Moore acknowledges that the directionality of causal laws is inherent in our concept of causation and can be used to reject the criticisms of the NESS account discussed in this section and the next section. However, he claims that referring to this directionality or to causal laws per se to elucidate the meaning of causation is viciously circular. He thus commends Mackie for treating this directionality, which Mackie calls "causal priority", as an addition to, rather than as an essential constitutive element of, the sense of sufficiency employed in causal analysis. Moore (n.1) 482–85. Mackie acknowledged the use of the more discriminating sense of causal sufficiency in common discourse, but he thought it better for clarity's sake to reserve "sufficiency" for mere lawful sufficiency. Mackie (n.9) 51–53. See Mackie (n.9) 190–92 for Mackie's analysis of causal priority.

79 See text to nn 25–34 above.

3.3 Epiphenomena (Collateral Effects of a Common Cause)

When a condition is a common cause of two different causal sequences, employing mere lawful strong sufficiency rather than causal sufficiency can result in erroneously treating conditions in one sequence as causes of the conditions in the other sequence, and vice versa.[80] A frequently mentioned example is Mackie's 'hooters' hypothetical, in which the horns ('hooters') at a Manchester factory and a London factory each sound at five o'clock every workday afternoon, signalling the stoppage of work at their respective locations. A few moments later, workers begin to exit from each factory. The sounding of the horn at the Manchester factory is lawfully strongly sufficient for its being five o'clock, and its being five o'clock is lawfully strongly sufficient for the sounding of the horn and the exodus moments later of workers at the London factory. Thus, the sounding of the horn at the Manchester factory is lawfully strongly sufficient for the sounding of the horn and exodus of workers moments later at the London factory.[81] But it is not a cause of these events at the London factory, as the NESS account correctly concludes, because it is not causally sufficient. Neither horn's sounding, nor even its existence, is part of the instantiation of the antecedent of any causal generalisation for which the consequent is the state of its being five o'clock. As we have empirically determined, the direction of causation runs the other way.[82]

3.4 Pre-emptive Causation

The NESS account has been criticised for allegedly being unable to handle properly some types of pre-emptive causation situations. Once again, the criticisms erroneously assume that the NESS account merely requires lawful sufficiency, rather than causal sufficiency.[83] Consider some common examples:

1. C is a traveller in the desert, whose only source of water is a keg full of water. A adds a fatal dose of undetectable poison to the water in the keg, for which there is no antidote. C remains unaware of the poison in the water. Subsequently, before C drinks any of the poisoned water, B dumps the poisoned

80 Collins, Hall and Paul, Introduction (n.9) 17–18; Fumerton and Kress (n.1) 93, 101; Lewis (n.53) 77; Mackie (n.9) 33–34.
81 Mackie (n.9) 83–86; Moore (n.1) 481–82.
82 Strevens (n.13) 108–09; Wright (n.5) 1808–09.
83 Fumerton and Kress (n.1) 100–02; Moore (n.1) 474; Thomson (n.1) 148–51.

water out of the keg. When C attempts to drink water from the keg, she discovers that it is empty. C dies due to dehydration.

2. C drinks a fatal dose of poison for which there is no antidote but which takes several hours to produce death. While C is still alive, D shoots C in the head. C dies a few minutes later from the bullet wound, well before the time at which the death by poisoning would otherwise have occurred.
3. A ship is traveling down a river to deliver goods to Metropolis by a specific date. The ship is unable to arrive by that date, since its crew must and does stop when it reaches bridge A, which had collapsed into and blocked the river. The ship would not have been able to reach Metropolis on time even if bridge A had not collapsed, due to another collapsed bridge, bridge B, of which the ship's crew was unaware, located on the river between bridge A and Metropolis.

If we merely require lawful sufficiency and do not qualify the consequence by the time of its occurrence – or, in examples 1 and 3, perhaps even if we do[84] – we would incorrectly treat the poison as well as the emptying of the keg in example 1, the poison as well as the shooting in example 2, and the collapse of bridge B as well as the collapse of bridge A in example 3 as duplicative causes of the relevant consequence (respectively, death, death, and failure to reach Metropolis on time). In each example, either condition guarantees the occurrence of the (abstractly described) consequence and thus is lawfully sufficient for its occurrence.[85] On the other hand, if we require strong necessity – that the condition 'made a difference' as a 'but for' cause – we would be forced to conclude that neither condition was a cause.

In the NESS account, we require *causal sufficiency* rather than strong necessity or mere lawful strong sufficiency. For causal sufficiency, the condition at issue must be part of the instantiation of a fully instantiated causal law that is part of a sequence of such fully instantiated causal laws that link the condition at issue with the consequence.[86] The instantiated causal laws that constitute the sequence are usually referred to incompletely and elliptically in the form of a causal generalisation.[87]

---

84 See text to nn 48–56 above.

85 See Fumerton and Kress (n.1) 100–02; Collins, Hall and Paul, Introduction (n.9) 18; Lewis (n.53) 80; J. Stapleton, 'Perspectives on Causation' in J. Horder (ed.), *Oxford Essays on Jurisprudence: Fourth Series* (Oxford, Oxford University Press, 2000) 61, 82–84; Thomson (n.1) 150–51; Wright (n.13) 298–300, 305.

86 See text to nn 27–29, 40 and 73 above.

87 See text to n.35 above.

In example 1, the causal generalisation for death by poisoning includes the victim's drinking the poison, a condition that was not instantiated since the keg was emptied before C was able to drink from it. On the other hand, the causal generalisation and the underlying causal laws for death by dehydration, which include as a necessary condition lack of water (and the physical bodily processes that occur as a result of the lack of water), were fully instantiated. Thus, B's emptying of the keg, but not A's poisoning of its contents, caused C's death, even though C may have lived longer due to the emptying of the keg.[88]

Jane Stapleton states that there is substantial disagreement about this conclusion.[89] Hart and Honoré initially rejected it, but only because they erroneously equated causing death with shortening life.[90] Honoré eventually focused on the details of the competing causal processes and applied a causal sufficiency analysis to reach the correct conclusion:

> [I]f we know enough about the stages by which the events came about we can generally tell, even in cases of over-determination, which causal process ran its course and which was frustrated. So in the case of the desert traveler .... it now seems to me that B causes C's death. .... B's conduct introduces a condition, lack of water, that in the circumstances .... is sufficient to bring about and does bring about C's death from dehydration.[91]

Stapleton initially claimed that A, instead of or in addition to B, can be treated as a cause of C's death, or that one can plausibly argue that neither was a cause of C's death – the occurrence of which thus is an unexplained miracle.[92] She later claimed (and apparently still does) that both A and B were causes. Her arguments for treating A as a cause fail to distinguish guaranteeing an outcome (here, death) from actually causing the outcome and erroneously assert that a lack of 'potable' or 'fresh' (unpoisoned) water is the same as a lack of water, while failing to focus on what actually caused C not to drink the water.[93] Even

---

88 Becht and Miller (n.53) 205–10; Mackie (n.9) 44–46; Wright (n.5) 1802. I now believe that my opposite conclusion, in Wright (n.5) 1802, for McLaughlin's original version of this hypothetical, in which A emptied the keg and refilled it with salt and B subsequently stole the keg before C attempted to drink from it, is wrong for reasons set out in section 3.1 below.

89 Stapleton (n.1) 439 fn 15. Since Moore refuses to treat negative conditions such as lack of water as causes or effects, he denies that either A or B caused C's death, thereby treating the death as an uncaused miracle. Moore (n.1) 144, 466–67; see section 3.8 below.

90 See Hart and Honoré (n.5) 239–41 and fn.74.

91 Honoré (n.1) 378; see Honoré (n.10) 7–133.

92 See Stapleton (n.85) 82–84.

93 Stapleton (n.85); J. Stapleton, 'Unpacking "Causation"' in P. Cane and J. Gardner (eds), *Relating to Responsibility* (Oxford, Hart Publishing, 2001) 145, 178–83. For further elaboration of

if we follow Stapleton by speculating about counterfactual scenarios rather than focusing on what actually happened, the poisoning of the water would not have caused C not to drink the water if the keg had not been emptied, since, under the usual understanding of the example, the poison was not detectable.[94]

A similar analysis applies in example 2, in which C actually drank the fatal dose of poison but was shot and killed before the poison had time to have fatal effect. The empirically derived causal generalisation for death by poisoning includes as a necessary condition, in addition to the person's drinking the poison, a minimum amount of time of the person's thereafter being alive: the time, determined empirically, that is required for the poison to have fatal effect, that is, for certain internal bodily processes to occur. (Strictly speaking, the occurrence of these bodily processes, rather than the passage of a certain amount of time, are the NESS conditions in the underlying causal laws; however, in causal generalisations we can and often do substitute for the bodily processes the time required for them to occur, especially when we have insufficient knowledge of the required bodily processes.) In example 2, the would-be poisoning victim is shot and dies after drinking the poison but before the specified required time of remaining alive in order for the poison to have fatal effect has elapsed. On the other hand, the causal generalisation and the underlying causal laws for death by shooting were fully instantiated.[95]

In example 3, the relevant causal generalisation for a ship's being delayed by a bridge's blocking the river includes the bridge's collapsing into and blocking the river, the ship's reaching the bridge while the bridge is blocking the river, and the ship's crew's seeing the bridge's blocking of the river and stopping the ship before it runs into the bridge. This causal generalisation was fully instantiated for bridge A, but not for bridge B. Although bridge B's collapsing into and blocking the river guarantees and thus is lawfully sufficient for the ship's being delayed and not reaching a point beyond the bridge by a certain time, it is not causally sufficient since all the antecedent conditions in the 'if' part of the relevant causal generalisation involving bridge B were not instantiat-

---

the flaws in Stapleton's arguments, see Wright (n.13) 298–300, 305; Wright, Once More (n.14) 1115–20.

94 See Stapleton (n.93) 178 (poison was 'odourless'). If C did not know that the keg had been emptied but did not attempt to drink from it because she knew the water in it had been poisoned, A's poisoning of the water rather than B's emptying of the keg was the pre-emptive cause of C's death. See section 3.1 below.

95 Fumerton and Kress (n.1) 100; Hart and Honoré (n.5) 124; Honoré (n.10) 7–130, 7–134; Thomson (n.1) 151; Wright (n.5) 1795.

ed: the ship did not reach bridge B, and the ship's crew did not see bridge B blocking the river.[96]

Michael Moore acknowledges that the NESS account reaches the proper conclusion in a non-circular, non-question-begging way in 'early pre-emption' situations. His examples of early pre-emption are a two-fires case, in which "the first fire burns all the fuel around the house, so the second fire cannot get to the house to burn it", and a case that is similar to example 1, in which "the shooter shoots the victim before he drinks any of the poisoned tea".[97] He states:

> One of the conditions needed to complete the set of which the second fire/poisoning was a part, was the fuel leading up to the house/the drinking of the tea by the victim. Therefore, there is no set (of which setting the fire/poisoning the tea are members) that is truly sufficient for death. Missing are some positive conditions, conditions not described in question-begging causal terms. Sufficiency theorists thus can get the right answers in cases of early pre-emption.[98]

However, Moore claims that attempts to use the NESS account to resolve the causal issue in 'late pre-emption' situations are circular and question-begging, because they allegedly simply amount to requiring that the effect was not already caused by something else.[99] His distinction between early pre-emption and late pre-emption is significantly different from the usual one. For Moore, early pre-emption situations are those in which "the pre-emptive cause removes something needed by the pre-empted factor to do any causal work", while late pre-emption cases are those in which "there is no last event needed by the pre-empted factor and prevented by the pre-empting cause, save the ultimate effect itself".[100] He treats the poison–shooting situation in example 2 above and a two-fires case in which the pre-empted fire approaches the already destroyed house from an opposite direction than the pre-emptive fire (and thus shares no fuel on the way to the doomed house) as late pre-emption cases,[101] and he

---

96 Fumerton and Kress (n.1) 100 – 01; Hart and Honoré (n.5) 250 – 51; Wright (n.5) 1796 – 97. Hart and Honoré agree that bridge A but not bridge B caused the boat's delay; however, they claim that bridge A did not cause any financial loss resulting from the delay if bridge B's collapse was not wrongfully caused. Hart and Honoré (n.5) 251. They have confused the causation issue with the normative issue of legal responsibility. Wright (n.5) 1797 – 98; Wright, Legal Responsibility (n.9) 1434 – 67.

97 Moore (n.1) 493.

98 Moore (n.1) 493.

99 Moore (n.1) 494 – 95.

100 Moore (n.1) 493. See text to n.69 above for the usual distinction between early pre-emption and late pre-emption.

101 Moore (n.1) 493 – 94.

claims that attempts to apply the NESS account in such cases by specifying, as alleged necessary conditions in the antecedent of the relevant causal generalisation, conditions such as "the house exists at the time the second fire arrived at the site" or "the poison remaining in [the would-be victim P's] body a certain amount of time while she is still alive" are simply disguised circularity, since

> the house existing, or [P's] still being alive, is just there not being a house destruction or a death – and this, in a deterministic universe, is to say nothing else (other than the putative cause we are testing) caused such destruction or death.[102]

Moore's argument ignores the distinction between the necessary conditions in the antecedent of a causal generalisation and the distinct condition that constitutes the consequent of the causal generalisation. Although to say that an entity exists or is alive at a certain time obviously entails (in our world) that nothing has caused the entity's destruction or death prior to that time, it should also be obvious that the entity's existence or being alive at a certain time is a state of affairs that is distinct from and not simply the converse of the destruction, death or non-existence of the entity at a later (remote or immediate) time;[103] rather, it is one of the necessary but by itself insufficient conditions for the occurrence of the later event or state of affairs. As Collins, Hall and Paul explain,

> When Suzy throws a rock at the window, breaking it, we naturally tend to think that there is just *one* sequence of events – the one initiated by Suzy's throw – converging on the effect. But it is far better, at least for the purpose of systematic metaphysics, to see this effect standing at the intersection of *two* sequences of events: There is the interesting sequence just mentioned, and then there is the quite boring sequence consisting in the continued presence of the window, up to the moment it shatters. More generally, a proper theory of events almost certainly must count as such things that we ordinarily would classify as states, or standing or background conditions.[104]

---

102 Moore (n.1) 494.

103 It is unfortunate that on this issue Moore fails to recognise or employ the rigorous distinction between distinct states of affairs that he correctly employs in distinguishing between acts and consequences to rebut various arguments by criminal theorists earlier in his book. See Moore (n.1) 14–19, 282.

104 Collins, Hall and Paul, Introduction (n.9) 44; see Fumerton and Kress (n.1) 90 ("John's stabbing Mary in the heart caused her death because it was a necessary element in a set of actual conditions—including her being alive at the time that she was stabbed"); Hall (n.14) 231 ("among the causes of the June [forest] fire is not just the lightning but also the very presence of the forest, filled with flammable material"); Hall (n.14) 244 (noting that the causal history of a bombing by a plane includes the process of the flying of the plane and "less conspicuously, the process consisting in the persistence of the target"); Strevens (n.13) 103–04 (a jar must be in existence when a ball reaches it in order for the throw of the ball to cause the shattering of the

In the two-fires example, the house's destruction is an instantiation of the consequent of the causal generalisation for destruction by fire, which will occur only if all of the necessary conditions in the antecedent of that causal generalisation and its underlying causal laws are instantiated. The existence of the house as fuel when a fire reaches it is one of those necessary antecedent conditions, as much as the existence of the other fuel along the fire's path to the house. All of the antecedent conditions were instantiated for the first fire to reach the house. At least one – the existence of the house when the fire reached it – was not instantiated with respect to the second fire, which arrived too late from the opposite direction.

The same analysis applies in the poison–shooting hypothetical. The NESS account requires that we empirically determine, as best we can, what set of conditions is minimally sufficient for a certain causal process to occur. By empirical observation and experimentation, we determine that a specific minimal amount of time is required for a specific poison to have fatal effect after the would-be victim drinks the poison. If we knew enough about the causal process involved, we could (but, as a practical matter, need not) replace this required elapsed time by the NESS conditions for which it is a placeholder: the steps of the physical process that must occur inside the victim's body during this elapsed time. The victim's remaining alive for the specified amount of time is included as one of the necessary conditions when specifying the causal generalisation. When we later investigate whether the poison caused the death in a particular situation, we check to see whether every one of the conditions specified in the antecedent of the causal generalisation was instantiated on the particular occasion. The elapsed time condition was not, so the complete instantiation required for causal sufficiency is not satisfied. Although we rely on our prior empirically derived causal generalisations, there is no circularity in our definition, identification or application of those generalisations.

Moore's examples of late pre-emption actually are instances of early pre-emption given his definitions of those terms. Indeed, there are no actual pre-emption situations that fit Moore's definition of late pre-emption, which rather is swallowed up by his definition of early pre-emption. Recall that he distinguishes late pre-emption situations from early pre-emption situations by the fact that, in the former, "there is no last event needed by the pre-empted factor

jar); Thomson (n.1) 149 (including in a causal generalisation for a thrown rock's breaking of a window the condition of the window's remaining in the place where it was when the rock was thrown for at least the amount of time it would take the rock, thrown at a specified velocity, to reach that place).

and prevented by the pre-empting cause, save the ultimate effect itself".[105] In both his two-fires hypothetical and his poison-shooting hypothetical, there *is* an 'event' (a state of affairs) needed by the pre-empted factor and prevented by the pre-empting cause – the existence of the house when the second fire reaches it and the would-be victim's remaining alive for a specific amount of time after drinking the poison, respectively – that is *not* the 'the ultimate effect itself' (the destruction of the house or the death of the victim, respectively) and may not even have been the last event or state of affairs needed by the pre-empted factor in order for it to be a cause. Consider, for example, the necessity of the house's not only still being in existence when the second fire arrives but also being sufficiently dry and remaining so for some period thereafter and with sufficient oxygen (necessary for combustion) being present and remaining present for some period thereafter.

Moore discusses a modified version of the two-bridges hypothetical as an example of a third, supposedly distinctive, 'trumping' type of pre-emption that he claims creates the worst problems for the NESS account, since pre-emption allegedly exists even though the pre-empted factor 'runs its whole course'.[106] Moore changes the hypothetical by having the boat's captain be aware of both collapsed bridges prior to the stopping of the boat, although he continues to assume that the captain stopped the boat solely because of the collapse of bridge A.[107] This is a plausible assumption, especially if, after becoming aware of the collapse of both bridges, the captain proceeded down the river until he reached bridge A. However, it could also be the case that the captain's knowledge of the collapse of bridge B was a duplicative, reinforcing positive reason for, and hence a cause of, his stopping the boat, rather than a pre-empted factor.[108]

The second, reinforcement rather than pre-emption, description of the causal situation seems more likely in the other example of 'trumping' pre-emption that Moore discusses, which also has been discussed by Jonathan Schaffer. In this example, a major and a sergeant each simultaneously order the same soldiers to advance. Schaffer and Moore assume that the soldiers advance solely due to the order of the major, although they normally would have obeyed the sergeant's order.[109] While the major's order will (or should) pre-empt the sergeant's

---

105 See text to n.100 above.

106 Moore (n.1) 494–95.

107 Moore (n.1) 495. Moore treats my previously published analysis of the original version of this hypothetical as if it were my analysis of his modified version of the hypothetical. Moore (n.1) 495.

108 See section 3.6 below.

109 Moore (n.1) 494–95; Schaffer (n.14) 67; see Coady (n.53) 333–35; Lewis (n.53) 81.

order when their orders conflict, when their orders are consistent it seems to me that the sergeant's order will continue to be a positive reason for advancing that reinforces the reason provided by the major's order, rather than its being completely without effect.[110]

Nevertheless, if we assume, along with Schaffer and Moore, that the soldiers advanced solely due to the major's order, no new type of pre-emption has been discovered and no new difficulties are created for the NESS account. The applicable causal generalisation is assumed to contain as a necessary antecedent condition for the effectiveness of an order that it be the highest-ranking relevant order. This antecedent condition was instantiated for the generalisation as applied to the major's order, but not for the same generalisation as applied to the sergeant's order, which thus, contrary to Moore's assumption, did not 'run its whole course'.[111] If the sergeant's order indeed had 'run its whole course' – that is, if the relevant causal laws were fully instantiated by a set of conditions including the sergeant's order but not the major's order – then the sergeant's order (as well as the major's order) was a cause of the soldiers' advance.[112] As John Collins states, examples like this offered to illustrate a supposed distinct type of pre-emption "owe what plausibility they have to a confusion of causes with norms – the only sense in which a major's order clearly *trumps* a sergeant's order rather than pre-empting it in some other way is a normative sense".[113]

For proper resolution of the two-bridges hypothetical, as modified by Moore, we need to know more about the thought processes in the captain's brain. If he was determined to proceed down the river until forced to stop by a physical obstruction, then the relevant causal generalisation includes as a necessary antecedent condition the boat's reaching the physical obstruction. This condition was instantiated with respect to bridge A but not with respect to bridge B, so

110 See section 3.6 below.

111 The same analysis applies to Schaffer's primary illustration of trumping pre-emption, which assumes that a necessary condition in the antecedent of the relevant causal law for the effectiveness of a magical spell is that it be the first spell cast during the relevant time period. Schaffer (n.14) 59; see Lewis (n.53) 81. It also applies to Collins, Hall and Paul's neuron example, which assumes a causal law according to which a neuron fires with the same polarity as the most intense incoming signal. Collins, Hall and Paul, Introduction (n.9) 27–28.

112 *Cf.* Strevens (n.13) 104 ("If there *were* a set of veridical conditions entailing that the mother's [supposedly pre-empted] ball hits the jar, it would indeed have hit the jar. But then it would, intuitively, be a cause of the breaking, in which case Mackie's [weak-necessity] account would be correct in deeming it so.")

113 Collins (n.69) 114. Schaffer acknowledges that this example could be a case of 'standard pre-emption', in which causal processes in the soldiers' brains filter out the sergeant's order or only respond to highest-ranked orders. Schaffer (n.14) 67.

bridge A's collapse, but not bridge B's collapse, was a cause of the boat's stopping and thus of the delay in reaching Metropolis. If, instead, the captain's learning of a blockage of the river was causally sufficient for his stopping the boat as soon as he learned of the blockage (or at the nearest convenient stopping point short of the first blockage), then bridge A's collapse and bridge B's collapse (more precisely, his knowledge of or belief regarding each collapse) were duplicative causes of the boat's stopping and the delay in reaching Metropolis. If, on the other hand, as implicitly assumed by Moore, the relevant causal generalisation includes as a necessary antecedent condition not only knowledge of an obstruction but also that the knowledge be knowledge of the nearest known obstruction, then (knowledge of) bridge A's collapse, but not bridge B's collapse, was a cause of the stopping of the boat and the delay in reaching Metropolis.

3.5 Duplicative Causation

It is generally acknowledged that the NESS account, by requiring causal strong sufficiency rather than strong necessity, properly handles situations involving duplicative causation by two or more independently strongly sufficient conditions, such as two independently sufficient fires or floods that merge and destroy a building, which the *sine qua non* account mishandles since none of the conditions 'made a difference' by being a 'but for' cause.[114] However, some have questioned the NESS account's handling of a condition that was not, or could not be proven to be, either strongly necessary or independently strongly sufficient – eg, each of 10 drops of poison or discharges of pollution when only three such drops or discharges were necessary for the occurrence of the relevant harm. Such situations are quite common – eg, in the frequent cases of multiple fires, flood waters, noises, weights, pollutants, toxic substances and other conditions that combine to cause a particular harm[115] or a more-than-sufficient number of individual affirmative votes under non-unanimity voting rules.[116]

My initial elaborations of the NESS account handled these situations by using subsets of existing conditions or 'at least so much' descriptions of an existing condition to construct minimally sufficient sets of existing conditions, for the sufficiency of which the inclusion of the non-independently-sufficient condi-

114 E.g. Fumerton and Kress (n.1) 96–97; Moore (n.1) 474. There is considerable disagreement over its ability to handle overdetermined *failure* of a causal process. See section 3.1 below.
115 Wright, Legal Responsibility (n.9) 1444–45; text to nn 10–11 and 40–41 above.
116 See Stapleton (n.1) 443.

tion was necessary.[117] Some critics have objected that doing so involves hypothetical, counterfactual reasoning – in particular, an assumption that the conditions not included in the described subset or the at-least-so-much nature of an included existing condition did not actually exist.[118] This is not true. The non-included existing conditions or greater-than-at-least-so-much nature of an included condition are simply 'roped off' while determining whether the described existing conditions constituted a minimally sufficient set. Indeed, I have always emphasised that one must double-check to make sure that the roped-off existing conditions or their roped-off nature did not prevent the complete instantiation of the antecedent of the relevant causal generalisation and its underlying causal laws.[119]

In any event, the objection to these methods of disaggregating existing conditions is mooted when the necessity aspect of the NESS account is confined, as it is in my later elaborations of the NESS account, to the relevant causal generalisations and their underlying causal laws. Under this simpler, more straightforward definition of a NESS condition, no disaggregation of existing conditions is necessary. A NESS condition need merely be part of the instantiation of one of the abstract conditions in the antecedent of an applicable causal law, all the conditions of which were at least minimally instantiated. It does not matter if some or all of them were more than minimally instantiated, although – I again emphasise – care must be taken to ensure that the more-than-minimal instantia-

---

117 Wright (n.5) 1792–94; Wright, Legal Responsibility (n.9) 1444–45; Wright, Once More (n.14) 1106–07; Wright (n.3) 1035–39. Fischer asserts that *Warren v Parkhurst* 92 NYS 725 (NY Sup Ct. 1904), affirmed 93 NYS 1009 (NY App Div 1905), affirmed 78 NE 579 (NY 1906), which I have used to illustrate judicial recognition of causation by conditions that were neither necessary nor independently strongly sufficient, is not a 'pure' example. Relying on the distinction between '[legal] injury' and '[actual] harm'—a distinction the *Warren* court did not make—Fischer argues that, although the pollution by each of the 26 defendants was neither necessary nor independently sufficient for the 'fixed threshold of stench' that constituted the required legal injury, each defendant's pollution was necessary for some separable part of the recoverable harm. Fischer (n.1) 285. He ignores the court's statements that each defendant's pollution by itself "would not cause any material change to the plaintiff by way of noxious smell" but rather would be "merely nominal" and would not support any liability.

118 Kelman (n.1) 603–04; D.A. Fischer, 'Causation in Fact in Omission Cases' (1992) *Utah Law Review* 1335, 1359, 1362; Fischer (n.1) 303–04, 307–08; Stapleton (n.85) 83–84.

119 E.g. Wright (n.13) 295–97; Wright, Legal Responsibility (n.9) 1444–45; Wright (n.3) 1035–37; see n.13 above. Strevens usefully discusses the difference between assuming the negation of some condition and simply setting it aside with no assumption as to whether or not it exists. Strevens (n.13) 96–97. Moore and Thomson recognise this distinction. Moore (n.1) 489–90; Thomson (n.1) 148, 156–59. Fischer and Stapleton do not. See Fischer (n.1) 303–04, 307–08; Stapleton (n.1) 472.

tion of some antecedent condition did not prevent the instantiation of some other antecedent condition.[120]

Moore acknowledges the validity and usefulness of the NESS account's ability to identify as causes conditions that were neither strongly necessary nor independently strongly sufficient, while also noting and criticising the consequent increased proliferation of causes.[121] David Fischer also objects to the proliferation of causes and questions the validity of recognising trivial contributions as causes – eg, a teaspoon of water added to a flooding river or a match added to a raging forest fire.[122] Yet the teaspoon of water and the match contributed to and are part of the flood and forest fire, respectively. What if the same flood or fire were caused by a million (or many more) different people all contributing a teaspoonful of water or a single match? Denying that any of the teaspoonfuls or matches contributed to the destruction of the property that was destroyed by the flood or fire would leave its destruction as an unexplained, noncaused miracle. As a pure matter of causation, it cannot possibly matter whose hands supplied the different bits of water, flame or fuel. What is driving the intuition of no causation is the judgment regarding attributable responsibility, which is especially brought to mind if the question is posed as "Did the teaspoon of water or match destroy the property?" rather than "Did the teaspoon of water or match contribute, even if only extremely minimally, to the flood or fire that destroyed the property?" What is generally agreed upon is that the trivial contributor should not be held liable when her contribution was trivial in comparison to the other contributing conditions and was neither strongly necessary nor independently strongly sufficient for the injury at issue, but this is a normative issue of attributable responsibility rather than causal contribution.[123]

Stapleton also acknowledges the validity and usefulness of this application of the NESS account, but she claims that I have failed to provide any reasons or justifications for it – or at least for the law's use of it – and have thereby (how?) made the NESS account 'incoherent'.[124] To the contrary, the reasons that Stapleton gives for endorsing it, and the NESS account as a whole as the proper 'algo-

120 See text to nn 40 – 41 above.

121 Moore (n.1) 487–91.

122 Fischer (n.1) 290 – 91; see Restatement Third (n.1) s.27 comment i (initially suggesting the correct causal analysis but then analogising these duplicative causation situations to quite different pre-emptive causation situations).

123 Restatement Third (n.1) s 36; Fischer (n.1) 289 – 90; Wright, Legal Responsibility (n.9) 1448 – 50 and fn.84.

124 Stapleton (n.1) 474 – 76.

rithm' for identifying causal 'involvement' or 'contribution',[125] are the same ones that I have repeatedly emphasised: the obvious need, in what is intended to be a comprehensive account of causation, to be able to identify all instances of causation, and the related need – especially in legal analysis – to distinguish the normative and context-specific purposive considerations that are often confused with the causation issue, which instead should be explicitly recognised, labelled and discussed as non-causal reasons for focusing on and attributing responsibility to only some of the many conditions that contributed to the occurrence of some consequence.[126]

It is Stapleton, rather than I, who has a history of failing to make this distinction.[127] Her failures have been encouraged by Fischer, who refuses to distinguish between causation as a purely scientific matter and attributable legal responsibility and instead seeks to have 'causal' judgments depend on intuitive judgments of legal responsibility, but who nevertheless ultimately agrees for practical reasons with the American Law Institute's finally making this distinction in the Restatement Third (after having confused students, lawyers and courts for deca-

125 Stapleton (n.1) 444, 474; Stapleton (n.93) 174. However, Stapleton's supposed elaboration of the NESS account differs greatly from that account by employing a doubly counterfactual 'duplicate necessity' analysis of strong necessity rather than a real-world analysis of causal sufficiency. She treats a condition as a cause if it would have been strongly necessary in the counterfactual world in which the condition(s) that prevented it from being strongly necessary in the real world did not exist. Stapleton (n.1) 433, 436, 441–44, 472–74, 479; J. Stapleton, 'Legal Cause: Cause-in-Fact and the Scope of Liability for Consequences' (2001) 54 *Vanderbilt Law Review* 941, 959–60; Stapleton (n.93) 175–85. This method of analysis, which unfortunately is adopted in s.27 of the Restatement Third, fails to distinguish duplicative causation from pre-emptive causation and is substantially over-inclusive and under-inclusive in both types of situation. See Restatement Third (n.1) s 27; Wright, Once More (n.14) 1110–15 and fn.149; Wright, Legal Responsibility (n.9) 1450–51 fn.86. The authors of the Restatement Third try to paper over these defects in comments that limit s.27 to duplicative causation situations, without providing any (non-viciously-circular) criteria for distinguishing the two types of situations, and that refer pre-emptive causation situations to supposed resolution by s.26's *sine qua non* test, which, however, cannot properly resolve pre-emptive causation situations. See Restatement Third (n.1) s.26 comment k, s.27 comments e and h. A recent case thus wisely moves past the blackletter sections of the Restatement Third to focus instead on the NESS-based 'causal sets' analysis that is employed in the comments to sections 26 and 27. *June v Union Carbide Corp* 577 F3d 1234, 1242–44 (10th Cir 2009); see Restatement Third (n.1) s.26 comments c, d, i and k, s.27 comments a, b, e, f, g, h and i, and related reporters' notes.

126 E.g. Wright (n.5) 1737–58, 1764 fn.121, 1781–83, 1791–92; Wright, Legal Responsibility (n.9) 1437–40; Wright, Once More (n.14) 1072–82, 1111, 1119–23; Wright (n.3) 1004–18; see Stapleton (n.1) 433, 441–42, 445–46, 455–58, 463–64, 473–77, 479–80; section 3.10 below.

127 See Stapleton, Legal Cause (n.125) 957 fn 38, 966–68 and fns 60 and 61; Stapleton (n.85) 61, 62–66 and fn.13, 77 fn.40, 79–80, 81–84; Wright, Once More (n.14) 1101 fn.108, 1111–13, 1119–23.

des by its failure to do so in the first and second Restatements).[128] Stapleton, while now claiming to support the distinction, instead abandons it and undercuts her primary argument – that the law should choose 'involvement' (as identified by the NESS 'algorithm') as the sole 'interrogation' regarding 'causation' in the law[129] – when she claims that there is no core empirical or metaphysical concept of causation, so that (as bluntly asserted by Lord Hoffmann at the conference at which the initial version of this chapter was presented), judges and others can and should define causation in any manner that suits their particular purposes:

> [Schaffer's attempt to provide an account of causation] is the same doomed concept of many other philosophers: a search for 'a broad and nondiscriminatory concept' of causation. In contrast to Schaffer's passing flirtation with the idea that such a concept might be 'a *philosopher's myth*,' the central argument of this article is that it is indeed a myth.[130]
>
> It is futile for philosophers to search for a coherent freestanding metaphysical account of 'causation' unless a choice of underlying interrogation (blame, explanation, physical role, any sort of involvement etc) is specified *at the outset.*[131]

Stapleton's seeming radical scepticism about there being any core concept of causation runs counter to her discussions of her concept of 'involvement', which she states is meant to encompass and be limited to the natural scientific relation that we call 'causation' and is determined objectively by reference to the physical laws of nature, excluding any normative considerations.[132] As she seems to recognise, all the other 'interrogations' (regarding blame, responsibility, contextual salience and so forth) that loosely employ causal language use this core

---

128 See Fischer (n.1) 284–92, 312–13, 317; Wright, Once More (n.14) 1074–80, 1121 fn.172.

129 Stapleton (n.1) 433, 441–44, 455, 473–74; see nn 125–26 above.

130 Stapleton (n.1) 439 fn 15 (quoting J.Schaffer, 'Contrastive Causation' (2005) 114 *Philosophical Review* 327, 350).

131 Stapleton (n.1) 439; 447 (same), 456 ('causal language can denote whatever we choose it to'), 459 (same).

132 Stapleton (n.1) 433–37, 444, 446, 452–53 and fn.45, 455, 474, 479–80. However, if by "physical laws of nature" Stapleton means the mathematical formulations of such laws, which do not incorporate the critical interrelated concepts of causal sufficiency and directionality, she is relying on the inadequate notion of mere lawful relation. See Collins, Hall and Paul, Introduction (n.9) 16, 34; text to nn 80–87 above. In a note, she refers to theoretical physicist Richard Feynman's description of physical laws in terms of 'the principle of least action' and restraints on and increasing entropy within a physical environment, but this is not a description that provides a basis for identification of singular instances of causation in law or ordinary life. See Stapleton (n.1) 440 fn.16 (citing R. Feynman, *The Character of Physical Law* (New York, Random House Modern Library, 1994) 46).

concept of causation but also use normative or other purposive or pragmatic considerations to focus on only some of the contributing conditions and to limit attribution of responsibility even for those contributing conditions.[133] While she often seems to argue otherwise,[134] the purposive considerations that determine the particular focus of the causal enquiry do not result in different concepts of causation being employed once the focus has been set.[135]

Stapleton's basic point seems to be that it is impossible to provide a comprehensive, non-circular account of this core concept of causation – even though she seems to assume that her concept of 'involvement' has succeeded in doing so. More specifically, she asserts that, although the NESS account (which she claims to employ and in tight spots does employ) is a very useful 'algorithm' for identifying all instances of 'involvement', it does not capture the essence or meaning of causation.[136] Yet, if, as she concedes,[137] the NESS account is able to identify all instances of causation (and its lack) given sufficient information about existing conditions and the relevant causal laws, hasn't it then (as she once stated[138]) captured the essence of causation and given it a comprehensive specification and meaning? Her claim that it has not seems to be based primarily on the charge that the NESS account, by referring to the interrelated concepts of 'causal sufficiency' and 'causal laws', engages in 'vicious conceptual circularity'[139] – a claim that I have rejected above,[140] but which applies to her own 'involvement' account.[141]

---

133 See Stapleton (n.1) 440–41, 444–46, 448–51, 455–64; Collins, Hall and Paul, Introduction (n.9) 36–37; Hall (n.14) 228–31; Fumerton and Kress (n.1) 87–88; Honoré (n.10) 7–49 to 7–53; Thomson (n.1) 160–63; Wright (n.5) 1741–50; Wright (n.3) 1011–14.

134 Stapleton (n.1) 437, 439–41 and fn 15, 444, 445–46, 447, 451, 476–77 and fn 149.

135 Wright (n.5) 1788–1803.

136 Stapleton (n.1) 472–74 and fn 145, 477; *contra* Honoré (n.1) 367 (treating the NESS account as capturing the meaning of natural causation as well as being a useful test for identifying natural causes).

137 Stapleton (n.1) 444, 474.

138 Stapleton (n.93) 174, 179.

139 Stapleton (n.1) 472–73 and fn 145.

140 See nn 25–34 above.

141 Stapleton asserts that her use of the term 'involvement' "avoid[s] circular causal terminology". Stapleton (n.1) 436. Yet not only does 'involvement' imply causal contribution, she explicitly defines 'involvement' as 'contribution' in her delineation of her three forms of 'involvement', states that 'involvement' is determined through our knowledge of "the physical laws of nature", for which she provides no usable definition or elaboration, and endorses the NESS account, with its allegedly circular reliance on causal laws, as the proper 'algorithm' for identifying all three forms of involvement. Stapleton (n.1) 433–37, 441–44, 446, 452–53 and fn.45, 472–74, 479–80; text to n.125 above.

3.6 Reasons as Causes

The NESS account's ability to identify conditions that were neither strongly necessary nor independently strongly sufficient as causes applies to and is especially useful for accounting for human decisions and actions, which often are based on multiple reasons, none of which may have been – or can be proven to have been – strongly necessary or independently strongly sufficient for the particular decision or action.[142]

Hart and Honoré acknowledge that loose generalisations apply to human decisions and actions, but they deny that these decisions and actions are governed by causal laws. They point out that it is not practically possible to specify all the conditions sufficient to produce a certain decision, and they deny that the same decision or action necessarily would be taken in the same situation by the same person at different times or by different persons at the same or different times.[143]

The first point is true, but it does not differentiate human decisions and actions from other causal processes. We can and do make plausible singular causal statements based on incomplete knowledge of the causal laws that underlie the causal generalisations that we employ.[144]

The second point also is true, but it is true only because all the relevant conditions are not the same. As Honoré notes, even for the same person, there is the additional information provided by the similar past experience.[145] There also is the additional information provided by other intermediate experiences, other sources of new knowledge, and possibly different decision criteria due to, eg, changed goals and attitudes towards risk. Two different persons have different experiences, genetic makeup and goals.

Honoré agrees that attributions of reasons for decisions or actions involve a belief that the (known and unknown) reasons in the aggregate were sufficient (along with other relevant conditions) for the decision or action, although none of them may have been strongly necessary or independently strongly sufficient. He treats such reasons as "necessary elements in a set of reasons together sufficient" for the relevant decision,[146] and he cites with apparent approval my

---

142 Wright (n.13) 297–98; Wright (n.3) 1035–37. Stapleton ignores these sources when she asserts that "Wright does not adequately address ... whether it is coherent, acceptable, convenient or wise notionally to disaggregate an individual person's decision". Stapleton (n.1) 476.
143 Hart and Honoré (n.5) xxxvii, 2, 22–23, 55–61; Honoré (n.1) 363, 382, 384; Honoré (n.10) 7–53, 7–168.
144 See text to nn 35–39 above.
145 Honoré (n.1) 382.
146 Honoré (n.1) 383.

application of the NESS account to such reasons.[147] However, he claims that the sense of sufficiency is different than for physical sequences.[148] The difference he seems to have in mind is the alleged lack of repeatability in the same circumstances, but this is contrary to the assumed sufficiency of the set of conditions, including reasons, on the particular occasion. As I have previously noted, if all the relevant conditions were jointly sufficient in the first instance, they will also be jointly sufficient in subsequent instances involving the same set of relevant conditions:[149]

> [I]f *all* the relevant conditions (accumulated experience and knowledge, beliefs, goals, mood, and so forth) were the same, surely the decision or action would also be the same. To assert otherwise is to assert that human action is random or arbitrary. Human action is less regular and predictable than physical events because humans learn from prior experiences and new information, the range of relevant conditions is much broader, and the applicable causal generalizations are much more complex and less well understood.[150]

The fact that the applicable causal generalisations and the underlying causal laws for human decisions are much more complex and less well understood than those for physical events often makes it especially difficult to determine what decision a person would have made if she had been provided with some information or opportunity that was not provided. In a recent essay, I erroneously stated that we need to have this question answered, and thus must use (highly restricted) counterfactual analysis, to resolve the causal issue in situations in which the defendant tortiously failed to provide some safeguard (information or device), which if provided and used would have prevented the injury that occurred.[151] The causal issue in such situations involving the failure of a preventive causal process instead should be resolved, without any counterfactual analysis, by using the method of analysis that is discussed in sections 3.8 and 3.9 below.

As is discussed in section 3.1, the lack of an attempt to access and use a safeguard pre-empts the potential failure of the preventive causal process (involving the successful use of the safeguard) at the subsequent stage in that process,

147 Honoré (n.1) 377 fn.40 (citing Wright (n.3) 1035–37).
148 Honoré (n.1) 383–85; see Honoré (n.10) 7–121.
149 Although Mackie argues for strong necessity rather than strong sufficiency when identifying singular instances of causation, see text to nn 19–22 above and nn 156–58 below, he agrees that there is a single basic concept of natural causation that applies equally to physical events and human decisions and actions. Mackie (n.9) 122–26.
150 Wright (n.13) 298.
151 Wright (n.13) 301–02; see V. Black, 'Decision Causation: Pandora's Tool-Box' in J. Neyers, E. Chamberlain and S.G.A. Pitel (eds), *Emerging Issues in Tort Law* (Oxford, Hart Publishing, 2007) 309.

never reached, in which the attempt would have failed due to the non-provision of the safeguard. However, the non-provision of the safeguard nevertheless was a cause of the non-prevented injury if (unlike the braking situation discussed in section 3.1) the lack of an attempt to use the safeguard was caused by its non-provision – for example, by knowledge of its non-provision or, conversely, by lack of knowledge of its possible availability due to its non-provision.

As in other overdetermined causation situations, the causal issue in these non-provided-safeguard situations unfortunately is often confused with the 'no worse off' limitation on attributable responsibility, which generally treats the defendant as not being legally responsible for an injury, despite having tortiously contributed to its occurrence, if the injury would have happened anyway due to non-liability-generating conditions – for example, if a plaintiff (who cannot sue himself) would not have used the information or safeguard even if it had been provided.[152] To resolve this attributable responsibility issue in these and other pre-emptive causation situations, (highly restricted) counterfactual analysis will be required.

Treating human decisions, like other biologically based mental processes, as subject to causal laws is not incompatible with a plausible conception of free will, given the very complex, goal-directed nature of human decision-making. Indeed, to treat human decisions as not being subject to causal laws would imply that they are arbitrary and irrational, rather than free in the sense of being based on one's interests and goals. On the other hand, as I will explain in the next section, the presence of a random or probabilistic element in human decision-making would not undermine the concept of causation or make it impossible to provide causal explanations of human decisions and actions.

3.7 Indeterminism and 'Probabilistic Causation'[153]

In a radically indeterministic world, in which nothing was (weakly or strongly) necessary or sufficient for anything else, the concepts of causation and probability likely would not exist due to lack of instantiation. Our world is at most only partially indeterministic – that is, probabilistic. A great many apparently probabilistic processes appear to be so only because we have insufficient knowledge of the underlying causal laws and turn out on closer examination to be determin-

152 See Wright, Legal Responsibility (n.9) 1434–78.

153 Portions of this section are taken, with minor modifications, from Wright (n.3) 1028–31.

istic.[154] As far as we know all apparently indeterministic processes may be deterministic. As Mackie stated, the difficulty one encounters in trying to describe truly indeterministic statistical 'laws of working' reinforces doubt about their existence. Such a law would seem to require an objective chance or propensity inherent in each individual occurrence of the antecedent conditions, but one can deny the existence of such objective entities with arguments similar to those used to deny the existence of objective causal qualities or powers in deterministic processes. Mackie concluded that the only workable formulation would be a limiting frequency on actual outcomes of a series of instances of a certain set of antecedent conditions. Yet, he noted, this formulation deprives such statistical laws of explanatory power. There is no apparent way to explain, without invoking deterministic laws, why an actual series does or should approach a limiting frequency. Truly indeterministic or probabilistic laws, therefore, are unintelligible and mysterious.[155]

However, Mackie and others have used the theoretical possibility of partially indeterministic processes to argue against the universal applicability of a strong-sufficiency account of causation and, indeed, for the preferability of the *sine qua non* account. Mackie postulates a candy machine L that never produces candy unless a shilling is inserted, but sometimes, due to indeterminism, does not produce candy even when a shilling is inserted. He assumes that this means that the insertion of a shilling in machine L is strongly necessary but not strongly sufficient for the machine's production of candy, and that, since whenever candy is produced we will treat the strongly necessary condition of the insertion of the shilling as a cause, strong sufficiency is not necessary for causation, but strong necessity is.[156]

154 See Mackie (n.9) 49–50, 76, 237–38, 242–46.
155 Mackie (n.9) 239–47; see Wright (n.3) 1029, 1042–49. Some believe that the notion of deterministic causation collapsed with the announcement in 1927 of Heisenberg's uncertainty principle. That principle, even if valid, merely states that it is impossible to measure simultaneously the position and velocity of an object so that the product of the uncertainties in measurement is less than an infinitesimally small constant—about 10 to the minus 34th power joule-seconds. 10 *Encyclopaedia Britannica, Micropaedia,*15th edn (1979) 253. While this might cause problems in hypothetical lawsuits between subatomic particles, it creates no problems at the macroscopic level of events in everyday life. Others believe that the notion of causation collapsed with the introduction of functional equations in science. Yet functional relationships in science are merely mathematically quantified statements of causal laws or generalisations, which usually are expressed through time-based derivatives of the regularities of succession that constitute ordinary causal generalisations. Mackie (n.9) 143–48, 153–54, 216–18. The concept of causation is alive and well in the natural and social sciences.
156 Mackie (n.9) 41–43.

Fumerton and Kress make the same argument using a similar example: a bomb activated by the indeterministic decay of a radioactive element, which has a very low probability of going off during the intended victim's lifetime but which nevertheless does go off a few minutes after being planted and kills the intended victim. However, countering Mackie, they note that even the *sine qua non* account will not properly identify the decay-activated bomb as a cause if there was a backup deterministically activated bomb.[157]

Mackie, Fumerton and Kress incorrectly assume that there is a lack of strong sufficiency in these examples. They seem to assume that the planting of the bomb or the insertion of the shilling must be sufficient all by itself – a situation that is rarely if ever true. The planting of the bomb or the insertion of the shilling need only be one of the conditions that are each necessary for the sufficiency of the set of conditions that constitutes the antecedent of the relevant causal law. Another of those conditions in each example is the occurrence of the specified indeterministic state or event: the decay of the radioactive element in the bomb or the unknown indeterministic state or event in the candy machine, respectively. When the bomb explodes or the machine produces candy, the planting of the bomb or the insertion of the shilling, respectively, was both strongly necessary and strongly sufficient for the occurrence of that result, as was the occurrence of the relevant indeterministic state or event.

Mackie's other candy machine hypothetical demonstrates, contrary to what he intended, that causation requires causal (rather than merely lawful) strong sufficiency rather than strong necessity. This machine, M, always produces candy when a shilling is inserted, but occasionally, as a result of some mysterious indeterministic process, produces candy even though no shilling was inserted. Mackie assumes that the insertion of a shilling in machine M is strongly sufficient but not strongly necessary for the production of candy. He asserts that when candy is produced by machine M following the insertion of a shilling, we will be unable to say whether the production of the candy by machine M was caused by the insertion of the shilling or by the indeterministic process. He concludes that strong sufficiency is not sufficient to establish causation; rather, strong necessity is required.[158]

Yet, when candy is produced after a shilling is inserted in machine M, we know by definition that the insertion of the shilling produced the candy through the deterministic process, if the insertion of a shilling is *causally* strongly sufficient for the production of candy. What we do not know is whether the probabil-

157 Fumerton and Kress (n.1) 97–98.
158 Mackie (n.9) 41–43.

istic event and its associated indeterministic process also occurred, since we have no knowledge of and cannot directly observe the probabilistic event or its associated indeterministic process. If the probabilistic event did not occur, the candy was produced solely by the deterministic process. If the probabilistic event did occur, then either the candy was duplicatively produced by both the deterministic and the indeterministic processes (if the probabilistic event also was causally strongly sufficient) or else the candy was produced solely by the deterministic process, which pre-empted the indeterministic process. Thus, no matter what happened with the indeterministic process, the insertion of the shilling was a (duplicative or pre-emptive) cause of the production of the candy.

This conclusion is logically compelled by the definition of causal strong sufficiency, if the insertion of a shilling is causally strongly sufficient for the production of candy in machine M. If that assumption is removed, so that we only have the empirical observation that machine M produces candy whenever a shilling is inserted, but sometimes produces candy although nothing was inserted, then Mackie is right when he insists that we cannot say on any particular occasion that the insertion of the shilling was a cause of the production of the candy. In the absence of the causal strong sufficiency assumption, it is possible that the deterministic process initiated by the insertion of the shilling was pre-empted by the indeterministic process. But this reinforces the argument that causation requires causal strong sufficiency. When we assumed that causal strong sufficiency existed, we were compelled to conclude that the insertion of the shilling caused the production of the candy. When we dropped the causal strong sufficiency assumption, we no longer could identify the cause(s) of the candy's production.

In sum, Mackie's indeterministic machine hypotheticals, and others like them,[159] demonstrate the reverse of what he claims. They demonstrate that attributions of causation, even in a partially indeterministic world, depend on the causal strong sufficiency requirement embodied in the NESS account rather than the strong necessity requirement embodied in the *sine qua non* account.

159 See e.g., Collins, Hall and Paul, Introduction (n.9) 26–27. Their examples nicely illustrate the defectiveness of attempts to define causation in terms of increased probability. See also Wright (n.3) 1042–49.

3.8 Omissions and Negative Causation

We routinely identify omissions, such as the failure to water a plant or to pay attention while driving, as causes of some result, such as the death of the plant or a traffic accident, respectively. However, there is reason to question whether omissions or other negative conditions can actually be causes or effects. As John Stuart Mill, who provided the philosophical foundation of the NESS account, observed, "From nothing, from a mere negation, no consequences can proceed".[160] Mill nevertheless saw the need to include negative conditions as causal (NESS) conditions:

> We say for example, The army was surprised because the sentinel was off his post. But since the sentinel's absence was not what created the enemy or put the soldiers asleep, how did it cause them to be surprised? All that is really meant is, that event would not have happened if he had been at his duty. His being off his post was no producing cause, but the mere absence of a preventing cause: it was simply equivalent to his non-existence. From nothing, from a mere negation, no consequences can proceed. All effects are connected, by the law of causation, with some set of *positive* conditions; negative ones, it is true, being almost always required in addition. In other words, every fact or phenomenon which has a beginning invariably arises when some certain combination of positive facts exists, provided certain other positive facts do not exist….
>
> The cause, then, philosophically speaking, is the sum total of the conditions positive and negative taken together; the whole of the contingencies of every description, which being realised, the consequent invariably follows. The negative conditions, however, of any phenomenon, a special enumeration of which would generally be very prolix, may be all summed up under one head, namely, the absence of preventing or countervailing causes.[161]

In this passage, Mill draws two important distinctions, without clearly distinguishing them or clarifying the precise nature of the second distinction. The first distinction is between 'positive' conditions and 'negative' conditions; the second distinction is between a 'producing' or 'positive' cause and a 'non-producing' or 'negative' cause. There seems to be general agreement on the first distinction: a 'positive' condition is the presence of some act, event or entity in a particular situation; a 'negative' condition is the absence of some act, event or entity in a particular situation. There is less agreement on the existence and nature of the second distinction.[162] I consider the distinction to be as follows: a

---

160 Mill (n.5) bk III ch.V s.3.

161 Mill (n.5) bk III ch.V s.3.

162 Jonathan Schaffer describes 'positive' causation as a 'physical connection' through transmission of some physical entity, structure or 'mark' between a cause and the consequence, 'producing' or 'positive' cause is a NESS condition that is connected to the consequence at issue by a causal process in which each step in the process has a positive condition as its consequence; a 'negative' cause is a NESS condition that is connected to the consequence at issue by a causal process in which at least one of the steps in the process has a negative condition as its consequence.

Many philosophers believe that a negative condition cannot be a positive cause, but rather, at best, can only be a negative cause.[163] Some argue that negative conditions cannot be part of any plausible account of reality and thus cannot be any sort of cause. Moore is most insistent on this point. He notes, correctly, that there are no negative conditions in the sense of the negative opposite of a positive condition, for example non-tramplings by non-elephants. Rather, a negative condition must be understood to be the absence of some positive condition, rather than the 'ghostly' reality of its negative opposite.[164] Moore and others agree that propositions about the absence of some positive condition can be included as NESS conditions in laws. However, Moore notes, again correctly, that such propositions, being mere abstractions rather than aspects of reality, cannot be concrete *instantiations* of the abstract conditions in causal laws and thus cannot enter into causal relations as causes or effects.[165]

---

without the involvement of any negative conditions, and 'negative causation' as counterfactual dependency of the consequence on the cause in the absence of any such physical connection. J. Schaffer, 'Causes need not be Physically Connected to their Effects: The Case for Negative Causation' in C. Hitchcock (ed.), *Contemporary Debates in Philosophy of Science* (Oxford, Blackwell, 2004) 197, 203–04, 214. Ned Hall makes a similar distinction between 'production' and 'dependence' as two different concepts or kinds of causation. His concept of 'production' focuses on the spatio-temporal contiguity and 'intrinsicness' (internal structure) of the causal process rather than physical transmission of some entity. Hall (n.14) 225–27, 253–54.

163 E.g. Hall (n.14) 253, 260; Schaffer 162) 197–98; Thomson (n.1) 163 fn.12.

164 E.g. Moore (n.1) 53–55, 399–400, 444–45, 460–61.

165 Moore (n.1) 303–04, 347–48, 351–53, 445, 461, 479. David Lewis agrees, but nevertheless treats absences as causes:

"Absences are bogus entities. Yet the proposition that an absence occurs is not bogus.... And it is by way of just such propositions, and only by way of such propositions, that absences enter into patterns of counterfactual dependence.... Should we conclude, then, that when we say absences are causes, really it is true negative propositions that do the causing?—No; in other cases, we distinguish between the cause itself and the true proposition that describes it.... [T]he proposition is a necessary being, 'abstract' in one sense of that multifariously ambiguous term, and doesn't cause anything.... I refuse to concede that facts—true propositions—are literally causes. So I have to say that when an absence is a cause or an effect, there is strictly speaking nothing at all that is a cause or effect. Sometimes causation is not a relation, because a relation needs relata and sometimes the causal relata go missing." Lewis (n.53) 100.

What Moore refuses to acknowledge is that the absence of some positive condition *is* an aspect of reality, a *fact* that makes the relevant proposition true or false, [166] that is as much a part of the real, existing state of affairs on a particular occasion as are the positive conditions in existence on that occasion.[167] Indeed, negative conditions often are positive or producing causes rather than negative causes, through the perception of the negative condition by a sentient being. For example, the absence of a salute by a soldier is a positive cause of an officer's perception of that absence and the consequent disciplining of the soldier, a baseball player's failure to touch a base is a positive cause of an umpire's perception of that failure and the consequent ruling that the player is out, the absence of a stop sign or signal is a positive cause of a motorist's perception of that absence and the motorist's consequent proceeding through the intersection with his foot pushing down on the accelerator, and the absence of a poison label on a container is a positive cause of a consumer's perception of that absence and consequent drinking, ingestion or handling of the contents of the container.[168]

Negative conditions also can be and often are effects. Indeed, a refusal to recognise negative conditions as effects makes it impossible to account for what is probably the most paradigmatic instance of an effect, to which Moore

---

166 I use 'fact' in the sense of a part of reality, a concrete property of a state of affairs, what Moore refers to as 'facta' to avoid confusing this sense with the different sense (that e. g. Ned Hall and David Lewis have in mind) of a true proposition about reality. See Hall (n.14) 254; Lewis (n.53) 100; Moore (n.1) 333, 341–47. It is not clear to me which sense Judith Thomson has in mind. See Thomson (n.1) 148, 150.

167 Moore (n.1) 352. At one point (only), to preserve his criticism of the NESS account's recognition of omissions as causes, Moore acknowledges that abstract negative conditions can be instantiated:

"When [NESS and other strong-sufficiency theorists] are asking after the truth makers for the negative conditions in laws, they are not looking for negative tokens of negative types. Rather, the truth-maker for negative conditions is the absence of any positive instances of some type. The law is 'instantiated' in this sense whenever its negative conditions are made true by the world. In that sense, negative conditions can be 'instantiated', and so omissions will be causes." Moore (n.1) 479.

168 Wright (n.13) 291; cf. Collins, Hall and Paul, Introduction (n.9) 48 ("Billy's failure to show up for their lunch date causes Suzy to become disappointed"); Schaffer (n.162) 201 ("One can perceive black holes or any other black entity, which is merely an absence of radiated light energy"). The same cognitive processes, which are limited and often biased, are involved in the perception of positive as well as negative conditions. A good example is the well-known optical illusion in which one sees either an old hag or a young, beautiful woman when looking at the drawing or picture of the woman, but never both at the same time.

repeatedly adverts: death. Although Moore argues otherwise,[169] death as an event is a transition between a positive condition, being alive (with a functioning heart or brain, depending on one's preferred definition) to a negative condition, the absence of life – which, unfortunately, for each of us is an ultimately certain real state of affairs. The relevant positive causal processes for the maintenance of life, at least as we know it, include as necessary positive conditions the presence of sufficient amounts of water, oxygen (for humans and other complex animals) and certain nutrients. The negative condition of an absence of the required amount of water, oxygen or nutrients, or of the blood that transports oxygen and nutrients to the brain and other parts of the body, is a negative cause of the negative condition of death (the absence of life).

As Jonathan Schaffer demonstrates, to deny that negative conditions participate in causation (generally but not always as negative causes or effects) is to blind oneself to the layers of the causal web and, more significantly, to deny that humans ever cause anything:

> The pattern of negative causation features in even the most *paradigmatically causal* cases. Suppose that the sniper feels murderous, pulls the trigger, fires a bullet through the victim's heart, and the victim dies. Here is a paradigmatic causal sequence, *every step of which* is negative causation.
>
> Working backwards, *surely* the firing of the bullet through the victim's heart causes the victim to die. But heart damage only causes death by negative causation: heart damage (*c*) causes an absence of oxygenated blood flow to the brain (~*d*), which causes the cells to starve (*e*) [and die]. ....
>
> At the next step backwards, *surely* the pulling of the trigger causes the bullet to fire. But trigger pullings only cause bullet firings by negative causation: pulling the trigger (*c*) causes the removal of the sear from the spring (~*d*), which causes the spring to uncoil, thereby compressing the gunpowder and causing an explosion, which causes the bullet to fire (*e*). ....
>
> At the third and final step backwards, *surely* the sniper's feeling murderous causes him to pull the trigger. But nerve signals only cause muscle contractions (such as that of the sniper's trigger finger) by negative causation: the firing of the nerve (*c*) causes a calcium cascade through the muscle fiber, which causes calcium-troponin binding, which causes the removal of [the inibitor] tropomyosin from the binding sites on the actin (~*d*), which causes myocin-actin binding, and thereby causes the actin to be pulled in and the muscle to contract (*e*). ....

169 E.g. Moore (n.1) 442 ("Dying is also a presence, even if it can be described as 'not surviving', and surviving is an absence, even if it sounds like it is referring to some actual state of affairs"); Moore (n.1) ibid 53–55, 303.

> Since all voluntary human actions are due to muscle contractions, it therefore follows that *all voluntary human actions* (perhaps the most paradigmatic of all causes) involve negative causation.[170]

As Schaffer's example illustrates, acts and other positive conditions often are negative causes. Acts of shooting, stabbing, strangling, removal of water or food, etc cause the negative condition of the absence of life by causing the negative condition of the absence of one or more of the necessary conditions (water, oxygen, nutrients, blood etc) for the positive causal process of maintaining life. Acts as well as omissions also cause positive conditions through negative causation, by preventing a positive causal process that would have prevented the occurrence of the positive condition. For example, the act of removing a safety device or damaging it so that it no longer works results in the same negative state of affairs – the lack of a working safety device, which if present and working would have prevented some injury – that exists if there is no working safety device in the first place. The act of removing the top X feet from a dam results in the same negative state of affairs – the lack of adequate height of the dam, which if present would have prevented a flood – that exists if the dam initially lacked those X feet of height.[171]

Thus, the critical distinction for purposes of causal analysis is not the distinction between positive conditions (eg, acts) and negative conditions (eg, omissions), but rather between positive causation and negative causation. This distinction is critical because the analysis of each type of causation, although based on the same underlying (NESS) account of causation, differs owing to their differing focus. A negative condition, eg, being dead, is the absence of a positive condition, eg, being alive. Such absences exist owing to the lack of oc-

---

170 Schaffer (n.162) 199–200; see 202 ("Biologists routinely invoke negative causation, such as in explaining diseases. What causes scurvy is an absence of vitamin D, what causes diabetes milletus is an absence of insulin, and what causes dwarfism is an absence of growth hormone, and so on. The way in which HIV causes death is by disconnecting the immune system"). Schaffer notes that "negative causation is supported by all the central conceptual connotations of causation, including counterfactual, statistical, agential, evidential, explanatory, and moral connotations". Schaffer (n.162) 202; see 198–203; D. Fair, 'Causation and the flow of energy' (1979) 14 *Erkenntnis* 219, 248 (noting that a shadow is an absence of light and that "ice on the road caused the auto accident because the road failed to transmit its usual frictional force to the tires").

171 Wright (n.13) 291–92. Negative causation by acts or other positive conditions is often referred to as 'prevention'—simple 'prevention' when the consequence is a negative condition and 'double prevention' when the consequence is a positive condition that occurred because the act prevented the occurrence of a causal process that, if not prevented, would have prevented the occurrence of the consequence. See Hall (n.14) 241; Moore (n.1) 54, 62, 130–31, 303, 459–61.

currence of the positive causal process(es) that would have produced the relevant positive conditions. Thus, while the analysis of positive causation focuses on the successful completion of the relevant positive causal process(es), the analysis of negative causation focuses on the failure of a positive causal process. To know that a positive causal process succeeded, we need to know that all of the necessary conditions in the antecedents of the relevant causal generalisations and their underlying causal laws were instantiated on the particular occasion. To know how one or more of them was instantiated, we need to go one or more levels deeper in the causal web. To know that a positive causal process failed, we need know that at least one of the necessary conditions in the antecedents of the relevant causal generalisations and their underlying causal laws was not instantiated. To know what caused its failure we need to know at what point it failed and go one or more levels deeper in the causal web to find out why it failed at that point.

As Mill noted, for any particular positive causal process, there are a multitude of possible preventing causes that could prevent its successful completion by preventing the instantiation of one of its necessary antecedent conditions. Mill's omnibus negative condition – the absence of any preventing cause – encompasses all the different possibilities, a listing of which is practically impossible.[172] If all the necessary conditions (which may include negative conditions)[173] for the positive causal process were fully specified, there perhaps would be no need to engage in any analysis of negative causation, since the instantiation of all of the fully specified necessary conditions would be inconsistent with the existence of any preventing cause. However, such a complete listing of all the necessary conditions is rarely if ever possible in practice. Mill's omnibus negative condition – the absence of any preventing cause – partially fills the gap, while also serving the useful purpose of emphasising the importance of always considering the possible existence of preventing causes.

172 See text to n.161 above. Moore properly criticises me for some 'incautious' references to this omnibus negative condition when engaging in some specific causal analyses, while generously granting that I do not place much reliance on it. Moore (n.1) 492, 494. In each of the cited analyses, I relied instead on non-instantiation of a specific necessary condition in the positive causal process. See Wright (n.5) 1795; Wright, Once More (n.14) 1129–30; text to nn 88, 95–96 above.

173 See text to n.168 above.

3.9 Overdetermined Negative Causation

Philosophers, including those who reject counterfactual dependency analyses of positive causation, generally believe that counterfactual dependency analysis is required for situations involving negative causation.[174] Yet, as with overdetermined positive causation, counterfactual dependency (*sine qua non*, 'but for', 'made a difference') analysis will not properly resolve situations involving overdetermined negative causation.

Philosophers have discussed a 'pre-emptive pre-emption' example in which a ball is thrown towards a window, is caught by B before it reaches the window and breaks it, but would have been caught by C, who was standing behind B with her arm raised to catch the ball, if B had not caught it. Neither B's nor C's conduct is a necessary condition for ('made a difference' with respect to) the window's not being broken, since the conduct of the other person guaranteed the ball's being stopped before it reached and broke the window. Nevertheless, when people are asked who prevented the ball's reaching and breaking the window, they almost always say B did. However, if C is replaced by a brick wall that would have stopped the ball if B had not caught it, many people's first reaction is that B did not prevent the ball's reaching the window, presumably because the fact that it would never have reached the window anyway is much more obvious although no more certain than in the original hypothetical. Yet, if they are then asked to identify who or what did prevent the ball's reaching the window, people again usually choose B. The options 'neither B nor the wall' and 'both B and the wall' are quickly ruled out, and choosing the wall

174 E.g. Hall (n.14) 248–53; Lewis (n.45) 281–85; Schaffer (n.162) 197, 214. Schaffer assumes this even though, when criticising Phil Dowe, he makes use of the fact that the counterfactual-dependency analysis cannot properly resolve situations involving overdetermined negative causation. Schaffer (n.162) 212–13. Surprisingly, Schaffer ignores overdetermined positive as well as negative causation when he states that even positive causation requires counterfactual dependency. Schaffer (n.162) 214. David Armstrong follows Dowe in using counterfactual dependency to provide an account of negative causes and effects as 'parasitic' on positive causation, without however accepting counterfactual dependency as an analysis of causation. D.M. Armstrong, 'Going through the Open Door Again: Counterfactual versus Singularist Theories of Causation' in Collins, Hall and Paul (n.9) 445, 447–49. Even Moore, despite all of his criticisms of counterfactual dependency analysis, uses it as a 'non-causal' basis for attributing moral and legal responsibility to what I and others call negative causes. Moore (n.1) 144, 302–05, 353, 451–53, 458–60.

is implausible given that the ball never reached the wall. This leaves B as the only plausible answer.[175]

B is also the correct answer in both versions of the example. As in the similar examples of pre-emptive overdetermined positive causation, eg, the destruction by fire A of a house that would have been destroyed anyway by the subsequent arrival of fire B, refusing to treat B's catching the ball as the cause of the ball's not reaching the window or, worse, choosing C or the wall as a pre-emptive or duplicative cause, confuses strong necessity or lawful strong sufficiency (guaranteeing an outcome), respectively, with causal strong sufficiency (actually causing the outcome). Although C's backstopping B or the presence of the wall guaranteed that the ball would stop its forward motion before it reached the window, and thus prevented B's catching the ball from 'making a difference' in the ball's not reaching the window, neither condition was guaranteed to be the actual cause of the ball's stopping, and neither condition actually stopped the ball. Instead, B's catching the ball stopped it. C or the wall would have stopped the ball, but only at a later and further point, which the ball did not reach, in the ball's movement towards the window. All of this is true even if the wall or C was in place, guaranteeing the ball's failure to reach the window, prior to B's arrival on the scene.[176]

This example illustrates the critical difference in the proper method of analysing positive causation and negative causation when there is causal overdetermination. In situations involving positive causation, we need to determine whether each possibly applicable positive causal process was fully instantiated. Only those that were fully instantiated in each step of the process were causes; the rest were pre-empted. Since the focus is on complete instantiation of every step in the process, not much attention needs to be paid to the sequencing of the steps. However, when analysing overdetermined negative causation, it is critically important to focus on the sequencing of the steps in the positive causal process that failed, in order to determine at which step it failed. As courts generally correctly hold, the failure at that step pre-empted any potential failure at subsequent steps, the occurrence of which is dependent on successful completion of all the prior steps.[177] In the thrown ball example, the positive causal process that failed requires, among other necessary conditions, the ball's continuing

---

175 M. McDermott, 'Redundant Causation' (1995) 43 *British Journal for the Philosophy of Science* 523, 525; see Collins (n.69) 107; Lewis (n.53) 102–03; T. Maudlin, 'Causation, Counterfactuals, and the Third Factor' in Collins, Hall and Paul (n.9) 419, 435–38.

176 See Wright (n.13) 298–300, 305; text to nn 84–96 above.

177 See Wright (n.13) 302–05; Wright, Once More (n.14) 1123–31; text at nn 152 and following n.171 above.

to move at each point along its line of travel in the direction of the window with sufficient speed to reach the window. The failure of the ball to continue along this line at the point where B caught the ball pre-empted its potential failure at the subsequent point along the line where C or the wall was located, which it never reached.[178]

One of the most discussed examples of overdetermined negative causation in the legal literature is the *Saunders* case, in which a vehicular collision occurred when a motorist driving a rental car did not attempt to brake until it was too late to avoid the collision, but the brakes were defective owing to a lack of proper inspection and maintenance by the rental car company and therefore would not have stopped the car in time even if the driver had applied them earlier.[179] Assume that there were two defects in the braking system: the lack of a bolt connecting the brake pedal to the lever rod between it and the master cylinder and the lack of sufficient hydraulic fluid in the master cylinder. There is considerable disagreement whether the defects in the brakes (for which the rental company's lack of proper inspection and maintenance was a negative cause), the driver's failure to attempt to use the brakes, neither, or both was a cause of the accident.

I have argued that the driver's failure to attempt to use the brakes was a negative cause of the collision, which pre-empted the potential negative causal effect of the defects in the brakes. David Fischer rightly criticised my initial analysis for making conclusory statements without elaborating (or, admittedly, clearly seeing) the distinct methods of analysis required for negative causation (which involves the failure of a positive causal process) and positive causation (which involves the successful completion of a positive causal process).[180] Fischer's criticism forced me to focus on and elaborate the distinction between these two types of causation and the distinct methods of analysis (both based on the

---

178 John Collins, confusing both guarantees and counterfactual dependency with causation, is "very reluctant" to say that B's catching the ball prevented the ball from breaking the window in the wall version of the hypothetical: "Given that the wall was there, the window was never in any danger of being broken. The presence of the wall really does seem to make [B's] catch irrelevant." Collins (n.69) 108. To persuade others of his position, Collins offers a third version of the hypothetical in which the Earth's gravitational force replaces the wall and the window is replaced by a point one hundred million miles from the Earth. However, this third version is critically different. Unlike the first two versions, Collins is assuming that the ball lacked sufficient speed when it was released to reach the stated end point. The lack of sufficient speed when it was released caused the failure of the positive causal process of the ball's reaching that very distant point the instant the ball was released and thus pre-empted the potential negative causal effect on that process of B's subsequent catching of the ball.

179 *Saunders System Birmingham Co v Adams* 117 So 72 (Alabama, 1928).

180 Fischer (n.118) 1357–59, criticising Wright (n.5) 1801.

NESS account) that are required for proper resolution of each, which I have restated above.[181]

The analysis of the failure of the braking-stops-car causal process is the same as in the thrown ball example. The braking process is a complex combination of a large number of more discrete causal processes, each of which is dependent for its occurrence on the occurrence of prior steps in the causal sequence. Some of the necessary events, in order of occurrence, are: (1) the driver's applying force to depress the brake pedal; (2) the depression of the brake pedal operating a lever to put pressure on the hydraulic brake fluid in the master cylinder; (3) the pressure in the brake fluid being transmitted through pipes and tubes to the brake cylinders; (4) the pressure in the brake cylinders pushing braking pads against the rotating brake drum or disc in the wheel assembly; and (5) the friction created by such contact slowing and stopping the rotation of the wheels. Each of these steps in the braking process, which occur in sequence, is itself a causal process; each has its own set of necessary antecedent conditions, mostly related to the structure and integrity of the mechanical, hydraulic and electrical components of the various parts of the braking system.

The failure of any step in the braking process prevents that process from progressing any further in the sequence of dependent events. It thus pre-empts the potential negative causal effect of any non-instantiated conditions in subsequent steps, which would have caused the braking process to fail if it had progressed that far. In *Saunders*, when the very first step in the braking process, the driver's depressing the brake pedal, does not occur, the braking process fails – actually never gets started – at that initial step in the causal sequence. The braking process does not get as far as step (2), although if it had got that far, it would then have failed owing to the missing bolt connecting the brake pedal to the lever, which in turn would have pre-empted the potential negative causal effect of the insufficient brake fluid in the master cylinder, which would have caused the braking process to fail at step (3) if it had progressed that far. But it never even got to step (1).

Duplicative as well as pre-emptive negative causation can occur. For example, if one mechanic put insufficient hydraulic brake fluid into the master cylinder for it to work and another failed to seal it properly so that whatever fluid was in it would leak out, their respective omissions, which negate required positive conditions for the occurrence of step (3) of the braking process, are duplicative

181 Wright (n.13) 302–07; Wright, Once More (n.14) 1128–31; text to nn 177–78 above. Allan Beever's criticism of my analysis of the *Saunders* situation fails to note my elaboration of the distinct nature of negative causation and the distinct method of analysis that is required when analysing overdetermined negative causation. See Beever (n.1) 423–25.

negative causes of the failure of the braking system to work, owing to the non-occurrence of step (3) in the braking process, when the brake pedal is subsequently depressed and there is no other defect.[182]

Fischer continues to assert that my detailed analysis of the situation in *Saunders* can be used to reach a conclusion opposite to the one that I reach: that the lack of proper inspection and maintenance of the brakes pre-empted the subsequent failure of the driver to attempt to use the brakes. He initially argues that this is true "because without good brakes an accident caused by a failure to stop became *inevitable* at the moment the car was given to the Driver".[183] This argument, like John Collins' arguments regarding the thrown ball hypothetical,[184] once again confuses guaranteeing the occurrence of some consequence with actually causing that consequence.[185]

Fischer also argues that the existence of working brakes can be viewed as a step in the braking process that is prior to the driver's pressing on the brake pedal, in which case, using the method of analysis that I claim is necessary for negative causation (failure of a positive causal process), the lack of working brakes due to the lack of proper inspection and maintenance caused the failure of the braking process and pre-empted the potential negative causal effect of the driver's failure to timely use the brakes.[186] Stapleton reiterates and expands on this argument. Without describing my analysis, she asserts:

> The only indication of how Wright arrives at [his] conclusion is his assertion that we 'must' look at the sequence of the causal process that did not take place.
>
> Two obvious objections to Wright's analysis can be made. First, it is not at all clear why we 'must' look at this sequence. After all, in the actual world our two specified factors (the failure-to-repair and the failure-to-attempt-to-brake) did not occur in sequence; omissions simply do not 'occur in sequence'; here both persisted at the time of the actual phenomenon of interest, namely the collision; so notions of one omission pre-empting another omission are, without more explanation, incoherent. Secondly, Wright merely stipulates that the relevant sequence would have started with 'the driver's depressing the brake pedal.' Yet we could just as easily have stipulated that the first step in the braking-stops-car causal process was the brake repair: after all, 'delivery' of the motorist's foot on a workable brake pedal *is not needed* in the braking-stops-car causal process *until* the working brakes are in place.
>
> Wright has no coherent rationale for choosing to stipulate the sequence in the way he does, and so, ironically, he stipulates *the exact opposite sequence* in a different example

182 Wright (n.13) 305 – 07.
183 Fischer (n.1) 310 (emphasis added).
184 See n.178 above.
185 See text to nn 84 – 96 and 176 above and following n.188 below.
186 Fischer (n.1) 310 – 11.

> concerning the failure of a house-building project. Here he asserts that if there was a simultaneous failure to deliver concrete for the foundation and lumber for the framing of the house, the failure to deliver the concrete, which results in the failure of the house-building causal process at the foundation-building stage, preempts the potential negative causal effect of the failure to deliver the lumber, which *is not needed until* the subsequent framing stage, the occurrence of which depends on the prior occurrence of the foundation-building stage.[187]

Stapleton's first objection puzzles me. As I have previously explained and have reiterated here, we must look at the physical sequencing of the braking process because we want to know how it failed, and determining that requires determining at what step in that process it failed. The failure at that step pre-empted the potential failure of the process at some later step that the process never reached. Stapleton erroneously states that the two relevant omissions in *Saunders* did not occur in sequence. She seems to have in mind temporal sequence. If so, she is wrong: the failure properly to inspect and maintain the brakes occurred prior to the driver's failure to timely attempt to apply the brakes. However, as I noted in my discussion of the thrown ball hypothetical, the temporal order of occurrence of the negative conditions at issue is not the sequence we need to consider.[188] Instead, we need to consider the physical sequence of the steps in the braking process.

Fischer's and Stapleton's argument that we could and perhaps should view the braking process as starting with working brakes or their proper inspection and maintenance fails to pay attention to the structure of the relevant causal web. The defects in the braking system, for which the lack of proper inspection and maintenance was a negative cause, are like the wall in the thrown ball example. Although the existence of the defects in the braking system occurred prior to the driver's failure to attempt to use the brakes and guaranteed the failure of the braking process, they did not actually cause the failure of the braking process. The defects in the brakes do not come into play in the braking process unless and until that process progresses to the steps, steps (2) and (3), at which those defects would actually cause the failure of the braking process. The braking process never reached those steps. Instead, it failed (never got started) owing to the driver's failure to (timely) use the brakes. The occurrence of steps (2) and (3) in the braking process is dependent on successful completion of each prior step in that process, including step (1), the driver's depression of the brake pedal. On the other hand, the occurrence of the driver's depression of the

187 Stapleton (n.1) 478, quoting Wright, Once More (n.14) 306 (emphasis by Stapleton).
188 See text to n.176 above.

brake pedal (step (1) in the braking process) is not dependent on the prior occurrence of steps (2) and (3) nor on the rental company's prior proper inspection and maintenance of the brakes.

Stapleton's third claim, that I inconsistently specify the sequencing of steps in different causal processes, apparently confuses my discussion of the dependency of occurrence of some steps in a causal process on the prior occurrence of other steps with claims regarding the strong necessity of various conditions. It is she, rather than I, who (unsuccessfully) attempts to use artificially constructed 'duplicate necessity'[189] rather than causal strong sufficiency to identify causes. Perhaps her misinterpretation of my statements would have been avoided if I had employed 'used' rather than 'needed'; when noting the step in the house construction process in which the presence of lumber becomes causally relevant.

Fischer also asserts that my analyses of causation in these and other situations are faulty because they fail to conform with many persons' intuitive 'causal' judgments, upon which he assumes I rely in all causally controversial situations.[190] However, I have never stated that the analysis of causation should conform to persons' intuitive 'causal' judgments in every case or even most cases. Indeed, I have often argued against taking persons' intuitive 'causal' judgments as reliable judgments regarding true (natural) causation, since such judgments often include normative or purposive factors in addition to the causation issue.[191] Instead, it is he and Stapleton who, while erroneously asserting that the NESS account privileges intuitive 'causal' judgments, continue to confuse intuitive judgments regarding liability with proper determinations of causation[192] and unfortunately have led others into similar confusion.[193] I have merely stated

189 See n.125 above.

190 Fischer (n.1) 299, 312–16.

191 See my articles cited in n.126 above.

192 See Wright, Once More (n.14) 1120–23 and fn.172; text to nn 92–94, 122–23, 127–35 above.

193 E.g. D.F. Partlett, 'Foreword: David Fischer, the Fox' (2008) 73 *Missouri Law Review* 281, 282–83, 286–87. Partlett and others have been led astray not only by Fischer's confusion of causation with liability judgments, but also by his careless and misleading use of causal terminology, some of which unfortunately has been employed in the Restatement Third. See Wright, Legal Responsibility (n.9) 1449 and fn.81, 1464 and fn.146; Wright, Once More (n.14) 1126. Fischer's misuse of causal terminology is particularly striking with his term, "dependently sufficient cause", which he defines as an omission that "is insufficient to be a 'but for' cause of the result because the other omitted act was necessary for sufficiency". Fischer (n.1) 279. This is a convoluted and highly misleading way of referring to a lack of strong necessity, which he misdescribes as a lack of 'independent sufficiency' and misapplies to situations like *Saunders*, in which each omission was not a 'but for' cause of but was "independently sufficient" (in the lawful guarantee sense that Fischer assumes) for the failure of the braking process and the consequent collision. See Fischer (n.1) 278–79. Stapleton uses without explanation a similarly

that, when attempting to determine the meaning of causation, including the proper senses of necessity and sufficiency, one should take into account our basic carefully considered intuitions regarding causation rather than policy considerations,[194] while also insisting that a theoretical account of causation is necessary to back up these intuitions and to prevent them from leading us astray:

> Despite the lack of an explicit comprehensive definition of causation, people from time immemorial have shown remarkable agreement in their causal judgments, at least once they are clearly focused on the causal issue rather than on some noncausal inquiry regarding *the* (most significant for some purpose) cause. In particular, judges and juries, when not confined by incorrect tests or formulas, consistently have demonstrated an ability to make intuitively plausible factual causal determinations.
>
> Some scholars rely heavily on this shared yet undefined concept of causation in their writings on causation and responsibility by grounding their arguments on intuitive responses to hypothetical situations. Yet intuitions that are not conjoined with theory in a search for underlying principles are often inadequate for the hard cases and sometimes may mislead even in the easy cases. In these situations in particular we would benefit greatly from elaboration of the concept that, unarticulated and imperfectly understood, underlies the intuitive judgments.[195]

I continue to believe that the NESS account provides the needed comprehensively applicable account of the concept of causation.

3.10 The Proliferation of Causes

As some critics have pointed out, the NESS account greatly increases the proliferation of causes.[196] The NESS account, like the *sine qua non* account, recognises acts and omissions as causes through negative as well as positive causation, which dramatically increases the number of causes. Moreover, the NESS account goes beyond the *sine qua non* account by recognising as causes not only strongly necessary conditions, but also independently strongly sufficient conditions and conditions that were neither strongly necessary nor independently strongly sufficient.

---

unhelpful and misleading term, "dependent double omissions", to refer to the omissions at issue in situations like *Saunders*. Stapleton (n.1) 477–78.

194 Wright (n.3) 1020.

195 Wright (n.3) 1018–19.

196 Collins, Hall and Paul, Introduction (n.9) 25; Fischer (n.1) 290–91; Fumerton and Kress (n.1) 98–99; Moore (n.1) 477–79, 486–95.

Even the *sine qua non* account is sometimes rejected by judges and others for treating as causes conditions that usually would not be identified as causes in ordinary speech but rather, if thought about at all, would be treated as 'background conditions' or as too remote in the causal web to even be acknowledged as background conditions. However, as I noted above,[197] this merely reflects a confusion of the causal issue with contextual salience, which in the law is appropriately handled by focusing the causal analysis solely on legally relevant conditions and by applying normative attributable responsibility limitations on the scope or extent of liability for the consequences of those conditions. Depending on the circumstances and purpose of the particular causal enquiry, something not ordinarily treated in common speech as a cause would easily be described as such – eg, oxygen as a necessary condition for a fire in circumstances where oxygen was not expected to be present.[198]

As most critics of the NESS account acknowledge, the proliferation of causes is not a significant problem in analyses of legal responsibility.[199] In law, as well as ordinary life, we are not interested in determining all of the practically innumerable immediate and remote causes of every event or state of affairs. In law, we are only interested in the possible causes of legally recognised injuries, and we are interested in only a very few of those possible causes: the aspect of the defendant's conduct that made the defendant subject to potential liability, the negligent aspect (if any) of the plaintiff's conduct (which may result in application of the defence of contributory negligence), and highly unexpected intervening necessary conditions or independently lawfully sufficient non-responsible conditions (which generally will result in denials of legal responsibility – misleadingly described as 'proximate' or 'legal' causation – despite tortious causation).[200] Legal responsibility may also be denied for legally relevant conditions that made only a 'trivial' contribution to a legally recognised injury[201] or that caused a legally recognised injury that was not the result of the actual or anticipated realisation of a risk that made the relevant party's conduct wrongful.[202] Moreover, failures to act to prevent a legally recognised injury generally are not considered to be wrongful (and thus legally relevant), or are considered wrongful only in very limited circumstances, if the person who failed to act

---

197 See text to nn 121–35 above.

198 See Hart and Honoré (n.5) 34–35; Wright (n.3) 1012–14.

199 Fischer (n.1) 289–90, 292; Fumerton and Kress (n.1) 87, 99; Stapleton (n.1) 440, 444, 448–51; Thomson (n.1) 150 fn 9; see Honoré (n.1) 367–69.

200 Wright (n.5) 1741–44, 1759–74, 1798–1801; Wright, Legal Responsibility (n.9) 1434–78.

201 See text to n.123 above.

202 Wright, Legal Responsibility (n.9) 1479–1528.

had no responsibility for any positive condition in the positive causal process that produced the injury (eg, the no- or limited-duty rules for 'nonfeasance').

4 Conclusion

While I do not claim to have addressed every possible objection to the NESS account, I have attempted to address all those of which I am aware. My consideration of the various objections has reinforced my belief that the NESS account is not merely a very useful tool for identifying singular instances of causation, which almost all of the critics of the NESS account admit, but that it does so precisely because it captures the essence of causation and gives it a comprehensive specification and meaning. I don't think the former is possible in the absence of the latter.

Ingeborg Puppe

The Concept of Causation in the Law

Introduction

All of someone's responsibility for an event is based on a relation of causality between his behaviour (doing or omitting) and this event. Whatever is required for justifying this responsibility and distinguishing degrees of it, it is a property of this causal relation or is connected to it. This holds for the law as well as for morality. So it is only natural that legal scholars have followed the attempts of philosophers to determine the relation of causality with great interest and with the readiness to learn from them. But philosophers could also have taken up some ideas from jurists. Modern philosophy of causality has only recently discovered the problem of determining a singular cause and its logical relation to the whole cause and its effect, namely in the mid-20th century. In contrast to this, legal scholars have always been concerned with this problem. It also seems to me that though philosophy deals very thoroughly with the problem of preempting causality, it somewhat neglects the problem of double or multiple causality. Multiple causality exists if several factors in a causal explanation can be substituted for each other without one preempting the other. This problem occurs in jurisprudence for example if in an accident, several people behave so wrong that each one's behaviour is sufficient to explain the accident.

In the last decades, philosophical discussion of causality has seen a turnaround. After centuries of a nearly unchallenged generalist notion of causality, according to which causality consists in the sequence of cause and effect being subsumable under a general law, philosophers and philosophically-minded jurists recently turned to the notion of a *causa efficiens*, in particular to a physicalist notion of causality. The physicalist notion of causality depicts the cause as a transfer of energy. Its proponents claim that it is more primitive and more robust than the generalist notion. According to the singularist conception of causality, the causal relation in particular cases is logically and empirically prior to the lawfulness of the causal process, even to the point to dispensing with the latter. What can we jurists learn from this new development in the philosophical discussion of causality?

In asking this question we must be aware of two points: Jurisprudence is bound, to a certain extent, to the everyday and scientific understanding of the world and must not get carried away too far from it. The notion of causality is, in general, that of natural science or perhaps even more that of technology.

On the other hand, the jurist needs the notion of causality for other ends than the natural scientist or the technician. The natural scientist needs it to explain a part of the world. The technician needs it to reach a certain aim or prevent a certain outcome. The jurist employs the notion of causality to justify responsibility for something that has already happened. So it is possible that the jurist suggests general rules for assessing causality that a natural scientist or a technician would never accept because they are not based on empirical evidence but on normative considerations. Present philosophical discussion is often content with a pluralism of causal notions that are supposed to co-exist. The jurist can concur with such pluralism only in the sense that there are different attributive practices according to different areas of attribution. For example, the jurist might accept that the notion of causality pertaining to the causation of human decision differs from that in the causation of natural events or that the notion pertaining to causation by actively doing something is different from that for causation by omission. But the jurist cannot accept that for one and the same case, the judge can choose between different notions of causality, so that he can decide as needed or as he sees fit which one is the basis of attribution.

From a mathematician I know the proverb that one may say that an egg is rotten even if one is not able to lay a fresh one. This is true for theoretical science and insofar for philosophy as well. In mathematics, it can be a significant scientific merit to falsify a long-accepted theory or proof, even if one cannot replace it with a new one. For practical sciences like medicine, engineering or jurisprudence, this is not true. The physician who rejects a therapy because it is not likely enough to succeed or produces too much side-effects must suggest a better one, unless he thinks the illness is incurable. The architect who rejects a method for fixing a leaking rooftop because he thinks it is then likely to leak again soon must propose a better one. Not to repair the leak is no alternative. Likewise, the jurist who rejects a procedure or criterion of deciding a legal issue needs to suggest a better one. He cannot end a lawsuit like the judge did in Lessing's *Nathan der Weise* by explaining to the parties that he cannot resolve their legal dispute and that they themselves should do it. So we will seek a single, philosophically justified notion of causality, that works across the board for at least one area, that of natural physical events. It will not be perfect, but there will be less objections against this conception than against others.

1 Short Sketch of the Development of the Notion of Causation

According to common practice and, by now, also to dominant scholarship in Germany and other countries, a singular cause must be a necessary condition for the occurrence of the result. We test for causality by asking whether we can think away the alleged cause, for instance human behaviour, without also having to think away the result. The action causes the result only if this question can be answered negatively. It is well known how this so-called *conditio-sine-qua-non* formula ('but-for rule') has made its way into German jurisprudence.[1] In the acclaimed but rarely read 1931 monograph "Die Kausalität als Merkmal strafrechtlicher Tatbestände", Engisch noted two problems with this formula: First, following David Hume and Stuart Mill, he pointed out that every causal relation between antecedent and consequent must be based on universal, empirically grounded laws.[2] In the current debate, this is called the regularity thesis.

Second, he showed with the aid of examples that the but-for rule yields a false description of the logical relation between antecedent and consequent, a relation that is necessary for the causality from the antecedent to the consequent.[3] If we were to require in earnest that, for instance, an action is only causal for a result if it is a necessary condition of the occurrence of the latter, then we would get the following: If several actions can be used interchangeably in the causal explanation of a result, none of them can be the cause of the result. For example, suppose each of several perpetrators contributes through his actions to a sufficient condition of the result instantiated in this case. Then they would relieve each other of the responsibility for the result. This would hold if all actions are causes as well as if one is only a seeming cause, a so-called pre-

---

1 J. Glaser, *Abhandlungen aus dem österreichischen Strafrecht*, Vol. I, 2. Abhandlung, (Wien, Verlag von Tendler und Comp, 1858), 298. From jurisdiction RGSt 1, 373 (374).

2 K. Engisch, *Die Kausalität als Merkmal der strafrechtlichen Tatbestände* (Tübingen, Mohr (Paul Siebeck), 1931) 18 ff.

3 K. Engisch, Kausalität (note 2), 15 ff. To detect preemptive and multiple causation Engisch developed the concept of causal chains, which he describes as follows: "A behaviour – at first we only think about positive action – proves itself as a cause for a concrete (positive) result, which is defined by a certain criminal provision, if chronologically later a number of changes in the outside world come along with this certain behaviour, which are bound to the behaviour and among each other in a (naturally) lawful way and if these changes lead into some kind of integral part of the concrete criminal provision, which is defined as result (Formula of lawful condition as opposite to the c. s. q. n. formula)." But thus nothing is said about how the logical connection between the single links of that chain should look like, since, at least, it cannot be a necessary condition.

empted cause (*Ersatzursache* in German law literature). Naturally, the scholarship and practice of German criminal law have never drawn this consequence. I have scrutinised the remedies intended to prevent it elsewhere.[4]

The notion that every causal relation, at least in the realms of so-called natural causality, must be based on universal laws was received by and by in German criminal law scholarship.[5] However, the second problem of determining the logically correct conditional relation between cause and effect was neglected for decades. At most, one substituted the term "necessary condition" with "lawful condition".[6]

To my knowledge, Hart and Honoré were the first to make a suggestion to determine this relation that was consistent with the assumption of multiple and preemptive causality in their book *Causation in the Law,* first published in 1959. Their starting point was the insight that a cause need not be a necessary condition for the result. It is enough that it is a sufficient one. Since a person's action can never be sufficient for a result but needs a multitude of other, additional conditions to be met in order to be sufficient, the action is only a necessary part of this set of conditions.[7] However, right from the start Hart and Honoré were not consistent in their conception of causality, because they dismissed the idea of the equivalent significance of all conditions of the result as causes in fa-

---

4 I. Puppe, 'Der Erfolg und seine kausale Erklärung im Strafrecht', ZStW 92 (1980), 863 (870 ff.) = I. Puppe, 'Der Erfolg und seine kausale Erklärung im Strafrecht', in: U. di Fabio, U. Kindhäuser & W.-H. Roth (eds), *Strafrechtsdogmatische Analysen* (Göttingen, V&R unipress, 2006), 101 (112); I. Puppe, 'Lob der Conditio-sine-qua-non-Formel', GA 2010, 551 (552 ff., 558 f.), I. Puppe, in U. Kindhäuser, U. Neumann & H.-U. Paeffgen (eds), *Nomos-Kommentar Strafgesetzbuch,* Bd. 1, 3rd ed., (Baden-Baden, Nomos, 2010), above § 13 par. 94 ff.

5 A. Kaufmann, 'Die Bedeutung hypothetischer Erfolgsursachen im Strafrecht', in: P. Bokkelmann & W. Gallas (eds), *Festschrift für Eberhard Schmidt* (Göttingen, Scientia Verlag, 1961), 200 ff. (209); C. Roxin, *Strafrecht Allgemeiner Teil,* Vol. I, 4th ed. (München, Verlag C.H. Beck, 2006), 11/12 f.; H. Jescheck & T. Weigend, *Lehrbuch des Strafrechts Allgemeiner Teil,* 5th ed. (Berlin, Duncker & Humblot, 1996), § 28 II 4.

6 H. Jescheck & T. Weigend, AT (note 5), § 28 II 4; C. Roxin, AT/1 (note 5), 11/15; G. Jakobs, *Strafrecht Allgemeiner Teil,* 2nd ed. (Berlin New York, de Gruyter, 1991), 7/12; G. Stratenwerth & L. Kuhlen, *Strafrecht Allgemeiner Teil I,* 5th ed. (Köln Berlin München, Vahlen, 2004), 8/19.

7 H. L. A. Hart & T. Honoré, *Causation in the Law,* 2nd ed. (Oxford, Oxford University Press, 1985), 112 ff.; T. Honoré, 'Die Kausalitätslehre im anglo-amerikanischen Recht im Vergleich zum deutschen Recht', ZStW 69 (1957), 465 (470); T. Honoré, 'Necessary and Sufficient Conditions in Tort Law', in: *Responsibility and Fault* (Oxford, Hart Publishing, 1999) 94 (96). Honoré again comes close to the 'but-for-rule' by thinking he has to give a hypothetical statement about the course of the world to prove causation in a single instance.

vour of a so-called individualized conception of causality.[8] Moreover, Honoré often reverted to the but-for rule in more complicated cases.[9]

Hart's and Honoré's idea was neither adopted in Germany nor, as it seems, in the English-speaking world. For both in Germany and apparently worldwide, the Australasian philosopher Mackie is nowadays regarded as having invented this conception of the logical relation between cause and effect. In an essay from 1965[10] and in his 1974 book "The Cement of the Universe", he adopted Hart's and Honoré's idea without giving his source, which he must have known as later citations show.[11] He coined the famous so-called INUS-condition, an acronym for "insufficient but nonredundant part of an unnecessary but sufficient condition". This is exactly the same logical relation that Hart and Honoré had described earlier. But Mackie was not only not the inventor of this solution, he neither was its advocat. He only regarded the INUS-condition as a causal link for types of events but not singular cases. He resolutely argued for using the but-for rule[12] in order to identify the cause of a result in a singular case. He even was explicitly against logically grounding the judgment that a cause is necessary for the effect on the regularity thesis. He noted: "A singular causal statement need not imply even the vaguest generalisation" (op.cit., pp.77 f.). So Mackie rejected the assumption of lawfulness even when using the *conditio-sine-qua-non* formu-

8 H. L. A. Hart & T. Honoré, Causation (note 7), 113; also T. Honoré, Kausalitätslehre (note 7), 463 (471 ff.). Although Hart and Honoré show subsequently that the *conditio-sine-qua-non* formula is misleading in cases involving a preempted cause or multiple causation of action and omission, they do not try to solve this problem by using the formula of a necessary component of a sufficient condition. Thus they do not demonstrate the benefit of their own findings clearly enough.

9 T. Honoré, Conditions (note 7), 94 (104 ff.).

10 J. L. Mackie, 'Causes and Conditions', in: American Philosophical Quarterly, Vol. 2, Number 4 1965, 245.

11 J. L. Mackie, *The Cement of the Universe* (Oxford, Oxford University Press, 1974), 59 ff., 62. But see R. Wright, 'Causation, Responsibility, Risk, Probability, Naked Statistics, and Proof: Pruning the Bramble Bush by Clarifying the Concepts', Iowa Law Review 73 (1988), 1017, (1023, note 113): "Hart and Honoré rather than Mackie were the original articulators and, until recently, the only advocates of the NESS test as opposed to the but-for test. [...] Unfortunatly, most lawyers and philosophers who refer to the NESS test cite Mackie rather than Hart and Honoré." R. Wright, 'The NESS Account of Natural Causation: A response to criticism', in: R. Goldberg (ed.) *Perspectives on Causation* (Oxford, Hart Publishing, 2011), 285 ff. (288): "Hart and Honoré's account had a significant impact on non-legal philosophers, a number of whom subsequently published analyses of causation similar to Hart and Honoré's account, although without citing Hart and Honoré." Maybe Mackie did not recognize how valuable this finding for a lawyer is – in contrast to the commonly known but-for-rule. Mackie developed the INUS-Condition in his essay 'Causes and Conditions' (note. 10), 245 in an easy and elegant manner.

12 J. L. Mackie, Cement (note 11), 39 f., 60, 76 f. 126 f.

la. Hence he proposed a singularist theory that determines the relation between cause and effect as a relation in a particular case, in the sense of an effective cause.

Therefore, it is quite incomprehensible that current criminal law and philosophical literature in Germany praise[13] and sometimes reprimand[14] Mackie of all people as the inventor of the doctrine of the lawful minimal condition. The reason for this could be that Stegmüller was the first to take up the problem of determining the logical relation between singular cause and result first in the second edition of his famous book about causal explanation. He presented Mackie's INUS-condition as the only solution.[15] It remained this way in German philosophical literature.[16] So jurists are willing to learn from philosophers after all, although it would seem that the opposite occurs only rarely.

I did not know Hart's and Honoré's solution when I set myself to the task of discerning the logical relation between singular cause and result in 1980, but it was clear from Engisch that as a necessary condition, this relation was ill conceived. I started with the so-called HO-schema. In the philosophy of science, this is the label for the schema of causal explanations by Hempel and Oppen-

---

13 U. Kindhäuser, *Gefährdung als Straftat* (Frankfurt am Main, Vittorio Klostermann, 1989), 85 ff.; U. Kindhäuser, 'Kausalanalyse und Handlungszuschreibung', GA 1982, 477 (486, 497); H. Koriath, *Kausalität, Bedingungstheorie und psychische Kausalität* (Göttingen, O. Schwartz Publication, 1988), 32 ff.; H. Koriath, *Grundlagen strafrechtlicher Zurechnung* (Berlin, Duncker & Humblot, 1994), 419 ff.; J. Vogel, *Norm und Pflicht bei unechten Unterlassungsdelikten* (Berlin, Duncker & Humblot, 1993), 150; F. Toepel, 'Hinreichende Mindestbedingung', in H.-U. Paeffgen, M. Böse, U. Kindhäuser, S. Stübinger, T. Verrel & R. Zaczyk (eds), *Strafrechtswissenschaft als Analyse und Konstruktion – Festschrift für Ingeborg Puppe* (Berlin, Duncker & Humblot 2011), 289 (290 note 5).

14 E. Samson, 'INUS-Bedingung und strafrechtlicher Kausalbegriff', in K. Rogall, I. Puppe, U. Stein & J. Wolter (eds), *Festschrift für Hans-Joachim Rudolphi* (Neuwied, Luchterhand, 2004), 259 ff.

15 W. Stegmüller, *Probleme und Resultate der Wissenschaftstheorie und Analytischen Philosophie, Vol. I Erklärung Begründung Kausalität*, 2nd ed. (Berlin Heidelberg New York, Springer, 1983), 584 ff.

16 M. Baumgartner & G. Graßhoff, *Kausalität und kausales Schließen* (Bern, Studies Verlag, 2004), 93; R. Rheinwald, 'Kausalität', in: H. J. Sandkühler (ed.), *Enzyklopädie Philosophie* Vol. 2 I-P, 2nd ed., (Hamburg, Felix Meiner Verlag, 2010), 1223 (1225); M. Carrier in: *Enzyklopädie Philosophie und Wissenschaftstheorie* Vol. 4 Sp-Z, 2nd ed., J. Mittelstraß (ed.) (Stuttgart Weimar, Metzler, 2004), 442. For recent anglophone literature see S. Psillos, 'Regularity Theories', in: C. Hitchcock, H. Beebee & P. Menzies (eds), *The Oxford Handbook of Causation* (Oxford, Oxford University Press, 2009), 131 (150 ff.); M. Strevens, 'Mackie Remixed', in: J. K. Campbell, M. O'Rourke & H. Silverstein (eds), *Causation and Explanation*, (Cambridge MA, MIT Press, 2007), 93 ff.

heim.[17] According to it, an event is causally explained if we know a sequence of preceding events that form a sufficient condition of this event in conformity with empirical laws. In the light of such an explanation, we can deduce the effect from the cause by using these laws, but not the reverse. The correct formulation of a causal law requires that it represents a minimal condition for an event or state of affairs and not contain superfluous elements. The causal explanation of an event or state of affairs is just its subsumption under such a correctly formulated causal law. A singular cause is nothing but a component of such a causal explanation. It is necessary in the sense that the explanation ceases to make sense in accordance with natural laws if this event is left out of the explanation.[18]

I do not hesitate to admit that this is identical in its logical structure with Hart's and Honoré's description of the conditional relation. It does not solve all problems, of course. What needs to be explained in legal contexts anyway? In any case, not a result in its specific form, like the prevailing doctrine has it in order to be able to rule out intuitively recognizable preempted causes.[19] Nor the fact that, for example, the proposition "X is dead" is true. For this proposition implies the fact that X has lived.[20] If the task was to causally explain the truth of this proposition, then the victim's mother and the doctor who once saved his life would be causal of his death. Therefore, what needs to be causally explained is a change in the given world that harms legally protected interests, hence not the fact that the proposition "X is dead" is true, but the change in the

17 See Stegmüller, Erklärung (note 15), 124 ff. However, T. Honoré (note 7), 94, 102 ff., approaches the but-for rule again by claiming that ascertaining causality in an isolated case requires a hypothetical statement about the course of the world.

18 I. Puppe, Der Erfolg, (note 4), 863, (876) = Analysen, (note 4), 101, (112); Puppe, 'Kausalität', SchwZStr 1990, 141 (151); Puppe, *Strafrecht Allgemeiner Teil im Spiegel der Rechtsprechung*, 2nd ed. (Baden-Baden, Nomos, 2011), 2/6; Puppe, Nomos-Kommentar (note 4), above § 13 par. 106; U. Kindhäuser, 'Risikoerhöhung und Risikoverringerung', ZStW 120 (2008), 481 (485 f.); T. Honoré, Conditions (note. 7), 94, 102 ff., R. Wright, 'Acts and Omissions as Positive and Negative Causes', in: J. W. Neyers, E. Chamberlain & S. G. A. Pitel (eds), *Emerging Issues in Tort Law*, (Oxford, Hart Publishing, 2007), 287 (296 ff.); see also Psillos, Regularity Theories (note. 16), 130, (148 ff.).

19 E. Hilgendorf, 'Zur Lehre vom "Erfolg in seiner konkreten Gestalt"', GA 1995, 515 (531). Formerly also F. Toepel, *Kausalität und Pflichtwidrigkeitszusammenhang beim fahrlässigen Erfolgsdelikt* (Berlin, Duncker & Humblot, 1992), 79; Toepel now differently in Hinreichende Mindestbedingung (note 13) 289 (302); critically I. Puppe, 'Naturalismus und Normativismus in der modernen Strafrechtsdogmatik', GA 1994, 297, (303), see also Puppe, Der Erfolg (note 4), 863, (870 ff.); T. Sofos, *Mehrfachkausalität beim Tun und Unterlassen* (Berlin, Duncker & Humblot, 1999), 68 ff.; S. Osnabrügge, *Die Beihilfe und ihr Erfolg* (Berlin, Duncker & Humblot, 2002), 50 ff.

20 See Hart & Honoré, Causation (note. 7), 115.

state of X from a living to a dead person.[21] How do we recognize that a lawful and in this sense sufficient condition of the result is not a cause but merely a preempted cause? How do we distinguish different, in this sense sufficient conditions of the result? How do we distinguish a mere variation of the causal chain from the substitution of one chain by another? I shall defer answering these questions here. The reason is that they have sparked criticism that has recently lead to a fundamental rejection of the thesis of lawfulness and to a renaissance not only of the formula of the necessary condition, but also of a singularist conception of the efficient cause.

In 1985, the American jurist Richard Wright coined the "NESS test", an acronym for "necessary element of a sufficient set". In contrast to Mackie, he wants to use this test particularly to assess causality in single instances. He explicitly referred to Hart and Honoré as the preeminent source for this.[22] However, he applied this theory much more consistently than Hart and Honoré did. He developed it further and defended it against the criticisms mentioned above.[23] We will deal with his defense later on, when we assess the objections to his theory.

2 Counter-concepts, Old and New

2.1 The Renaissance of the But-For Rule

An old concept that has been rejected by some scholars, but now again is the dominant opinion in Germany, is the application of the so-called *conditio-sine-qua-non* formula. The application of this formula is supposed not to be based on general laws.[24] Authors defending this conception can rely on Mackie, who intended his INUS-condition, as argued above, for universal laws, but based the assessment of causality in singular cases on a necessary condition the ascertainment of which does not require any generalisation of conditions.[25]

---

21 Puppe, Der Erfolg (note 4), 863, (880) = Analysen (note 4), 101, (115 f.); Puppe, Lob (note 4), 551 (559); consenting Kindhäuser, Risikoerhöhung und Risikoverringerung (note 18), 481 (483).

22 R. Wright, 'Causation in Tort Law', California Law Review 73 (1985) 1745 (1788 ff.), recently Wright, The NESS Account (note 11), 2 ff. (286 ff.).

23 Wright, Causation, Responsibility, Risk, (note 11), 1001, (1028 ff.); recently Wright, The NESS Account (note 11), 286 ff.

24 W. Frisch, 'Defizite empirischen Wissens und ihre Bewältigung im Strafrecht', in R. Bloy, M. Böse, T. Hillenkamp, C. Momsen & P. Rackow (eds), *Gerechte Strafe und legitimes Strafrecht – Festschrift für Manfred Maiwald zum 75. Geburtstag* (Berlin, Duncker & Humblot, 2010), 239, (258); Toepel, Hinreichende Mindestbedingung (note 13), 289, (297 f.).

25 Mackie, The Cement (note 11), 77 f.

This theory purports to have two advantages: Necessity in isolated cases is supposed to enable the assessment and ascertainment of causality in areas in which we do not assume there to be universal laws, particularly for the so-called psychological causality. More exactly, the area concerned is that of motivational causality. Here, the aim is a verdict on the question whether a person's decision and ensuing action can be causally attributed to another's influence, for example an instigator's influence on the principal offender or a fraud's on the enacting person.[26]

The second advantage is to consist in the fact that the theory can do without universal laws even in the assessment of relations of natural causality, as in physics, chemistry, medicine or biology. Therefore, this theory has first to prove itself in simple cases in which the causal relations are obvious. If the coroner sees strangulation marks on the victim's neck, he can base the causality of the defendant's strangulation on the supposition that the death would not have occurred but for the strangulation, without recourse to general laws.[27] But this method of assessing causality is also supposed to work if the causal laws governing the area concerned are not yet known or not with sufficient certainty. Cases of this nature have occurred particularly in criminal and civil product liability, where the scientific opinions concerned did not agree on whether a certain product caused damage to the consumers' health.[28] Here, it is supposed to be enough that the judge observes a "normative relation" between action and result that enables him to maintain that the damage to the consumers' health would not have occurred without any contact with the product.[29]

Let us turn first towards the so-called psychological causality, or better motivational causality. According to the view in question, it is supposed to be pos-

---

26 Frisch, Defizite empirischen Wissens (note 24), 239 (255).

27 W. Frisch, 'Die Conditio-Formel: Anweisung zur Tatsachenfeststellung oder normative Aussage?', in: V. Erb & D. Dölling (eds), *Festschrift für Karl Heinz Gössel zum 70. Geburstag* (Heidelberg, C.F. Müller Verlag, 2002), 57 (66 f.), see also Toepel, Kausalität (note 19), 53 f.

28 Contergan case, LG Aachen JZ 1971, 507; see also A. Kaufman, 'Tatbestandsmäßigkeit und Verursachung im Contergan-Verfahren', JZ 1971, 569 ff.; Leather protective spray case (Lederspray), BGHSt 37, 106; Spanish rapeoil case, NStZ 1994, 37 ff.; Timber preservative case, BGHSt 41, 206.

29 Frisch, Defizite empirischen Wissens (note 24), 239 (258): "Since the ascertainment of the quality of conditions of the behaviour in any singular case can be done differently than through proof of a recognized lawful regularity, the legal practitioner is not forced to [...] identify any lawful relation between action and result, although special science cannot (yet) give a corresponding law. The legal practitioner can restrict himself to the observation that the law, by its own standards, regards a normatively sufficient relation as given – without thereby making any statements about lawful regularities." (Translation BK).

sible to establish that the influence was a necessary condition for the influenced person's decision by claiming that the latter would not have behaved as he did if no influence had been exerted on him. Therefore, the view concludes, the negation of the influence is to be a sufficient condition for the absence of his action. This is supposed to be established by asking the influenced person whether he would have behaved as he did if he had not been under the influence.[30] This question is a so-called counterfactual conditional in the form of a sufficient condition. The conditional is counterfactual because it contains the statement that both the premise which is to be the sufficient condition and the consequent are false. The claim that in a singular case, a state of affairs is a sufficient condition for another one, is only false if the first state of affairs is not true but the second one is. But if the sufficient condition is explicitly false, nothing follows for whether the consequent is true or false. The counterfactual conditional then is true no matter whether the consequent is true or false.[31] Therefore, an counterfactual conditional only makes sense insofar it refers to universal laws that are also valid for fictional states of affairs, or as some philosophers say, in possible worlds. If, as presupposed by law, for motivational causality such laws do not exist, nobody, not even the person concerned, can answer the question how he would have behaved if he had not been subjected to the influence he was in fact subjected to.[32] So the claim to necessity in an isolated case and its explication by means of an counterfactual conditional are unsuitable to establish causality where there are no universal laws.

Then, the second advantage of the but-for rule in singular cases is also illusory: It neither enables us to ascertain causality in particularly simple cases nor in cases where we cannot adduce or prove causal laws. Here, causality is to be ascertained by claiming that the result would not have occurred but for the defendant's action.[33] But without recourse to universal regularities, so-called causal laws, such a claim makes no sense in physical, chemical or medical contexts. It can only be plausible insofar the claimant presupposes that there are sure to be some universal laws, and that these laws license his inference that under the

30 Frisch, Defizite empirischen Wissens (note 24), 239 (255 f.); Frisch, Die Conditio-Formel (note 27) 57, (67 f.); L. Kuhlen, 'Ausschluß der objektiven Erfolgszurechnung bei hypothetischer Einwilligung des Betroffenen', JR 2004, 227 f.
31 Stegmüller, Erklärung (note 15) 329 f.; see also Puppe, Der Erfolg (note 4), 863, 867.
32 Puppe, Nomos-Kommentar (note 4) above § 13 par. 132; I. Puppe, 'Hypothetische Einwilligung bei medizinischen Eingriffen', Anm. zu BGH, Urt. v. 20.01.2004 – 1 StR 319/03, JR 2004, 470 (471).
33 Frisch, Defizite empirischen Wissens (note 24), 239 (256); Toepel, Kausalität (note 19) (1992), 53 f.

given circumstances the result would not have occurred but for the action. This then counts as proof of the claim that the action is a necessary condition of the result. But actually, it is only a logical reformulation of this claim by the inference rule of contraposition.[34]

So if we cannot adduce a causal law according to which the action is a necessary element in the causal explanation of the result, we cannot justifiably maintain that the result would be nullified without the action, or more precisely that it would not be causally explainable without it. If the coroner finds strangulation marks on the victim's neck and thereupon maintains that the defendant strangulated the victim, he refers to a causal law, namely that if somebody throttles somebody else for a certain time, the latter dies of oxygen deprivation.[35] It is a further question whether the coroner is well advised to be content with this piece of evidence in order to use this causal law to explain the victim's death or whether he should investigate other causes of death.

Still, if the relevant natural science cannot provide us with a universal law in accordance to which the defendant's action, together with other facts, is sufficient for the result, then the claim that this is the case, i.e. that the result would not have occurred but for the action, is nothing but mere speculation that there is some such law. There may be evidence for this speculation and it may have a certain plausibility. But it is a proof-theoretic question whether this, conjoined with the fact that another explanation of the result could not be found, is enough to prove the lawful conjunction between action and result that is causality.[36]

The bottom line is this: Neither the conception of a cause as a singularly necessary condition nor its ascertainment through the claim that the result would not have occurred without it make sense without the presupposition of universal laws. The hope that we could solve the problem of psychological causality by

34 I. Puppe, *Kleine Schule des juristischen Denkens*, 2nd ed. (Stuttgart, UTB, 2011) 163; Puppe, Lob (note 4), 551f.

35 However, Frisch thought that the coroner does not need any causal law for this observation and that this is precisely the advantage of the *conditio-sine-qua-non* formula, Die Conditio-Formel (note 27), 66f.

36 Jurisdiction and current doctrine in Germany are in favour of this, BGHSt 37, 106 (111f.); R. Bloy, 'Die strafrechtliche Produkthaftung auf dem Prüfstand der Dogmatik', in: R. Bloy, M. Böse, T. Hillenkamp, C. Momsen & P. Rackow (eds), *Gerechte Strafe und legitimes Strafrecht – Festschrift für Manfred Maiwald zum 75. Geburtstag* (Berlin, Duncker & Humblot, 2010), 51 (65ff.); Frisch Defizite empirischen Wissens (note 24) 239 (254f.) critically I. Puppe, Anm. zu BGH, Urt. v. 6.7.1990 – 2 StR 549/89 (BGHSt 37, 107), JR 1992, 27 (31); W. Hassemer, *Produktverantwortung im modernen Strafrecht* (Heidelberg, C.F. Müller Verlag, 1994), 42f.; E. Samson, 'Probleme strafrechtlicher Produkthaftung', StV 1991, 181, (182f.).

means of the so-called *conditio-sine-qua-non* formula, without assuming that there are universal laws in the realm of physics or using them without having to know them, has turned out to be an illusion.

The conception of a cause as necessary condition of the result turns out to be logically false as soon as, in a causal explanation, there are two or more factors that can be substituted for each other. For then, neither factor is a necessary condition of the result. Then, according to the *conditio-sine-qua-non* formula, neither is a cause.[37] Mackie, who is not willing to make an exception to the but-for rule in this case, says that the necessary condition is that either the one or the other factor has to occur.[38] First of all, we do not know how to use such a conception of causality, neither in ethics nor in jurisprudence. After all, it makes no sense to praise or reprimand (A or B), to fine (A or B) to compensation for damages or to sentence (A or B) to a punishment.

If we now take both disjunctively connected facts, A as well as B, as causes, we can bring every fact into a causal relation to every consequence in the following way: We connect it disjunctively with a fact that is really a necessary condition for this effect. If the fact F is a necessary condition for the consequence C then the fact "F or X" is a necessary condition, too. Or if we weaken a necessary condition for a consequence we get another necessary condition for it. By the way, if we strengthen a sufficient condition by adding any fact to it, we get another sufficient condition.

In Germany, criminal science tries to avoid this result by adding the following requirement: None of the single facts connected in the disjunction is on its own a necessary condition for the result. So they get the so-called "formula of alternatives"(*Alternativenformel*): "If several actions can be thought away alternatively, but not cumulatively, without the result becoming void, each is causal."[39] But this so-called "formula of alternatives" is not just an extension of the necessary condition (but-for rule), but a direct contradiction to it.[40] Such a

37 Engisch Kausalität (note 2), 15 ff; Hart & Honoré, Causation (note 7), 124; Honoré Conditions (note 7), 94, 111ff.; Puppe Der Erfolg (note 4), 868f; Wright, Causation (note 22), 1735, (1791 ff).
38 Mackie, Cement (note 11), 47.
39 K. Kühl, *Strafrecht Allgemeiner Teil*, 6th ed. (München, Vahlen Franz, 2008), 4/19; J. Wessels & W. Beulke, *Strafrecht Allgemeiner Teil*, 40th ed. (Heidelberg, C.F. Müller Verlag, 2010), Rn 157; J. Baumann, U. Weber & W. Mitsch, *Strafrecht Allgemeiner Teil* (Bielefeld, Gieseking, 2003), 14/41. The idea is from L. Traeger, *Der Kausalbegriff im Straf- und Zivilrecht* (Marburg, N.G. Elwert, 1904), p. 45f., the formulation from M. L. Müller, *Die Bedeutung des Kausalzusammenhanges im Straf- und Schadensersatzrecht* (Tübingen, J.C.B. Mohr, 1912), p. 17, who himself rejects this formula because it fails even for preemptive causes.
40 Puppe, Kleine Schule (note 34), 179; Puppe, Lob (note 4). 553; Puppe, Nomos-Kommentar (note 4), above § 13 marginal number 92.

contradiction can be removed by giving meta-rules which determine in which case one of the opposed sentences is to be used and in which case the other. As such meta-rules are missing in German legal dogmatic, there is a danger that so-called alternative causation, or better double causation, is not detected. Therefore, the original but-for rule is used, but only one of the competing causes is thought away. The result is that the other one of the competing causes is not a cause, or even that neither one is a cause. In German jurisdiction, this mistake occurred several times in cases of double causation of negligent behaviour of two participants in a road accident.[41] In other cases, in which the German Federal Supreme Court (BGH) intuitively felt that one participant of the accident could not excuse himself by pointing to the misbehaviour of the other, they developed bizarre constructions to get the right result from the but-for rule.[42]

In the case of multiple causation, however it may have been detected by means of the but-for rule, this doctrine is forced into inconsistency. In such a case, the causality of the competing factors is supposedly assessed by the so-called formula of alternatives: If several actions can be thought away alternatively but not cumulatively without the result being nullified, every action is causal.

Finally, the theory of the necessary condition does not provide any means to distinguish a preempted cause from an actual cause, since if it is supposed to do without universal laws after all. Because if there exists a preventive cause the real cause is no necessary condition for the result.[43]

The predominant doctrine in Germany tries to mitigate this problem by enriching the description of the result with facts that are consistent with a causal explanation containing the actual cause but not with a causal explanation containing the preempted cause. This description is called the result in its concrete form.[44] But once again, we need universal causal laws to determine that an al-

---

41 The most famous case of this kind is the so-called lorry-bicyclist-case BGH 11, 1 see also BGH VRS 25, 262; Puppe AT (note 18), 3/13 ff.

42 See BGHSt 24, 31 and correspondingly Puppe AT (note 18) 3/23 ff.

43 Engisch, Kausalität (note 2), 15 ff.; Hart & Honoré, Causation, 122 ff.; Honoré, Conditions (note 7), 95; Puppe, Der Erfolg (note 4), 868 ff.; Puppe, Lob (note 4), 553 f.; Wright, Causation, Responsibility, Risk (note 11), 1022.

44 RGSt 1, 373; BGHSt 1, 332; Frisch, Die Conditio-Formel (note 27), 61; C. Jäger, 'Die notwendige Bedingung als ereignisbezogener Kausalfaktor', in: R. Bloy, M. Böse, T. Hillenkamp, C. Momsen & P. Rackow (eds), *Gerechte Strafe und legitimes Strafrecht – Festschrift für Manfred Maiwald zum 75. Geburtstag* (Berlin, Duncker & Humblot, 2010), 345, (356); E. Mezger & H. Blei, *Strafrecht Allgemeiner Teil*, 15th ed. (München, Beck, 1973), 74 f.

H. Welzel, *Das Deutsche Strafrecht*, 11th ed. (Berlin, C.F. Müller, 1969), 43; Jescheck & Weigend, AT (note 5) § 28 II 4; Roxin, AT/1 (note 5), 11/21; Kühl, AT (note 42), 4/13 ff., T. Walter in: H. W. Laufhütte, R. Rissing-van Saan & K. Tiedemann (eds), *Strafgesetzguch Leipziger Kommentar*, 12th

leged cause is inconsistent with a certain specification of the result and therefore with a preempted cause. What is more, if we enrich the description of the result with such a specification, the consequence is that everyone who is causal for this specification is also causal for the result as a whole. An example: A ministry official of the German federal government is sent a letter bomb to his home address in Bonn that explodes there. But the ministry official is in Berlin at this time and there, he dies from a heart attack. So the bomb was not causal for his death, because it was not causal for his death in Berlin. But our official's superior who called him to Berlin was causal for his death because he was causal for his death in Berlin.[45]

2.2 The Renaissance of the Concept of Efficient Cause, or the Cause as Energy Transfer

The problem of distinguishing preempted from actual causes is the starting point for the second counter-conception to the idea of a lawful minimal condition, namely the doctrine of efficient cause. Without any theoretical foundation, German jurisdiction and law literature have coped with this problem for a long time by pointing out that one just has to figure out which cause really was "effi-

---

ed. (Berlin, de Gruyter, 2007), above § 13 par. 79; H.-J. Rudolphi & J. Wolter (eds), *Systematischer Kommentar zum Strafgesetzbuch*, Carl Heymanns Verlag, above § 1 marginal number 41; V. Erb, *Rechtmäßiges Alternativverhalten und seine Auswirkungen auf die Erfolgszurechnung im Strafrecht* (Berlin, Duncker & Humblot, 1991), 41 ff.; V. Erb, 'Die Zurechnung von Erfolgen im Strafrecht', JuS 1994, 449 (452); E. Schlüchter, 'Grundfälle zur Lehre von der Kausalität', JuS 1976, 378 (380); H. Walder, 'Die Kausalität im Strafrecht', SchwZStr 1977, 113 (130); Baumann, Weber & Mitsch (note 42) 14/10 ff; R. Maurach & H. Zipf, *Strafrecht Allgemeiner Teil*, vol. 1, 8th ed. (Heidelberg, C.F. Müller, 1992), 18/54; restricting Jakobs, AT (note 6) 7/15 ff; H. Koriath, *Kausalität und objektive Zurechung* (Baden-Baden, 2007), 145; Hilgendorf, Zur Lehre (note 19), 515, (531). This method to exclude preempted causes falls for a vicious circle: Some fact belongs to the result "in its concrete form" because the action was causal for and the action, not the preempted cause, was causal for the result because this fact belongs to the result in its concrete form, Puppe, Naturalismus (note 19), 297, (303); Puppe, Der Erfolg (note 4), 863, (870 ff.); Puppe, Lob (note 4), 551, (558 ff.); Sofos, Mehrfachkausalität (note 19), 68 ff.; Osnabrügge, Beihilfe (note 19), 50 ff.; Wright, Causation in Tort Law (note 22) 1745 (1978 ff.); Wright, Causation, Responsibility, Risk (note 11) 1735, 1778 ff.; Wright, The NESS Account (note 11), 285 (293 f.)

45 Puppe, Lob (note 4), 559 f.; Puppe, Nomos-Kommentar above § 13 (note 4) marginal number 99; see also Wright, Causation in Tort Law (note 22), 1779.

cient"[46]. Indeed, we cannot distinguish actual and preempted cause if we are satisfied with causal explanations that skip distances in space and time. For the preempted cause provides a prediction that the effect will occur just like the actual cause does. A temporally and spatially distant cause must be connected to the effect through a continuous process[47] with limited propagation speed. Now most people cannot imagine such a continuous process otherwise than as a movement of something through space and time.[48] If we cannot see an object that the cause sets in motion and that moves through space and time towards the effect and finally causes it like one billiard ball moving towards the others until it hits them, there has to be another conserved physical quantity, for instance "energy, impulse or a more complicated extension or combination of both"[49].

Now many processes of natural causality, though presumably not all, can be described as a spread or transfer of energy, although it remains quite unclear what energy is supposed to be. Such a description of the process, however, does not guarantee its continuity, because there are often gaps in transfers of energy. When the executioner releases the trap door under the gallows, he triggers a process in which energy is transferred. But the energy that affects the delinquent's body and that finally breaks his neck stems from a completely different

---

46 BGHSt 39, 195, 197 = NStZ 1993, 386 (387); G. Spendel, *Die Kausalitätsformel der Bedingungstheorie für die Handlungsdelikte* (Heidelberg, 1951), 38 (44 ff); E. A. Wolff, *Kausalität von Tun und Unterlassen* (Heidelberg, 1965), 14; Erb, Rechtmäßiges Alternativverhalten (note 44), 46; U. Murmann, *Die Nebentäterschaft im Strafrecht* (Berlin, Duncker & Humblot, 1993), 148 ff; W. Lenckner & J. Eisele in: A. Eser, G. Heiner, W. Perron, D. Sternberg-Lieben, J. Eisele, N. Bosch, B. Hecker & J. Kinzig (eds), *Strafgesetzbuch Kommentar*, 28th ed. (München, C.H. Beck, 2010), above § 13, marginal number 75; G. Freund in: W. Joecks & K. Miebach (eds), *Münchener Kommentar zum Strafgesetzbuch* (München, C.H. Beck, 2003), above § 13, marginal number 309 f; H. Otto, 'Die Unterbrechung des Zurechnungszusammenhangs als Problem der Verantwortungszuschreibung', in: D. Dölling (ed.), *Ius Humanum Grundlagen des Rechts und Strafrecht. Festschrift für Ernst-Joachim Lampe zum 70. Geburtstag* (Berlin, Duncker & Humblot, 2003), 491 (493), D. Dölling, *Grundkurs Strafrecht, Allgemeine Strafrechtslehre*, 7th ed. (Berlin, de Gruyter, 2004), 6/22 ff.; Roxin AT/1 (note 5)11/21; Jakobs AT (note 6), 7/13 and 21; M. Köhler, *Strafrecht Allgemeiner Teil* (Berlin Heidelberg New York, Springer, 1997), 140.

47 See Stegmüller, Erklärung (note 15), 155 ff.; This was actually the meaning of the so-called formula by Engisch, see the quote in note 3.

48 M. S. Moore, *Causation and Responsibility An Essay in Law, Morals, and Metaphysics* (Oxford, Oxford University Press, 2009), 500 ff.; V. Haas, *Kausalität und Rechtsverletzung* (Berlin, Duncker & Humblot, 2002), 182; R. Merkel, 'Über einige vernachlässigte Probleme des Kausalitätsbegriffs im Strafrecht und Ingeborg Puppes Lehren dazu', in: H. U. Paeffgen, M. Böse, U. Kindhäuser, S. Stübinger, T. Verrel, R. Zaczyk (eds), *Strafrechtswissenschaft als Analyse und Konstruktion – Festschrift für Ingeborg Puppe zum 70. Geburtstag* (Berlin, Duncker & Humblot, 2011), 151 (165).

49 Merkel, Vernachlässigte Probleme (note 48), 151 (165).

source, namely from the gravitation of the earth. Both energy transfers are merely related through a lawful condition, namely that the trap door not longer carries the delinquent's weight.

If the perpetrator shoves a knife in his victim's body and the latter bleeds to death because of the wound, the infliction of the wound may be explainable as a transfer of the power the perpetrator exerted by his stabbing. But the energy that causes the flow of blood and thereby the wounded to bleed to death has a different source, namely gravitation and the pumping of his heart. Strictly speaking, both energy transfers are related only through a negative fact, namely that the cut vein no longer hinders the blood to flow into body tissue or out of the body. At the end of the causal chain, there is another negative fact, namely that not a sufficient amount of blood reaches the brain and so brain cells die due to lack of oxygen. It is the same, in the end, with every causation of the death of an organism.[50] When I switch on an electric device, I close a circuit. Yet the energy that powers the device does not spring from my hand but from the power plant. The only thing that connects the different transfers of energy in our examples are universal causal laws. If the support for a heavy body is taken away, the body falls. If a vein of a living animal is cut open, blood flows out. Electric current only flows if the circuit is closed.

So there is no reason to think that a condition of the activity of a process is not a cause just because the condition cannot be described as the depletion or transfer of energy to a body or something similar. Whoever takes away the water from travellers in the desert causes them to die of thirst. Whoever turns off the sprinkler system of a building causes it to burn down due to a later lightning strike or arson.

These examples show that we have to recognize so-called negative facts, i.e. the prevention of conditions interrupting a causal chain (the so-called hindrance of a rescuing event), as causes. Therefore, there is no reason not to treat the omission of a certain prescribed behaviour as cause. This has always been countered by the observation that an omission "has no real existence"[51]. Behind this is the image that a proposition that contains a negation does not describe something real or even "a Nothing" (how many Nothings are there, anyway?), "that a prop-

---

50 J. Schaffer, 'Disconnection and Responsibility: On Moore's Causation and Responsibility, Legal Theory' (forthcoming), note 5.

51 Toepel, Hinreichende Mindestbedingung (note 13), 298; an omission is something "that is not" Jakobs AT (note 6), 7/25, or omissions are "bogus entities", Moore, An Essay in Law (note 48), 444. Critically with regard to this Schaffer, Disconnection and Responsibility (note 50), note 5; J. Stapleton, 'Causation in the Law', in: C. Hitchcock, H. Beebee & P. Menzies (eds), *The Oxford Handbook of Causation* (Oxford, Oxford University Press, 2009), 744 (760 ff.).

osition contains a negation is not yet a characteristic of its sense"[52]. The proposition "four is dividable by two" refers to something "existing", the proposition "three is not dividable by two" not? The proposition "The tortured did not betray his knowledge" has the same meaning as the proposition "The tortured withheld his knowledge". And the tortured's "not-doing-something" is a great achievement. Sometimes, a rhetorical question from Hartmann is quoted in this context: "How can something that does not exist participate in the structure of that which exists?" Here the logical mistake that lies at the bottom of all these formulations is apparent: the confusion of the negation and the negated proposition. What is not, what does not exist is the negated proposition. The negation of this proposition is, insofar it is true, real as well.[53] Thus, there is no ontological reason not to accept negations that are conditions for the occurrence of a result or for the activity of a causal process as causes. However, there are a couple of things that such negations are not: They are not changes, not events and not transfers of energy. So the conception of a cause as a transfer of energy is too narrow to be suitable for grounding attribution in law or morality.

A further problem of attribution that forces us to assume and check causal factors that are not energy transfers is the problem of the causality of tortuous aspects of the act. The task here is to verify the causality not of the action as a whole but of certain aspect of actions, for example the aspect of riding a car that has a defective blinker or braking system. Now if there is a car accident in which the driver needed to use neither blinker nor brakes, for instance a rear-end collision, he is not responsible for the accident, although his driving is causal for the accident and also negligent. This is a problem of causality and, in principle, Hart and Honoré already recognized that.[54] We verify the cau-

---

52 L. Wittgenstein, *Tractatus logico-philosophicus* (Frankfurt, Suhrkamp, 1963) 4.0621: "Dass in einem Satz die Verneinung vorkommt ist noch kein Kriterium seines Sinns."

53 Puppe, Der Erfolg (note 4), 897; Puppe, Nomos-Kommentar (note 4) above § 13 marginal number 57.

54 Hart & Honoré, Causation (note 7), 118 ff; also Honoré, Conditions (note 7), 94, 100 ff.; Wright, Causation in Tort Law (note 22), 1745 (1759 ff.); R. Wright, 'The Grounds and Extent of Legal Responsibility', San Diego Law Review 40 (2003), 1425 (1494 ff.); I. Puppe, 'Die Beziehung zwischen Sorgfaltswidrigkeit und Erfolg bei den Fahrlässigkeitsdelikten', ZStW 99 (1987), 595 (599 ff.); I. Puppe, 'Negligence and Responsibility in German Road Traffic Law', European Journal of Crime, Criminal Law and Criminal Justice, 2003, 151 ff. The US courts express this problem as a problem of causation but they do not agree whether the negligent part of the action has to be causal or whether it is enough that the action itself is negligent and is causal for the damage, see Moore, An Essay in Law (note 48), 328 ff. Moore himself misses a statement by the law about that. § 222 of the German Criminal Code contains the phrase "Who causes the death of another person by negligence [...]". The German doctrine agrees that someone is not guilty if also

sation of the tortuous aspect by concealing these aspects from the causal explanation of the accident and checking whether the explanation remains plausible without these information.[55] If we insisted that only an energy transfer can be a cause, in this case only the action of driving as a whole, only the whole action of driving could be checked as a cause and then it would prove to be one. German courts and the prevailing doctrine try to solve these cases by putting a non-tortous act of the defendant in the place of the tortuous one. But it is not clear and precise whether the defendant has several possibilities of behaving correctly. In our example, he could have taken his wife's car, and then the rear-end collision would have happened as well, or he could have taken the tram, then it would not have happened.[56] So we have to be able to separate the tortuous aspects of an action from the action itself. But we cannot do this if we define a cause as an energy transfer, since a property of an energy transfer is not itself an energy transfer.

Finally, we have to be able to base the legal attribution of a result on regular processes that cannot be described as energy transfers at all. This holds for example for the causality of information. Without going into the problems of psychological causality and human freedom of choice, we can state the following rule: If someone does not have a particular piece of information, he cannot use it. If someone used a particular piece of information, for instance in executing a criminal act, the person who gave this information to him contributed a necessary component of a sufficient condition of the execution of the criminal act. Hence, this person is causal for the criminal act as instigator or assistant.

Particularly in jurisprudence we have to use institutional regularities to ground responsibility. These institutional regularities are juridical procedural prescriptions for the validity of an act of law. The parties agreeing on a contract cause, in this sense, the existence of the rights and duties from this contract, even though a physicist would not regard this as a cause. Submitting an application to an administrative body causes the existence of an administrative act.

---

his lawful behaviour would have caused the death but they do not see this as a problem of causation; instead they call it a requirement of avoidability.

Hence, they fail when judging cases of multiple causation through negligent behaviours of different persons, since they first consider the lawful behaviour of the defendant and than recognize that the damage would also have occurred. But so does Honoré, Conditions (note 7), 114 f.

55 Puppe, Negligence and Responsibility (note 54), 151 (155 ff); Puppe, AT (note 18), 3/13 ff; I. Puppe, 'Die Lehre von der objektiven Zurechnung und ihre Anwendung', ZJS 2008, 140 (144 f.). So it is not allowed to replace the tortuous aspect of the action by any correct aspects of the action or by another action at all, see Strevens (note 16), 96.

56 Puppe, Negligence and Responsibility (note 54), 151 (152); I. Puppe, AT (note 18) 3/4.

Voting for a certain motion in a committee causes the legal validity of this motion insofar there is the required majority for it. The same holds for the parliamentarian who votes for a law or for the judge who votes for a judgment. All of these causal relations are governed by regularities, but they cannot be understood as transfers of energy.

It seems to me there is a convincing argument for regularity as the basis of explanation and in particular for the attribution of institutional change: It works even though the regularities do not have the dignity of laws of nature or necessity (in any sense), but it is only we who establish them. We establish them by making them regularities that hold in the prevailing legal system.

The concept of energy transfer or of efficient causes also contributes little towards solving the problem of distinguishing actual and preempted cause, since even critics of Hume do not get around one of his insights: Generally, we cannot perceive with our senses the powers that connect cause and effect. Even imagining a causal process as transfer of energy or impulse from one point in spacetime to another, we can only reconstruct it by tracing universal laws that govern such a process. If the conditions of these causal laws are fulfilled, this process is a cause and not merely a preempted cause of the result. Though the causal process reconstructed in this way may be completely describable as a transfer of energy – which is, as shown, not always the case – it has no epistemic value in order to decide whether it is a cause or a preempted cause. Moreover, the notion of the *causa efficiens* is still quite unclear, which renders the ones applying it vulnerable to the criticism of falling into a cause-theoretic anthropomorphism.[57] Likewise, the notions of efficient cause, productive cause, ability or force are suspicious. Is it not circular that an efficient cause is something that has an effect, that a productive cause is something that produces an effect etc.?

We can be content to delegate the task of constructing the concept of a cause as the transfer of a conserved physical quantity, in particular the transfer of a certain quantum of mass or energy, to the philosophy of nature. In any case, as a basic concept of legal attribution, such a notion of cause is not enough.

---

57 See R. Carnap, *An Introduction to the Philosophy of Science: Philosophical Foundations of Physics*, (New York London, Basic Books, 1966), 188 f.

3 Objections to the Doctrine of the Lawful Minimal Condition and the Cause as Its Necessary Component

3.1 The Recent Discussion of the Regularity Thesis

Haas raises the epistemic problem of incomplete induction against the regularity thesis (once more).[58] In principle, this problem is known since Hume.[59] How many observations we may ever make that a phenomenon P1 is followed by another P2, they do not justify the logically sound conclusion that it will be the same for the next observation. We cannot logically infer a universal law from a finite number of observations. Haas, however, illustrates the problem with an example that is obviously not a causal law because it is not a universal conditional. The conditional concerned is: "If there is a ball in this box, it is red". Haas is right in claiming that the fact that one, several or many balls drawn from the box are red does not even increase the probability that the next ball drawn is also red.[60] Whoever filled the box with balls could have cunningly put in a single black ball. But if we have a correctly formulated regularity hypothesis and assume that there are regularities in the world, then a high number of observations that the alleged consequent follows the alleged antecedent increases the probability that we found a regularity, although we can never be certain of it.

The establishment of a causal law always begins with a causal hypothesis that there is a causal relation between a first event and a second one. We are entitled to this hypothesis only by already accepted causal laws and theories and sometimes also by the observation that an accepted causal law is false: We would not put forward the suggestion that the colour of a ball depends on the box in which it lies to begin with. Without the formulation of hypotheses, we would not be in a position to design experiments to verify or falsify a causal regularity. Which logical methods are apt to verify or falsify causal hypotheses is a

58 Haas, Kausalität und Rechtsverletzung (note 48), 175 f.

59 D. Hume, *A Treatise of Human Nature*, reprinted from the original edition in three volumes (Oxford, Clarendon Press, 1955), book I, part III, VI 86 ff., see also D. Hume, *Enquiries Concerning the Human Understanding and Concerning the Principles of Morals*, reprinted from the posthumous edition of 1777, 2nd ed. (Oxford, Clarendon Press, 1955), section V, part I, 42 f., where he derives the assumption that an often perceived succession of results will reappear in the future under equal conditions from custom. See also D. Hume, Enquiries, section VII, part II, 74 f.

60 Haas, Kausalität und Rechtsverletzung (note 48), 176.

subject of the philosophy of natural science. In the latter, it is accepted that all these methods only yield preliminary results but not ultimate certainty. This problem of incomplete induction has prevented neither engineers nor physicians nor physicists, insofar as they work in a branch of applied physics, to accept and apply universally valid causal laws. So we jurists may as well delegate the problem of incomplete induction to epistemology and the philosophy of natural science and may continue to accept and apply general causal laws.[61] We should take care not to confuse the epistemological question of the possibility of attaining empirical certainty at all with particular problems of forensic proof as may occur in product liability law or medical law.[62]

A causal law is generally of the form "if...then...". Rarely, it refers to a necessary condition. The first part of the extensive implication, the antecedent, describes a state of affairs that precedes the consequent. We can accept this in the present context as an element of the conception of a cause without having to enter into the philosophical discussion about the nature of time or the physical discussion about the reversibility of time or the possibility of time travel. The possibility of affecting the past is not within our experience.[63]

Now there are conditionals that fulfil these criteria but that we nevertheless do not accept as causal laws. There are different groups of such conditionals. To the first, group A, belong propositions like the following: "If today is Friday, then the next day always is Saturday", or "If a husband dies, then his wife always becomes a widow".[64] For the second kind of conditional, group B, the following is an example: Given that we know that all balls in a box are red, we can say "If a ball is in this box, then it is red".[65] A third kind of conditional, group C, is illustrated by different authors with the following example: There is a tower or flag

---

61 M. Maiwald, *Kausalität und Strafrecht Studien zum Verhältnis von Naturwissenschaft und Jurisprudenz* (Göttingen, Otto Schwartz, 1980), 47 ff.; J. Stapleton, 'Choosing What We Mean by 'Causation' in the Law', Missouri Law Review, Vol. 73, No. 2, 2008, 433 (447).

62 Bloy makes this mistake in Die strafrechtliche Produkthaftung (note 34), 35, 51 f., by entrusting it to the judge to regard a causal law as empirically proven due to the problem of incomplete induction.

63 The possibility that later events can be INUS conditions for earlier ones has led philosophers like Mackie to back off from a regularity thesis. So philosophically, the point remains to be argued, but as jurists we can simply postulate this direction of causality without getting into a vicious circle, Stapleton, Choosing What We Mean (note. 61), 433 (447); Wright, The NESS Account (note. 11), 285 ff. (296). In contrast: R. Fumerton & K. Kress, 'Causation and the Law – Preemption, Lawful Sufficiency, and Causal Sufficiency', in: Law and Contemporary problems, Vo.l 64, No. 4, 2001, Duke University School of Law, 83 (102 f.).

64 Examples follow Merkel, Vernachlässigte Probleme (note 48), 157.

65 Example follows Haas, Kausalität und Rechtsverletzung (note 48), 167.

pole, the sun is in a certain position and the tower throws a shadow of a certain length. Universal laws of optics and geometry allow us to calculate the height of the tower. We can formulate the conditional thus: "If, for a certain position of the sun, the shadow of the tower or flag pole has the length L, then the tower or flag pole always has the height H".[66] The following are examples for conditionals of group D: "If the gate of the level crossing is closed, then a train always passes the crossing" or "If the factory hooters sound at 6 p.m. in Manchester, the Londoners stop their work".[67] Or else "if the barometer falls suddenly, then sometime later a storm gathers".[68] We would not accept the antecedent of these conditionals as cause of the consequent.

In recent times, a solution to these problems is thought to lie in the notion of power or efficient cause, which has been ridiculed as metaphysical and circular for a long time.[69] The solution is supposed to work in one of two ways: Either the regularity thesis is rejected as a foundation for causality and the notion of a transfer of power is adopted in its stead, which yields a singularist theory of causation[70]; or the notion of the *causa efficiens* as transfer of energy or any other conserved physical quantity is employed to distinguish conditionals that are causal laws from those that are not. So a conditional, by virtue of which we

---

66 Example from Moore, An Essay in Law (note 48), 476 f.; Fumerton & Kress, Causation (note 63) 83, (93 f.); Merkel, Vernachlässgte Probleme (note 48), 162; Toepel, Hinreichende Mindestbedingung (note 13), 293. Further similarly structured examples can be found at S. Bromberger, 'Why-Questions', in R. Colodny (ed.), *Mind and Cosmos: Essays in Contemporary Science and Philosophy* (Pittsburgh, University of Pittsburgh Press, 1966), 86 (92 f.).

67 Example from Mackie, Cement (note 10), 83 ff.; Fumerton & Kress, Causation (note 63), 83 (93); Moore, An Essay in Law (note 48), 481 ff.; Toepel, Hinreichende Mindestbedingung (note 13), 293.

68 Example following Fumerton & Kress, Causation (note 63), 83 (93); Merkel, Vernachlässigte Probleme (note 48), 158.

69 For example Carnap Introduction (note 57), 188; The idea goes back to D. Hume, A Treatise of Human Nature, (note 59): "For what does he mean by production? Can he give any definition of it that will not be the same with that of causation? If he can; I desire it may be produc'd. If he cannot; he here runs in a circle, and gives a synonymous term instead of a definition" D. Hume, *Enquiries Concerning the Human Understanding and Concerning the Principles of Morals*, reprinted from the posthumous edition of 1777, 2nd ed. (Oxford, Clarendon Press, 1955), section V, part I, 42 f.

70 Haas, Kausalität und Rechtsverletzung (note 48), 182, who defines cause as energy transfer. Fumerton & Kress, Causation (note 63), 83 (103), who are unclear what this thing named cause is supposed to be in any particular case.

can infer the consequent from the antecedent, is a causal law only if it describes a transfer of energy or other efficient entity from antecedent to consequent.[71]

Let us see whether we need the still rather unclear notion of a *causa efficiens* or a restriction of the concept of a cause to a transfer of quanta of energy in order to argue that we do not accept the four groups of conditionals introduced above as causal laws.

Group A: This proposition contains two proper names, Friday and Saturday. Proper names must not occur in causal laws since causal laws are universal.[72] Replacing these proper names by abstract descriptions yields expressions like "the sixth and seventh day of the week". The proposition then is "if the sixth day of the week ends, then always the seventh follows". This proposition is analytically true. The example concerning the widow is no different. Becoming a widow means loosing a husband through death. So our example proposition is synonymous to "if a wife's husband dies, then she loses her husband through death". Alas, we do not need any efficient causes or energy transfers to gain these profound insights from the concept of a causal law. Propositions that are true due to logical or semantic reasons do not refer to reality and so cannot be causal laws.[73]

The example for group B concerning the red balls neither contains any universal law. The expression "this box" refers to an individual, the expression "the balls in this box" refers to a closed class. So although the proposition "if a ball is in the class of balls that lie in this box, then it is red" is based on experience, it is by its mere form not a universal law and therefore no causal law. Banning expressions for closed classes from use in causal laws should practically solve the problem of distinguishing causal laws from accidental successions of events. If there is a succession of two events for an open class of events, it cannot be accidental. However, the assertion of a non-accidental succession can only be based on a limited number of observations, hence a closed class. Therefore, we transcend observational insight by claiming the validity of this succession for open classes. This is the so-called problem of incomplete induction that we discussed above.

Group C: One can view the calculation of the height of the tower from the length of its shadow as a measuring process. Each measuring process permits

---

71 Moore, An Essay in Law (note 48), 498 ff. For Merkel, Vernachlässigte Probleme (note 48), 164 ff. that is "[e]nergy, impulse or complicated enhancement or connection of both". See also M. Esfeld, *Einführung in die Naturphilosophie* (Darmstadt, Wissenschaftliche Buchgesellschaft, 2002), 95 f.

72 Stegmüller, Erklärung (note 15), 320 ff.; Moore, An Essay in Law (note 48) 476 f.

73 See with a very similar example Hart & Honoré, Causation (note 7), 114 f.

inferring the measured phenomenon from the indicator, even though the indicator is not the cause of the phenomenon but the other way round. This relies on the fact that every good measuring instrument is constructed in such a way that in error-free operation, it displays a certain reading if and only if the phenomenon to be measured is in contact with its receptors. This is why one can infer the measured phenomenon from the measuring. But the fact that the phenomenon is measured is not a minimal condition for its existence. Rather, its existence is a prerequisite for its being measured and for the measuring process to yield a certain value. The length of the shadow is a sufficient condition for the height of the tower, if there is a tower. If there is a tower, it has to have a certain height. Thus the shadow is superfluous for the sufficient condition for the height of the tower, which we will recognize at sunset at the latest.[74] This argument is no relapse into the *conditio-sine-qua-non* account. A singular cause need not be *per se* a necessary condition for the result. But a fact that is in no case connected to another which is in turn necessary for the result does not belong to any minimal condition for the occurrence of the latter, even if it is, together with other facts and general rules, the basis for an inference to this result.[75] This is one of several scientific methods for distinguishing causal laws from other regular successions.

Group D deals with cases in which we do not explain the succession of phenomena by the first causing the second, but rather by both having a common cause. If we did not know about the common cause, we could think that the first phenomenon causes the second. If we did not know about the proceedings of rail traffic at level crossings, we could think that the closing of the gate causes the train to approach and not the other way round. If we did not know why the London workers cease to work at 6 p.m., we could think they do it because the Manchester hooters sound. This criticism of the regularity thesis is based on a very simple conception of how causal laws are discovered, namely that an observer sees event A followed by event B sufficiently often to come up with the causal law that A causes B.

However, discovering causal laws is not that simple. They are part of a more comprehensive causal theory that is supposed to explain a piece of the world. The propositions of such a theory must fit together, they must not be inconsistent with each other or with other recognized laws. Therefore, it is easy to falsify the

74 Haas, Kausalität und Rechtsverletzung (note 48) (2002), 174 f. makes a logical mistake when claiming that every sufficient minimal condition also is a necessary condition since it does not contain any superfluous elements. For if there are several sufficient minimal conditions, none of them is necessary, or more precisely: the elements not contained in both sufficient conditions are not necessary.

75 Baumgartner & Graßhoff, Kausalität und kausales Schließen (note 16), 104.

causal law with the content "If the factory hooters sound at 6 p.m. in Manchester, the Londoners stop their work" by noting that no human being reacts to a phenomenon that he cannot perceive, that the Manchester hooters cannot be heard in London and that the position of the sun in London does not depend on the Manchester hooters sounding.[76]

A causal law with the content that the shadow of a tower causes its height is incongruous with the general laws of optics, although these laws justify inferring the height of the tower from the length of its shadow given a certain position of the sun.[77] An argument against the hypothesis of such a law is the observation that the length of the shadow varies with the position of the sun but that the height of the tower does not. This is one of several experimental methods for falsifying causal hypotheses.

Another method to test experimentally whether a phenomenon is the cause of a succeeding one or whether both have a common cause consists in removing the prerequisites for the first. If the second phenomenon still occurs, the first cannot be its cause. If one destroys the barometer and the storm still forms, this shows that the falling of the barometer cannot be the cause of the storm.

Theoretical concepts like energy, energy transfer, energy transformation and mass play an important role in the development of causal theories, at least in physics. So these concepts can, in particular cases, help to discern whether the succession of two phenomena is an instantiation of a causal law that renders the first phenomenon the cause of the second, or whether both have a common cause or whether the one only accidentally follows the other. This does not mean that only energy transfers can be considered as causes. Nor does it mean that we can forego the application of universal causal laws in order to determine causality in singular cases in favour of a conception of causality as energy transfer.

It is essential for a causal law that it is part of a more comprehensive explanation of a part of our world.[78] By accepting only those conditions as lawful minimal conditions that can be subsumed under a causal law[79], the doctrine of the lawful minimal condition refers to such a part of the empirical-scientific explanation of the world. It does not claim, however, that it provides all of the explanation in question by itself. This is why it is accused of circularity. The challenge for this doctrine that it should give a general criterion when a proposition of the

76 See Wright, The NESS Account (note 11), 285ff. (297); Wright, The NESS Account (note. 11), 285ff. (297f.); Puppe, Der Erfolg (note 4), 863 (874).

77 Wright, The NESS Account (note 11), 285ff. (296).

78 Psillos, Regularity Theories (note 16), 130 (141ff.); See Esfeld, Einführung (note 71), 90f.

79 Wright, The NESS Account (note. 11), 285ff. (297f.); Puppe, Der Erfolg (note 4), 863 (874).

form "if...then" is a causal law[80] is about as reasonable as asking a logician for a general criterion to recognize that a proposition has the property of being true.[81] We jurists can and may answer the question whether a regular succession is a causal law: A causal law is a regular succession of events that the relevant natural science acknowledges as causal law.

Stapleton denies that the NESS conception has the quality of a definition because of its supposed circularity. Instead, she sees it as a useful formula for finding causes in singular cases.[82] This does not do justice to the aim and concern of the NESS conception. The NESS theory is nothing more or less than the logically correct determination of the relation between singular cause, causal law and effect, under the presupposition that we can know and name causal laws. Without this presupposition, it is not possible to set result and action in a relation that grounds attribution of the result to the agent; a random singularist notion of causality would be inapt for this. Fumerton and Kress think that the but-for rule would be applicable in a stochastic world.[83] But that is inconsistent. In a stochastic world, it is not only uncertain whether a result will occur subsequently to an event, but also whether it will not occur without the event.

80 Fumerton & Kress, Causation (note 63), 83 (102): "Professor Wright is caught between a rock and a hard place. To avoid the charge that he cannot handle certain cases of causal preemption, he must come up with a way to distinguish lawful (or law-like) sufficiency from causal sufficiency without relying on the concept of causation, a task that has eluded all philosophers to date."

81 See I. Kant, *Critique of Pure Reason*, Cambridge Edition of the Works of Immanuel Kant (transl. P. Guyer and A.W. Wood): "The old and famous question with which the logicians were to be driven into a corner and brought to such a pass that they must either fall into a miserable circle, or else confess their ignorance, hence the vanity of their entire art, is this: What is truth? The nominal definition of truth, namely that it is the agreement of cognition with its object, is here granted and presupposed; but one demands to know what is the general and certain criterion of the truth of any cognition. It is already a great and necessary proof of cleverness or insight to know what one should reasonably ask. For if the question is absurd in itself and demands unncessary answers, then, besides the embarassment of the one who proposes it, it also has the disadvantage of misleading the incautious listener into absurd answers [...]" (AA A57–58/B82)

82 Stapleton, Causation in the Law (note 51) 744 (765); Stapleton, Choosing What We Mean (note 61), 433, (472f.). It is not quite intelligible that Stapleton follows Fumerton and Kress in accussing Wright's reference to causal laws as circular, since she earlier (note 61), 433 (447) allowed the jurists to leave the epistemological problems of causal laws to philosophers and natural scientists. If the accusation has bite that one is caught in a vicious circle in spelling out the difference between causal laws and other regularities, it also hits Stapleton herself, for she uses causal laws in her three forms of involvement.

83 Fumerton & Kress, Causation (note 63), 83 (97f.).

3.2 Objections to the Sufficient Condition

Every sufficient and true minimal condition of the occurrence or endurance of an event that we use in practice is incomplete, even rudimentary. Our attention is focussed on a small part of the specifications that are needed to give a sufficient condition in its entirety. The others we implicitly presuppose as so-called background conditions.[84] Mackie calls these background conditions the "causal field"[85]. The only difference between the explicit elements of the causal explanation and the causal field is that we are currently more interested in the former. After an accident, the traffic policeman or the judge will be interested in the causes relating to the tortuous behaviour of a driver, the civil engineer in those relating to the road surface, the car mechanic in those relating to the state of the brakes and the meteorologist in those relating to the weather conditions.[86] We must and can live with this deficiency of causal explanations.[87] But we have to see that it is a source of error. For if under the countless elements of the sufficient condition that we implicitly presuppose, there is one that does not in fact occur, our causal explanation is wrong and we did not notice it.

However, we have the means to counter this threat, even if it is not immune to error. We check whether certain events that, according to our causal hypothesis and common empirical knowledge would have to occur before, during or after the result to be explained, did not actually occur. For example, our causal hypothesis is falsified if under the assumption that it is true, the result would have occurred at an earlier time, at a later time, at another place or under other circumstances than it actually did. If, in the example above, the ministry official dies in Berlin, the bomb that detonated in his house in Bonn could not have killed him. However, the current doctrine in Germany commits the mistake to count the circumstances of a result that confirm the causal explanation to

84 Fumerton & Kress, Causation (note 63), 83 (98 f.) Moore, An Essay in Law (note 48), 475; Carnap, Einführung (note 57), 191 f.

85 Mackie, Cement (note 11). 34 f.

86 Example from Carnap, Introduction (note 57), 191 f.

87 In any case, this is not a substantial argument against the NESS-condition. Fumerton & Kress, Causation (note 63), 83, (98 f.). Other causal theories have the same problems, Moore, An Essay in Law (note 48), 478. Keil however thinks contrafactual and singularistic concepts of causation do not have this problem. "The reason for this is, that the sentence 'Y would not have occurred if X did not occur' can be understood as an implicit reference to the further factual circumstances, which the generalist is obliged to enumerate (without coming to an end). So the contrafactual sentence is to be interpreted as including the ceteris paribus clause" (translation IP). Keil, *Handeln und Verursachen*, (Frankfurt a.M., Vittorio Klostermann, 2000), 274. But why doesn't Keil allow the generalists to refer on the *ceteris paribus* clause as well?

this result “in its concrete form”. The consequence is that everyone who is causal for such a circumstance is also causal for the result that grounds compensation or criminal liability.

The causal field grows significantly if we accept so-called negative facts as elements of the sufficient condition. This is cited as the reason why negative facts, like for example the fact that a certain person omits to fulfil his duty, cannot be a cause.[88] But if we refuse to take negative facts into account for causal explanations, we run the risk of accepting a wrong causal explanation with an interfering condition. Thus, in order to find true causal explanations, we have to check and negate every possible interfering condition. Since we can never check all background conditions, theoretically there is always the danger that we overlook one or that we overlook an interfering condition that falsifies our causal explanation. Mill rightly pointed out that every causal explanation is only valid under the condition that no interfering conditions are present.[89]

Moore accuses Mill of circular reasoning by imputing to him that he includes into a causal explanation the negation of all possible interfering conditions.[90] This is only possible in the following way: The sufficient minimal condition is causal if there are no conditions present that interfere with its causality. However, this formulation would not only be circular, but completely useless for the verification of a causal minimal condition. For this verification requires checking one by one the absence of interfering conditions that are possible according to universal laws. Was the sprinkler system out of order when the fire broke out? If not, why did it not start working? We cannot avoid the possibility that we miss an interfering condition that actually obtains and that falsifies the causal explanation. An overtaking or superseding causal chain may be an interfering condition as well, because it reveals the condition that appears to be a cause as a preempted cause. So it is theoretically possible that we miss an overtaking causal chain. Every criminalist and every coroner and every crime author knows this.

But it does not follow that the criminalist or the coroner must add to each of his causal explanations “if there isn’t another causal explanation”. That would

---

88 Moore, An Essay in Law (note 48), 475 f.; Toepel, Hinreichende Mindestbedingung (note 13), 291 f.

89 J. S. Mill, *A System of Logic Ratiocinative and Inductive*, 9th ed. (London: Longmans, Green, Reader, and Dyer, 1875), book III, chapter V, section 3; Carnap, Introduction (note 57), 190 ff.; Stegmüller, Erklärung (note 15), 434 ff.; also Puppe, Der Erfolg (note 4), 898 f.

90 Moore, An Essay in Law (note 48), 492 and Toepel, Hinreichende Mindestbedingung (note 13), 298.

render a causal explanation circular.[91] In Karl May, there is the hilarious trapper Sam Hawkins, who, every time he is completely convinced he is right, adds to his statement "if I'm not mistaken". This renders his statement circular. If Sam Hawkins was a philosopher, he would not say that he can always be mistaken. Mill was a philosopher.

The but-for rule is supposed to have the advantage over the doctrine of the lawful minimal condition that one does not need to discuss the countless background conditions (the causal field) that belong to the complete description of a sufficient condition. For all one has to do is to name the one condition that was necessary for the occurrence of the result.[92] But this is an illusion. If one really wants to argue that the action cannot be thought away without the result being nullified, one has to try to give a causal explanation of the result without the action. Doing this confronts one with the countless background conditions (the causal field) just as much as the doctrine of the lawful minimal condition does. The only difference is that the attempt to explain the result without the action is required to fail, instead of the attempt to explain it with the action being required to succeed. The argument for the claim that a state of affairs, for example an action, is a necessary condition for the occurrence of a harmful result is as rudimentary and incomplete as the claim that it is a necessary element of a sufficient minimal condition of the result.

Anglo-American literature discusses a logical objection to the conception of the lawful sufficient condition. It aims at showing that any fact can be made a necessary element of a sufficient condition. In order to do this, one only has to link the negation of a fact with a part of the true sufficient condition of the result through a disjunction.[93] So, for example, one writes: V died because either D cut off his head or Napoleon did not marry Joséphine.[94] This is not a sufficient condition of V's death, because this condition would still be true if Napoleon did not marry Joséphine. To make it a sufficient one, one has to add the fact that Napoleon married Joséphine. This would prove that this fact is a necessary element of the sufficient condition of V's death. Moore declares such disjunctions of conditions as inadmissible for causal explanations because he rejects negations as

---

91 See Moore, An Essay in Law (note 48), 444 f.; Toepel, Hinreichende Mindestbedingung (note 13), 298.

92 Toepel, Hinreichende Mindestbedingung (note 13), 289, (301).

93 Fumerton & Kress, Causation and the Law (note 63), 83 (95); J. Thomson, 'Some Reflections on Hart and Honoré, Causation in the Law', in: *The Legacy of H.L.A. Hart* (Oxford, Oxford University Press, 2008), 151 f.

94 Example from Wright, The NESS Account (note 11), 285 ff. (295).

constituents of causal conditions.[95] Since we accept negations as causes, this is no solution to the problem for us. Wright thinks this prohibition is implicit in the NESS test, because the latter may only contain true states of affairs and the proposition "Napoleon did not marry Joséphine" is not true.[96] Still, the proposition "either D cut off V's head or Napoleon did not marry Joséphine" is still true insofar D really did cut off V's head. But the inadmissibility of disjunctions in minimal causal conditions is revealed by linking a cause to an arbitrary true state of affairs. For this provides the means to falsify any causal explanation. So we write: "V died because either D cut off his head or Napoleon married Joséphine." This condition is too weak to be sufficient for the explanation of V's death, since it is already true due to the fact that Napoleon married Joséphine, even if D would not have cut off V's head. To sharpen this condition into a sufficient one, we have to claim that Napoleon did not marry Joséphine. But this proposition is obviously false. Therefore, the whole causal explanation of V's death would be false if we would allow such disjunctions in causal explanations.

This might mean that the criterion of the sufficient minimal condition can likewise be indefinitely manipulated, so that everything can be deduced from it, both false and true. Let us take a closer look at the technique. Our sufficient minimal condition is supposed to consist, among others, of the following two propositions:

1. D cut off V's head or Napoleon did not marry Joséphine.
2. Napoleon married Joséphine.

If proposition 2 is true, we can eliminate from proposition 1 the part "or Napoleon did not marry Joséphine". This yields the following sufficient condition:

D cut off V's head and Napoleon married Joséphine → V is dead.

In this sufficient condition for V's death, the proposition "Napoleon married Joséphine" is superfluous.

This attempt to reduce the NESS conception to absurdity is simple. It can also simply be refuted by completely spelling it out. However, more sophisticated methods can be conceived of establishing artificial dependencies between condition by means of logic. One could add the requirement that a NESS condition only contains elementary propositions. At the least, the following rule holds

95 Moore, An Essay in Law (note 48), 487 ff. However, Moore uses a complicated example that combines this problem with so-called problem of boards.

96 Wright, The NESS Account (note 11), 285 ff. (295).

true: A condition is a NESS condition only if it is a necessary element in every logical form in which the sufficient minimal condition can be put.

3.3 The Requirement of the Minimal Condition

Since a singular cause can at most be a necessary part of a sufficient condition, one may very well wonder whether we really need the requirement that a condition is minimal. For if the sufficient condition contains an element that goes beyond a minimal condition, its lack of causality will show if we think it away from the sufficient condition and see that the condition remains sufficient. Despite this, we do need the requirement that a sufficient condition is minimal. We need it to preclude the case that there are several elements in the sufficient condition that can be substituted as causes, i.e. multiple or preemptive causality. If one were to think away the alleged cause from the sufficient but not minimal condition in this case, one would have to conclude that it is not a cause, because the sufficient condition remains sufficient due to the remaining causal factors or the preempted cause.[97] It is just in these cases in which the doctrine of the sufficient minimal condition shows its practical superiority to the *conditio-sine-qua-non* formula.[98] Furthermore, we have shown above (pp.56–57) that there is a danger of wrongly accepting a relation of sufficiency as causal law if one neglects the requirement of the necessity of each of its elements.

Dencker objects to the requirement of the minimal condition that it is nothing but the abbreviation of the specific state of affairs in question. For how a minimal law is made out depends on the circumstances of the specific case. The minimal lethal dose of a poison depends, for example, on the victim's height, weight, age and health.[99] Dencker's observation is correct, but no objec-

97 The challenge from C. Knauer, *Die Kollegialentscheidung im Strafrecht Zugleich ein Beitrag zum Verhältnis von Kausalität und Mittäterschaft* (München, C.H. Beck, 2001), 197, Koriath, Kausalität (2007) (note 44), 110, and E. Hilgendorf JURA 1995, 514, 516, that the reason for the requirement of the minimal condition "remains in the dark", only shows "that some authors did not yet logically penetrate the method", E. Kraatz, *Die fahrlässige Mittäterschaft Ein Beitrag zur strafrechtlichen Zurechnungslehre auf der Grundlage eines finalen Handlungsbegriffs* (Berlin, Duncker & Humblot, 2006), 337.

98 Moore, An Essay in Law (note 48), 486, denies the doctrine of the sufficient condition this benefit since both could contain competing causes. The reason for this is that he neglects the requirement of minimality.

99 F. Dencker, *Kausalität und Gesamttat* (Berlin, Duncker & Humblot, 1996), 113f; L. Greco, 'Kausalität- und Zurechnungsprobleme bei unechten Unterlassungsdelikten', ZIS 2011, 674 ff (686).

tion against the requirement of the minimal condition. Naturally, the formulation of the minimal law that is supposed to be used in a specific case must account for all circumstances of this case. If a child receives a dose of poison lethal for its body, one can of course give a minimal condition that contains a dose lethal for an adult by concealing the victim's age and height. Then, the actual dose would not be sufficient. However, it is enough to be able to give a condition of the result that is sufficient under the given circumstances and that includes the alleged cause as a necessary element. It is possible to do this in Dencker's example by citing the victim's age, height, weight, etc.

The requirement of the minimal condition provides the means to resolve the so-called problem of committees (*Gremienproblem*). An illegal motion is passed with a majority greater than would have been necessary for it to pass. Against the background of all other votes, a particular single vote is neither necessary for the motion to pass nor, taken in isolation, sufficient. However, we get a minimal condition that contains the vote of committee member M as a necessary element by pooling together his vote with so many other actual votes that they suffice for the motion to pass.[100] It does not do any harm that the different minimal conditions are not discrete but possess common elements, namely the votes that, together with M's vote, are needed for the required majority. It is unavoidable that several competing and sufficient minimal conditions have common elements. Likewise, it is harmless that one can arbitrarily choose other votes in addition to M's in order to formulate the sufficient condition. The crucial point is that it is possible to formulate one or several such sufficient conditions that are true and that contain M's vote as a necessary element.

100 Wright, Causation (note 22), 1792f.; Puppe, JR 1992 (note 36), 30 (33); Puppe, Nomos-Kommentar above § 13, (note 4),par. 108; likewise Sofos, (note 19), 160f.; Rodrigues-Montanes, 'Einige Bemerkungen über das Kausalitätsproblem und die Täterschaft im Falle rechtswidriger Kollegialentscheidungen', in: B. Schünemann, H. Achenbach, W. Bottke, B. Haffke & H. J. Rudolphi (eds), *Festschrift für Claus Roxin zum 70. Geburtstag* (Berlin New York, de Gruyter, 2001), 307 (313f.). Stapleton, Causation in the Law (note 51), 744 (747); Stapleton, Choosing What We Mean (note 61), 433 (435ff.) deems it necessary to acknowledge three forms of causation (involvement): the necessity, the double necessity and – to solve the committee problem – a third from which she calls contribution. The NESS-Account handles all three constellations. Stapleton, 444. Moore is ambiguous on that solution. He applies it to another example, An Essay in Law (note 48), 487: Five environmental offenders each discharge a certain amount of a poisonous substance into a river that on their own are not harmful to the river. But the effluents of three of them put together are poisonous enough to damage the river. Moore admits that the NESS account is able to solve this problem correctly, though a few pages later, 510, he claims that the NESS account can only lead to a wrong answer in these cases.

4 The Hindrance of Rescuing Events and the Causality of Omissions

If there is a condition that interferes with a causal chain, everyone who removes this condition causes the result of the causal chain. In Germany, we call this a hindrance or prevention of rescuing events. Samson came up with the following illustration: A sick person lies in the jungle and can only be saved by a certain serum. On the next airfield, a plane and the required serum stand ready to depart. However, the plane is lacking the necessary cooling equipment, so that the serum will go bad during the flight. While loading the plane, an inattentive worker spills the serum. Is he causal for the sick person's death?[101]

One could answer affirmatively by constructing a causal chain from the preparation of the serum and the plane to the patient's death and introducing as a link the fact that the serum is spilled. This is how Wright would proceed. He supposes that there is an interfering condition, here the condition that the sick person receives a serum, and goes on to ask why this did not occur. The answer is that the worker spilled the serum. That the serum would have gone bad during the subsequent flight anyway is a causally irrelevant preempted cause. For the causal chain that would have led to the serum going bad is cut by it having been spilled.[102]

However, before constructing this chain, one has to justify that the proceedings on the airfield have to be taken into account for the sufficient minimal condition of the sick person's death. Alternatively, one could formulate a sufficient condition only containing the illness and the prerequisites of its aggravation to death. But this minimal condition is not complete if somewhere in the world there would be preconditions ensuring that the aggravation of the illness would be prevented. If the plane had carried the necessary cooling equipment, all conditions for preventing the aggravation of the illness would have been fulfilled at the point of loading the plane. Then, the worker would have been causal for the patient's death through his inattentiveness.

Here we indeed come across a peculiarity of negative facts. In every world, there are many more negative than positive facts. We can therefore think of a variety of conditions for the rescue of the sick person that do not exist and that would then be cumulatively causal for the absence of the rescue. We could, for example, say: It is causal for the sick person's death in the jungle that

101 E. Samson, *Hypothetische Kausalverläufe im Strafrecht. Zugleich ein Beitrag zur Kausalität der Beihilfe* (Frankfurt, Alfred Metzner, 1972), 95f.

102 See Wright, Acts and Omissions (note 18), 287 (303ff.).

first, A did not supply a serum, second, B did not charter a plane, third, C did not buy cooling equipment and fourth, the pilot P was not available to fly the plane. The question "What was the cause for something that did not happen?" only makes sense if, at some time, all conditions for it to happen are fulfilled. Then, the action that removes the first of these conditions is the cause for its not occurring, hence for the hindrance of rescuing causal chains and so for the harm. There is cumulative causality only if several conditions simultaneously remove a necessary condition for the hindrance.

If it is correct that the fact that something does not occur is to be included in a causal explanation only if at some time the conditions exist for it to occur, this vindicates a principle for the responsibility of an offender by omission that is used in Germany: A duty to perform the omitted act and the causality of the omitted act for the result presuppose that the act actually could have prevented the result. This is not a relapse into the doctrine of the necessary condition. There certainly are cases of multiple causality of omissions, namely if several omissions happen at the same time and each of the omitted actions would be an interfering condition for the occurrence of the result. For example, both the pool attendant and the father who has been trained as a lifeguard omit to rescue the drowning child. According to what has hitherto been said, if several simultaneously omitted actions only jointly constitute an interfering condition for the result, each omitting agent could argue his exoneration by pointing out that because of the other's omission, the conditions for his action to be an interfering event for the occurrence of the result do not obtain. But if this condition consists of another person fulfilling his duty at the same time, none can claim the other's violation of his duty for his exoneration.

The famous politburo case of the German Federal Supreme Court (BGH) concerned the responsibility of members of the defence council of the German Democratic Republic, who took office after the construction of the Berlin wall, for the death strip and firing orders which led to the killing of fugitives. Everyone was accused of violating their duty in omitting to abolish this border regime of the GDR and thereby being causal for fugitives' deaths at the border. Here, our rule that an omission can only be part of a minimal condition of a result if the preconditions for the prevention of the result through dutiful action are fulfilled must be restricted: In answering this question, others' duty-violating behaviour must not be taken into account, although it is actually present and although this makes the prevention of the result impossible for any particular defendant.[103]

103 BGHSt 48, 77, 95, see Puppe AT (note 18), 30/1ff.

Consider the following case: A and B are under a certain duty. A omits to warn B of a danger relevant to their duty. A's capability to prevent the result in question depends on B's doing his duty to prevent the result later on. In such a case, the causality of A's omission cannot depend on whether B would have fulfilled his duty if A had given him the chance. For firstly, this question can in principle not be answered, as long as we assume that human beings act freely. Secondly, nobody may call upon another's fictional violation of duty for his exoneration. So we have to presuppose that B would have fulfilled his duty if he could when assessing whether A's omission to warn of the danger is causal for the harm because of normative reasons.[104] Since there are normative reasons for this rule of assessing causality of omissions, it is valid independently of empirical acceptance.

These problems of the joint occurrence of several omissions do not only exist for the NESS algorithm as a definition of causality. They also exist for the but-for rule and every counterfactual account of causation (or quasi-causation) of omissions. All these accounts must suffer the normatively motivated restriction that a defendant who has violated a duty cannot be exonerated by another's actual and even less hypothetical violation of duty. So these problems are no reason to discard the NESS algorithm as a definition of causality.[105]

5 The Problem of Detecting Preempted Causes

5.1 Causal Chains

In contrast to the *conditio-sine-qua-non* formula, the conception of the cause as a necessary element of a sufficient and true minimal condition can solve the problem of multiple and preemptive causality logically correct.[106] Now a preempted cause is a true sufficient minimal condition for the occurrence of the result as well, so that the result can be predicted from the presence of the preempted cause. The *conditio-sine-qua-non* formula already has its problems to represent the actual cause as such if several causal explanations come into consideration. The challenge for the doctrine of the sufficient minimal condition is to reveal the preempted cause as a merely alleged cause.

104 See Puppe AT, (note 18), 2/27 ff., 30/12 ff.

105 Contra Stapleton, Choosing What We Mean (note 61), 433 (477 ff.).

106 Hart & Honoré, Causation (note 7), 124; Honoré, Conditions (note 7) 94, 107 ff.; Wright, Causation in tort law (note 22); Wright, The NESS Account (note 11), 285 ff. (293;); Puppe, Der Erfolg (note 4), 863, (870 ff.); Puppe, Nomos-Kommentar above § 13 (note 4) par. 108.

As mentioned above, there would be no difference between genuine causes and preempted causes if one would accept as cause every sufficient minimal condition that exists at any time before the occurrence of the result and therefore allows a prediction of the result. We only recognize such a condition as cause of the result if it is linked to the latter through a chain of events that are spatially and temporally contiguous and in which each link is a sufficient minimal condition for the subsequent link. Figuratively, we call this a causal chain.[107]

Now here, opponents of the doctrine of the sufficient minimal condition believe to have spotted its Achilles' heel. They ask what connects the links of this chain if not energy or some other thing that is transferred from one link to the next.[108] But the spatially and temporally contiguous states are linked by the lawful succession into a chain. The causal explanation of two sequential states of this chain has the same structure that we presuppose for the causal explanation of a result by its antecedents, only that the distance between cause and effect is very short.

Opponents object that it is not possible to give a complete description of this chain of causes and effects, because between two states it is always possible to find a third.[109] They suppose that the only way to solve this problem is by using the notion of an energy transfer or an impulse propagating along the way of the chain. But such propagation can neither be completely described, because between two points, between which energy or impulse spread, we can always find a third. Since Euclid, the impossibility of their complete description has not prevented us from representing and working with continua like lines, areas, spaces and movements of bodies. So why not work with lawful connections of events?

The requirement of linking cause and effect by proximate causal laws entails that every causal process has a determinate speed of propagation. This does not only hold for processes of energy transfer, but for lawful relations of all sorts. So if I know a causal chain through its lawful minimal conditions, I can determine

107 Puppe, Der Erfolg (note 4), 863, 888 ff.; Wright, The NESS Account (note. 11), 285 ff. (298).
108 Moore, An Essay in Law (note 48), 500 ff., does not commit to a certain entity which connects the links of the chain, unlike others who make commitments to more or less specified entities. Haas, Kausalität und Rechtsverletzung (note 48), 102: "Macrophysically, this relation corresponds to a transfer of energy based on the propagation of power"; Merkel, Vernachlässigte Probleme (note 48), 165: "What else could be the specific origin in a lawful development of the links of a causal chain than the transfer of energy or impulse, which means physically efficient powers?"; Toepel, Hinreichende Mindestbedingung (note 13), 297: "Causal chains acquire unique reality, as does the concept of the cause as efficient power."
109 Erb, Die Zurechnung von Erfolgen (note 44), 449, 451; Haas, Kausalität und Rechtsverletzung (note 48), 182; Toepel, Hinreichende Mindestbedingung (note 13), 289.

the time at which the result must occur if I have to do with a cause and not merely with a preempted cause. This is not a privilege of singularist or physicalist theories of causation. If the result occurs at a different time, I am dealing with a preempted cause. If the result occurred earlier, there is an even simpler method for discerning the cause in question as a preempted cause. A corpse can no longer die, a destructed building no longer be destructed and a burnt-down house can no longer be burnt solely by lack of inflammable materials.[110]

Moore uses just these examples to charge the doctrine of the sufficient minimal condition with a insoluble problem and circular reasoning.[111] The only reason I can imagine why he does this is that he does not concede to this doctrine the ability to construct causal chains.[112] In his opinion, one needs something that runs through a causal chain and connects its links in order to establish such a chain, may it be power, impulse, shape or some other identical entity. I suspect this also to be the reason why he so vehemently argues against accepting negative facts as causes. For in a negative fact, there is no such entity. Thus, Moore finally opts for a singularist theory of causation, though not clearly a physicalist one. He claims that the doctrine of the lawful minimal condition must treat both a genuine cause and a cause preempted by a genuine one as causal. But "[s]ingularist theories slick through these cases like the proverbial hot knife through butter"[113].

Yet the doctrine of a lawful minimal condition has much less trouble to construct causal chains than a singularist theory. For the singularist theory must first identify the mysterious entity supposed to connect the links of the causal chain. If we take an exertion of power as this entity, this theory is in trouble as soon as the flow of power is interrupted (see the above example concerning the executioner and the murderer). In the end, every human being dies because his brain cells do not get enough oxygen. In contrast to this, the doctrine of the

---

110 Toepel, Hinreichende Mindestbedingung (note 13), 289 (296) regards this as a break with a generalist notion of causality, because one considers in a singular case that the house is already burned down or that the victim hit by the bulled is already dead. But this is to consider the events in accordance with general causal laws as the law is relevant that a burned-down house can no longer burn down and that a dead man cannot be killed, where at least the least proposition is analytic. Contrary to Moore, An Essay in Law (note 48), 494 f., considering these circumstances is no vicious circle, even if they only occurred shortly before the presumed causal process reaches the object, so-called late preemption, Wright, The NESS Account (note 11), 285 ff. (301 ff.); Wright, Causation in Tort Law (note 22) 1795.

111 Moore, An Essay in Law (note 48), 493; likewise Toepel, Hinreichende Mindestbedingung (note 13), 289, (296).

112 Moore, An Essay in Law (note 48), 491 ff.

113 Moore, An Essay in Law (note 48), 510.

lawful minimal condition is capable to construct a causal chain in all of these cases. What connects its links is the fact that every event is a sufficient, lawful condition for the subsequent one.[114] To take Moore's picture: The doctrine of the lawful minimal conditions slicks through the proverbial butter like a laser beam. The following example will illustrate this.

It is conveniently possible to construct causal chains backwards, from the result to the alleged cause, where every state in the chain is a sufficient, lawful condition for the subsequent one. Since the description of one single sufficient condition cannot be complete, the description of the whole causal chain can neither be complete. Let us reconstruct the causal chain that led to the collapse of the ice rink in Bad Reichenhall.[115] On January 2nd, 2006 at 15.55, the roof of the ice rink collapsed suddenly, killing 15 ice-skaters. We suspect construction shortcomings and the age of the over 30-year-old roof as causal factors. In the days preceding the accident, unusually great amounts of snow had fallen. This load of snow crushed the roof. Why could the roof not carry it any more? The roof did no longer possess full carrying capacity, because the glue required for a stable assembly of the wooden elements was no longer there. By the way, this is a negative fact. Yet I could give Moore the "truth-maker"[116] for the negative condition that there was not enough glue to hold the construction together. It was not any non-glue, but the rainwater that seeped into the wood and dissolved the glue. With passing years, water had entered the wooden construction and effectively dissolved the glue. This was possible because the builders used water-soluble glue in the construction of the roof. For such a building, this was an offense against the rules of architecture.

Even though some parts of this causal chain can be described as processes of energy transfer, this does not hold for all segments. So it is not necessarily an energy transfer that connects the links of this causal chains. What connects the links is just that every state is a sufficient, lawful minimal condition for the subsequent one. If a rooftop that is no longer held together by glue is laden with at least X kilogrammes of snow, it collapses. If the glue dissolves, it does no longer

114 Stegmüller, Erklärung (note 15), 156 f.; Puppe, Der Erfolg (note 4), 888 ff.; Wright, The NESS Account (note 11), 285 ff. (299).

115 BGH JR 2010, 353, comments Puppe, 355.

116 By demanding to be shown the "truth-maker" of this state of affairs, i. e. the non-glue that did not hold the elements together, Moore An Essay in Law (note 48), 445 commits an indeed classical anthropomorphism, see Carnap, Introduction (note 57) 189. If the wind blows, there must be someone who blows, namely the wind. 'Was macht der Wind, wenn er nicht weht?', E. Kästner, *Kurz und Bündig*, Epigramme (Deutscher Taschenbuch Verlag, 1950), see Puppe, Sorgfaltswidrigkeit und Erfolg (note 54), 609.

hold the rooftop together. If the glue is water-soluble and water enters into the roof, the glue dissolves, etc.[117]

Now, in order to test the method for discerning preempted causes, we imagine that a terrorist installed a bomb on a bearing element of the ice rink, carrying a time fuse that is set to the January 2nd, 15.55. The installation of the bomb would only be causal for the collapse of the ice rink if the collapse would be preceded by a shock wave, the shock wave by an explosion and the explosion by the activation of the fuse. If one or all of these preliminary states that are lawfully linked with the destruction of the ice rink by the bomb did not in fact occur, the installation of the bomb is revealed as a preempted cause.[118] The exact time of the occurrence of the result can provide a hint as to whether a certain causal chain is only a preempted cause, for every process of causation propagates with a certain speed. If, for example, the time fuse of the bomb was set to a time earlier or later than 15.55, we can see that the bomb cannot be the cause of the collapse of the ice rink at exactly 15.55. To argue this point, we do not need include the time of the occurrence of the result in the definition of the result. So we need not adopt the thesis that every harm consists in reducing the period of existence of the object harmed. There is a difference between the acceleration of a causal process and its replacement by another one.

5.2 Separation and Substitution of Risk

There may be cases in which it is not clear whether the perpetrator changed the circumstances of a causal process or replaced it with another. For this can depend on the terms in which we describe the causal process. To a natural scientist, this does not make any difference, because he is only interested in providing any causal explanation of the result at all. But for the jurist, this question can be crucial. For in general opinion, the substitution of risk grounds the perpetrator's responsibility for the result, whereas the variation of circumstances does not.

In Germany, jurists have been discussing Samson's switchman case for a long time.[119] A landslip has blocked both tracks of a railroad. A train approaches

117 Toepel objects that such a connection between intermediate states is superfluous. His reason for thinking this is that this connection is already contained in the requirement that the first, spatially and temporally distant cause is a sufficient minimal condition, see Toepel, Hinreichende Mindestbedingung (note 13), (297). However, he is wrong, which every case of cut or overtaken causal chains shows. These are just the merely seeming or preempted causes.

118 Puppe, Der Erfolg (note 4), 863, 888ff.

119 Samson, Hypothetische Kausalverläufe (note 101), 68.

the landslip on track A and the switchman reroutes it to track B. Most authors in Germany take it for granted that in describing the cause of the train accident, we have to distinguish between track A and B. Then the switchman is causal for the actual causal process.[120] But one can disagree. If we describe the causal chain not in terms of track A and B, but in terms of the railroad instead, the causal explanation of the accident no longer contains the switchman's behaviour. The reason for this is the ambiguity and flexibility of our language.[121] Only a language that has standardized expressions of all objects and states of affairs, so that every state of affairs only allows for one explanation, yields clear-cut results. Think, for example, of classical geometry, that clearly defines the characteristics of a triangle or circle, and so under which conditions two descriptions of a triangle refer to the same triangle.

However, this problem only occurs in the rare cases in which we disagree about whether to use wider or narrower terms in describing a state of affairs. Still, some authors regard this as ample justification to dismiss the method of identifying preempted causes through constructing causal chains and the doctrine of the sufficient minimal condition. They return to the *conditio-sine-qua-non* formula and the result "in its concrete form".[122] This grants the arbitrariness of descriptions of states of affairs in natural language the status of a general principle for distinguishing substitution of risk from mere variation of risk. If one wants to represent a state of affairs as substitution of risk, one includes the change in the world affected by the perpetrator in the description of the result in its concrete form. If one wants to depict this change as irrelevant, one omits this.

But we cannot escape our language and in most cases, our descriptions will be sufficiently clear to determine whether a perpetrator's intervention replaced an existing causal process with another one or merely changed an inessential circumstance of this process. Anglo-American literature has been discussing the following case for a long time[123]: A traveller through the desert carries only one canister of water. Perpetrator 1 mixes it with a lethal but colour- and tasteless poison. Later, perpetrator 2 secretly drills a hole in the canister so that it

120 Samson, Hypothetische Kausalverläufe (note 101), 68; Kindhäuser, Risikoerhöhung und Risikoverringerung (note 18), 499 f.

121 See, with another example, Puppe, Der Erfolg (note 4), 863, 894 f.

122 Erb, Rechtmäßiges Alternativverhalten (note 44), 41 ff.; M. Binns, *INUS-Bedingung und strafrechtlicher Kausalbegriff. J. L. Mackies Kausalanalyse und ihre Übertragung auf das Strafrecht* (Baden-Baden, Nomos, 2001), 109 ff.

123 Mackie, The Cement (note 11), 44 ff.; Honoré, Conditions (note 7), 111 f.; Wright, Causation in Tort Law (note 22) 1802; Wright, The NESS Account (note 11), 285 ff. (298).

drains. The traveller dies of thirst. We could describe the cause of his death as lack of drinkable water. Then perpetrator 1 would be causal for the death. However, we could not include death by thirst with death by poisoning in one causal process, first because the two would have occurred at different times, and second because we need to apply completely different causal laws for their explanation. Only perpetrator 2 caused the death by thirst by simultaneously cutting the causal chain to death by poisoning. In every substitution of causes, the original causal chain is either cut or overtaken, so that the result occurs before the preempted cause could have affected it. In the present case, perpetrator 2 even postponed the traveller's death, because the latter would have died sooner from poison than from thirst. This example shows that we cannot put the causation of the destruction of an object of a legally protected right on a par with the reduction of its period of existence.[124]

6 Conclusion

There are significant theoretical objections against the generalist theory of causation, especially in the form of the lawful, sufficient minimal condition. This theory employs regularities, so-called causal laws, which cannot be proven with 100 % certainty (the problem of incomplete induction). It requires a whole net of theoretical causal propositions in order to decide whether a frequently observed sequence of states is based on a causal law or is accidental. It only focuses on a small part of the sufficient minimal condition and takes the significantly larger part, the so-called causal field, as given. Because of this it runs the risk of accepting false causal explanations, which occur when one of the conditions in the causal field does not obtain or an interfering condition obtains. Overtaking or superseding causal chains are such interfering conditions. In rare cases, the elasticity of our language prevents us from telling apart the substitution of a causal process from a modification of circumstances.

It is remarkable how seldom these theoretical problems are of practical significance. In practical life, in technology, in medicine, we are content with the certainty of causal laws that incomplete induction grants. Why should we jurists demand more than that? In most cases, we actually do have a theoretical net of causal laws which permits us to see whether a sequence of events can be ex-

124 Although this is claimed by: Samson, Hypothetische Kausalverläufe (note 101), 99, 165f., Kindhäuser, AT (note 43) see 10/24 for preemptive causation and 10/4 for the shortening of the life span as a result; Toepel, Hinreichende Mindestbedingung (note 13), 302. Contrary Wright, Causation in Tort Law (note 22). 1802; Wright, The NESS Account (note 11) 298f.

plained by one state being the cause of the following or whether both have a common cause or whether it is an accidental succession. The world we live in is relative stable, so that we can take a significant part of the sufficient condition of a result, the causal field, for granted. If we lived in a universe in which conditions perpetually change, this would not be the case. To raise the problem of distinguishing the substitution of a causal process from the mere modification of circumstances, one has to make up quite strange cases like the one of the switchman, which, sure enough, are then discussed all the more eagerly.

Singularist theories of causation do not have these problems. They have the simplest answer to the question what causes an event in a particular case: The cause causes the event. If they do not want to be tautological, singularist theories have to construct a general notion of a singular cause that has to apply to every case of causation. To my knowledge, only physicalist theories of causation have succeeded in this. According to them, a cause is a transfer of quanta of energy from one point in space-time to another. With this notion of a cause, many natural processes are no longer causally explainable, because they do not consist in a constant flow of energy. Social processes, for example the exchange of information and other institutional processes, cannot be causally explained in this way at all. So-called negative facts like the removal of interfering conditions or an omission contrary to obligation would neither be causes – not because they are nothing, but because they are not energy transfers. This shows the physicalist notion of a cause to be a pure conceptual definition according to definitional taste. It is unfit for many purposes that require the notion of a cause. In particular, it is unfit as the sole basis of the juridical and moral attribution of results.

If we ask further how to discover such a cause as energy transfer, we are often merely pointed to methods of measuring energy. Simple cases like the hitting of billiard balls remain the exception to this. Except for these simple cases, we just cannot see the flow of energy. But all methods of measurement presuppose causal regularities. The epistemological problem of the regularity thesis that the singularist theory shoved out of the front door re-enters through the back door.

Singularist theories do not provide a general method for ascertaining causality in particular cases. The generalist ones do this. However, the counterfactual generalist theory of causation provides a logically wrong method. The doctrine of the sufficient minimal condition suggests the right one, or at least the one that every technician, every practically working physicist, every physician and every criminalist uses in practice. This is, practically and ultimately, its theoretical benefit.

If a conception of causality is to be apt to ground the attribution of results in the law, it is crucial that it gives the reason for this attribution. But the singularist conception does not achieve this, at least not if it goes without regularities. For if we imagine the workings of powers and energies without regularities, there is no reason to attribute the consequence to whoever set free these energies. Attributing the consequence of an action to a perpetrator is based on his knowledge or his ability to know the consequences of his actions. So he has to know universal rules which actions yields which consequences. But if the perpetrator does or can know such rules, his responsibility does not depend on the fact that he set free certain energies. It depends on the fact that he established certain conditions that, in combination with other existing conditions, are sufficient for the occurrence of the result, and he did or should have known this. Acceptance of this generalist conception of causality as the basis of attribution in the law does not even depend on whether we accept, in principle, Hume's account of causality.

Abbreviations

Anm	comment
AT	Allgemeiner Teil
BGH	Bundesgerichtshof (German Supreme Court)
BGHSt	Entscheidungen des Bundesgerichtshofs in Strafsachen (Official collection of decisions of the Supreme Court concerning Criminal Law)
GA	Goltdammer's Archiv für Strafrecht
JR	Juristische Rundschau
JuS	Juristische Schulung
NK	Nomos Kommentar
RGSt	Entscheidungen des Reichsgerichts in Strafsachen
SchwZStr	Schweizerische Zeitschrift für Strafrecht
SK	Systematischer Kommentar
StV	Strafverteidiger Zeitschrift
Urt.	Judgement
VRS	Verkehrsrechts-Sammlung Zeitschrift
ZIS	Zeitschrift für Internationale Strafrechtsdogmatik
ZStW	Zeitschrift für die gesamte Strafrechtswissenschaft

Friedrich Toepel

Causal Overdetermination

1 Introduction

The majority of the arguments concerning causation in Michael S. Moore's book on 'Causation and Responsibility' sounds completely convincing to me.[1] Particularly, his chapter on generalist theories should reduce the attractiveness of generalist theories which seem to be sort of a favourite among many legal scholars all over the world who have made themselves a name in the field of causation.[2] This paper is motivated by two factors which made me think it might be worthwhile to write a paper on causation even after 'Causation and Responsibility' has been published.

First, I do not like Moore's conclusion that singularist theories win by default because there is no better account.[3] To leave the possibility open that causation may not be more than a mysterious entity of which we can say nothing than with Jeremiah Smith that we will know causation when we see it[4], seems to me to be no more than a declaration of the bankruptcy of reason. I think we should be very reluctant to give up the idea of being able to explain causation in terms of a precise conditional analysis. I just have the feeling – which may be wrong, of course – that Moore has been a bit too quick to accept the impossibility of an adequate conditional analysis. What seems to confirm my impression is the comparatively small space that Mackie's concept of causation occupies in Moore's book.[5] That brings me to my second point. I am convinced that Mackie's work 'The Cement of the Universe' contains the key to a standard of causation applicable in a legal context for which until now an adequate full-fledged anal-

---

1 I use the term cause in this paper exclusively in the narrow sense referred to by Moore as the 'cause-in-fact' in contrast to a 'proximate cause', Michael S. Moore, *Causation and Responsibility* (Oxford, Oxford University Press, 2009), 83.

2 Like Ingeborg Puppe, Introduction before Section 13 in the Nomos Commentary to the German Criminal Code, 3rd ed. 2010, para. 80 – 134, in Germany and Richard Wright, 'Causation in Tort Law', California Law Review 73 (1985), 1788 – 1803; 'Causation, Responsibility, Risk, Probability, Naked Statistics and Proof: Pruning the Bramble Bush by Clarifying Concepts', Iowa Law Review 73 (1988), 1001 – 1077, in the U. S.

3 See Moore (note 1) x, xii.

4 Jeremiah Smith, 'Legal Cause in Actions of Tort', Harvard Law Review 25 (1911 – 1912), 103 – 128, 223 – 252, 303 – 327; referred to in Michael S. Moore, (note 1) 505.

5 At least he calls Mackie's discussion 'refreshingly honest', Moore (note 1) 482.

ysis has never been given. In this paper, I just wish to outline how in my opinion the hints to be found in 'The Cement of the Universe' need to be connected while at the same time avoiding crushing arguments from 'Causation and Responsibility'.

2 Mackie's View Concerning Symmetrical Overdetermination

To me, a good starting point seems to be the constellation which Moore calls symmetrically overdetermined concurrent-cause cases[6]. I refer particularly to situations of the following kind:

> (1) A and B shoot C in the head. Each shot would by itself have caused death at the exact moment t_1 at which it happened in reality even if the respective other shot would never have been fired.

Before we try to analyse this example, we have to set aside complaints about its artificiality. It will always be difficult to imagine a real situation where the problem of symmetrically overdetermined concurrent-cause cases materializes, and therefore the practical relevance of symmetrically overdetermined concurrent-cause cases is negligible. One might take the view that all examples could be dissolved if a more fine-grained description of the circumstances would be possible. It may be, for example, that on the microscopic level the two bullets in (1) never hit an equal amount of molecules and that this difference always causes one shot to bring about death a tiny split-second later than the other. Then, the problem of symmetrically overdetermined concurrent-cause cases would coincide with pre-emptive overdetermination.

In practice, the problem of symmetrically overdetermined concurrent-cause cases will not occur because the situation will regularly not be observed by an expert witness with a stop watch. Therefore, nobody will be able to exclude the possibility that one potentially causal factor pre-empted the other. There is general agreement that in case of pre-emptive overdetermination only the pre-emptive, not the pre-empted factor should be a cause of the effect. Even if all of the rivelling factors in symmetrically overdetermined concurrent-cause cases would be deemed causes, the presumption of innocence would forbid simply

6 Moore (note 1) 414, 486.

to insinuate that the effect would have been brought about simultaneously by all potential causes.

However, the theoretical problem will always remain that of two cause candidates which separately would be necessary conditions each is no longer necessary if they occur simultaneously and if there is an equal chance for both to cause the result. This theoretical problem is the reason why symmetrically overdetermined concurrent-cause cases may become the touchstone by which to discern the differences between the various causal concepts, and that makes it worth the pain to cut through the thicket of theories that has developed around this problem.

If we therefore take the example (1) at face value, the two shots in (1) are each sufficient but not necessary to bring about the victim's death. Some scholars think this result would be evidence for the superiority of the sufficiency criterion which most generalist theories of causation share.

Moore cites Mackie's early paper on 'Causes and Conditions' as endorsing a sufficiency criterion in order to solve the problem of symmetrically overdetermined concurrent-cause cases[7], and he also rejects Mackie's theory along with the rest of generalist theories in chapter 19 of his book. To my mind, however, we should distinguish between the early Mackie of 'Causes and Conditions' and the late Mackie of *The Cement of the Universe*. We should further note that it is correct for the early but not for the late Mackie that he endorsed an unrestricted INUS[8]-condition account – i.e. a sort of sufficiency analysis. Even the early Mackie indicated that he did not regard his sufficiency criterion as wholly satisfactory in cases where two INUS-conditions are present at the same time. Rather, Mackie concedes in 'Causes and Conditions' concerning symmetrically overdetermined concurrent-cause cases that we are unsure how to use the word cause. He supports his decision to assume causation by each of the candidates in the following way:

> Our ordinary concept of cause does not deal clearly with cases of this sort, and we are free to decide whether or not to add to our ordinary use, and to the various more or less formal descriptions of it, rules which allow us to say that where more than one at-least-INUS-condition, and its conjunct conditions, are present, each of them caused the result.[9]

---

7 John L. Mackie, 'Causes and Conditions', American Philosophical Quarterly Vol. 2 (1965), 245, 251; cited by Moore (note 1) 416.

8 Mackie's abbreviation for 'insufficient necessary part of an unnecessary sufficient condition', Mackie, (note 7) 245, see also below. Note that Mackie here uses INUS conditions as a test for singular causal statements.

9 Mackie (note 7) 251.

Thus, the early Mackie already seems not to see his result as dictated by the sufficiency concept he then endorsed but rather as the reasonable consequence of an evaluation where the sufficiency criterion leaves us in the dark.

Interestingly, Mackie did not repeat this argument later in *The Cement of the Universe*. He changed his concept insofar as he preferred the necessity over the sufficiency criterion for an account of singular causal statements[10], and he reserved INUS conditions for an account of causal regularities.[11] The main reason for his rejection of the sufficiency criterion was the adoption of the term causal field. A causal field are the circumstances in which a cause event occurs. If the causal field by itself would have caused the effect event, it is undecidable whether the candidate for a cause was responsible for it.[12] It is quite natural under these presuppositions to demand that a cause ought to make the difference with respect to the result and therefore should be necessary 'in the circumstances' (in the causal field) for the result.

However, the late Mackie of *The Cement of the Universe* does think a modified sufficiency account is appropriate for causal regularities like the laws of nature discovered by science.[13] To my mind, Mackie's different treatment of general and singular causal statements is justified, and it seems for me to be easy to supply an account regarding the background of such differences.

In the following sections, I try to show that the two-pronged concept of the late Mackie presents a feasible and more precise alternative to Moore's default solution which at the same time evades the critique of 'Causation and Responsibility'. I shall do this in three steps: I shall show first why none of the serious concerns Moore enumerates is fatal for the necessity-criterion if it is restricted to singular causal statements (section 3), then how the INUS-account may evade Moore's criticsm if it is restricted to general causal statements (section 4) and finally how the different standards for singular and general causal statements may be linked in a unified concept (section 5).

10 John L. Mackie, *The Cement of the Universe* (Oxford, Oxford University Press, 1974), 29–58.
11 Mackie (note 10) 59–87.
12 Mackie (note 10) 42–43, 47.
13 Mackie (note 10) 59–87.

3 Meaning of Singular Causal Statements: Condition Sine Qua Non

As I mentioned before, Mackie takes the view that the necessity criterion ought to be preferred over a sufficiency criterion regarding singular causal statements. An event should not be called a cause if the causal field in which the event occurs by itself would be able to produce exactly the same effect without the event as with the event. Mackie tried to illustrate this point by his chocolate automats L and M. Automat L works in such a way that inserting a coin into the slot sometimes induces the machine to produce a bar of chocolate and sometimes it does not, but it never produces a bar of chocolate without a prior inserting of the coin. Automat M differs from automat L because it regularly produces a bar of chocolate when a coin is inserted, but sometimes even produces a bar of chocolate by itself when no coin has been inserted. For Mackie, inserting a coin into automat L is a cause for the appearance of a bar of chocolate, but not inserting a coin into automat M because inserting a coin into L is a necessary condition for the appearance of a bar of chocolate but inserting a coin into M is not.[14] Once again, we should not complain about the artificiality of the example or contend that this particular example does not work[15]. Even if this example has not been well constructed, the theoretical problem remains that it is odd to call a factor a cause if it does not bring about a change in the world in any sense we would call relevant.

I think the following are the main objections against the necessity criterion with which I shall deal one by one:

- The necessity criterion cannot plausibly explain that in symmetrically overdetermined concurrent-cause cases like example (1) each of the cause candidates caused the result (section 3.1)
- The necessity criterion forces those who endorse it to accept fine-grained individuations of results which cannot be successfully restricted to relevant descriptions without becoming circular (section 3.2).
- It is counterintuitive that none of the cause candidates should be a cause in symmetrically overdetermined concurrent-cause cases (section 3.3).
- Those who endorse a necessity criterion are forced to accept a highly controversial possible-worlds account (section 3.4).

---

14 Mackie (note 10) 41.

15 See also Wright (note 2, 1988) 1029 – 1031.

3.1 Symmetrical Overdetermination: Cause Candidates are Not Causes

It is striking that the overwhelming majority of legal scholars regardless whether they come from the Anglo-American or the Continental legal tradition are not willing to accept the result that neither of the shots in the example (1) above is a cause of the victim's death. This reluctance to accept non-causation in symmetrically overdetermined concurrent-cause cases is particularly interesting because the dominant test for the courts in both legal traditions is the condition sine qua non or but for test.

I want to recapitulate here shortly the pains and twists German scholars have chosen to avoid the result of non-causation. Those adhering to the condition sine qua non in Germany formulate the test for the condition sine qua as a counterfactual conditional:

> x caused y if x cannot be eliminated out of the situation without y failing to occur as well.[16]

The traditional German approach to symmetrically overdetermined concurrent-cause cases is to ward off criticism with a supplementary formula:

> Of several conditions which can be eliminated separately but not cumulatively without the effect failing to occur, each is a cause.[17]

However, this step marks an unwitting departure from the sine qua non criterion. Translated into the language of conditions, the supplementary formula has to read:

> Of several conditions which are not separately but cumulatively necessary for the effect, each is a cause.

The formula indicates that a factor does not have to be necessary in itself in order to be called a cause. It rather suffices if the factor together with some other factor does become part of a necessary condition. Such inconsistency has lead many scholars in both legal traditions to embrace the concept of causes as sufficient conditions.[18]

---

16 See Friedrich Toepel, 'Condicio sine qua non und alternative Kausalität' – BGHSt 39, 195, JuS 1994, 1009, 1010.

17 This formula can be traced back to Ludwig Traeger, *Der Kausalbegriff im Straf- und Zivilrecht* (Marburg, N. G. Elwert, 1904), 47–48.

18 E. g. the authors cited above (note 2).

I think that there is no way of convincingly maintaining that each shot by itself would be a necessary condition for the victim's death in example (1) above, but I do not take the view that such a result would constitute a reason legitimately to reject the condition sine qua non-formula. To the contrary, if – in a thought experiment – we eliminate A's shot out of the situation, B's shot will still cause the same effect, C's death, as the same concrete event as it would be with A's shot. Therefore, A's shot apparently makes no difference in the world with respect to A's death. What needs an explanation is not our hesitation to call something a cause which makes no difference in the world, but rather our affirmation of causation although the cause candidate is not necessary at all for the result.

Why should someone affirm causation in these cases? An imaginable objection would be that if we deny causation in symmetrically overdetermined concurrent-cause cases, we also would have to deny it in the following variation of (1):

> (2) A and B shoot C in the head like in (1). Again, each shot would by itself have caused death, but this time not exactly at the same moment at which it happened in reality. A fired a second before B and caused instant failure of all brain functions, i.e. instant death at t_1, while B fired a second later and his bullet hit C's head at t_2 when C was already dead.

Do we not have to say that A did not cause C's death in (2) if he did not do so in (1)? No, with respect to (2) we are able to differentiate. Our answer depends a bit on the causal relata we choose.[19]

If we are dealing with fact-results in explanatory causal statements, for example, we are able to say that A's shot caused the fact that C's life ended at t_1, but not the fact that C's life ended at all because A's shot does not explain that C has to die at all. C is human and therefore has to die one day. Facts are generic. They therefore may be expressed by imperfect nominals[20], propositions[21] or in other words 'that'-clauses. The more explanatory a factual cause statement is, the more differences count between expressions describing facts.

---

19 Discussed in depth in Moore (note 1) Ch. 14, 327–368.

20 Mackie (note 7) 249, Zeno Vendler, 'Causal Relations', Journal of Philosophy 64 (1967), 704–713.

21 John L. Austin, 'Truth' in: J. O. Urmson & G. J. Warnock (eds), *Philosophical Papers* (Oxford, Oxford University Press, 1979), 117, 122–124. A thorough discussion of propositions, also illuminating for factual issues, is contained in Georg Henrik von Wright, 'Demystifying Propositions', in: *Truth, Knowledge and Modality* (Oxford, B. Blackwell, 1984), 14–25. See Willard van Orman Quine, *Word and Object* (Cambridge MA, MIT Press, 1960), 247–248 on the connection between propositions and facts.

I agree with Mackie[22] that a scientifically ideal causal explanation reduces the description of the situation in such a way that everything causally relevant about it is expressed in general terms. These explanatory general terms are unique and may not be replaced salva veritate within the context. A construction consisting of such terms as well as the terms themselves are therefore also called referentially opaque.[23] Referentially opaque terms may not be replaced salva veritate within a context.

The lawyer's task of subsuming concrete situations under general norms cannot be accomplished by using referentially opaque terms. It does not help us in (2), for example, that we know that A's shot caused the fact that C's life ended at t_1, but not the fact that C's life ended at all because the law prohibits bringing about the death of another person and not just bringing it about at t_1. Legal descriptions therefore make use of a language which allows the matching of a very general description of things with a more specific description. Lawyers describe concrete things and thus make use of referentially transparent constructions.[24] Some terms within a referentially transparent context may be replaced salva veritate. Referentially transparent causal effects are called events.[25]

---

22 Mackie (note 10) 260 – 262.

23 Concerning the term referential opacity see Quine (note 21) 146 – 156. Quine refers in his examples for the distinction between referential opacity and transparency exclusively to characteristics of persons and objects within descriptions of propositional attitudes. Therefore it seems as if he in reality wants to talk about the contrast between 'de dicto' and 'de re' descriptions which is usually associated with characteristics of objects. There is a close relationship between the referential transparency/referential opacity dichotomy on the one hand and the de re/de dicto dichotomy on the other. However, the application of the terms de re and de dicto to other things than objects is controversial, see Thomas McKay & Michael Nelson, 'The De Re/De Dicto Distinction', Supplement to 'Propositional Attitude Reports', in: Edward N. Zalta (ed.), *Stanford Encyclopedia* (Winter 2010 ed.), http://plato.stanford.edu/entries/prop-attitude-reports/dere.html. Therefore, I prefer to use Quine's terms referential transparency and opacity which permit the broader understanding of referential transparency as the possibility of substituting co-referring terms salva veritate and of referential opacity as the impossibility of substituting the terms salva veritate, see also Mackie (note 10) 250, 254. This allows me to apply the distinction not only to objects, but also to events which are relevant in the causal context.

24 See concerning the term referentially transparent note 23. It should be noted, however, that factual language also has an important function for the lawyer, particularly in connection with procedural law, and that there are close relations between facts and events, despite their difference, see Mackie (note 7) 266 – 267. A separate paper would be needed to exhaustively explore the relationship between the two notions in a legal context.

25 During the Aachen Symposium on Moore's *Causation and Responsibility*, 15 – 17 March 2010, Professor Geert Keil referred to Arthur Danto's view that calling a cause an event would mean committing a category mistake. Although I cannot agree that it would be wrong to call a causal chain a relation between events and consequently the cause to be one of the events – Mackie

If we think of C's death as a concrete event, C's death at t_1 is the same event as C's death on day x or simply C's death. Consequently, if we are able to give a description fine-grained enough to say that A's shot caused C's death at t_1, we are also able to say that A's shot caused C's death. And as we are able to say that A's shot caused C's death at t_1 in (2), we may assume a causal chain in that example.

Not so in (1), where no more detailed account is able to differentiate between the consequences of A's and B's shot with respect to C's death. Perhaps one is tempted to say that if we eliminate A's shot out of situation (1), a different death will occur because C's death will be a death with only one bullet in C's head, while there will be two bullets in his head when A fires his shot as well. Ergo, we are able to differentiate and A's shot is after all a necessary condition for C's death?

To my mind, such a differentiation would be fatal since we would then either say that any causally irrelevant circumstance could supply the necessary differentiation or we would just unwarrantedly assume the causal relevance of the presence of each bullet in C's head – something which we wanted to find out in the first place with the help of our criterion of the necessary condition. If any such differentiation would suffice, there would be no problem of causal overdetermination. Something is always different in the world if a second factor is added.

To my mind, it is acceptable in principle to differentiate between events with the help of detailed descriptions. But servants must not become masters. We may never use detailed descriptions for a differentiation between effects which we have already used to describe the cause candidates whose causal role we yet wish to examine. We also must never assume the causal relevance of a factor before we have examined it. In both cases we would be begging the question. Therefore, we may not differentiate between the effects in (1) by describing the consequence of A's shot as 'C's death after A's shot' because A's shot is exactly the causal factor we want evaluate as candidate for a cause. We also may not use the description of 'death with A's bullet in C's head' because whether A's bullet in C's head is relevant for A's death in the concrete situation is precisely what we wish to find out.

The dilemma of the condition sine qua non in symmetrically overdetermined concurrent-cause cases therefore consists in the following: We have no fine-grained individuation of the event effects left over which would be a description

(note 10), in particular 257–267, evidently considered it to be harmless to construct causation as a relation between events – I leave this issue open. It is sufficient for the concept outlined here to treat the result of a cause as an event, and I do not see how this could be plausibly criticized.

independent of the cause candidates and would not assume the causal relevance of factors we have yet to check. Therefore, the question asking for a discrimination between the alternative cause candidates has no answer.[26]

3.2 Relevant Fine-Grained Individuations of Events

Some, like Moore, have concluded we should not go down the road of fine-grained individuations at all.[27] We would have to agree with these scholars if allowing any fine-grained individuations meant that we would not be able to restrict such individuations to relevant and non-circular descriptions.

I think, however, that accepting some relevant fine-grained individuations does not force us at all to accept any individuations whatsoever. We rather should have to decide separately for each kind of individuation whether it may be admitted or not. In the field of law we should find out by interpretation whether the causing of results prohibited in a provision implicitly refers to a difference between individual features of a certain kind. Only those kinds of individuations should be allowed which we are able to determine by interpretation as relevant in advance. If we stick to these rules we should not be in danger to run into trouble.

In my opinion, there should be agreement that shortening lives is an essential feature of killing and that therefore time differences are always important for the prohibition of killing. To my mind, the same applies for other violations of a person's integrity or for destroying or damaging another person's property. It is not the destruction of the property as such or the transition from life to death as such for which the law holds transgressors responsible. All things draw to an end at some time. If punishing someone for killing another person would involve holding the perpetrator responsible for the fact that the person died at all, no one could ever be punished for such a crime because each person is mortal and will die at some time whether killed by another human being or not. We rather think a perpetrator should be held responsible for making the life of a human being shorter than it would be without his interference. That is what we usually mean by killing someone, and that necessarily involves time differences between the actual life of the victim including the perpetrator's activity and the hypothetical life of the victim without that activity. If we have agreed with the

26 See also Mackie (note 10) 47.

27 Moore (note 1), 412–414; in Germany primarily Ingeborg Puppe (note 2) paras. 62–71, though for different reasons than Moore.

argumentation so far, no other solution seems to be possible than to reject causation in example (1) because the question whether each shot was responsible for the shortening of the victim's life "has no answer" as Mackie[28] rightly says. At least, there is no affirmative answer to that question.

Sometimes it is considered to be contradictory[29] that Mackie thinks both shots together are a cause of the result[30] while each shot by itself is not. I can detect no contradiction at all in Mackie's view. On the one hand, each shot by itself was not responsible for the shortening of the victim's life because the circumstances were such as to produce the result at time t_1 by themselves without the perpetrator's interference. On the other hand, both shots taken together were responsible for the victim's death because there are no indications that the circumstances in which they occurred as a unit were such as to bring about the victim's death at time t_1 by themselves. For this reason, I think that each of the perpetrators may be held responsible for the whole unit of two shots if both acted as accomplices on account of a common plan so that each of the perpetrators made the other's contribution his own and therefore both contributions could be imputed to each of them[31].

I concede to have reached the decision for the relevance of time differences on account of an evaluative interpretation of the result description in the provision involved, not on account of intrinsic features of causation. Nonetheless, it seems to be hardly possible to find reasons for a different interpretation.

The relevance of other concrete descriptions is not so clear, for example differences of location. To my mind, here remains room for evaluation. To me, it seems to be unclear whether the railroad employee's action in the following example has become a cause for the passengers' death:

(3) A railroad track has been destroyed by a landslide. The railroad employee works the switches so that the passenger train is redirected on another track. This track, however, has also been destroyed by a landslide. As a consequence, the passenger train is derailed, and the passengers die on the second track – by chance just at the exact moment at which they would have died on the first track.

---

28 Mackie (note 10) 47.

29 For example, Moore (note 1) 354.

30 Mackie (note 10) 47.

31 In Germany we call the commission of a crime where the contributions are mutually imputed to the perpetratrors acting in 'Mittäterschaft' (complicity). It is, however, controversial whether such mutual imputation may also take place with respect to causation or whether each perpetratror himself has to be a cause of the result.

If by killing we only mean shortening the life of another person, then the railroad employee's action has not changed anything. The passengers were doomed to die at t_1 independent of whether the train took the first or the second track. If however, death at a different location makes it a relevantly different event, then we have good reason to include differences of location into our list of relevant concrete features and thus to conclude that the railroad employee's action was a cause of the passengers' death. But we have to be careful to restrict our decision to include differences of location and not to include mere differences concerning the intermediary stages leading to the passengers' death. There ought to be agreement, for example, that in the following variation of (3) the railroad employee did not cause the passengers' death:

> (4) As in (3), the railroad track has been destroyed by a landslide. The railroad employee works the switches so that the passenger train is redirected on another track. This track, however, joins the first track before the place where the landslide has destroyed the track. As a consequence, the passenger train is derailed, and the passengers die on the original track – by chance just at the exact moment at which they would have died without the railroad employee's interference because the second track has exactly the same length as the first before the two tracks join again.

3.3 Counterintuitive Results

Moore's main reason for rejecting the necessity-account even if supplemented by an acceptance of fine-grained individuations seems to be that it yields counterintuitive results.[32] Moore in this respect joins the majority of legal scholars around the world. I do not wish to dispute that there are such intuitions. I rather wish to dispute their reliability. Intuitions appeal to our emotional responses more than to our intellects, and emotions are bound to be vague and to blurr fine distinctions.

My following remarks concerning our intuitions should not be taken to mean that no other interpretation of them but mine would be possible. I only wish to point out what could possibly lie at the heart of such intuitions and that therefore we should not let our decisions depend on them at all. I thus would not consider myself defeated if someone can suggest the possibility of a different explanation of the intuitions but only if he would prove that my interpretation is totally unjustified.

32 See Moore (note 1) 86, 415.

If we change the situation of symmetrically overdetermined concurrent-cause cases in a suitable way, we are able to see that the object of such intuitions may not be causation itself but the fact that a person should go free on account of mere coincidence although the occurrence of a damaging result is an undisputable reality. No scientist would count an experiment as successfully completed if he could not single out a necessary factor as responsible for his results. He would never say: "I want to test whether factor x generally is a cause for factor y. I have introduced factor x into the laboratory set z. As a result, y obtains. I do not know whether factor x is responsible for the result y or whether the laboratory set z was able to produce y by itself. However, I do not care. I only do not know whether x was a necessary condition for y. But I do know that either the laboratory set z itself or the factor x in the laboratory set z were sufficient to produce the result. For here we have result y. So, let us just say, both x and z were a cause for y. At any rate, x and z together were one necessary condition for the result, and that suffices to call each, x and z a cause of y. Thus, I can congratu late myself, for I have found (with the help of some reasoning) that x is a cause of y." According to my intuition, such a scientist should be called a madcap scientist, and not without reason.

To get the counterintuitive effect, we have to change the scientist's example to a criminal or tort law setting. There it seems to become plausible that the legal scholar argues parallel to the madcap scientist: "I cannot say exactly whether person x has brought about the damaging result y or whether the circumstances including another person z would have been able to produce the same damaging result by themselves. However, it is unjust to let x go free merely because there happened to be these circumstances including z. x and z have both done enough to bring about y. Therefore, sufficient conditions must be sufficient for the assumption of causes here."

Moore also refers to another example which in his view is even more convincing to support the idea that the necessity criterion is counterintuitive:

> (5) The Major's Order: A major and a sergeant both simultaneously order troops under their command to advance and the men begin to move forward. The men hear both persons, but they obey the higher officer. If the major would not have given the order, the men would still have moved forward on account of the sergeant's order.[33]

To my mind, the intuition that the men moved forward on account of the major's order is just another example of our emotions blurring fine distinctions. I think

33 Moore (note 1) 423–424, citing Jonathan Schaffer, 'Trumping Preemption', Journal of Philosophy 97 (2000), 175.

second thoughts should tell any discerning scholar that the major's order is not the cause for the men's beginning to march at t_1.[34] This is so because with respect to the physical motion of marching at t_1, the person giving the order is an irrelevant individuation. The case being formulated as above under (5), the person of the major is no non-redundant factor for the result that the men begin to move forward. One might say that the existence of at least one order shortly before t_1 was the cause for the result that the men moved forward at t_1. But it is not possible to say that the *major*'s order caused this result because the world being as it was and including the sergeant's order would foreseeably have produced the same result by itself without the major's help.

Finally, intuitions are unreliable because they tend to be contradictory. I find it very surprising that people deny causation when confronted with examples (3) and (4) above much more often than when confronted with (1). In (3) as well as in (4) the railroad employee has done enough to ensure the result – death of the passengers. True, the world itself would have brought about just the same effect without the railroad employee's help. However, if such consideration is to be relevant in (3) and (4), it also has to be relevant in (1). Additionally, the real and the hypothetical result are not quite the same in (3). The real death occurred at another location and on account of another landslide than the death that would have occurred if the train would have continued the journey without the railroad employee's interference. I personally would think it could be reasonably argued that the railroad's employee caused the passengers' death in (3) depending on whether we are ready to accept the relevance of location differences for the result or not. I believe that we only need to evaluate the circumstances consistently in such a case.

Nonetheless, I also believe that one cannot consistently deny causation in (3) and (4), but at the same time assume causation of each shot in (1). I think that there should be no controversy about the fact that time differences are more relevant than location differences. The relevance of time differences can be made plausible by pointing out the task which causation has to fulfil. When we ask for the cause of a result like the death of a human being or the destruction of an object, we want to know what shortened the human life or the duration of the object. It is more difficult to find a similar argument for mere location differences. Why should we consider as relevant what destroyed an object which would have ceased to exist without the interference? Perhaps because of the po-

34 I presuppose here that even men with free will may be caused to do something, see Mackie (note 10) 43; Friedrich Toepel, 'Free Will and Infinite Regress', in: Toepel (ed.), *Free Will in Criminal Law and Procedure*, ARSP 120 (2010), 29, 36 note 14.

tential of that same cause candidate to cut short the object's span of existence and because we wish to avoid such a causation. But this argument would be the argument of a preventive approach, parallel to the argument why we punish an attempt: because of the potential harm which the perpetrator would have caused if he would have been successful. The distinction between attempted and completed offences with respect to result crimes is – at least mostly – dependent on just the criterion that in case of a completed result crime the perpetrator has caused the result while he did not cause that same result in case of a mere attempt. Such a correspondence between an argument concerning the relevance of location differences and an argument for the penalization of attempts suggests that the denial of causation is correct rather than the opposite evaluation.

If therefore causation is denied because of insufficient location differences in (3) and (4), causation should a fortiori be denied in case of lacking time differences in (1). If our intuitions want to teach us otherwise, we should not give heed to them.

3.4 Non-Controversial Possible Worlds Account?

Another argument presented by Moore against the condition sine qua non-formula is that it involves a possible worlds account. Moore's main argument against the availability of a plausible possible worlds account is the vagueness of such an account. Moore gives the example: "If the rocket were to have gone less than 18,000 miles per hour, it would not have escaped the gravitational pull."[35] He points out that it would be an illusion to think that the possible world that is overall closest to the actual world would be one where only the state of affairs referred to in the antecedent would change. The rocket in his example would not only have to go much slower, but at the very least, we would need some laws not to hold in this possible world, namely all the laws that connect the rocket going over 18,000 miles per hour in the actual world to earlier events that caused it to go that fast in the actual world.[36]

Yet, to my mind, the difficulties pointed out in Moore's argument do not arise in legal contexts. We are not required to give an account of the whole possible world in order to be able to answer the question of causation. It is rather sufficient to postulate that the same laws hold in the possible worlds to be compared

35 Moore (note 1) 373.
36 Moore (note 1) 387.

from the moment on in which the cause candidate occurred. We only compare how the possible worlds run on from that moment onwards. It is also not always impossible to answer how the worlds would have run on from a certain moment under a certain presupposition.[37] To the contrary, historians as well as lawyers try to answer such questions all the time. If we have no indications for certain assumptions, we have to deny causation due to the lack of evidence. But that is not as often the case as scepticists want to make us believe.

If, for example, a member of the rocket crew injured himself because he had expected the gravitational pull which did not happen because the commander pulled the lever down too quickly so that the rocket went too fast, then there is room for a reasonable prognosis what would have happened if the rocket would have gone less than 18,000 miles per hour. We do not have to be interested at all in the world before the commander pulled the lever. We just have to compare the chunks of two worlds in one of which the commander pulls down the lever quickly and in the other of which he pulls it down with appropriate care. We just have to watch these two worlds from time t_1 – the pulling of the lever – until time t_2 – the crew member's injury and postulate the exact identity of both worlds except that the lever was pulled differently in these worlds.

Moore[38] also suspects that the counterfactual conditionals which we need for the condition sine qua non-formula could only be satisfactorily explained by a 'full-blown modal realism' like the controversial theory of David Lewis[39]. A separate paper or book would be necessary to refute such an objection satisfactorily. I am only able to state here that I do not consider it necessary to endorse Lewis' controversial view in order to give a satisfactory account of causes as necessary conditions. I believe that we can avoid Lewis' extravagant realism as well as the desert landscapes of linguistic ersatzism if we accept a theory like Theodore Sider's ersatz pluriverse view[40]. To my mind, Sider has successfully solved the problem of world reduction on the one hand and retaining descriptive power on the other.

---

37 As Moore (note 1) 389 wonders concerning his example (26): "If the Soviets had pushed the button to unleash a nuclear response to the blockade of Cuba in 1962, the world would have experienced a nuclear winter."

38 Moore (note 1) 385.

39 David Lewis, *Counterfactuals* (Cambridge MA, John Wiley & Sons, 1973), 85–86; David Lewis, *On the Plurality of Worlds* (Cambridge MA, John Wiley & Sons, 1986), 136–142.

40 Theodore Sider, 'The Ersatz Pluriverse', Journal of Philosophy 99 (2002), 279–315; or the very similar account by David P. Nolan, *Topics in the Philosophy of Possible Worlds* (London, Taylor & Francis, 2002), 77–174.

4 Standard for General Causal Statements: INUS-Conditions

4.1 The Problem of Set-Construction

The meaning of regularity statements and of singular causal statements is fundamentally different: The natural sciences have set strict standards which must be met by test arrangements. The causal field must be defined as clearly as possible, ideally clinical conditions must obtain. In such a purified causal field the candidates for causes are introduced, the experiment is repeated without these candidates and the difference between the results can be observed minutely, for example in the double blind tests of the medical sciences. The very opposite situation is typical for singular causal statements, especially if they are about the past as it frequently happens to be the case in legal contexts. Here, the causal field cannot be purified completely from uncontrollable influences. Here, it is only possible to remember similar situations like the one to be evaluated and then imagine what would have happened in a situation resembling as closely as possible the real one. Such a thought experiment can never lead to the same degree of certainty as an experiment under clinical conditions.

Also the purpose of the proposed causal hypothesis is different in both situations. Whoever states a causal regularity intends to explain the connection between cause and effect as clearly as possible, but he who makes a singular causal statement has the primary objective to track a causal chain back to a cause.[41]

Therefore, it is natural for a scientist to ask what exactly would be minimally sufficient to bring about a certain observed effect. Mackie intends to give a detailed account of precisely that criterion: A condition is minimally sufficient if each of its parts is necessary to make the whole cluster sufficient to produce the effect. The insufficient but non-redundant parts of the whole unnecessary sufficient condition are the generic causes for Mackie.[42]

In contrast to the test arrangement with regard to which regularity statements are appropriate, singular causal statements are focused on the quest for the necessary element which was responsible in the circumstances for a certain effect.

---

41 See more in detail Friedrich Toepel, 'Legal Proof and Scientific Explanation', in: E. Attwool & P. Comanducci (eds), *Sources of Law and Legislation*, ARSP Beiheft 69 (1998), 80, 82–83, referring to the distinction between explanation-seeking and reason-seeking why-questions by Carl G. Hempel, *Aspects of Scientific Explanation* (New York, Free Press, 1965), 335.
42 Mackie (note 10) 62.

After we have accepted this distinction, we are able to explain why INUS conditions do not adequately express the meaning of a cause in a singular causal statement. If a causal field contains only one INUS condition, there is no difficulty in identifying it as the necessary condition for a concrete effect. But if the causal field contains more than one INUS condition, the question which would be the responsible element for the effect has no obvious answer. We must differentiate between all conditions in order to find the candidates which were necessary for the effect in the concrete situation.

All causal theories transplanting the INUS criterion to singular causal statements must somehow cover up this shortcoming. Moore correctly identifies such difficulty as the problem of set construction.[43] Moore sees the main predicament in the circularity of argumentation and the necessity to introduce features of singularist causation into the generalist account when deciding whether a subset is 'really' a sufficient condition for the result.[44]

I do not wish to dispute the validity of Moore's argumentation here. However, I am of the opinion that there is another aspect of the problem of set construction to which not sufficient attention has been given until now and which I therefore wish to illustrate with the following example. This example shows to my mind that also in the context in which the INUS criterion is appropriately applied, namely regarding the identification of causal regularities by observation of tests, natural scientists would reasonably view an experiment as showing no positive indication for a causal chain if more than one INUS condition would be present.

> (6) Let us assume, the toxic properties of a certain chemical would be investigated by animal testing. The animal is kept in a cage and the experimentalists take care that it eats only a certain amount of the chemical which they presume would be sufficient to kill the animal. A saboteur smuggles another dose of the poison into the cage which contains the same amount which the experimentalists fed to the animal. The animal eats all of the chemical and dies.

The scientists who would learn all the facts would take the view that the experiment has failed because the causal field has been contaminated by the saboteur. The ex-

---

43 Moore (note 1) 486, 491–495. He rejects the trivial way in which Mark Kelman, 'The Necessary Myth of Objective Causation Judgments in Liberal Political Theory', Chicago-Kent Law Review 63 (1987), 579, 603–604, understands the objection and rather identifies it as a circularity problem on pages 491–495 of his book. Moore uses his argument in connection with preemptive cause cases. However, to my mind, the argument can without loss be transferred to the symmetrically overdetermined concurrent-cause cases. I even think that the argument is more relevant there because generalists often boast they alone are able satisfactorily to solve cases of symmetrically overdetermined concurrent-cause cases.

44 Moore (note 1) 491–495.

periment has not shown that the dose fed by the experimentalists was sufficient in the circumstances to kill the animal. They would have to repeat the experiment with other comparable animals slowly reducing the whole amount of poison until they have identified the necessary minimum for a deadly dose. But even now, looking back they could not say that in the failed first experiment the dose fed to the animal by themselves killed it after all. For in a causal field thus contaminated, there is no unambiguous way how to construct the sufficient set of the INUS condition. It could be constructed in such a way that it contains only the experimentalist's dose. Then all would seem to be well for the moment although the real problem only has been postponed – how to deal with the other INUS condition contained in the causal field. Yet, at the same time no compelling reason would hinder to construe the sufficient set as comprising both doses together, and then, how could we identify each dose as a non-redundant part of the sufficient set? We would have to deny causation because neither dose was necessary and could have been eliminated without any difference for the causal effect. There is no cogent reason for constructing the sufficient set in one way rather than the other, and therefore the question which would be the cause of the animal's death "has no answer", just as it would be if we were working with necessary instead of INUS conditions.

4.2 The Typical Clinical Situation

This result can be easily explained. The INUS condition has been developed for laboratory conditions where care has been taken to keep the introduced candidate for a cause as clearly separated from the rest of the test arrangement as possible and the causal field as precisely defined as possible. Only then are we able to observe differences clearly. The scientist is not interested in a test arrangement which contains more than one INUS condition at the same time. He considers his experiment as successful only if he believes to have been able to isolate one necessary condition within the test arrangement. Suspected overdetermination is not wanted and counts as failure and as a reason to repeat the experiment. Therefore overdetermination does not present a problem in the typical clinical situation. The INUS condition as a tool fit for such a test situation is no appropriate instrument for the solution of overdetermination cases and does not need to be because it was not created for such a purpose.

Puppe argues that a continuous causal chain can be observed from both candidates which are sufficient in themselves for the effect.[45] However, thereby she not

45 Puppe (note 2) paras. 114–115.

only introduces another criterion in addition to the INUS condition which cannot be explained with the notion of the INUS condition. Puppe's account also becomes inconsistent because she gives up her declared decision to endorse a generalist account[46] and mixes it with the singularist idea of a 'causal chain'.

5 Linking the Two Prongs of the Causal Concept

We have ended up with two different meanings of causes, singular causal statements stating conditions sine qua non and general causal statements stating INUS conditions. Is there a connection between them?

In my opinion, Mackie gives us a clue how the two kinds of causes are linked in an argument. He takes the view that in most cases there are laws to back up singular causal statements, but that singular causal statements do not entail laws.[47]

I think that this relationship of regular support of singular causal statements by regularity statements, yet of lacking complete entailment can be best explained with the help of Toulmin's old argumentation scheme. Toulmin distinguished the parts of a substantial argument in the following way:[48]

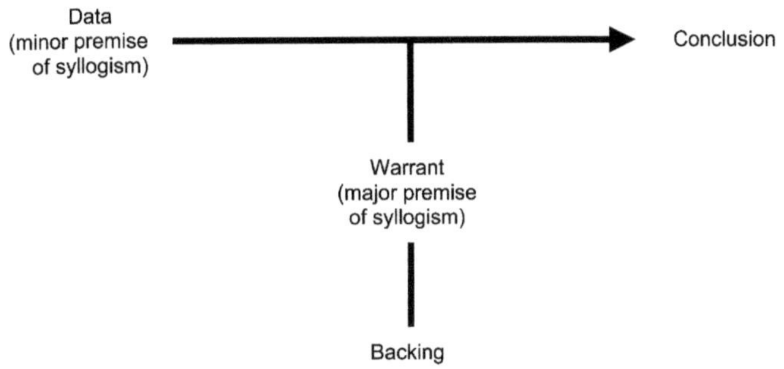

He located all elements contributing to the meaning of the conclusion with the conclusion itself on the right side of the arrow. Modal terms like probably or possibly he took to be qualifying the meaning of the conclusion. He therefore located these terms with the conclusion on the right side. While data and warrant to-

46 See Puppe (note 2) paras. 66–67 concerning her critique of the assumption "that reality is given to us in concrete features" (dass uns die Wirklichkeit in konkreten Gestalten vorgegeben ist).

47 Mackie (note 10) 267–269.

48 Stephen E. Toulmin, *The Uses of Argument* (Cambridge, Cambridge University Press, 1958), 103–107.

gether entail the conclusion because of their formulation, these parts of the argument do not determine whether an argument is substantial. It is rather the backing of the argument which makes it substantial. However, the data and the backing, unlike the data and the warrant, never entail the conclusion of a substantial argument.[49] The backing could not fulfil its role to support the warrant and indirectly the conclusion if it together with the data would merely entail the conclusion. The explanatory content of the backing hinders a relationship of entailment between backing together with data, and conclusion.

In my view, regularity statements expressing INUS conditions function as the backing in an argument supporting singular causal statements as conclusions. In case (2) above, the desired conclusion of our causal argument would be "A's shot caused C's death". The data would consist in statements describing how exactly A pointed the gun in the direction of C and pulled the trigger and how C died. The warrant would state the data in its antecent and link them to the conclusion in its consequent. If the warrant would be challenged however, the substantial support for the argument would have to come from the backing which would have to contain all the laws of ballistics needed to explain how the conclusion could come about in the concrete circumstances. The conclusion could be rephrased as a counterfactual conditional "If A would not have pulled the trigger at the time he did, C would not have died at t_1". The condition sine qua non expressed by the counterfactual therefore reflects the meaning of the conclusion and is to be located on the right side of the argument.

Only the element of the backing, however, is a relevant place for the INUS conditions in the argumentation scheme. The laws of ballistics, for example, may be expressed by such INUS conditions or by approximations to INUS conditions.[50] The INUS condition therefore is not part of the meaning of the singular causal statement in the conclusion. It rather supports the conclusion substantially which it can only do because it is not entailed in the conclusion.

This model helps us also to justify that courts in product liability cases like the famous German thalidomide case[51] have tended to hold evidence for causa-

---

49 Toulmin (note 48) 224.

50 I acknowledge that it often may be difficult to formulate pure INUS conditions because of the lack of exact knowledge. But this is a problem for the natural sciences in the first place. I do not think it problematic to use approximations to INUS conditions to be able to solve our everyday problems as long as we have nothing better. Of course, we then incur the difficulty where to draw the borderline between an insufficient and a sufficient backing. However, we have to cope with this problem in our everyday decisions anyway. If we would only act when scientific evidence tested under laboratory conditions would be available, we would probably die soon because we could not even make elementary decisions. Evaluations are an indispensable part of our lives.

51 LG Aachen JZ 1970, 507.

tion sufficient even if the expert witnesses professed not to be able to affirm a causal connection between certain events like the taking of thalidomide pills and certain results like prenatal deformities because they had not yet been able to observe such a connection under clinical conditions. The conclusion to be proved in such cases is the counterfactual stating a condition sine qua non in a certain case. But this conclusion may be supported by various sorts of backing. Toulmin identifies the backing as a field-dependent part of the argument.[52] In the academic field of medicine, more precise formulations of INUS conditions may be necessary therefore than the approximations to INUS conditions needed for the purposes of legal proof.[53]

Thus we are able to distinguish between different functions of the causal notions of condition sine qua non and INUS condition with respect to singular causal statements. The condition sine qua non expresses the meaning of the singular causal statement. The INUS condition explains why we reach the singular causal statement contained in the conclusion.

Such a theory seems to be preferable to me compared to the alternatives available at the moment because it combines the precision of conditional analysis with the explanatory power of the INUS condition account. A conditional analysis also has the advantage that we are able to avoid unnecessary complications connected with a denial of the possibility of causation by omission, prevention or double-prevention[54] and that we do not have to defend ourselves against the charge of an implausible ontological commitment.

Abbrevations

BGHSt	Bundesgerichtshof für Strafsachen (Official collection of decisions of the Supreme Court)
JuS	Juristische Schulung
ARSP	Archiv für Rechts- und Sozialphilosophie

52 Toulmin (note 48) 104.
53 See Toepel (note 41) 80 – 86.
54 See Michael S. Moore (note 1) 444 – 451.

Dieter Birnbacher and David Hommen

Omissions as Causes – Genuine, Quasi, or not at All?

1 Negative causation by non-action: a metaphysical puzzle

Michael S. Moore's *Causation and Responsibility* (2009) is an all-encompassing examination of prevalent legal doctrines of causality and its connection to legal liability and an outstanding achievement in philosophical systematization and argumentation. The author deftly reconstructs and discusses the law's demands on the concept of causation and conceptualizes a theory of causality to accommodate both the metaphysical implications of legal doctrines and the theoretical standards of intelligibility, coherence and stringency called for in philosophical analysis. All this is done with expertise, clarity and consistency.

In this contribution, we focus on one distinctive aspect of Moore's theory of causality, namely his treatment of omissive or negative causation. Moore is one of the many law theorists who doubt that omissions can operate as factors in the causation of events and that in cases in which potential agents remain passive in spite of an obligation to intervene ascriptions of responsibility are justified exclusively by non-causal factors. We argue that this is an uneasy and essentially unstable position. We show, furthermore, that Moore himself does not consistently follow, in *Causation and Responsibility*, his exclusion of a causal role of omission in the context of casuistic analysis. Though Moore is to be praised for the clear stance he takes on the issue of negative causality it is argued that an analysis of the reasons given for the negation of causality by omission shows that these do not carry enough weight to compensate for the sacrifices of theoretical coherence necessitated by the special treatment given to negative responsibility in cases of special obligation. It is argued, instead, that an alternative explanation for the responsibility for omissions is called for.

In many situations we assume that non-action plays the role of a cause or a causal factor. This assumption derives particularly from three kinds of cases where it seems natural to speak of omissions and forbearances as having causal impact:

1. Whenever an agent A fails to act though he is *morally or legally required* to act, it is natural to say that his failure is causally relevant to what follows.

For instance, if A fails to pay back his debts to B, this is naturally assumed to be the cause for B's sending A an angry letter.
2. Causality is attributed to non-action in cases where the agent fails to act in the way he is *expected* to act. If A does not drink his usual morning coffee, this is assumed to cause B's asking A what is wrong with him.
3. Causality is attributed in cases of *deliberate* non-action with the intention to harm, as when A fails to provide insulin to the bed-ridden B with the intention to let him die, and B consequently dies from diabetes. Especially in this case, the justification of attributing moral or legal responsibility to A seems to depend on the existence of a causal relation between the omission and the harm at least to the extent that A's failure to provide insulin causally contributes, among other causal factors, to the occurrence of B's death.

However, prevalent as these ways of speaking (and thinking) may be, they seem to harbour inconsistencies when considered with more scrutiny. How can an event be caused by a non-existing event? How can a non-doing *make* something happen? Is it not that we introduce a *creatio ex nihilo* of sorts if we presume omissions to be causally efficacious? Nothing can come from nothing, or so it seems. Call this the *argument from nothingness.* It has led many legal theorists to reject the causality of omissions altogether, as for example expressed by the German legal theorist Karl Larenz (1953, 686): "Unterlassen kann für nichts kausal sein." But also among philosophers there has always been a certain reluctance with regard to negative causes. John Stuart Mill, though he was quite clear about the fact that negative conditions are indispensable for the production of an effect along with positive ones, was far from thinking that negative conditions can be *literally* causes:

> From nothing, from a mere negation, no consequences can proceed. All effects are connected, by the law of causation, with some set of positive conditions; negative ones, it is true, being almost always required in addition. (Mill, System of logic III, V, § 3)

Mill's Solomonic solution is to take "cause" as a philosophical term and to equate it with the

> sum total of the conditions positive and negative taken together ... which being realized the consequent invariably follows. (§ 3)

In this way, Mill recognizes the causal role of negative causes without dignifying them by the name "cause" in their own right. The price he pays for this move is that the terminology he proposes runs counter to common ways of speaking. Normally, "cause" is not used for the sum total of causally sufficient conditions of an event but for each of the more or less salient causal factors that are not identical with but relevant parts of the set of conditions sufficient for the consequent event.

As Mill's treatment of the problem suggests, one should distinguish three senses in which the question of negative causation may arise:

1. The first question is if there can be negative causes in Mill's interpretation of "cause", i.e. in understanding "cause" as "total cause": Can there be (sets of) causally *sufficient* conditions for subsequent effects that are purely negative?
2. The second question is if there can be negative causes in the sense of causal factors, i.e. in the sense of *necessary* or *non-redundant parts* (in Mackie's terms) of causally sufficient sets of conditions: Can there be purely negative causal factors that are not sufficient for the effects by themselves but without which the sufficiency of the totality of conditions of which they are parts would not be guaranteed?
3. A third question is suggested by Mackie's concept of "causal field". As Mackie (1974) points out, so-called "sufficient" causal conditions are generally sufficient only within the context of a "causal field", i.e. a set of background conditions, positive and negative, not all of which can always be specified in the circumstances but all of which have to be present for the effect to invariably follow from the cause. For example, presence of oxygen and absence of humidity are generally taken to be background conditions which have to be fulfilled for a match to ignite when struck against the surface of a matchbox. Formally, these background conditions are necessary or non-redundant conditions in the same way as the "causes" properly so called. Unlike the causal factors, however, they enter into causal explanations only rarely, partly because they are not manageable, partly because they constitute the normalcy conditions that form the background of more or less all our practices. Without knowing all of them, their presence is usually taken for granted. Hence, the third question we have to deal with is if there can be causal background conditions of a purely negative kind.

If we were to allow for negative causes, it is clear that this would not be in the first, but only in the second or third of these senses. Making room for negative causes would not constrain us literally to accept a *creatio ex nihilo*. The idea that there might be purely negative *total* causes seems, to say the least, odd. If there are any totally negative total causes at all, they should be very rare. In reality, almost every effect seems to be caused by both negative and positive factors.

The more pressing questions then are the second and the third one. The third question concerning the possibility of purely negative background conditions is motivated by the fact that it seems impossible to banish negative conditions from the causal field since they typically consist in the nonappearance of *disturbing factors* that would otherwise interfere with the causal process and prevent the effect (e.g. somebody wetting the match so that it will not ignite when struck against the matchbox). This question is of interest in the metaphysics of science. More relevant in the context of moral and legal theory is the second question concerning the possibility of negative causal factors. In many cases, particularly in the cases of omissive actions mentioned at the beginning, negative factors seem to be able to play the role not only of background or enabling conditions but also of full-fledged causes in the everyday sense. Quite often, negative actions are even assigned the status of "the" or the "crucial" cause of some – usually undesired – outcome, as in cases of omissive forms of manslaughter or murder. It appears that we cannot but suppose that negative actions – and by extension negative events, for that is what negative actions ultimately amount to – are, if not causally sufficient, at least causally *relevant*. Yet, the argument from nothingness remains a head scratcher even for that supposition. The question remains, how a nothing, as it were, can be causally relevant. The intuition persists that what can be done causally can be done by positive factors only, leaving negative ones causally inert.

2 Three positions on the causality of omissions

Given this exposition of the problem, what are the options on the causal status of omissions and other negative factors? One option is to *deny*, another to *accept* that omissions can be causes. Michael S. Moore clearly opts for the first option, whereas we are going to argue for the second. However, a majority of legal theorists and a bunch of philosophers take a third position on the issue: They assert that omissions, though they cannot be causes, can be causes *in a wider sense* (Fair 1979), *quasi*-causes (Dowe 2001), or *hypothetical* causes (many legal theorists). The central idea is that negative factors such as omissions are hypothetically causal or quasi-causal or causal in a wider sense for some effect, e.g. some harm, if and only if the unrealized corresponding positive events or actions *would* have prevented the effect or harm. It should be noted that this conception of *hypothetical* causality has nothing to do with a counterfactual analysis of causation. While it presupposes the notion of causation in the analysans, it is indifferent to the question of how causation is analyzed. As hypothetical causes, negative events or actions refer to their positive counterparts, the "real" causes under hypothetical circumstances. Thus, according to this account, our cases of omissive action should be redescribed as follows: A's failure to pay back his debts to B quasi-causes B's sending A an angry letter because if A paid back his debts, B would not send him the angry letter; in the same vein, A's not drinking his usual morning coffee quasi-causes B to ask A what is wrong with him because if A drank his coffee, B would not ask him what is wrong. Finally, A's failure to provide insulin to the bed-ridden B quasi-causes B's dying from diabetic shock because if A provided insulin to B, B would survive.

This third position is open to an obvious but nevertheless crucial objection: Hypothetical causation is not genuine causation. After all, the "real" causality of the considered positive events or actions exists only in the imagination and not in reality. The positive events or actions actually do not take place. All there is are negative events or actions. But these – as the proponents of hypothetical causation are eager to insist – are not able to "really" cause anything. Thus, speaking of hypothetical causation here seems delusive at best. The term "hypothetical" in "hypothetical causation" is syncategorematic in the sense that it does not qualify its determinative further but in fact partly annihilates it. Hypothetical causation is not a type of causation, but no causation at all. It relates to causation in the same way as apparent truth relates to truth.

Despite this problem the theory of hypothetical or quasi-causation has been quite popular among legal theorists and those causal theorists who think their causal theories cannot straightforwardly account for negative causation. Its attraction lies in its diplomatic quality.

It purports to do justice both to our common sense ways of thinking and speaking, in the case of omissions, of causal powers, and to the intuition that omissions cannot be genuinely causal. But this compromise amounts to nothing more than a verbal trick. Assigning hypothetical causality to omissions is pretending to bestow causal relevance on them, but in fact it is depriving them of any relevance. It is not solving the problems surrounding negative causation but burying them under mere rhetoric. It testifies to Michael Moore's intellectual honesty that he denies negative causality outright and does not go into the camouflage of talking about "hypothetical causality" or quasi-causality. In that he is more consistent than many other sceptics concerning negative causality. Nonetheless, his arguments for the denial of negative causation need to be inspected.

3 Are there good ontological reasons for excluding omissions as causes?

Moore offers several arguments for the conclusion that omissions cannot be causes. His first and prime argument is ontological: In the case of omissions, there is no event or state of affairs to cause anything. This is the argument from nothingness reprised. If causes are categorised as *events* and not as *facts*, this seems to be a real difficulty. As Moore notes, it could be a *fact* that no elephants trampled the grass in the park today. "But it boggles the mind to think that the truth-maker for that negative proposition is some particular non-elephant and particular non-trampling 'done' by that non-elephant" (Moore 2009, 445). As negative *events*, omissions are "bogus" (Lewis 2000, 195).

What is the content of this argument? On one reading, the contention that in the case of negative actions there are no events or states to cause anything could mean that there are, in these cases, no entities that are apt to causally relate to other entities. On this reading, the picture of omissions as a "nothing" is based "on an intuitive view of the causal *relation* and then, because of that view, only secondarily on an intuitive view of causal *relata*" (Moore 2009, 446, emphasis in the original). What is found wanting in the idea of negative causes is that this idea is not compatible with a certain view of the causal relation. In consequence, the worth of this argument essentially depends on the view of the causal relation presupposed.

One view with which the idea of a negative cause is clearly incompatible is the view of causality as *productivity*. On the productivity view, causation requires that causes produce their effects. Causes do so by transferring (physical or metaphysical) power, energy or momentum onto their effects. The causal chain is conceived as a chain of dynamically connected events, held together by a flow of physical or metaphysical energy, or of some other quality running through the links of the chain.

The productivity view of causation conforms to a common understanding of causes as "pushers" and "pullers". Causation, on this conception, plays the role of the metaphysical "oomph" that drives the world. Taking Hume's example of one billiard ball striking another as a paradigm, this account seems indeed convincing. In these and many other empirical cases it is plausible to think of causation as involving the transmission of power, impulse or physical energy – or, in Dowe's more generalized formulation, the transference of a physical magnitude. One merit of the conception seems that it allows us to distinguish causal processes from accidental coincidences (i.e. the *propter hoc* of causality from the *post hoc* of the successive symptoms of a common underlying process). What bestows on causal processes their specifically causal character is, according to the productivity view, the transference of a physical magnitude. This magnitude, then, constitutes the "glue" Moritz Schlick thought philosophers were looking after in the causal relation (Schlick, 1932, 522; cf. Moore 2009, 446). In many cases this test works perfectly all right. If the presence of a virus in an organism leads to two kinds of symptoms that are constantly conjoined (e.g. fever and rash with measles), there typically will be a line or chain of transmission from the virus to each of the symptoms but not from one symptom to the other. We take the lack of such a line of transference as evidence that there is nothing more than a correlation between the symptoms. The correlation indicates that there may be an underlying causal relation, but does not by itself constitute such a relation. Likewise, questions of priority or suspicions of plagiarism, as e.g. whether Leibniz or Newton invented the calculus, are clarified, among other things, by retracing the transmission of energy (here: information) that may have led from the actual discovery of the one to the apparent discovery of the other. If such a pathway cannot be made plausible or proven, we assume the discoveries to constitute a coincidence of causally unrelated events.

It is evident that on the productivity view, omissions cannot take the role of causes because they are unable to confer energy or momentum on other events. Nor can they confer any kind of metaphysical energy or force. There is neither a point of origin from where the energy flow could get started nor a proper medium that could conduct the flow. Therefore, speaking of omissions as causes cannot be justified in that picture. Omissions cannot be considered as pushers and pullers and hence have to be regarded as causally inert. This reading, however, is only one reading of Moore's ontological argument. Another reading is even stronger since it does not depend on any particular view of the causal relation. On this second reading, there is, in the case of omissions, not only no event or state required by a particular view of the causal relation, but there is no event or state in the first place, independently of how the causal relation is conceived. As Moore says, omissions "are literally no things at all" (2009, 129). Not only are there no items that would be apt to causally produce other items – there do not exist any items whatsoever. This, if true, makes for a stronger argument because the claim that omissions cannot be causes then does not depend on a productivity view of causation. If there are no events or states at all in the case of negative actions or events, then there are in the end no relata to causally relate, no matter how the causal relation is construed – for there are simply no relata to relate (causally or otherwise). This is what David Lewis – who is not known to be an adherent of the productivity view of causation – called the "problem of the missing relatum" (Lewis 2001, 281). On this stronger reading, the ontological argument plagues any account of negative causation that construes causation as a relation, at least as a relation between entities in the world. If successful, it will be fatal for any conception of causation by omission realistically construed.

It may be thought that both the weaker and the stronger conclusion of Moore's ontological argument can be avoided if omissions are construed not as purely negative items but as sets of positive items described, for pragmatic reasons, in negative language. If this should prove to be possible the ontological problem would no longer arise. If causation is interpreted as transmission of energy, for example, the positive events or states of an agent might serve as the point from where the transfer of energy required by causality originates in the case of criminal omissions. Such an attempt has been undertaken, among others, by Gross (1979). Gross's proposal amounts to shifting the reference of the negative act-description to the positive acts that the agent actually undertakes while omitting. Consider A who goes on vacation without recruiting somebody to water his plants. B could water the plants but fails to do so. Consequently, the plants wither. If B's behaviour is to be regarded as causally relevant to the plants' withering then this (on the sceptic's view) cannot be because B did *not* water the plants but because B pursued his usual business *without* watering the plants. B is to be blamed for the plants' withering not insofar as he did *not* do certain things but only insofar as he *did* certain things without doing other things (cf. Gross 1979, 64).

Again, Moore testifies to his intellectual integrity in rejecting such strategies of reducing omissions to simultaneously undertaken positive acts. He rightly thinks that attempts on this line are pseudo-solutions. First of all, the semantic shift of reference that is implied in the envisioned reduction does not correspond to what normal speakers intend when they attribute moral and causal responsibility for omissions. Even if the agent does something while he fails to do something else, the focus in attributing responsibility for omissions is on the causal consequences of his non-doings, not on the consequences of his doings. In the case of the withered plants, grounding B's responsibility on the positive acts he does misses the point (cf. Moore 2009, 141). What matters are the acts he does not do, or so it seems. In fact, most of the items of the totality of positive acts of B are irrelevant to the occurrence of the effect. Suppose B watches television instead of watering the plants. What has watching television to do with withering plants? If there are positive causes for the withering then they will probably have nothing to with what B actually does – solar radiation, for instance. But then, how can B's positive acts ground any responsibility of B for the withering of A's plants?

Second, the totality of positive acts does not pick out the particular non-act for which B is to be blamed. Even a full description of the acts that B undertakes does not determine the act he omits. This holds at least as long as B does not do things which are logically, nomologically or otherwise incompatible with the particular act he fails to do. B's watching television, in any case, need not be inconsistent with his watering the plants, so just referring to this does not tell whether B actually fails to water the plants. Therefore, reference to positive actions does not single out, and cannot replace, the negative factor that is considered to be a cause of the plants' withering and to ground B's responsibility. This is different if B, instead of watching television, goes on vacation himself. This would be logically incompatible with his watering the plants, and hence would logically imply his not-watering. In this case, it would be in order to shift the attribution of causal relevance, if there is any, to the positive action.

Third, for many omissions, there are no simultaneous positive acts. Even if talk of omission presupposes an agent who has both the capacity and the opportunity to act in the relevant circumstances, the agent need not actually act when he omits something – neither in the sense of outer bodily action nor in the sense of inner mental action. B does not need to do anything while failing to water the plants. He may lie stock-still and thoughtless in his hammock. As Gross concedes: "Some crimes of omission may be committed when all is quiet on the mental front" (Gross 1979, 62).

Another misguided reduction or "reference-shifting" strategy has been proposed by Trapp (1988, 417). Trapp attempts to replace the causality of omissions by the causality of the *intention* not to act. The weaknesses of this proposal are obvious. True, intentions not to act may be regarded as positive actions that can be causally efficacious. But omissions are not necessarily intentional. The majority of acts that we fail to do though we could do them is not intended. Though omitting to act in a certain way generally requires that the agent knows or at least suspects that he could prevent a particular consequence by acting in that way, it does not require that the agent has the intent not to act in the sense that he consciously makes a decision or performs an act of will to that effect. Omitting as well as acting does not have to be deliberately controlled in every single case. What is required is only that it *can* be deliberately controlled if necessary, for instance if circumstances ensue during the course of action which call for an instantaneous modification of behaviour. In our case: If B fails to water A's plants, this does not imply that B *decides* or *wills* not to do so. B omits to water the plants even if he does so unintentionally. Moreover, intentions not to act are not sufficient for omitting to act. Even in cases in which the actor consciously intends not to act, the intention constitutes only one aspect of the omission as a whole. In order for B to omit to water the plants, it does not suffice that B *decides* not to water the plants. (Nor does it suffice that B *tries* not to water the plants.) For he may decide (and try) not to water the plants yet end up watering the plants – just like the one who decides not to smoke may end up smoking. What counts is that B actually fails to water the plants. In sum, intentions not to act, both unnecessary and insufficient for non-action, cannot account for omissions and their purported causal relevance.

Omissions and other negative events, then, do not reduce to positive acts or events. But what are they? Are they really "no things at all"? It is our conviction that negative actions are less of a "nothing" than Moore supposes. To begin with, in order for an omission to take place, there must be a) an agent, b) an opportunity for action, and c) a capacity to act. Likewise, negative events are almost always embedded in situations that comprise a bunch of positive factors. We have seen, on the other hand, that negative action or event descriptions refer to something further than the positive agential or situational factors. This is not to say that negative descriptions refer to spooky entities that exist in some barely intelligible mode of existence: things that somehow exist though they actually do not exist. To see this, it is crucial to remind ourselves that the distinction between negative and positive events or actions is first and foremost *not* an ontological distinction, but a *logical* distinction between forms of linguistic expressions we use to describe the world. First and foremost, it is the expressions that have the form of negation, not the things referred to by these expressions. Our linguistic resources may be such that there are properties for which we have no simple predicates in our language and which we have to pick out by negative predicates satisfied by the objects or events that have these properties. That does not imply that the properties designated by negative predicates are negative by themselves. Negative expressions may refer to suitable entities, or entities *bona fide*, in no way other than positive expressions. They may describe aspects of the world in no different way than positive predicates. They, too, refer to how the world is, not how the world is not. Saying that B fails to water A's plants is specifying, by means of negation, the way B behaves or the way B is. It is picking out a particular and in the circumstances explanatorily relevant aspect of what B *does* or how he *is*.

That said, it is an open question whether negative descriptions always correspond to something in the world. But the answer to that question is not prejudged by the negativity of linguistic form. Nor is it that negative actions and events become trivialized on the ground that, linguistically, any entity can be described as a negative entity – for example as the negation of its negation. The concession that not all negative act or event descriptions correspond to real aspects of the world brings with it the non-trivial task to specify the criteria that have to be fulfilled in order for negative actions or events to be real. One obvious criterion would be that negative actions or events are real if they are explanatorily necessary. Whenever epistemological theory – pruned by principles of parsimony, simplicity, coherence etc. – has to presume negative factors in order to account for the phenomena, we have a strong reason to suppose the reality of negative factors. Many putative negative entities like non-objects or non-persons (or non-elephants, for that matter) will fail this test; but many negative states, events and actions will pass it. Think of Jones who does not come to a party. It would be absurd and useless to say that someone else, Non-Jones, comes to the party and enjoys herself. Nevertheless, there *is* a negative factor, namely Jones's failing to come to the party, that very well may be relevant for explaining the ensuing commotion (cf. Thomson 2003, 81–82). The role of negative factors is here not only one of a fact-like condition (a condition in the logical sense) but that of a causal condition (a condition in the metaphysical sense).

These considerations suggest how the strong reading of Moore's ontological argument can be circumvented. It consists in thinking of omissions as real aspects of agents that enter into explanatory relations. Ontologically, non-actions need not to be any spookier than actions, even if linguistically they are accessed and individuated by formally negative descriptions.

This does not, however, meet the challenge of the weaker reading of Moore's argument. One might still suspect that omissions and absences, even if real, lack causal *productivity:* that they cannot initiate transferences of energy or momentum to other items and therefore cannot be causally efficacious. Even though omissions may be respectable ontologically, they might still be unsuited to take over the role of causal pushers and pullers.

As we have said, this reading of the argument from nothingness depends very heavily on a productivity view of causation. In reply, we contend that this account of causes is one-sided and should be resisted. As far as productivity is tied to physical impact (as in the majority of theories) it cannot account for forms of causation that are far from unthinkable, even if they are rejected as descriptions of anything in the real world, such as causal action of *mental* on physical phenomena as in mind-body interactionism or causal action of *spiritual* on physical phenomena as in theism. In these constellations, we have causation with non-physical events as relata. Since physical magnitudes like energy or impulse are not applicable to non-physical mental events like volitions, or spiritual events like acts of God, theories that tie causality to processes that involve exchanges of such magnitudes cannot adequately handle these cases. This difficulty cannot be by-passed by denying, for example in the case of mental causation, the mind-body-dualism implied in the concept of psychophysical causation. Even if one denies (as materialists do) that the mental occupies an independent realm of reality besides the reality of neuronal processes, one has to concede that the hypothesis of dualism, though it may turn out to be false, is nevertheless meaningful. The same holds for the hypothesis that the mental causally acts on the physical. Héctor-Neri Castañeda's proposal to make room for the transference of a physical magnitude of amount zero in the case of psychophysical causation (Castañeda 1980, 99) should be resisted. Transference of a magnitude of amount zero is just as little a transference of anything, as a body with the extension zero is a body.

Theses difficulties can be overcome if one chooses a radically different perspective on causality: one that does not link genuine causation to a flow of energy or some other persisting mark that connects the items of a causal chain but that conceives causes as *conditions*. This alternative picture is partly derived from John Stuart Mill who developed it, not least because of the necessity to account for the actual scientific practice of causal reasoning. Causation, according to this view, is a relationship of nomological determination whereby effects abstractly *result* from certain constellations of temporally prior conditions without necessarily being actively *produced* by them. A condition view of causality not only loosens the grip of the anthropomorphic overtones of talking of causes as "producing", "making" or "acting on" their effects but also makes room for negative causes. Though negative actions or events cannot actively produce anything, they may nevertheless enter into nomological relationships with subsequent events by combining with positive factors to form sets causally sufficient for their effects. Logically, they are perfectly on a par with positive causes. They, too, are rarely sufficient and rarely necessary for their effects. They are causes only in the sense of causal factors. Thus, passive euthanasia for example, i.e. letting a terminally ill patient die by not intervening into the progress of the illness, has to count – though it is often and perhaps understandably denied by physicians – as a cause of the death of the patient in the same way as a hypothetical active intervention to the same effect.

A conception of causes as conditions no longer invites the criticism of one-sidedness. Furthermore, it accounts for the many functions causality serves in our world-view as well as the productivity view (cf. Schaffer 2004):

1. Causality may still be conceived of as the "cement of the universe". It still may be thought of as the glue that perpetuates the "go" of the world, with the crucial difference that the glue is not made of productivity and transference but of nomological connectivity. Nomological connections need not necessarily involve transferences of physical or metaphysical magnitudes.
2. Causation still serves as an epistemic concept for use in explanation and prognosis. Causal hypotheses are regularly employed to explain *ex post* why a certain event has occurred, and to predict *ex ante* that a certain event is bound to happen. This employment is not impaired by the fact that the conception of causation as a productive process is replaced by a conception of nomological connection. On the condition view, causal statements still provide legitimate answers to questions about why future or past

events can or could be expected. Besides, by allowing for negative causes along with positive causes, the condition view conforms better to common explanatory practices. In most contexts, we find explanations of events that refer to negative causes no less satisfactory than explanations that quote positive factors. Normally we do not find anything odd in explanations that mention B's failing to water the plants as a cause of A's plants withering. The same applies to predictions based on causal hypotheses.

3. The justificatory role of causal relations in the attribution of moral or legal responsibility is in no way diminished by conceptualizing causation on the lines of a condition view of causality.
4. A condition view of causality is fully compatible with the most convincing explications of the causal relationship such as the counterfactual analysis or the nomological analysis of causation. It can even be accommodated to the interventionist theory. According to that account, proposed e.g. by Gasking (1955) and von Wright (1971), causes are conditions which can or could in principle be realised by humans in order to bring about or to alter states of affairs. The paradigm in this conception is human action with the intent of achieving some desired goal. The attribution of causality to non-human processes is then conceived of as a projection of this archetype onto non-intentional systems. At first sight, it may appear paradoxical to say that omissions can be integrated into the conception of causes as interventions because interventions are typically active. But it is easy to see how interventionism can be aligned to omissive causation. Omissions and non-doings can be contents of intentions, plans and strategies as well as actions. One can intend *not* to act, with the goal of realising a certain outcome, just like one can intend to *act* to achieve a certain outcome. Thus, B can achieve that A's plants wither, if he wants to, by intentionally not watering them. Omissions can function as means of realising or altering certain states of affairs no less than actions or act-like interventions.

In sum: The case for the rejection of the productivity view in favour of a condition view of causation seems to be able to dispel Moore's argument from nothingness even in its weaker reading.

4 Are there other metaphysical reasons for excluding omissions as causes?

Moore, in several places of *Causation and Responsibility*, refers to what Dowe (2000, 218) has called the *intuition of difference*, i.e. the feeling that there is *some* kind of essential difference between doing and letting happen, changing things by actively intervening in the course of events and passive letting things take their course (cf. Moore 2009, 445). What does this intuition exactly amount to? On one interpretation, the intuition of difference is rooted in nothing less than the argument from nothingness, either in its weaker or in its stronger reading. With Dowe, the intuition of difference is nurtured by a physicalist variant of the productivity view that binds causality to the transference of a physical magnitude. With Moore, the intuition is not bound to such a narrow view of causality. As Moore says, "That omissions cannot push, pull, or make things happen ... may seem intuitive, but only on an illegitimate picture of the causal relation. The intuition of difference remains after excising these extraneous features." (Moore 2009, 454) The question is whether there is not a perfectly innocuous explanation for the remaining intuition of difference. After all, even on a condition view of causality, there is a difference between positive and negative causes: negative causes are negative, whereas positive causes are positive. This difference seems perfectly sufficient to explain the "intuition of difference". No "deeper" difference seems to be called for.

There are suggestions in the literature, however, that this simple answer may be too simple.

One suggestion is that the intuition of difference alludes to the distinction between causal background conditions and causal factors we have introduced in the first section. The intuition might be understood as pointing to the fact that negative factors may be apt to take over the role of background or enabling conditions, yet, due to their negativity, are unsuited for the part of proper causal factors. Several authors have hinted at this suggestion. Thus, Martin (1996, 94) writes: "Absences and voids are causally *relevant* but not causally *operative*." Another way of interpreting the intuition is by saying that negative factors are somehow *passive*, whereas positive factors are somehow *active*. But this is an eventually unstable position. On the one hand, if a productivity view is adopted, then, by the same instance, negative factors not only cannot be actively operative but they cannot be passively relevant either. They are legitimate neither as causal factors nor as causal background conditions. On the other hand, if a condition view is accepted, there is no difference between background conditions and causal factors in respect to activity and passivity and no reason to withhold from negative factors the possibility of being assigned the status of a causal factor. If both negative and positive items are legitimate as causal background conditions, they are both legitimate as causal conditions proper. Hence, they can both enable and realise the coming into existence of certain effects. There is no sense, within the condition view, in distinguishing the "merely relevant" from the "operative", or the "merely passive" from the "active".

Another, related way of formulating the intuition of difference is that negative conditions merely *prepare* the effect whereas positive factors *trigger* it. Thus, Judith Thomson (2003, 83) writes:

> A [negative] state of affairs lies there, placidly and quietly. If a [negative] state of affairs is to cause an outcome O, some non-boring event has to occur, such that it causes O.

Similar proposals are that negative factors are *states* whereas positive ones are *events*, or that negative factors are *static* whereas positive ones are *dynamic*. (But: states are not always static and events are not always dynamic. There may well be static events – e.g. a movement of constant velocity – and dynamic states – e.g. nervousness.) The common denominator of these proposals seems to be that negative factors, unlike positive ones, are only poorly datable. Negative factors may supply a relevant causal background, but they do not operate as causal factors "here and now". But if this is the intuition of difference then it is not universally true. Negative causal conditions sometimes *are* event-like and datable and may be selected as the triggering causes of an event. Admittedly, many negative normalcy conditions like the absence of disturbing factors are – by the very nature of the concept of normalcy – static conditions with diffuse temporal boundaries. But sometimes one can readily locate a negative event or action within the course of time. When A permanently talks and then suddenly falls silent, this pops up as an omission that may trigger B to ask A what is the matter with him. Negative actions and events are even more probably perceived as punctual items and not just as states whenever the omitted actions and the unrealised events have been expected, as if A omits to drink his usual morning coffee or if the collapse of computer networks on the turn of the millennium does not take place.

Moore's own rendition of the intuition of difference argument seems even more clearly ill-conceived. As we have seen, Moore rejects omissions as causes or causal conditions *tout court*. Yet strikingly, he does acknowledge that non-actions, and non-events, too, "enable", "aid" or "make it easier for" other factors in the situation to operate as causes. Negative states "provide opportunities" to causal processes to get off the ground: "'Making possible' ... seems different than 'causing', is the intuition" (2009, 461). One of Moore's pertinent examples is that of leaving the keys in the ignition of a bulldozer that some vandals then run down a hill into a house. Leaving a key in the ignition of a bulldozer is clearly an omission and not a positive act. Moore, consistently with his position on omission, denies that such an opportunity-providing omission causally contributes to the harm. Rather, the liability of the opportunity-provider is, in these cases, said to be non-causal:

> I am held liable for making it easier for the harm to be caused; I am not liable for causing the harm, because intervening between my act of aiding and the harm is the free choice of the murderer (Moore 2009, 128).

However, it is difficult to think of "enabling" or "opportunity-providing" conditions in other than causal ways. In normal contexts of speech, these conditions are commonly held to be causal conditions or at least causal background conditions. In fact, there are a number of points at which Moore himself has difficulties in avoiding causal ways of speech in connection with non-action. Thus, in the context of the example of leaving the keys in the ignition of a bulldozer, he writes:

> ... if the defendant's culpability consisted in providing an opportunity to another to cause harm ... then such opportunity-providing acts are the cause of the harm despite the intentional act of those who seize the opportunity. (Moore 2009, 126)

Furthermore, thinking of enabling and opportunity-providing conditions as non-causal implies considerable complications. If a causal interpretation of these notions is ruled out, some non-causal dependence relation has to be created *de novo* to account for the enabling or opportunity-providing role of negative factors within the causal mechanism. This, in turn, is at odds with Moore's own ontological argument from nothingness, at least in its strong version, according to which negative factors are pure nothings and are unable to enter into any relations whatsoever. How could a non-action aid or enable some state of affairs to get caused, if it really is, as Moore has it, nothing at all? In the least, the introduction of a specific enabling-relation is at odds with Moore's general strategy of ontological parsimony and simplicity that led him to reject negative causes in the first place.

This means that our first conclusion can be upheld even in the light of further arguments: There seems to be nothing in the "intuition of difference" that is coherent and is able to compensate for the weaknesses of the ontological argument from nothingness.

5 Are there normative reasons for thinking that omissions cannot be causes?

Moore's third reason for rejecting the causality of omissions is ethical: We (i.e. the lawyers, philosophers, laymen) make a moral distinction between an action and a failure to act or to prevent. Therefore, Moore concludes, there must be a causal distinction between positive and negative acts. In other words, Moore postulates a link between the *causal* role of pieces of behaviour and *liability*. Positive acts are generally linked with full liability whereas omissions and pieces of aiding (active or passive) are typically correlated with reduced liability.

It goes without saying that a metaphysical account of causality must be indifferent to the purposes the concept of causality serves in its various contexts. One consequence is that the account must be ethically neutral. The concept of cause must be explicated in a purely descriptive way, so that it becomes maximally independent of questions of norms and values. It would be a mistake to make normative issues a conceptual ingredient of causation and to deductively conclude differences in causality from differences in liability. Normative issues of the degree of culpability cannot influence the causal structure of an action, or omission, and its consequences. We do not wish to attribute this rather elementary mistake to Moore. A more charitable interpretation of Moore's argument of a link between causal role and liability is to understand it as an inference to the best explanation: The best way to account for the obvious differences in our attribution of liability in cases of non-action compared to cases of positive action is to assume objective differences in causality between non-action and action. This seems to be what Moore actually aims at. He asks,

> ... how we can explain the usual absence of legal or moral duties not to kill, etc., by omission? ... The easiest, most intuitive way to draw the distinction is by using causation to mark the difference. (2009, 140)

This reading no longer invites the criticism of a "converse naturalistic fallacy", i.e. the erroneous application of normative criteria to a descriptive concept.

But even if interpreted as an abductively valid inference, Moore's ethical argument seems flawed. Moore himself concedes that differences in the strength of causation do not always correlate with the moral responsibilities involved. That is, he admits that active or passive aiding, for instance, can ground full liability in special cases even though aiding is, in Moore's picture, a non-causal condition of liability: "We can relax our normal causation requirement ... only because of the high level of culpability with which the aider acts" (Moore 2009, 139). Moore even goes so far to admit that there is full liability at least for some omissions, namely in cases of special obligations (*Garantenpflichten* in German law; cf. Moore 2009, 141). On the other hand, he quotes examples of causally efficacious positive acts for which liability is reduced, such as the case of the non-intentional bumping of the chair that makes someone else fall to the floor (Moore 2009, 151). Clearly the bumping of the chair would be selected as "the cause" of the accident. Nevertheless, liability is reduced, though not because the bumping is not causal, but because it is non-intentional. One might add other cases in which two actions are causally equivalent yet accompanied by different degrees of liability. For instance, A might try to rescue a drowning person but fall short of achieving it, whereas B does not start trying in the first place.

If the correlation between causation and liability breaks down in certain significant cases, this is to the discredit of the argument from moral difference even if it is *not* interpreted as a deductive inference from a normative to a descriptive distinction. The reasons why liability is reduced in some cases are not consistently to be found in some sort of reduced or missing causality but in other morally relevant factors, such as intentions and motives. Causation and liability are not logically symmetrical. Causation is, arguably, a condition of liability. But liability cannot be a condition of causation. Nor is it a reliable indicator of a certain *degree* of causation. But then, the inference that the moral difference between acts and omissions is best explained by causal differences does not follow abductively. Linking the distinction between (causal) action and (non-causal) omission to that between full liability and reduced liability invites difficulties in explaining, among other things, the full liability for omissions in case of special obligations. A more promising approach to account for moral differences is on purely non-causal grounds. (We shall pursue this strategy in more detail in the last section.)

Taken all in all, Moore's argumentation from moral differences runs counter to his overall strategy of systematicity. In fact, systematicity is one of the central themes of his book. Moore's aim throughout the book is to prune the legal concept of causation from pragmatic relevance principles alien to the purity of a metaphysical theory. But in spite of his rightly thinking that "the law has mixed too many extrinsic elements into what it calls 'causation'" (Moore 2009, 136), Moore is still very much impressed by legal ways of speaking. Even if Moore tries hard not to "let the moral tail wag the metaphysical dog" (Moore 2009, 448), the law very often does fall prey to this fallacy, and Moore tends to import this bias into his own theoretical framework in taking the law's demands too seriously and failing to recognize that they are infected with what he calls an "aphrodisiac effect" (Moore 2009, 136) of culpability on causal potency.

6 Reasons for thinking that omissions can be causes

We have already suggested some reasons for thinking that omissions can be causes in the introductory section. First, negative causality, including causality by non-doings, is well-entrenched in common ways of thinking and speaking. Causal talk, moreover, is practically unavoidable in connection with omissions and negative events more generally. We have already observed that Moore himself has difficulties avoiding causal speech in connection with non-doings, his speaking of "aiding" and "opportunity-providing" being clearly infused with causal idioms and connotations. Second, "the cause" selected in ordinary speech to focus attention on one or more of the causal factors can be a negative cause (negative event or omission), e. g. in cases of failures to act in the expected or required way. In the example of the angry letter, for instance, it is highly probably that A's not paying back his debts would be selected as "the cause".

There are further reasons for accepting negative causation. If omissions are unsuited to take the position of causes, they should likewise be unsuited for the position of effects. If omissions are literally a nothing that can cause nothing, they should not qualify as events that can be caused by anything either. In fact, Moore rejects prevention along with the causality of omissions. His first and most important reason is, again, that "there is no event or state of affairs to be caused in cases of prevention" (Moore 2009, 453). This, however, is highly counterintuitive. In ordinary language and thought, omissions and absences occur as a matter of course not only in the position of causes but also in the position of effects – as for instance when A, prior to his vacation, forgets to instruct B to water his plants, and B as a result fails to water A's plants though he would have watered them if A had instructed him to do so. Things would be even worse if we were to reject preventions. Not even death could be an effect, being an absence of life functions. The bizarreness of this is substantially admitted by Moore, though only with hesitation. He concedes no more than that "many people find it more acceptable to think that something real can produce an absence than vice versa" (Moore 2009, 454). In fact, Moore concedes, in taking up an example of Schaffer's, that "common intuition tells us that A *caused* the death of his victim". He also concedes that causal processes often involve negative intermediaries, such as the lack of oxygen that precedes cellular death in the case of A's shooting B. But though Moore concedes as much, his own premises make him deny that A's shooting causes the lack of oxygen in B's brain. Furthermore, Moore's rejection of prevention as a form of causality is hostage to his own ethical argument that there are moral differences between human behaviours involving causation, such as ordinary actions, and behaviours not involving causation, such as omissions and preventions. His own example of suffocating tells against his theory. Is there really a normative difference between squeezing a person's neck so as to block air from reaching his lungs (a positive event, caused by a positive act) and causing the absence of air entering the lungs (a negative event, *not* caused by a positive act)? Though this is an example of a case in which Moore himself thinks that the intuition of difference between causing and preventing "tends to evaporate", it is highly implausible that anyone would be prepared to make a moral difference between these acts on causal grounds.

Rejecting omissive and preventive causation thus implies severe complications of theory. Attributions of moral responsibility are commonly associated with causal involvement. The same seems to be true for criminal liability (though not for other kinds of legal liability). At least in criminal law it is generally assumed that the attribution of liability or culpability is legitimate only insofar as the one who is attributed liability has directly or indirectly participated causally in the generation of a particular harm. We rightly do not accept to be made responsible for events the causation of which we were not involved in. Likewise we find it amiss to be praised for pleasant happenstances to which we did not contribute in any way. The association of causality as a necessary condition of responsibility is no less valid in drastic cases of omissions in which somebody *intentionally* lets someone else suffer through non-acting. (Recall A who lets the bed-ridden B die from diabetes by not supplying him with insulin.) In cases of omissions, too, we do not accept to be made responsible for letting a certain harm occur, if our omitting actually has not made, and would not have made, any difference to the occurrence of that particular harm. If causality is no longer accepted as a necessary condition of moral responsibility and criminal liability in law that means a considerable complication of the theory of responsibility. One should have to introduce, as Moore does, some *sui generis* relations in order to accommodate common moral and legal intuitions. One is inclined to ask, *pace* Moore, if this is really the "most intuitive way" of marking the moral weight of certain acts and omissions. The more one can show how negative causation can be integrated into an overall theory of causation, the more this alternative strategy appears to be *ad hoc*.

7 How to explain the difference in moral stringency of negative and positive duties

Causation, or the degree or lack thereof, cannot be what accounts for the gradient between the moral and legal responsibility for actions and omissions. That there *is* such a gradient is beyond doubt. Moore rightly observes that

> I have a strong negative duty not to kill you even though you are a stranger to me; I ... have ... a considerably less stringent duty to prevent your death when compared to my duty not to cause your death. (Moore 2009, 447)

So what accounts for this moral gradient?

The first candidate for an explanation is that there are a number of "hidden parameters" (cf. Birnbacher 1995, 129–212) in the distinction between actions and omissions that tend to aggravate active in contrast to passive harming. The following list combines different attributes suggested by Glover (1977), Singer (1984), and Feinberg (1984), and is tailored to actions and omissions that have consequences which are, in general, judged negatively:

	Commission		Omission
		Agent parameters	
1	more effort required (more "criminal energy")		less effort required (less "criminal energy")
2	intentional		non-intentional
3	awareness		unawareness
4	individual responsibility		shared responsibility
		Recipient parameters	
5	harming		failure to benefit
6	certain harm		uncertain harm
7	immediate harm		delayed harm
8	recipients identified		recipients unidentified
		Third parties parameter	
9	perceived threatening		less perceived threatening

The list may be read as a polarity profile representing the divergent connotations of actions and omissions with roughly equivalent main (harmful) consequences. The list comprises three categories. First, there are parameters that concern typical attributes of the agent who acts or omits. Acting, as a rule, goes along with more effort required (more "criminal energy"), more intentionality, more awareness and more individual responsibility on the side of the agent, whereas omitting, as a rule, goes along with less effort required (less "criminal energy"), less intentionality, less awareness, and more shared responsibility on the side of the agent. Second, there are the parameters concerning the recipient side. Acting is associated, on the side of the recipient, with harming, where the occurrence of the harm is relatively certain, immediate and the recipient identified. Omitting, in contrast, is more associated with failing to benefit, where the failure to benefit is relatively uncertain, delayed and the recipient unidentified. Finally, there are parameters concerning third parties, i. e. parties that are not directly involved in the course of action or omission either as agents or recipients. From their point of view, acting, as a rule, is more likely to be perceived as threatening, whereas omitting is less likely to be perceived as threatening.

The listed attributes do not designate polar opposites but continuous scales. Given two behaviours equivalent with respect to their main consequences, active behaviour is, as a rule, assigned a comparatively higher degree of effort, intentionality, efficacy etc., whereas passive behaviour is normally assigned a lesser degree of effort, intentionality, efficacy, etc. How robust these correlations are is, of course, an empirical question that would have to be dealt with by appropriate psychological and psycholinguistic studies. If actions and omissions were indeed robustly correlated with the listed agent, recipient and third party parameters, this would make for at least a partial explanation of our spontaneous inclination to sanction harmful actions more strongly than harmful omissions. Absent systematic evidence, however, it seems to us that only the first and the last pair of correlations can probably be substantiated. Only the assignments of comparatively more effort and perceived threat to actions and of comparatively less effort and perceived threat to omissions seem to apply to a range of cases general enough to plausibly ground differences in attribution of moral and legal responsibility for actions and omissions. All other mentioned correlations seem too weak or too unstable to justify that we generally give so much more normative weight to negative than to positive duties.

More plausible than an explanation by statistical correlations of active forms of harming with aggravating factors is an explanation of the asymmetry of negative and positive duties by two *pragmatic* factors. There are two grounds on which negative duties might be held to be more important in social morality:

1. Positive duties tend to be more demanding than negative duties. Saving someone is, as a rule, more demanding than not hurting, maiming or killing him. A schematic differentiation of positive and negative duties might be justified because it is likely to avoid excessive moral demands. If we had to feel responsible for all the things that we could actively turn to the better we would be crushed by this responsibility up to a total incapacitation to act. In the real world, responsibility has to be limited if we want to be sure that it will be accepted and followed. A full-grown ethical parity of positive

and negative duties would be practical only for a utopian society of ideal agents but not for real humans who would collapse under the burden of their positive duties.

This point conforms with Aquinas's justification of the different moral weights of positive and negative duties in his *Summa theologica* (II-II, q. 79). Aquinas argues that it is easier not to do something bad (to abstain from an infringement) than to do something good. Therefore, one can more promisingly demand from someone not to do something bad than to do something good. Therefore, the one who does not do something good is to be less criticised than the one who does something bad (or who does not abstain from an infringement). Alas, Aquinas does not presuppose, as he should, in his example of *denigration* versus *missing reverence*, that the consequences of the active and the passive form of harming are equivalent. The one who fails to respect his parents as he should acts less sinfully than the one who insults them. But denigration will offend the parents more gravely than missing reverence; so there is no equivalence in consequences in these cases. Be it as it may, Aquinas's principle of the lesser culpability of omissions can be read as a tendency statement: though in individual cases acts of omission can be morally worse than acts of commission, in general it is the other way round.

2. Another pragmatic factor that may explain the asymmetry of positive and negative duties is the fact that for positive duties there are significantly fewer cases than for negative duties in which their observance becomes relevant. Hence negative duties play a more important and more stringent role in social morality. You can only let someone die if he is already about to die, whereas you can kill him at any time. You can only deceive someone by not informing him about a state of affairs if he already holds a false belief. This explains why we naturally associate killing, maiming, deceiving etc. with the active modes of these harms. However, this asymmetry is contingent. It holds in this world, but not in other possible worlds. In our world, responsibility is attributed wherever a point can be identified in the causal continuum that can serve as a lever, as it were, for negative and positive sanctions. In our world, this point is predominantly the transition from evil intent to active harming. One can speculate that in another world in which refraining from harming others were extremely demanding, responsibility for saving and coming to the aid of others would be far more stringent. For example, in a society where everyone were dependent on insulin for his survival, passive harming by not providing insulin in cases of immobility would be far more of a risk. One can expect that, in this world, omissions would be sanctioned much more severely by law and morality.

References

Birnbacher, Dieter (1995). *Tun und Unterlassen.* Stuttgart: Reclam.

Castañeda, Héctor-Neri (1980). Causes, energy and constant conjunctions. In Peter van Inwagen (ed.): *Time and cause. Essays presented to Richard Taylor.* Dordrecht, 81–108.

Dowe, Phil (2000). *Physical causation.* Cambridge: Cambridge University Press.

Dowe, Phil (2001). A Counterfactual Theory of Prevention and 'Causation' by Omission. Australasian Journal of Philosophy 79, 216–226.

Fair, David (1979). Causation and the flow of energy. Erkenntnis 14, 219–250.

Feinberg, Joel (1984). *Harm to Others.* New York: Oxford University Press.

Gasking, Douglas (1955). Causation and Recipes. Mind 64, 479–487.

Glover, Jonathan (1977). *Causing death and saving lives.* Harmondsworth: Penguin.

Gross, Hyman (1979). *A Theory of Criminal Justice.* New York. Oxford University Press.

Larenz, Karl (1953). Ursächlichkeit der Unterlassung. Neue Juristische Wochenzeitschrift 6, 686–687.

Lewis, David (2000). Causation as Influence. Journal of Philosophy 97, 182–197.

Lewis, David (2001). Void and Object. In John David Collins, Edward Jonathan Hall & Laurie Ann Paul (eds.), *Causation and Counterfactuals.* Cambridge, MA: MIT Press, 277–290.

Mackie, John L. (1974). *The Cement of the Universe.* Oxford: Oxford University Press.

Martin, C. B. (1996). How It Is: Entities, Absences and Voids. Australasian Journal of Philosophy 74 (1), 57–65.

Moore, Michael S. (2009). *Causation and Responsibility.* Oxford: Oxford University Press.

Schaffer, Jonathan (2004). Causes Need Not Be Physically Connected to Their Effects. The Case for Negative Causation. In Christopher Hitchcock (Ed.), *Contemporary Debates in Philosophy of Science.* London: Blackwell, 197–216.

Schlick, Moritz (1932). Causality in Everyday Life and in Recent Science. In Herbert

Feigl & Wilfried Sellars (Eds.). *Readings in Philosophical Analysis.* New York: Appleton-Century-Crofts 1949, 515–533.

Singer, Peter (1984). *Praktische Ethik.* Stuttgart: Reclam.

Thomson, Judith J. (2003). Causation: Omissions. Philosophy and Phenomenological Research 66(1), 81–103.

Trapp, Rainer W. (1988). *"Nichtklassischer" Utilitarismus. Eine Theorie der Gerechtigkeit.* Frankfurt/M: V.Klostermann.

Wright, Georg Henrik von (1971). *Explaining and Understanding.* Ithaca, NY: Routledge & K. Paul.

Geert Keil

Making Causal Counterfactuals More Singular, and More Appropriate for Use in Law

1 Introduction

Unlike any other monograph on legal liability, Michael S. Moore's book *Causation and Responsibility* contains a well-informed and in-depth discussion of the metaphysics of causation. Moore does not share the widespread view that legal scholars should not enter into metaphysical debates about causation.[1] He shows respect for the subtleties of philosophical debates on causal relata, identity conditions for events, the ontological distinctions between events, states of affairs, facts and tropes, and the counterfactual analysis of event causation, and he considers all these issues relevant to law.

Part V of the book deals with the metaphysics of causal relata. In the final analysis, Moore opts for fine-grained states of affairs as the "true" relata of the causal relation, while he concedes that legal liability should rather turn on coarse-grained Davidsonian events. In Part VI, Moore discusses the major philosophical theories of causation, including Humean regularity theories, nomic theories, probabilistic theories and various singularist and primitivist theories. Most attention is paid to David Lewis' influential counterfactual theory. Moore argues that the counterfactual theory founders for several reasons (Ch. 17). He argues, however, that counterfactual dependency is rightly regarded as a "desert determiner" both for moral responsibility and for legal liability, although it is neither a necessary nor a sufficient condition for causation (Ch. 18).[2] In cases of omissions, for example, the negligent person is often held responsible, both morally and legally, although omissions resist an event-causal analysis. Moore himself favours a singularist account while being non-committal about which

1 Here is an oft-quoted assessment: "The lawyer cannot afford to adventure himself with philosophers in the logical and metaphysical controversies that beset the idea of cause." (Pollock 1901, 36)

2 "[T]hose who mistakenly identify causation as counterfactual dependence can have most of the bottom-line conclusions about responsibility that they want, if they will but recognize counterfactual dependence to be a desert-determiner independent of causation." (CR, 426)

version of singularism is "closest to the legal presuppositions of what causation must be like" (CR, x–xi).

In this contribution, I shall argue that an amended version of the counterfactual theory of causation can be defended against Moore's objections, that such a theory best captures our pretheoretical intuitions about causation, and that it is the most suitable theory for use in law. Moore maintains that all generalist theories of causation "founder on the same seven arguments that doom the counterfactual theory as well" (CR, x), "so that singularism wins by default" (CR, 507). I agree with Moore about many of the shortcomings of generalist theories. I shall however argue that rightly conceived, the counterfactual theory is a singularist theory, and that it enjoys all the advantages that Moore reserves for such theories.

2 Causation in Law, Science and Common Sense

To begin with, a number of Moore's general assumptions about the connections between causation in law, in science and in common sense deserve attention. "The central idea that organizes the book", says Moore, "is that causation as a prerequisite to legal liability is intimately related to causation as a natural relation lying at the heart of scientific explanation" (CR, vii). Hence, jurisprudence would be ill-advised to limit itself to its own homespun conceptions of causation. Now while the role that causation plays in advanced physical science has been a matter of controversy since Russell called it into question, the indispensability of the notion of cause in common sense explanations can hardly be denied. Moore approvingly quotes John Carroll's dictum that "with regard to our total conceptual apparatus, causation is at the center of the center" (Carroll 1994, 118).[3] As to the relation between causation in law and causation in common sense, Moore holds a second continuity thesis: "The law's implicit concept of causation differs little from a concept of causation embedded in common sense explanations and evaluations of human behavior" (CR, viii).

The picture that emerges is that of a unitary and intuitive concept of causation that plays a pivotal role in common sense, in science and in law. This pic-

3 Davidson has even pleaded for a reversal of the received wisdom: "It is often thought that scientific explanations are causal, while explanations of actions and mental affairs are not. I think almost exactly the reverse is the case: ordinary explanations of action, perception, memory, and reasoning, as well as the attribution of thoughts, intentions, and desires, are riddled with causal concepts; whereas it is a sign of progress in a science that it rids itself of causal concepts." (Davidson 1990, 22–3)

ture, albeit quite optimistic, has much to recommend it. One reason why the law's implicit concept of causation should be both intuitive and consistent with our descriptive metaphysics of causation, is that citizens must be able to know the conditions for legal liability. If legal liability presupposed a highly technical notion of causation, this constraint would be violated.

At first sight, there is a tension between the intuitiveness constraint and Moore's view that metaphysical subtleties are relevant for establishing the best theory of causation. This tension is relieved by the fact that mastery of a concept does not require being able to analyse it. It is one thing to be able to employ the concept of cause correctly, i.e., to have a good grasp of its extension in a vast number of cases. It is quite another thing to be able to spell out its logical structure, let alone provide necessary and jointly sufficient conditions. It takes a lot of hard and sophisticated work to make explicit the concept of causation implicit in our descriptive metaphysics.[4]

3 The Counterfactual Theory of Causation

As regards relevance to law, the counterfactual theory of causation is not just one theory among many. It underlies the dominant test for causation in many legal traditions, namely the *but for* test, also known as *sine qua non* test or *necessary condition* test. In Moore's words: "Such a test asks a counterfactual question: But for the defendant's action, would the victim have been harmed in the way the criminal law prohibits?" (CR, 83 – 4)

The idea that a cause is simply a necessary condition in the way the counterfactual account suggests is very intuitive. It is so intuitive that Hume took it to be equivalent with his regularity account, which is a blunder that no freshman student would get away with today:

> We may define a cause to be an object, followed by another, and where all the objects similar to the first are followed by objects similar to the second. Or in other words where, if the first object had not been, the second never had existed. (Hume 1748, sc. VII)

4 "Descriptive metaphysics", according to Peter Strawson, aims "to describe the actual structure of our thought about the world". It examines "the commonplaces of the least refined thinking", which "are yet the indispensable core of the conceptual equipment of the most sophisticated human beings. It is with these, their interconnexions, and the structure that they form, that a descriptive metaphysics will be primarily concerned" (Strawson 1959, 9 – 10).

Far from putting the first definition "in other words", the second sentence introduces a distinctively new idea. Today's standard version of the counterfactual theory was presented by David Lewis in 1973. Here is Lewis' original definition:

> If *c* and *e* are two actual events such that *e* would not have occurred without *c*, then *c* is the cause of *e*. (Lewis 1973b, 167).

I neglect Lewis' distinction between causation and causal dependence, because I do not share the main motivation for this distinction, namely his assumption that the causal relation is transitive. Note that in this analysis the question of causal relata is already prejudged in the *analysandum:* The variables "c" and "e" range over events, and the statement to be analysed is the singular causal statement "event *c* has caused event *e*". Further note that *c* and *e* have actually occurred, a fact that is implicit in the grammar of counterfactual statements. A statement can only be contrary to fact if the facts themselves obtain. Counterfactual dependence is always stated and evaluated *ex post factum*, in view of events that actually occurred. A future conditional such as "If the wrong wire is cut, the bomb may explode" is hypothetical, but not counterfactual. This trait of the counterfactual analysis completely changes the subject, compared with Hume's way of putting the problem. This change of subject often goes unnoticed. Hume asked which properties an object or event must possess so that we can infer that another event will occur. He found none, drew his sceptical conclusions and sought a psychological explanation in terms of expectations, associations and habits. The counterfactual theory, on the other hand, asks of two events that actually obtained whether they were related as cause and effect or not. Hume, in asking two predictive questions at once – Will *e* occur? Will *e* be caused by *c?* –, tied the analysis of causation to the problem of induction and thus put the whole debate about the *metaphysics* of the causal relation on the wrong track. If we bracket Hume's empiricist assumptions, there is no good reason to burden the theory of causality with the problem of induction.

4 The Case for Singularism

The primary task of a theory of causality, I submit, is to make explicit the truth conditions for uncontroversial cases of singular causal statements. In doing so, we start with a given *pair* of events and ask whether they were related as cause and effect. Incidentally, this is precisely the situation in the courtroom. Some damage or harm or other violation of rights has occurred, and the pivotal question is whether the defendant's conduct was causally responsible for that harm.

Thankfully, what makes most sense in the courtroom makes most sense for a theory of causation in general. What philosophical and legal *theories* of causation add to the factual question of whether *e* was caused by *c* or not is the search for truth conditions for statements of the form "*c* caused *e*".

The *sine qua non* test indicates the law's leanings toward the counterfactual theory. The courtroom situation also brings into the open the law's leanings toward singularism. The court's primary task is not to find out whether fast driving in general causes accidents or whether smoking causes cancer. The cases to be decided are particular incidents, and the causal claims to be assessed are singular causal statements.

Quite a number of theories of causation pursue different projects, rather than specifying truth conditions for singular causal statements. Process theories and transfer theories try to sort out what distinguishes causal from non-causal processes. Interventionist theories look for recipes, i.e. for manipulations that work as means to bring about certain kinds of effects. The probabilistic theory either fails to give the correct truth conditions for singular causal statements, or does not address the issue in the first place. Lewis' counterfactual theory is quite special in being unmistakably clear that the *analysandum* of a theory of causation are singular causal statements. Before going into the details we should pause to praise this insight.

What makes a theory of causation singularist, however, is not the nature of the *analysandum*, but that of the *analysans*. Generalist theories may well accept singular causal statements as starting points, but they attempt to analyze them in terms of general relations such as regularities, lawful connections or relations of necessitation between universals. Since there is no generally accepted view about the exact nature of the singularist/generalist distinction, I refer to Moore's explanation. Moore distinguishes between an extreme and a moderate form of singularism, the "axis of difference between those forms" being "the degree of commitment to there being causal laws whenever there are singular causal relations" (CR, 496). Extreme singularism "holds that singular causal relations can (and even do) exist even if there were no true causal laws that connected types of events of which these causes and effects are instances" (CR, 496). Moderate singularism leaves open whether there are such covering laws. Singularists may grant that such laws exist "because the more pertinent axis here is not accompaniment, but reduction. [...] Singularism can be best seen as the account that does not reduce singular statements to statements of causal laws. Such a non-reductionist-defined singularism can then be agnostic about whether such laws are always present where there exist singular causal relations" (CR, 497).

The view that every singular causal statement implies a strict law that covers the case in question has been held by Kant, Mill, Popper, Hempel, Stegmüller and Davidson, among others. Davidson has called this view, somewhat clumsily, "the principle of the nomological character of causality" (1970, 208), or, later and less clumsily, "the cause-law thesis" (1995). In Davidson's version, the cause-law thesis says that if two events "*c* and *e* are related as cause and effect, there exist descriptions of *c* and *e* that instantiate a strict law" (1993, 312–3).[5] We neither need to know this strict law nor the event descriptions, but they must exist. Strict laws, according do Davidson, are exceptionless generalizations that support counterfactuals and that do not contain *ceteris paribus* clauses or other open-ended phrases.[6]

The cause-law thesis is arguably false. The reason for rejecting it is simply that, for all we know, strict laws of the required kind do not exist. All candidates are falsified by counterexamples. As Cartwright (1983, 46) bluntly puts it: "there are no exceptionless quantitative laws in physics [...]. In fact our best candidates are known to fail". Two decades before Cartwright's book *How the Laws of Physics Lie* made the sceptical perspective on laws popular, Scriven had opened a paper with the remark: "The most interesting fact about laws of nature is that they are virtually all known to be in error" (Scriven 1961, 91).

This bold claim is in need of qualification, of course. For the present purpose, the claim should be restricted to those kinds of laws that the cause-law thesis must rely on. Not just any connection between laws and causation suffices for the cause-law thesis. A *causal* law must exist that actually covers the case, causal laws being "laws that do subsume cause-effect pairs" (Cummins 1983, 5). In this paper, I assume without argument that only events, rather than aspects thereof, or facts, or properties, or tropes, can be causally related. Under this assumption only laws about the succession of events can be causal laws, i. e., laws that state, crudely put: "Whenever an event of the type *c* occurs, it is followed by an event of the type *e*". Such laws make a claim about what regularly happens. Most of the laws of physics do not. For example, the law of the pendulum says something about the relationship between the length of a pendulum and its period of swing. Boyle's Law makes a statement about the ratio between the pressure, tempera-

5 Or, more precisely: "'*A* caused *B*' is true if and only if there are descriptions of *A* and *B* such that the sentence obtained by putting these descriptions for '*A*' and '*B*' in '*A* caused *B*' follows from a true causal law." (Davidson 1963, 16) Here is Moore's version: "Singular causal statements are thus unpacked as referring to *instantiations* of causal laws by spatio-temporally located particulars" (CR, 471).

6 "Laws must be true universally quantified statements. They also must be lawlike: they must support counterfactuals, and be confirmed by their instances (these conditions are not independent). To qualify as *strictly* lawlike, they should contain no singular terms referring to particular objects, locations or times [...]. Strictly lawlike statements do not contain open-ended phrases like 'other things being equal', or 'under normal conditions'" (Davidson 1995, 265).

ture and volume of a fixed amount of an ideal gas. These laws are laws of *coexistence*, not laws of succession. They say something about simultaneous, or rather timeless, relations between properties or physical quantities.[7]

Hence, rejecting the cause-law thesis does not amount to the bold claim that there are no laws of any kind with any role to play in determining the truth conditions of singular causal statements. The claim is that no *causal* laws of the required kind exist, i.e., no true, exceptionless generalizations that subsume cause-effect pairs. "Scepticism about laws" is an unfortunate expression of this claim, for no distinctly sceptical attitude is required in order to notice that laws of succession which state empirical regularities are plagued with exceptions. True, the philosophy of science is bristling with counter-reactions[8], but far from disputing the diagnosis that series of events do not exhibit exceptionless regularities, most of these "Yes, but" reactions change the *concept* of law in the face of the problem of exceptions. Woodward, for instance, argues that "if we demand that all genuine laws must be exceptionless, it follows that we know very few laws" (Woodward 2000, 228). So, if we know quite a number of laws, the laws of physics must be conceived differently.

Another often overlooked *prima facie* argument against the cause-law thesis is this: If strict causal laws that subsume cause-effect pairs were available, then these would plausibly yield the truth conditions for singular causal statements. There would be no need to develop alternative theories of causation. It is precisely because such laws are not at hand that philosophers search for alternative theories that analyze causal relations in terms of energy transfer, counterfactual dependence, probabilities, experimentation, etc.[9]

Moore gives the no-causal-laws view short shrift. He addresses one of the weakest defences of this view, an article of Anscombe's, who indeed fails to mount much of an argument.

---

7 The distinction between laws of succession and laws of coexistence goes back to Mill: "The phenomena of nature exist in two distinct relations to one another; that of simultaneity, and that of succession", and accordingly they obey two kinds of laws (Mill 1843, 323 [III, v, § 1]). Thereupon, Mill makes a crucially important remark: "[U]nless there [are] laws of succession in our premises, there could be no truths of succession in our conclusions" (Mill 1843, 325). Mill correctly states that no truth about what actually happens can be derived from truths about simultaneous relations alone.

8 For an overview, see (Keil 2000, 182–240).

9 Lewis once rightly suspected that he did not exhaust the potential of the counterfactual analysis: "Perhaps by ignoring indeterminism I squander the most striking advantage of a counterfactual analysis over a regularity analysis: that it allows undetermined events to be caused." (Lewis 1973b, 162–3). For the benefits of an indeterministic interpretation, see (Keil 2009, 22–25).

The cause-law thesis is only the strongest version of a generalist theory of causation. For a more moderate form of generalism, a number of options are still left. Moore frames the singularism/generalism distinction in terms of "degree of commitment to there being causal laws whenever there are singular causal relations" (CR, 496). I suggest to draw the distinction between extreme and moderate generalism in this way: *Extreme* generalism claims that *causal* laws exist that *subsume* the cause-effect pairs of ordinary singular causal statements. *Moderate* generalism is not committed to these restrictions. First, there are other kinds of general statements that may back singular causal statements, e.g., statements about dispositional properties, about non-nomic general facts, about non-nomic correlations or about symmetries. Secondly, physics knows other kinds of laws, apart from causal laws of succession. Thirdly, these laws may play other, less crude roles in the truth conditions of singular causal statements than the cause-law thesis imposes on them.

As for the counterfactual theory of causation, it is not clear whether according to Moore's criterion it counts as a generalist or as a moderate singularist theory. In some places, Moore classifies it as singularist, because "causal laws play no essential role in the truth conditions of the relevant counterfactuals" (CR, 502f.). Irritatingly, however, he claims that the counterfactual theory and generalist theories founder on exactly the same arguments (CR, x). Mostly, he works with a tripartite classification of singularist, generalist and counterfactual theories.

In Lewis' theory, laws do play an important role in evaluating the relevant counterfactuals. But since there is no consensus about *which kind* of laws must play exactly *what* role in order to make a theory of causality a generalist one, short of *causal* laws that *subsume* cause-effect pairs, it is best to leave the terminological issue open as to whether the counterfactual theory is a generalist theory.

5 Moore's Criticism of the Counterfactual Theory

Moore raises numerous objections to the counterfactual theory of causation. His discussion consists of two parts. In chapter 16, he discusses the question of what makes counterfactuals themselves true. In chapter 17, he inquires whether causation can be analyzed in terms of counterfactuals. He calls both topics "two distinct parts" of the counterfactual theory (CR, 392). I am not so sure. Moore does not seem so either, for already chapter 16 deals primarily with causation. The reason for this amalgamation is that in Moore's view, the counterfactual theory of causation makes an identity claim:

> On the construal I favor, the counterfactual theory purports to tell us the nature of causation. Thus, it is best construed as an identity claim, namely causation is counterfactual dependence. (CR, 394)

Accordingly, the first group of objections[10] turns on this identity claim:

> (1) Overbreadth I
> Counterfactual dependence is not sufficient for causation. Many counterfactuals have no causal interpretation. Counterfactual dependence relates things that are not causally related (394–6).
>
> (2) Overbreadth II: Promiscuity
> The counterfactual analysis multiplies the number of causes for an event beyond plausibility (396–403). In reaction to counterexamples the theory must admit as causes an immense number of finely individuated events, facts and properties. Furthermore, it must admit absences and omissions as causes, since effects are counterfactually dependent on them.

Two further objections concern basic tenets of Lewis' possible worlds metaphysics and semantics:

> (3) Modal realism
> The metaphysics of modal realism is "extravagant" and "difficult to accept" (385). Belief in the literal reality of possible worlds is counterintuitive.
>
> (4) Similarity standard
> Lewis' metric of overall similarity between possible worlds lacks an independent justification. Lewis gerrymanders his idea of a "closest possible world" to get the desired results, i.e., to make the causal conclusions come out right (401–2). The same holds for Lewis' claim, insufficiently argued for, that all backtracking counterfactuals are false (403–9).[11]

The last two objections concern specific problems with the counterfactual analysis of causation:

> (5) Counterexamples
> The counterfactual theory cannot adequately handle many cases of overdetermination and pre-emption. It yields intuitively implausible results in these cases (410–25).
>
> (6) Nontransitivity
> "Counterfactual dependence across chains of causes does not, as causation seems to, weaken or peter out" over time (399).

---

10 I slightly rearranged and renumbered Moore's list (see CR, 508–12), which comprises objections to all generalist theories of causation, not just to the counterfactual theory.
11 "Backtracking" counterfactuals are those where counterfactual dependence goes back through time, i.e., where earlier events allegedly depend on later events.

For the present purpose, not all of these challenges need to be addressed in detail. As to Lewis' modal realism, I claim that the counterfactual analysis of causation does not depend on this metaphysical foundation. In everyday life we constantly engage in counterfactual reasoning about causes and effects without being committed to the belief that possible worlds exist, or are real.[12] Neither common sense nor jurisprudence need take a stance on the metaphysics of modal realism.

Pre-emption cases are commonly regarded as a challenge to the counterfactual analysis. Moore discusses the historical case where two fires burned their way to the plaintiff's house. Both fires were big enough to burn down the house, but the first was faster, so that when the second arrived, there was no house to burn down (see CR, 412). In such a case, Moore holds, "our causal intuitions are very clear: a pre-emptive cause causes all of the damage, and a pre-empted 'cause' is no cause at all" (CR, 419). I agree. It is anything but clear, however, that a properly refined counterfactual analysis cannot handle these cases and yield the same result. In the vast recent literature on overdetermination, trumping and pre-emption, there are promising efforts to handle these alleged counterexamples. From a truly singularist perspective, the method of choice is the "fragility strategy" (see below, sct. 7).

My strategy for discussing the remaining objections follows a simple maxim: Do everything in the correct order!

6 Do Everything in the Correct Order!

Judging from Lewis' work, the correct order for developing a theory of causality seems to be this: First elaborate a general possible world semantics, analyse counterfactual dependence in terms of similarity between possible worlds, devise a metric for overall similarity, and then apply the results to the analysis of causation. Moore, too, thinks that the counterfactual theory of causation has to accomplish all these tasks. In thinking this he ignores the fact that Lewis' philosophical agenda is shaped by many motives that have nothing to do with causation, let alone with the role that causation plays in legal liability.

Let us take a step back. I suggested above that the primary task of a theory of causality is to make explicit the truth conditions for uncontroversial cases of sin-

12 The issue is partly terminological. Lewis holds that possible worlds "exist" in an innocuous sense, though not "actually". The *actual* world is distinguished from other possible worlds by the fact that we inhabit it (see 1973a, 84–6). Roughly speaking, in Lewis' modal realism, "being actual" plays the role that "being real" or "exist" play in other metaphysical systems.

gular causal statements, such as "The cause of her death was poisoning" or "The explosion caused the bridge to collapse", or "The cause of the capsizing was the shift of cargo". If there are such uncontroversial cases, then their being uncontroversial should supervene on some fact. It is contentious, however, whether the factual basis of that consensus consists of anything over and above our descriptive metaphysics of causation as reflected in our linguistic intuitions and the causal judgements we actually make. As competent speakers of a natural language we share a number of implicit assumptions about causation. Among them there are bedrock intuitions that no philosophical analysis can overturn without changing the subject.[13] The method of counterexamples is telling in this respect: The very fact that philosophical theories about causation are being tested by citing and trying to accommodate counterexamples shows that we expect philosophical theories to account for our intuitions, rather than the other way round. There seems to be a certain class of core concepts in our descriptive metaphysics, which may include "causation", "knowledge", and "truth", where we are more confident of our linguistic intuitions than of the correctness of any philosophical definition or theory that purports to analyse those concepts. We are firmly convinced that Gettier cases are not cases of knowledge, and if our judgment that Jones, in Gettier's original case, does not know who will get the job clashes with the best available philosophical definition of "knowledge", then the definition has to go, not our judgment.[14]

Moore also assumes that there are "firm intuitions about causation" (CR, 507), even "bedrock intuitions" (403), though he does not enumerate them. I submit the following list:

- Causation is a relation between two items, called "the cause" and "the effect".
- Causation is something that happens in space and time.
- Causation does not work backwards in time: Effects cannot precede their causes.[15] (The additional issue as to whether cause and effect must be tem-

13 "The first step in providing a [...] definition of the causal relation is to set down the central tenets of our folk theory of causation – the platitudes about causation which are common knowledge among us." (Menzies 1996, 97)

14 What holds for "knowledge" and "causation" does not seem hold for natural kind terms like "gold" or "tiger". Chemical elements and biological species, it is said, have an essence, constituted by an underlying microstructure, that empirical science can study and that competent speakers may be wrong about. While linguistic intuitions trump philosophical theories, scientific essences trump linguistic customs. Moore resolutely sides with Kripke's and Putnam's scientific essentialism and even extends it to "social kinds" and "legal kinds".

15 Note that the intuition against backward causation is neutral about the proper direction of explication. It does not rule out a causal theory of time.

porally contiguous or whether they may be separated by a temporal gap is contentious.)

- The Humean intuition about *spatial* contiguity is not a bedrock intuition, but a little more fragile. Action at a distance has never been regarded as absurd as backward causation.
- The causal relation is asymmetric and irreflexive. Of course, ordinary speakers need not know these technical terms. These logical properties of the causal relation are best seen as being abstracted from our actual causal judgments, which in turn are informed by the bedrock intuition of temporal succession. Nothing can be the cause of itself, and effects do not bring about their causes.
- There is some kind of necessity involved. Mere co-occurrence does not suffice for causation. This modal intuition is firm, but notoriously hard to specify.
- Finally, there is the commonplace that causal chains can weaken or thin out over time, in the same way that ripples from a stone dropped in a quiet lake fade out towards the lakefront. This commonplace, which implies that the causal relation is not transitive, is a particular challenge to philosophical theories of causality, which teach, in the majority, that the causal relation is transitive.

Given these commonsense intuitions, some of them bedrock, some of them soft rock, what can we reasonably expect from a philosophical theory of causation? According to Moore, the counterfactual theory aims at a "metaphysical reduction" of the causal relation to the relation of counterfactual dependence:

> On the construal I favor, the counterfactual theory purports to tell us the nature of causation. Thus, it is best construed as an identity claim, namely causation is counterfactual dependence, either direct or linked down a chain. As an identity claim, the theory is committed to an equivalence corollary, namely, anything predicable of causation is equivalently predicable of counterfactual dependence, and vice versa. (CR, 394)

Now if both relations are meant to be identical and hence have to share all their properties, then the counterfactual theory is doomed to fail from the outset, for the simple reason that there are lots of non-causal counterfactual conditionals. Counterfactuals like "If today were not Tuesday, then yesterday would not have been Monday", or "If the word 'dog' had one letter more, it would have four letters" have no causal reading. This argument from non-causal counterfactuals is well-known from Kim, and Moore restates it as the objection of overbreadth: "Counterfactual dependence relates things that causation does not" (CR, 396). The very expectation that the counterfactual theory must be able to rule out cases of non-causal counterfactual dependence, however, rests on the identity claim that Moore has foisted on the counterfactual theory. The identity claim is hopeless, and Lewis does not make this claim, as his original definition witnesses: "If *c* and *e* are two actual events such that *e* would not have occurred without *c*, then *c* is the cause of *e*." (Lewis 1973b, 167) The statement to be analyzed is the singular causal statement "*c* is the cause of *e*". The variables *c* and *e* ranging over events in the analysandum, Lewis need not bother about Mondays and Tuesdays, or the spelling of words, or about Verdi and Bizet being compatriots[16], or about kangaroos without tails.[17] These troublemaker cases need not be considered in the first place, because they do not belong to the class of counterfactuals that could fit the bill, causation being a relation between distinct events.[18] Admitting only events as causal relata rules out many alleged counterexamples, the distinctness condition rules out even more, Davidsonian individuation of events (see below) rules out the rest.

From Moore's perspective, such a "stipulated narrowing down of the class or relevant counterfactuals" (CR, 395) is illegitimate. But the problem is self-created. Neither Lewis nor any other serious proponent of the counterfactual theory endorses the identity claim.

Moore also considers it illegitimate to add the constraint about temporal succession:

> The persuasive power of the truism that you cannot change the past is already loaded with the asymmetry of the causal relation precisely because causation does not work backwards in time. (CR, 404)

Any additional restrictions on the counterfactual analysis "have to be shown to follow from the counterfactual nature of causation", according to Moore (CR, 404). Again, they have to if we impute to the counterfactual theory the assumption that the causal relation *is* simply the relation of counterfactual dependence. Once we give up this unreasonable demand, we need not expect that the relation of counterfactual dependence alone yields all the commonplace features of causation. Once we give it up, we can grant that our intuitions do not and need not follow from the counterfactual analysis. If our preanalytic descriptive metaphy-

16 If Bizet and Verdi had been compatriots, would Bizet have been Italian or would Verdi have been French? (see Quine 1950, 15)

17 If kangaroos had no tails, would they topple over or would they walk around on crutches? (see Lewis 1973a, 8–9)

18 "Two events are distinct if they have nothing in common: they are not identical, neither is a proper part of the other, nor do they have a common part." (Lewis 1973b, 212)

sics of causation is such that, among other things, effects cannot precede their causes, so that we know in advance that no analysis is correct that disregards this feature, then we do not need a general argument to the effect that all backtracking conditionals are false, which Moore accuses Lewis of not having provided.

It is as clear as daylight that the relation of causation is not identical with the relation of counterfactual dependence. The existence of countless non-causal counterfactuals suffices to refute this claim. All there has to be is a partial overlap: On the counterfactual theory, the class of causally related pairs of events is a proper subset of the class of counterfactually dependent items. Causation is not counterfactual dependence *simpliciter*, but at most counterfactual dependence between distinct events that follow one another. This is how Moore's first charge of overbreadth of the counterfactual theory should be countered.

Not only do many counterfactuals lack a causal interpretation, many of them do not even seem to have a truth-value. Quine's Verdi-Bizet example was meant as a *reductio ad absurdum* of the assumption that counterfactual conditionals have a truth-value. But Quine was overstating the point. What the example shows is that *some* counterfactuals are too indefinite to have a truth-value. Now, if only a subset of counterfactual conditionals is truth-apt, it suggests itself to delineate and examine that set, i.e., to determine what distinguishes those cases from the others.[19]

It should have transpired by now what I mean by "doing everything in the correct order":

First step: Make up your mind what the primary task of a theory of causality is. I suggest that it is to provide truth conditions for uncontroversial cases of singular causal statements. If there are such cases, their being uncontroversial should supervene on commonsense intuitions about the nature of causality.

Second step: Collect those intuitions and commonplaces.

Third step: Turn them into constraints for the class of counterfactuals that a counterfactual analysis of causation has to consider.

There are remarkable concessions by Lewis that point in the same direction. In particular, he despairs of finding an independent justification for the appropriate similarity relation:

> [W]e must use what we know about the truth and falsity of counterfactuals [...] to find out about the appropriate similarity relation – not the other way round. (Lewis 1979, 43)

19 Elsewhere I have tried to specify five measures to ensure the truth-aptness of counterfactual conditionals. See Keil 2000, 431–457.

> It is fair to discover the appropriate standards of similarity from the counterfactuals they make true, rather than *vice versa*. (Lewis 1973b, 211)

Moore objects that Lewis lacks a general standard for the similarity of possible worlds that the counterfactual theory of causation can apply. Lewis, however, does not claim that we have independent resources to develop such a similarity metric. Rather he recommends what may be called the method of clear cases. He seems to think that we are more confident about, or that have we better epistemic access to, the truth of certain counterfactual judgements than to general similarity standards that purportedly fix their truth conditions. With regard to causal counterfactuals, the method of clear cases concerns the second of the three steps I suggested: In order to collect intuitions and commonplaces about causation, we first gather a sample of clear cases of causal counterfactuals (such as: "If I had not opened my hand, the pencil would not have fallen on the table"), then we figure out what these cases have in common, and thereby abstract the commonplace features of the causal relation from the sample.

"Collecting clear cases" of singular causal statements and causal counterfactuals does of course not mean collecting only *true* statements. This demand would indeed be circular. The counterfactual "Had Michael Jackson not been administered an overdose of Propofol, he would not have died that day" is a clear case of a statement amenable to causal interpretation, since it relates entities of the right kind. Whether it is true is another matter.

7 Singular Causes as Necessary Conditions?

Now I wish to defend the claims that counterfactual dependence between events is a singular relation, that the counterfactual theory of event causation is best construed as a singularist theory, and that only a singularist construal brings out its superiority over the INUS and NESS theories.

The biggest obstacle to the singularist construal is the myth that the antecedent of a causal counterfactual cites a necessary condition. Moore shares this myth: "On the counterfactual theory, for *c* to be the cause of *e c* must be necessary for *e*" (CR, 354). This cannot be true because strictly speaking, calling an event a necessary condition is a category mistake. The logical notions of necessary and sufficient conditions are not defined for dependency relations between events.[20]

20 "Obviously, given the usual definition of necessary conditions, namely through implication

On a less pedantic and more charitable reading, calling the striking of the match a necessary condition for its lighting is easily translated into the general statement that every time a match lights, it has been struck. Calling the striking a sufficient condition for the lighting is easily translated into the general statement that every time a match is struck, it lights. Now my claim is that the singular counterfactual "If this match had been struck, it would have lit" is anything but a singular instance of some general necessary relation.

In what follows I employ the standard notions of "necessary condition" and "sufficient condition".[21] One might object that the dependency relation to be analysed is *causal* necessity and/or sufficiency, and that these relations are different from *logical* necessity and sufficiency. As long as we are concerned with the logic of conditionals, this comment is out of place. The distinction between causal and logical modality concerns the non-logical question *by virtue of what* does the conditional become true. Take the textbook example: "If it rains, the street gets wet". In calling rain a sufficient condition for wetness and wetness a necessary condition for rain, the logician *stipulates* that the conditional is true. If, on the other hand, we assert a *causal* connection between rain and wetness, the truth of the assertion depends on whether the regularity actually holds. Arguably, it does not. (Think of Wimbledon's Centre Court that gets covered as soon as it starts raining.) What distinguishes "causal" from "logical" necessity is not the meaning of the modal terms, but rather the source of the alleged necessity. Analyses of the causal relation in terms of necessary and sufficient conditions do not invoke some special relation of dependency between particular events, rather they express the fact, if it is one, that events of a certain *kind* occur in constant conjunction. There is no second, independent, non-logical sense of "necessary and/or sufficient conditions" that would be explicable without the universally quantified conditional "Whenever *c*, then *e*".

The distinction between causal and logical necessity tends to blur the all-important difference between the related items. Events can be causally related, but not logically. For statements, the converse holds. I do not only find fault, as Danto does, with the naïve application of the idiom of necessary and sufficient conditions to relations between events. There is a deeper issue related to that

---

and denial, it is strictly a mistake in category to speak of *events* as necessary conditions. I do so in fact only in a semantical respect, viz. as instantiating a description." (Danto 1973, 94)

21 "If a conditional of the form 'If *p*, then *q*' is true, then the state of affairs expressed by *p* is said to be a sufficient condition for the state of affairs expressed by *q* and, correlatively, the state of affairs expressed by *q* is said to be a necessary condition of the state of affairs expressed by *p*." Entry "necessary and sufficient conditions" in the *Oxford Companion to Philosophy*, ed. by Ted Honderich, Oxford 1995, 608.

fault, raised by Mill's objection that the striking of the match is not sufficient for its lighting. The logic textbook calls the striking a sufficient condition for the lighting, insofar as it assumes the conditional "every time a match is struck, it lights" as true. Mill, in denying that a particular striking was sufficient for a particular lighting, denies that the universally quantified conditional is empirically true. Further conditions have to be fulfilled: The match must have been dry, there must have been enough combustible air, etc., hence the striking cannot have been the cause of the lighting. No striking has ever caused a lighting, since, according to Mill, only "total causes" are causes proper: "The cause, then, philosophically speaking, is the sum total of the conditions [...] which being realized, the consequent invariably follows".[22] Mill's comment is related to the sceptical view on the laws of nature discussed above. While the logician simply stipulates the truth of the conditional, the causal theorist makes an empirical claim about what always happens, and if no true, exceptionless generalizations that subsume cause-effect pairs should be available, then "nomic sufficiency theories", as Moore calls them, are in trouble. They are rightly "accused of parochialism in an indeterministic universe" (CR, 476).

Such theories are in trouble for another reason: On the one hand, no exceptionless causal laws seem to be available, on the other hand, the *sine qua non* test yields too many causes. Being a necessary condition does not seem to be sufficient for being a cause. Both Mill and the extensive discussion on causation in the law focus more on the second problem than on the first.

Sufficiency theories are in trouble, but not helpless. Mill distinguished between "total causes" and "partial causes", recent philosophy of science distinguishes "proximate" from "distal" causes, Hart/Honoré and Mackie refined the sufficiency theory to an ingenious combination of necessary and sufficient conditions. Causes are neither necessary nor sufficient for their effects, rather they are INUS conditions: insufficient but necessary parts of conditions which are themselves unnecessary but sufficient for the effect. The acronym NESS, introduced by Richard Wright and more widespread in legal theory, means the same: a cause is a necessary element of a sufficient set.[23] INUS theorists often introduce a special kind of "weak necessity", sometimes called "necessity-in-the-circumstances", and claim that "a cause is ordinarily taken to be necessary in the circumstances for its effect, and perhaps sufficient in the circumstances as well" (Mackie 1974, 50). I insist that this hybridization of the relation of causation

22 Mill 1843, 332 (Bk. III, Ch. V, § 3)

23 Usually, Mackie (1965, 245) is credited for having invented the INUS analysis. Actually Hart and Honoré (1959, 112ff.) were the first to articulate it. Wright (2013) emphasizes the differences between the INUS account and his NESS account.

and the logical relation of being a necessary and/or sufficient condition does nothing to alleviate but rather confirms the worry about categorical confusion.

As to the problem that the events we call causes fall short of being sufficient conditions, Mill introduces a pragmatic element into his analysis. Often we cite something as "the cause", he says, which is only a partial cause. Only "philosophically speaking", the cause is "the sum total of the conditions [...] which being realized, the consequent invariably follows".[24] Outside of philosophy, it is not. Mill mocks "the absence of any scientific ground" and "the capricious manner in which we select from among the conditions, that which we choose to denominate the cause".[25] The *selection problem*, as it has been labelled, is notorious both in the philosophical debate as well as in the literature on causation in the law.

Again, Mill's objection that alleged causes are not sufficient conditions rests on the confusion between the singular relation of causation and the general relation of sufficiency. Causation is a relation between events, sufficiency is not. Davidson got things straight:

> The inevitable comment (since the time of Mill anyway) is that the striking may have been *part* of the cause, but it was hardly sufficient for the lighting since it was also necessary for the match to be dry, that there be enough oxygen, etc. This comment is, in my opinion, confused. For since this match was dry, and was struck in enough oxygen, etc., the striking of this match was identical with the striking of a dry match in enough oxygen. (Davidson 1969, 172)

The striking of the dry match in the circumstances did cause the lighting, notwithstanding the fact, or rather the counterfact, that if the match had not been dry, or if the obtaining circumstances had been relevantly different, the striking would not have caused the lighting. The lighting would not even have occurred then, and *a fortiori*, it would not have been caused. Davidson makes clear:

> The difficulty has nothing to do with Mill's sweeping view of the cause, but attends any attempt of this kind to treat particular causes as necessary or sufficient conditions. (Davidson 1967, 150 – 1)

Davidson insists that the match did not have to be dry *in addition to* its being struck, rather its striking *was* the striking of a dry match. It should be noted that this way of putting it takes it for granted that causal relata are "coarse-

24 Mill 1843, 332 (Bk. III, Ch. V, § 3).
25 Mill 1843, 329 (Bk. III, Ch. V, § 3).

grained" events, rather than Kimian or Lewisian events.[26] What I suggest in order to make the counterfactual analysis more singular is basically to do the analysis with Davidsonian whole events rather than with poorly individuated *aspects* of events or property-exemplifications. The striking of the match that caused the lighting was a dated, unrepeatable particular with innumerable properties. Lewis calls such events "fragile", but this way of putting it only obscures the plain fact that if events are spatiotemporal particulars, then no two events with ever so slightly different properties can be numerically identical. Wright argues for "causally relevant instantiated properties" ("abstract events", "features of possible events") as causes, and he adds that "the law is not ambivalent between event-causation and aspect-causation, but clearly requires the latter" (Wright 2013, 15). He underestimates the metaphysical complications of this view of causal relata, though. He maintains that abstract relata stand in "successional relations", but neglects to explain how temporal relations between abstract entities should be possible.[27]

A strong argument for Davidsonian "whole events" as causal relata is the linguistic fact that singular causal statements are extensional contexts, i.e., contexts that permit substitution of co-referring expressions *salva veritate*. If a blow with a cane was the cause of the wasp's death, then by the same token, a blow with my grandfather's heirloom caused the death of the second largest animal in my office. To be sure, not every arbitrarily chosen event description has the same *explanatory* value. Here is where causation and explanation come apart. Causal explanations are intensional while singular causal statements are extensional. Sometimes the mere citing of the causing event helps to explain why the effect occurred, sometimes it does not. The lethal blow with the cane had many unmentioned properties, but it was causally effective regardless of how it was described, and regardless of whether a different blow with different properties would have been lethal, too.[28]

Linguistically, the inclusion of further properties and circumstances is achieved by the device of demonstrative reference. Davidson does not mention

---

26 Lewis argues that in order to be causally related, events must not be too "fragile". A fragile event is one that "could not have occurred at a different time, or in a different manner. A fragile event has a rich essence." (Lewis 1973b, 196)

27 "A causal law is an empirically derived statement that describes a successional relation between a set of abstract conditions (properties or features of possible events and states of affairs in our real world) that constitute the antecedent and one or more specified conditions of a distinct abstract event or state of affairs that constitute the consequent [...]" (Wright 2013, 19).

28 Moore's perplexed question, "How can causal explanations be so intensional if causal relations are not?" (CR, 357), indicates that he has not fully grasped Davidson's point.

this fact, so I must fill in. Singular causal statements refer to pairs of events either via definite descriptions, or via proper names, or demonstratively. In most real-life cases, the reference is demonstrative or even indexical: "The striking of this match caused its lighting", "Opening my hand caused the fall of the pencil". Often it is not necessary to use demonstrative articles, because already the definite article, as Frege, Russell and Quine have observed, works as a uniqueness operator.[29] In many contexts, the definite article is used in the function of a demonstrative article. And in referring to a particular event demonstratively, its countless properties and the circumstances in which it occurred are included without having to be mentioned or described. Goodman, in his early discussion of counterfactuals, got it right:

> Notice especially that our assertion of the counterfactual [sc. "If that match had been scratched, it would have lighted"] is *not* conditioned upon these circumstances obtaining. We do not assert that the counterfactual is true *if* the circumstances obtain; rather, in asserting the counterfactual we commit ourselves to the actual truth of the statements describing the requisite relevant conditions. (Goodman 1954, 8)

It is only because a particular match in particular circumstances is referred to that we accept the counterfactual as true, for in general, strikings are not sufficient for lightings of matches. But in the case at hand, the match *was* dry enough, the atmosphere *did* contain enough oxygen, etc. These circumstances do not get described, but they obtained, and the demonstrative reference exploits their determinacy. Though Goodman does not lay emphasis on the fact that his example sentences contain demonstratives, this fact strikes me as essential. The reader understands that in the given situation the requisite conditions obtained, so that explicit conditioning upon certain circumstances is redundant.

Danto and Davidson are right to claim that particular events cannot be necessary or sufficient conditions. And if the causal relation relates events, then causes cannot be necessary or sufficient conditions for their effects to occur. To think otherwise is to commit a category mistake. Furthermore, a singular cause is not any combination of necessary and sufficient conditions; the NESS analysis as such obviously does not remedy the category mistake.

Let us apply this result to cases of preemptive overdetermination, which seem so difficult to handle for the counterfactual theory. Remember the case of the two fires: "Our causal intuitions", says Moore, "are very clear" in this

29 In appropriate contexts, terms like "the river" work as "degenerate demonstrative singular terms" (Quine 1960, 102). "Now *the*, when it is strictly used, involves uniqueness." (Russell 1905, 481)

case: the first fire caused "all of the damage", and the second fire, the "pre-empted 'cause' [was] no cause at all" (CR, 419 and 412). Agreed. Our intuitions are correct, and the counterfactual theory delivers the goods: Both *c* and *e* occurred, and had the first fire been absent, the effect would not have occurred. Those who object that the house would have been destroyed nonetheless forget that the variable "e", both in the singular causal statement to be analyzed and in the counterfactual analysis, has a particular, concrete event as its value. No ever so slightly different event could have been numerically identical with the actual destruction. A particular causal counterfactual cannot be refuted by claiming that under slightly different circumstances, another destruction of the same or similar kind would have occurred instead. A different counterfactual would have come true then, but this does not eliminate the counterfactual dependence of the actual destruction on the actual fire. If the analysandum is about tokens, the analysis cannot relate types. Here I part company with Lewis. His reluctance to accept the fragility strategy (see 1973b, 193–9; 1981, 247–54) shows that he is not prepared to consider counterfactual dependence between events as a truly singular relation between spatiotemporal particulars.[30]

The trouble begins if the true counterfactual that *e* would not have occurred absent *c* is rephrased in terms of necessary conditions. Only then the counterfactual provokes the confused comment that the first fire was not necessary, since the second stood in reserve. If the first fire had been absent, the second would not have done *this* job, i.e. the actual job that the effective fire performed, but a slightly different job. Hence, the first counterfactual is not rebutted by the counterfact that if the first fire had been absent, the second would have stood in reserve to make another causal statement true.

There is an open problem with the fragility strategy, however. While the numerical non-identity of events that do not share all their properties follows directly from Leibniz' law, *counterfactual reasoning* about fragile "whole events"

---

30 Lewis' later account of "causation as influence", however, contains moderate revisions. In the face of the hard problem of where to "draw the line between *C* not occurring at all and *C* occurring differently in time and manner" (Lewis 2000, 91), Lewis introduces the new technical term of an "alteration" of an event. Alterations are "different versions of the very same event" (90), which allow for new kinds of counterfactual dependence: "Then we look at the pattern of counterfactual dependence of alterations of the effect upon alterations of the cause" (91). While ordinary causation amounts to "whether-whether-dependence", causation as influence gets analysed as "a pattern of counterfactual dependence of whether, when, and how on whether, when, and how" (91). Still, Lewis does not accept modally fragile Davidsonian events as causal relata. The new technical term precisely allows him to circumvent the problem of identity conditions and to remain "indecisive about the distinction between alterations that are different versions of the very same event and alterations that are different but similar events" (90).

can lead to unwanted results. Not just any relational property of *c* and *e* seems to be relevant to their counterfactual dependence, on pain of making the counterfactual conditional trivially true. Presence of oxygen in the surroundings is clearly relevant to the striking of a match, relations to events outside the "light cones" of *c* and *e* are clearly not. Generally speaking, it is not the whole history of an event that contributes to its individuation, but only its causal history. The challenge is to single out its causal history in a non-circular way.

To sum up: It is not true, as Moore claims, that "on the counterfactual theory, for *c* to be the cause of *e* *c* must be necessary for *e*" (CR, 354), at least not if "being necessary" means "being a necessary condition". Asserting a counterfactual dependence between singular events does not amount to specifying a necessary and/or sufficient condition or any combination thereof. The counterfactual conditional $\neg c \mathrel{\Box\!\!\rightarrow} \neg e$ does not say or imply that in all cases where an *e*-like event occurs, an *c*-like event must have occurred, nor does it say or imply that in all cases where a *c*-like event occurs, an *e*-like event follows, nor does it say that *c*-like events are necessary elements of a sufficient set (NESS) for *e*-like events to occur. It does not state any general dependence between *c*-like events and *e*-like events whatever.

The widespread view that the antecedent of a counterfactual expresses a *conditio sine qua non* is untenable. The counterfactual (i) "Had the match not been struck, it would not have lit" states a necessary condition only if it is tacitly understood as implying the universally quantified indicative conditional (ii) "Every time a match lights, it has been struck beforehand". But, singular counterfactuals do not carry such implications. (i) can be true without (ii) being true.

8 Causal Necessity without Necessary Conditions?

Now what about the modal intuition that the effect could not have failed to occur, given the cause? Causal connections are supposed to have some kind of modal force. Can a singularist counterfactual analysis account for the intuition that a cause *produces* the effect, rather than merely being followed by it, or that it makes the effect *inevitable?* Even if accounts in terms of necessary and/or sufficient *conditions* are untenable, the intuition will not go away that some kind of necessity is involved, perhaps a distinctive causal necessity.

The problem is where to get this necessity from, in the absence of strict causal laws. Armstrong's necessitarian account of the laws of nature provides an instructive example. In Armstrong's account, some physical properties *F* and *G* are such that, as a contingent fact, the property of being F *necessitates* the property of being G. As Lewis and many others have observed, the necessitation relation N remains mysterious if not backed by something else:

> Whatever N may be, I cannot see how it could be absolutely impossible to have $N(F,G)$ and Fa without Ga. (Unless N just is constant conjunction, or constant conjunction plus something else, in which case Armstrong's theory turns into a form of the regularity theory he rejects.) The mystery is somewhat hidden by Armstrong's terminology. He uses 'necessitates' as a name for the lawmaking universal N; and who would be surprised to hear that if F 'necessitates' G and a has F, then a must have G? But I say that N deserves the name of 'necessitation' only if, somehow, it really can enter into the requisite necessary connections. It can't enter into them just by bearing a name, any more than one can have mighty biceps just by being called 'Armstrong'. (Lewis 1983, 366)

Causal necessity does not come cheap, hence the view that "on the counterfactual theory, for *c* to be the cause of *e* *c* must be necessary for *e*" (CR, 354), faces a dilemma. Either the counterfactual theory succeeds in specifying causal laws that yield necessary conditions. In that case it collapses into a generalist theory. Or, in the absence of necessary conditions, some non-standard relation of causal necessitation is needed that no one has spelled out yet.

In a loose, preanalytical way of speaking, causal counterfactuals themselves express the sought-after modal force. The locution that a cause is necessary for its effects may be seen as an innocuous stylistic variant of the claim that *e* would not have occurred but for *c*. No harm is done unless this talk of necessity, which awaits analysis, is confused with the technical, logical notion of a necessary condition. Note again that without this confusion, the necessity claim cannot serve as a reason to deny the counterfactual in cases of overdetermination. In the circumstances, the second fire being too slow, the first fire caused the destruction. But as soon as it is argued that the first fire cannot have been necessary, because in its absence the other fire would have done the job, the logical notion of "necessary condition" is being employed that has no application to singular causal relations.

It has been suggested that the modal intuition about causality is fully captured by the counterfactual statement itself: "The 'causal glue' is the *truth* of the counterfactual statement, one could perhaps say" (von Wright 1976, 384). This move is unsatisfying, in leaving open what *makes* the counterfactual true. Many philosophers argue that counterfactual dependencies must be *grounded* in something factual, since they are not ground-floor properties of the physical world.

Well, they are grounded in facts. The truth-*conditions* for singular causal statements may be given by the counterfactual analysis, but the truth-*maker* for the counterfactual conditional must include something factual. Truth-makers, if there are such things, are non-linguistic entities.[31] Usually, they are conceived as facts, i.e., as states of affairs that obtain. The truth-makers for singular causal statements and for the causal counterfactuals that analyze them are the same, of course, if the analysis is correct. Here are some tentative and unoriginal suggestions: It is pivotal that the substances involved in the causing event have certain physical properties. As soon as we go beyond the metaphysics of causation and ask for a causal *explanation*, we will have to mention these properties. Claiming that the litmus tincture would not have turned red, had the acid not been poured into the test-tube, will fail to enlighten anyone who has witnessed the experiment. In science, we rarely ask for the triggering cause and leave it at that. Often it is obvious enough which event caused the effect. What we want to know, in addition, is why the effect produced was *F*, rather than *G*. For such a contrastive explanation, we must refer to the physical properties of the substances involved, to further facts about their arrangement and the physical forces present, and about contingent particular circumstances. These facts are what ground both the singular causal statement and its counterfactual analysis. To be sure, referring to those facts does not replace the counterfactual analysis, but supports it.

Plausibly, these facts are the source of the assumed necessity of causation. If a singular cause in some sense necessitates its effect, then this necessity does not derive from a strict causal law but from a number of general and particular facts which, taken together, account for the truth of the causal statement and its counterfactual analysis.

9 How to Explain the Petering Out of Causation

The last of Moore's six objections to the counterfactual theory was that "counterfactual dependence across chains of causes does not, as causation seems to, weaken or peter out" (CR, 399). The objection has force only if causation does peter out with time. In the philosophical debate, the majority view is that it

---

31 It is a matter of controversy whether the idea of truth-making is theoretically fruitful. Moore thinks so, Quine, Strawson and Davidson think otherwise. See Stepanians (2013) for an argument that Moore's "states of affairs" cannot do both jobs that Moore imposes on them, i.e., function as truth-makers for singular causal statements and as causal relata.

does not. Most theorists of causality, including Lewis, hold that the causal relation is transitive, and transitivity is incompatible with petering out.[32]

On this matter, I side with Moore. Both in real life and in legal contexts we often judge that causal chains weaken over time, and with good reason. An adequate theory of causation should account for these judgments. This challenge is not easily met. It is much easier to explain transitivity. Most theories of causation – regularity theories, nomological theories and transfer theories, in particular – explain transitivity naturally, at the price of adopting a concept of causation that is neither part of our common sense picture nor appropriate to determine legal liability.

In the remainder of this paper, I will expound and defend the view that a singularist counterfactual theory can account for the nontransitivity both of counterfactual dependence and of causality. And only if the causal relation is not transitive, can causation weaken or peter out over time, as it plausibly does. My concern is limited, though. I shall not argue for the claim *that* the causal relation is not transitive – arguably, the burden of proof is on those who adhere to transitivity – but only that *if* it is not transitive, a singularist counterfactual theory has a nice explanation for this.[33]

I once encouraged a student to spend an academic year in Norway. He heeded my advice. In Norway, he died from a heart attack during a swim in an icy mountain lake. When I was informed about the fatal accident, I felt sad, but not guilty. Now assume that the following counterfactuals are true:

(A) If I had not encouraged him, he would not have gone to Norway.
(B) If he had not gone to Norway, he would not have taken the swim in the icy mountain lake.
(C) If he had not taken the swim, he would not have died.

Further assume that all three conditionals relate distinct events and have causal interpretations.[34] If we add transitivity, we get the result that my advice caused the student's death. But in real life, we seldom attribute causal or moral respon-

32 But remember that Lewis distinguishes between *causal dependence*, which is not transitive, and *causation*, which is transitive by stipulation: "If *c* and *e* are two actual events such that *e* would not have occurred without *c*, then *c* is the cause of *e*. But I reject the converse. Causation must always be transitive; causal dependence may not be; so there can be causation without causal dependence. Let *c*, *d*, and *e* be three actual events such that *d* would not have occurred without *c* and *e* would not have occurred without *d*. Then *c* is a cause of *e* even if *e* would still have occurred (otherwise caused) without *c*." (Lewis 1973b, 167)

33 Recently, the broad consensus that causation is transitive has started to crumble; see Hitchcock (2001) and Maslen (2004), who both refer to the counterfactual analysis.

34 One might well deny that (B) has a causal interpretation.

sibility over long and winding causal chains, even if the agent's contribution passes the *but for* test. As Moore puts it: "Caesar's crossing the Rubicon may well be a necessary condition for my writing this chapter, but so many other events have also contributed that Caesar's causal responsibility has long petered out" (CR, 102). The issue is all-important for theories of legal liability. The literature is vast, but manageable causal criteria that help to avoid implausible attributions of legal liability are hard to find. (There may be *normative* criteria, of course.) The standard theories of causation are deplorably unfit to yield such criteria. The *sine qua non* test fares particularly badly in this respect. Moore argues that "the sheer size of Caesar's contributions disqualifies Caesar's act as a cause" (CR, 398).[35] I agree, but Moore's quantitative consideration echoes rather than explains the intuition.

In order to avoid holding agents with causally remote contributions responsible, German legal theory has devised the doctrine of "adequate causation", according to which not just any *conditio sine qua non* of a given harm establishes legal liability, but only those factors that caused the harm with some degree of foreseeability, hence "adequately".[36] This theory, however, has never been convincingly elaborated and lacks theoretical rigour. In the philosophical debate, the situation is not much better. Terminologically, causes have been distinguished from "boundary conditions", "proximal" or "direct" causes have been distinguished from "remote" or "distal" causes, "complete" from "partial" or "contributory" causes, but as soon as causal responsibility is to be judged in complicated cases, the matter is usually left to pragmatic considerations.[37]

An easy way out is to dissever moral and legal responsibility from causal responsibility. I follow Moore in dismissing this easy way out. The petering out of causal chains needs to be explained somehow, even if having caused harm does not suffice for being morally responsible or legally liable.

In order to demonstrate how chains of counterfactual dependence between events can break, although the events are pairwise linked, one further element needs to be added to the counterfactual analysis, or rather to be made explicit. Suppose that I throw a heavy stone against a window, the window breaks, and I maintain: "If I had not thrown the stone, the window would not have broken". An observer objects: "That's not true. I could have thrown the stone as well. Or a sudden earthquake could have shattered the window." The proper reply, to my

35 "My own suggestion is that [...] when there are too many event-links in the causal chain, it becomes too attenuated to support judgments of transitivity." (CR, 122)

36 Compare Moore's extensive discussion of the related "harm-within-the-risk" test in the Anglo-American legal tradition (CR, 178 – 225).

37 Lewis is no exception (see 1973b, 162).

mind, would have to be: “You might have, but you didn’t. And no earthquake was imminent.” What is sought is an analysis that supports this reply.

The standard view is that only a possible world semantics can yield such an analysis. One must find out whether the closest world that we have to consider contains earthquakes or not, and which standards of similarity between worlds to apply. In my singularist view, the case is much simpler. Using the possible worlds jargon, in the nearest possible world in which I do not throw the stone there is no earthquake, but simply an unbroken window. The reason is that in evaluating the counterfactual, we do not consider a certain *kind* of situation, and then figure out which kinds of changes in such situations constitute necessary conditions for which kinds of further changes. Rather we refer to the situation that actually obtained. This is only possible *ex post factum*. In an indeterministic universe, it was not written in the stars that no earthquake was nigh, and if it was written, I did not know this when throwing the stone. But since the truth-value of the counterfactual is being assessed in retrospect, my prior epistemic situation is irrelevant. This holds quite generally: An incalculable number of interferences *might* have occurred, but when we evaluate a causal counterfactual, both events being present, we already know whether any of these interferences did occur.

The *ex post factum* character is not only built into the grammar of truly counterfactual conditionals (in contrast to hypothetical ones), as mentioned above: A statement can only be contrary to fact if those facts obtain. It follows already from the logical form of the singular causal statements to be analyzed. It is no accident that all the textbook examples of singular causal statements are in the past or perfect tense. Singular causal statements of the form “*c* (has) caused *e*” assert the holding of a relation, whereas they *presuppose* the existence of the relata. Compare the relational statement “Adam is Bill’s brother”, which presupposes that two persons, Adam and Bill, exist, while it asserts that both are related as brothers. Taking the logical form of singular causal statements seriously, it is definitely unwise to burden the business of giving truth conditions for such statements with the problem of justifying induction. It is unwise to ask two questions at once, as Hume did. If it remains to be seen whether *e* will occur in the first place, the question as to whether *c* and *e* will be related as cause and effect is premature. The situation in which singular causal statements are being evaluated is different: Both events have occurred, and the open question is whether they were related as cause and effect. Whether *e* was caused by *c* is being examined *ex post factum*, in view of events that actually occurred. The counterfactual analysis only brings the nature of this task into the open. (For this reason, it is the congenial theory for lawsuits, which are backward-looking, too.)

In defending the counterfactual “If I had not thrown the stone, the window would not have broken” against the objection from alternative causation or overdetermination, we refer to the situation that actually obtained. We compare the happenings to a counterfactual situation in which the stone’s throw is missing while preserving as much as possible from the actual situation. In order to make this strategy explicit, the counterfactual analysis must be supplemented with a *ceteris paribus* clause that was implicit in it all along (recall Goodman’s observation). The clause is neither open-ended (like “under normal conditions”) nor vacuous (like “provided nothing interferes”), but has a determinate content. The cp clause fixes the prehistory of the causing event and the circumstances that actually pertained when it occurred, so that the hedged counterfactual reads: “If *c* had not occurred, *and if everything else had been as it was when c actually occurred*, *e* would not have occurred”.

This move is not original, of course. Lewis himself suggests it, as one among many other suggestions he makes to maximize similarity: “To get rid of an actual event *e* with the least overall departure from reality, it will normally be best not to diverge at all from the actual course of events until just before the time of *e*” (Lewis 1973b, 171). This is the right line to take in causal contexts, but Lewis cannot explain why. He considers a number of competing respects of similarity between possible worlds, which have to be traded off against one another. In particular, he suggests a trade-off between “similarities in matters of particular fact” and “similarities of law” (163). This trading off of similarity respects, however, and hence the fixing of truth conditions for counterfactuals, he says, “are a highly volatile matter, varying with every shift of context and interest” (1973a, 92).[38] Far from developing a similarity standard that deserves the name of a “metric” (Moore), Lewis employs only a loosely knit network of similarity respects. No general, context-independent similarity standard being available, Lewis calls the relation of comparative overall similarity among possible worlds “primitive”.

At least in causal contexts, we can do better to motivate the demand to leave the past unaltered, I think. The cause is the factor that made the difference, and this factor is where the divergence from actuality must be located. In evaluating causal counterfactuals, we do not brood over standards of comparative overall similarity, rather we simply refer to the facts that actually obtained up to the moment described in the antecedent. When trying to identify singular causes, we ask what would have happened *in that very situation*, if only the putative

38 “Overall similarity consists of innumerable similarities and differences in innumerable respects of comparison, balanced against each other according to the relative importances we attach to those respects of comparison.” (Lewis 1973a, 91)

cause had been absent. That is, we do not make assumptions, but we refer to facts that obtained. What does the trick, linguistically, is the *indexical* reference of the *ceteris paribus* clause. The clause "and if everything else had been as it was when *c* actually occurred" refers directly to the actual situation, and not via some general description of it.

Notably, the indexical nature of the cp clause precludes its being used to restore the truth of causal *laws* in the face of counter-instances. Genuine laws must not contain singular terms referring to particular objects, locations or times. Hence, if cp clauses have an indexical content, there can be no such things as cp laws. Indexical cp clauses need singular propositions as their habitat, so that they cannot be used to defend the cause-law thesis in the face of counter-instances. But they can do something better for the theory of causality, as I just pointed out. They are perfectly intelligible if combined with singular counterfactuals.[39]

Adding this indexical cp clause to the counterfactual analysis, an easy explanation for the nontransitivity of the causal relation is available. (Lewis is well aware that counterfactual dependence is not transitive, but he does not use this insight to abandon the transitivity of causation.) Three events *c*, *d* and *e*. Assume that the counterfactuals $\neg c \;\Box\!\!\rightarrow \neg d$ and $\neg d \;\Box\!\!\rightarrow \neg e$ are true. The cp clause in the wording giving above being added, it becomes clear that the clause does not fix the same circumstances in both cases. In the first conditional, it fixes the history of event *c*, in the second conditional, it fixes the history of event *d*. So it is not the case that *c* and *d*, and *d* and *e*, respectively, are connected by the same dependence relation, as they would have to be, by definition, if the relation is supposed to be transitive. Both pairs of events are related by counterfactual dependence, but not by the same *particular* dependence relation. On closer examination, counterfactual dependence between events is not an ordinary relation like "bigger than" or "older than". It can be instantiated only once, because it is a relational property of a particular pair of events, which cannot be detached from that pair. In other words, it is not a universal, as ordinary relational properties are. Asserting a counterfactual dependence between events is making a direct reference to a particular situation, namely to the actual history and circumstances of an actual event. This reference to actual circumstances provides a nice explanation of *why* counterfactual dependence is not transitive.

Reasoning through a chain of counterfactual conditionals is to commit the so-called fallacy of the ambiguous middle term, or four-term fallacy (*quaternio*

39 See Keil (2005) for a more thorough discussion and a defence of this clause against competing translations of the Latin phrase "ceteris paribus".

terminorum). The presence of this fallacy has been noticed before,[40] but neither Mackie nor Lewis draw the conclusion that *causation* is not transitive, nor do they recognize the value of an indexical cp clause.

As I said before, none of this amounts to compelling evidence *that* causation is not transitive. But given Lewis' theory, it strikes me that the burden to prove the contrary is on him. Instead of shouldering the burden, he simply *defines* that causation is transitive.[41] That is a pity, given that the counterfactual analysis nicely explains non-transitivity. In the cases at hand, there *is* an unbroken chain of counterfactual dependencies, just as Lewis requires for causal chains: *c* and *d*, *d* and *e*, *e* and *f*, respectively, are pairwise linked. But since each antecedent in the series refers to different circumstances, the unbroken chain of pairwise counterfactual dependencies does not amount to transitive closure. Lewis does not claim that it does, but he cannot explain how such a chain of *non-transitive* counterfactual dependencies should generate, without further assumptions, the transitivity of causation.[42]

10 Conclusion

The title of my paper, "Making causal counterfactuals more singular", is a misnomer. Counterfactual dependence between particular events *is* a singular relation. True causal counterfactuals do not require the existence of strict causal laws, i.e., laws of succession that subsume cause-effect pairs. All the counterfactual analysis can do is to bring the singularist character of causal relations into the open. In this contribution, I defended an amended version of the counterfactual theory of event causation both against Moore's criticism and against some traits of Lewis' version of the theory. The dialectical situation was somewhat complicated. Moore holds that all generalist theories fail, but wavers as to

40 "The non-transitivity of counterfactuals is nothing surprising: it is merely a variant of a very old form of fallacy, a syllogism with an ambiguous middle term." (Mackie 1980, 53) Similarly, Lewis explains the nontransitivity of counterfactual dependence by the fact that often "the closest worlds where the first antecedent holds are different from [...] the closest worlds where the second antecedent holds" (Lewis 1973a, 33). See also Moore (CR, 393).

41 "We extend causal dependence to a transitive relation in the usual way. Let *c*, *d*, *e*, . . . be a finite sequence of actual particular events such that *d* depends causally on *c*, *e* on *d*, and so on throughout. Then this sequence is a *causal chain*. Finally, one event is the *cause* of another iff there exists a causal chain leading from the first to the second." (Lewis 1973b, 167).

42 "But if all there is to direct causation is counterfactual dependence, and if all there is to transitive causation is the iteration of direct causation, there just is no room to add anything more to counterfactual dependence in order to generate transitivity." (Rosenberg 1992, 308)

whether the counterfactual theory is generalist or singularist or *sui generis*. I take him to think that the theory is ultimately generalist, since he claims that the counterfactual theory founders on the same arguments on which all generalist theories founder. It is not surprising that these arguments cut no ice against a singularist version of the counterfactual theory.

On a number of counts, I simply defended Lewis' theory against Moore's misdirected criticism. Moore's claim that according to the counterfactual theory, causation simply *is* counterfactual dependence (CR, 394) does not even do justice to Lewis' *analysandum*. Moore's unreasonable demand that all the commonplaces about causation have to *follow from* the counterfactual analysis rests on the identity thesis. His claim that on the counterfactual theory, the cause "must be necessary for the effect", suffers from an ambiguity: The logical notions of necessary and sufficient *conditions* are not defined for dependency relations between particular events. A distinctive kind of *causal* necessity might be involved, but is notoriously hard to pinpoint and does not seem to figure in the counterfactual analysis.

In other respects, I had to part company with Lewis in order to highlight some underrated strengths of the counterfactual approach. The common denominator of my revisions is that they make the counterfactual theory unambiguously singularist. The suggested revisions comprise: performing the counterfactual analysis with Davidsonian rather than with Lewisian events, taking seriously the ex post-character of singular causal statements, making explicit the indexical *ceteris paribus* clause that fixes the actual circumstances of the causing event, abandoning the alleged transitivity of causation, and, last but not least, doing everything in the correct order. The correct order is to start with bedrock intuitions about the nature of causality rather than with a general possible world semantics, and then to turn these intuitions into constraints for the class of counterfactuals that a counterfactual analysis of causation has to consider.

References

Armstrong, David M. (1983). *What is a Law of Nature?*, Cambridge: Cambridge University Press.

Carroll, John (1994). *Laws of Nature*, Cambridge: Cambridge University Press.

Cartwright, Nancy (1983). *How the Laws of Physics Lie*, Oxford/New York: Oxford University Press.

Collins, John D., Edward J. Hall and L. A. Paul (Eds.) (2004). *Causation and Counterfactuals*, Cambridge, MA: MIT Press.

Cummins, Robert (1983). *The Nature of Psychological Explanation*, Cambridge, MA: MIT Press.

Danto, Arthur C. (1973). *Analytical Philosophy of Action*, Cambridge: Cambridge University Press.

Davidson, Donald (1963). Actions, Reasons and Causes. In his (1980), 3–19.

Davidson, Donald (1967). Causal Relations. In his (1980), 149–162.

Davidson, Donald (1970). Mental Events. In his (1980), 207–225.

Davidson, Donald (1980). *Essays on Actions and Events*, Oxford: Clarendon Press.

Davidson, Donald (1990). Representation and Interpretation. In K. A. Mohyeldin Said et al. (Eds.), *Modelling the Mind*, Oxford: Oxford University Press, 13–26.

Davidson, Donald (1993). Replies. In: R. Stoecker (Ed.), *Reflecting Davidson*, Berlin/New York: de Gruyter.

Davidson, Donald (1995). Laws and Cause. *Dialectica* 49, 263–279.

Goodman, Nelson (1954). The Problem of Counterfactual Conditionals. Repr. in his *Fact, Fiction, and Forecast*, Cambridge, MA: Harvard University Press 1983.

Hart, Herbert L. A. and Honoré, Anthony M. (1959). *Causation in the Law*, Oxford: Oxford University Press.

Hitchcock, Christopher (2001). The Intransitivity of Causation Revealed in Equations and Graphs. *Journal of Philosophy* 98, 273–299.

Hume, David (1748). *An Enquiry Concerning Human Understanding*, ed. by T. H. Green and T. H. Grose, Repr. Aalen: Scientia 1992.

Keil, Geert (2000). *Handeln und Verursachen*, Frankfurt am Main: Klostermann.

Keil, Geert (2005). How the Ceteris Paribus Laws of Physics Lie. In Jan Faye, Paul Needham, Uwe Scheffler and Max Urchs (Eds.), *Nature's Principle*, Berlin/Heidelberg/New York: Springer, 167–200.

Keil, Geert (2009). Making Something Happen: Where Causation and Agency Meet. In Siri Granum Carson and Kjartan Koch Mikalsen (Eds.), *Nature and Rational Agency*, Frankfurt am Main: P. Lang, 9–28.

Lewis, David (1973a). *Counterfactuals (2nd ed.)*, Oxford: Oxford University Press 1986.

Lewis, David (1973b). Causation. In his (1986), 159–213.

Lewis, David (1979). Counterfactual Dependence and Time's Arrow. In his (1986), 32–66.

Lewis, David (1981). Events. In his (1986), 241–269.

Lewis, David (1983). New Work for a Theory of Universals. *Australasian Journal of Philosophy* 61, 343–377.

Lewis, David (1986). *Philosophical Papers*, Vol. II, New York/Oxford: Oxford University Press.

Lewis, David (2000). Causation as Influence. Repr. in Collins, Hall and Paul (Eds., 2004), 75–106.

Mackie, John L. (1965). Causes and Conditions. *American Philosophical Quarterly* 2, 245–264.

Mackie, John L. (1974). *The Cement of the Universe. A Study of Causation*, (2nd ed.) Oxford: Oxford University Press 1980.

Mackie, John L. (1980). The Transitivity of Counterfactuals and Causation. *Analysis* 40, 53–54.

Maslen, Cei (2004). Causes, Contrasts, and the Nontransitivity of Causation. In Collins, Hall, and Paul (Eds., 2004), 341–358.

Menzies, Peter (1996). Probabilistic Causation and the Pre-Emption Problem. *Mind* 105, 85–117.

Mill, John Stuart (1843). *A System of Logic, Ratiocinative and Inductive*, [= *Collected Works*, Vol. VII/VIII], ed. by J. M. Robson, Toronto: University of Toronto Press 1973/4.

Moore, Michael S. (CR). *Causation and Responsibility. An Essay in Law, Morals, and Metaphysics*, Oxford: Oxford University Press 2009.
Pollock, Frederick (1901). *Torts*, New York: Macmillan (6th ed.).
Quine, W. v. O. (1950). *Methods of Logic*, New York: Holt.
Quine, W. v. O. (1960). *Word and Object*, Cambridge, MA: MIT Press.
Rosenberg, Alexander (1992). Causation, Probability and the Monarchy. *American Philosophical Quarterly* 29, 305–318.
Russell, Bertrand (1905). On Denoting. *Mind* 14, 479–493.
Scriven, Michael (1961). The Key Property of Physical Laws – Inaccuracy. In Herbert Feigl and Grover Maxwell (Eds.), *Current Issues in the Philosophy of Science*, New York: Holt, 91–101.
Stepanians, Markus (2013). Moore on "the true metaphysics of causation". In this volume.
Strawson, Peter F. (1959). *Individuals. An Essay in Descriptive Metaphysics*, London: Routledge.
von Wright, Georg Henrik (1976). Replies. In Juha Manninen and Raimo Tuomela (Eds.), *Essays on Explanation and Understanding. Studies in the Foundations of Humanities and Social Sciences*, Dordrecht: D. Reidel, 371–413.
Woodward, James (2000). Explanation and Invariance in the Special Sciences. *British Journal for the Philosophy of Science* 51, 197–254.
Wright, Richard W. (2013). The NESS Account of Natural Causation: A Response to Criticisms. In this volume.

Markus Stepanians

Moore on "the true metaphysics of causation"

Explaining metaphysics to the nation –
I wish he would explain his explanation.
Lord Byron, *Don Juan*

The question Professor Moore tries to answer in part V of *Causation and Responsibility* (= CR) is central to any theory of causation: What kind of entities are said to be the causes and effects in true singular causal statements of the form 'a causes b'? Moore does so against the background of two plausible assumptions:

(I) Essential Relationality: Causation is a dyadic relation between causes and effects.[1]

(II) Causal Realism: Causation is something 'in' the (mind-independent) world.

Together these two assumptions imply that the causal relata must be denizens of the mind-independent word. For, if causation is a dyadic relation between causes and effects, and causation takes place in the mind-independent world, its relata must be part of this word, too. Moreover, Moore takes the world to be the totality of spatio-temporal particulars. This narrows the class of possible causal relata considerably. They must be spatio-temporal particulars, and the only remaining question is: What type of spatio-temporal particulars?

CR argues that the decision as to which spatio-temporal particulars qualify for the title of "true causal relata" depends on causal as well as non-causal considerations. Obviously, candidates have to fit the causal data, but this is not enough. According to CR, a further condition of adequacy is that there should be plausible *causation-independent* reasons for belief in the existence of the entities in question. That is, we should admit as candidates for causal relata only entities in "... whose existence we have reasons to believe independent of any role such entities may or may not have as causal relata" (CR, 332). For shortness, I will refer to this condition of adequacy as the requirement of plausible causation-independent ontological credentials.

1 This assumption is usually taken for granted, but it is worth noting that not everybody agrees: "Sometimes causation is not a relation, because a relation needs relata and sometimes the causal relata go missing" (Lewis 2000, 100). It is mysterious, though, how some instances of causation could be relational and others not.

However, the first question is this: Which spatio-temporal particulars provide the best fit with requirements stemming from causal considerations? According to CR, among all possible candidates, property-instances ('tropes') and real or actual states of affairs answer best to our causal intuitions. But Moore argues that, for the purposes of the book's general argument, there is no need to decide between these two candidates. However, Moore tells us that, if we had to break the tie between real states of affairs and property-instances, the additional requirement of plausible non-causal ontological credentials would do so in favor of state of affairs. At least champions of 'traditional' ontological tastes – like the author of CR – will prefer real states of affairs over property-instances for their choice of the true causal relata: "Those who favor the traditional ontology of particulars and universals will favor states of affairs; those with more revolutionary ambitions will favor the nominalist ontology of ardent tropism. This is not an issue we need to resolve here, although my sympathies are with the traditionalists on this one" (CR, 366). Moore complains that arguments for the existence of tropes too often rely on their alleged role as causal relata and thereby violate the requirement of plausible causation-independent ontological credentials. Thus, although Moore does not think that the issue needs to be resolved for the purposes of CR, he does provide a causation-independent argument for resolving it in favor of actual states of affairs, and it is this argument I would like to scrutinize – and ultimately reject – in this paper.

Ramsey's Argument for states of affairs

What are those tie-breaking "general ontological considerations" that tip the scales in favor of real state of affairs for followers of the traditional ontology of particulars and universals? Here is CR's answer: "The traditional metaphysical view divides existents between particulars ... and abstract universals. Seemingly such a metaphysics requires that one also admit *states of affairs* into one's ontology" (CR, 341). CR argues that the pressure on the traditional ontology of particulars and universals to admit states of affairs stems mainly from the theory of truth. More precisely, it stems from the ontology of 'truth-making', and it pushes (not just for any notion of states of affairs but) for *real* states of affairs, that is, states of affairs that exist as spatio-temporal facts.

According to CR, the beginnings of an argument to this conclusion are due to Frank Ramsey. Call this 'Ramsey's Argument'[2]: "The traditional metaphysical view divides existents between particulars ... and abstract universals. Seemingly such a metaphysics requires that one also admit *states of affairs* into one's ontology. For as Ramsey pointed out, neither particulars nor abstract universals correspond to true sentences. Rather, it is the *having* (or the *being*, or the *instantiating*) of the universal by the particular that can correspond to a true sentence. 'The dog is wet' is not made true by there being the dog referred to and there being the abstract property, wetness; rather, the sentence is true only if in addition the dog has the property, wetness" (CR, 341). Generalized, Ramsey's Argument seems to be this: If a statement of the atomic form 'a is F' is true, neither the particular a, nor the property F, nor the mere aggregation of both correspond to the statement 'a is F' as a whole. The particular and the property have to be depicted as standing in the right relation. What corresponds to 'a is F' is a's-*having*-the-property-F. Thus, each truth of the form 'a is F' presupposes the existence of a complex spatio-temporal particular: a particular-having-a-property. According to CR, this truth-making particular-having-a-property is a real ("actual") state of affairs, a spatio-temporal fact: "'[S]tates of affairs' [is] the label for the complex, a-particular-having-a-universal, which complex makes a statement true when that complex exists. 'Facts' we can also deal with briefly: facts are simply actual states of affairs" (CR, 341).

In short, the upshot of Ramsey's Argument is that truth is correspondence with reality; that the converse of the dyadic correspondence relation is the truth-maker relation; and that truth-making presupposes complex truth-makers: real states of affairs. Therefore, truth-maker correspondence forces on us the ontic recognition of real states of affairs.

CR's strategic argument for recognizing spatio-temporal facts as the ultimate causal relata proceeds in two steps: First, an argument that truth-theoretical considerations along the lines of Ramsey's Argument force the admission of spatio-temporal facts into our ontology. It is clear, then, that the plausible causation-independent reasons demanded by the requirement of causation-independent ontological credentials are provided by the ontology of truth. The second step is an argument to the effect that these spatio-temporal facts can and do play the role of primary causal relata.

2 Strictly speaking, of course, it should be called Ramsey's Argument *according to Moore*, but we can leave open the question whether Moore's attribution to Ramsey is historically correct.

Against spatio-temporal truth-maker correspondence

My doubts about CR's argument for spatio-temporal facts as the primary causal relata concern mainly the first step. I would like to suggest that Ramsey's Argument for spatio-temporal facts – like all considerations based on the idea of spatio-temporal truth-maker correspondence – fails; and that, because of this failure, CR's argument for spatio-temporal facts does not meet its own requirement of plausible causation-independent ontological credentials.

The main source of my misgivings is CR's reliance on (what I think is) a particularly dubious version of the correspondence theory of truth, viz. spatio-temporal truth-maker correspondence. We already saw that spatio-temporal facts (alias 'real states of affairs', alias 'facta', alias 'situations') are introduced in CR as what 'corresponds to' and 'makes true' true statements. I will try to show that CR does not give us sufficient reasons to believe that there is a single class of entities that can do both jobs, that of 'truth-makers' *and* of causal relata. Generally speaking, it seems to me that a general theory of causation and causal relata should not be based on such highly controversial metaphysics; and that CR is flouting this condition of adequacy with its strong commitment to spatio-temporal truth-maker correspondence.

Many philosophers look askance at the 'tractarian' metaphysics presupposed by truth-maker correspondence, and some even urge the wholesale rejection of such theories. David Lewis asks us in the title of his 'tirade' against all types of correspondence theory to "[f]orget about 'the correspondence theory of truth'" (= Lewis 2001), and I sympathize with Lewis for two general reasons.

Although correspondence theories of truth have been around and discussed for more than a millennium, it is still a mystery (1) what that relation of 'correspondentia' (alias 'adaequatio', 'commensuratio', 'concordia', 'conformitas', 'convenientia') of a truth to something in the world consists in; and (2) what that something in the world is to which a truth is supposed to 'correspond' and which 'makes' it true – the 'truth-maker'. The truth-maker for a truth is the worldly relatum of the dyadic correspondence relation. There is no doubt that truth-maker correspondence has intuitive appeal as an account of empirical and atomic sentences of the form 'a is F'. However, since spatio-temporal truth-maker correspondence aspires to be a *general* theory of truth, it must also give an account of logically more complex statements – and here the trouble begins. To see the problem, just ask yourself: What is the spatio-temporal truth-maker for the following truths (supposing that that's what they are)?

(1) If today is Monday, Jill has to get up early.

(2) Everything is identical with itself.
(3) Two is a smaller than three.
(4) Causation is in the world.
(5) There are wombats.
(6) It rains.
(7) I exist.

As we have seen, CR takes the truth-making states to consist of a particular having a property. But in (1) there are two particulars (Monday, Jill), two properties, (being Monday, having to get up early) and the logical if/then-relation, which is not a property, and an unlikely denizen of the spatio-temporal world. So which particular-having-a-property makes it true? In (2) no particular and no spatio-temporal property is mentioned – what does it correspond to? (3) is a truth that seems not to be about the spatio-temporal world at all, which makes it difficult to see how it is made true by it. (4) Is a basic metaphysical assumption endorsed in CR about the spatio-temporal framework called "the world", which therefore seems not to be about a particular-having-a-property *in* the world. Again, logical analysis suggests that (5) does not ascribe a property to any particular, but makes a second-order claim about a property, viz. that it is instantiated. A truth like (6) is certainly about the spatio-temporal world and seems to ascribe a property, but to which particular? Truth (7) has the reverse problem. (7) is about a particular, alright, but there seems to be no property that gets ascribed – at least not, if the logicians' view is accepted that existence is not a (first order) property.

Ramsey's Argument without truth-makers

As the explicit invocation of 'correspondence' and 'truth-making' shows, CR's rendering of Ramsey's Argument presupposes the correctness of (some version) of truth-maker correspondence. However, it seems to me that whatever is right about Ramsey's Argument is better formulated without talk of 'correspondence' and 'truth-making'. At best, Ramsey's Argument shows the need for a notion of propositional facts, not of spatio-temporal facts.

Here is (what I think is) a metaphysically less loaded statement of Ramsey's Argument that works without appeal to the concept of spatio-temporal truth-maker correspondence: If a statement of the form 'a is F' is true, neither the existence of the particular a nor the existence of the property F nor their mere aggregation of a and F is sufficient to explain its truth. The reason is that, for 'a is F' to be true, the particular a must *have* the property F. With other words, F-ness must be true of a; or, alternatively: it must be the case that a is F; or: it must be a fact that a is F.

Note that, in this alternative rendering of Ramsey's Argument, 'fact' is just another word for 'true proposition' or 'truth'. 'Facts' in this sense are the propositional contents of true sayings and true thinkings. Propositional contents can be true or false. They are what is said to be true or false; what is thought to be true or false; what is true or false (the truth-bearers). The metaphysical basis of true and false propositional contents and therefore of propositional facts is logic. Propositional contents are 'entia rationis' or logical entities. They are the primary relata of inference relations. They are what logical operators (¬, &, ⊃, etc.) operate upon.

There are, then, two very different notions of 'fact', which should be distinguished carefully. On the one hand, we have propositional facts: truths or true propositional contents. These are abstract, logical entities with no place in space and time. On the other hand, there are spatio-temporal facts. They are 'truth-making' spatio-temporal entities, i.e. particulars-having-a-property. These are concrete existents in the spatio-temporal world.

Do propositional facts 'correspond to' true statements? Yes and No. Yes – if 'correspondence' is construed as a relation between true statements and the true proposition they express – call this 'propositional correspondence'. No – if 'correspondence' is construed as a relation between a true statement and a complex particular in the spatio-temporal world. Call this 'spatio-temporal correspondence'. Do propositional facts 'make' to true statements 'true'? Yes and No. Yes – if 'truth-making' is construed as an *explanatory* relation between true statements and the true propositions they express – call this 'propositional truth-making'. For example: What makes my true statement "Yes berliniz chem" true? Why is it true? Because it expresses a fact, viz. that I'm not a Berliner. No – if 'truth-making' is construed as a relation between a true statement and the spatio-temporal world it is about. Call this 'spatio-temporal truth-making'. The following diagram is an attempt to capture the relevant relationships:

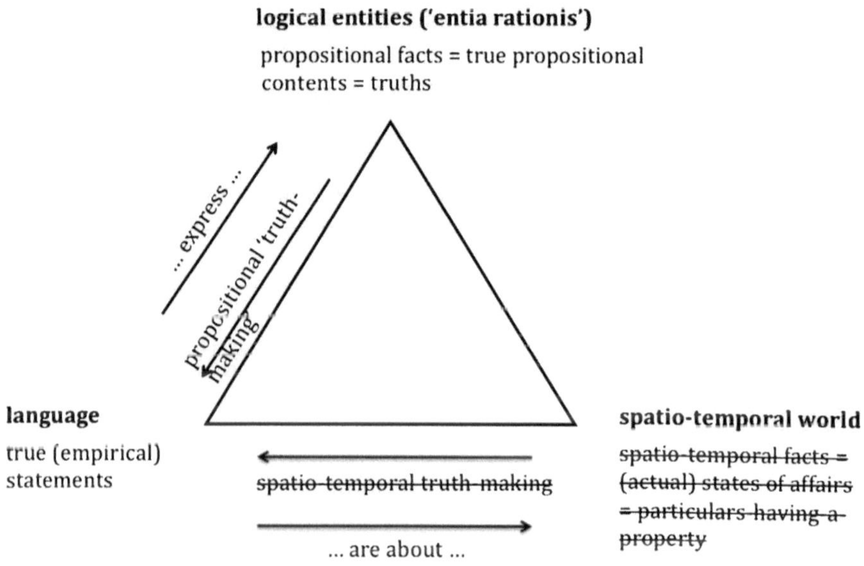

This picture, I think, stands in the background of Strawson’s view:

> What ‘makes the statement’ that the cat has mange ‘true’ is not the cat, but the *condition* of the cat, i.e. the [propositional] fact that the cat has mange. The only plausible position of what (in the world) makes the statement true is the [propositional] fact it states; but the [propositional] fact it states is not something in the world (Strawson 1950, 135).

Shortly thereafter Strawson adds that “the [propositional] facts which statements (when true) state can neither be located nor dated” (Strawson 1950, 140). Davidson seems to have the same point in mind when he says:

> Nothing ... no *thing*, makes sentences and theories true: not experience, not surface irritations, not the world, can make a sentence true. *That* experience takes a certain course, *that* our skin is warmed or punctured, *that* the universe is finite, these [propositional] facts, if we like to talk that way, make sentences and theories true. But this point is put better without mention of facts. The sentence ‘My skin is warm’ is true if and only if my skin is warm. Here there is no reference to a fact, a world, an experience, or a piece of evidence (Davidson 1974, 16).

My main point here is that the notion of propositional fact can account for the truth-theoretical intuitions about ‘truth-making’ and ‘correspondence’ underlying Ramsey’s Argument, and does an even better job. It has no problems to identify the ‘truth-makers’ of true statements, no matter how logically complex. For example ‘If today is Monday, then Jill has to get up early’ is made true by the propositional fact that if today is Monday, then Jill has to get up early. 'Everything is identical to itself' is made true by the propositional fact that everything is identical to itself, etc. Moreover, the notion of propositional fact accounts for these truth-theoretical intuitions without the need to postulate additional complex spatio-temporal particulars-having-a-property, that serve as spatio-temporal truth-makers / facts. If so, reasonable requirements for ontological austerity ('Ockham's Razor') suggest that the theory and ontology of truth should do without spatio-temporal facts.

CR's misconstrual of propositional facts as "linguistic"

To sum up so far: I have argued that the truth-theoretical intuitions invoked by Ramsey's Argument are better explained by admitting propositional instead of spatio-temporal facts into our ontology; that propositional facts have impeccable causation-independent metaphysical credentials – logic! And that propositional facts therefore meet CR's condition of adequacy for candidates of causal relata (even though, as we will see, they are causally impotent). On the other hand, spatio-temporal facts become to that extent redundant and fail to meet CR's condition of adequacy for candidates of causal relata. So far, we have not been given sufficient causation-independent reasons to believe in their existence.

Needless to say, CR is fully aware of this alternative, propositional understanding of facts, and raises no doubts about the metaphysical credentials or legitimacy of belief in propositional facts (or propositions in general). Nonetheless, CR denies that invoking the notion of propositional fact can satisfactorily account for our 'Ramseyan' intuitions about 'truth-making' and 'correspondence, insists that spatio-temporal facts are needed over and above propositional facts, and denies therefore that the notion of propositional fact makes the concept of a spatio-temporal fact redundant.

But why? Why are propositional facts not enough? Whence the need to postulate spatio-temporal facts above and beyond propositional facts? The root of this insistence, it seems to me, is CR's realism about causation combined with a serious misconstrual of propositional facts as "purely linguistic entities". As a result, CR mistakenly suggests that the propositional interpretation of 'facts' is incompatible with a realist understanding of truth in general and causation in particular. This mistake is manifest in CR's "too linguistic" alias "too propositional" objection against propositional facts (cp. CR, 343f). Clearly, *if* propositional facts were linguistic entities, they would be human artefacts, and would as such not qualify for the role of mind-independent, i.e. 'real' spatio-temporal causal relata. The objection "is that [propositional] facts, etc. are too propositional in nature to do any causal work. How, after all, can a sentence or a statement move a mountain?" (CR, 342). Moreover, the truth-maker relation, no matter how conceived, is dyadic: It takes two to 'make' a truth, and the truth-maker relation is irreflexive: nothing can make itself true. Thus, *if* propositional facts were linguistic entities, they would not qualify as spatio-temporal 'truth-makers', for the reason that propositional facts would be identical with the true statements they are supposed to 'make true'. In CR's words:

> [Propositional] facts cannot be what makes true statements true. [Propositional] Facts cannot play this role because of their propositional nature; [propositional] facts *are* true propositions. They thus do not have a sufficiently independent existence to *make* such statements true. Facts 'make' true statements true only in the trivial sense that the truth of a true statement 'makes' that statement true (CR, 342).

However, the 'too linguistic / too propositional'-objection misfires. There is nothing linguistic about propositions in general and propositional facts in particular. They are as language-independent as it gets. For, propositional facts are what is expressed in true statements. They are not those statements, as Dummett emphasizes:

> No philosopher has proposed to *identify* facts with true statements ... [S]tatements are made in particular languages, whereas a fact may be stated in many languages; this unfits true statements to be what facts are (Dummett 2006, 3).

For example, these three distinct statements non-trivially express one and the same propositional fact, viz. that I'm not a Berliner:

1. "Yes berliniz chem"
2. "No soy berlinés"
3. "Ich bin kein Berliner"

Moreover, it is entirely contingent that the propositional fact that I'm not a Berliner has been expressed in any language, and there are literally infinitely many propositional facts (= truths) that will never be expressed in any language.

However, even if propositional facts cannot be identified with linguistic entities, isn't it still true that their existence depends on language? CR sympathizes openly with an argument to this effect by Peter Menzies. It says that, even though propositional facts are not 'purely linguistic', they are nonetheless 'quasi-linguistic'. According to Menzies, propositional facts

> ... are quasi-linguistic entities that are posited merely to provide extralinguistic correlates to true statements. On this conception, [propositional facts] are completely parasitic on a language, with the different languages carving up the world up into different totalities of [propositional facts] (Menzies 1989, 68).

Such a view of propositional fact arouses suspicion. For, as CR puts it,

> ... then it looks like one is simply positing the existence of an extra level of entities, stipulating that these entities are *not* linguistic while nonetheless urging that their boundaries are exactly those of linguistic entities (CR, 343).

However, propositional facts are not 'quasi-linguistic' either. None of the philosophers who explicitly (such as Frege, Strawson, Dummett, D. Lewis, and, arguably, Davidson) hold this view of propositional facts believe that propositional facts are individuated linguistically, or that their boundaries are "exactly those of linguistic entities". On the contrary, these philosophers never tire of warning us that we should not confuse the linguistic / grammatical structure of our statements with the logical structure of the propositions stated.

Conclusion

Where does all this leave us concerning the question with which we started, i.e. the true metaphysics of causal relata? I said at the beginning that CR's general argument proceeds in two steps: First, an argument that truth-theoretical considerations along the lines of Ramsey's Argument force the admission of spatio-temporal facts into our ontology. And second, an argument to the effect that these spatio-temporal facts can and do play the role of primary causal relata. I tried to show that the first step is not successful: Ramsey's Argument and similar truth-theoretical considerations demonstrates at best the need for propositional facts, but not for spatio-temporal facts. Propositional facts can account for all intuitions about 'correspondence' and 'truth-making' that deserve respect, without postulating yet another layer of fact-like entities in the spatio-temporal world. Moreover, I argued that CR is right about the causal impotence of propositional facts – but for the wrong reason. I conclude therefore that CR has given us no plausible reason to believe that there are entities that can do both: function as truth-makers and play the role of causal relata. It therefore seems to me that CR has not proved its case that spatio-temporal facts (alias 'facta' alias 'situations' alias 'states of affairs') are the true causal relata.

References

Davidson, Donald (1974). On the Very Idea of a Conceptual Scheme. *Proceedings and Addresses of the American Philosophical Association*, *47*, 5–20.

Dummett, Michael (2006). *Thought and Reality.* Oxford: Oxford University Press.

Lewis, David (2000) Causation as Influence. *The Journal of Philosophy, 97 (4)*, 182–97.

Lewis, David (2001) Forget about the ‘correspondence theory of truth. *Analysis 61 (4)*, 275–80.

Strawson, Peter F. (1950). Truth. *Proceedings of the Aristotelian Society, Supplementary Volumes*, Vol. 24, *Physical Research, Ethics and Logic*, 129–156.

Philipp Hübl

Events over Facts. Why Metaphysics Matters for Law

In his book *Causation and Responsibility*, Michael S. Moore gives a detailed analysis of the metaphysics of causation that can be used to make legal debates more explicit. The connection between causation and responsibility seems obvious. We change the world when we act. We can be held responsible for our actions, the effects of our actions, and for our omissions, namely when we had the duty to bring about an effect and failed.

Naturally, the legal and the philosophical theory of causation have the same starting point. The law, or its interpretation, need to presuppose a theory of causation, that matches our pre-theoretic causal intuitions, otherwise it is not transparent or understandable for normal people. A philosophical theory starts with our pre-theoretic intuitions as well. It aims at making causal claims and causal explanations explicit. Explication starts at the surface of ordinary language, but does not consider it sacrosanct.[1] For one thing, words in everyday utterances can be ambiguous. Thus, the philosophical analysis focuses on what is *said* by speaker's utterance, on the conceptual deep structure so to say. Moreover, there is a difference between what is literally said and what is implied or presupposed. Thus, our everyday explanatory practice must be *disciplined*, that is, turned into unambiguous explicit statements. A theory of causation should systematise those statements from everyday talk and from the sciences.

Since I agree with large parts of Moore's line of argument, I will focus on a few controversial cases of causal explanation. Moore convincingly argues that causal relata, namely cause and effect, have to be construed as something concrete, as something occupying space-time regions.[2] Causal claims are about what happened at particular locations at particular times. That is the reason why it is hard to see how abstract entities could ever be related as cause and effect, since they are not in space and time. Most theories of causation opt for events of one kind or another as causal relata, but some have considered facts as promising candidates. On one reading "fact" refers to something abstract, namely a true proposition. However, there is a concrete reading of "facts" as "facta", as Mellor calls them, namely as those entities true propositions are about. [3] Another term

1 What Quine calls "regimentation", see (Quine 1960, 157 f); see also (Lewis 1973a, 88).
2 (Moore 2009, 330 f)
3 (Mellor 1995)

would be "states of affairs" or "real situations".[4] In the legal system of the United States, theorists favour events over states of affairs, but according to Moore events are, in fact, ultimately derived from states of affairs. He furthermore claims that Lewis' counterfactual theory of causation, which seems to capture an important sine-qua-non-intuition in legal practice, is flawed for many reasons.

As a counter strategy to Moore's approach, I want to make a case for Davidsonian events.[5] I believe that they are not derived from states of affairs, or concrete facts at all. Concrete facts play a role in causal explanation, because they sometimes comprise events and the respective circumstances, but they are not literally causes. If causation is a relation between Davidsonian events, we can accommodate two intuitions about causation at the same time. First, our intuition about counterfactual dependence, and second, our intuition, that the behaviour of objects in the world is constant over time, or law-like, if you will. Treating concrete facts, namely states of affairs, as causes stems from cross-fading causes with causal factors that are cited in causal explanations.

In order to make my point I proceed in five steps. First, I will make a few remarks on concepts and causal relata that will prove useful for the second step, namely making explicit the conceptual deep structure of causal explanations. In a third step, I will briefly sketch how causation and counterfactual dependence are related, drawing on arguments developed by Keil.[6] In the fourth step, I apply these arguments to cases of overdetermination that seem to either confound types with tokens of events, or causation with causal explanation respectively. Finally, a similar problem appears with regard to omissions. Both problematic cases seem to have the same spring: intuitions about moral and legal practice typically override our basic metaphysical intuitions. If I am right, it should be reversed. Metaphysics comes first. Law has to follow.

The Concept of Cause and the Nature of the Causal Relata

I follow Carroll, Davidson, and others in holding that the concept of cause is one of the most basic concepts we have in everyday life and the sciences.[7] The con-

4 For "real situations" see (Menzies 1989, 70); for "states of affairs", see (Armstrong 1997).
5 (Davidson 1969); (Lombard 1986)
6 (Keil 2000); (Keil 2006)
7 (Davidson 1995); (Carroll 1994)

cept of cause not only lies at the bottom of how we explain and see the world, it is also necessary for having an indefinite number of other concepts like *love bite*, *trace*, or *evolution*, as well as most mental concepts like *perception* or *anger*. For example, one can only grasp the concept of a love bite, if one assumes that a person has kissed another in a peculiar way that caused a tiny bruise. Leaving a trace, in general, is causing a change in the structure of an object like a footprint in the sand or a scratch on the table. And so on.

As with many other philosophical concepts, it seems hopeless to analyse the concept of cause in more basic concepts, if one understands "analysis" as a definition comprising necessary conceptual components that are jointly sufficient to determine the concept. Nevertheless, we can specify the nature of the causal relation itself, for example that it is asymmetric and non-reflexive, and very likely non-transitive. So I am with Moore in holding that there is no "reduction" in the sense of a complete conceptual analysis of the concept of cause.[8] Yet this does not foreclose what Strawson called a "connective analysis", namely relating one concept to other basic concepts we have, such as *object*, *event*, *space*, and *time*.[9] Such an analysis refrains from the view that concepts are structured as definitions. It employs a network of conceptual relations instead. Some concepts may be so basic that they can only be analysed in large conceptual circles comprising many other concepts.

Causal Relata

If causation is a relation, what are the relata? Roughly, a causal claim is an answer to the question what happened or what was going on at a particular region in space and time. And this is the best indicator that only concrete things in the world can be causes, as Moore has shown in detail. The nature of those relata is important, because what causation is heavily depends on what they are. Or as Moore puts it, the question for the relation and the relata can only be answered together.[10] Moore opts for states of affairs understood as concrete space-time regions. However, he points out that in the legal practice in the United States, events are favoured over states of affairs. On his account, events are ultimately derived from facts.

8 (Moore 2009, 392)
9 (Strawson 1992, Chapter 2)
10 (Moore 2009, 327)

I believe a stronger case can be made for events, if understood correctly. According to Davidson, events are particulars that are stretched over space and time. They are unrepeatable, they can be picked out by many descriptions and as opposed to states, they are not divisible into equal parts. Quite the opposite: their parts can in turn be events.[11] However, in his later work, Davidson gave a second characterization of events, which has not been discussed in detail in Moore's book, namely that events are *changes*.[12]

Talk of "change" raises the question about what changes, when there is a change. This question paves the way of relating events as changes to objects and their properties. Events are changes of states. The notion of change appeals to something that underwent that change. Typically, these are objects. One can say that an event is a change of a state of an object. Objects are in states if they have the same properties at two consecutive points of time. And if some properties change from t_1 to t_2, the object has changed. In other words, the concept of change can only be explicated in relation to a concept of constancy, or stable state-behaviour.[13] Moore acknowledges this relation in highlighting the origin of this debate can already be found in Aristotle's notion of change. However, he claims that according to "the standard version, an event is a concrete particular consisting of an object undergoing change over an interval of time".[14] This analysis needs a slight modification. Events are particulars, but they are not objects undergoing change, they *are* the changes themselves.

How can one distinguish between what is constant and what changes? Cummins has argued that there is a pragmatic aspect in picking out changes, because what is constant and what is a change is to a certain extent relative to our description or knowledge.[15] He gives an example from physics. Aristotelian physics needed a constant cause for an object to show "uniform rectilinear motion", but modern physics considers it a *state* of motion or an "inert process", that only needed a cause for its onset. Another of Cummins' examples is "constant proper acceleration" as in the case of the planetary orbits, which modern physics considers it to be a state. Again, this phenomenon was thought to require a causal explanation before.

---

11 For a detailed discussion, see (Simons 1987).
12 (Davidson 1969); (Lombard 1986)
13 I take it that Hüttemann proposes a similar view by distinguishing between "inert processes" (which can be called "states") as opposed to "interferences" or "disturbances" (which can be called "changes"); the discussion has a long tradition, see for instance (Hart & Honoré 1959); (Mach 1905).
14 (Moore 2009, 335)
15 (Cummins 1976)

Now, it appears to me that these two cases from the sciences are only two examples for a much more general attitude we exhibit towards causation in non-scientific contexts, namely that if a behaviour is sufficiently regular, it does not require a causal explanation. Only changes of states need a cause.

The Deep Structure of Causal Explanations

Singular causal explanations aim at more than simply stating a singular causal relation. They often refer to the *circumstances* of the causes, more narrowly the objects, states, and regularities that were changed or disturbed. Ultimately, any explicit causal explanation has to specify two things. First, two changes related as cause and effect and second, some object that has changed. The first specification answers to the question of *what* happened. The second specification is about the objects involved, in particular their properties. Only because objects have certain properties, they could be subject to this particular type of change. Here is an example, if someone asks "Why did the window break?", one can answer in at least two ways. Either with "Someone has thrown a stone". This statement explicitly mentions the event, but leaves the properties of the objects implicit. Or with "The glass of the window was fragile". This mentions the properties of the object, but leaves the event implicit. Any explicit causal statement contains precisely two elements: *changes* of objects and something *constant* about the object, namely its causal properties. Both can be mentioned as "causal factors" in a causal explanation, but only the event is the cause.

Davidson stresses the difference between causation and causal explanation. The former is an *extensional* relation between events, which obtains no matter how we describe them. The latter is an *intensional* relation between propositions. Singular causal claims are true or false depending on how the world is, namely whether the causal relation in fact obtains. Yet in explanation, we typically give an answer to a wh-question using pronouns like "what", "why", "who", and so on.[16] Not only may we want to know what caused the sinking of the Titanic, but also why it sank so fast, why it broke in the middle, or why the outer shell of steel plating could not withstand the impact.

In calling Davidson's argument a "flight to explanations", Moore makes it sound as if Davidson made the distinction between intensional and extensional relations up in order to defend his approach.[17] But Davidson only drew our atten-

16 (van Fraassen 1980)
17 (Moore 2009, 357)

tion to a linguistic fact. Causation in itself is not explanatory, *pace* Moore's summery of Davidson's view, though mentioning a causal relation is a common element in causal explanations. Cross-fading causation with causal explanation is common in everyday explanation and the sciences. It may be the reason for treating states of affairs or properties as causes instead of causal factors cited in explanation.

Here is an example for what seems to me a merging of causes and others causal factors in Moore's book, namely about the "presence of oxygen" in the Apollo capsule. In referring to a legal discussion, Moore says "when there was a fire in an Apollo test capsule years ago, the presence of oxygen was cited as the cause of the fire. This was appropriate because that presence was surprising, given the oxygen-free environment both usual and required in such settings."[18] Here, it seems to me, that when we refer to the presence of oxygen, we refer to a state of the capsule. This state had certain dispositional properties that explain why for example changes in the capsule then could lead to a chemical reaction that caused the explosion. But this does not turn the state into a cause. We can say that the presence of oxygen was a "causal factor" or that it "causally explains" the explosion, but it is not a cause, because it is not a change of an object. In short, it is not an event. Of course, we can give "presence" an event reading, when we talk about the onset of the presence, say if a leak in the capsule caused the entering of oxygen into the chamber. Yet, this is a change of topic, since the presence itself is not a change, but a state. Of course, events as changes can cause the onsets of states. For example, after some change, objects at hand are left in a new state, say of being broken, or of being angry, or of being sweetened. However, the mere presence of oxygen in the capsule can never answer the question why the explosion took place at a certain area of space and time.

Two Kinds of Counterfactual Dependence

Suppose events are the only causal relata, construed along the lines of Davidson and Lombard.[19] Then we still have to specify the nature of the causal relation itself. Legal practice often refers to the sine-qua-non-test, which finds is philosophical counterpart in Lewis' counterfactual theory of causation.[20]

18 (Moore 2009, 398)
19 (Davidson 1969); (Lombard 1986)
20 (Lewis 1973b)

At first sight, we have strong confidence that counterfactuals about particular events are true. If we claim "This event has caused that effect", then we are certain that this particular effect would not have taken place, had the cause not have taken place. So, in particular cases, counterfactual dependency characterises at least one aspect of causation. Note that the effect also depends counterfactually on the circumstances of the cause. Had the condition of the window been different, for example had it been made of bullet proof glass, or had the condition of the stone be different, for example had a porous stone been used, the effect would have been different. A little crack might have occurred, but not the breaking of the window.

Now, Moore raises a number of objections to the counterfactual theory. For him, the counterfactual theory does not say what causation is, but only gives a "heuristic" of causation.[21] He seems to presuppose that any theory of causation should give something like a "reduction" of the concept of cause in the sense of replacing it by something more fundamental or better understood. However, if the concept of cause lies at the bottom of our conceptual structure, we might strive for a less ambitious aim. Counterfactual dependence is wider than causation, but if we restrict counterfactual dependence to singular events, it captures an important intuition about causation, namely that it is an asymmetrical dependence. We believe that the effect depends in some sense on the cause. It is not mere coincidence that the effect occurred. And we take the effect to follow the cause.

Keil has developed a counterfactual theory that focuses on singular causal claims and differs from Lewis' approach in some respects.[22] Keil argues that a singular causal claim is true, if the respective counterfactual is true. He also holds that our confidence in the truth of the counterfactual rests on knowledge about the substances or objects the causal claim was about. It does not rest on alleged laws of event succession or cross-world comparisons.

Keil suggests improving Lewis' approach by putting some restrictions on his counterfactual theory. I will mention only two. First, the revised counterfactual theory is only about Davidsonian event tokens, but not about events in the spirit of Lewis, which are cases of property exemplification as construed by Kim, and even less about types of events.[23] This is a natural suggestion, since a causal claim is made *after* both particular events have taken place. The important feature of this approach is that the event tokens are pinpointed by indexicals. All

21 (Moore 2009, 411)
22 (Keil 2000)
23 (Lewis 1979); (Lewis 1973b); (Kim 1976)

singular causal statements contain an *indexical* element. In its most obvious demonstrative form it says for example: "this shooting" caused "this death". Even giving events proper names presupposes a demonstrative act of baptizing the event, as Kripke has shown in detail.[24]

However, the indexical has a second function. By using indexicals one also refers, though often *implicitly,* to the circumstances of the event as in "this shooting of this particular gun with all its particular properties" and "the death of this man with his particular physiological attributes". Or, more generally: this change of this object with its given properties caused the change of that object with its given properties. Keil expresses this point in terms of an "implicit ceteris-paribus clause" saying "under the conditions that actually obtain" or "with the circumstances being the same". So, his revised counterfactual analysis reads, "*e* caused *c* if and only if, *e* and *c* have taken place, and if *c* had not occurred and the circumstances had been the same, *e* would not have occurred." The indexical is a tool that allows nailing down events and circumstances in one breath.

Keil's second suggested improvement of Lewis' counterfactual theory is this: The temporal gap between the two events should be as small as possible, because the larger the temporal gap, the stronger does the causal influence rarefy or, as in Moore's terms, they "peter out".[25] If one thinks of causes as changes of objects, or of disturbances of regularities, one can give "rarefying" or "petering out" a straightforward temporal interpretation. The longer the time lapse between two events, the more can happen in between. The larger the *funnel of possibilities*, the thinner is thus the basis for our intuition about counterfactual dependencies.

The tricky question is, where does our counterfactual intuition come from, the confidence with which we make such claims to be true, or respectively, the lack of confidence, if the gaps are too large?

The Basis of Our Counterfactual Confidence

There is a *nomic basis* for our counterfactual confidence, but it does not derive from cross-world comparisons or causal laws, namely laws about the succession of events, but rather indirectly from the law-like dispositions of the objects that enter the causal relations. From our knowledge about the properties of sugar and our knowledge about water, we infer that generally dropping the sugar into the

24 (Kripke 1972)
25 (Moore 2009, 327)

water will cause it to dissolve. This causal generalisation itself is *not* exceptionless of course, because something could intervene between dropping and dissolving, for example someone catching the sugar or quick-freezing the water. However, the properties of water and sugar are exceptionless in that they define them as natural kinds. The microstructure of natural kinds is nothing but their dispositional structure like their mass, the binding properties of the elements, their crystalline patterns, or their charge.

Of course, not all objects entering causal relations are natural kinds. Artefacts may have no essence at all. However, when considering their causal role, we believe that it ultimately depends on their microstructure, such that they can be manipulated or changed in a certain way, or that they would have remained in a certain way, if they had not been changed. For example, we are not only confident that vases typically shatter, when they hit the ground, we also believe that it has to do with the material of vase and floor, and the relative distance between them, even though vases and floors can be made of different materials. Only closer examination, the dispositions are a function of the material and its form, say the crystalline structure. Aristotle seems to have had that in mind when he considered form and material as "aitia".[26] Translating "aitia" as "causal factors" instead of "causes", as it is commonly done, makes Aristotle's view congruent with the approach proposed here.

Events qualifying as cause and effect are changes in objects made of certain materials that have certain dispositions. They have these dispositions over a longer period of time. This constant dispositional structure is what is stable or regular in the world, relatively to which we pick out events as changes of those regularities.

Sometimes dispositions are distinguished into "active dispositions" or "powers" as opposed to "passive dispositions" or "liabilities".[27] An active disposition would be "being poisonous", and a passive disposition would be "being fragile". However, this does not mean that dispositions can cause anything by themselves as some theorists would have it.[28] Dispositional terms must be read as characterising the object's or the material's contribution to a cause or effect, when they interact: We know that hard things can break fragile things and we know that fragile things break, when hit by something hard. Yet, they do not break if noth-

26 Aristotle, *Metaphysics*
27 (Harré & Madden, 1975)
28 (Mumford 1998, chapter 6)

ing happens. They require an "initiating stimulus", for example bringing the stone into motion, and this is clearly another term for an event.[29]

To conclude this section, if we relate counterfactual claims to our knowledge about the properties or structures of the objects involved in those claims, we can do justice to the observation that the world is stable, and that events are changes of those regularities. One does *not* thereby explicate causation in terms of sufficient conditions for events, since the occurrence of one event does not necessitate another, because something could intervene. In the next section, I want to apply this approach to the case of overdetermination.

The Case against Overdetermination

Moore argues that cases of overdetermination show that counterfactual dependence is not necessary for causation. The argument focuses on the so-called "symmetrically overdetermined concurrent cases": if, for example, two fires are sufficient to burn down the house each on its own, the effect does not counterfactually depend on any of them, and thus the theory that identifies causation with counterfactual dependence is false.

According to Moore, one popular move to counter this objection is to combine both fires into a single event of a huge fire. In some cases, this manoeuvre may be appropriate, in others, however, it seems problematic. To my mind, there is another way out of the objection from overdetermination, if one distinguishes between token events and types of token events. If we take the starting point of any causal theory to be singular cases, as the law typically has in mind, namely cases where two events that have taken place, then we say "The first event caused the second, and had the first not occurred, the second would not have occurred".

Again, the argument from overdetermination says: In the symmetrically overdetermined concurrent case, two fires burn down a house, but one fire would have sufficed for burning down the house. However, as Davidson and others have pointed out, if only the first or only the second fire had burned down the house, it would have been a *different* burning.[30] All cases, the actual case and either one of the counterfactual cases, fall under the type reading "burning", but they are different tokens of burning. To reconsider another of Moore's

29 Mumford admits this, but seems to propose a wider notion of cause comprising dispositions next to events, see (Mumford 1998, 126–127).
30 (Davidson 1967)

examples: a soldier who dies of two wounds dies a different death than dying of one wound. Both are of the type "death by deadly wound", but we do not talk about the same death.[31]

According to Moore, one possible countermove against the charge from over-determination is a strategy of fine-grained individuation that makes more and more details necessary for the event to occur. I am with Moore that this is dubious for metaphysical reasons, because the details are endless. However spelling out all details is not needed if we use *indexicals*. We can say "This particular fire at this particular place and time has caused this destruction of the house". The indexical refers to the event and objects involved in the event – in all their detail. In other words, if we use indexicals, there is no finer graininess available, since we refer to everything there is, not to some aspects of it.

Moore argues that such a view on events faces a problem about numerical identity. He compares the persistence of persons or objects through time with the cross-world identity of events.[32] Of course, everything depends on what events exactly are, but if they are changes of objects at space-time positions, then all their properties at this space-time position are essential. Persons or objects can change their space-time positions, they are not fixed to them. Now I sit on my desk in my apartment, but tomorrow I will walk down the street. Yet events, like the event of the fire of the house, are fixed to a given space-time-position. They cannot change their position, because events have their space-time positions essentially. Objects and persons can undergo some change and remain the same, as Moore points out. But events cannot undergo changes and remain the same, because they *are* changes.

Moore's third argument against the type-token distinction says that "surely it is possible that in every detail, save causal genesis, the 'three' house-burnings [the defendant's fire, the natural fire, and both together] are qualitatively identical".[33] But quite frankly, I cannot imagine such a case. The burning patterns would surely be different, depending on where and when the flames reach the house. This objection may sound slightly scholastic, so let us consider an event comprising a smaller space-time region, say, a case of two bullets being fired at someone. A death with two bullets in the heart is surely different from one with one bullet. The bullets could not have been on the same trajectory at the same time, for there is trivially only space for one.

31 (Moore 2009, 417)
32 (Moore 2009, 414)
33 (Moore 2009, 414)

Now, in order to make the events even smaller, consider a science fiction device of two laser light beams in space fired at the same time in close parallels hitting a light-sensitive button of a perfectly shielded vacuum chamber that activates an electromagnetic field within the chamber causing an electron to move. We may say that had the first light beam not activated the button, the second would have activated it at exactly the same time and the effect would have been qualitatively exactly the same at the same space-time region. All the same, the effects in the counterfactual scenario may be qualitatively identical to the one in the actual world, but this is not *numerical identity*, because we make singular causal claims about events that have already happened. The singular counterfactual is not touched by what could have happened instead.

Types and Tokens in Moral Contexts

It appears to me that in moral causal judgments, we often switch from considering token events to considering token events in virtue of falling under a given type. It is not only bad or blameworthy to cause "this particular death", but to case "a death" in general, namely a particular effect that falls under the type "death". The reason, why many moral and especially legal cases are about the type, any particular token falls, seems to be that it is important to know whether a given deed falls under the law or not, for example if it is a murder or not. Singular causal claims and counterfactuals are about *particular* fires, but responsibilities are about fire in general, or how to handle inflammable materials in general. Any instance of arson requires legal consequences, not only this particular case.

Moore gives an interesting example about differences in American tort and criminal law.[34] Apparently in some cases, when a defendant's fire caused a house to burn down, and thereby pre-empted another fire that would have burned down the house, the defendant is only held responsible for the interim loss between the two fires. However, in criminal law, this is not always the case. There seem to be no real overdetermined cases. This is clearly a difference in the type-token reading. Arguably, this difference has to do with the nature of the receiver of the harm or damage. Human beings are treated differently from houses.

I think the inconsistency in treating these cases in legal practices shows that moral or even legal consideration often cloud metaphysical distinctions, espe-

34 (Moore 2009, 429)

cially when it comes to actions and causes. For example, some *experimental philosophers* have shown that we apply terms like "intentionally" differently in morally relevant contexts than in morally irrelevant contexts. Here is an example that could easily be a case in tort law. Knobe asked subjects questions in order to elicit their intuitions about applying the term "intentionally" by using vignettes that differed in the moral status of the consequences of action.[35] Compare the following two stories

> (1) The Harm Story
> "The vice-president of a company went to the chairman of the board and said, 'We are thinking of starting a new program. It will help us increase profits, but it will also harm the environment.' The chairman of the board answered, 'I don't care at all about harming the environment. I just want to make as much profit as I can. Let's start the new program.' They started the new program. Sure enough, the environment was harmed."

If one replaces "harm" by "help", one gets the Help Story.

> (2) The Help Story
> "The vice-president of a company went to the chairman of the board and said, 'We are thinking of starting a new program. It will help us increase profits, and it will also help the environment.' The chairman of the board answered, 'I don't care at all about helping the environment. I just want to make as much profit as I can. Let's start the new program.' They started the new program. Sure enough, the environment was helped."

In an experiment, Knobe asked subjects in the first case "Did the chairman of the board *intentionally* harm the environment?" and in the second "Did the chairman of the board *intentionally* help the environment?"[36] Surprisingly, 82 % of the subjects receiving the Harm Story said that the chairman harmed the environment intentionally. Only 23 % said this about helping the environment intentionally.

Suppose the attribution of "intentionally" is morally relevant. Then it appears to be that the same causal story, or more precisely, the same story about side-effects or omissions, has different interpretation depending on the moral or legal relevance. The findings pose many general problems about concepts and philosophical method. However, they also have an important methodological flaw. The forced-choice paradigm is known to distort judgements. Subjects may choose the best alternative between two or more fairly bad choices. In

---

35 (Knobe 2006); (Knobe 2003a)
36 (Knobe 2003b)

this sense, it is like voting for a political party. Once the options are "intentionally" versus "knowingly", the effect disappears almost entirely.[37]

At any event, the tests reveal that moral intuitions, in particular our tendency to ascribe blame or responsibility to a person, sometimes clouds our general causal judgement. I suppose that the same happens in cases of omissions. We want to blame the plaintiff for what happened, even though she did not cause the change. Nevertheless, the blame rests on a causal intuition. Had she caused a change, the event would not have taken place. The only failure is to treat the omission as cause in order to assure that the person omitting is responsible, as some interpretations of the law do. Yet, omissions cannot be causes, because they are not events, located in space and time. Every second, we omit an infinite number of actions. For some omissions, we are responsible, yet since the application of responsibility differs from the application of action and causation, we need not treat omissions as causes, even though counterfactuals are needed in order to spell out why some omissions are in fact blameworthy.

The moral I would draw from this fact is to do the metaphysics of non-moral singular cases first and then look at the moral and legal contexts.

References

Aristotle, *Metaphysics*

Armstrong, David (1997). *A World of States of Affairs.* Cambridge: Cambridge University Press

Carroll, John (1994). *Laws of Nature.* Cambridge: Cambridge University Press.

Cummins, Robert (1976). States, Causes, and the Law of Inertia. *Philosophical Studies* 29: 21–36

Davidson, Donald (1967) Causal Relations. Reprinted in Davidson, Donald (1980), *Essays on Actions and Events.* Oxford: Oxford University Press, 149–162

Davidson, Donald (1969). The Individuation of Events. Reprinted in Davidson, Donald (1980), *Essays on Actions and Events.* Oxford: Oxford University Press, 163–180

Davidson, Donald (1995). Laws and Cause. *Dialectica* 49: 263–279

van Fraassen, Bas (1980). *The Scientific Image.* Oxford: Oxford University Press

Harré, Rom and Madden, Edward H. (1975). *Causal Powers.* Oxford: Blackwell

Hart, Herbert L. A. and Honoré, A.M. (1959). *Causation in Law.* Oxford: Oxford University Press

Keil, Geert (2000). *Handeln und Verursachen.* Frankfurt am Main: Vittorio Klostermann

Keil, Geert (2006). La cause d'un événement: Éléments d'une métaphysique descriptive de la causalité entre événements. *Philosophie* 88: 21–39

37 I gather that from own experiments conducted in German using Knobe's vignettes. The results are not published yet.

Kim, Jaegwon (1976). Events as Property Exemplifications. In Brand, Myles and Walton, Douglas (Eds.) *Action Theory*. Dordrecht: Reidel, 159–177

Knobe, Joshua (2003a). Intentional Action and Side Effects in Ordinary Language. *Analysis* 63: 190–193

Knobe, Joshua (2003b). Intentional Action in Folk Psychology: An Experimental Investigation. *Philosophical Psychology* 16: 309–324

Knobe, Joshua (2006). The Concept of Intentional Action: A Case Study in the Uses of Folk Psychology. *Philosophical Studies* 130: 203–231;

Kripke, Saul (1972). Naming and Necessity. In Davidson, Donald and Harman, Gilbert (Eds.) *Semantics of Natural Language*. Dordrecht: D. Reidel: 253–355

Lewis, David (1973a). *Counterfactuals*. Oxford: Blackwell

Lewis, David (1973b). Causation. Reprinted in Lewis, David (1986), *Philosophical Papers, Vol. II*. Oxford: Oxford University Press

Lewis, David (1979). Counterfactual Dependence and Time's Arrow. *Noûs* 13: 455–476. Reprinted in Lewis, David (1986), *Philosophical Papers II*. Oxford: Oxford University Press, 32–66

Lombard, Lawrence B. (1986). *Events. A Metaphysical Study*. London/Boston: Routledge

Mach, Ernst (1905). *Erkenntnis und Irrtum*. Leipzig: Barth

Mellor, D.H. (1995). *The Facts of Causation*. London: Routledge

Menzies, Peter (1989). A Unified Account of Causal Relata. *Australasian Journal of Philosophy* 67, 59—83

Moore, Michael S. (2009). *Causation and Responsibility. An Essay in Law, Morals, and Metaphysics*. Oxford: Oxford University Press

Mumford, Stephen (1998). *Dispositions*, Oxford: Clarendon Press

Quine, Willard Van Orman (1960). *Word and Object*. Cambridge (Mass.): MIT Press

Simons, Peter (1987). *Parts. A Study in Ontology*. Oxford: Clarendon Press

Strawson, Peter F. (1992). *Analysis and Metaphysics: An Introduction to Philosophy*. Oxford: Oxford University Press

Stephen Mumford and Rani Lill Anjum

With Great Power Comes Great Responsibility

On Causation and Responsibility in Spider-Man, and Possibly Moore

Preface

Omissions are sometimes linked to responsibility. A harm can counterfactually depend on an omission to prevent it. If someone had the ability to prevent a harm, but didn't, this could suffice to ground their responsibility for the harm (Moore 2009, 304).

Michael S. Moore's claim is illustrated by the tragic case of Peter Parker, shortly after he became Spider-Man. Sick of being pushed around as a weakling kid, Peter became drunk on the power he acquired from the freak bite of a radioactive spider. When a police officer called to Spider-Man to stop an escaping burglar, which he could have done easily, he failed to act. He was through taking orders. The omission was followed by a crime. That very same burglar later robbed Peter's own house and when challenged he shot dead Peter's Uncle Ben. Later, Spider-Man tracked down the killer and, when seeing his face close up, the possibility of prevention dawned on him. He could have stopped this crook and had he done so Uncle Ben would still be alive. Stan Lee's tale of power finished with a Shakespearean twist. Young Peter realised the truth of the WGPCGR-thesis: With Great Power Comes Great Responsibility.

We too will endorse the WGPCGR-thesis. There is a close connection between our notions of moral and legal responsibility and the powers we have as causal agents. This will be particularly important when it comes to the case of omissions: where we had the power to act but failed to do so. We hope to show the connections between the notions of power, cause, act, omission and responsibility but also some of the nuances. We will do so with particular reference to Moore's account in *Causation and Responsibility* (Moore 2009).

1 Power and responsibility

The burglar exercised a power in killing Uncle Ben and thus certainly has responsibility for his death. He caused the death. But why should Spider-Man take any of the blame too? He didn't cause anything. He failed to act. His was an omission. And it seems an omission has no causal powers. That is all well and good but that doesn't mean that Peter Parker was wrong to blame himself. An omission can sometimes have just as much moral significance as an act as Moore says and we will back that claim in this paper.

The WGPCGR-thesis has an intuitive attraction through its connection of the notions of power and responsibility. In the first place, one can only be held responsible for something not happening if one had the power to bring it about. No human can have a responsibility to jump to the moon or breathe (unaided) underwater. Without the power, the responsibility makes no sense. In the second place, the WGPCGR-thesis also draws a connection between degree of power and degree of responsibility. When a man is drowning in a lake, the stronger swimmer in attendance has more responsibility to jump in and save him than does a weaker swimmer. If a woman is knocked down by a car, a trained medical doctor who is present has more responsibility to assess and care for her than does an onlooker with mere first aid training or no training at all.

Blame can then attach to persons who fail to act when they have the power and responsibility to do so. No one was to blame for the earthquake off the coast of Japan in 2011 because no one had the power to stop it. But someone could be to blame for an assault or a theft or even an accident if negligence played a role. Blame comes from neglect of responsibilities. It doesn't always come from the failure to exercise a power, however, because some of them we have no responsibility to exercise. Responsibility is a normative matter whereas power need not be. We have the power to talk all day non-stop but we have no responsibility to do so. We also have the power to strangle a passer-by. We have no responsibility to do so and indeed in almost all conceivable cases have a responsibility not to do so. It is up to moral and legal theory to tell us which of our powers we have a responsibility to exercise and on what occasions. What it cannot fairly tell us, however, is that we have a responsibility to do something that we simply cannot.

An apparent exception is not really one. You may not know first aid and thus have no power to save a collapsed man. But perhaps you had a moral responsibility to have learnt first-aid in the first place, just in case of needing it. Hence, it might be argued, you have a responsibility to save the man even though you don't have the power to do so because, for instance, you don't know the recovery position. But this apparent responsibility without power arises only by conflating first and second-order powers. If you don't have the power to administer first aid you have no responsibility to do so as you could do harm if you make a clumsy attempt (you may nevertheless have a responsibility to offer general assistance and reassurance). But you had the power to learn first aid and it is conceivable that you could have had a responsibility to do so. You might then be blamed if you don't. One may, therefore, have a second-order responsibility to do something (to acquire a power to act) while at the same time lacking the corresponding first-order responsibility (to exercise the acquired act). This is no real exception to the WGPCGR-thesis then.

2 Powers and Causal Dispositionalism

We aim to explore further the connections between causation and responsibility and we do so using the framework of causal dispositionalism, a theory of the metaphysics of causation developed in Mumford and Anjum 2011. We will explain the basics of the theory in order to show its application to the issue of responsibility.

Causal dispositionalism is a theory of causation based on a metaphysics of real causal powers or dispositions. Such a philosophy of nature is associated with Aristotle and Aquinas and is non-Humean. It is not a reductive analysis as the notions of cause and power are too closely connected. It accounts for causes in terms of the exercise of powers, where effects are typically produced by many powers acting together. When we have multiple powers producing an effect it is called polygeny. We model polygenic powers acting together using vector diagrams (whereas the conventions of standard neuron diagrams – the other main way of representing causal situations – allow only one immediately prior cause for each effect). Moore also allows that many factors can work together to produce an effect. He calls them concurrent causes (Moore 2009, 486). Figure 1 shows us an example of multiple concurrent powers at work.

We model powers as vectors because powers have a direction: there is something towards which they dispose. Vectors also have a direction, which we show in the figure by plotting them on a quality space that ranges from the property F to the property G. These could indicate the properties of being hot and being cold, for instance, and the powers that emanate from a central vertical line – the current temperature – indicate powers towards raising the temperature, F, or lowering the temperature, G. Powers can also have a magnitude or intensity, which the vector indicates by its length (the longer, the stronger). Again this is important but frequently overlooked. We should allow that causation is scalar (Moore 2009, 105). Both causes and effects can occur to some degree. What produces an effect is all the concurrent powers working together. They compose, indicated by resultant vector *R*, into one big power: how the overall situation disposes. Powers thus become the truthmakers of all the causal truths. All effects are produced by powers exercising themselves in various combinations.

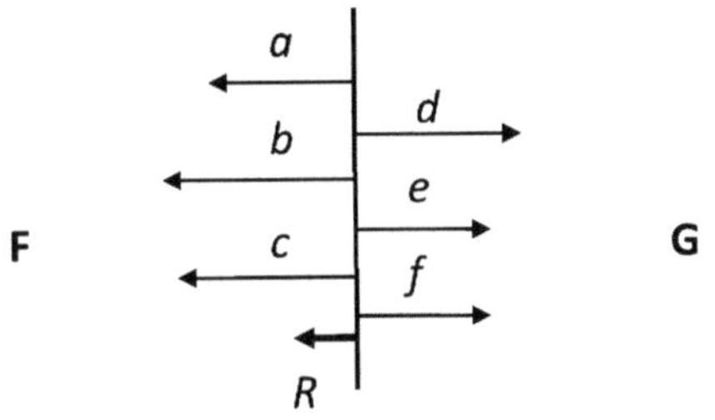

Figure 1: Multiple powers at work

An upshot of causal dispositionalism is that we should separate the notion of causal production from that of causal necessitation. Powers produce their effects without guaranteeing them. Instead we have tendencies towards certain outcomes. A cause is thus something that tends or disposes towards its effect. This is something more in the world than Humean regularity: we have real powers that bring with them a genuine modal connection between causes and effects. But the modal connection is one of tendency, short of fully-blown necessity, as Aquinas saw (see Geach 1961, 102). The polygeny depicted in figure 1 shows us that if there had been a further power, *h*, disposing towards G, powers *a*-*f* might not have brought about a movement towards F. We call this additive interference, which shows that causes do not necessitate their effects, even on the occasions they succeed in producing them.

3 Causation and Responsibility

The law often seeks to apportion blame or responsibility according to the degree of a cause. This seems to be one area in which the metaphysics of causation has much to learn from the philosophy of law. The importance of the scalarity in causation is often neglected or indeed ignored completely. Lewis's influential counterfactual dependence account (Lewis 1973), for example, suggests an account in which causes and effects are all or nothing. The accompanying neuron diagrams are able to show only that a cause or effect happened or it did not: not that they might happen to some degree.

Degrees of cause and responsibility are important matters in law. Because of the polygenic aspect of causation, in which an effect is typically produced by many causes working together, one might need to single out what was the main cause of the harm before judging responsibility. The main cause is the biggest contributor for the harm: what in figure 2 would be represented as the longest vector. In apportioning legal or moral responsibility, therefore, we might judge whether a particular factor was only a small part of the total cause, or instead the main contributor.

But in judging responsibility, there are further factors to be considered. A small factor can nevertheless by highly significant. Someone who has developed lung emphysema might, for instance, blame the factory that they worked in for over 30 years, exposing the employees for damaging dust particles. But if in court it emerges that the worker was also a heavy smoker and genetically predisposed for the disease, the defence could argue that the smoking was the main cause and not the dust particles from the factory. Does this mean that the factory owner is without responsibility? No. It might still be that the exposure to the dust particles from the factory was what tipped the situation over the threshold of the lung emphysema. This might have been just a small contributor, but one that made the outcome radically different (represented by power *f* in figure 2). The factory owner could then be responsible and held liable for partial damages.

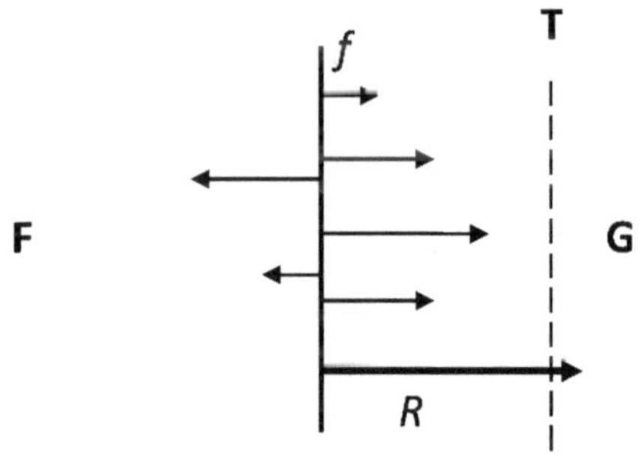

Figure 2: A cause, f, that is not the main cause

A tiny contributor can thus make a large difference for the outcome if we have a so-called tipping case (figure 3). Where we have a tipping case situation the operating powers are very close to a threshold at which something happens: they are all lined up and ready to go such that just a very small addition would be enough to reach that threshold. Hence, a very small extra input could lead to a huge difference in outcome. If a rock is balanced on a cliff edge, for instance, just a push from a passing ant might be enough to send it hurtling down a ravine (see Moore 469).

It is conceivable that major legal and moral responsibility could be allotted to a small causal factor if it is indeed the one that tips a causal situation over a threshold. Instead of a rock and an ant at the cliff edge, we could easily imagine a man standing there, struggling against the wind to keep his balance. If a bystander then comes and gives him a push – even a very slight push – they might have major responsibility for a subsequent death.

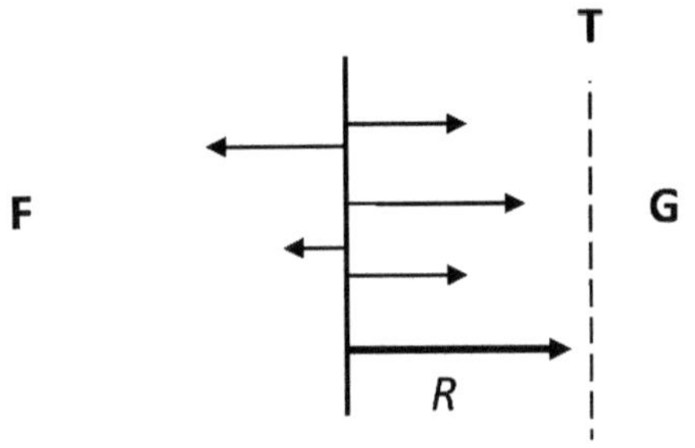

Figure 3: The set-up for a tipping cause

So much for causation. But we also know that responsibility comes from omissions. How does that work? In the next section, we argue that an omission is an occasion for an effect, not its cause.

4 Omissions: Responsibility without Causation

Omissions prima facie create a problem for causal dispositionalism. It looks like they produce outcomes and yet they are not actions: they are lacks of action, where a lack of something is nothing at all. We take it that agency involves people causing effects through exercise of their powers. If that is anywhere near right, then omissions are thus the agency version of causation by absence. Some philosophers accept that absences can be causes (Schaffer 2004), citing commonplace examples such as lack of water killing a plant, a horse shoe falling off for want of a nail and the guillotine causing someone to die through lack of a head. Causal dispositionalism, however, tells us that effects are produced by powers exercising themselves. Absences, lacks and omissions are not real things in any way, however. They are precisely something not being there. If we have nothing, therefore, we cannot have causal powers. We thus want to agree with Moore when he says that omissions cannot be causes (Moore 2009, 54). Nothing comes from nothing: we reject causation *ex nihilo*. But then we owe a metaphysical account of how causation by absence appears to happen. What is really going on in such cases?

Fortunately, the vector model allows us to explain causation by absence entirely in terms of what there is: the powers of things that really are, rather than any alleged powers of nothingnesses. The account will also show why we can attribute responsibility without causation, in the cases of omissions.

In abstract terms, what is suggested is that in cases of putative causation by absence removal of a power is the occasion on which powers disposing in the opposite direction win out. In figure 4, we have two powers disposing towards

F and two towards G. If they are jointly of equal strength, we will have an equilibrium situation in which nothing happens. But if we now remove one of the powers disposing towards F (represented by vector *a*), then the powers disposition towards G will be the stronger. Overall, the situation will then dispose clearly towards G (indicated by the broken resultant vector *R*). The crucial insight, from a metaphysical point of view, is that it is the remaining powers towards G that do the causal work of producing G. The absent power *a* is no longer there and does nothing. We try to indicate this by saying that the removal of *a* was the *occasion* for the causing of G without being one of the causes of G. When *a* was removed, the remaining powers towards G were able to do their work: but it was the remaining powers towards G that did all the causing, not the absent *a*.

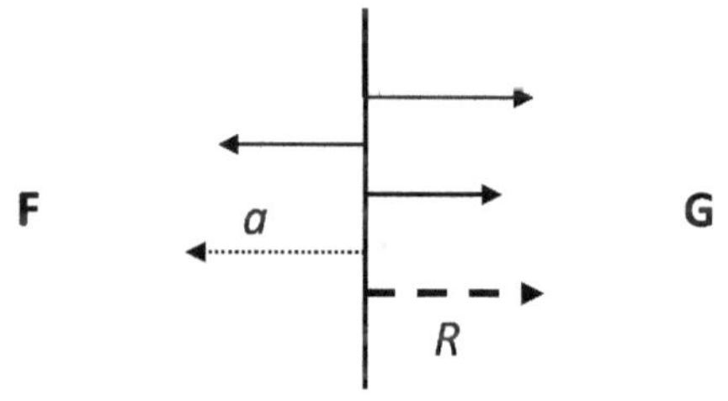

Figure 4: 'Causation by absence'

A concrete example will illustrate the abstract account. Consider a game of tug of war between philosophers and theologians. The sides are equally matched and the rope goes nowhere. One weak-willed philosopher gives up and leaves the contest, whereupon the theologians achieve a quick victory. Did the absent philosopher cause the theologians' win when he left the contest? No. All the causing of that result was due to the forces exerted on the rope by the theologians pulling. But the philosopher giving up was the occasion for their victory insofar as he had previously been holding them back. The philosopher's teammates may well apportion responsibility to their weak-willed colleague. Would they have avoided defeat had they remained at full strength? If so, they would be right to think of their team-mate giving up as the occasion for the theologians win, even if the giving up was not the cause.

Peter Parker was obviously mindful of all this. He didn't cause his uncle's death, even though he has mistakenly thought so since. The burglar's bullet did the causing. But he rightly has understood that his omission occasioned the killing to the extent that it would probably not have happened if he had acted. What he had in mind was thus a *sine qua non* rather than a real cause: a distinction we will examine further.

5 Overdetermination and Prevention: Responsibility without Counterfactual Dependence

An attractive explanation of this would be in terms of counterfactuals. Had the philosopher remained, the theologians would not have won. In that case, blame is apportioned. This story, which Moore (2009, 304) endorses, is basically right (see also Dowe 2001). But it needs to be nuanced in various ways because the connection between causes, omissions and counterfactual dependences is not a simple matter, certainly if one accepts the insights of causal dispositionalism.

The counterfactual truths, such as they are, can indeed be made true by the worldly powers rather than, for instance, the plurality of worlds (Lewis 1986). The counterfactual situation really is contrary-to-fact, though: contrary to all facts. There are no facts – not even in other worlds – that they are about. Mere possibilities are fictions and their ontological status is thus akin to truth in fiction. But a power gives us more than a mere possibility of its manifestation. As stated above, there is a more than Humean modal connection involved in causation, according to causal dispositionlism, such that if a cause occurs, its effect will also *tend* to occur. As we stated, however, this is not a matter of necessitation of the effect.

The dispositionalist view thus has implications for how we understand any associated counterfactuals. Two counterfactuals interest us when it comes to causation:

i. *C* and *E* occur and *C* caused *E*. *C* had the power whose manifestation was *E*, such that *had there not been C, there would not have been E.*
ii. Neither *C* nor *E* occur. But *had there been C, there would also have been E,* because *C* was the power whose manifestation was *E*.

According to causal dispositionalism, however, we have reasons to accept neither i nor ii. In the case of ii, a thoroughly dispositionalist account cannot say that if C occurs, E will occur: only that it will be disposed to occur. In the case of additive interference, something is added that can prevent E even though C. Hence, even if Spider-Man had exercised his powers and tried to stop the Burglar, he cannot know for sure that he would have succeeded. Causal prediction is fallible and for a good reason. Even Spider-Man's action could have been prevented, for instance if the incredible Hulk had restrained him.

We reject i because of the possibility of overdetermination. Many causes do make a difference to the world. Had they not occurred, something else might not have occurred. But not all causes make a difference. Some effects are overdetermined (Moore 2009, 411–25). They have more than one cause or set of causes each of which alone could have produced the effect. Two assassins, for instance, working independently each put a deadly dose of poison in their victim's drink. The victim consumes it and dies. If we thought of causation and responsibility in terms of counterfactual dependence, each assassin could claim innocence. Their poison made no difference given that the other dose was lethal. Neither assassin's action was a *sine qua non* for the victim's death. There is no shortage of other examples. For example, two brain neurons N_1 and N_2 fire simultaneously and each would alone have been enough for the passing of the threshold for N_3 to then fire (Moore 2009, 416; example from Lewis). The firing of N_3 is overdetermined.

Defenders of the counterfactual dependence theory of causation have gone to great lengths to explain away the possibility of overdetermination. It threatens the core difference-making intuition of the theory. And yet there seems nothing unintuitive about overdetermination itself. In that case, it looks as though the amendments to the theory that have been designed to avoid the problem are *ad hoc* with no greater motivation than to salvage the theory. In contrast, the causal dispositionalist theory can accept the intuitive possibility of overdetermination without any further amendment or cost to the theory. We simply accept that two powers *a* and *b*, or sets of powers, each could get the situation over a particular threshold for an effect to occur (figure 5).

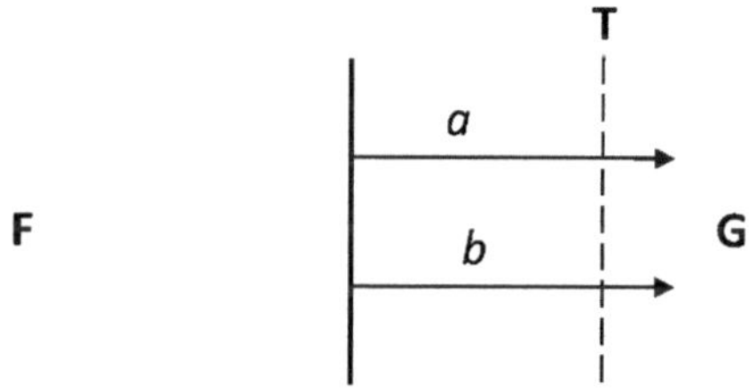

Figure 5: Causal overdetermination

What we need to do, therefore, is recast both our counterfactuals in dispositional terms, which we can do:

i*. *C* and *E* occur and *C* caused *E*. *C* had the power whose manifestation was *E* such that *had there not been C, it would not have disposed towards E (though something else might have).*

ii*. Neither *C* nor *E* occurs. But *had there been C, it would have disposed towards E*, because *C* was the power whose manifestation was *E*.

Despite these amendments, i* and ii* can still serve as a basis for responsibility. An agent's actions do not necessitate an outcome and nor can we be sure that their action made a difference, if the effect was overdetermined. But we can still hold people responsible for actions that dispose towards an outcome. Someone who sells a dangerous drug, for instance, can still be responsible for a death it subsequently produces even if it did not guarantee the death. Producing it is enough. Similarly, if would be a weak defence to argue that only half of those who took the drug died and death was not therefore within the control of the drug seller. Had Spider-Man tackled the burglar, it would have disposed strongly towards them being apprehended and committing no murder that evening. The fact that the Hulk had the power to restrain Spider-Man does not affect his responsibility through omission. And it would further be a bad defence that one's own poison made no difference to the victim because they were ingesting the other assassin's lethal dose. More to the point is that the first assassin's dose was lethal: it had the power to kill the victim whether or not anyone else had also introduced a lethal dose.

6 Transitivity and Responsibility

Despite what we take to be the inadequacies of a counterfactual dependence theory of causation, the counterfactual or difference making notion of cause still holds some power (Moore 2009, 371). But we will argue that this *sine qua non* notion is clearly distinguishable from genuine causation. If it really were causation, there would simply be too many causes: many things will be a *sine qua non* for an effect without being a cause of it. In this and the next section we will try to resolve the issues of causal chains, transitivity and necessary conditions and it should then be clear how a cause differs from a *sine qua non.*

Causal responsibility often works via intermediaries. This can result in causal responsibility that stretches back many years. One may be responsible for someone's death even if one caused it via a series of intermediate steps. Perhaps one 'only' pushes a rock, but if the rock is on the edge of a cliff under which one's enemy is stood then one may be guilty of murder, depending on the circumstances. And if that works with just one intermediate cause, there seems no reason why one couldn't murder someone via many steps, as with a Heath Robinson or Rube Goldberg machine for instance (an elaborate mechanical contraption with many operating stages).

As soon as we allow causation to transfer through intermediate causes we get into the issue of the transitivity of causation. A common metaphor that is used is the causal chain, which conveys the idea that causation consists in a sequence of events or links with strong connections between each of those links. A causal dispositionalist has reasons to be suspicious of that metaphor, however.

In the first place, the idea of links in the chain suggests something strong and unbreakable but we have already said that causes do not necessitate their effects but tend towards them only. The links of the chain are far from unbreakable. But the metaphor also ignores what we take to be an essential feature of causation, namely its polygeny. Neuron diagrams, it will be recalled, show us only one cause for every effect. Lewisians do not think that this is the case for causation generally: they allow that causes can be complex. But their project is to explain what it is to be *a* cause of an event (among others) and there cannot be more than one, in the circumstances, that was sufficient for the effect; that is, upon which the effect counterfactually depends. As we saw above, a counterfactual dependence theory cannot allow effects to be overdetermined. The image of a chain is thus particularly suited to the conventions of neuron diagrams, which in turn is particularly suited to the two-event-plus-relation model of Humean and Lewisian theories of causation (see Martin 2008, 46 and Mumford and Anjum 2011, ch. 2).

Moore offers us a better metaphor: one that shows the polygeny of effects. We should think instead of a backwards causal cone (Moore 2009, 276). A particular effect has three causes, say, but then each of those three causes has three causes, and so on. We can see that the further back in time one goes, the more causal ancestors an effect will have. We endorse the idea of the causal cone metaphor instead of the causal chain. What bearing does this have on responsibility?

Moore allows that:

> Causation is then pictured as an inverted cone. The further up the cone from *e* is some *c*, the less causal contribution it makes to *e* (because it is joined by so many other causes). Thus later is usually greater, when it comes to degrees of causation. (Moore 2009, 72)

This gives Moore, he thinks, a reason to put limitations on transitivity of causation. If c_1 cause c_2, and c_2 causes c_3, and so on to c_n, we cannot always say that c_1 caused c_n. The reason is that causation weakens and then peters out through time (Moore 2009, 121–3, 224 and 397–9) and thus need not always transfer from an earlier causal transaction to a later one in the same causal cone. An earlier cause will be one among more than a later cause so it has less of a responsibility for the final effect. And we can go so far back in the causal history that we reach *de minimis* causes, which are among so many that they should not properly be thought of as causes at all. Causation and thus responsibility are not always transitive, therefore. Some causes will have petered out with respect to some later effect. We can think of causes as petering out over time insofar as time is a good indicator or proxy for how many causal transactions have occurred (Moore 2009, 122).

We accept that transitivity can fail but not for the reasons Moore gives. He is right that we do not generally consider, for instance, a distant event such as the Big Bang to have been the cause of someone speeding or being involved in a car accident even if we accept that it is part of its backwards causal cone (arguably a part of everything's backwards causal cone). But there are two problems with Moore's account. First, the limit at which a cause moves from just being one small cause among many others to not being a cause at all – one that has petered out – would seem to be arbitrary. It would not be something dictated by nature but only by our decisions. Do we say c can be a cause of e if it is one among a thousand causes of e but not if it is one among a thousand-and-one causes (or 'no-longer causes') of e? Do we say that the causes of e must have occurred within its previous ten years but no longer? The world and its causal cones seem to involve a smooth continuity of degrees of influence rather than any sharp and obvious cut off between being a cause and not being a cause. Second, Moore's diagnosis would seem to imply that factors in e's backwards causal cone of equal temporal distance from e are either both causes of e or both not causes of e. But it seems a possibility that we think of one thing c_a as a cause of e even though c_b, which occurred at the same time as c_a and is also in e's causal cone, is not a cause of e. A cause of a bridge collapsing might be the use of a batch of weak rivets 50 years previously. At the same time and elsewhere on the bridge some adequate and strong rivets could have been used. The latter seems to be within the causal cone of the bridge's collapse but would not be thought of as one of its causes.

This last example gives a clue as to what we think the right answer is for why transitivity can fail and the answer is within the spirit of dispositionalism. Clearly, some factors in the causal history of an event dispose towards the effect in question and others don't, even though they are indeed parts of its causal cone. Weak rivets dispose towards the bridge's collapse (even if it takes them 50 years to manifest their disposition) while strong rivets don't. And the Big Bang, while it is a part of everybody's backwards causal cone, does not dispose towards anybody speeding (or slowing down). It is not merely that the causal effects of the Big Bang have faded away over time (Moore 2009, 121 uses the metaphor of emanating ripples in a lake caused by the dropping of a stone and fading away to nothingness over the lake's surface). Indeed, there are still things happening now for which the Big Bang can be identified as the major cause: the ongoing expansion of the universe, for instance. Geological causes can also stretch over a lot of time. Temporal distance does not automatically exclude causation, therefore. Rather, causes are selective about what it is, at a certain distance, they cause and what they don't. Dispositionalism can explain the difference. Causes dispose towards some manifestations rather than others, even if it takes them a long time to manifest those dispositions.

We have an alternative to Moore's account of causes petering out but we have not yet ruled on the issue of failures of transitivity generally. Are we saying that causation is transitive or not? Our answer is that causation can indeed pass through intermediaries but it need not always do so. In that case, causation should be regarded as non-transitive. If causation were transitive, then if *a* causes *b* and *b* causes *c*, then *a* causes *c*. In explaining why some parts of an event's backwards causal cone were not properly causes, we said that such parts were not counted as causes because they did not dispose towards the event in question. The Big Bang disposed towards the expanding of the universe but not towards someone speeding. And we can now see the good sense in accepting this as a general principle. Many factors can be involved in the timing, manner or degree of an effect without being causes of it. Causal dispositionalism explains how. If a doctor attempts to save a patient, they may delay their death but be unable to prevent it. The time and manner of death is significantly affected by that intervention. But did the doctor cause the death? No. The patient died despite the doctor's efforts not because of it. We should not count as causes of an effect those powers that were disposing away from it (the exception to this being where equally balanced opposing powers produce equilibrium). Adoption of this principle explains to us why there can be failures of transitivity in causal sequences. We can have a case where *a* disposes towards *b* and succeeds in producing it, *b* then disposes towards *c* and succeeds in producing it, but where *a* had no disposition towards *c*. To take a simple example, an arsonist sets fire to a building. The fire starts the sprinkler system which then puts out the fire. Did the arsonist put out the fire? Clearly not: they started it. Starting fires does not in general dispose towards them being extinguished. In our example, of course, the fire occurs in a particular context in which a building is sprinkler protected. It is only through the further intervention of this system that events lead to the fire's extinguishing, which is a matter extrinsic to the arsonist's actions.

It might assist if we represent the powers at work in our case in two successive vector diagrams. Figure 6 shows the cases where *a* at t_1 disposes towards F: the arsonist's actions dispose towards fire, for example. But the fire then reaches a certain threshold that triggers the sprinklers. At t_2 the sprinklers extinguish the fire. The sprinklers dispose in the opposite direction to the arsonist's actions. The result is G instead of that towards which the act of arson disposed, F.

It should be obvious that the dispositional account does not suffer the same defects as the petering-out account of why transitivity does not hold. We do not have to specify arbitrary points of temporal or causal distance at which causa-

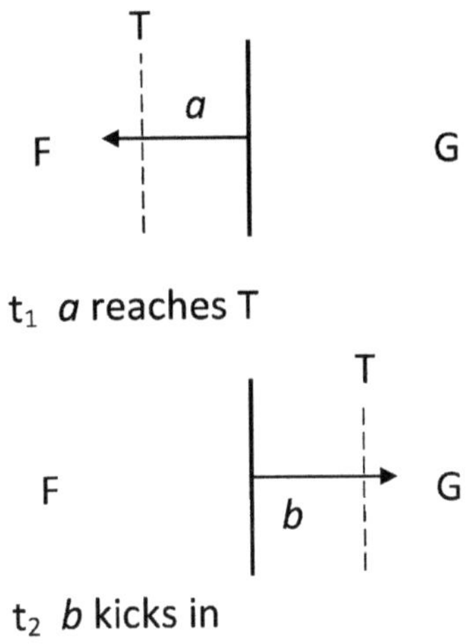

Figure 6: Transitivity failure

tion fades. And nor do we have to say that distinct factors in a causal cone that are at equal temporal or causal distance from an effect are either both causes of that effect or both not causes.

7 Sine Quibus Non

Transitivity clearly bears on the issue of responsibility. If transitivity has failed it shows that someone, event or thing can be a part of an effect's backwards causal cone without being a cause of it. Just as an arsonist cannot claim credit for putting out the fire, nor should a doctor necessarily take blame if an intervention that should produce one outcome is part of the causal history of an opposite outcome. Both these instances would not have had those effects without the further intervention of some further factor and we assume that the action was taken in ignorance of that factor. The arsonist did not want a sprinkler system to intervene and nor should our doctor have known that a complicating factor would produce the unintended consequence.

What should we say of these parts of a causal cone that are nevertheless not causes of the effect? A distinction is sometimes drawn between causes and background conditions. Striking the match caused it to light. The presence of oxygen was just a background condition. We cannot make much sense of that as it is traditionally outlined. Oxygen is just as much a cause of a match lighting as is its striking and the distinction seems a purely epistemic or pragmatic one rather than a metaphysical one. But we do not have a more metaphysical basis for drawing a distinction of this ilk. Instead, while we may couch it simply in terms of causes versus conditions the conditions that we have in mind are *sine qua non* conditions. A *sine qua non* is a *without-which-not* and this seems a simpler way of referring to what we have so far described as being within the causal cone of *e* without being one of the causes of *e*. Again the Big Bang example provides a good illustration. Without the occurrence of the Big Bang, someone could not have been speeding, nor slowing down, but that does not mean it is a cause of such an event. The Lewisian counterfactual dependence theory conflates causes with *sine quibus non* and thus has to rule that someone speeding is caused by the Big Bang. Similarly, someone's death counterfactually depends on their birth and someone's sneezing counterfactually depends on the conception of one of their grandparents. But none of these are cases of causation. The earlier event does not dispose towards the latter. Birth does not dispose towards death, for instance. Certainly it is a precondition for it – a *sine qua non* – but that is not the same. Some mortal danger is what causes death, or some further biological process, but not the birth itself.

This brings us back to the issue of causes, omissions and responsibility. Although a *sine qua non* is not a cause, it may still be a basis for responsibility. One might do something that did not cause an accident but without which the accident would not have happened, or would not have been disposed to happen. The case of omission is clearly of this kind. We had principled reasons for saying omissions could not be causes and yet Peter Parker feels, probably correctly, that his uncle's death would not have occurred without his omission. We need not limit our cases to omissions. There could be some positive factors that were necessary conditions for an effect without being a cause of it. Nevertheless, we can have responsibility for a *sine qua non* if it is considered negligence. If a man leaves a dangerous and unmarked chemical where others have access, for instance – such as keeping turpentine in a reused water bottle – he has not caused someone to drink it but his action might have been a *sine qua non* for them doing so. The judgement of negligence would be on the basis that he had needlessly and carelessly created a condition for harm being done, without any precaution being taken against the possibility of someone using it in a harmful way.

8 Dispositionality: A Modality for Moral Agency

We have already mentioned that dispositions bring with them a modality that is short of necessity but still more than mere contingency and we think it reducible to neither. Dispositions or tendencies are more than mere possibilities because they are directed towards a particular outcome. Intentionality has such a directedness. Amongst all the things that are possible to do one intends to do only some of them. The dispositional modality is a selection function that picks out some of the many possible outcomes (Mumford and Anjum 2011, 189–90). But an intention to do *x* does not guarantee *x*. One might intend to swim 600 meters, for instance, but without succeeding in doing so.

In figure 1 we saw that the effect is a result of many powers working together, sometimes with each other, and sometimes against each other. For any tendency towards F, there could be a counteracting tendency, disposing away from F. This is why a cause is never sufficient for its effect. There could be something added that disposed away from and interfered with the effect. This is an essential feature of powers and also of causation. But it is also an essential feature of responsibility. In order to be responsible for one's acts, one must be able to produce the act. But perhaps equally important is that one is able to not produce the act, or even to counteract it. This is what we mean when we say that an act needs to be voluntarily for us to be held responsible for it. If an act is forced, involuntary, or we weren't able to control it, we could not be held responsible for it. Someone who causes a harm but in a psychotic state was indeed able to produce the harm. The morally and legally relevant question is whether they were also able to prevent the harm.

What we cannot avoid is beyond our moral blame or praise. If one had to act, or couldn't act, one is not responsible for the action. A result of this is that the same type of act can be both blameworthy or not depending on who produced it. A kick to the body can certainly cause harm, and is usually something we would consider blameworthy. But we only think it's blameworthy if it was intentional: something that one could choose not to do. A kick caused by a spasm is an involuntary act because it lacks at least one of the two elements of the dispositional modality. There was the power to produce the effect, but not the power to prevent it. There might not even have been a directedness, as there was no intention to kick. So although the intentional and accidental kicks have the same effects, there is a modal difference, hence also a moral difference.

The dispositional modality must also hold for omissions. If we had no power to act, then our omissions cannot be blameworthy. We must both be able to omit and to not omit: that is, the omission must be voluntary for us to be held responsible for it.

The dispositional modality is thus an essential part of our notions of responsibility and moral agency. Without it our actions would either be necessary or purely contingent. In the first alternative, we would not be able to prevent our own actions, in the second they would be mere accidents.

9 Greater Power, greater Responsibility

We hope to have vindicated the general idea that responsibility is based on power, and not on causation as such. Specifically, an agent can be held responsible for an act only under certain modal conditions: if it was within their power to act but also not to act. They could be responsible causally for some effect when it was their action that produced it. They might be responsible for something non-causally when they had the power to prevent it and failed to do so. We have also seen that they could be non-causally responsible for something if their action was a *sine qua non* for something else.

This provides a foundation for supporting a part of the WGPCGR-thesis. But the thesis also says something more. It suggests that responsibility can come in degrees and the degree of responsibility is proportional to the degree of power. The former, we take it, is uncontroversial. Courts of law regularly apportion degrees of responsibility, for instance on the degree of causal contribution or effect. This concerns the exercise of power but also of unexercised power. The strongest swimmer present, we contend, has more responsibility to jump in the lake and save the drowning man than weaker swimmers. Having a power to do something does not always produce a responsibility to exercise it (an ability to dance, for instance) but on some occasions it does. It is relevant that our strong swimmer has a better chance of performing the rescue successfully. The weaker swimmers are more likely to fail or, indeed, get themselves into trouble in the water. The stronger swimmer is likely to make the rescue quicker, minimising a chance of injury to both parties. Similarly, Spider-Man can prevent the burglar's escape almost effortlessly. If someone else attempts it they might fail or put their own safety at risk. These are factors that have some moral significance and there is hence no reason why they shouldn't also have legal significance. For the case of omissions, the more one is able to do, the more negligent one is in not doing it, if the moral features of the situation dictate that it should be done. If donations are required to relieve famine, for instance, the rich man has a power to relieve more famine than a poor man. If morality dictates that famine should be relieved, therefore, clearly there is more obligation on someone of rich means than on someone of poor. And if both the rich and poor man fail to act, in full knowledge of the moral features of the situation, then both are to blame but the richer man more.

What philosophical principle is behind this judgement, we are not sure. Moral and legal theory tells us what should and shouldn't be done and we have not entered into that discussion. Our claim is rather that if there is a responsibility to do something, then the more one is able to do it, the more responsibility one has to do it.

There are certain things this does not mean. An ability to do good doesn't always create a responsibility to do so. Some acts may be supererogatory: praiseworthy if performed without being blameworthy if not performed (Urmson 1958). If an athlete 'comes out' as gay it may be praiseworthy, because they may make a good role model for others, but we wouldn't necessarily blame a gay athlete who chose not to do so because we realise it could be at a personal cost. We also do not mean that it is better to exercise more of a power than less. One can kill a plant by overwatering it and, similarly, one has to find the appropriate amount of good to do, otherwise it could do harm. Giving someone too much assistance, for instance, might stifle their independence and thus their own capability. And giving away all our money to the poor might harm our own families. As Aristotle's ethics showed, being the good person also involves knowing how much of a certain virtue it is appropriate to exercise.

These cases aside, then, the principles we would want to support, in both the legal and moral case, are that:

a. Without the ability to do *x*, but also to prevent *x*, one cannot be responsible for doing *x*.
b. With the ability to do *x*, one can (but need not necessarily) have a responsibility to do *x*.
c. The more able one is to do *x*, if one should do *x*, then the greater the responsibility to do *x*.

Peter Parker is right to blame himself for the death of his uncle even though he didn't cause it. He had the power to prevent it. This is based on the connection we feel exists between our causal powers and responsibilities. We are also responsible for our omissions where we had the power to prevent some outcome. And the greater our power, the greater our responsibility.

We argued, however, that the connections between power, omission and responsibility need to be carefully set out. In speaking in terms of powers, we are deliberately making use of a causal dispositionalist thesis. But we hope to have justified this by showing the use to which it can be put in solving certain philosophical problems. We have shown what really occurs in the cases of omissions, which are a class of 'causation by absence'. We have shown that the counterfactual thinking that bases our attributions of responsibility in the cases of omission has to be cast in dispositional terms. We then explained how causation and thus responsibility was not always transitive: not for the reasons Moore gives, of petering out, but on the basis that only those things that disposed towards an effect could be causes of it. We then used this as a principled basis on which to distinguish causes from (*sine qua non*) conditions. We hope that all of these claims are useful and that those not yet persuaded of a dispositional approach to causation will here see some of its attractions.

References

Dowe, Phil (2001). A Counterfactual Theory of Prevention and "Causation" by Omission. *Australasian Journal of Philosophy*, 79: 216–26.

Geach. Peter T. (1961). Aquinas. In G. E. M. Anscombe and Peter T. Geach, *Three Philosophers*, Oxford: Blackwell, 1961: 65 125.

Lewis, David (1973). Causation. In *Philosophical Papers*, ii, Oxford: Oxford University Press, 1986: 159–213.

Lewis, David (1986). *On the Plurality of Worlds*. Oxford: Oxford University Press.

Martin, Charles B. (2008). *The Mind in Nature*. Oxford: Oxford University Press.

Moore, Michael S. (2009). *Causation and Responsibility: An Essay in Law, Morals, and Metaphysics*. Oxford: Oxford University Press.

Mumford, Stephen & Anjum, Rani L. (2011). *Getting Causes from Powers*. Oxford: Oxford University Press.

Schaffer, Jonathan (2004). Causes Need Not be Physically Connected to Their Effects: the Case for Negative Causation. In Christopher Hitchcock (Ed.), *Contemporary Debates in Philosophy of Science*. Oxford: Blackwell, 197–216.

Urmson, JO (1958). Saints and Heroes. In A. Meldon (Ed.), *Essays in Moral Philosophy*. Seattle: University of Washington Press, 198–215.

Alex Broadbent

Explanation and Responsibility

1 Introduction

"Causation matters to legal liability", says Michael Moore at the beginning of *Causation and Responsibility* (Moore 2009, 3). So does money, in the sense that it is one of the factors that determines who is in fact held liable. But this descriptive sense of "matters", for Moore, is secondary to the normative sense. Moore thinks causation *ought* to play a determining role in liability, in a moral sense of "ought". This normative thesis is the focus of Moore's book, and the analysis of the role causation does in fact play in determining legal liability is conducted with a view to assessing to what extent the law is right.

The reason that causation ought to be a determinant of legal liability is that it is a determinant of moral responsibility, in Moore's view. One might be tempted to criticise Moore for confusing law and morality. Indeed it does not follow directly from the fact that a person is morally responsible that they (morally) ought to be held legally liable. However, even if Moore said nothing at all about the relation between the two (and he does of course have something to say about this), it would be hard to accept the conclusion that causation is a determinant of moral responsibility without conceding that it (morally) ought to play some role in determining legal liability. To resist conceding this would require conceding instead that legal liability (morally) need never reflect moral responsibility. This is implausible, implying that the law is above moral evaluation, and that proper legal judgements have no moral significance. Moore's underlying view, I take it, is that law is subject to moral evaluation and ought to carry moral weight, and it is hard to disagree.

The two principal obstacles facing Moore's normative thesis are these. First, there is the problem known as *moral luck*. Imagine two exactly similar agents Able and Baker who independently set out to commit exactly the similar heinous murders. Each breaks into the intended victim's house and raises the Samurai sword (say) over the hapless victim. Able brings the blade down and beheads his victim, but Baker is at that moment savaged by his intended victim's honey badger (say).[1] Is Baker a better person than Able, merely because his victim kept a honey badger? Does Baker deserve a lesser punishment merely be-

1 Honey badgers are small but fearsome animals famous for eating extremely poisonous snakes, raiding bees nests, and fighting much larger would-be predators when attacked.

cause the honey badger intervened? If so, then there is a sense in which Baker is lucky: a moral sense, because through no act of his own, he was saved, by the honey badger, from doing something bad. (This is compatible with admitting that what he did so far was bad, of course; the point at issue is whether what Able did was worse.) But a significant number of commentators deny that there is any moral difference between Able and Baker, since the honey badger's intervention was entirely independent and unforeseen. (This is compatible with admitting that there is a difference in the desirability of the eventual outcome, of course.) Cases like this suggest that moral responsibility arises not from a causing a bad outcome, but from something else.

Backing up a little, the *reason* for the problem of moral luck is that causes are rarely, if ever,[2] *sufficient* for an effect to occur. It follows that, if causation is a determining factor in moral responsibility, then the degree or kind of an agent's moral responsibility depends on many factors beyond her control, and in this sense is partly a matter of luck.

The second major obstacle to Moore's thesis concerns the nature of causation. Moore must provide some positive characterisation of causation, one which explains the fact that causation matters to moral responsibility and thus to legal liability. There are several reasons why he must. First, it is implausible to suppose that causation is either necessary or sufficient for moral responsibility, or for legal liability; so the relation between the two must be a complex one. An account is called for simply to help us understand the proposal. Second, and this is my main interest in this essay, Moore must face the fact that most philosophers and legal theorists regard it as settled that the relation between law and morality is in fact much *less* intimate than we ordinarily suppose. Thus the theory of causation that he needs must be radical and unorthodox: it must be a theory of something which, in the eyes of most (but not all) philosophers, is not causation at all, strictly speaking. That thing is *causal selection,* consisting in our exceptionless habit of mentioning only some of the many events that are, in some loose sense, causally (or perhaps nomically[3]) responsible for a given effect.

The strange fact is that Moore does not realise that he needs a theory of causal selection. Indeed he explicitly agrees with those philosophers who have dismissed it – philosophers like David Lewis:

> We sometimes single out one among all the causes of some event and call it 'the' cause... We may select abnormal or extraordinary causes, or those under human control, or those

2 For a powerful critique of the notion of causal sufficiency see (Russell 1917).

3 Where "nomically connected" means connected by laws of nature.

> we deem good or bad, or just those we want to talk about. I have nothing to say about these principles of invidious discrimination. I am concerned with the prior question of what it is to be one of the causes (unselectively speaking). My analysis is meant to capture a broad and non-discriminatory notion of causation. (Lewis 1973, 558–9)

Moore cites (part of) this passage with approval. Yet in this passage, Lewis denies that the distinction between morally significant and insignificant "causes" (in his unselective sense) has any significance for the "prior" question of what it is to be "one of the causes (unselectively speaking)".

In this essay, therefore, I want to argue the following: In Section 2 I will argue that Moore's stance on the role of causation in legal liability and moral responsibility requires him to provide a theory of causal selection, and moreover a theory which makes selection a causal fact and not a mere pragmatic overlay. In Section 3 I will argue that Moore is confused about causal selection, failing to see that he needs a theory of selection; and thus, unsurprisingly, his theory of causation does not provide one. In Section 4 I will espouse my own theory of causal selection, which I think does enable the "unified" analysis of causation that Moore seeks.

2 Causal Selection

Richard is fiddling with his radio while driving his car. He swerves off the road and hits a pedestrian, Jane. The impact breaks her leg. It is natural to suppose that Richard has done something wrong, while Jane has not; and moreover it is natural to characterise the difference by saying that Richard caused the injury while Jane did not. We can even imagine Richard leaping from his car and seeking to blame Jane, and Jane replying (through gritted teeth) that it's not her fault but his, because he caused the accident. She will regard herself, not only as morally blameless, but also as causally blameless.

This is an instance of *causal selection.* It is hard to give a neutral characterisation of causal selection. A common, but not entirely accurate, way to characterise the difference is by distinguishing *necessary conditions* for an effect from the event(s) we call, or treat as, the cause(s). This is not entirely accurate because the so-called conditions may not be necessary at all; just as there may be redundancy among causes, there may be redundancy among so-called conditions. A more general characterisation, assuming the causal relata are events, might be that selection occurs whenever our causal judgements differentiate between events which, in some broader sense, lie in the causal or nomic history of the effect.

Either way, selection does not require anything as strong as what Jane asserts. Jane's presence on the pavement is either causally necessary for the injury, or on my preferred characterisation, lies in the causal history of the injury. Either way there is *some* causal connection. But there is a difference between that connection, and Richard's connection with the injury.

There are two attitudes we might take to this difference. We might say that it is intrinsic to the causal relation (assuming causation is a relation) – that there is a causal difference between Richard's fiddling and Jane's walking. Or we might deny that, and say that there is no causal difference, only a difference of attitude towards the underlying causal relations.

The dominant view among philosophers since John Stuart Mill has been the latter. Mill writes:

> it is very common to single out one only of the antecedents under the denomination of Cause, calling the others merely Conditions. The real Cause, is the whole of these antecedents; and we have, philosophically speaking, no right to give the name of cause to one of them, exclusively of the others. (Mill 1843)

Lewis implies something very similar through his righteous disinterest in the principles governing selection in the passage previously cited (Lewis 1973, 558–9).

As I mentioned in the introduction, Moore explicitly agrees with Mill and Lewis. He writes:

> Lewis and Mill are on solid ground in refusing to grant semantic status to the discriminatory principles by which we select amongst the various causes [...] These are merely pragmatic features of causal utterances which are dependant on the context of the utterance and the speaker's intent [...] (Moore 2009, 397)

This stance generates a question, namely: is it compatible with the various other claims Moore makes about what causation is like, or must be like if it is to do what morality and the law require of it?

There is compelling evidence for the answer "No".

First, Moore admits that "the law presupposes some criterion for distinguishing causes from merely necessary conditions" (114). And notwithstanding the remark just cited from several hundred pages later (Moore 2009, 397), this feature of law's causal concept survives the "pruning" of Chapter 6: "Not every condition necessary for the happening of some harm *y* is a cause of *y*" (Moore 2009, 152). Unless this claim is trivial, "necessary" must given a nomic or causal rather than logical reading. And thus it appears that Moore does endorse some kind of selective view of causation.

Second, more substantively, Moore explicitly seeks a "unitary" legal approach to causation – one which does not distinguish between "cause-in-fact" and "cause-in-law". He writes:

> The problems with the conventional analysis of causation – in terms of a bifurcation into cause-in-fact and proximate causation – have tempted some legal theorists to abandon the conventional analysis, root and branch. This generates a search for a unitary notion of causation that is much more discriminating (in what I allows as a cause) than the hopelessly promiscuous counterfactual cause-in-fact test of the conventional analysis. (Moore 2009, 104)

The standard, bifurcated view is one on which the causal inquiry (properly) has two stages. First, it is asked whether the wrongful act is a cause-in-fact of the harm. If (and only if) so, it is then asked whether the cause-in-fact is a *sufficiently proximate* cause to incur liability, or in alternative terminology a *cause-in-law.* The standard analysis of these two elements holds that cause-in-fact concerns the objective causal status of the relation between wrong and harm, while cause-in-law concerns the legal question of whether this kind of causal relation is one which attracts liability.

The standard, two-part legal approach to causation is strongly reminiscent of the orthodox philosophical view of causal selection. According to Lewis and Mill, there is a prior question as to whether one event causes another, unselectively speaking. This is strongly reminiscent of the legal question, whether a wrong is a cause-in-fact of a harm. Then, say Lewis and Mill, we commonly ask a secondary question as to whether the event in question is a salient, or morally relevant, or explanatory, or otherwise interesting cause. This is strongly reminiscent of the law's question, whether the cause-in-fact is a cause-in-law. It is natural to say that cause-in-fact is, as the name suggests, a question of the causal facts; and whether a cause-in-fact is a cause-in-law is essentially a normative question as to whether this is the sort of cause (or the sort of causal link) which ought to attract liability, a question not settled by deciding whether the wrong is in fact a cause of the harm. On this view, some of the doctrines of legal causation must be interpreted metaphorically – particularly *novus actus interveniens*, the notion that some sorts of events can "break the chain of causation" (see e.g. *Knightley v Johns* [1982] 1 W.L.R. 349). But given the difficulty of making literal sense of *novus actus* in terms of the causal facts (notwithstanding some heroic efforts; see Hart and Honoré 1985), this might be considered an advantage. Moreover, the other most important doctrine of legal causation, namely the issue of remoteness of damage, is determined by asking whether the damage was reasonably foreseeable (*The Wagon Mound No. 1* [1961] A.C. 388). This is strongly suggests that the doctrine concerns whether the defendant ought to be held liable, rather than whether some objective causal fact obtains.

So it seems that Moore does not agree with Lewis and Mill about causal selection, even if he thinks he does. It is central to his entire project that many facts about moral responsibility are determined by causal responsibility; and given the sorts of facts he has in mind, the only way this can be true is if causal responsibility is a lot more discriminating than philosophers like Mill and Lewis allow. If causal selection were not a part of causation, but a matter of "pragmatics", as Moore wrongly thinks, he thinks, then moral judgements would not after all be grounded in causation, but in pragmatics. The unselective, prior notion of causation is far too unselective to ground moral responsibility. It makes Jane as morally responsible as Richard.

Moore holds that it is holds that it is "rare" for the law to discriminate between "*temporally co*-present, equally necessary conditions" (Moore 2009, 114). But this seems to be simply wrong. The case of Richard and Jane is not rare but *typical*. Victims of wrongs are *typically* necessary conditions for those wrongs to occur. Thus the law discriminates between temporally co-present, equally necessary conditions extremely commonly.

To lean heavily on the notion of temporal co-presence at this point would be a mistake, because it would be tantamount to admitting that temporal, not causal, relations determine liability. Likewise, Moore would be ill-advised to insist that there is some other, non-causal reason for Jane's innocence – for example, the fact she is not in breach of a duty. This would be hard to reconcile with the general stance on the centrality of causation to moral responsibility: Moore would be conceding that, in this case, causation does not explain why we hold Richard and not Jane liable in law or morality. Moreover, elsewhere I have developed this example so as to block this response, by making Jane in breach of a duty too (Broadbent 2009).

Perhaps there remains some theoretical space for Moore to have his cake and eat it. But it is a small space, and rather than expend further effort trying to eliminate it, let us ask a fresh and more charitable question. Notwithstanding Moore's explicit stance on causal selection, and its relation to causation, does Moore's positive theory make causation selective enough to ground moral responsibility?

3 Primitivism is too primitive

According to Moore, causation is "a natural relation lying at the heart of scientific explanation" (Moore 2009, vii). Even if it is not a relation, Moore holds it legitimate in the legal context to speak as if causation were a relation between events (Moore 2009, 366–8). His tentative proposal is that this relation (if relation it be) is "a metaphysical primitive", meaning "it is not reducible to any other sort of thing or things, and thus there is little by way of an *analysis* that one can say about it" (Moore 2009, 104–5). Despite lack of analysis, Moore identifies several advantages of primitivism, perhaps the main one being its alleged invulnerability to the problems that causal redundancy creates for other philosophical accounts.[4] He also identifies some of the properties of this primitive relation. He tentatively suggests it is "singular", where a singularist theory, for Moore, is one which "does not reduce singular causal statements to statements of causal laws" (Moore 2009, 497). Much firmer is Moore's view that causation is "a scalar relation, which is to say, a matter of degree" (Moore 2009, 105).

Moore believes that the standard procedure, though it represents a conceptual confusion and is standardly analysed in a confused way, nonetheless generally gets the *extension* of just findings roughly correct. Between them, primitivism and scalarity are supposed to be better accounts of the *real* nature of the judgements underlying doctrines of legal causation. They are also supposed to offer a better explanation of why the law is morally justified. The idea is that causal relations are determinants or constituents of certain moral facts, and the law is morally justified to the extent that it finds liability where causal relations obtain and withholds it where they do not.

Does the account achieve the selectivity, or discrimination, which I sought to require of it in the previous section?

Moore does not provide a direct answer to the question, of course, because he does not think he needs to. But both, the primitivism (or, more exactly, primitivist singularism) and the scalarity in his account could be of use. Regarding primitivism, he writes:

> Primitivists of course have the license to shape causation to their pre-theoretical intuitions, so their theory cannot suffer from overbreadth. (Moore 2009, 508)

Probably this is not intended as a solution to the problem of identifying principles governing causal selection; but let us suppose it were. Would it be promising?

---

4 "Causal redundancy" is an umbrella term for various cases including those known as overdetermination, pre-emption, characterised by the fact that at least one cause is "redundant" in the sense that without it, the effect still would have occurred. The lights in the hospital are on, thanks to the national grid; but the national grid is a redundant cause because if the grid went down, a generator would kick in, and the lights would still be on.

The answer is No, for two reasons. First, it is hard to see how it could advance our understanding of this puzzling phenomenon to say that causation is a primitive, unanalyzable relation. We would need to say something else *about* the relation, and primitivism by itself does not do this.

Second, more importantly, the answer takes no notice of the main *reason* that philosophers have mostly (but not all) considered selection to be a matter of pragmatics and not of causal facts themselves. As Mill puts it:

> Nothing can better show the absence of any scientific ground for the distinction between the cause of a phenomena and its conditions, than the capricious manner in which we select from among the conditions that which we choose to denominate the cause. (Mill 1843)

In other words, causal selection is "capricious"; or, in modern terminology, context-sensitive. One of Hart and Honore's examples is a fire in a factory where procedures are usually conducted in a vacuum. In such circumstances we might well say that the oxygen caused the fire, even if under more normal circumstances we would not mention the oxygen and say that the spark caused the fire (Hart and Honoré 1985, 10).

This context-sensitivity undermines Moore's vision of the happy primitivist declaring that the causal relation obtains wherever he intuits it. For the primitivist must still explain how a relation can hold between oxygen and fire (to continue that example) in one context, but between oxygen and spark in another, even if the two fires are chemically identical. Likewise he must explain why the pedestrian, not the driver, is "selected" as cause when an impact with identical physical properties to the Richard-Jane impact occurs due to the pedestrian running haphazardly into the path of a careful driver. The primitivist who is also a singularist, as Moore is, will be at liberty to say that causation holds in this case but not in that. But in doing so, she will cut causation entirely free of the physical properties and events which we usually take to be causes and effects. Physically similar situations will be causally different, due to the differential distribution of this primitive causal relation. The picture may be consistent, but it is almost supernatural; it is hardly one on which causation lies "at the heart of scientific explanation" (Moore 2009, vii). So we must conclude that Moore neither ought to nor would want to develop the suggestion that primitivist singularism can provide an account of causal selection.

The other element of Moore's account which might ground an account of causal selection is *scalarity*. According to Moore, causation "peters out" over long causal chains. The question of whether causation is transitive has received more recent philosophical attention than the relatively neglected question of whether it is selective, but there are some links between the two; I have sought to analyse these elsewhere (Broadbent 2011). The most obvious link is that we often ignore events that are very distant from a given effect, even if they are necessary conditions for the effect, or lie in its causal history; and thus the apparent failure of causal transitivity constitutes a case of causal selection, on either of the definitions offered in the previous section. To this extent, an account of the apparent failure of causal transitivity will be at least a partial account of causal selection.

Does Moore's claim that the causal relation is scalar provide such an account? Again, the answer is No. The mechanism for "petering out" is described as follows:

> Causation diminishes over the number of events through which it is transmitted. This makes the causal relation one of only limited transitivity. (Moore 2009, 153)

The idea is that each event has multiple causes, and the contribution that a given event makes to an effect will be less the more other events are involved. If the putative cause is a long way back along a causal chain, then there will be more such events than if it is close. Eventually, the contribution will be so minimal as not to attract legal liability, even if there is in fact still a small contribution, strictly speaking.

This suggestion conflates the notion of a relation obtaining with a much less well-defined notion, something like *contribution*. Whether a relation obtains is usually understood as a yes/no matter. Moore needs a logic of relations which supports his claim that relations can obtain in greater or lesser degrees. Relatedly (but less technically), it does not seem that causation *does* peter out, as Moore claims. *If* several short causal links add up to one long one, we don't regard that long link as somehow "weaker" than the constituents. Just because the marksman is a more *distant* cause of the President's death than the bullet entering her heart, it does not follow (in ordinary thought) that the marksman is somehow a *lesser* cause. And the solution ignores the fundamental question about causal transitivity, which I have elsewhere described as the "adding up" problem. When a cause of a cause of an effect is also a cause of that effect, this seems to be *because* of the obtaining of the intervening causal relations. On Moore's account, we have a string of causal relations, but no explanation of how, and when, they can "add up" into one big causal relation.

The conclusion of this section, then, is that Moore's positive characterisation of causation does not provide an account of the principles governing causal selection, which I argued in the previous section that it must. In the next section I will briefly outline an alternative and more promising account.

4 Contrastive Explanation

Moore hopes "to relate two contexts in which causation figures, that of legal and moral responsibility on the one hand, and that of scientific explanation on the other" (Moore 2009, vii). Theories of scientific explanation offer a promising starting point for this endeavour. This is because at least some scientific explanation involves citing causes, and causal explanation, like the attribution of moral responsibility is an instance of causal selection. If I explain that I am late because of the concentration of oxygen in the atmosphere you will not be impressed, even though oxygen is a cause of my (late) arrival.

One promising way to account for the irrelevance of the presence of oxygen is to understand (at least some) causal explanations as answers to contrastive questions, perhaps implicit. Thus your question, fully stated, would be "Why are you late *rather than on time?*" Peter Lipton argues for the following necessary condition on contrastive explanation:

> To explain why P rather than Q, we must cite a causal difference between P and not-Q, consisting of a cause of P and the absence of a corresponding event in the case of not-Q. (Lipton 2004, 42)

Thus to explain why I am late rather than on time, I must cite a cause that features in the history of my being late, *but not* the history of my being on time (whether that is the actual history of other on-time arrivals, or the counterfactual history of this on-time arrival, as Lewis prefers (Lewis 1986)). The presence of oxygen, though a cause of late arrival, is not a difference between late and timely arrival; hence it is a poor explanation. But my missing a train is a difference, and hence a good explanation.

Notice a couple of nice things about this account. It allows us to locate a distinction between subjective and objective features of explanation, which otherwise appears troublingly split between the two. Surely it is neither entirely up to us what counts as a decent explanation, nor entirely independent of us, our interests, our background knowledge, and so on. The contrastive account helps because the choice of foil with which to contrast the fact we are asking about is entirely up to us; but once a contrast has been drawn, it is an objective matter whether a given event is a causal difference between them.

A related point is that the account allows for the goodness of an explanation can depend upon context. Different why-questions amount to different verbal contexts; and as well as variation in the explicit question, the other elements of the context may suggest further implicit detail in the contrast. There is a way for context to determine how good an explanation is, namely, by playing a role in determining the question to which the proffered explanation is an answer, without threatening to make the question of what a good answer is totally subjective. The context-sensitivity of explanation arises from the context-sensitivity of the why-question; once the why-question is fixed, it is an objective matter how well a putative answer answers it.

What happens if we do not restrict this approach to causal explanation, but seek to apply it to causation quite generally? Elsewhere I have argued that we can derive both a general account of causal selection (Broadbent 2008; 2011) and an alternative, unitary formulation of the law's causal inquiry. The latter is as follows:

> **Contrastive Condition on Causation in Law:** For a defendant's breach of duty to satisfy the causal element of liability with respect to a given harm to the claimant, the breach must be a difference between the instant case and the legally appropriate foil in which the claimant did not suffer that harm. (Broadbent 2009, 187)

I do not want to repeat the arguments I have made for this condition elsewhere. Rather let me confine myself to identifying some advantages over Moore's view.

First, my proposal explicitly links causation in legal contexts with causal explanation in science. If we accept a contrastive theory of scientific explanation, and we also accept something like my contrastive condition on causation in the law, then there is an apparent parallel between scientific explanation and the causal inquiry in law. Moore says he wants to link these two contexts, and this proposal does so, in a more direct and explicit way than Moore's own theory.

Second, my proposal seeks to provide, or at least integrate with, an account of causal selection. I argued in Section 2 that an account of selection was necessary for the success of Moore's approach, and in Section 3 that his account of causation was inadequate in this respect. In particular, the account my proposal provides handles the *context-sensitivity* of selection. The legally appropriate foil will depend on the context; and moving up a level, the fact that it a *legally* appropriate foil is employed arises from the legal context. The basic selective mechanism is the same across contexts, scientific, legal, or otherwise; only the choice of foil varies with context. (I am happy to allow that *how* context determines foil is a "pragmatic" matter, that is, not a causal one.)

Third, my approach is "unitary". The legal inquiry should be understood as answering one question, namely, whether the contrastive condition above is satisfied. Regarding the status of selection, on this view it is an integral part of causal judgements, and not a pragmatic overlay. Like Ducasse, I think that picking out an element from a background is a crucial point of making a causal judgement. But unlike him, I do not think that the difference is one between cause and background condition. Rather, a cause is an event which is a difference between the occurrence of the effect in question, and its non-occurrence, as contextually specified; while events that we do not call causes are present in both cases. A cause makes a difference to its effect by being the difference between its occurring and not, where "not" is contextually specified.

Finally, and most specifically to Moore's proposal, my proposal is more informative. No doubt my Contrastive Condition is a long way from anything that could ever be used as a legal test. However, it is a good deal closer than Moore's. "Look for the primitive causal relation" is never going to form the basis of a legal test, even a bad test; whereas the Contrastive Condition just might.

5 Conclusion

Moore sets out to show that causation matters to legal liability. I have argued that, to establish this claim, Moore needs an account of causation which shows how causal and moral responsibility are linked. I argued that, given the work Moore envisages for causation, he needs an account of causal selection, and moreover an unorthodox account: one on which causation is a matter of the causal facts themselves, not merely a sort of pragmatic overlay. Moore does not clearly see this need, I argued, and moreover, I argued, that his account of causation does not satisfy it. I outlined an alternative, my Contrastive Condition on Causation in the Law, and briefly advertised some alleged advantages of this account. I have not, however, offered anything like a full exposition or defence.

References

Broadbent, Alex (2008). The Difference Between Cause and Condition. Proceedings of the Aristotelian Society 108: 355–364.

Broadbent, Alex (2009). Fact and law in the causal inquiry. Legal Theory 15: 173–191.

Broadbent, Alex (2011). Causes of causes. Philosophical Studies, 2012. Volume 158: pages 457–476. doi:10.1007/s11098-010-9683-0.

Hart, H.L.A., and A. Honoré (1985). *Causation in the Law.* 2nd ed. Oxford: Clarendon Press.

Lewis, David (1973). Causation. The Journal of Philosophy 70 (17): 556–567.

Lewis, David (1986). Causal Explanation. In *Philosophical Papers, Volume II*, 214—241. Oxford: Oxford University Press.

Lipton, Peter (2004). *Inference to the Best Explanation.* 2nd ed. London and New York: Routledge.

Mill, John Stuart (1843). *A System of Logic, Ratiocinative and Inductive.* 8th ed. New York and Bombay: Longman's, Green, and Co.

Moore, Michael S. (2009). *Causation and Responsibility: An Essay in Law, Morals, and Metaphysics.* Oxford: Oxford University Press.

Russell, Bertrand (1917). On the Notion of a Cause. In *Mysticism and Logic.* London: Allen and Unwin.

Cases

Knightley v Johns [1982] 1 W.L.R. 349

The Wagon Mound No. 1 [1961] A.C. 388

Benedikt Kahmen

Intentions, Intentional Actions and Practical Knowledge

Does the law require a specific philosophy of action? Michael Moore (1993, 2009) prominently argues that it does and that it demands a volitional causal theory of action. However, when this theory is tested against a legal requirement for intentional actions, it turns out to be inadequate. This requirement is that agents have to know their intentional actions. The reason why the volitional causal theory does not meet this requirement is that this knowledge must be practical knowledge in a certain sense. At least, this is what I argue.

1 The Knowledge Requirement for Intentional Actions

When you act, a variety of causal relations is at work. Your actions have more immediate and more distant effects that are commonly attributed to you as your deeds.[1] But causal relations may also be crucial for whether you are acting at all: According to the causal action theory to which Moore (1993, 136) subscribes, whether something is an action depends on its mental cause. This cause may lead to actions that are intentional, but also to ones which are unintentional. Because of the special interest morality and the law have in intentional actions, I will concentrate on the latter in what follows.

In law, there is a requirement for intention and intentional action that can be used to test the plausibility of a theory of action: For an intentional action, the agent has to have concurrent knowledge of his present actions.[2] It is not enough that he had this knowledge at an earlier time or that he could have had it, he must actually have it at the time of action. But it is not required that the agent knows his actions in all detail, only that he knows his action under a generic description φ where agents are legally liable for φ-ing. Neither is he required to be continuously, consciously aware of his intentional action – his knowledge must only be available to him at the time of action. For the sake of simplicity, I will call this requirement of continuous knowledge of one's present intentional actions the *knowledge requirement*. In the following, I will assume

1 The well-known "accordion effect", see (Feinberg, 1967).

2 See, for an example on this requirement in German law, (Wessels, 2009, 87–88).

that the knowledge requirement is true. The question I want to discuss is whether Moore's version of the causal action theory satisfies the knowledge requirement.

2 Volitions, Intentions and Active Agents

Moore (1993, 113–155) argues that actions are bodily movements caused by volitions. Volitions, for him, are individual functional states that conclude our practical reasoning and connect our motivations to our bodily movements. They are non-actional states that have non-actional descriptions of bodily movements as their content.

Moore's argument for his claim that actions are caused by volitions proceeds in two stages: First, he argues that actions must be caused by "bare intentions" that are distinct from pro-attitudes and beliefs. Second, he argues that the bare intentions initiating actions are intentions to move one's body and that such bare intentions are volitions. In what follows, I will focus on the first stage of Moore's argument in order to test whether the volitional theory he develops meets the knowledge requirement.

Moore thinks that the causes of actions are not the Davidsonian combinations of pro-attitudes and beliefs, but mental states in their own right. He sees four reasons for this conclusion. They arise from Davidson's (1969, 22–3) claim that conflicts between desires to act are resolved by differing strengths of the competing desires. But first, Moore argues, in resolving such a conflict, we as agents experience a state that goes beyond the respective desires. Second, in cases of weakness of will we resolve such conflicts in favour of a weaker desire. Third, there may be Buridan's ass-style situations in which none of the competing desires is stronger than the other. Still, we can act in such situations. Fourth, resolve of such a conflict exhibits diachronic stability: Agents tend to stick with their earlier decisions. These arguments are supposed to justify the need for a mental state beyond pro-attitude and belief as the cause of action. The propositional content of this state are the more immediate bodily movements that the agent regards as instrumental to attaining the larger goal contained in his pro-attitude. Thus, they constitute a volition in Moore's understanding.[3]

However, these arguments do not force a Davidsonian to adopt a volitional theory.[4] First, perhaps sometimes we experience resolve of conflict, but there are

3 See (M. S. Moore 1993, 149–155).

4 I defend Davidsonian causal action theory against these objections to motivate the approach below, without myself endorsing such a theory.

equally times in which the conflict continues even beyond the action. Secondly, if we act from weakness of will, we act against stronger desires. But, as Watson (1977) observes, only against evaluationally stronger desires, not against motivationally stronger ones. Davidson's claim, however, is only concerned with the latter. Third, in a situation in which our desires are equally strong, the causally effective desire might not be one of the desires in conflict, but a meta-desire. Fourth, it is open to the Davidsonian to claim that the strength of desires is responsive to earlier resolve and thus creates diachronic stability.[5]

A stronger case for volitions builds on the contention that volitions are crucial for a *person's* agency. Consider again the Davidsonian picture of agency: Reasons cause an intention and the intention causes a bodily movement. But somebody has been left out: the agent. As Davidson himself concedes:

> Some causes have no agents. Among these agentless causes are the states and changes of state in persons which, because they are reasons as well as causes, constitute certain events free and intentional actions. (1963, 19)

In this story about agency, nobody does anything. Rather, as Velleman (1992b) suggests, "[p]sychological and physiological events take place inside a person, but the person serves merely as the arena for these events: he takes no active part" (461). This shortcoming needs to be mended. Improving it does not necessarily require to regard the agent as an irreducible element in an account of agency; so it does not require the appeal to sui generis "agent causation". But it requires at least that some mental state can take the functional role of the agent in action, which includes interactions with his reasons for action.[6] This mental state may just be a volition which is not just a function of the agent's reasons.[7] So volitions would serve the function of rendering the agent active in his intentional actions.

But an agent is only active in his intentional actions if his actions are integrated with his conscious thinking, even when he has appropriate volitions. Consider a cruel husband who intends to ridicule his wife's new dress, forms the appropriate volitions and executes them. However, this man is a self-deceiver: He does not believe that he has such an intention, nor that he intentionally offends his wife. Such a man may, perhaps prompted by the subsequent row with his

---

5 Volitions need not provide reasons of their own, but may support already existing reasons in future decisions. Therefore, this proposal does not yet lead to familiar boot-strapping problems.

6 See (Velleman 1992b, 463).

7 Velleman claims that the meta-desire to act in accordance with reasons takes this role. However, I believe but cannot argue here, nothing short of volitions will suffice his own criteria.

wife, reflect on his own behaviour and notice that some of its aspects cannot be explained by his intention merely, say, to give honest feedback. This may force him to the conclusion that he both intended to insult his wife and that he did so intentionally.

Such a man is not active in his intentional action. What this man announces as his intention is one thing, what he intends is another. His intention is formed, broken down into volitions and executed without his awareness.[8] He only learns of his intention and corresponding volitions by reflecting on his action. But what he announces as his volitions *after* reflecting on his action he does not announce with any distinctive authority. After all, his wife has the same epistemic warrant for her opinion about her husband's volition.

The problem with this is not just that this man's volition occurs somewhere out of sight of his conscious thinking, but that his intentions are immune to his conscious thinking because they run out of sight of his consciousness.[9] The man consciously only sees reasons for giving his wife honest feedback, not for offending her, but still he forms the intention to ridicule her dress. His consciously held reasons are not merely outweighed by his unkind inclinations. Rather, they do not even get a grip on the formation of his intention to offend, because this formation takes place entirely without his acknowledgment. He cannot reason against offending his wife because he is not aware that there is any possible intention to reason against. Such a man is not only irrational because he deceives himself about his will. He is also reduced to a mere bystander of his intentional action, because his action is disconnected from the influence of his conscious thinking. So even though the cruel self-deceiver has the right volitions, he is passive in his action. Therefore, an agent's being active requires the integration of his action with his conscious thinking, even when he has appropriate volitions. Volitions can hence only render the agent active in his action if they derive from an intention that is embedded in the agent's conscious thinking. This, it seems, is only the case if an agent knows his intention in a distinctively first-personal way. In what follows, I will attempt to spell out why this is so and what this first-personal way of knowing looks like.

---

8 A subtlety: Moore suggests that not only volitions, but also intentions are mental states in their own right. I do not share this view about intentions, but cannot argue against it here. Still, even if intentions are not mental states in their own right, I will argue below that they can be known in a distinctively first-personal way.

9 Compare (Moran 2001, 123).

3 Knowing One's Intentions

Why do agents not know their intentions just like everyone else knows them? The suggestion that they do looks like a non-starter. According to Ginet (1990), forming intentions (including volitions) is an exercise of one's agency, which is accompanied by immediate awareness of it, an "actish phenomenal quality" (13).[10] Evidence for the existence of this phenomenal quality is supposedly found in an agent's high reliability to correctly distinguish his intentional bodily movements from bodily movements as brought about by external neurological manipulation. But even without immediate phenomenal awareness, prospects look dim for the suggestion that agents know their intentions like everyone else does. I argued above that if an agent does not know his intention from a distinctively first-personal point of view, he is not active in his intentional action, despite having the appropriate volitions.

So volitions can only serve their purpose – rendering an agent active in his intentional actions – if they derive from an intention that the agent can know in a distinctively first-personal way. This does not mean that agents cannot make reflective discoveries about their intentions like the cruel man in our example. But such self-discoveries cannot be the normal case. A global failure in an agent's direct awareness of his intentions would not only lead to their isolation from his conscious reasoning, but his resulting actions could only be called intentional in an impaired sense of the word, because they would lack the agent's active participation. This might even lead to a psychopathological diagnosis.[11] Therefore, the knowledge requirement does not only demand knowledge of one's intentional actions, but also first-personal knowledge of intentions.

This can be captured in the knowledge requirement by a condition of simultaneity. The requirement, in the above form, demands concurrent knowledge of present intentional actions. By extending this to the demand for concurrent knowledge of intentions, reflective self-discovery is excluded as a way of meeting the knowledge requirement. Here is why. There must be something on which to reflect in order to make such self-discoveries. Even if such reflection does not take place in a 'cool hour', but more immediately in the heat of the action, the agent needs a basis for his reflection. But if intentions are only known from action – even if they are known merely from the earliest stages of the action – then they cannot simultaneously cause the action and be known by the agent.

---

10 See also (M. S. Moore 1993, 151).
11 See (M.S. Moore 1984, ch.11).

Agents have to know their own intentions in a way that is different from how everyone else knows them. Different in what way? If knowledge of intentions is only based on observational self-discovery, this undermines the intentionality of an action, because it renders the agent passive in his action. It excludes the agent from active participation by isolating his intentions from his conscious reasoning. Therefore, the relation of this knowledge to the agent's conscious reasoning is the pertinent difference: An agent's knowledge of his intentions must be directly responsive to his conscious practical reasoning. This makes the agent's knowledge privileged because of his agency towards his own intentions – no one else can directly change or maintain this agent's intentions on the basis of what he takes to be reasons for action. The kind of privilege relevant for our purposes is hence an essentially practical one, as opposed to the more theoretical privilege often associated with avowals of one's mental states.

How can agents have this privileged knowledge under a functionalist conception of intentions? Functionalism specifies mental states by their causal roles. This suggests to construe the relation between intentions and knowledge of them as causal. One way in which this relation might be established is that intentions are coupled with the experience of the actish phenomenal quality mentioned above, on the basis of which agents form beliefs about their own intentions.

Does the functionalist version of privileged knowledge meet the requirement for first-personal knowledge of intentions? On the functionalist construal, the relation between intentions and knowledge about them is contingent. As Moore (1993, 161) observes:

> There is no necessary link of subjective experience to functional states, since the nature of such states is given by their functional roles and not by their accessibility to consciousness.

However, there is a necessary connection between intentions and first-personal knowledge about them, as argued above (p. 256): Without knowledge of one's intentions that is directly responsive to an agent's conscious thinking, his intentions are immune to his conscious reasoning. Though such rationally isolated intentions are psychologically possible, as in the above example of the self-deceptive husband, they are irrational. Therefore, having first-personal knowledge of one's intentions is a requirement of rationality – it may not be strictly necessary, but it is *rationally* necessary.

The functionalist construal, however, does not capture the rational significance of an agent's knowledge of his intentions. I argued above that this knowledge must be directly responsive to conscious practical reasoning. But being directly responsive in the relevant sense requires that consciously held reasons for action constitute reasons for belief about one's intention. If they are not, and reasons for action are one thing, but reasons for belief about one's intention another, then it is possible that an agent finds reasons to believe that he has an intention to φ although he consciously sees only reasons not to φ. If this agent's belief is knowledge, then the intention contained in this knowledge – the intention to φ – is isolated from the agent's conscious practical reasoning, because his conscious practical reasoning only speaks against φ-ing.

Although such a case follows the letter of the knowledge requirement, it neglects its spirit: The agent knows his intention, but he does not know it in the way that is rationally required for intentional action. Now even if intentions cause knowledge about them, as the functionalist suggests, this does not yield the required notion of knowledge of one's intention, unless this knowledge is also directly responsive to reasons for action. If this knowledge is directly responsive to reasons for action, then it does not matter whether intentions cause knowledge about them or not. An agent's knowledge of his intentions is not first-personal in virtue of its causal relation to his intentions. It is first-personal in virtue of being formed on the basis of what the agent takes to be reasons for action.

4 Knowing One's Intentional Actions

If an agent acts intentionally, he has reasons-responsive knowledge of his intentions. But what about his knowledge of his intentional actions?

One way to extend knowledge of intentions to knowledge of intentional actions is to claim that agents intentionally do whatever they think they do on the basis of their intentions. What actually happens around the agent is irrelevant, because the essential thing in action is the intention or the derived volition.[12] Actions, then, are only mental events. But this is no viable option in legal contexts. For firstly, it would undermine the existence of unintentional actions where an agent does something without having the corresponding intentions. If an action is essentially a kind of intention, then it does no longer make sense to regard the agent as doing something for which he lacks an intention. Consequently, there could be no legal liability for unintentional actions, for instance in cases of negligence. Furthermore, this view would render the physical elements of an offence completely irrelevant for its assessment. The corresponding ethical theory of

12 Anscombe (1957, 52) discusses and rejects a related view as one that Wittgenstein might have had in the *Tractatus*.

which such assessment would be based[13] would have to be an extreme form of an agent-relative view in which nothing but intentions count for moral blameworthiness – causation would not matter at all. At least Moore rejects this view explicitly.[14] Finally, the legal knowledge requirement explicitly includes not only knowledge of intention, but also of the physical elements of an offence.[15] Therefore, we should refrain from this way of extending knowledge of intentions to knowledge of actions.

But how then would an agent's knowledge of his intentional actions on Moore's volitional causal theory look like? In his view, actions are those bodily movements that are caused by volitions. So in knowing his intentional actions, an agent knows his volitions, his bodily movements and that the volitions cause the movements. As argued above, an agent's knowledge of his intentions, and presumably of the derived volitions as well, should be privileged to meet the knowledge requirement. His bodily movements are probably known to him by his proprioception and observation, since only in this way the agent can know that none of the causal chains concerned are cut, that he indeed moves his body.

Does this conception meet the knowledge requirement? I will argue that it does not, because agents are rationally required to have non-observational and non-proprioceptive knowledge of their intentional actions. Consequently, I shall suggest that Moore's volitional theory does not satisfy the knowledge requirement for actions.

The conception considered here is that agents know their own intentions and volitions with privilege and the effects of their volitions by proprioception and observation, where the latter is without privilege – anyone can, in principle, see whether bodily movements occur and have certain effects.[16] There is a somewhat similar view that Anscombe discusses in her *Intention*. The view she considers is that "[...] what one knows as intentional action is only the intention, or possibly also the bodily movement; and [...] the rest is known by observation to be the *result*, which was also willed in the intention" (1957, 51–2). She continues:

> But that is a mad account; for the only sense I can give to 'willing' is that in which I might stare at something and will it to move. People sometimes say that one can get one's arm to move by an act of will but not a matchbox; but if they mean 'Will a matchbox to move and

13 According to Moore, at least, legal assessment needs moral grounds. See, for example, (M. S. Moore 2009, 20–1).

14 See (M. S. Moore, 2009, 36–41).

15 See (Wessels 2009, 87).

16 Falvey (2000) labels this position the "two-factor" view and opposes it to Anscombe's "one-factor" view.

> it won't', the answer is 'If I will my arm to move in that way, it won't', and if they mean 'I can move my arm but not the matchbox' the answer is that I can move the matchbox – nothing easier. (1957, 52)

The "mad account" under consideration resembles Moore's theory. On his view, the bodily movements that are actions are the effect of the agent's volitions, which are a species of intention and, as I argued above, need to be derived from an intention known in a distinctively first-personal way. Does the possibility of proprioceptive knowledge of one's bodily movements in Moore's account make a relevant difference that Anscombe's objection neglects? Like Hursthouse (2000, 103) and Moran (2004, 48), I do not think that it does, for reasons I will point out below.

So if Anscombe's argument against the "mad account" is relevant for our question, then what is her argument? She seems to think that if an agent only knows his intentional action by observation, then we can only speak of him as 'willing' his action at best in a forced, artificial sense. This sense, if not outright implausible, is at least disconnected from the agent acting intentionally. But why should that be?

Anscombe's argument, set out below, is based on a distinction between what has come to be called "directions of fit" of a propositional attitude.[17] She (1957, 56–7) illustrates this distinction with her famous example of a man going around town with a shopping list. If he fails to bring home some of the items on the list, his action is mistaken, but not the list. She contrasts this with a detective following this man and making a record of the things he buys. If the detective's record diverges from what the man buys, the mistake is in the record, not in the man's purchases. So if the detective's record is to be knowledge of the man's actions, it has to be what Anscombe calls speculative knowledge, knowledge that "must be something that is judged as such by being in accordance with the facts. The facts, reality, are prior, and dictate what is to be said, if it is knowledge" (56–7). She suggests that this knowledge is knowledge by observation, and contrasts it with an agent's practical knowledge that he has in intention. So, presumably, the man's knowledge of what items he buys, if he buys them intentionally, is supposed to be practical rather than speculative. On the

---

17 "Directions of fit" is not Anscombe's own term, but is now commonly used to refer to Anscombe's distinction. For a more detailed account of the origin of this notion, see (Humberstone 1992). "Directions of fit" is of course a metaphor, and I will assume throughout that this metaphor can be sufficiently spelled out in non-metaphorical terms. This assumption is not trivial. For some attempts to vindicate it, see (Platts 1979), (Smith 1987) and (Velleman 1992a).

basis of the distinction between directions of fit, Anscombe's argument is, I believe, the following:

(1) If an agent's knowledge of his intentional action is observational, then it must fit with the facts.
(2) The facts must fit with an agent's knowledge of his intentional action.
So an agent's knowledge of his intentional action is not only observational.

This argument presupposes that an attitude cannot have both directions of fit, and so that knowledge cannot be both speculative and practical. It also presupposes that the concept of knowledge, or perhaps its subjective component of belief, is a normative notion that lends itself to characterisation in terms of what it "must" do or what the facts "must" do with regard to it. Both presuppositions are controversial, but I am going to side-step these debates here and concentrate on premise (2) in order to spell out Anscombe's "mad account" argument.

Why must the facts fit with an agent's knowledge of his intentional action? Let us make this question more precise. What sense of 'must' does Anscombe aim at in premise (2)? She thinks that without an agent's non-observational knowledge of his action, the latter is not intentional. The knowledge is the "cause of what it understands"[18]. So the facts 'must' fit with an agent's knowledge of his intentional action, because if they do not, then the action is not intentional. Being known in a certain way, in Anscombe's view, is an essential ingredient in intentional action. Therefore, practical knowledge is supposed to fix the descriptions under which an action is intentional.[19]

Still, our question remains: Why must an agent have knowledge of his intentional action that fixes the descriptions under which the action is intentional? To start with, it seems odd to say that it is an agent's knowledge that fixes these descriptions. It would be more natural to think that an agent's intention does this: An agent φs intentionally if his action is the execution of his intention to φ. But as Bratman (1987, 113–6, 122–3) points out, there are intentional actions that are not intended. An anticipated but unintended side-effect of one's intended action is one example, intentional success in one of several, jointly unintended attempts is another. So intentions do not seem to fix the descriptions under which an action is intentional in all cases. But anticipated side-effects and attempts are known to the agent. So Bratman's examples might even support Anscombe's claim that practical knowledge fixes these descriptions.

18 (Anscombe 1957, 87).
19 See (Hursthouse 2000, 103) and (Moran 2004, 54).

But not all knowledge can determine the descriptions under which an action is intentional. An agent may unintentionally be φ-ing and know it, but his knowledge that he is φ-ing does not render his φ-ing intentional. So which knowledge sets the descriptions under which an action is intentional? Consider actions that are both intentional and intended. Here, the intention fixes these descriptions: If your action is the execution of your intention, but you do not do what you intend, you act unintentionally. If the man in Anscombe's example goes around town with the intention to buy the things on his list and he does not buy all of them, for example because he forgets one of the items on the list or confuses it with something else, then he acts unintentionally.[20] In such a case, the intention fixes the description under which the action is intentional. This is just what Anscombe's practical knowledge is supposed to do. But it is not sufficient for knowledge to be practical that the action is known under the same descriptions under which it is intended.[21] An agent may intend to φ, know that he is φ-ing, but still φ unintentionally – agents may unintentionally achieve what they intend and know it.[22] The man in Anscombe's example may intend to buy all the items on his list, he makes only the mistake to confuse the Grana Padano on the list with Parmesan, but what he thinks is Parmesan is really Grana Padano, only wrongly labelled, so that he manages to buy all the items on his list, only unintentionally. Opening the package labelled "Parmesan", he discovers that he has bought all the items on his list. But such knowledge cannot be practical, because the agent's action is not intentional. What's missing is a tighter integration of the agent's knowledge of his action with what makes the action intentional under a certain description in the first place, i. e. the intention. To have practical knowledge, the agent not only needs to know his action under a description under which he intends it, he also needs to acquire this knowledge in a way that fixes the description under which the action is known also as one under which it is intended. Practical knowledge, then, must be knowledge *by intending*. If Anscombe is right that there is such a thing as practical knowledge, then intending must be a way of knowing one's action.

---

20 The consequent only follows if the agent does not change the list, or some of the things were not to be had anyway. See (Anscombe 1957, 56).

21 "Known under a description": There may be several true descriptions of my action, but I need not know all of them. Characteristically, if I do not, then my action will neither be intentional under this description. Contra (M. S. Moore 2009, 348), this does not carry a commitment to a coarse-grained view of action individuation. See (Anscombe 1979, 222–3).

22 Deviating from the example that follows, it may even be that the agent does not realise that he acts unintentionally. See (Hursthouse 2000, 101).

Even in intentional but unintended φ-ing, the agent has an intention, just not one for φ-ing, as Bratman (1987, 122–3) admits. In forming such a further intention, the agent may notice that his action will have unwelcome side-effects but form the intention nevertheless, or he may see it as maximising his chances of success to form an intention to attempt several things at the same time that cannot all succeed. So even the unintended actions with which Bratman is concerned can be part of the practical reasoning on which an agent's intention is based. As I am going to sketch below, such actions can therefore also be known by intending.[23]

If intending is a way of knowing that covers one's intentional actions, then it is possible to explain why and in what sense agents are required to know their intentional actions. I argued above that if an agent has an intention, he is rationally required to know it. If he is rationally required to know his intention and intending is a way of knowing one's intentional actions, then the agent is rationally required to know his intentional actions. More precisely, the agent is rationally required to know his intentional actions *by intending*. To clarify: My proposal is not that the normativity of the rational requirement to know one's intentions is somehow transmitted to knowledge of one's intentional actions via knowledge by intending. My proposal is that, given that intending is a way of knowing that covers one's intentional actions, knowledge of one's intention constitutes knowledge of one's intentional action.

However, I assumed throughout that intending is indeed such a way of knowing. How can this be? Intending to φ does not yet guarantee that one is φ-ing – one may simply not be φ-ing yet, or something might go wrong so that one does not manage to φ at all. There are, roughly, two ways in which intending can be a way of knowing, divided along the lines of Anscombe's distinction between directions of fit. The first is one in which beliefs about one's intentional actions are made to fit the facts: Because of the epistemic situation the agent is in, his intention is a sound basis for forming reliably true beliefs about one's intentional actions. In other words, in favourable epistemic situations, intentions are reliable evidence of corresponding intentional actions. This is, I take it, the gist of Grice's (1971) inferentialist approach and Paul's (2009) neo-Gricean account, as well as of Falvey's (2000) view. The second way in which intending can be a way of knowing is one in which the facts are made to fit the agent's beliefs about his intentional actions: Because the agent exercises his capacity to do what, on the basis of his intention, he believes he

23 Though ex hypothesi not by intending *these actions*, because these actions are not intended.

does, he reliably makes his belief true and thus[24] knowledge. This, in my view, is the core of Velleman's (2000), Moran's (2004) and Setiya's (2008) proposals and, arguably, Anscombe's own account. I said above that the distinction of these two ways how intending can be a way of knowing is only rough, because there are accounts that reject the need for an epistemic warrant for practical knowledge.[25]

I will not try here to decide between one approach or the other. However, the above discussion suggests that taking intentions as evidence of intentional actions does not suffice for practical knowledge. I argued in section 3 that an agent's knowledge of his intentions must be responsive to apparent reasons. If the above suggestion is correct that knowledge of one's intention constitutes knowledge of one's intentional action, given that intending is a way of knowing that covers one's intentional actions, then knowledge of one's intentional actions must also be reasons-responsive to be practical. But if intentions are taken as evidence on which knowledge of one's action is based, then this knowledge is not responsive to apparent reasons for action. It is only responsive to apparent reasons for belief – the evidence of one's intentional action – and these apparent reasons for belief are not also apparent reasons for action. So, if the argument of section 3 is correct, then taking one's intention as evidence for one's intentional action undermines one's taking an active part in one's intentional action. This suggests that the second kind of approach is more plausible: Intending is a way of knowing because agents make their beliefs knowledge through their capacity to act in the way they intend. Here, the agent's action does the heavy epistemic lifting, not the intention or belief formation. This explains why this way of knowing is restricted to one's intentional actions. It also enables us to see how intentional but unintended actions can be known by intending. As argued above, such potential actions can figure in an agent's practical reasoning that concludes with the formation of an intention. In executing this intention, the agent can knowingly make true not only the description under which he intends his action, but also the descriptions under which he merely anticipates it or the ones that are only a part of an overarching intention.

We are now in a better position to understand why an action is not intentional if an agent knows it only by observation. An agent is rationally required to know his intentional action by intending it. If he does not, then either he is irrational in the sense of the self-deceiver who, at most, knows his action like a by-

24 This does not follow trivially. Rather, this conception of practical knowledge needs to explain how we can speak of knowledge without evidence, or alternatively explain how evidence figures in practical knowledge without rendering it speculative knowledge. See (Velleman 2007, xxi – xxv). I will not discuss these issues here.

25 At least this is how I read (Rödl 2007, ch.2).

stander, or he does not act intentionally, because the action is disconnected from an intention. If the agent knows his action only by observation, he does not know it by intending. For knowledge by observation is not responsive to apparent reasons for action, while knowledge by intending is.[26] So if a rational agent only has observational knowledge of his action, then his action is not intentional under the description under which he knows it.

This conception of practical knowledge also shows, with regard to premise (1) of Anscombe's argument, that the relevant point about the agent's practical knowledge is not merely that it is non-observational, but that it is based on the agent's intention. This is why Anscombe thinks that the action is unintentional not only if the agent knows it solely by observation, but also if it is solely known or believed by "inference, hearsay, superstition or anything that knowledge or opinion are ever based on" (1957, 50). Since these ways of knowing are not based on the agent's own intention, the knowledge they provide is not the one an agent is rationally required to have of his intentional actions.

The point carries over to proprioceptive knowledge. An agent can have proprioceptive knowledge of bodily movements that are not intended, like a twitch or reflex movement. So, proprioceptive knowledge of the action is not acquired by intending. Therefore, it does not qualify as practical knowledge, but is rather speculative in that it has to fit with the facts. As Moran observes:

> Even if immediate, and not grounded on observational evidence, the claim that one's knee is bent is still something corrected by the fact of one's straightened leg. Hence the immediate knowledge of one's bodily position cannot be an example of what Anscombe means by "practical knowledge" [...]. (2004, 48)

However, the fact that if proprioceptive beliefs and actual performance diverge, the mistake is in the belief, is only a consequence of proprioceptive knowledge not being knowledge by intending. Otherwise, it would still be open for a friend of proprioceptive practical knowledge to argue that if one believes, with straightened legs, that one's knee is bent, then this belief is either not arrived at by proprioception or something is amiss with one's leg, so that this example would not show that proprioceptive knowledge is not knowledge with which the facts have to fit.

26 See (Anscombe 1957, 53). For some actions, observational knowledge is mandatory: Even if, as Anscombe claims, writing is done without the eyes, reading is not. But though one needs to look to read, one needs to look at the text, not at *oneself*. It is only the latter, observational self-directed knowledge, that is under attack here.

Back to the "mad account". Agents cannot know the results of their intentions and volitions only by observation, because these results are their actions and rational agents cannot know their actions only by observation unless they do not intend them. In such a case, their "willing" or "intending" has nothing to do with willing or intending as it figures in intentional action. Any sense then given to "willing" or "intending" has to be a completely artificial one that is detached from action. The only sense left is one in which "I might stare at something and will it to move" (Anscombe 1957, 52). But that is indeed mad, to call something a "willing" or "intending" that is not a willing or intending.

These results for the "mad account" show that a view like Moore's volitional causal theory does not meet the knowledge requirement for actions. For the requirement is that a rational agent does not have exclusively observational or proprioceptive knowledge of his intentional action. But this is just the conception that, as argued above, best fits a volitional theory like Moore's. So agents do not only know their own intentions with privilege, they also know their actions in a way that is different from that available to everyone else: Only the agent can know his action by intending, because only the agent can make his action intentional under a description by executing his intention. As Moran (2004, 68) points out, this yields a practical sort of privilege, not the epistemic one usually associated with knowledge of one's mental states. The privilege of practical knowledge is not, Moran argues, marked primarily by the agent being infallible about his intentional actions, but by the fact that without the agent's non-observational knowledge of his action, what others could observe would not be an intentional action. However, I have argued above that the pertinent privilege in knowledge of one's intentions is also practical rather than epistemic: Only the agent can change or maintain both his intention and his knowledge about his intention on the basis of what he takes to be reasons for action. Since his practical reasoning is also the basis for his intentions, the privilege in his knowledge of his intentions and the privilege in his knowledge of his intentional actions have the same source.

More generally, the knowledge requirement for actions casts doubt on the plausibility of a purely causal theory of action. On such a theory, actions are intentional in virtue of being caused in a certain way by certain mental states. The mental states in question are typically propositional attitudes, and the descriptions under which the action is intentional is then determined by the propositional content of these attitudes.[27] But as Hursthouse (2000 102) observes, an agent's knowledge of his action then only tracks the causal relations underlying intentional action. It is not the agent's knowledge of his actions that determines the descriptions under which his action is intentional, but only the propositional content of the causally efficient mental states. But the agent is rationally required to have knowledge that determines these descriptions. Therefore, causal action theory does not capture this rational requirement to know one's intentional actions.

The only way for friends of the causal theory to circumvent this problem is to claim that the mental state that causes intentional action is practical knowledge. But even if such a proposal is developed into a causal account of practical knowledge, the causal efficacy of practical knowledge does not capture the rational requirement associated with it. In any case, Moore does certainly not adopt a causal theory of practical knowledge. To the contrary, he explicitly eschews what might be a first step in this direction, namely regarding volitions as explanatorily self-referential states.[28] He thinks that such a move would render volitions more complex than they seem to be. One might raise the same doubts about practical knowledge. We do not seem to ordinarily think that it is the cause of what it understands. However, the parallelism between self-referential volitions and practical knowledge does not carry very far. While the former are supposed to have self-referential content, the content of practical knowledge is not specified as being caused (in any sense) by this knowledge. Nevertheless, we seem to be aware of the fact that practical knowledge is necessary for intentional action when we refuse the request to give the reasons for our actions, and thereby deny that we act intentionally, by the answer "I was not aware that I was doing that".[29] Another possible Moorean worry with practical knowledge can also be dissolved quickly: Practical knowledge intuitively is, at least partly, a kind of belief. But this seems to him an implausible candidate for a state necessary for intentional action, because even if an agent believes hat some act of his is desirable or that he will do it, this it is consistent with his decision not to act and his subsequent refraining from acting in this way.[30] However, I have argued above that practical knowledge is knowledge by intending, and that this way of knowing is not consistent with a failure to intend the action known.

27 See, for example, (Davidson 1963, 7): "To know a primary reason why someone acted as he did is to know an intention with which the action was done".
28 See (M. S. Moore 1993, 159–60).
29 See (Anscombe 1957, 11).
30 See (M. S. Moore 1993, 120, 145–6).

So does the law require a specific philosophy of action? Yes, it calls for a philosophy of action in which rational agents have practical knowledge of their intentional actions. But Moore's volitional action theory does not meet this requirement. What is needed instead is an account of intentional agency that incorporates the agent's knowledge of his action.[31]

References

Anscombe, G. E. M. (1957). *Intention.* Cambridge, MA: Harvard University Press.

Anscombe, G. E. M. (1979, May). Under a Description. *Noûs, 13*(2), 219 – 233.

Bratman, Michael (1987). *Intentions, Plans, and Practical Reason* (Reprint 1999 ed.). Stanford, CA: CSLI Publications.

Davidson, Donald (1963). Actions, Reasons and Causes. In *Essays on Actions and Events* (2nd ed., p. 3 – 20). Oxford: Oxford University Press, 2001.

Davidson, Donald (1969). How is Weakness of the Will Possible? In *Essays on Actions and Events* (2nd ed., p. 21 – 42). Oxford: Oxford University Press, 2001.

Falvey, Kevin (2000). Knowledge in Intention. *Philosophical Studies, 99*, 21 – 44.

Feinberg, Joel (1967). Action and Responsibility. In M. Black & W. P. Alston (Eds.), *Philosophy in America* (2nd ed., p. 134 – 160). Ithaca, New York: Cornell University Press.

Ginet, Carl (1990). *On Action.* Cambridge: Cambridge University Press.

Grice, H. Paul (1971). Intention and Uncertainty. *Proceedings of the British Academy, 57*, 263 – 279.

Humberstone, Lloyd (1992). Directions of Fit. *Mind, 101*(401), 59 – 83.

Hursthouse, Rosalind (2000). Intention. In Roger Teichmann (Ed.), *Logic, Cause and Action: Essays in Honour of Elizabeth Anscombe* (p. 83 – 105). Cambridge: Cambridge University Press.

Moore, Michael S. (1984). *Law and Psychiatry: Rethinking the Relationship.* Cambridge: Cambridge University Press.

Moore, Michael S. (1993). *Act and Crime.* Oxford: Oxford University Press.

Moore, Michael S. (2009). *Causation and Responsibility.* Oxford: Oxford University Press.

Moran, Richard (2001). *Authority and Estrangement.* Princeton, NJ: Princeton University Press.

Moran, Richard (2004). Anscombe on 'Practical Knowledge'. In John Hyman & Helen Steward (Eds.), *Agency and Action (Royal Institute of Philosophy Supplement: 55)* (p. 43 – 68). Cambridge: Cambridge University Press.

Paul, Sarah K. (2009). How We Know What We're Doing. *Philosophers' Imprint, 9*(11), 1 – 24.

Platts, Mark (1979). *Ways of Meaning.* London: Routledge and Kegan Paul.

Rödl, Sebastian (2007). *Self-Consciousness.* Cambridge, MA: Harvard University Press.

Setiya, Kieran (2008). Practical Knowledge. *Ethics, 118*, 388 – 409.

31 I am indebted to Rüdiger Bittner and Erasmus Mayr for generous and extensive comments. An earlier version of this essay was presented at the "Causation and Responsibility in the Law" workshop at RWTH Aachen. I thank the audience, especially Michael Moore, for helpful discussion.

Smith, Michael (1987). The Humean Theory of Motivation. *Mind, 96* (381), 36–61.

Velleman, J. David (1992a). The Guise of the Good. *Noûs, 26* (1), 3–26.

Velleman, J. David (1992b). What Happens When Someone Acts? *Mind, 101* (403), 461–468.

Velleman, J. David (2000). *The Possibility of Practical Reason.* Oxford: Oxford University Press.

Velleman, J. David (2007). *Practical Reflection (The David Hume Series).* Stanford, CA: CSLI Publications.

Watson, Gary (1977). Skepticism about Weakness of Will. *The Philosophical Review, 86,* 316–339.

Wessels, Johannes (2009). *Strafrecht allgemeiner Teil: Die Straftat und ihr Aufbau* (39th ed.). Heidelberg: C.F. Müller.

Erasmus Mayr*

The Problem of Consequential Waywardness: Between Internalism and Externalism about Intentional Agency

In his book *Causation and Responsibility*, Michael Moore has rightly warned against the danger of failing to properly distinguish between metaphysical questions of causation and questions of culpability, commenting ironically on the tendency of some legal philosophers to treat "increased culpability (...) as a kind of aphrodisiac to causation, enhancing the latter's reach and power" (2009, 135). In the following, I am going to address a topic which can also invite confusions of this kind, namely the problem of consequential waywardness in the philosophy of action. In its most important form, this problem concerns the causal connection between what people do 'directly' and more distant consequences of their actions, and the impact of certain unforeseen 'anomalies' or 'freak occurrences' within this connection for the assessment of an action as intentional or unintentional.

While the problem of consequential waywardness is not a problem about causation – or so I will argue – it touches many questions which Michael Moore has been dealing with in his writings over the years.[1] The problem, however, will not merely concern me for its own sake, nor because, as I am going to argue, it is a problem which standard causalist theories of action are unable to cope with. More fundamentally, I believe, this problem highlights a general difficulty – a fundamental theoretical choice which is required – in action theory, namely how externalist or internalist an account of intentional agency can and must be. Dealing with the problem of consequential waywardness requires, as I will argue, that one accepts a substantial degree of externalism with regard to the assessment of intentionality of actions, since this assessment not only depends on the present psychological states of the agent or causal processes taking place during the action, but also on its normative background. If this is right,

* A large part of this paper is based on (and some passages are taken from) my Ph.D. Thesis *Understanding Human Agency*, sect. 3.1., though I have, in some respects, significantly changed my views since then.

1 In particular, there are close connections to questions about the foreseeability criterion for proximate causation and about moral luck, which Michael Moore has addressed at length in (1997), ch. 5 and 8.

then this will clearly have important consequences for assessments of responsibility as well, at least on the level of culpability assessments.

I will start off by briefly sketching the central elements of today's most influential account of agency – to one version of which Michael Moore, too, subscribes – , before turning to one particular kind of challenge to this account, the so-called problem of causal waywardness, of which one sub-type will concern me in the following, namely consequential waywardness. I will go on to discuss and criticise the standard approach to this kind of problem within contemporary philosophy of action, the so-called 'action-plan' analysis, before briefly turning to two alternative attempts to deal with the problem. As these latter attempts, as well, will turn out to be unsuccessful, I will then consider what one may call a 'normative-externalist' treatment of these cases, which takes them to show that intentional agency is a notion which cannot be analysed in purely non-normative and internalist, especially causal, terms. The resulting view may appear both (1) 'poor' in explanatory value, and (2) overly 'externalist', but, as I am going to argue, it allows us to deal with some of the problems which have proved fatal to the causalist analysis, and it provides just the right measure of 'externalism' about intentional agency.

1 The Standard Picture of Human Agency

While the picture of human agency which is still predominant in action theory today traces its ancestry back to the 17th century and to philosophers like Thomas Hobbes, it was only through the work of philosophers such as Donald Davidson and Alvin Goldman in the 1960's and 1970's that it acquired its contemporary status as *the* default theory of agency (esp. Davidson 1980, Goldman 1970). Roughly, this picture goes like this: Human actions involve bodily movements of the agent, and in order for a bodily movement to qualify as an action, it must be caused by the right mental antecedents. Thomas Hobbes had thought that these right mental antecedents must simply be desires – or 'appetites' – of the agent which 'constitute his will', but Donald Davidson has convinced the majority of theorists of agency that these antecedents must include both a desire and a belief of the agent, namely a desire to perform an action of kind X, and a belief that by moving his body in a specific way, e.g. by raising his arm, he will perform an action of this kind. The belief-desire pair, which, on the Davidsonian account, is required for an intentional action, plays a twofold role: On the one hand, it must cause the bodily movement, and on the other hand, it must 'rationalize' this movement, by providing the premises of a practical syllogism which has, as its conclusion, the verdict that a movement of this kind should be performed. If both these conditions are fulfilled, i.e. if the bodily movement is caused by a belief-desire pair with the right kind of content, the ensuing movement qualifies as an action.

Philosophers after Davidson, who have followed his general approach, have usually postulated additional elements along the causal pathway between belief and desire, on the one hand, and the bodily movement, on the other. In particular, prior intentions as 'coordinating' mental states (cf. Bratman 1987), and immediate intentions or volitions as 'executive' mental states have widely been accepted as states which must obtain and play a causal role whenever an intentional action is performed (cf. e.g. Searle 1983, Moore 1993). The version of the standard model which I am going to address in the following,[2] will, in consequence, be one that considers an action to be a bodily movement[3] which is caused by a volition to perform a bodily movement of this kind; the volition, in its turn, being caused by a prior intention.

The ensuing picture of human agency is, crucially, both internalist[4] and non-normative: For it only relies on 'local'[5] psychological, physical and causal facts about the agent himself, which obtain during the time of the action, and it is developed on the assumption that we can analyse (intentional) agency in such purely factual, non-normative terms.[6] Where normative aspects come in, on this assumption, is only during the evaluation and justification of actions, but not at the stage where we have to decide whether something qualifies as an action, or as an intentional action, in the first place.[7]

---

2 Without, however, subscribing to this account myself.

3 As Hornsby (1980), ch. 1, has famously pointed out, the term 'bodily movement' is used both in a transitive and an intransitive sense; this distinction is crucial when it comes to analyzing agency simpliciter, for then 'bodily movement' within the analysans could only be used in the intransitive sense, on pain of already presupposing an unanalyzed notion of agency. We can, however, leave this distinction aside here, since we will only be concerned with the analysis of intentional *non-basic* action, and can thus already presuppose that the underlying basic action is an (intentional) action.

4 This does not mean, though, that an adherent of this picture cannot be an externalist about the content of the mental states involved. The crucial point is, rather, that once the content of the mental states is fixed (somehow or other), the further explanation of (intentional) agency involving these states does not refer to (further) 'nonlocal' or normative facts.

5 I.e. it is internalist in the sense of 'local', not in the sense of only involving internal states of the agent (which would be absurd in the case of actions involving bodily movements and further results).

6 At least insofar as we can analyse the possession of the relevant mental states in those terms, that is – an assumption which would not have been shared by Davidson himself.

7 This view is very clearly illustrated, e.g., in Garcia's reaction to Harman's point that our view about whether the action performed is morally bad has implications for our judgement of

Two clarificatory remarks have to be added here: First, the introduction of an intention in this analyis ties agency to *intentional* agency. If, whenever a person acts, she must have an intention, it seems that an agent cannot act without (also) acting intentionally. And this latter is indeed just what philosophers like Davidson have thought.[8] What is important for our purpose is that this means that the analysis of action which we have just presented, can serve just as well as an analysis for intentional action – and it is intentional agency, rather than agency simpliciter, which is going to concern us here.

Second, so far we have only been talking about what qualifies a bodily movement as an (intentional) action, but it is far from clear whether all actions consist in bodily movements.[9] To keep things simple, I'll avoid any commitment on this latter question here, but I will, for the following, assume that all, or almost all, *basic* actions are bodily movements. The distinction between non-basic and basic actions turns on the fact that some actions are performed by performing other actions – e.g. a murderer kills his victim *by* shooting him, he shoots him *by* pulling the trigger of his gun etc. – , while other actions are not performed by doing something else, but directly. E.g. when I raise my arm, under normal circumstances, I don't do anything else in order to raise my arm, but simply raise it. Leaving aside cases of 'pure' mental actions, I will focus, in the following, just on those basic actions that are bodily movements.

How the connection between basic and non-basic actions is to be spelled out in general,[10] need not concern us here, for we can restrict our attention to one important kind of case, where the connection is causal:[11] I.e. where what the agent does directly[12] causes some further result – e.g., the murderer's moving

whether it was performed intentionally. For Garcia, in making the assessment of intentionality partly depend on an evaluative judgement about the action, Harman clearly "gets backwards the relation", Garcia (1990), 202.

8 Cf. Davidson (1971), 46.

9 The thesis that all actions are bodily movements, which was most famously defended by Davidson (1971), 49, is questionable on two counts: First, it depends on Davidson's view about the identity-conditions for actions, namely that when an agent performs a non-basic action by performing a basic action, the basic and the non-basic action are one and the same action; and second, it seems very hard to describe mental actions – such as intentionally doing a sum – as 'bodily movements' without overly stretching the meaning of the term.

10 Cf. Goldman (1970), 22ff., for the different forms in which a non-basic action can be 'generated' by a more basic one.

11 In Goldman's terms, cases of "causal generation", (1970), 22ff.

12 Some philosophers would deny that it is, strictly speaking, what the agent does directly that causes the further consequences, but rather the *result* of what he does directly; but we can set aside this distinction for the purpose of our discussion here.

his finger causes the trigger of his gun's to move, which, in turn, causes the gun's going off and the victim's being hit by the bullet.

When we restrict our attention to this class of non-basic actions, the following causalist analysis of intentional agency in non-basic actions seems prima facie plausible, given the general causalist view of intentional agency we have encountered earlier:

> (A) An agent intentionally brings about X iff X is caused by a basic action of his and he intends to bring about X.

2 The Problem of Causal Deviance

However, as philosophers familiar with the contemporary debates in the philosophy of action know only too well, none of the causalist analyses of intentional agency in basic and non-basic actions we have just sketched works in its original version.[13] For the mental antecedents may cause the bodily movement 'in the wrong way' – deviantly – , i.e. not in the way required for agency. For instance, the intention to move his finger in order to pull the trigger of his gun may so unnerve a would-be murderer that, from sheer nervousness, he starts trembling and jerks his finger against the trigger. The movement[14] of his finger is the movement he intended to produce, and it was caused by his intention; but, since agency requires control over the bodily movement in question, and since the causal pathway from intention to movement is, in this case, of a kind to preclude agential control by running through control-preempting nervousness, the agent did not perform an action of moving his finger. He would only have done so, had his intention caused the movement 'in the right way' – and the possibility of wayward or deviant causal chains shows that this extra requirement is indispensable.

The problem of causal deviance arises in different versions, which concern different aspects of the general causalist approach to intentional agency. One version concerns the pathway from the mental antecedents to the bodily movement, as in the example just described. When causal deviance occurs along this pathway, the ensuing behaviour of the agent doesn't qualify as an action (or an

---

13 Analysis (A) has also come under criticism from a different direction, namely as to whether foreseen, though not intended side-effects of an action count as being intentionally brought about. These cases have been discussed at length in Harman (1976) and Bratman (1987), and I will not go into them here.

14 'Movement' in the intransitive sense, if we use Hornsby's distinction, cf. fn. 3.

intentional action) at all. This kind of waywardness is usually called antecedential, or primary, waywardness. But, clearly, causal deviance can just as well occur on the causal path starting off from the basic action itself, i.e. on our earlier assumption, between the bodily movement, and the more 'distant' consequences of the agent's behaviour, as the following famous example by Davidson demonstrates (1973, 78): A murderer wants to shoot his victim in order to kill him. His shot misses the victim, but stampedes into action a horde of wild pigs which trample the victim to death. Even though the would-be murderer did something intentionally – shoot at his victim – which caused the result he intended to bring about – his victim's being killed – he did not intentionally kill the unfortunate victim, because the causal route to the intended result was too far off from anything he had foreseen, for the result to be, from his point of view, anything more than 'mere luck'.

Cases, where the causal deviance occurs on the causal pathway from the more basic action to the further result, are usually called cases of consequential or secondary waywardness.[15] They don't concern the basic causalist analysis of agency, but 'only' the analysis of *intentional* agency in *non-basic* action. While the problem of antecedential waywardness has also given rise to a very extensive philosophical literature,[16] it will only be the problem of consequential waywardness that will interest us here.[17]

In claiming, as I just did, that cases of consequential waywardness only concern the question of whether a non-basic action of the agent was performed intentionally, I have presupposed that, in these cases, it is neither in doubt that

15 Distinguishing between antecedential and consequential waywardness goes back to Brand (1984), 18.

16 Moore (1993), 159f., has advocated solving it by the requirement that the volition must proximately or directly cause the bodily movement when an action is performed.

17 In addition to antecendential and consequential waywardness, Mele has proposed a third category, tertiary waywardness (1987). This kind of waywardness occurs, he argues, when the agent makes a mistake prior to the action with the result that when he later does what he intends to do, he does so only by coincidence. E.g. take the case that I want to take the train to Frankfurt on the Main and board a train which is destined for Frankfurt on the Oder, because, out of complete ignorance of German geography, I don't know the difference between the two cities. To my very good fortune, however, and without my noticing it, the train is diverted to Frankfurt on the Main on this day. In this case, I didn't go to Frankfurt on the Main intentionally – my earlier mistake just, accidentally, turned out to be lucky. Cases of tertiary waywardness differ from cases of consequential waywardness, in that the causal deviance occurs on the causal pathway before the action; but, as with consequential waywardness, tertiary waywardness can threaten the causalist analysis of non-basic intentional action. For the latter reason, some of the things I am going to say will also concern the phenomenon of tertiary waywardness, though I will, explicitly, only be talking about consequential waywardness.

this action was performed by the agent at all, nor that he brought about the further result. This assumption may seem doubtful, especially when one considers these cases in the context of criminal law or law of torts. In German criminal law, for instance, some of the cases discussed as cases of consequential waywardness would be treated as raising questions of objective ascribability (*objektive Zurechenbarkeit*) of the result to the agent,[18] and denial of criminal responsibility would then rest on denying objective ascribability rather than *intentional* performance.

Furthermore, relying on a background theory of causal responsibility according to which a cause relevant for criminal responsibility must be a *proximate* cause of the effect, rather than a mere necessary factor, it might be argued that, at least in many cases of consequential waywardness, the agent does not even – in the relevant sense – cause the effect in question.[19] This kind of reasoning can appear especially plausible if one adopts a foreseeability test for proximate causes, i.e. claims that a defendant causes (in the sense relevant for legal responsibility) a certain harm only if the harm was foreseeable to him when he acted.[20] For once one adopts a foreseeability requirement for proximate causes, it may appear tempting to extend this requirement to the way in which the effect is brought about. Nonetheless, I think that the right place to deal with the problem of consequential waywardness is the topic of *intentional* agency (which means that, in criminal law, it will be a question of culpability rather than causation). For it is the *intentional* character of an action which is incompatible with the effect's being brought about merely by luck or 'by pure accident'. As far as the purely metaphysical question of causation is concerned, there is no parallel implication from the effect's being brought about 'by luck', from the agent's point of view, to its not being brought about by the agent at all. We can easily see this by reminding ourselves that the mere ignorance of the actually obtaining causal connections on the agent's part may turn the causal chain into a deviant one, without severing these connections themselves.

Accepting an implication from 'mere luck' to 'not caused by the agent at all' would amount to attributing to missing intentional control a 'negative' "aphrodisiac effect", which would be the counterpiece of the positive one Moore has so aptly mocked (2009, 136). The only independent systematic reason for denying

---

18 Namely those which involve extremely 'atypical' causal chains (*atypische Kausalverläufe*), cf. Wessels / Beulke (2011), 75 f.

19 Mitchell (1982) has proposed such a solution to the problem of antecedential causal deviance.

20 For a discussion and criticism of the foreseeability test cf. Moore (1997), ch. 8, and (2009), 98 f.

that, in cases of consequential waywardness, the agent – or defendant – , by his basic action, *caused* the effect in question, would be to consider all such cases as cases of intervening causation, where the additional unforeseen factors in the freak causal chain from basic action to further effect – i.e. in Davidson's example, the trampling of the herd of wild pigs – act as intervening causes which block the causal influence of the basic action itself. But even besides the fact that the legal doctrine of intervening causation has not gone unchallenged,[21] the cases we are considering here cannot, even on the traditional doctrine, be plausibly construed as cases of intervening causation. For they fail the condition generally accepted for intervening causes that these must not themselves be caused by the agent.[22] Looking at Davidson's case of the wild pigs, we easily see that this condition is not fulfilled, since the trampling of the wild pigs is itself caused by the agent's shot.

3 The Action-Plan Analysis of Consequential Waywardness

Given that the problem of consequential waywardness is a particular problem for the standard causalist analysis of *intentional* agency, how can an adherent of this approach react to this problem? Defenders of the standard approach have not been slow to propose modifications of the original analysis, (A), to deal with cases of consequential deviance, trying to spell out what it means that an effect is caused 'in the right way' by the agent's more basic action. While these modifications have included the introduction of new elements into the original account of intentional agency, they have tried to remain true to the central tenets of the internalist, non-normative approach to intentional agency: What makes behaviour an intentional action has to be spelled out in purely factual, non-normative terms and must include only 'local' factors about the agent and his action.[23]

21 For an overview and discussion cf. Moore (2009), part IV.

22 Cf. Moore (2009), 236 ff.

23 For the relevant sense of 'internal', cf. above p. 273. The 'locality' requirement will, necessarily, be construed somewhat more broadly for non-basic actions, because the relevant actions also involve the causal chains issuing from the agent's basic actions. But this does not undermine the main point that it will only be non-normative facts either about what happens during the time of the action (or shortly before) to the agent, or regarding the causal chain itself, that are considered as relevant for whether his action is intentional or not.

The by far most influential account of this kind is the so-called action-plan analysis. The core idea of this analysis, which goes back to Goldman and Gilbert Harman,[24] is that when an agent performs a non-basic action, he must have a more or less definite 'action-plan' about how he is going to perform this action, which includes (i) which basic actions he is going to perform, and (ii) how these basic actions are going to produce the more distant consequence he intends to bring about. This action-plan is usually thought to be part of the content of the agent's intention,[25] i.e. the intention is not just 'to do X', but 'to do X by doing Y, Z ...'. What goes wrong in cases of consequential waywardness, on this view, is that the agent, though bringing about the intended effect, fails to bring it about in accordance with this plan. E.g. in our earlier case, the would-be murderer had planned to kill his victim by shooting him, and did not successfully execute this plan when he killed him by getting him trampled to death by a herd of wild pigs.

Now, it is easy to see that successfully executing an action-plan requires more than that one executes the basic actions specified in this plan and these actions cause the intended results in the envisaged way. This is demonstrated by the following example. Killer A intends to kill B by running him over with his car when B takes his evening stroll. When he drives along the street looking for his unsuspecting victim, A's murderous intention awakens his long-slumbering homicidal instincts, and seeing a pedestrian walking at the side of the street, whom he does not recognize, he decides to run him over just for fun. The pedestrian is, as chance has it, none other than B. In this case, though A, in killing B, performed just the actions he had specified in his action-plan, and though he did kill his victim intentionally, he did not kill B intentionally qua this particular person, i.e. qua B, – since he did not know he was killing B at the time – , but, as it was, 'by mistake'.

This case demonstrates that intentional performance of a non-basic action F requires that the agent, in bringing about the intended result, not only acts, as Myles Brand put it in Wittgensteinian terminology, in accordance with his action-plan, but that he *correctly follows* his action-plan (1984, 23). He must, in acting, intend of his action that it be the execution of the relevant step in his action-plan. In purely causalist terms, which remain true to the internalist spirit of the standard model, this requirement can be spelled out as follows:

---

24 Goldman (1970), 59; Harman (1976), 160. More recent adherents include Searle (1983), 138, Brand (1984), 23ff.; Thalberg (1984); Alston (1986) and Bishop (1989), 128ff.

25 E.g. Thalberg (1984), 256; Bishop (1989), 129; Mele / Moser (1994), 229; Gibbons (2001), 588.

(A') (1) the agent has an action-plan (contained in his intention) of how to F, (2) performs all the basic actions specified therein, (3) intentionally,[26] (4) with the intention thereby to F, and (5) these basic actions lead to the intended result (of the F-ing) via the causal routes foreseen in the action-plan.[27]

Promising as it may seem, this account of non-basic intentional action is not going to work, though. There are four, partly interconnected, difficulties which, in my view, this analysis cannot satisfactorily deal with, and which I will, in the following, briefly go through.

a) The first problem concerns the question of the required content of the action-plan. This difficulty arises from the fact that the action-plan, as we've just seen, is supposed to be part of the intention's content and that the intention, on the standard model, must cause the basic actions by which the agent performs the non-basic action. When the intention causes the basic actions, it must plausibly be the case that its content is relevant to what basic actions are being caused – the alternative would be subscribing to a version of epiphenomenalism about intentional content.[28] While content epiphenomenalism has, for some time, been hotly debated in the philosophy of mind, I cannot go into its possibility any further here, and will simply leave it aside, given its unpalatable consequences for a theory of action. But even on the assumption that the intentional content of the intention *can*, in general, be causally relevant for what basic actions the agent performs, there are some additional conditions which must be met in order for the content of the intention to be so relevant. These conditions include, at least, that (i) the intention with the action-plan it (allegedly) contains must be present before or at least at the beginning of the basic action,[29] and that (ii) this plan must be 'psychologically real', i.e. we must be able to realistically ascribe a mental state with this (explicit or implicit) content to the agent.

(One might want to raise doubts about condition (i) on the basis of cases of where action-plans are adapted to changing circumstances by informational updating, so that the action-plan is changed while the action is being performed, or on the basis of cases of action-plans which are fully specified only during the

26 This condition does not – as it may appear – make the whole analysis circular, since (3) only requires that the *basic* actions are performed intentionally, while the analysandum is intentional agency in non-basic actions.

27 Cf. Bishop (1989), 130.

28 Such as the one explored – though not espoused – by Dretske (1989).

29 Ruling out the possibility of backward causation.

course of an action.[30] In both these kinds of cases, one might want to argue, the action-plan need not be fully present at the beginning of the action, but can change or be fully developed during the course of the action. However, even when both kinds of cases are admitted as possible, condition (i) still makes sense: For condition (i) only concerns the causal relevance of the action-plan for each *particular* basic action which the agent performs. And, plausibly, for the action-plan to be causally relevant for a particular basic action, it must be present at least at its beginning. This is completely compatible with the possibility that when a non-basic actions includes several basic actions, not *all* of them are specified at the beginning, i.e. that the agent, in performing the first basic action, doesn't yet know which step he will perform next.[31])

Once we start looking at the content of intentions we can plausibly ascribe to agents we can quickly see that it is not generally true that we can ascribe to agents who intend to perform a non-basic action a plan comprising all the basic actions to be performed, nor one comprising all the causal paths from their basic actions to the more distant result to be brought about. E.g. when killer A intended to kill his victim B by running him over with his car, he did not, realistically, have a plan which broke down the more encompassing action of killing into sub-parts so fine-grained as specific basic actions, i.e. bodily movements. More realistically, the plan only included such sub-stages as 'driving to the place where the victim takes his evening stroll', 'finding the victim', 'turning the steering wheel of the car' etc. Requiring more detail in the action-plan would, for most agents and most actions, amount to massive cognitive over-burdening.

Furthermore, assuming that the action-plan must always break down the non-basic action into basic ones to be performed, presupposes that, for all non-basic actions, descriptions of the corresponding basic actions *as basic actions* – 'simplex' descriptions[32] – must be available to the agent, when the non-basic action is performed intentionally. And this assumption is highly dubious: For it is quite conceivable that, for instance, in tying my shoelaces I am unaware of which specific bodily movements I am about to perform – I may only be aware that I am about to perform movements normally involved in tying my shoelaces. And since it is also quite conceivable that if I were asked before or after the action which bodily movements were involved, I would be unable to

---

30 Some philosophers think that in cases of sustaining causation of behaviour by an intention it is one of the main functions of the feedback to enable this 'altering' and 'filling' out of intentions, cf. McCann (1998), 123.

31 And it is fully compatible with the possibility that the way in which the basic action is performed is changed during its performance.

32 The term is from Hornsby (1980), 43 fn. 3; though here usage of the term is slightly different.

provide 'simplex' descriptions of them, it is very often even unrealistic to ascribe an action-plan to me which at least implicitly spells out the basic actions to be performed as such.

If this is right, then generally requiring for intentional non-basic actions an action-plan which specifies which basic actions the agent must perform, turns out to be incompatible with conditions (i) and (ii) for the action-plan to be causally relevant to which action is performed. Now, a causalist might react to this point by admitting that action-plans need not always be so fine-grained as to specify basic actions to be performed. It will be sufficient that they specify actions the agent knows how to perform. E.g. in our case, A, as an experienced car-driver, will know how to turn around the steering wheel, even if he does not know which basic actions he performs in doing so.

However, specifying actions the agent knows how to perform, rather than basic actions, will not always be enough for an action-plan which is sufficiently specific for the performance of an intentional action. For there are cases where intentional agency does require being in possession of a very detailed action-plan which breaks the non-basic down to the basic actions. A safe-breaker who performs the tricky task of opening a bank-safe with his instruments, with an alarm going off the moment he will make a wrong movement, will need a detailed plan which specifies how he has to move his fingers etc. and will have to execute this plan faithfully, in order to count as having opened the safe intentionally, and not just by luck.

So, the problem for the causalist analysis with regard to the content of the action-plan turns out not to be that the original proposal about the content – i.e. the one that demanded that the basic actions to be performed were spelled out – was too demanding. The problem is, rather, that there seems to be *no* general standard (at least not one to be spelled out in non-normative terms) for how specific the content of the action-plan has to be which is required for intentional action.

This lack of a general standard presents a major stumbling-block for the causalist analysis in those cases where the agent lacks any explicit action-plan and where, if the causalist 'action-plan analysis' of intentional non-basic action is right, we must be able to ascribe to him one which has been formed only implicitly. If the agent had no explicit idea of what basic actions he was going to perform, then how are we to decide which to include in his implicit action-plan? The ones by which he normally brings about the intended results? But this would be too strict, for it would rule out *tout court* the possibility of intentionally doing something in an unaccustomed way when one does not specifically plan to do so.

b) The second problem, which is, in a way, the 'reverse side of the coin' from the first, concerns the degree of 'match' or 'fit' with the action-plan required for an intentional action. Obviously, not all deviations from the action-plan make the non-basic action which is performed non-intentional, but only relevant ones. When a killer shoots his victim in the head though he had intended to shoot him in the neck, he has, despite his 'mistake', killed him intentionally.[33] Similarly, I may have completely misguided conceptions of the causal processes I set in motion when I ring someone on the phone, without my ringing him up being therefore unintentional.

So, we clearly don't always need perfect fit with the action-plan for the non-basic action to be performed intentionally. Causalists such as John Bishop have tried to accomodate this insight by arguing that the action-plan usually contains not just one set of basic actions to be performed and causal pathways to the further result, but a disjunction of several different routes to the intended result. Alternatively, one might argue that all relevantly similar routes are acceptable to the agent; i.e. when the actually obtaining causal route is sufficiently similar to the envisaged one, any mismatch will count as irrelevant. But which routes are to be included within the disjunction, or are to be counted as relevantly similar? Bishop has advocated ruling all those routes that the agent "could have considered in reasoning toward his or her action-plan" (1989, 131) as being more or less covered by the plan; only when the actual sequence of events leading to the result is not one the agent could have considered is there a relevant mismatch which leads to the action's being unintentional.[34]

The 'could-have-considered' criterion can be interpreted in similar ways as the 'foreseeability test', used for deciding whether harm not brought about intentionally can be ascribed to the agent. As this latter test, the 'could-have-considered' criterion can either be given a normative or a non-normative, purely psychological reading.[35] Clearly, for a causalist the latter reading will be more appealing, because it gives the proposed criterion a reassuringly internalist and non-normative ring: What the agent could have considered is, it seems, a purely psychological question about the particular agent and his actual mental capaci-

33 Even though the action was not intentional under the more specific description of 'a killing-by-a-shooting-in-the-head'; cf. Bishop (1989), 131. The case would be different, however, if the killer had, when shooting, positively thought that he could only kill his victim by shooting him in the neck – then the deviation from his plan would clearly be relevant.

34 Similarly Zimmerman (1984), 128, for whom the result must not be brought about in a manner 'surprising' to the agent.

35 Or a statistical one; cf. Moore (1997), 364, for different readings of the foreseeability test.

ties.[36] But even though it is plausible to accept that when an agent could not even have envisaged the ensuing scenario, he has not brought about the result in question intentionally,[37] this criterion is much too permissive to distinguish intentional from non-intentional non-basic actions. For the converse does not hold, because not all cases where the agent could have envisaged the ensuing causal pathway – and not even all cases where he did envisage it (but then rejected it as too improbable) – count as cases of intentionally bringing about the result in question. Consider, again, the case of the experienced safe-breaker, who tries to open a safe, under conditions where one false movement of his may set off the alarm. The safe-breaker may very well have considered the possibility that a mistake on his part need not necessarily be disastrous, because there is the slight possibility that it is counterbalanced by a minor defect in the safe's set-up. Nonetheless, when he makes a mistake and, by pure coincidence, he succeeds because of such a minor defect, his success will still count as too lucky to have been brought about intentionally.

Even worse for the defender of the causalist, internalist analysis of intentional agency, there is a strong reason for positively expecting that we cannot spell out the standard of similarity – or relevant difference – for the required fit between action-plan and ensuing scenario in non-normative terms. This is the heavy dependence of assessments of intentionality on the normative contexts of the action in question, which entails that even when the factual and psychological conditions of two actions are completely the same, the assessment may still differ. For illustration, compare a case of moral wrongdoing with the case of a skill-contest. When a marksman kills a victim he intends to kill, but knows, when firing, that his shot has only a very small chance[38] of hitting the victim, he is plausibly considered to have killed him intentionally. When a player in a darts contest intends to hit a bulls-eye and knows that he has a very small chance of hitting it – which may be as small as in the case of the marksman – we plausibly consider his success, when he does succeed in hitting the bull's-eye, to

36 Very differently from the influential, avowedly normative interpretation of the criterion used in German criminal law: "was nach der Lebenserfahrung in Rechnung zu stellen war", BGHSt 3, 62.

37 However, for intentional agency he must only have been able to envisage, in some vague form, the actually ensuing scenario – for otherwise we would wrongly rule actions which involve the use of technical equipment about whose precise functioning the agent is completely ignorant as generally unintentional.

38 Of course, the chance must, even in cases of moral wrong-doing, not be extremely low; e. g. even if winning a non-rigged lottery were, in a certain context, morally wrong, the chances of winning would be too small, for one to count as having intentionally won when one has bought one ticket, which turned out to be the winning one.

have been 'too lucky' to count as intentional.[39] Crucially, both actions will still be assessed differently with regard to their intentionality, even when all the psychological and causal features of both cases that, on an internalist view, can plausibly determine whether the action is intentional or not, are the same. Thus, you can assume that the objective likelihood of success in both cases, the abilities of both persons with regard to hitting their aims, as well as their psychological characteristics regarding their views about how likely they were going to succeed and how much they wanted to hit their aim are exactly alike, and that the actual course of events is similar to the envisaged one to the same degree in both cases. So, no factor which, on the internalist approach to agency, can plausibly be relevant for determining whether the action is intentional or not remains to account for a different assessment. The only factor which can explain this difference is the different normative background of both actions, on which the assessment of intentionality depends.

When I speak of 'normative background' here, this can be understood in two ways: Either regarding the normative (or good) reasons[40] which apply to the agent, or regarding the normative practices before whose background the action takes place. Whenever we have a normative background of the former kind, we will also have one of the latter kind, but not vice versa: When an agent takes part in football game, for instance, this is a social practice with an inherently normative structure – it contains rules which provide the persons who intend to play the game reasons for behaving in a certain way – , but one can obviously deny that it generally provides an agent with normative reasons to act, since it might, e.g., be better if he did not play this game at all. When talking of normative background, in the following, I will understand it in the latter – 'normative practices' – sense, which is the less demanding notion, so that what I am claiming here is that normative practices are connected to different standards for when an action counts as intentional.

This result should not be very surprising. Context-dependence of assessments of actions with regard to their intentionality, and especially dependence on the moral valence of the action, are rather well-investigated phenomena, primarily in the field of side-effects which are not brought about on purpose (the so-called Knobe cases).[41] For instance, it is a well established result of investiga-

39 This point about the 'lower' standards for cases of moral wrong-doing to count as intentional has already been pointed out by Harman (1976), 151.

40 Using Dancy's distinction between 'normative' and 'motivating' reasons, cf. his (2000), ch. 1.

41 On Knobe's own understanding of his cases, the 'normative background' in the stronger – normative reasons – sense is relevant to the assessment of intentionality. I can remain agnostic

tions into the actual practice of ascriptions of intentional agency that such side-effects are much more readily ascribed to the agent as something intentionally brought about by him if causing these results is regarded as morally blameworthy, than if this causing is regarded as morally praiseworthy.[42] In the Knobe-cases, this difference can arguably be explained by some particular aspects of what it is to act on a *moral* rule or from moral reasons. But as cases of consequential waywardness show, the context-dependence of the assessment of a non-basic action as intentional generalizes to (i) cases of acting on purpose and (ii) to non-moral cases. For instance, the same difference between the assessments as in our earlier two cases would hold if one case was an instance of playing a pure skill-game ('reines Geschicklichkeitsspiel'), and the other of a game essentially involving an element of luck. For the standards of what successes count as 'too lucky' to have been brought about intentionally by the agent are different in these two kinds of game. In a pure skill-game, often nothing less than a manifestation of a generally reliable skill of the agent will suffice for intentionality. Thus, when a go player uses a very fallible and unreliable strategy in order to capture an enemy piece, and succeeds because his opponent makes a minor mistake, we would hardly consider this capture as intentional rather than as 'pure chance'. On the other hand, in a football game, even when a player shoots the ball in a way that does not reliably get the ball into the goal, and scores only because the goalkeeper makes a slight mistake, we would not deny that the player has scored intentionally, at least if he had envisaged what happened as a 'live' possibility. So, in general, in games inherently involving an element of luck, we do not require a reliable skill, but only fulfilment of a 'did-consider-as-possible' criterion (or even only of a 'could-have-considered' criterion).[43]

This shows that the standard for assessing whether a mismatch between the agent's action-plan and the actual process which led to the result is relevant to

about this stronger claim, since, if it is true, we can also trace the different assessments to different normative backgrounds in the normative practice sense.

42 Cf. Knobe (2003).

43 Mele / Moser (1994), 246, advocate a disjunctive analysis of the form "(a) at the time of S's actual involvement in A-ing at t, the process indicated with significantly preponderant probability by S's on balance evidence at t as being at least partly constitutive of her A-ing at t does not diverge significantly from the process that is in fact constitutive of her A-ing at t; or (b) S's A-ing at t manifests a suitably reliable skill". Even apart from the problem that Mele and Moser have not dealt with the standard for significance in (a), their basic oversight lies in simply neglecting the context-dependence of application of a standard like (a) or (b) – it is not, as if in cases, where standard (b) is applicable, fulfilment of condition (a) might also suffice for intentional action.

the question of intentionality or not, depends on the normative context or background within which the action is being performed, and cannot be determined independently from this background.

It is questionable, however, whether this result already puts an end to the hope which underlies the causalist action-plan analysis of non-basic intentional action, namely the hope of getting a purely internalist account of intentional agency. For might not the causalist reply, at this point: 'Well, it's true that the normative background is relevant, but *only* if it is somehow incorporated into the agent's intention, i.e. only if the agent intends to hit the bull's eye as part of a contest of skill etc. Which normative background is relevant then, still depends on the agent's intention, and so we can still hope to spell out the conditions for intentional non-basic agency in purely internalist, non-normative terms – even if the whole story will be more complicated than we had originally thought.'

But this escape-strategy for the causalist is not viable: Were the standard for when an action or causal process is to count as conforming to the content of an intention to be itself determined by the intention's content, this would lead to an infinite regress. For assume that the intention not only contained an action-plan, but also a standard for when the evolving processes 'matched' the action-plan: How could we then decide whether the relation between action-plan and evolving processes 'matched' this further standard? To decide this, yet a further standard would be needed and so on ad infinitum.[44]

Furthermore, we should keep in mind that there are clearly cases where the agent's intention does not determine which standard is relevant, namely in moral contexts: The marksman who kills his victim with a chance shot, need not intend the shooting of his victim to be assessable by moral norms in order for the more encompassing criterion for which causal chains count as covered by his intention to apply. Thus, he cannot escape blame for intentionally killing his victim by arguing that, as he tried to shoot his victim as part of a skill-contest, his hit was too lucky to count as intentional.

c) A further problem for the action-plan answer to the problem of consequential waywardness, has been pointed out by Geert Keil (2000, 92f.). Keil has argued that even if we make the action-plan extremely fine-grained, – even to the point of risking wild psychological implausibility in ascribing such a detailed plan to the agent – we can never make it fine-grained enough to ex-

44 This problem is, basically, the very same as the regress problem concerning the application of rules or plans, which has been pointed out by Kant, Critique of Pure Reason, B 172, and by Wittgenstein (concerning the 'grasping' of rules) PI, §§ 139, 141, 201.

clude the possibility of deviance. For in whatever detail an action-plan specifies a causal scenario, the actual scenario that ensues could always be described with infinitely more detail. This is a simple consequence of the 'ontological density' of the world, which can never be totally captured by a linguistic or mental representation of it. For each actual process will have an infinitude of features which cannot all be captured by us, given the finitude of our minds. Therefore, every expectation an agent has of the process which will lead to the result will have 'gaps' or 'indeterminacies' in comparison with the latter, actual course of events. And these gaps will always be opportunities for possible deviant causal chains to be inserted, however narrow we succeed in making them: The causal chain, as far as the characteristics specified in advance are concerned, will then be the same, because the waywardness only appears at an intermediate stage which has not been captured by the ex-ante specification. But even though the chain therefore fits precisely the ex-ante specification, it will still be wayward. So, for no causal chain imagined in advance, we can know before its evolving whether it will count as a fulfilment of our intention or not (even if the standard of relevant mismatch is assumed to be known).

d) Lastly, the action-plan analysis, as presented above, also faces the problem of rational constraints on the formation of action-plans. Even if the agent acts as he intends, and even if his more basic actions lead to the further consequence he intends to bring about, he will not have brought about this further consequence intentionally, if his (correct) beliefs about how he would bring it about were completely arbitrary, in lacking any epistemic justification. This means that the action-plan is subject to substantive rational and epistemic constraints, regarding both its content[45] and formation. Take the following case for illustration (after Ginet (1990), 81):

A comes into a room with the intention to kill B, who is sitting on a sofa in an adjacent room; as yet, A lacks any idea of how to achieve his aim. He suddenly discovers an electrical button on the wall, and acquires, completely unjustifiedly and without any evidence in favour of this view, the belief that this button is connected to the sofa next door, and that by pressing it he can fatally electrocute B. As it happens, this is the case – i.e. when A does press the button, he kills B just in the way he happened to imagine. Both his basic actions and their causal connection to B's death may have exactly matched A's action-plan, which means that the causal analysis would have to assess this as a case of intentional killing.

45 For a case where it is the action-plan's content, which is 'too mad' for the action to count as intentional, even though the intended aim is reached, cf. Moya (1990), 127.

But this result is clearly false: A didn't kill B intentionally, because, from the basis of the evidence available to A, it was a mere coincidence that he succeeded, given that he was not justified in forming the belief that he could kill him in this way, in the first place.

This shows that the agent's epistemic situation – i. e. what he is epistemically entitled to believe – and not merely his actual psychological situation, play a decisive role in determining whether his action is intentional or not. While this point has been recognized by several philosophers who have attempted to offer a causalist analysis of intentional non-basic action,[46] they have, mostly, overlooked the fact that answerability of the action-plan to external standards of justification – such as the requirement of the right kind of evidential connection to the outside world – presents a major obstacle to providing a purely causalist, internalist analysis of intentional agency. For accordance with these rational requirements is not something that can be spelled out in terms of causal connections and degrees of fit between the agent's actual mental states and the ensuing action.

4 Alternative, Non-Standard Analyses

These four considerations – the problem of specification of the action-plan's content, the context-dependence of standards of relevance for deviations, the problem of the ontological density of the world, and the problem of rational constraints on the formation of action-plans – show that adding the condition that an action-plan is being successfully followed by the agent, at least so long as this condition is understood in purely factual, non-normative and internalist terms, will not enable the causalist analysis of intentional action to deal with the problem of consequential waywardness. But there are other, non-standard accounts, which might stand a better chance of success and which might still be compatible at least with the basic tenets of the standard analysis of intentional action. We must briefly look at two of these accounts here.

a) First, the analysis of intentional non-basic action in terms of knowledge. As has been recognized right from the beginning of the discussion on consequential waywardness,[47] there is an obvious analogy between this latter problem

46 Who have tried to adjust their analyses accordingly, cf. Ginet (1990), 87; Mele / Moser (1994), 253.
47 This parallel has been urged by Danto (1973), 8 ff.

and the Gettier problem in epistemology, which makes it appear an attractive move to argue that what goes wrong in cases of consequential waywardness is that the agent only believes, but does not *know* that he will bring about the result in question.[48] But while it is true that the agent, in cases of consequential waywardness, does not know that he will bring about the further effect, it is not true that this distinguishes these cases from cases of non-deviance. For also in these latter cases, often the agent does not know, but only believes that he will bring about (or is bringing about) the further effect; just think about our earlier case of the marksman killing his victim with a shot he realizes may well go awry.

This objection to a knowledge analysis, however, primarily applies to knowledge of the further effects conceived of as theoretical knowledge about what will happen, and might be circumvented if we turn to practical knowledge, instead i.e. the agent's knowledge of what he is doing, which, as Elizabeth Anscombe famously argued, is non-observational.[49] But, without being able to go into details of this account here, I don't think this line of approach will work, either. For, at least as I understand it, practical knowledge is more or less knowledge of what one is up to, which, at least in the cases we are considering here – i.e. cases of non-basic actions – roughly amounts to knowledge of what one is trying to do. And it seems clear that an agent, even in a case of consequential waywardness, may very well have this kind of knowledge – without thereby knowing whether he will succeed in bringing about the effect he tries to bring about.

b) A different approach has been developed by Keil, who, as we have seen, takes the problem of the ontological density of reality to be decisive against the action-plan analysis. In consequence Keil thinks that what deviant causal chains deviate from cannot simply be a prior action-plan. However, once the causal process has terminated in the result, the problem of ontological density can be circumvented, because the agent can now – instead of describing the different stages of the process – refer to this process 'ostensively'. I.e. he can now, retrospectively, make the judgement: '*this* is what I wanted to happen (or not)'. Consequently, Keil argues, what deviant causal chains deviate from is the counterfactual course of events that would have matched the agent's retrospective, post actum specification of his own intention (2000, 102).

48 Cf. Gibbons (2001), 591: "if your means-end belief does not constitute knowledge, you will not do it intentionally". The situation is slightly complicated by the fact that Gibbons regards this rather as a case of knowing-how, than of knowing-that, but his examples clearly suggest that what he takes to be relevant for intentional action is knowing that one can do p by doing q.
49 Cf. Anscombe (1957), §§ 45–48.

Now, first, notice, how far this proposal is off from the original causalist view we have started with. We had argued that in order for the intention and its content to be causally effective, the latter had to be 'psychologically real' *in advance* of the action – and an ex post actum specification of the intention's content is, obviously not sufficient for this. So, accepting Keil's analysis would eventually force us to abandon the causalist approach.

But, second, even Keil's proposal, when construed in this non-causalist way, will not work. For we sometimes don't accept an agent's retrospective specification of his intention as correct, but regard it, on occasions, as mistaken, an instance of self-deceit, or even a dishonest attempt to escape blame. This is a possibility that Keil's account doesn't allow for once he turns the agent's post actum assessment into the only constitutive criterion for deviance.

5 An 'Externalist' and 'Normative' Alternative?

So, from the different analyses which we have been going through so far, we have been able to extricate, at best, one necessary condition for intentional agency in non-basic action – that it must not have been psychologically impossible for the agent to consider the way in which the result was brought about – and one sufficient condition – that he knows that he will bring about the result in question. But for the largest chunk of cases of bringing about a result, which lie in between the fulfilment of the necessary and the fulfilment of the sufficient condition, we are still without any satisfactory criterion for distinguishing cases of waywardness from cases of intentionally bringing about the intended result.

Given the failure of the earlier analyses, what is the alternative? I think that in order to find a solution to the problem of consequential waywardness we have to retrace our steps and look again at where precisely the causalist analysis has gone wrong. We have seen that the causalist was forced to modify his original, simple condition of match with the action-plan by adding that the agent not only acts in accordance with the plan, but that he correctly follows the action-plan. What the discussion of the different causalist attempts to analyse the notion of 'following a plan' has shown is that causalists have no such analysis merely in terms of purely psychological and 'local' facts available.[50] What it

50 Moya (1990), 125 f., has advanced another powerful argument to the result that the notion of (correctly) following an action-plan is not amenable to a purely causal analysis. He considers a case where the agent is working on a complicated and long addition problem, and his step-by-step adding is guided by his plan – the plan is causally guiding his behaviour –, but he makes a series of mutually compensating mistakes. Even though, as a result of this compensation, he

has not given us reason to doubt, however, is that acting intentionally (in non-basic actions) can be spelled out in terms of following an action-plan correctly – so long as we accept that the latter notion cannot be spelled out in purely factual and internalist terms.

This simple insight, I take it, constitutes the basis of a successful analysis of consequential deviance. Whenever an agent forms an intention, his pursued aim forms the standard of success, by which his behaviour is to be assessed with regard to success or failure. For non-basic actions, forming the intention to perform them must include, as causalists have rightly argued, that the agent has a plan of how to achieve his aim. In cases of causal deviance, the agent tries to follow the plan, and his action and the process involved are, outwardly, partly in accordance with it – since he does reach the aim he has set himself, and has, so far, been successful – , but the agent is not following the plan correctly. For either in acting he is not following this plan at all – think of our earlier case of killer A discovering his long-slumbering homicidal instincts – or , though following the plan, he makes a mistake. What is crucial is that the key notion of following an action-plan correctly cannot be understood in the terms proposed by the causalist defenders of the action-plan analysis, i. e. in terms of (i) a mental state encompassing the action-plan causing the basic actions and their further consequences and (ii) the actual events objectively corresponding (to some specified degree) to the content of this plan. For, as our arguments have shown, further factors, in particular the normative background of the action, have to be taken into account as well.

If this is right, and if the basic approach of relying on the notion of correctly following an action-plan in explaining intentional non-basic agency is sound, this means that a purely non-normative and internalist account of intentional non-basic agency is not to be had, for we cannot reduce this notion to 'local' non-normative facts about the agent and his action. Taking into account the action's normative background involves, at least, taking into account existing social practices within whose framework the agent acts, which introduces an externalist element. While this externalist element does not, strictly speaking, imply that the notion of intentional agency, must be an irreducible *normative* notion – for one could still hold that normative facts could globally be reduced to non-normative ones[51] – , it does mean that, in the context of explaining intentional *individual* action, the notion has to be treated as an irreducible normative notion.

arrives at the correct result, he does so only by accident, not intentionally. (In the terminology developed by Mele (1987), this is a case of 'tertiary waywardness'.)

51 This is a possibility which I cannot go into here.

For in the context of explaining individual agency, only local reducibility would ensure that we could dispense with the normative aspects of the notion of correct plan-following in favour of a purely factual account. (Treating intentional agency as an irreducibly normative notion seems attractive for other reasons as well, especially given the already noted parallels between the cases of consequential waywardness and the Knobe-cases, which latter cases Knobe himself took to establish that our concept of intentional agency has an irreducible normative component.) So what our considerations about consequential waywardness show is that we are committed to what might aptly be called a 'normative externalism' about intentional agency.

Now, even if one agrees that following a plan cannot be analysed in purely non-normative terms, but is, instead, best understood, e.g., in non-causal terms, one might still object that analysing intentional non-basic action in terms of correct plan-following does not really advance our understanding of this notion in any way. It merely provides a redescription of the same phenomenon, with the added claim that a proper analysis is impossible, though without any additional explanatory value. But this objection can be met, since there is a fruitful non-causal model of following a plan, provided by a Wittgensteinian non-causalist account of rule-following. What makes it especially natural to turn to this account in our case, is the parallel between Wittgenstein's insight that a mental representation connected to an utterance cannot by itself determine what this utterance means, and our insistence that an intention in itself, even when connected to an action, cannot determine whether this action is intentional.[52] I.e. as mental representations don't, in isolation, determine meaning, so intentions, by themselves, don't determine the intentionality of actions. Wittgenstein's insistence on this earlier point makes it seem promising to look to the lessons of his account of rule-following. And, indeed, once we apply these lessons to our understanding of following an action-plan, I think we are able to deal with the problems which beset the causalist analysis of intentional agency. I just want to show this briefly for two of these problems, namely the context-dependence of assessments of intentionality, and the problem of the ontological density of the world.

The context-dependence of our judgements about whether a causal chain is deviant or not can be accounted for by the fact that the forming of an intention does not normally occur 'in a vacuum' or 'in isolation', but is embedded in a pre-existing background of normative practices which contribute to determining both the content of the action-plan itself and whether the action-plan is correctly

52 Cf. Wittgenstein PI, §§ 138 ff.

executed or not. E.g. when someone takes part in a prize-shooting he is participating in a contest whose point it is for the participants to prove their skills at shooting; and such a contest-practice has some constitutive rules without which it simply would not count as a practice of this kind. For example, the very notion of a skill-proving contest excludes the possibility that the winner is decided on by a mere random procedure (that is the difference between 'Glücksspielen' and 'Geschicklichkeitsspielen').

The preset standards intrinsic in such a contest-practice necessarily form the background for the agent's own, more specific, intention of hitting the target when he willingly takes part in the contest. We could express this point by saying that he intends not merely to hit the target, but (at least implicitly) to hit it as a participant of the contest; this way of putting it would highlight tho point that the agent implicitly 'incorporates' the pre-set standards into his own intention. What is important, though, is that such an 'incorporation' is, often at least, a mere fiction. Regularly, the agent does not think about which standards will be relevant, and it is more apt, in these cases, to accept that the mere fact of consciously participating in the practice is sufficient for the connected standard to be relevant.

The insight that agents form their intentions normally against a background of pre-existing normative practices also accounts for the fact that deviance may occur even when the agent had not consciously thought about one way of achieving the aim in question, or that his plan is only very sketchy. In such cases, causalists have to postulate some implicit reasoning on the part of the agent, which is psychologically real enough to play a causal function on the particular occasion; this move appears very much ad hoc. The non-causalist account of non-deviance as correct rule-following does not need this questionable assumption: The normative standard is already there, provided by the normative practices, and we therefore need not assume that the agent must consciously or unconsciously adopts this standard for each occasion.

The problem of the 'ontological density' of the world, due to which we cannot exclude all possible cases of waywardness in advance, does not arise for the non-causalist analysis advocated here, either. For in order to follow a rule, it is not necessary that we are able, for a given type of action, to tell in advance whether it will constitute an instance of correct following of the rule or not. For precisely in virtue of the 'ontological density' of the world, there can be features of the action which we have not specified in advance, and which can invalidate our first assessment of the action as correct rule-following: i.e. the assessment of an action as correct rule-following is, very often, defeasible. For illustration, take an (to my knowledge, fictional) rule in tennis, that a player must refrain from shouting during play, when he thereby unfairly distracts his opponent.

Can we tell in advance which kinds of cases will necessarily count as violations of this rule? No, because we cannot be sure that aspects which speak prima facie in favour of the player's unfairly distracting his opponent – such as shouting very loudly – won't turn out to be defeated by other considerations. (E.g. when the player is always shouting very loudly when hitting the ball, so that his opponent can be expected to be no longer distracted by these shouts.)

6 Conclusion: The Price of Externalism about Intentional Agency

Now, even if we accept that understanding intentional non-basic action along the lines of a non-causal Wittgensteinian account of rule-following advances our grasp of the former notion, because it allows us to deal with some important difficulties, there will remain the worry that these advantages have been purchased at too high a price: Namely the price of externalism about intentional agency.

While the original account of intentional agency was strictly internalist, in trying to determine the intentionality of the action merely by the agent's psychological states and their causal upshots, the account we have arrived at now is substantially externalist. For remember, on the view I have been advocating, the normative background of the practices in which the agent participates becomes directly relevant for determining whether an action has been intentional, simply in virtue of the agent's participating in this practice, and *without any explicit intention of his* with regard to the standards encoded in the normative background. (The ensuing externalism is, it should be noted, related to, but different from externalism about the intentional content of mental states.[53] For, as we have seen, the need for accepting this former externalism arises even if we assume the content of mental states already to be fixed, since this fixing doesn't yet account for the standard of relevant deviance or the rational constraints on plan-formation.)

One obvious worry about this form of externalism is that it makes ascriptions of intentionality in general, and assessment of whether a causal deviation is relevant in particular, too subject-*independent* – i.e. dissociates it too much from the agent's intention, which seems to become almost irrelevant to determin-

53 There is a particularly close parallel to Burge's 'anti-individualistic' arguments to the effect that the social environment inevitably co-determines what mental states we can attribute to someone, and what contents these mental states have, cf. Burge (1979).

ing the relevant standard for a success to be too lucky to count as being intentionally brought about. And this seems to overly remove control of what his action is, or is supposed to be, from the agent. For it implies that when an agent consciously takes part, for instance, in a skill-contest, the normative background of this contest automatically determines the standard of correct plan-following – and thereby also, implicitly, determines what kind of action the agent is performing. But cannot, one might ask, the agent, even if he outwardly participates in a skill-contest, still reject 'for himself' the idea that he should prove his skill, and merely intend to hit the target, no matter how? And will not the standard of relevance then have to be determined independently from the normative background of the practice in which he is outwardly taking part?

I think this is indeed possible, but cases of this kind are exceptional. For normally we presuppose that the agent, even when he does consciously think about the standard in question, accepts – albeit reluctantly, sometimes – that his performance is to be judged according to the constitutive rules of the contest, even if his primary aim is different from 'winning according to the rules'. I.e. even if the marksman in the shooting-contest wants to 'win by all possible means', he will still be conscious of participating in a skill-contest and of the standards of this contest which apply for judging his behaviour, whether he likes it or not. It is only when an agent consciously dissociates himself from a standard that this standard is sometimes no longer relevant for determining whether his action was intentional;[54] and conscious dissociation regularly requires not only that the agent thinks that achieving his own objects is more important than following the rules of this practice, but that he rejects the practice as a whole, because e.g. he thinks that it is morally unacceptable. However, even these exceptional cases don't undermine our central point that normally intentions are formed on the background of existing normative practices, for regularly the agent who rejects the standards of the practice in which he is outwardly participating will implicitly use the pre-existing normative standards of another practice. E.g. when an explorer reluctantly, and in order to save his own life, takes part in a cannibals' skill contest which consists in shooting war-prisoners over a longer distance, he will consciously dissociate himself, for moral reasons, from participating in a skill-contest, and the standards connected to this contest in assessing whether his hitting a prisoner was intentional or not will no longer apply to him. But, at the same time, the standards connected with the practice of moral blame and determining whether a morally blameworthy action was intentional will

54 Even in these cases, dissociation does not automatically make it irrelevant, as one can see in cases of moral wrongdoing.

apply to his action. So, while the possibility of conscious dissociation from a normative practice one outwardly participates in does provide an internalist corrective to the externalist story about intentional agency we have been urging so far, this corrective is limited.

If this is right, externalism about intentional agency will stay with us, for better or for worse. But given the bad job internalists about intentional agency have been doing in dealing with cases of consequential waywardness over the past forty years, this is just as it should be.[55]

References

Alston, William (1986). An Action-plan Interpretation of purposive Explanation of Actions, *Theory and Decisions*, 20, 275ff.

Anscombe, Elizabeth (1957). *Intention*. 1st ed. Oxford: Oxford University Press

Bishop, John (1989). *Natural Agency. An Essay on the Causal Theory of Action*. Cambridge: Cambridge University Press.

Brand, Myles (1984). *Intending and Acting. Towards a Naturalized Action Theory*. Cambridge, MA: MIT Press.

Bratman, Michael (1987). *Intentions, Plans and Practical Reason*. Cambridge, MA: Harvard University Press.

Burge, Tyler (1979). Individualism and the Mental. *Midwest Studies in Philosophy* 4, 73ff.

Dancy, Jonathan (2000). *Practical Reality*. Oxford: Oxford University Press

Danto, Arthur (1973). *Analytic Philosophy of Action*. Cambridge: Cambridge University Press

Davidson, Donald (1971). Agency, repr. in Davidson (1980)

Davidson (1973). Freedom to Act, repr. in Davidson (1980)

Davidson (1980). *Essays on Actions and Events*, Oxford: Clarendon Press

Dretske, Fred (1989). Reasons and Causes. *Philosophical Perspectives* 3, 1ff.

Garcia, J.L.A. (1990). The Intentional and the Intended. *Erkenntnis* 33, 191ff.

Gibbons, John (2001). Knowledge in Action. *Philosophy and Phenomenological Research* 62, 578ff.

Ginet, Carl (1990). *On Action*. Cambridge: Cambridge University Press

Goldman, Alvin (1970). *A Theory of Human Action*. Princeton, NJ: Princeton University Press

Harman, Gilbert (1976). Practical Reasoning. *Review of Metaphysics* 79, 431ff.

Hornsby, Jennifer (1980). *Actions*. London: Routledge and Kegan Paul

Kant, Immanuel (1781). *Kritik der reinen Vernunft*. ed. Heidemann, I., Stuttgart: Reclam 1966

Keil, Geert (2000). *Handeln und Verursachen*. Frankfurt a.M.: Klostermann

Knobe, Joshua (2003). Intentional Action and Side-Effects in Ordinary Language, *Analysis* 63, 190ff.

55 For very insightful comments on earlier drafts of this paper, I am much indebted to Erich Ammereller, Benedikt Kahmen, and Franz Knappik. An earlier version of this paper was presented at a workshop in Aachen with Michael Moore; I am grateful to him and the audience for their helpful comments.

McCann, Hugh (1998). *The Works of Agency. On Human Action, Will, and Freedom.* Ithaca & London: Cornell University Press

Mele, Alfred (1987). Intentional Action and Wayward Causal Chains: The problem of tertiary waywardness. *Philosophical Studies* 51, 55 ff.

Mele, Alfred & Moser, Paul (1994). Intentional Action. Repr. in Mele (ed.), *The Philosophy of Action*, Oxford: Oxford University Press

Mitchell, Dorothy (1982). Deviant Causal Chains. *American Philosophical Quarterly*, 19, 351 ff.

Moore, Michael (1993). *Act and Crime: The implications of the philosophy of action for the criminal law*, Oxford: Oxford University Press

Moore (1997). *Placing Blame: A general theory of the criminal law*, Oxford: Oxford University Press

Moore (2009). *Causation and Responsibility*, Oxford: Oxford University Press

Moya, Carlos (1990). *The Philosophy of Action. An Introduction*, Cambridge: Cambridge University Press

Searle, John (1983). *Intentionality*, Cambridge: Cambridge University Press

Thalberg, Irving (1984). Do Our Intentions Cause Our Intentional Actions. *American Philosophical Quarterly* 21, 249 ff.

Wessels, Johannes & Beulke, Werner (2011). *Strafrecht Allgemeiner Teil. Die Straftat und ihr Aufbau.* 41th ed., Heidelberg et al.: C.F. Müller

Wittgenstein, Ludwig (1984). *Tractatus logico-philosophicus. Werkausgabe Band I.* 9th ed., Frankfurt a.M.: Suhrkamp

Zimmermann, Michael (1984). *An Essay on Human Action.* New York: American University Studies

Thomas Schmidt

How to Understand the Problem of Moral Luck

1. Acts of negligence which do not lead to bad results do not appear to be morally on a par with otherwise identical instances of negligence which cause significant harm to others. The same is true with regard to similar cases in which we at least seem to make our moral assessment of agents dependent on factors which are not, or not entirely, up to them. A much-discussed example is the case of reckless driving. If a reckless driver, in addition to and as a consequence of his driving recklessly, hits a child, this can hardly be denied to be a morally significant matter. Plausibly, however, whether a child crosses the road right in front of the driver is something beyond his control.

Bernard Williams, in his paper "Moral Luck" (Williams 1976), and Thomas Nagel, in his reply to Williams which was published under the same title (Nagel 1976), have both famously argued that these and similar moral phenomena are philosophically significant. Following Nagel, many see them as giving rise to what has come to be called the *problem of moral luck*. According to the by now canonical way of putting this problem, there is a tension between the *control principle*, i.e. the claim that

> people cannot be morally assessed for [...] what is due to factors beyond their control (Nagel 1976, 25)

and our moral practice if, as it seems plausible to many, upholding this very practice commits us to believing that there are instances of *moral luck*, i.e. cases in which that for which agents are to be morally assessed at least partly depends on factors which are not, or at least not fully, within their control.[1]

---

1 Dana Nelkin is among the many who conceive of the claim that there is moral luck, *cum grano salis*, in this way (Nelkin 2008, § 1). Nagel, however, uses the term *moral luck* in order to refer to situations in which "a significant aspect of what someone does depends on factors beyond his control, yet we continue to treat him in that respect as an object of moral judgment" (Nagel 1976, 26). Nagel, that is, does not require that the relevant moral assessment is *appropriate*. Under his understanding, moral luck is involved whenever we, as a matter of fact, do make differences in our moral assessments of the sort in question, regardless of whether making these differences is justifiable. Given this understanding, there is no contradiction between the control principle and the claim that there is moral luck. Rather, the control principle and the claim that there is moral luck together imply that our moral practice is, as far as the control principle is concerned, not as it ought to be.

A number of writers believe that this is a deep and unsettling problem of moral philosophy which requires specific philosophical attention. Not all agree, however. A line of thought which has already been pursued by Nagel seems to imply that the problem of moral luck is not a genuine problem in its own right, but that it instead boils down to issues which are addressed in the free will debate.

The main objective of this paper is to show that this claim is false. Moreover, it will turn out that if one does not appreciate that the problem of moral luck is to be distinguished from issues about free will, then one arrives at a distorted picture of the issues which have to be addressed, of the theoretical resources which need to be brought into play, and of the theoretical options which are plausible when it comes to tackling the problem of moral luck.

2. Nagel suggests that if the claim that moral blameworthiness does not depend on results is defended with reference to the fact that results are, at least partly, influenced by luck, then it is difficult to see why the very same thought would not also apply to all other aspects of our agency which also depend on factors which are subject to luck.[2] It would then follow, however, that "nothing or almost nothing about what a person does seems to be under his control" (Nagel 1976, 26).

According to Nagel, if we accept the idea that blameworthiness only depends on what is free from luck in the sense of not being influenced by external factors, then we are forced to accept that the "area of genuine agency, and therefore of legitimate moral judgement, seems to shrink [...] to an extensionless point" (Nagel 1976, 35). The core of the reasoning leading to this result is as follows:

(1) Blameworthiness does not depend on results (since results are not within the scope of control).
(2) If blameworthiness does not depend on results, then we are not blameworthy for anything (if results are not within the scope of control, then nothing is, and blameworthiness depends on control).
(3) Therefore there is nothing for which we are blameworthy.

2 Nagel claims, in other words, that *resultant luck* (i.e. "luck in the way one's actions and projects turn out") is, as far as its relevance for blameworthiness is concerned, not different from *circumstantial luck* (or, as Nagel calls it, "luck in one's circumstances") which occurs when the circumstances of one's actions were such that one acts in non- (or less) objectionable ways, nor from *constitutive luck* (i.e. luck with regard to "the kind of person you are"), nor from *causal luck* ("luck in how one is determined by antecedent circumstances", all quotes in Nagel 1976, 28).

Nagel does not accept the conclusion of this *modus ponens* but believes the situation to be paradoxical (Nagel 1976, 27). As he sees it, the view that this is the case

> is not a *mistake*, ethical or logical, but a perception of one of the ways in which the intuitively acceptable conditions of moral judgment threaten to undermine it all. (Nagel 1976, 27)

3. Michael Moore, in his 1994 paper "The Independent Moral Significance of Wrongdoing", turns the *modus ponens* just presented into a *modus tollens*, thus arriving at a *reductio* of the claim that results do not affect blameworthiness. Suppose this claim were true for the reason that results are beyond our control due to the possibility of intervening causal chains. Intentional bodily movements, rather than events further down the causal road, then appear to be better suited as candidates for what is under our control. Yet with regard to the relation between bodily movements and their causal antecedents, the situation is, says Moore, in relevant aspects analogous to the relation between consequences and bodily movements:

> Just as a number of events could intervene between the movement of the trigger finger and the death of the victim that would rob the bullet of its normal capacity to kill, so a number of events could intervene between each of these mental states [*sc.* the mental states causing the movement of the trigger finger] and their normal effects so as to rob them of their normal causal power. (Moore 1994, 272)

Moving backwards in the chain of the mental states causing our actions ultimately leaves us, so the argument goes, with nothing at all which is in our control and, therefore, with nothing for which we are blameworthy. This, says Moore, is an unacceptable conclusion, and he therefore rejects the initial assumption of the argument. Results, then, do matter to blameworthiness. Rather than inferring (3) from (1) and (2), Moore infers not-(1) from (2) and not-(3).

4. Whether one has no alternative to going for either the *modus ponens* from (1) and (2) to (3) or for the *modus tollens* from (2) and not-(3) to not-(1) depends on whether premise (2) is true. Nagel and Moore back up this premise by a reflection on the notion of control which seems to establish that, with regard to control, there are two and only two options:

Either, the fact that an aspect of an agent's action is at least partly due to causal factors which are not up to him implies that the aspect in question is beyond the agent's control. Then nothing is under an agent's control, since for any action there are aspects causally relevant to it which are not up to him. When conjoined with the control principle, this implies that there is nothing at all for which agents could be morally responsible and blameworthy and, in particular, that blameworthiness does not depend on results (in other words, (1) and (3) come out as true). In our moral practice, however, we nevertheless do hold one another, at least by and large, responsible for at least some aspects of what we are doing. The 'problem of moral luck', accordingly, would not be a tension between *some* of our ascriptions of moral responsibility and blameworthiness on the one hand and the control principle on the other, but between this principle and our *whole* practice of ascribing responsibility and blameworthiness.

Or, it is possible (and, indeed, often the case) that we are in control of both our actions and their results (in other words, (1) and (3) are false), even though both are, at least partly, caused by factors external to us. Then taking seriously our moral practice does not seem to commit us to the claim that there is moral luck, since the scope of control is wide enough such that there is no reason even to suspect that results are, in principle, *beyond* what we can control. Consequently there is no tension worth being called the 'problem of moral luck' at all.

If there were no other options than the ones just described, then there is *either* a tension between the control principle and *all* of our ascriptions of responsibility and blameworthiness, *or* there is no deep conflict between the control principle and *any* of our ordinary ascriptions of responsibility and blameworthiness (at least to the extent to which they are based on the view that results are among the sorts of things which can influence blameworthiness). If these were the only options, then there would be no *specific* problem of moral luck, since either *all*, or *none* of our ordinary practice would be dubious, as far as the control principle is concerned.

Observe that these options are exactly the standard ones in the traditional debate about free will and responsibility, if determinism is assumed to be true: if incompatibilists are right in claiming that determinism rules out control, then the control principle implies that none of our ascriptions of responsibility and blameworthiness are justified. If compatibilists are right, then there is no conflict between determinism and control, and consequently no fundamental problem with any of our standard ways of ascribing responsibility and blameworthiness, as far as the control principle is concerned. This is, indeed, the way Moore views matters. Accordingly, he writes, somewhat harshly, that there

> is nothing new going on in the badly labelled 'moral luck' debate not already going on (for centuries) in the free-will debate. (Moore 2009, 25)[3]

3 Moore's view that there is no independent problem of moral luck is also reflected by his

5. If what is commonly referred to as the 'problem of moral luck' were to collapse into issues concerning compatibilist and incompatibilist conceptions of free will and responsibility in general, then this would have significant consequences for assessing the standard options for dealing with it which have been proposed in the literature.

If the control principle is upheld, then – on pain of inconsistency – one needs to deny that there is moral luck. There are three ways of harmonizing this with the fact that our moral practice seems to suggest otherwise:

> *Reinterpretation.* The phenomena which might be taken to indicate that there is moral luck can, and ought to be, interpreted such that they are consistent with the denial of moral luck. One might, for instance, be able to explain and justify differences in reactions by pointing to epistemic asymmetries. When something bad has happened as a consequence of some act, this might be taken to be an *indicator* for (a greater degree of) blameworthiness rather than as something which *in itself* is able to influence the degree of blameworthiness. Also, part of the relevant phenomena could be interpreted, to use a term proposed by David Enoch and Andrei Marmor, as "blame-related reactions" (Enoch/Marmor 2007, 412), the justification of which might consist not only in considerations about blameworthiness but also involve, for instance, reference to pragmatic reasons (see Enoch/Marmor 2007, 413 ff.).

> *Revision.* Given certain aspects of our moral practice, we are indeed committed to the view that there is moral luck. Since, in these respects, our practice is not as the control principle says it ought to be, our practice is in need of revision.

> *Wide control.* As with *revision*, the relevant differences in reactions are indeed grounded in the thought that results can *in themselves* be relevant for the degree to which an agent is blameworthy. This, however, does not conflict with the control principle, since, understood correctly, no relevant aspect of human action is *ex ante* excluded from the scope of control.

Going for the *modus tollens* from (2) and not-(3) to not-(1) amounts to adopting the *wide control* strategy. If this were the right view about control, then there

calling the two above distinguished views about control 'incompatibilist' and 'compatibilist' (Moore 2009, 24–25) (see also § 7 below).

would be no tension between the control principle and our practice of assuming that blameworthiness depends on results, since these are not in principle excluded from the scope of control.

If one believes that, according to an appropriate understanding of control, we do not control anything at all, then one is committed to the *modus ponens* version of the reasoning introduced above, i.e. to inferring (3) from (1) and (2). Then one can, in general, either opt for *reinterpretation* or for *revision*. Reinterpreting our differing reactions in the way indicated above might indeed seem like a promising approach with respect to moral distinctions we make given differences in results. It is, however, difficult to see how *all* of our relevant reactions could be interpreted as being grounded in something other than judgements about responsibility and blameworthiness. This effectively leaves the proponent of the *modus ponens* version of the above reasoning with the *revision* strategy. Yet revising our whole practice with regard to ascriptions of responsibility and blameworthiness such that it conforms to the control principle would – under the assumption that nothing at all is under our control – amount to giving up that practice entirely. Even if this were possible (which is highly doubtful), it would be a move more drastic than most people would be able to accept (see, in particular, Strawson 1962).

These considerations can be seen as corroborating Moore's view that the above *modus tollens*, rather than the *modus ponens*, is the most promising option to go for if premise (2) is accepted. Given that results are not in principle excluded from the scope of what agents can control, and given that the only alternative is that we can control nothing at all, the former is definitively the more attractive view.

6. To summarize: If one thinks about control in the way Nagel and Moore do, then one is committed to accept premise (2). As a consequence, one is forced either to accept (1) and (3), or to reject both. In both cases, there is no moral luck, and the most pressing issues are those discussed in the debate about free will.

Whether there is an alternative understanding of the problem of moral luck to the one forced on us by Nagel's and Moore's reasoning crucially depends on whether premise (2) can successfully be criticized. In what follows, it will turn out that this can indeed be done: even if agents do not control results, it does not follow that they do not control anything at all.

Suppose that R is the relation which needs to hold between an agent A and some X in order for A to have control over X. Without presupposing any specification of R, a generic notion of control can be defined as follows:

An agent A has *control* over some X if, and only if, A stands in relation R to X.

With this notion of control in place, a notion of partial control can be defined as follows:

> An agent A has *partial control* over some X if, and only if, A stands in relation R to at least one (or sufficiently many) of the factors which are causally relevant for the occurrence of X.[4]

The scope of control depends of course on the control-constituting relation R, and the same is true for partial control. However R is fleshed out in detail – for which there are several different theoretical options[5] – it is obvious that R, and with it control, will not extend to all consequences of our choices, no matter how remote they are. It is even possible that control does not extend to results *at all*, and that R and control only extend to intentional bodily movements. Of course, it is also possible that there is *nothing* at all which stands in relation R to any agent, and, consequently, that nobody has control over anything.

The question of which view about the scope of control is correct depends on how the control-constituting relation R is to be understood. Even so, the purely structural points just made already show that premise (2) and the arguments given in its favour rely on a distorted view of control. Recall that Moore and Nagel base their defence of premise (2) on the assumption that if results are not within the scope of control, then nothing is. This conditional, however, has just shown to be false: even if results are not within the scope of control, it is nevertheless possible that things causally closer to the agent are (intentional bodily movements being a case in point).

7. In passing, it is worth noting that Moore's own way of setting up the matter also commits him to accepting the conceptual framework just introduced. In a passage from his 2009 book *Causation and Responsibility*, Moore takes what he refers to as a 'compatibilist' notion of control to be characterized by the thought that in order for there to be control over some result,

> [w]e do *not* need to control *every* factor making [a] result possible [...]. (Moore 2009, 25, emphasis added)

4 This notion of partial control can be straightforwardly modified such that partial control comes in degrees: the more of those factors which are causally relevant for the occurrence of some X stand in relation R to some agent A, the higher the degree of partial control which A has over X.

5 Such as e.g. some version of agent-causality, or the notion of reasons-responsiveness as worked out in detail by Fischer/Ravizza (1998).

If what he calls an 'incompatibilist' notion of control is presupposed, by contrast, then

> we control some results only when we can make causally efficacious choices about *every* factor that could cause or prevent this result. (Moore 2009, 24–25)

In a passage from his 1994 paper, he ascribes to incompatibilists essentially the same idea, using the notion of control instead of referring to the ability to make causally efficacious choices:

> Incompatibilists have long sought to show that we must be in control over *all* factors that cause our choices in order for us to be responsible for both those choices and the wrongdoings such choices initiate. (Moore 1994, 257, emphasis added)

In order to avoid either conceptual circularity or a regress, the notion of control invoked in the *definiens* of these two definitions has to be different from the notions of 'incompatibilist' and 'compatibilist' control which they are, respectively, meant to define. As Moore sets up the matter, whether there is some sort of control – be it, in his terminology, a 'compatibilist' or an 'incompatibilist' one – over a result X, depends on whether we have control in some *other* sense over all or some of the factors leading to X. 'Incompatibilists' in Moore's sense thus believe that in order to control anything at all, we need to be in control over all factors influencing it. 'Compatibilists' deny this.

'Compatibilist' control in Moore's sense is partial control as introduced above. In order to define any of these two concepts, one needs to bring into play another, more basic notion of control: there is no partial control in the sense introduced above, and no 'compatibilist' control in the sense of Moore, without some more basic sort of control with regard to which partial control can meaningfully be defined. Apart from the fact that the above definitions require this to be so, the point can also informally be put as follows: when one starts thinking about results of actions as events or states of affairs, the occurrence of which is caused by a number of factors, then responsibility and control have not even begun to enter the picture. In order for control to be involved in some element in the causal chain of events, control has to enter the story at some earlier point.

Clearly, what Moore labels 'incompatibilism' is a highly implausible view, and there is much reason to reject it. A position which is 'compatibilist' in the nonstandard sense introduced by Moore, however, is open for both an incompatibilist and a compatibilist understanding of control, when these terms are used in the way which is standard in the debate about free will and responsibility. As already indicated above, the control-constituting relation R can be spelled out in a number of different ways – and, in particular, such that relation R's holding is either compatible, or incompatible with determinism. In the former case, one's understanding of control (and, as a consequence, of partial control) is compatibilist. In the latter case, it is incompatibilist. It thus turns out that the contrast between compatibilism and incompatibilism is misconceived when it is seen as concerning the question of whether there is control over all, or only over some of the factors leading to some result.

8. The distinction between control and partial control which has been introduced in § 6 above has provided a basis for a criticism of premise (2) and, with it, of the thought that the problem of moral luck collapses into issues about free will. Given that control and partial control can (and, indeed, must) be distinguished conceptually, premise (2) is refuted, and so is the idea that, as far as control is concerned, there are only two options – either we control nothing at all, or all of those things which are potentially relevant for blameworthiness are within the scope of control.

If our understanding of control should, as has been argued above, be more nuanced, then the same is true of our understanding of the theoretical options with regard to the problem of moral luck. In order to assess whether certain elements of our moral practice are not in line with what is required by the control principle, relying exclusively on considerations about control does not suffice. What, if anything, is ruled out by the control principle depends both on what is within the scope of control *and* on what is a legitimate basis for moral assessment. Hence, in order to be able to assess how the distinction between control and partial control bears upon the appropriate understanding of the problem of moral luck, two sorts of considerations have to be brought together. For one thing, a more worked-out conception of control is required. In particular, the extent to which there is a tension between our practice and the control principle will depend on whether (and if so, why) control extends only to things causally close to the agent, such as intentional bodily movements, or whether (and if so, why) it also covers results. For another thing, at least the first steps towards a normative theory of blame need to be undertaken. In particular, it is of crucial importance whether blameworthiness depends only on things within the scope of control, or whether blameworthiness can also depend on what happens within the scope of partial control. One needs, in other words, to know whether control, or rather partial control, is the relevant notion figuring in the control principle.[6]

---

6 Note that this would be different if the scope of control is either void or else such that none of

Suppose that it turned out that control extends to results, or that blameworthiness attaches to partial control (or both). Then there would not even be the appearance of a fundamental tension between our moral practice and the control principle. Furthermore, *wide control* (as introduced above in § 5) would be the appropriate way of dealing with the problem of moral luck.

Correspondingly, there is only a tension between the control principle and our moral practice if the scope of control is restricted to intentional bodily movements (or something else causally close to the agent), and if, at the same time, blameworthiness is only dependent on factors within our control. Then certain elements of our moral practice would seem to violate what is implied by the control principle. To the extent to which this is so, both *reinterpretation* and *revision* are conceivable strategies. Note that also a combination of these two options offers an attractive perspective: while certain reactions might indeed be out of place and should be abandoned, others might be appropriate but misinterpreted if understood as being based on the idea that blameworthiness depends on results.

9. The task of developing reasonably worked-out conceptions of both control and of (the normative grounds of) blameworthiness cannot be accomplished in this paper. Even so, here shall be told at least the beginning of a plausible theoretical story supporting the view that the scope of control and the scope of what blameworthiness depends on coincide.

As a number of authors have observed, it is a worthwhile project to spell out the notion of control by fleshing out the thought that those sorts of things which are within the scope of what agents can control are exactly those things with re-

---

the relevant items are beyond what agents can control (and that, in particular, results are within the scope of control). Then the control principle either implies that none of our moral assessments are acceptable, or it does not constrain them at all, and other sorts of considerations can be brought into play. This is indeed why Moore believes that he can do without both a worked-out conception of control and a normative theory of blame in dealing with the problem of moral luck. The view that the blameworthiness of an agent is increased, *ceteris paribus*, when the agent's action has caused some harm could then be backed up with reference to the way we react in situations of the kind in question. This is precisely what Moore does using what he calls an "experiential argument" (Moore 2009, 29), which allegedly allows to infer that

> we *are* more blameworthy when we cause some evil, than if we merely try to cause it, or unreasonably risk it (Moore 2009, 30)

from the fact that

> we experience greater guilt when we have caused some harm that we either tried to cause, or unreasonably risked, than we experience when we have been equally culpable but we have not caused such a harm (Moore 2009, 30).

spect to which agents can be said to be responsive to reasons. The *prima facie* attractiveness of this idea is supported by the following pair of considerations: for one, being an agent does seem to be closely related to being able to recognize and to being guided by reasons for action. For another, the scope of control is the sphere of agency.

Given that we consider only agents to be potential candidates for appropriate blame, there is reason to believe that blame is, in a sense to be worked out, essentially tied to agency. This observation at least suggests that blameworthiness will have something to do with what is, or could have been, the case with regard to things within the scope of control. This idea gains additional support by the observation that retrospective blame can be understood as something like a temporary shifted correlate of demands – i.e. a correlate of speech acts which are meant to influence agents by giving them, or pointing out to them, certain reasons.[7]

There is, thus, reason to believe that the scope of control and the scope of what our blameworthiness depends on coincide. Moreover, it is not implausible to assume that actions, and not results, are the sorts of things with regard to which agents are responsive to reasons and which, consequently, are relevant for our (degree of) blameworthiness.

This is, to be sure, nothing more than a very brief hint at an argumentative strategy supporting the view that blameworthiness and control – as opposed to partial control – are intimately connected, and that the scope of both includes actions, and not results. If this strategy can be successfully developed, then the tension at the heart of the problem of moral luck is that our moral practice

---

7 It is instructive to consider the case of criminal law and criminal responsibility. With regard to criminal law, Stephen Morse points out that

> a crucial aim of the criminal law is to guide and thus to prevent certain *actions*, because only actions can culpably produce harms. (Morse 2004, 367)

Given that, according to Morse,

> legal rules [...] guide actions primarily because they provide an agent with good moral or prudential reasons for forbearance and action (Morse 2004, 368)

and also given that

> intentional action or forbearance is the only aspect of the human condition that is fully 'up to us', that is fully within our control, and that can be fully guided by and produced by our reason (Morse 2004, 368)

(the degree of) criminal responsibility should depend on actions, and not on their results, since results cannot be controlled by reason(s) in the same way as actions. These ideas cannot, however, be straightforwardly transferred to the case of moral blameworthiness, since a purely instrumentalist interpretation of moral blame is, at least initially, not as plausible as it is in the case of criminal law.

sometimes seems to rest on a view which cannot be maintained. Attempts to reinterpret our reactions in accordance with the idea that upholding our practice does not commit us to the view that blameworthiness depends on results, or attempts to revise our practice to the extent to which it violates the control principle, or a combination of these two strategies, are the only theoretically feasible options.[8]

References

Enoch, David & Marmor, Andrei (2007). The Case Against Moral Luck. *Law and Philosophy* 26, 405–436.

Fischer, John M. & Ravizza, Marc (1998). *Responsibility and Control. A Theory of Moral Responsibility.* Cambridge: Cambridge University Press.

Moore, Michael S. (1994). The Independent Moral Significance of Wrongdoing. *Journal of Contemporary Legal Issues* 5, 237–281.

Moore, Michael S. (2009). *Causation and Responsibility. An Essay in Law, Morals, and Metaphysics.* Oxford: Oxford University Press.

Morse, Stephen J. (2004). Reason, Results, and Criminal Responsibility. *University of Illinois Law Review*, 363–444.

Nagel, Thomas (1976). Moral Luck. Quoted from the revised version reprinted in Thomas Nagel, *Mortal Questions.* Cambridge: Cambridge University Press 1979, 24–38.

Nelkin, Dana (2008). Moral Luck. In E. N. Zalta (Ed.), *The Stanford Encyclopedia of Philosophy (Fall 2008 Edition)*, URL = <http//plato.stanford.edu/archives/fall2008/entries/moral-luck/>.

Strawson, Peter F. (1962). Freedom and Resentment. *Proceedings of the British Academy* 48, 187–211.

Williams, Bernard (1976). Moral Luck. Quoted from the revised version reprinted in Bernard Williams, *Moral Luck*, Cambridge: Cambridge University Press 1981, 20–39.

8 I have presented versions of this paper at workshops and colloquia in Aachen, Berlin, and Potsdam, and I have profited a great deal from the discussions which took place on these occasions. I also received very helpful comments on a draft by Anne Burkard, Simon Gaus, Jan Gertken, Benjamin Kiesewetter, Leo Menges, Christian Neuhäuser and Eduardo Rivera Lopez.

Alexander Aichele

Causation to Culpability: Why Imputation Matters

German Theory of Law, Michael Moore's Causation-Based Approach to Singular Moral Judgment, and Some Kantian Criticism*

Thanks to his moral realism[1] and a certain number of fitting intuitions[2], Michael Moore's theory of singular moral judgments, especially of the ones reached in criminal law, goes without the time-honoured concept of imputation. The phrase was introduced and defined at first by Samuel Pufendorf.[3] Ever since, it lies at the core of German theory of criminal law even if, unfortunately, most of its schools have left the solid foundations of law of nature respective reason. This historical fact is no accident, because the concept of imputation does the whole moral work to hold a person culpable for something done. Imputation is a systematically crucial issue, because it puts the moral or legal blame for something that has happened, usually some harm, on a person who is held, in this way, responsible for it. Hence imputation denotes a moral judgment which ascribes to a person to have done wrong by violating a natural or positive law so that she has to be punished just for this reason.[4] If causation is regarded as a not a moral concept but only a theoretical one, applied to physical objects, causation can't accomplish that task on its own; or anyway, so the story goes. Indeed, I want to defend this old story showing that ascribing blame to somebody and holding her responsible for the wrong she has done involves, at least, two different judgments: On the one hand, a universal one about causality, which is theoretical respective speculative, and on the other hand a singular one about guilt, which is practical respective moral, the latter not being reducible to

---

* Concerning the German practice of academic teaching in criminal law I am indebted, above all, to the front-line reports of Joachim Renzikowski, to whom I am also grateful for many discussions and suggestions of improvement, as I am to Jenny Nolting, Arthur Ripstein, and Erich Roth.

1 See for example (Moore 2009, 30 ff., 41 f., 448).

2 See for example (Moore 2009, 30 ff., 58 f., 140 ff., 337 f.).

3 See (Aichele 2011d).

4 I agree with Moore (2009, 95 f.) on the solely retributional nature of punishment, however for a different reason: The justification of punishment by its assumed function of deterring crime degrades the offender by using her just as a means to some other purpose and, in this way, violates her subjective rights. Of course, deterrence may be a welcome side-effect of punishment.

the first.[5] To cut it short: Imputation, closely connected to causation as it is, cannot be reduced to causation, imputation does not just substitute causation,[6] and causation is, presumably, neither a metaphysical nor, surely, a moral concept.

Since even contemporary German theory of law is therefore right in sticking to the systematic relevance of imputation and its close connection to causation, the first part of the paper shall present the standard doctrines concerning these topics presently taught up and down the country. The situation nicely parallels the one in the U.S. as Moore sees it: "These common legal sayings are all false, and because false, probably misleading to legal fact-finders."[7] Having visited these theoretical waxworks I am going to discuss Kant's way of solving the issue. I am going to analyze his definition of imputation in the *Metaphysics of Morals* and the role his transcendental concept of causation plays in it, although it has found no place in Moore's work. I will close with some hints to another problem which seems to lurk at the heart of moral, that is both juridical and ethical, judgment.

1 Theoretical Waxworks

The following will sketch the so-called theories of causality and imputation presently used in German criminal law.[8] Even better, they are the ones taught at any faculty of law as using them is, normally, necessary or, at least, extraordinarily useful for passing the exams, since the highest courts apply these theories for themselves, too. So, I will concentrate on the teachings called the 'ruling doctrine' (*herrschende Lehre*). This represents the theoretical standard that should be applied as learned, and it is indeed done so in practice, as evidenced by court opinions. Of course, there are some partisans of other, perhaps more systematical theories carefully developed by, presumably clandestine, study of philosophical books or other spooky scientific issues. These partisans take the standards of ruling doctrine for nonsense. But I won't speak of those minority opinions

5 Analyzing culpability like that should indicate the way to get rid of the "general problem with general theories" (Moore 2009, 493), which is their being general since, then there is no need for such a tricky thing as a metaphysical theory of singular causation surrounded by an "aura of mystery" (Moore 2009, 505).

6 The model I support seems to resemble the "old 'ascriptivist' view" (Moore 2009, 4). Right at the beginning of this book, Moore tries to knock down this view. But, as I said before, imputation does not denote simply a "moral usage" (Moore 2009, 4) of causation.

7 (Moore 2009, xii).

8 It has to be emphasized that these doctrines miss the logical and epistemological standards of scientific theory building by far; see (Aichele 2011b).

(*Mindermeinungen*)[9], as most lawyers ignore them. Concerning causation, ruling doctrine in German criminal law is centered around a special counterfactual concept which requires a particular juridical theory of imputation. The former is called 'theory of equivalence' (*Äquivalenztheorie*), the latter 'doctrine of objective imputation' (*Lehre von der objektiven Zurechnung*). I will present both according to one of the standard textbooks on German criminal law, Claus Roxin's *Strafrecht, Allgemeiner Teil.*

1.1 Causation: The Ruling Doctrine

First of all, some theory on causation is needed in jurisprudence, especially in criminal law, as imputation presupposes causation: If and only if someone has caused some event in the outer world which meets the physical elements of some offence, it is possible to hold him responsible for that event.[10] Unfortunately, according to Roxin, neither metaphysics nor transcendental philosophy nor epistemology nor the theory of science are able to assist the law's longing for theory. For causal issues are still in dispute, or to put it differently: There is no such thing as a ruling doctrine in philosophy.[11] Thus, jurisprudence is willy-nilly forced to develop some apt theory on its own. Moreover, even if juridical theory-building, in its spare-time, would look on present philosophy and theory of science, it will find itself quite ahead of these efforts anyway.[12] The mentioned theory of equivalence is a result of the own work of criminal law. Maximilian von Buri first presented it in the middle of the 19th century.[13] The supreme court of the Reich commonly used it afterward, and the Federal High Court (*Bundesgerichtshof*) hallowed it with 'undisputed use' after the second world war,[14] and held fast onto until now.[15]

9 On of the most renowned examples widely known even in the English speaking scientific community may be Joachim Hruschka. On our topic see for example (Hruschka 1976).

10 (Roxin 2006, Vol.1, §11, Rn. 1): "Erste Voraussetzung der Tatbestandserfüllung ist immer, dass der Täter den Erfolg verursacht hat." Since imputing omissions presents no special problems I will omit their discussion. See (Nolting 2011).

11 (Roxin 2006, § 11, Rn. 4).

12 (Roxin 2006, § 8, Rn. 50). Roxin's example for present philosophy in this context, which is action, is G.E.M. Anscombe's "Intention" which was first published in 1956.

13 (von Buri, 1873).

14 (Roxin 2006, § 11, Rn. 9).

15 (Roxin 2006, Rn. 8 f.). Concerning the history of the theory of equivalence see (Haas 2002, 144 ff.).

Roxin presents and the average German law student knows, learns and reproduces the theory of equivalence as follows: 1. Any condition necessary for some offence to happen must be considered as the cause of the same offence – no matter what kind of condition that may be. Any of them – be it logical, metaphysical, natural, moral, normative and so on – has the same value, since it plays a causal role for the offence to happen. The theory is named, thus, after the equivalence of necessary conditions insofar all of them are taken for causes. For example: If someone is murdered by shooting, causes are, in the same way, the person who shot, the murderer's and the victim's parents, grand-parents, great-grand-parents etc. as well as the gunsmith having made the weapon and his parents etc.; but also the circumstances under which all those people met, fell in love etc.; and also the law forbidding to shoot people etc.; and also cosmic contingence that made earth a place where iron to make guns is found and so on – one gets the general idea.[16] It is, clearly, the same thing which Moore in his penetrating discussion of the sufficiency of counterfactual dependence for causation dubs nicely the "promiscuity" of causes.[17]

2. According to this theory, any offence has an infinite number of causes. Therefore it is impossible, from a causal point of view, to discriminate culpable human action from other, natural events. The law, however, is interested solely in man-made conditions, that is, those which are actions.[18] Action here is, as Roxin has it, any possible external expression of personality made willingly and consciously – whatever these strong metaphysics of personality may, precisely, say.[19]

3. Conditional necessity and therefore causality is stated, solely, by forming negative counterfactuals of the form "If A hadn't happened then B wouldn't have happened" or "If X hadn't done A, then B wouldn't have happened to Y". These counterfactuals, obviously, presupposes some law-like regularities typically connecting certain classes of events. But even if natural sciences[20] might provide such 'covering laws', the laws cannot solve the 'problem of indeterminacy' of

16 (Roxin 2006, § 11, Rn. 6).
17 (Moore 2009, 396).
18 (Roxin 2006, § 11, Rn. 7).
19 (Roxin 2006, § 8, Rn. 44): "Handlung ist zunächst einmal alles, was sich einem Menschen als geistig-seelisches Aktionszentrum zuordnen läßt." Moore, as well, seems to be comitted to quite strong metaphysics of personality insofar as he hints at the possibility of "truly essential properties" (2009, 435) making up personal identity, on the one hand, which are kept unfortunately completely in the dark. On the other hand, the job seems to be done by some kind of infallible emotion- or intuition-based self-knowledge, which Moore calls "*sense of* identity" (435), but that, indeed, "is not yet much of an argument" (435).
20 (Roxin 2006, § 11, Rn. 8–17).

causation as counterfactual dependence, as Moore shows.[21] And in general, there can be no counterfactual-based positive concept of causation, which, at the same time, excludes univocity.

4. The theory of equivalence does not say anything about the connection of logical entities. It neither aims at explaining classes of events. So it seems to be what Moore calls a "counterfactualist/singularist theory"[22] – but this happens, so to speak, behind its own back, since it does not reflect on its ontological commitments concerning a solid possible-worlds-realism which actual protagonists of the German law's equivalence of causes certainly would despise. Anyway, causality in the law deals with concrete actions of actual persons bringing about concrete effects.[23] So, in the law, in contrast to natural science, single external events must be linked by causation, despite the fact that the only way of testing such a connection involves only logical entities. It is necessary to conceptualize negative counterfactuals, may they be in accordance with law-like regularities or not, if one wants to know what they denote – real names do not entail what their subject is. Therefore, the negative counterfactuals must be general. Since general propositions include general concepts and general concepts are universals and universals do not exist independently from some kind of thinking, universals are no real metaphysical entities respective substances like singular things, but logical objects. Obviously, Moore rejects such nominalistic metaphysics. And, like him, 'I shall not undertake a general defense of nominalism versus realism'[24] – this was done most convincingly by William of Ockham or Leibniz for example.[25] But, at least, it should be emphasized that apart from other rather unclear metaphysical and epistemological points, it seems quite strange to endorse at the same time both a materialistic ontology and realism concerning universals, as Moore does; the latter point needs no further evidence,[26] the former is corrobated by the conviction that "(i)t is up to" – probably: natural – "science to tell us what there is and what there is not".[27]

But back to the theory of equivalence in German law. It is developed as a means to ascertain efficient causation as a relation between singular and man-made modifications of the physical world. At any rate, such a theory

21 See (Moore 2009, 372–382).

22 (Moore 2009, 503).

23 (Roxin 2006, § 11, Rn. 4, 21, 24).

24 Vice versa (Moore 2009, 444).

25 Against Hobbesian hyper-nominalism, which Moore may have in mind, see (Leibniz 1670, 427 f.). On Ockham see for example (Kaufmann 1993).

26 See for example (Moore 2009, 444).

27 (Moore 2009, 443), see also (Moore 2009, 263, 273).

rests on metaphysics. These metaphysics, however, remain obscure. The truth it seeks is like Moore's metaphysics, namely it exists independently from being recognized or being thought of.

5. Discovering causality between an action and an event is not sufficient but necessary for imputation. There must not be any choice between causal factors during the juridical examination of possible causal connections of said events. Consequently, there is no singling out of certain causes according to individual relevance.[28] So the whole infinity of causes counting for possible reasons for imputation, that is, any actions or man-made circumstances or possible influences of natural circumstances before or during the event examined, has to be considered. For, if investigating some possible causality is concerned with singular events, and assessing the relevance of causes is not part of the causal investigation, according to the principle of equivalence any action and any event that occurred until the event in question actually occurred has to count as a possible reason for imputation, since it is, obviously, a possible cause of it. If this preliminary investigation is to be completed at all, clearly a theory of imputation has to carry the burden of defining causal relevance. If it were to do this without at the same time providing sufficient reason for imputation, causality would have no place in law; it wouldn't be a necessary condition but, simply, superfluous.

Before turning to the mentioned theory of imputation, let us take a short look from the outside on this theory of causation as it is represented by Roxin's textbook. Even if one doesn't look too closely, the diagnosis is devastating. The theory of equivalence commonly taught and used in German criminal law is as alien to common sense as it is impracticable, dysfunctional, and self-contradicting.[29]

1. That the theory of equivalence is alien to common sense goes without saying: No one will accept or believe without having been vigorously indoctrinated for a long time that his own beloved grandmother is the cause of the brutal murder committed by his sister's son, who was born seven years after grannie's decease.

2. The theory is impracticable: Since there is an infinite number of causes, there is an infinite number of possible sufficient reasons for imputation. A decision which one is or which ones are actually sufficient for imputation only can be made after a full exposition of all possible reasons. Therefore, this decision has to be postponed until infinity ends. So, either actions are imputed regardless

28 (Roxin 2006, § 11, Rn. 21/22).

29 The following objections are, concerning their formal structure, in principle the same as the ones put forward by Joachim Hruschka, who is one of the most prominent legal critics of the equivalence of causes; see (Hruschka 1998, 588–594).

of equivalent causation and the theory is, evidently, superfluous or it is done with regard to it and the whole process is at loss.

3. The theory is dysfunctional: The law's interest is focussed on man-made external action, which is willing and conscious expressions of personality. However, if we hold equivalent any condition for some event taken as offence, there is no possibility to distinguish such expressive action from other another one. The only feature that will serve legitimately to distiguish natural events and actions can be the mere fact that the latter ones are motions of human beings, whereas the former ones are not. Consequently, any motion of any human being has to be taken for an action. Then the intended distinction cannot be established, and motions of human beings necessitated by nature like breathing, eating, sleeping and so on are not distinguishable from actions. Therefore, equivalence of causes treats natural events and human actions as the same.

4. The theory is self-contradicting: As Joachim Hruschka rightly insists,[30] it defines, on the one hand, a cause explicitly and exclusively as any necessary condition. But makes use of it, on the other hand, in a way only a sufficient condition allows. This is because contributing somehow to the possible occurence of an event and bringing it about by efficiently causing it is simply not the same thing.[31] So, it is not just a question of names leading to vain discussions about words which philosophers notoriously are prone to, as Roxin deigns to insinuate when shortly touching on Mackie's INUS construction.[32] On the contrary, it is a matter of different phenomena. This difference may be ignored and eliminated semantically but, having done so, mustn't be used factually.

Obviously, the reason why the equivalence of causes collapses, in the first place, is its vain refusal to draw a difference between necessary and sufficient conditions. This difference cannot be restored even by some magical theory of imputation. This failure was and is, surely, not unavoidable. For, firstly, it is at the latest since Leibniz quite common to ask for a sufficient reason if one wants to know why some single event occurs. Secondly, all problems put aside, classical theories of causation as different as, for example, the ones of Kant and John Stuart Mill, agree that the concept of cause denotes the condition determining and bringing about the state of affairs identifiable as effect – always supposing that there are some laws of nature. And as it shall be pointed out later, treating causes as sufficient conditions holds good even if we accept the possibility of free action. In sum, the complete failure of German criminal

30 (Hruschka 1998, 589–591).

31 See also (Hart & Honoré, 1959, 393).

32 (Roxin 2006, § 11, Rn. 8, especially fn. 13).

law's homemade ruling doctrine of causation simply seems to be a matter of ignorance – may it result from modesty towards the depths of philosophical discourse or sheer indifference towards non-juridical issues.

1.2 Imputation: The Ruling Doctrine

Doubtlessly, any issues concerning the ruling doctrine of objective imputation could be finished off without even looking at its content, since it rests on the equivalence of causes. Leading protagonists like Roxin consider the relation between the two theories strict enough to refute objections against objective imputation on the grounds that denying objective imputation entails denying equivalence of causes.[33] Both theories are treated logically equivalent, and that would be that. However, the informational content transferred on the subject of the doctrine would then be poor. So, it shall be exposed here to some extent. Even if the following criticisms sound similar to the points Moore rightly makes against the harm-within-the-risk analysis,[34] it should be noted that its German cousin has its fief in criminal law.

Objective imputation responds to the vastness of the causal ocean opened by the equivalence of causes. It has the task of picking out the causes that make mere causation into an action which fulfills the elements of some offence.[35] Such causes are the ones endangering a legally protected right by giving rise to some illicit risk. If that risk is actualized by bringing about a certain effect which completes an offence, the risk-producing actions are to be imputed to the person who has given rise to said risks.[36] The equivalence of causes requires this artificial sounding construction: If person A aims at person B, pulls the trigger of the Magnum and shoots B in the heart, it is neither the pulling of the trigger which kills B nor the shooting nor the hitting him. For B, obviously, dies from a bunch of mysterious physio-physical reasons. Therefore, aiming, trigger-pulling, shooting, and hitting must be considered as illicit risks to kill someone. They are realized only when B actually dies, since otherwise it would be impossible to make a risk-based distinction between committing and attempting some crime. Although it is hidden in the abysses of the causal ocean what, precisely, has caused B to meet his maker, at the same time, it is quite clear from a look into the penal code that it is forbidden to kill people intentionally. However, ac-

---

33 (Roxin 2006, Rn. 46, fn. 105).
34 (Moore 2009, ch. 7–10).
35 (Roxin 2006, § 11, Rn. 46).
36 (Roxin 2006, Rn. 47–49).

cording to objective imputation, the penal rule forbidding murder cannot refer to causation but, in truth, refers to illicit risks.[37] So, it is not forbidden to kill people by shooting them, but it is forbidden to shoot someone because he might die by it – whether that is done with intent of murder, again, is another matter. And, of course, it is not correct, in the legal sense, to say “A shot B to death”. Rather, stating the fact runs: “By shooting B, A gave rise to a certain legally illicit risk which has become real as B died by a gunshot wound.” Therefore, clearly, perpetrator A cannot be condemned for shooting B dead. Rather, A must be condemned for giving rise to said risk which, unfortunately or intentionally, has become real.

Now, the concept of risk implies possible future events respective future contingents. So, in order to establish some possible offence judgement, it cannot be based on simple *ex post* causal assumptions. For from that point of view, due to equivalence of causes, each prior event or action caused the effect – B’s lying dead with a hole in him – and, on this ground, would have to be culpable even if it was completely unapt to bring about said effect.[38] This way, the aim of causal restriction could not be reached. Consequently, any sentence must evidently be based on the possible perpetrator‘s fictional *ex ante* point of view, which has to be constructed by the judge according to the defendant’s actual and possible knowledge of the circumstances of the action.[39] It is A’s epistemic state which does or doesn’t meet the penal norm, precisely because that person will be condemned for giving rise to some risk and not for bringing about some effect. This is the reason why the whole thing is called *objective* imputation, for A is obliged to know the risks her actions give rise to in the same way as any other person. There is no place for individual gaps of knowledge, since what a person has to know is prescribed by law reflecting the generally knowable state of natural science. Therefore, not the actual state of knowledge person A was in at the time when giving rise to the risk is relevant, but the epistemic state she should have been in while having done so.

In order to compensate for the oversupply of causes bringing about the death of B, objective imputation eliminates concrete respective individual causation in favour of abstract risks originating from A’s acting. If however, according to the equivalence of causes, any action of A prior to B’s death is actually a cause of B’s being dead, then, again according to the equivalence of causes, any action of A before that event gives rise to the illicit risk which is realized by B’s being

37 See (Haas 2004, 199).
38 See (Mir Puig 1996, 766); (Jakobs 1999, 55).
39 (Renzikowski 1997, 120 f).

dead. Therefore, giving rise to legally illicit risks while performing legally permitted actions is not only possible but should be affirmed emphatically by supporters of objective imputation. Doing so can be seen in general as acting negligently. According to Roxin, willful acting even implies negligent acting straightaway.[40] Therefore the same offence, that is giving rise to a certain illicit risk, is simultaneously committed intentionally and negligently, although it remains, of course, still possible to commit the offence just by negligence.

Ignoring the blatant contradiction apparently involved in that idea of intentional offence, the upshot of objective imputation is obviously this: Since it is obviously possible to commit offences by any action, even permitted or due, the possibility of giving rise to some illicit risk performing any action must be and can be known by any person *ex ante*. Any realization of such a risk is at least an offence by negligence, forbidden by law and therefore culpable. Any person has to know *ex ante* whether an action is in some way apt to give rise to an illicit risk. Therefore, any permitted action might be, at the same time, forbidden, if it could be in some way apt to give rise to an illicit risk – whenever this risk is realized somehow, since its realization evidently cannot be caused by the risk itself.

One may then ask why an effect, the realization of a risk, is needed at all. If the offence is always committed prior to that effect, and if the offending character of the action performed is likewise prior to said effect, and if the latter is subject to objective *ex ante* knowledge, which can be constructed independently of *ex post* knowledge by any judge, there seems to be no reason to wait for risks becoming real events. So, A would not need to have killed B to murder him and even to be sentenced for murder, since the offence is the risk that A gives rise to. The law, by means of the doctrine of objective imputation, should be able to create heaven on earth: No criminal effect would have to be caused by some perpetrator to get him off the streets and to put him in jail. Even better, no victim would have to be harmed. This is obviously not the case. The sheer fact should actually surprise supporters of objective imputation, provided that they cling to their theoretical viewpoint. No one does that, of course. Rather, even supporters of objective imputation – wisely but without logical reasons – insist that realizing illicit risks forms a necessary condition for prosecution.[41]

---

40 (Roxin, 2006 § 11, Rn. 49): "In der Erfüllung des objektiven Tatbestandes realisiet sich stets schon eine fahrlässige – wenngleich meist nicht strafbare – Erfolgsherbeiführung, so dass in jedem vorsätzlichen Delikt ein fahrlässiges darinsteckt."

41 (Roxin, 2006 § 11, Rn. 49): "Man kann also zusammenfassend sagen, dass die Zurechnung zum objektiven Tatbestand die Verwirklichung einer vom Täter geschaffenen, nicht durch ein erlaubtes Risiko gedeckten Gefahr innerhalb der Reichweite des Tatbestandes voraussetzt."

But this concession to common sense amounts to a tacit admission either that the offending risk is neither recognizable nor identifiable in any way without its realization having happened or that defining those actions prone to give rise to illicit risks is completely at random.[42] Unfortunately, none of this can explain away the unfortunate consequence that no one has to be killed if someone is murdered.

2 A Better Theory of Singular Moral Judgment: The Kantian Analysis of Imputation

If one does not turn a blind eye to the complete failure of ruling doctrine in German criminal law – as, in general, its protagonists do – we could ask what we can learn from it. There are two answers: Firstly, concerning causation, dismissing the difference between necessary and sufficient conditions seems not advisable; secondly, concerning culpability, establishing causation, fundamental as it is in most cases, is never enough for declaring culpability. And, indeed, even German authors saw that long before German theory of criminal law fell into the maelstrom of philosophical indifference, which may have been provoked by the rise of German idealism on the one side and historicism on the other side during the 19th century, which have been influential enough to pulverize in between themselves the traditional philosophical roots of German legal theory. Actually, the average relevant theories which were developed throughout the tradition of universal jurisprudence of German Elightenment from Pufendorf to Gottfried Achenwall and Alexander Gottlieb Baumgarten integrate both answers into systematically sound and practicable doctrines. So the Kantian solution concerning imputation as it shall be presented now is not really original. On the contrary, Kant drew heavily upon Achenwall and Baumgarten.[43] His definition of imputation is just best known and, perhaps, the systematically most developed approach in the line of this tradition which, unfortunately, has come to a temporary end with Kant's classical theory. Causation, however, is quite another story, since it was, as it is widely acknowledged, Hume's skeptical empiricism, especially concerning causation, which has set Kant on the tracks of transcendental philosophy. It is not possible, of course, not even necessary to give a full blown analysis of Kantian causality here. Instead, I will deliver just a

42 See (Haas 2004, 210 ff.).
43 See (Hruschka 2004); (Aichele 2008); and (Aichele 2011c).

rough sketch[44] and focus, first and foremost, on imputation. I will try to point out why causation alone is not enough in order to arrive at singular moral judgements, as Moore wants – even if a true singularist theory of causation would be at hand, which is obviously not the case at present, as Moore himself concedes.[45]

2.1 Universality of Causal Judgment

In the *Critique of Pure Reason,* Kant distinguishes two different concepts of causality, which complement each other in judgments of experience.[46] The first is a formal one. According to this pure category, a cause is defined as a necessary and sufficient condition of some effect, where both are expressed by categorical propositions. So, the logical meaning of causality entails the equivalence of antecedent and consequent in a hypothetical judgment.[47] This cannot be any other way because pure formal relations do not involve intuitional elements, that is, material content arranged according to the general forms of intuition (*Anschauung*), which are time and space. The second concept encloses such content, presupposing the pure category and at the same time modifying it. Therefore, schematized causality entails reality. That is, it refers to a determined object of possible experience which has been perceived or is, at least, perceptible by intuition.[48] Now perception and determination of different objects, expressed by different categorical judgments and linked hypothetically, entails succession in time.[49] In this way, the pure category and its logical meaning of equivalence are modified into strict implication[50]: They are applied to succeeding conceptual determinations of perceptible objects. This may well be called the material sense of schematized causality, where the scheme consists in the rule of hypothetically linking categorical empirical propositions: "Das Schema der Ursache und der Kausalität eines Dinges überhaupt ist das Reale, worauf, wenn es nach Belieben

---

44 On this issue I shall constantly refer to (Schnepf 2006), which, as far as I see, is not only the most penetrating and conclusive systematic analysis of Kantian causality, but even has the merit of relating it to empiricist – and therefore antirealist – models of causal explanation from Hempel to van Fraassen presently discussed in theory of science.

45 See (Moore 2009, 506 ff.)

46 See (Schnepf 2006, 360 ff.)

47 See (Schnepf 2006, 334 ff.)

48 See (Heidegger 1989, §§ 7–9); (Grapotte 2004).

49 See (Schnepf 2006, 347 ff.)

50 See (Schnepf 2006, 357 f.)

gesetzt wird, jederzeit etwas anderes folgt. Es besteht also in der Sukzession des Mannigfaltigen, in so fern sie einer Regel unterworfen ist."[51]

Kantian causality, therefore, involves a categorical rule that allows to decide which one of two categorical judgements about objects of possible experience must be given priority when both are linked by an asymmetrical if-then-connection. In other words, a rule like that just makes it possible to identify antecedent and consequent of empirical conditionals in such a way that their relation itself, on account of the universality of the linked propositions, has to be necessary. At the same time, this makes it even possible to determine the truth-values of negative counterfactual conditionals.[52] Clearly, such a rule does not have to contain anything about the way events, existing independently of our experience, are linked in or by nature. But it enables finite minds like ours to order the ever-flowing stream of intuitions moulding it into regular and identifiable, that is, causally determined, changes of objects of experience.

Why, now, do causal judgments have to be necessarily universal ones, according to this model? To put it bluntly: Because the possible parts of the categorical propositions, which the conditionals in question are made of, are not intuitions but concepts. And, according to Kant – who merely continues reasonable traditional teaching on this matter –, there are only two sorts of mental contents, namely intuitions and concepts. Of these only one, which is intuition, is singular by extension, whereas concepts are absolutely universal.[53] Since individuals – even as it seems[54] in Moore's opinion – and, therefore, the mental contents representing them, too, are ineffable meaning not completely analyzable by a finite mind, intuitions must be conceptualized in order to say what it is they represent. So, in order to know which or what kind of events are causally connected, both propositions forming a causal judgment have to be universal. Therefore, causal judgments must be universal by extension, too. Or, trying to put it in terms more akin to Moore's preferred terminology: Surely, singular events are conceptualized and expressed as tokens of some general types which entail all there is to know about the properties making an event a token of a certain type. But that, firstly, does not rule out the possibility of relating one singular event to another type; secondly, it does not explain how a type, which must be given already to apply it to some event, is given; thirdly, it does not explain how some singular event can be identified as a token of this certain type but not another one; fourthly, there is no reason to make such a type an

51 (Kant 1781/1787, A 144/B 183)
52 See (Schnepf 2006, 372ff.).
53 See (Kant 1800, 521 §1); (Kant 1781/1787, A 50ff./B 74ff.)
54 See (Moore 2009, especially 348 and 334 ff, 363, 511f.)

object existing independently from being thought of or formed by thinking on grounds that could be called pragmatical – if its contingent content is meant – and transcendental – if its formal necessity is meant – as well. Therefore, there seems to be no difference between such types and universal empirical concepts applied to singular intuitions. But that leads to the result that singular events are defined as tokens of some type by applying a type to a singular event. That leaves the type-defined token formally universal by extension, although it will be much richer in content. According to its logical status, such tokens should behave like Aristotelian last species which might be specified *ad infinitum*, if one wishes or if further differentiation is required, without ever reaching the singularity of *infima species*. So, any singular event may, even necessarily if seen from an epistemological point of view, become a token by subsumption under some type. But certainly, metaphysically speaking, it has not to be in itself just a token of that type. However, all this does in no way make these concepts merely "illusory".[55]

2.2 Singular Moral Judgements: Imputation

Suppose we were to share Moore's robust moral realism and its natural connection to moral sense, and, therefore, we were hopefully to be able to answer, for example, the question why the guilt felt by some survivors of concentration camps for surviving their nearest and dearest is not real and true guilt.[56] Even then, the possible acceptance of the universality of causal judgements shows that the thesis "causation of the harm is sufficient for liability for that harm"[57] does not hold, whereas, as Moore also claims, "culpable causation"[58] is sufficient. This is because of a difference between causation and culpability. This difference is due to the fact that causal judgments are universal and indicate regularities of changes in the world. Judgments about guilt, however, refer to something which a single person did or should have done, impose the blame for it on her if that action was ethically or legally wrong, and put that person to ethical or legal punishment. In short: Judgments about guilt are singular moral judg-

55 (Moore 2009, 444).
56 I am indebted to Jenny Nolting and Joachim Renzikowski for this example. See for Moore's "experiential argument" (Moore 2009, 29) on guilt (Moore 2009, 29 ff.).
57 (Moore 2009, 430).
58 (Moore 2009, 431).

ments.[59] Even Moore acknowledges this.[60] The concept of imputation fulfils the requirement of a theory of such judgments.

Kant defines the concept of imputation in the *Introduction to the Metaphysics of Morals:* "*Zurechnung* (imputatio) in moralischer Bedeutung ist das *Urteil*, wodurch jemand als Urheber (causa libera) einer Handlung, die alsdann *Tat* (factum) heißt und unter Gesetzen steht, angesehen wird."[61]

Notice first Kant's emphasis on the moral meaning of imputation. This is no pleonasm, since traditionally imputation is divided in two greater steps.[62] These two steps are called imputatio facti or imputatio physica and imputatio legis or imputatio practica. Kant follows that tradition in such a way that he treats the first one as a judgment about the relation of two different events in the physical world, that is, as a causal judgment. A pure causal judgment does not entail ascriptions of freedom to the objects involved in bringing about the related events since "every action can be seen either as some physical event or under the condition that we have a certain obligation to act".[63] And only if this condition is met an action is imputable.[64] Therefore, practical imputation leads to a certain moral judgment which is made with regard to a change in the physical world, because, as Kant emphasizes, mere volitions are not imputable, at least legally.[65] Since imputation presupposes physical change, an imputative judgement follows the logical structure of a causal judgment, which is hypothetical.

So imputation does not only link two concepts, but two categorical judgments, which can be true or false according to an antecedent-consequent- or cause-effect-relation. Concerning its modality, such a hypothetic judgment is problematic. That is, it is affirming or negating the merely possible. Therefore, it at least can be true. Now an imputative judgment is not focussed on the logical relation of its arguments, that is, the truth-value of their conditional connection. Rather, the parts of that connection are propositions about non-logical objects, which only can be linked hypothetically in accordance with a cause-effect-relation. Thus, in virtue of being based on some causal judgment, imputative judgment in principle connects empirical propositions, propositions that cannot be

---

59 See (Joerden 2010, 337).
60 See (Moore 2009, 173 f.).
61 (Kant 1797, 334).
62 After Joachim Georg Daries' *Institutiones Jurispridentiae Universalis* (1740), these greater steps usually are methodically subdivided in smaller ones, see (Hruschka 1991, 449–452). On the corresponding differentiations in Baumgarten's *Initia philosophiae practicae primae* (1760) which Kant used as textbook see (Aichele 2005, 6–20).
63 (Kant 1793/4, 503).
64 (Kant 1793/4, 503).
65 (Kant 1793/4, 564).

acquired without experience.[66] While doing so, it ascribes, presupposing the succession of time, to the cause that it is "so etwas, woraus sich auf das Dasein eines anderen schließen läßt."[67] However, if it is of the imputative kind, such causal judgment must be understood in different way than the judgment that ascribes to the shining sun, being the cause, the warming of a stone, being the effect. For it does not concern theoretical or rather physical issues. On the contrary, it has moral meaning, that is, imputative judgment refers to "Kausalität aus Freiheit" to be sought for "immer außer der Sinnenwelt im Intelligibelen"[68], meaning that freedom can never be an object of experience. The possibility of freedom concerning free causation just says that a natural cause can do nothing but bring about its adequate effect, whereas the cause which is the subject of imputation is capable of refraining from bringing about a certain effect.[69] So the truth-value of such judgment only can be assertively defined for singular cases.[70] From this, it follows firstly, that the truth-value of any imputative judgment is contingent,[71] secondly, that it cannot be turned into modal necessity, and thirdly, that any imputative judgment, strictly speaking, must remain probable. Any imputative judgment, therefore, is singular and can consequently be formed only retrospectively. Imputative judgement ascribes freedom to the cause, precisely in this sense, that it is up to the possible cause being an actual cause, that is to say, to result in some effect. So finally, the subject of imputative judgment is spontaneity of the cause, since it asserts that it has become a cause on its own.

Kant calls causes of that kind "Urheber" (author) or *causa libera*. An author brings about some effect by an action which is called "Tat" (deed) and also falls under a practical law. Kant defines 'deed' in the *Introduction to the Metaphysics of Morals* likewise: "*Tat* heißt eine Handlung, sofern sie unter Gesetzen der Verbindlichkeit steht, folglich auch, sofern das Subjekt in derselben nach der Freiheit seiner Willkür betrachtet wird. Der Handelnde wird durch einen solchen Akt als *Urheber* der Wirkung betrachtet, und diese, zusamt der Handlung selbst, können ihm *zugerechnet* werden, wenn man vorher das Gesetz kennt, kraft welches auf ihnen eine Verbindlichkeit ruhet."[72]

An action is to be considered a deed if and only if it can be subsumed under some given ethical or juridical rule which is, in itself, absolutely necessitating

66 See (Kant 1781/1787, A 198 ff./B 243 ff.; A 243 ff./B 301 ff.).
67 (Kant 1781/1787, A 243/ B 301).
68 (Kant 1788, A 188).
69 (Kant 1788, A 174 f.)
70 (Kant 1781/1787, A 75/B 100 ann.).
71 (Kant 1781/1787, A 74 f./B 100.).
72 (Kant 1797, 329).

the will, that is, it obliges by pure reason alone. Without such obligation no action can be considered a deed and consequently must not be imputed to any author. It follows that imputation strictly presupposes a deviation from a moral rule.[73] Just doing one's duties, therefore, never results in imputation. So only supererrogation and violation give possible objects of imputation, which either lead to ethical respect or disdain or to juridical reward or punishment.[74] Therefore, only imputation leads to culpability. Any imputative judgement is formed, retrospectively, on occasion of some singular event that is ascribable to a free cause and related to a certain moral duty which applies to the given situation. So, it is only by imputation that an ethical rule or a positive law can be applied to a physical change in the world, which has no moral meaning in itself if it would just be seen from the causal point of view. Single actions are brought about – or can be brought about, in the case of omissions which I shall ignore here[75] – by certain acting subjects labeled as the author of the action by a singular imputative judgment. Imputative judgment, therefore, does neither refer to the possibility of freedom in general, which must be taken for granted until the opposite is proven, nor to an acting subject's maxims which are, in principle, universal. Since each imputative judgment is a singular moral judgment, and each singular moral judgment has to be an imputative judgment, any acting subject's prerequisite for being subject to practical imputation is "freie Willkür" (free arbitrariness).

Skipping detailed analysis, arbitrariness is basically defined as a faculty "*nach Belieben zu tun oder zu lassen*" connected "mit dem Bewußtsein des Vermögens seiner Handlung zur Hervorbringung des Objekts".[76] Thus, the general concept of arbitrariness already implies prospective knowledge of causal processes respective rules, that is, a knowledge of means appropriate to achieve the end intended, but it doesn't entail that this end is a moral one.[77] Arbitrariness is free only if that faculty in "Unabhängigkeit ihrer *Bestimmung* durch sinnliche Antriebe" "zu Handlungen aus reinem Willen bestimmt werden (kann)".[78] This is the mark of human arbitrariness. It is potentially free since, though nec-

73 Immanuel Kant, AA vol. 19, Refl. 7124 "1. Was ich gutes thue, ob ich gleich nicht schuldig bin es zu thun, das kann mir imputirt werden. / 2. Was ich gutes nicht thue, ob ich zwar schuldig bin es zu thun, das kan mir imputirt werden. (...)/ 1, Was ich gutes nicht thue und auch nicht schuldig bin es zu thun, das kann mir nicht imputirt werden. / 2. Was ich gutes thue und auch schuldig bin es zu thun, daß kann mir (nicht) imputirt werden."

74 See (Kant 1797, 334); (Hruschka 1998, 105 ff.).

75 See fn 10.

76 (Kant 1797, 317).

77 See Kant's own instructive example in (Kant 1793/4, 502).

78 (Kant 1797, 318).

essarily affected by sensual stimulation, it is not, necessarily, determined by affection.[79] And according to Kant, just an acting subject of this sort, which is capable to obey to the laws of practical reason, is considered a person. The subject's personality is referred to with assertive judgments of imputation only,[80] for mere accountability in general has to be taken for granted until the opposite is proven.

To summarize, Kant's analysis of imputation contains the following elements: 1. Imputation is a judgement concerning a special relation of causality wherein the cause brings about some effect from itself, that is, it acts freely. 2. Such a judgement ascribes to some subject authorship of a deed, that is, deviation from some moral rule. 3. Therefore, the factual reason for imputation is the acting subject's free arbitrariness. 4. Ascription of practical authorship qualifies the acting subject as a person. 5. Since causation as such is morally neutral, because it is a physical issue which does not stand under moral rules, only imputation involving application of such rules leads to culpability. 6. From the logical point of view an imputative judgment is: a) in quantity: singular, b) in quality: either affirmative or negative, c) in relation: hypothetical, d) in modality: problematic-assertive.

As remote from Moore's strictly causal model as a Kantian theory of imputation seems to be, it might cast some light on a point which could be seen as a discrete weakness of Moore's conception. Since it is permanently present between the lines of this very paper it should be brought in the open, too: It seems at least to me as if in Moore's *Causation and Responsibility,* there is no extra-intuitional argument for strict – that means: nothing else needed – sufficiency of causation for culpability. And far from banning intuition from scientific or rather philosophical research, intuition, as pure and simple it may be and as necessary as a heuristic starting-point it is, does not amount in itself to an argument. And, as it is, even intuition may deceive, as it seems intuitively perfectly clear that the sun circles around the earth. To be sure, any of these intuitions about the equivalence of causation and culpability could be subject to a cast-iron proof based on a true singularist metaphysical theory of causation. Yet in the present lack of such theory, a generalist one, of course supplemented with Kantian imputation, will do quite well, perhaps just until the desired metaphysics are at hand – whenever that may be.

---

79 See (Kant 1797, 318).
80 This Kantian claim seems to resemble strongly Tony Honoré's (Honoré 1999) model of moral personality.

3 The Heart of the Matter

If Kant's analysis just roughly hits the mark, it might also serve to open the view on a – or perhaps the – crucial problem lurking at the heart of the matter as I see it. It was well-known in the 18th century and it lies hidden behind Kant's definition of a deed, too. I just want to describe it in short, since I am not aware of a completely convincing solution – except a few attempts to alleviate it by pragmatically developing some rules of thumb. That was done, for example, quite conclusively by Baumgarten,[81] which might explain Kant's silence about the problem of subsuming single events under general rules respective of applying general rules to single events.

Since single events occurring in the external world are not conceptualized in themselves, they must be brought under some categories. I don't want to enter and, presumably, get lost in the discussion about origin, kinds, and application of categorical forms. But, obviously, the last point bears the largest difficulties in a theory and the practice of imputation, physical and practical. For, if a single event must be distinguished from a universal concept, which may or may not be used to determine it, that event becomes a case of a certain rule only by applying a certain concept. And, as not only Kant's analysis of imputation shows, doing that should come up to some, hopefully, higher level of probability concerning correspondence between logical and metaphysical entities, but it will never reach certainty. Now one might find these remarks quite boring, since there are well-known problems with truth as correspondence that may tempt one to give up the whole idea. But, even then, there has to be some approach to that problem, especially concerning criminal judgment. At this point, procedural or similarly formal theories seem to come in handy. However, fifteen years or more in jail is a long time, and to pass such a sentence just on formal grounds without some reference to, let us say, extralinguistical reality leaves, at least, a stale taste. So, it might be desirable to find ways to legitimate imputation on individual reasons which seems to entail some kind of correspondence-seeking. At any rate, German law, notwithstanding its theoretical output in form of ruling doctrines, is bound to do so, since the objective of every trial is truth, and the truth, which is found out by the court, is revealed by the juridical or rather penal rule under which an action is subsumed. So some theory of subsumption is at least as important as the causal analysis if questions of moral or juridical responsibility are to be fully discussed. However, I am afraid that

81 See (Aichele 2011a).

the result won't go beyond pragmatical and empirically corroborated rules of thumb. At the moment, we should be content with that.

References

Aichele, Alexander (2005). Die Ungewißheit des Gewissens. Alexander Gottlieb Baumgartens forensische Aufklärung der Aufklärungsethik. *Annual Review of Law and Ethics 13* (2005), 1–21.

Aichele, Alexander (2008). Persona physica und persona moralis: Die Zurechnungsfähigkeit juristischer Personen nach Kant. *Annual Review of Law and Ethics 16*, 1–21.

Aichele, Alexander (2011a). Enthymematik und Wahrscheinlichkeit. Die epistemologische Rechtfertigung singulärer Urteile in Universaljurisprudenz und Logik der deutschen Aufklärung: Christian Wolff und Alexander Gottlieb Baumgarten. *Rechtstheorie 42* Sonderheft Rechtsschutz 495–513.

Aichele, Alexander (2011b). Ex contradictione quodlibet – Die Untauglichkeit der Äquivalenztheorie zur Erklärung von Kausalität, die Untauglichkeit der Lehre von der objektiven Zurechnung zur Rechtfertigung von Zurechnungsurteilen und ein Vorschlag zur Güte. *Zeitschrift für die gesamte Strafrechtswissenschaft,123*, 260–283.

Aichele, Alexander (2011c). Zurechnungsmetaphysik? Samuel Pufendorfs Begriff der *imputatio* als Realitätsgrund von Moralität. *Annual Review of Law and Ethics, 19*, 325–346.

Aichele, Alexander (2013) Personalität und Individualität in der Philosophie der Aufklärung: Locke, Leibniz, A. G. Baumgarten. In Stephan Kirste (Ed.), *Person und Rechtsperson.* Tübingen: Mohr.

von Buri, Maximilian (1873). *Causalität und deren Verantwortung.* Leipzig: J.M. Gebhardt's Verlag.

Grapotte, Sophie (2004). *La conception kantienne de la réalité.* Hildesheim: Georg Olms.

Haas, Volker (2002). *Kausalität und Rechtsverletzung.* Tübingen: Mohr.

Haas, Volker (2004). Die strafrechtliche Lehre von der objektiven Zurechnung – eine Grundsatzkritik. In Matthias Kaufmann & Joachim Renzikowski (Ed.), *Zurechnung als Operationalisierung von Verantwortung.* Frankfurt/M. et.al.: Peter Lang, 193–224.

Hart, Herbert L. A. and Honoré, Anthony M. (1959). *Causation in the Law*, Oxford: Oxford University Press.

Heidegger, Martin (1989). *Die Grundprobleme der Phänomenologie.* 2nd ed. Frankfurt a. M.: Klostermann.

Honoré, Anthony M. (1999) *Responsibility and Fault.* Oxford: Oxford University Press.

Hruschka, Joachim (1976). *Strukturen der Zurechnung.* Berlin: de Gruyter.

Hruschka, Joachim (1991). Verhaltensregeln und Zurechnungsregeln. *Rechtstheorie 22*, 449–460.

Hruschka, Joachim (1993). Regreßverbot, Anstiftungsbegriff und die Konsequenzen. *Zeitschrift für die gesamte Strafrechtswissenschaft 110*, 581–610.

Hruschka, Joachim (1998). Supererogation and Meritorious Duties. *Annual Review of Law and Ethics* 6, 93–108.

Hruschka, Joachim (2004). *Zurechnung seit Pufendorf. Insbesondere die Unterscheidungen des 18. Jahrhunderts.* Kaufmann & Renzikowski 2004, 17–27.

Jakobs, Günther (1999). Bemerkungen zur objektiven Zurechnung. *Festschrift für Hans-Joachim Hirsch*. Berlin/New York: de Gruyter, 45–63.

Joerden, Jan C. (2010). *Logik im Recht. Grundlagen und Anwendungsbeispiele*. 2nd ed. Heidelberg et al: Springer.

Kant, Immanuel (1781/1787). *Kritik der reinen Vernunft*. In *Werkausgabe* (Wilhelm Weischedel ed.), Frankfurt a. M.: Suhrkamp 1977, Vol. III/IV.

Kant, Immanuel (1788). *Kritik der praktischen Vernunft*. In *Werkausgabe* (Wilhelm Weischedel ed.), Frankfurt a. M.: Suhrkamp 1977, Vol. VII.

Kant, Immanuel (1793/4). *Metaphysik der Sitten Vigilantius*. In *Kants gesammelte Schriften. Akademie-Ausgabe*, vol. XXVII. 2,1, 477–732.

Kant, Immanuel (1797). *Metaphysik der Sitten*. In *Werkausgabe* (Wilhelm Weischedel ed.), Frankfurt a. M.: Suhrkamp 1977, Vol. VIII.

Kant, Immanuel (1800). *Immanuel Kants Logik, ein Handbuch zu Vorlesungen*. In *Werkausgabe* (Wilhelm Weischedel ed.), Frankfurt a. M.: Suhrkamp 1977, Vol. VI, 417–582.

Kaufmann, Matthias (1993). *Begriffe, Sätze, Dinge. Referenz und Wahrheit bei Wilhelm von Ockham*. Leiden: Brill.

Leibniz, Gottfried Wilhelm (1670). *Dissertatio praeliminaris, De alienorum operum editione, de Scopo operis, de Philosophica dictione, de lapsibus Nizolii*. In Marii Nizolii, *De veris principis et vera ratione philosophandi* libri IV. In *Sämtliche Schriften und Briefe*, AA 6.2, 401–444.

Mir Puig, Santiago (2009). Objektive Rechtswidrigkeit und Normwidrigkeit im Strafrecht. *Zeitschrift für die gesamte Srafrechtswissenschaft 108*, 759–784.

Moore, Michael S. (2009). *Causation and Responsibility*. Oxford: Oxford University Press.

Nolting, Jenny (2011). *Theorien der Unterlassung – Gegenwärtige Ansätze zur Lösung des Problems von Kausalität und Schuld*. Zulassungsarbeit, Halle.

Renzikowski, Joachim (1997). *Restriktiver Täterbegriff und fahrlässige Beteiligung*. Tübingen: Mohr.

Roxin, Claus (2006). *Strafrecht. Allgemeiner Teil*. 2 Vol. 4th ed. München: Beck.

Schnepf, Robert (2006). *Die Frage nach der Ursache. Systematische und problemgeschichtliche Untersuchungen zum Kausalitäts- und Schöpfungsbegriff*. Göttingen: Vandenhoeck & Ruprecht, 257–395.

Michael S. Moore

Further Thoughts on Causation (and Related Topics) Prompted By Fifteen Critics

It is a pleasure to respond to the rich array of thoughts, suggestions, and criticisms contained in the foregoing thirteen papers. It was also a pleasure listening to their oral presentation and defense at a variety of events held in Germany in 2010 and 2011. These events consisted of: a three day seminar on my book, *Causation and Responsibility*,[1] held at RWTH University in Aachen in 2010 and organized by Markus Stepanians of that faculty; a vigorous "disputation" between myself, Richard Wright, and Ingeborg Puppe, given at the Faculty of Law of Bonn University in 2011 organized by Ingeborg Puppe of that faculty; a seminar on my book held at Cologne University in 2011; and another seminar on my book, held again at RWTH University in Aachen in 2011. Each of these exchanges was both enjoyable and profitable to my understanding of causation and I am pleased to here thank the participants and commentators for their many excellent thoughts.

The thirteen papers collected here are far too rich in their detail, broad in the scope of issues covered, and nuanced in their argumentation, to be given an adequate reply by me here. What I can do is highlight some of the issues raised in these papers, giving some thoughts along the way as to where the cutting edge of our collective understanding currently rests on these issues and pointing out further directions in which we might collectively take the discussion of them. Because of the largely non-overlapping nature of the issues raised in these papers, I have not sought to organize this reply by topic; rather, I respond to each author in the order in which their papers appear. The two exceptions are the common responses I give to Richard Wright and Ingeborg Puppe, and to Geert Keil and Philipp Huebl. With regard to Wright and Puppe, their views of causation, while developed independently of one another, nonetheless significantly overlap, and in light of this overlap I have discussed some issues about their common NESS view of causation in the context of both of their articles. Similarly with Keil and Huebl, the similarities of their whole-event, singular counterfactual views of causation are great enough that problems with those views are conveniently discussed together.

---

1 Michael S. Moore, *Causation and Responsibility: An Essay in Law, Morals, and Metaphysics* (Oxford: Oxford University Press, 2009), paperback edit, 2010, Spanish edition, *Causalidad Y Responsabilidad: Un Ensayo Sobre Deracho, Moral y Metafisica* (Madrid: Marcel Pons, 2011).

1 Richard Wright and Ingeborg Puppe on the NESS Conception of Causation

Broadly speaking, both Professor Wright and Professor Puppe write in the Millian tradition on causation.[2] They like Mill reject Hume's notion that causation is to be identified as counterfactual dependence; rather, they (again like Mill) focus on the *sufficiency* of causes rather than their *necessity*, which was the focus of Hume.

As David Lewis remarked decades ago,[3] there are really two Humes on causation, Hume the counterfactualist and Hume the regularity theorist. Different as Millians are from the first Hume, Puppe and Wright do share some views with the second Hume, prominent amongst which is the view that singular causal statements ("this spark caused this explosion") are elliptical for, and can be reduced to: some statements of causal laws ("sparks cause explosions") together with statements of space/time locators. In a phrase, for Millians and Humeans (of this second kind), causes are instantiations of the antecedent clauses of causal laws.

The difference between Millians and Humeans of this second kind lies in their view of causal laws. Humeans (which *may* have included Hume himself)[4] reduce laws to uniformities ("regularities") in nature, whereas Millians would analyze causal laws in terms of nomic sufficiency. The "whole cause," as Mill used to say, is the entire set of conditions lawfully sufficient for the effect, even though in idiomatic English we usually only single out one or two members of such set as "the cause" of that effect.[5] Latter day Millians such as Hart, Honoré,[6] Mackie,[7] Wright,[8] and Puppe[9] add that each member must be a necessary member of the

---

2 I summarize the Millian tradition, *id.*, chap. 19.

3 David Lewis, "Causation," *Journal of Philosophy*, Vol. 70 (1973), pp. 556–567, at p. 556.

4 On whether the historical David Hume really subscribed to the "Humean" regularity theory, see Galen Strawson, *The Secret Connexion: Causation, Realism, and David Hume* (Oxford: Clarendon Press, 1989).

5 John Stuart Mill, *A System of Logic* (8th edit., London: Longmans, 1872), Book III, Chapter V, sec. 3.

6 H.L.A. Hart and Tony Honoré, *Causation in the Law* (2d edit., Oxford: Oxford University Press, 1985).

7 J.L. Mackie, *The Cement of the Universe: A Study of Causation* (Oxford: Clarendon Press, 1974).

8 Wright's initial foray into causation was his "Causation in Tort Law," *California Law Review*, Vol. 73 (1985), pp. 1735–1828. See, most recently, Wright, "The NESS Account of Natural Causation: A Response to Criticisms," this volume, originally published in Richard Goldberg, ed., *Perspectives on Causation* (Oxford: Hart Publishing, 2011), pp. 285–322.

9 Ingeborg Puppe, "The Concept of Causation in the Law," this volume.

set, that is (in the phrase now favored by Wright), each member must be "necessary for the sufficiency of the set."

In my book, and echoed in my presentation at Bonn in 2011, I leveled essentially seven charges at Millian theories of causation.[10] Without any attempt to explicate them here, they were:

1. Mill's nomic sufficiency is as poor a reduction base for causal laws as was Hume's counterfactual necessity, since there are many instances of both nomic sufficiency and counterfactual necessity that do not look to be in any way causal in nature.
2. Being a necessary member of a set of conditions sufficient for some effect, is as non-discriminating ("promiscuous") as is counterfactual necessity; more specifically, neither notion does well with:
   a. The notion that causation is scalar;
   b. The notion of insubstantial or *de minimus* causes in both asymmetrical overdetermination and other cases;
   c. The notion that causation "peters out" over time, space, and numbers of intervening events;
   d. The residual selectivity of what is eligible on a given occasion to be considered a cause of a particular effect.
3. Nomic sufficiency (at best construed, at least) countenances absences as causes and effects; it is thus unable to distinguish causation from:
   a. Omissions that fail to prevent some harm;
   b. Preventions of some harm that did not happen;
   c. Allowings and other double-preventions, viz, a prevention of a would-be preventer of some harm from doing its preventative work and thus allowing that harm to take place.
4. Nomic sufficiency not only wrongly treats omissions, preventions, and double-preventions as causal, but it also gets the wrong conclusions (about causation and about responsibility) for all three with respect to:
   a. Concurrent overdetermination omission (or prevention, or double prevention) cases; and
   b. The supposed pre-empting omission (or prevention or double prevention) in supposed pre-emptive overdetermination omission (or prevention, or double prevention) cases.
5. Nomic sufficiency, again like counterfactual necessity, prima facie treats the relationship between the horns of an epiphenomenal fork as causal when

10 Moore, *Causation and Responsibility*, chap. 19.

such co-effects of a common cause ("epiphenomena") are paradigmatically non-causal.

6. Nomic sufficiency has an even more difficult time than counterfactual necessity in accounting for three rock-bed features of causality, namely, that the causal relationship is asymmetrical (c may be a cause of e only if e is not a cause of c), irreflexive (c may not be a cause of e if c = e), and temporally ordered (c may be a cause of e only if c does not succeed e in time).
7. Although nomic sufficiency does better with concurrent overdetermining causation than does counterfactual necessity, it does equally poorly (although differently so) with pre-emptive overdetermination cases.

Given the length and the richness of the discussion of these seven issues in philosophy these past 150 years, there is no way I can in short compass in these pages bring my readers up to speed on the ebb and flow of the argument hitherto. Those readers coming in "half-way through the movie," as we say in Hollywood, would do well to view the original "films"[11] and then consider what follows.

About issues one, five, six and to some extent seven, I can be brief. For Wright and Puppe respond to me here as they have responded before on these issues to others, which is to blatantly beg the question. If the question (to which NESS is supposed to be the answer) is, "What is the nature of causation?," their answer reduces to the circular answer of the causal primitivist: "causation is what it is – causation – and no other thing." Wright embraces such circularity explicitly, when he eschews lawful sufficiency as his reduction base and tells us, unhelpfully, that causation is *causal* sufficiency: "The required sense of sufficiency... I call 'casual sufficiency' to distinguish it from mere lawful strong sufficiency..."[12] Wright's circularity is particularly blatant in his attempt to smuggle the asymmetricality and time-directionality of causation into his notion of sufficiency: "Another critical feature of ... the concept of causal sufficiency as distinct from mere lawful sufficiency ... is [its] successional or directional nature..."[13]

11 My introduction to this discussion of these issues may be found, respectively, at:
1. *Id.*, pp. 394–396, 475–477.
2. *Id.*, pp. 85–86, 396–399, 468–469, 477–478, 489–491.
3. *Id.*, pp. 399–400, 444–451, 453–459, 460–467, 478–480.
4. *Id.*, pp. 449–451, 457–459, 466–467.
5. *Id.*, pp. 400–403, 481–483.
6. *Id.*, pp. 403–409, 483–485.
7. *Id.*, pp. 410–425, 486–495.

12 Wright, "The NESS Account," p. 18.

13 *Id.*, p 19.

Despite the blatant circularity of using *causal* sufficiency to define causal laws, which are then used to define singular causation, Wright assures us that "there is no conceptual circularity here."[14] In the next breath he assures us that, if there is circularity here, "it would not be 'vicious.'"[15] Let me consider these two thoughts of Wright's one at a time.

Wright's conclusion of non-circularity stems from his present definition of causal laws (and thus of causal sufficiency), which, he assures us, makes do "without any use of causal language:"[16]

> A causal law is an empirically derived statement that describes a successional relation between a set of abstract conditions (properties or features of possible events and states of affairs in our real world) that constitute the antecedent and one or more specified conditions of a distinct abstract event or state of affairs that constitute the consequent such that, regardless of the state of any other conditions, the instantiation of all the conditions in the antecedent entails the immediate instantiation of the consequent, which would not be entailed if less than all of the conditions in the antecedent were instantiated.[17]

This is a recognizable description of the Millian view that causal laws describe sets of conditions minimally sufficient for the existence of some other condition. Yet notice, first, that asymmetricality and temporal order ("successive relation," "immediate") are merely stipulative add-ons to nomic sufficiency that in no way follow from the supposed nature of causation (viz, nomic sufficiency). Sure, causation is an asymmetrical and time-ordered relation; and nomic sufficiency as such is not. But *causal* sufficiency has these features – once one by fiat adds these features of causation to nomic sufficiency. As I point out in my book,[18] this *ad hoc* strategy is available to the counterfactualist about causation as well, and with about as much plausibility. One can fairly demand of both theories that they show us how an asymmetric and time-ordered relation (causation) can be identified as a seemingly different relation (nomic sufficiency, counterfactual dependence) that is neither. Ad hoc stipulations, such as Wright's – causation is such nomic sufficiencies as are asymmetrical and time-ordered – do not answer this demand.

The second thing to notice about Wright's definition is that it does not rule out treating epiphenomenal relations as causal. Let c be a common cause of e_1 and e_2; let c occur at t_1, e_1, at t_2, and e_2 at t_3; let t_3 succeed t_2 by as small an interval

14 *Id.*, p. 20.
15 *Id.*
16 *Id.*
17 *Id.*, p. 19.
18 Moore, *Causation and Responsibility*, pp. 403–404, 484–485.

of time as Wright means by "immediate." The occurrence of e_1 can be sufficient of the occurrence of e_2 (the cases are legion – use your imagination); unless "successive" means something causal (Wright's "causal process"?),[19] Wright has no way not to conclude that e_1 causes e_2, contrary to what we all know to be true.

The third thing to notice about Wright's definition is that (again by mere stipulative fiat) it stipulates away examples of nomic sufficiency that are not plausibly construed to be causal. Like Lewis and other counterfactualists about causation, Wright adds the requirement that the sufficiency relations eligible to be the reduction base for causation, be between distinct events.[20] This rules out, as Wright notes, the kinds of mereological and other counter examples Jaegwon Kim first put to Lewis' counterfactual theory.[21] As with the temporal stipulation, this may avoid circularity, but again seems ad hoc in that it is unmotivated by the nature being attributed to causation.

Finally, notice that Wright's definition does not rule out (as being causal) pre-empted factors in pre-emptive overdetermination cases. In the case of the poisoned victim about to die from his poisoning who is then shot dead immediately by a second wrongdoer, the "poison leads to death" causal law was about to be instantiated in however small an interval of time as Wright means by "immediate." (It's my hypo, so I can assure of this with the certainty of an omniscient novelist.) The "instantiation of the consequent" (i.e., here, death) immediately followed the set of conditions (of which poison was here a necessary member) sufficient for death, and that set (in this case of the latest of late pre-emptions) was "fully instantiated." Yet we know that the even more immediate-acting bullet killed here, pre-empting the poison.

In a moment of perhaps only *arguendo* concession, Wright admits that perhaps there is circularity in his definition of causal laws but then denies that any such circularity is vicious. Wright:

> Even if some circularity should be found to exist in these definitions, it would not be 'vicious.' The NESS account provides a description of the structure of causal laws and their instantiation that is acknowledged, even by its critics, to be illuminating and very useful for proper identification of singular instances of causation.[22]

---

19 Wright, "The NESS Account," p. 19.

20 *Id.*, p. 35.

21 Jaegwon Kim, "Causes and Counterfactuals," *Journal of Philosophy*, Vol. 70 (1973), pp. 520–572.

22 Wright, "The NESS Account," p. 20.

Admissions of illumination by critics, and usefulness for verification of causation in particular cases, are hardly grounds for exoneration on a charge of vicious circularity. NESS purports to be an account of the nature of causation. This is a matter of the correct metaphysics of the relation. Epistemic virtues, such as heuristic or verificationist usefulness, are not germane to this metaphysical project except on old and long-discarded views of metaphysics.

I have deferred my discussion of Puppe because, although she and Wright share a common answer ("NESS"), it is not clear that they share a common question. Indeed, Puppe's shifting of the question may supply just the corrective to the circularity charge that Wright needs and should adopt.

Like Wright, Puppe addresses the first, fifth, sixth, and seventh problems for the NESS test while being sensitive to the charge of circularity in both hers and Wright's previous answers to those problems. Occasionally Puppe sounds just like Wright in claiming the supposed ability to stipulate restrictions on lawful sufficiency so as to carve out some such category of *causal* sufficiency. With regard to problem six, the asymmetry and temporal directionality of causation, for example, Puppe urges that "we can simply postulate this direction of causality without getting into a vicious circle."[23]

Yet mostly Puppe's instincts are different than Wright's. She treats the question (to which NESS is supposed to be the answer) as a scientific question of contingent fact, not as a question of either metaphysical necessity seeking real essences, or analytic necessity seeking nominal essences. Thus, her considered answer to the worry about the mismatch between causation and lawful sufficiency in the dimension of symmetry and temporal direction, is this:

> A causal law is generally of the form, 'if...then...? the antecedent...precedes the consequent. We can accept this in the present context as an element of the conception of a cause without having to enter the philosophical discussion about the nature of time or the physical discussion about the reversibility of time or the possibility of time travel. The possibility of effecting the past is not within our experience.[24]

Puppe likewise answers the fifth problem, that having to do with epiphenomenal relations looking like causal relations under the NESS theory, by adverting to how we test to see if the relationship between two events is epiphenomenal or causal. We use "one of several experimental methods for falsifying causal hypotheses,"[25] and we rely on well-established scientific facts such as the facts

23 Puppe, "The Concept of Causation," p. 87 n. 63.
24 *Id.*, p. 87.
25 *Id.*, p. 91.

that "no human being reacts to a phenomenon that we cannot perceive..."[26] and that "the position of the sun in London does not depend on the Manchester hooters sounding."[27]

Likewise with regard to the seventh problem, that of pre-empted factors looking like causes under the NESS test, Puppe relies on the scientific fact that "every causal process has a determinate speed of propagation."[28] (She uses this fact to rebut claims such as mine above, that pre-empted factors can be followed by their "results" in as small an interval of time as one wants to imagine, thus foreclosing (under NESS) the possibility of a pre-empting factor intervening.)

One's first reaction to all of these responses by Puppe is to think that she has missed the point of each of these challenges. After all, the common structure of the challenges to NESS is that causation has certain features or has certain clear applications, yet NESS seems to lack just such features or applications. Being told that we have reliable methods to rule out epiphenomena and to detect pre-emptions, and that we never really face instances of backwards causation, all seem to miss the fundamental nature of these challenges.

Yet Puppe in effect refuses to regard these as problems for her NESS theory. She refuses the task of restricting lawful sufficiency to that subset of the class of lawful sufficiencies that captures all and only causal laws. As she puts it: "The challenge for this doctrine [NESS] that it should give a general criterion when a proposition of the form 'if...then...' being a causal law, is about as reasonable as asking a logician for a general criterion to recognize that a proposition has the property of being true."[29]

Puppe goes too far in regarding as senseless the legitimate demand for a criterion restricting lawful sufficiency to causal sufficiency. One does not indeed demand a criterion of truth from a logician, although one might from an epistemologist; but one can quite sensibly ask such a logician for a criterion of *logical* truth. Not only is such a demand sensible; but the completeness proof in modern logic shows that we have two pretty good criteria for logical truth, one in terms of truth tables and the other in terms of a complete axiomatic system.

If we eliminate the hyperbole, however, we can see that Puppe is entitled to answer a different question than one asking into the essence, real or nominal, of causation. As to *that* metaphysical question, she is happy with circularity: "A causal law is a regular succession of events that the relevant natural science ac-

26 *Id.*
27 *Id.*
28 *Id.*, p. 102.
29 *Id.*, pp. 91–92.

knowledges as causal law."[30] Puppe's different question is one of scientific practice: as we currently practice science, do we have the resources with which to distinguish epiphenomenal from causal relations, pre-empted from pre-empting causes, and resources with which to deal with all experienced cases of genuine (versus backwards) causation? And is NESS a useful part of our epistemic arsenal in these tasks? Puppe is satisfied in her defense of NESS if it possesses this epistemic virtue. At times, in truth, Wright sounds like he might be too.[31]

A critic of NESS as a metaphysical theory about the nature of causation (such as myself), need have no objection to this defense of NESS's epistemic usefulness in verifying when there is or is not a causal relation. A "wild-eyed" singularism that countenances the existence of singular causal relations where there are no causal laws, is as much an anathema to my "moderate singularism" as it is to Wright's and Puppe's generalism about causation.[32] Given the omnipresence of laws for all three of us, sufficiency is often a good test for the presence of causal laws. But this happy agreement comes at a price for the Nessies: when limited in ambition to epistemic usefulness, theirs is not a theory of causation, in the usual sense of the phrase.

I thus far have said little about challenges two, three, and four to the NESS theory, so let me do so now. About number two, the embarrassing prolixity of causes under the NESS conception of causation, both Wright and Puppe make the rejoinder long used by counterfactual theorists as well: causes *are* prolix, but they only give the appearance of not being so because of the extreme narrowing done by pragmatic factors of appropriate causal utterances in particular contexts. *Some* relegation of discriminating power to pragmatics and context is surely quite plausible, and virtually every causal theorist endorses this to some extent. So any disagreement here can only be a matter of degree.

Yet I think the disagreements outlined earlier to be significant: (a) my scalar notion of causation will grade causes by the size of their contribution to some effect, whereas (without some fancy footwork, at least)[33] any necessary member of any sufficient set is equally a cause with any other member of that set, and any sufficient set is equally a cause with any other sufficient set. (b) Very small contributions are non-causal when they reach the de minimus line on

---

30 *Id.*, p. 92.

31 Wright, "The NESS Account," p. 20.

32 Moore, *Causation and Responsibility*, pp. 361–364, 506.

33 I myself attempt such footwork in my own use of a scalar counterfactual dependence as a desert-determiner independent of causation. See Moore, "Moore's Truths About Causation and Responsibility: A Reply to Alexander and Ferzan," *Criminal Law and Philosophy*, Vol. 6 (2012), pp. 445–462, at pp. 449–450.

my account, whereas these can be full-fledged necessary members of sufficient sets, on the NESS account. Wright attempts a reductio here on me (and on David Fisher, another critic of NESS): what if the same de minimus contribution was made by a million defendants, would we conclude that the harm in question was caused by none of them and so was "an unexplained, non-caused miracle?"[34] Wright's rhetorical flourish here is not as conclusive as he seems to think. If it is not the case that defendant_1 caused it, not defendant_2, not...not defendant one million, it doesn't follow that it is not the case that (defendant_1 *and* defendant_2 and...and defendant one million) did not cause the harm in question. The harm was caused by the conjunction of all of their acts, even while not being caused by any one of their acts individually. The harm is thus in no sense an "unexplained, non-caused miracle."

With regard to challenge number three, Wright and Puppe defend the view I attribute to NESS in my book: most favorably construed, and recognizing that Mill and later Millians have equivocated here, NESS in Wright's and Puppe's hands is committed to regarding absences as causal relata, both causes and effects. This makes omissions, preventions, and double preventions all causal. I think this counts against the NESS view because I think each of these three items is not causal but counterfactual in nature.

Whether omissions, etc., are causal is a large topic. It is also raised later by the Birnbacher/Hommen paper so I shall defer discussion until later. I note preliminarily here, however, that both Wright and Puppe rely extensively on my former ANU colleague and sometime critic Jonathan Schaffer,[35] for the idea that absences can be the relata of singular causal relations. Actually Schaffer's considered view is not that, as both I[36] and Markus Stepanians[37] have taken some pains to point out. Schaffer's actual view is that items that look like absences are really positive presences, which no one including me would deny are eligible to serve as causal relata.

The fourth set of challenges relate to omissive (and *mutatis mutandis*, to preventative and to doubly preventative) overdetermination cases; NESS theorists

---

34 Wright, "The NESS Account," p. 41.

35 The Schaffer paper on which both Puppe and Wright rely is Schaffer, "Causes Need Not Be Connected to Their Effects: The Case for Negative Causation," in Christopher Hitchcock, ed., *Contemporary Debates in Philosophy of Science* (Oxford: Blackwell, 2004). Schaffer's deployments of these arguments against me specifically may be found in Schaffer, "Disconnection and Responsibility," *Legal Theory*, Vol. 18 (2012), pp. 399–435.

36 Moore, "Four Friendly Critics: A Response," *Legal Theory*, Vol. 18 (2012), pp. 491–542, at p. 512.

37 Markus Stepanians, "Why Schaffer's Solution to the Problem of Absence Causation Fails," under submission 2012.

like Wright and Puppe rightly see that their theory commits them to the conclusions that:

(a) each of two omitters in concurrent omissive overdetermination cases is both causally and morally responsible for the harm each omitted to prevent; and
(b) there are pre-emptive kinds of omissive overdetermination cases and in such pre-emptive cases only the supposedly pre-empting omitters bear causal and moral responsibility for the harm, not the pre-empted omitters.

Since neither of these conclusions is sustainable, that counts against the NESS theory that implies them.

I have elsewhere dealt at length with both issues (a)[38] and (b)[39] and will not here recapitulate these analyses. More useful in this context is to pursue Wright's response here to issue (b). I am not alone in finding Wright's conclusions here to be either normatively implausible, incoherent, or false as a matter of causal metaphysics,[40] but let me put the arguments in my own terms.

Imagine a simple case of omissive overdetermination. Some harm H can be prevented, but only if two individuals, A and B, each push their "Prevent" button; if one of them pushes his button while the other does not, then H occurs. In actual fact both A and B omit to push their respective buttons and H occurs. In

---

38 Moore, *Causation and Responsibility*, pp. 449–451, 457–459, 466–467. My conclusion (of there being only an inchoate responsibility for each overdetermining omitter) has been challenged by both Carolina Sartorio and Phil Dowe. See Sartorio, "Two Wrongs Do Not Make a Right: Responsibility and Overdetermination," *Legal Theory*, Vol. 18 (2012), pp. 473–490; Dowe, "Moore's Account of Causation and Responsibility, and the Problem of Omissive Overdetermination," *Jurisprudence*, Vol. 4 (2013), pp. 115–120. I have continued the discussion in Moore, "Four Friendly Critics," pp. 534–542; and Moore, "Author's Reply," *Jurisprudence*, Vol. 4 (2013), pp. 121–137, at pp. 133–137.

39 Moore, *Causation and Responsibility*, pp. 140, 466–467. Chris Hitchcock and Gideon Rosen have both critically probed my thoughts here. See Christopher Hitchcock, "The Metaphysical Bases of Liability: Commentary on Michael Moore's Causation and Responsibility," *Rutgers Law Journal*, Vol. 42 (2011), pp. 377–404, at 395–404; Gideon Rosen, "Causation Counterfactual Dependence, and Culpability: Moral Philosophy in Michael Moore's Causation and Responsibility," *Rutgers Law Journal*, Vol. 42 (2011), pp. 405–434, at pp. 423–424. I continue the discussion in Moore, "Causation Revisited," *Rutgers Law Journal*, Vol. 42 (2011), pp. 451–509, at pp. 479–482 (for Hitchcock), and pp. 501–507 (for Rosen).

40 See David Fischer, "Causation in Fact in Omission Cases," *Utah Law Review*, Vol. [1992], pp. 1335–1384, at pp. 1357–1359; Fischer, "Insufficient Causes," *Kentucky Law Journal*, Vol. 94 (2006), pp. 277–317, at p. 310; Jane Stapleton, "Choosing What We Mean by 'Causation' in the Law," *Missouri Law Review*, Vol. 73 (2008), pp. 433–480, at p. 478; Horacio Spector, "The MMTS Analysis of Causation," in Richard Goldberg, ed., *Perspectives on Causation* (Oxford: Hart Publishing, 2011), pp. 339–359, at pp. 354–359.

which event A's omission was sufficient for H to occur, as was B's omission. Hence the name for these kinds of cases: "omissive overdetermination."

Now suppose three variations of this omissive overdetermination case: (1) both buttons needed to be pushed simultaneously if H is to be prevented; (2) only if button A is pushed first, then button B, will H be prevented (this is because B's button does its work through the circuit opened by A); (3) only if button B is pushed first, then button A, will H be prevented (this is because A's button does its work through the circuit opened by B). Wright's resolution of both causal metaphysics and moral responsibility for these cases is as follows: (1) both A and B are (causally and morally) responsible for H; (2) A is responsible for H, B is not; (3) B is responsible for H, A is not. This, because according to Wright: (1) is a case of concurrent omissive overdetermination, where (just like ordinary, non-omissive concurrent overdetermination) both "actors" are responsible for H; whereas (2) and (3) are cases of pre-emptive omissive overdetermination, (2) being a case of A's omission pre-empting B's from having any "causal effect" on H's, whereas (3) is a case of B's omission pre-empting A's from having any "causal effect" on H.

My first objection is that I find these conclusions normatively unmotivated. In cases (1), (2), and (3), neither A nor B has, individually, the ability to prevent H. Only if his opposite number acts does he have such ability. Where A does not push his button, then *no matter when B needed to push his button to help to prevent H*, B never had the ability to prevent H. And ditto for A when B does not push his button. Such cases of two "actors" omitting are morally indistinguishable from cases where: one actor, say A, omits to push his button, but the other actor's button, B's button, is: stuck and can't be depressed; or it is short-circuited by lightning; or it doesn't exist because it was never installed; etc. In cases where actors lack the ability to prevent some harm H, their omissions to try to prevent H do not make them morally responsible for H's occurrence. I thus find Wright's analysis peculiar in its moral motivation.[41] Even if there is a causal or other metaphysical distinction to be made between variations (1), (2), and (3) – of which, more below – such factual distinction is without normative significance.

Secondly, let us press Wright's analysis to see if there really is even a factual distinction in cases like (1), (2), and (3) above. One is tempted to reconstruct Wright's intuition in this way: in cases like (2), when A omits to press his button at t_1, then B at t_2 has no ability to prevent H. Whereas in cases like (2) B's non-

41 For a more extended version of this objection, see my responses to Carolina Sartorio and Phil Dowe, in Moore "Four Friendly Critics: A Response," at pp. 534–542, and in Moore, "Author's Response," at pp. 133–137.

pressing of his button at t_2 does not deprive A of his ability at t_1 to prevent H because B's omission to push his button has not yet "occurred" at t_1 when A omits to press his. (I argued above that this is wrong, but at the moment I am trying to make Wright's intuition even marginally intelligible.) So on Wright's view, it matters which omission "occurred" first.

Yet this intuition is broken-backed from its inception. Omissions are not particulars that occur at some time; they are absences of there being any particulars that instantiate a type.[42] A and B omitted to press their buttons at all times from the Big Bang that began this show to the heat death of the universe that will apparently end it. There is no sequence of omitting in such cases, as a matter of the metaphysics of what omissions are. It is for this reason that Jane Stapleton finds Wright's analysis here to be "incoherent."[43]

Wright sees this and thus eschews temporal order of omissions as the sequence in which he is interested. Instead he proffers a criterion based on causal sequence in a possible world. What Wright wants to know is how harms like H would have been prevented in the possible world where, contrary to actual fact, both A and B pressed their respective buttons. As Wright puts his causal sequence criterion:

> [I]t is critically important to focus on the sequencing of the steps in the positive causal process that failed, in order to determine at which step it failed...the failure at that step pre-empted any potential failure at subsequent steps, the occurrence of which is dependent on successful completion of all the prior steps.[44]

So in scenario (2), where A's button must be pressed first to open the circuit allowing B's button to prevent H, A's omission (for Wright) pre-empts B's omission from having any "causal effect" on H.

One question is whether Wright really wants to say this. In order to see the puzzlement here, let us pry apart the temporal order of omissions criterion from the possible causal sequence criterion. Suppose B's omission was a failure at t_0 to inspect his button, which, as it turns out, had never been connected to the relevant circuit. At t_1 A again omits to push his prevent button, but at t_2 B now push-

---

42 Moore, *Causation and Responsibility*, pp. 436–444. Chris Miller's recent defense of Wright on this point makes the same mistake. Miller argues "that the only distinguishing characteristic [between these pairs of omissions] now comes from temporal order: the first to occur is not only sufficient, it is pre-emptive in that it makes any subsequent failure(s) redundant." Miller, "NESS for Beginners," in Richard Goldberg, ed., *Perspectives on Causation* (Oxford: Hart Publishing, 2011), pp. 323–337, at p. 329.

43 Stapleton, "Choosing What We Mean," at p. 428.

44 Wright, "The NESS Account," p. 58.

es his button (but of course with no effect, because of its lack of connection to the circuit). Now B's omission (to inspect) is prior (if we date it by when he first had a duty not to omit) to A's; yet the failure in the causal sequence (of what would have happened if both A and B had done what they should) is in reverse order, according to Wright: A's omission to press his button at t_1 removes the opening of the circuit so that B's button never gets to the point of using this unopened circuit. I find it unmotivated to choose Wright's "possible causal sequence" criterion over a "temporal order of duty not to omit" criterion.[45]

One can perhaps sense the oddness of Wright's choice here with the more extended example he both gives in his paper and which we both used in the debate that he, I, and Puppe had at the Bonn University Faculty of Law.[46] Suppose H is some harm to a pedestrian, occurring because a car didn't stop at an intersection and struck that pedestrian. Wright imagines the following causal sequence that would occur if, contrary to fact, the driver of the car had applied pressure to the brake pedal at t_1: the brake pedal pressure at t_1 would produce fluid pressure at t_2; the fluid pressure at t_2 would produce pressure in the brake cylinders at t_3; the pressure in the brake cylinders at t_3 would produce movement of the brake pads against (brake drum or brake disc) at t_4; such pad movement would produce friction at t_5; and such friction would stop the car at t_6. Now suppose that what actually happened is this: the driver omits to push the brake pedal, but had he pushed the pedal, it would have failed to slow the car because: the pedal would have broken off (it was badly cracked); there was no brake fluid; the brake cylinders could maintain no pressure because they were broken; the brake pads were missing; *and* the discs or drums were greasy and incapable of producing any friction. Further, suppose that all of these defects were findable by a reasonable inspection, and that Inspector-one ("I_1"), was charged with inspecting the discs and drums, I_2, with inspecting the brake pads; I_3, with inspecting brake cylinders; I_4, with inspecting brake fluid; I_5, with inspecting brake pedals. Further, suppose that the inspectors are required by their contract to inspect in the order given – I_1 first, then I_2, etc. – because that is the easiest way to access each of the relevant parts. Finally, of course, suppose that each inspector omits to inspect.

45 Miller, despite his sympathetic agreement with Wright, actually prefers the temporal criterion over the causal-priority-in-a-possible-world criterion, on the ground that the latter is circular (on its use of "depends"). Miller, "NESS for Beginners," at pp. 328–329.

46 Faculty of Law, Bonn University, May 27, 2011.

The situation thus is:

	t_1	t_2	t_3	t_4	t_5	t_6
Causal Priority:	driver puts pressure on brake pedal →	brake fluid pressure builds →	pressure in brake cylinders builds →	brake pads move against brake drums →	friction provided →	car stops

	t_1	t_2	t_3	t_4	t_5
The Time at Which the the Duty Arises to Inspect:	Brake drums	Brake pads	Brake cylinders	Brake fluid	Brake pedals

The order in which the duty not to omit begins is the reverse of the order in which the causal sequence would have taken place if everything worked as it should and if the driver hit the brake pedal. I see nothing to be said for Wright's choice of the latter ordering over the former, and thus see nothing in Wright's conclusion that the driver's omission pre-empts all of the inspectors' omissions (rather than the brake drum/disc inspector's omission pre-empting all other omissions). But then, I am also at a loss to motivate distinguishing between any of the five inspectors. It would be more plausible to hold all of them or none of them responsible for the collision. But if both of these non-discriminating solutions is put aside, as Wright does, I am at a loss to motivate Wright's holding the driver alone (versus holding the drum/disc inspector above). When both prongs of a choice are arbitrary, the choice, whatever it is, is also bound to be arbitrary.

Passing this point, however, can we even make consistent sense of Wright's possible causal sequence criterion? What is the possible world Wright is imagining when he constructs the counterfactual that gives the sense to his causal priority criterion? The relevant counterfactual is: "If both A and B had pressed their buttons, H would not have occurred." In particular, how is he imagining the sequence of steps in this possible world? If A's button is stuck, are we imagining it to be not only upushed but also unstuck? If A has no button, are we imagining a causal process where he has a button that would open the circuit for B's button? And if we are allowed these degrees of freedom in imagining causal processes, why not also the freedom to imagine causal processes where it is B's button that opens the circuit for A's button to have effect? It will not do for Wright to respond here by pretending that he never imagines possible worlds, sticking only to the actual world. His counterfactual test, stating what would happen if, contrary to fact, both buttons were pushed, belies any such pretense by him.

One can amplify this last point by returning to Wright's more complicated overdetermined omission example, that of the car that can't stop because of six omissions (by its driver and by five independent inspectors). Given all six omissions in the actual world, Wright's counterfactual here is: If the driver had pressed the pedal, and if there was a pedal to press, and if there was brake fluid in the system, and if there were brake cylinders that could hold pressure, and if there were brake pads, and if there were discs or drums with no grease on them, then in this possible world the car would have stopped. But in what possible world would Wright have us test this counterfactual? If we are going to imagine a car changed this much from what was actually the case, why stop here in our construction of possible worlds in which to test the counterfactual? If we are going to give this imagined car brake pedals, fluids, cylinders, pads, and discs/drums that it in actuality didn't have, why not also give it other sorts of stopping mechanisms? E.g., a wire and pulley braking system? Or an anti-theft device that disables the brakes? Or redundancy mechanisms that need to be engaged before the car starts to work? Or a reverse thrusting jet engine braking system? Drag chutes too? Different systems will have different causal sequences, and in some of the sequences the driver's imagined push on the pedal will not come first.

My conclusion is that there is no coherent distinction between concurrent and pre-emptive omissive overdetermination cases. There is no metaphysical distinction. And if there were, it would be a metaphysical difference making no moral difference to responsibility. These same two points apply, *mutatis mutandis*, to Wright's supposed distinctions between concurrent and pre-emptive overdetermined preventions and double-prevention cases.[47] If the NESS analysis of causation demands that there be such distinctions – and I agree with Wright that it does – so much the worse for the NESS theory of causation.

2 Friederich Toepel's Revised Millianism

Professor Toepel's paper is the natural one to next discuss after the above discussion of Wright and Puppe. For Toepel both celebrates my book's demolition of

47 As I explore in Moore, "Causation Revisited," pp. 479–482, there are some differences here between overdetermining omission cases, on the one hand, and overdetermining prevention and double prevention cases, on the other. Such differences ultimately are immaterial to this issue, however.

generalist theories of causation like Mill's, Wright's, and Puppe's,[48] and yet amends the Millian account in order (he thinks) to circumvent the very objections he applauds when they are directed at unreconstructed Millianism.

Toepel takes his cues on reconstructing Mill from the late John Mackie.[49] Toepel interprets Mackie to be a causal dualist. Toepel's Mackie takes singular causal statements – such as, "this spark caused this explosion" – to be counterfactual in their meaning. Thus: "if the spark had not occurred, the explosion would not have occurred." Whereas Toepel's Mackie interprets statements of causal laws to be as Mill described, where causes are identified as sets of minimally sufficient conditions (rather than necessary conditions). E.g.: "Sparks when introduced into a mixture of hydrogen and oxygen are sufficient for an explosion."

Toepel's is a possible interpretation of Mackie. Toepel recognizes that his is not my interpretation of Mackie in my book, where I lump Mackie in with unreconstructed Millians like Puppe and Wright.[50] Toepel attributes the differences in our interpretation of Mackie to early Mackie (Moore) as opposed to later Mackie (Toepel). Yet that is not where Toepel's and my differences lie. The "early Mackie" of the 1965 "Causes and Conditions" article[51] had not seen clearly the distinction between general (causal and conditional) statements, dealing with *types* of events or perhaps facts about events, and singular (causal and conditional) statements dealing with event-tokens. As Mackie acknowledges,[52] it was Jaegwon Kim's criticism[53] on this point that lead him eventually to the separate discussions of the two types of causal statements in his book.

I took all of this into account in my interpretation of "later Mackie." The problem is that Mackie's discussion is very nuanced and open to multiple interpretations. In favor of Toepel's dualist interpretation we find Mackie saying things like, "our concept of causation is not primarily a concept of the instantiation of regularities: we locate causation in singular cause-effect sequences, and assume that there is some distinctively causal relation...in each sequence taken on its own."[54] Further, Mackie spends the chapter Toepel cites analyzing the or-

---

48 Moore, *Causation and Responsibility*, chap. 19.

49 Mackie, *The Cement of the Universe*.

50 Moore, *Causation and Responsibility*, chap. 19.

51 John L. Mackie, "Causes and Conditions," *American Philosophical Quarterly*, Vol. 2 (1965), pp. 245–264.

52 Mackie, *The Cement of the Universe*, at p. 59 n. 1.

53 Jaegwon Kim, "Causes and Events: Mackie on Causation," *Journal of Philosophy*, Vol. 68 (1971), pp. 426–441.

54 Mackie, *The Cement of the Universe*, p. ix.

dinary concept of singular causation in terms of counterfactuals, but then analyzes general causal statements in terms of minimal sufficiency.[55] Yet against this, note that Mackie characterized his counterfactual analysis of the meaning of singular causal statements as only "an initial analysis,"[56] one that could not literally be true or false,[57] and one that was only of the *meaning* of our *ordinary* concept of causation, not of the actual metaphysics of the causal relation.[58] I thus interpret Mackie's seeming dualism about the causal relation the same as I interpret his seeming dualism about the relata of the causal relation (in terms of both facts and events):[59] one is the common sense, ordinary way of thinking (counterfactuals about events) whereas the other is the sophisticated, theory-dependent, and correct way of thinking (minimally sufficient conditions relating facts about events).

That said, Toepel's is a possible interpretation of Mackie, and whether it was Mackie's actual view should not here detain us. For Toepel-Mackie (my name henceforth for Toepel's interpretation of Mackie) has a view worth considering on the merits.

Toepel rightly focuses on the symmetrically overdetermined concurrent cause cases to illustrate how Toepel-Mackie differs from Millians like Wright and Puppe. Toepel sees that a main advantage claimed by Millians for their theory, over and against the counterfactual theory, is that their theory correctly concludes that each of two sets of sufficient conditions is a cause of some harm in such cases. Where each of two fires join to destroy a house, where each fire was (with other conditions) sufficient without the other for the destruction, Millians conclude that each fire caused the destruction. Counterfactualists have a problem about such cases, by contrast, because seemingly no one fire was necessary to the destruction, given the sufficiency of the other fire for that destruction.[60]

True to his theory, Toepel-Mackie regards this as no advantage for the traditional Millians. In contrast to them, Toepel-Mackie defends the view that in cases of symmetrically overdetermining concurrent causation, neither fire caused the destruction (although the set constituted by both together did). This was also the historical Mackie's actual view – not just applying the "common," "ordinary," or "primitive" concept of causation to be found in common sense,[61] but also

---

55 *Id.*, chap. 3.
56 *Id.*, pp. 59, 270.
57 *Id.*, p. 38.
58 *Id.*, pp. 77, 80 – 86.
59 *Id.*, chap. 10. Moore, *Causation and Responsibility*, p. 350.
60 Moore, *Causation and Responsibility*, pp. 414 – 417, 486.
61 Mackie, *The Cement of the Universe*, pp. 46 – 47.

in the "sophisticated," "explanatory," "fact-relating" concept of causation employed by reflective theorists.[62] Like David Lewis,[63] Mackie thought that we lack any definitive causal intuitions in symmetrically overdetermined concurrent cause cases. As Mackie says, the common sense question (of whether one of such overdetermining factors was a cause) "has no answer."[64] In this Mackie and Lewis are poor sociologists. Toepel is better. He recognizes that common intuition regards each overdeterming factor, considered separately, to be a cause. This sociological fact is evidenced by the well-nigh universal legal fact that cause-based liability is imposed on each such overdetermining factor, in German as well as Anglo-American legal systems.[65]

Toepel thus recognizes that he and Mackie have an uphill battle here. Toepel's maneuvers in this battle seem to be four. First, he seeks to show how it is at least not contradictory to believe that the set of both overdetermining factors is a cause of some harm, while yet also believing that it is not the case that either of such factors is by itself a cause. Toepel seeks to show, in other words, that his and Mackie's view is at least a possible view to hold. I am cited as one who believes that it is not.[66]

Mill himself articulated one sense in which a set of items may be a cause of some harm H even while no part of that set is a cause of H. The term "whole cause," Mill said, was properly reserved for the entire set of minimally sufficient conditions on some occasion. While in ordinary, common sense discourse it was idiomatic to pick out one factor in such a set as "the cause" of some harm, in reality and "strictly speaking," only the whole set was the cause.

Yet this is not what is wanted here by Toepel and Mackie. For in overdetermination cases sets S_1 and S_2 are each minimally sufficient sets for the production of some harm. Yet the claim they make is that only the set of sets $\{S_1, S_2\}$ is the cause, that in no sense is S_1 or S_2 by itself the cause. This should be seen for the extraordinary claim that it is.

Consider what Mackie calls cases of quantitative overdetermination.[67] Mackie's example is crushing a chestnut with a hammer blow when the force or number of blows is greater than was needed to crush the chestnut. Although we may properly say, "the blow(s) caused the crushing of the chestnut," we surely are

---

62 *Id.*, p. 265.

63 Lewis, "Causation," at p. 191. For Lewis' equivocation on this point over the course of his career, see Moore, *Causation and Responsibility*, at p. 414 n. 49.

64 Mackie, *The Cement of the Universe*, p. 47.

65 Fredrich Toepel, "Causal Overdetermination," this volume.

66 *Id.*, at. p. 121.

67 Mackie, *The Cement of the Universe*, pp. 43–44, 265.

also committed to the truth that some part of the set of blows was a cause too. For by hypothesis there was more than needed to do the job. The same is true for symmetrically overdetermined concurrent cause cases, where, for example, two simultaneous blows are delivered to the chestnut, each being sufficient to crush it by itself. There was more than was needed to do the job, so surely a part or parts of the set constituting the two blows was also a cause. As I say in my book,[68] only in cases where the set $\{S_1, S_2\}$ is minimally sufficient will it be plausible that no part of that set is itself a cause. But the set $\{S_1, S_2\}$ is by hypothesis not minimally sufficient.

The second argument I use in my book to show how odd is the Toepel-Mackie position on these cases begins by noting that sets like $\{S_1, S_2\}$ above for hammer blows, are ambiguous between two quite different possibilities.[69] In the ordinary, garden-variety concurrent cause case, S_1 and S_2 are each only individually necessary for some harm H; they are only jointly sufficient. Whereas in the overdetermination concurrent cause cases, S_1 and S_2 are each individually sufficient and only jointly necessary for H. A natural thought is that in the first, garden-variety concurrent cause case, S_1 and S_2 are conjunctive; whereas in the second, overdetermination concurrent cause case, S_1 and S_2 are disjunctive. As I note in the book,[70] conjunction and disjunction are properties of propositions, not of events; in particular, the idea of a disjunctive event seems to make little sense. But Mackie (although not Toepel) regards the ultimate relata of causation to be facts (in the sense of true propositions) anyway. So we may reconstrue S_1 and S_2 to be the facts that a certain hammer blow occurred. And now we can unproblematically distinguish the conjunction of S_1, S_2 from the disjunction of S_1, S_2.

In a sense this will generate the accusation of contradiction that Toepel attributes to me[71]. If we represent causation in terms of sufficiency, itself symbolized by the material conditional, we may represent the Toepel-Mackie belief in causation by the set $\{S_1, S_2\}$ in cases of overdetermination as follows:

(1) If (S_1 or S_2), then H. (Where S_1, S_2, and H are all propositions about their respective events occurring).

Yet Toepel-Mackie also believe:

68 Moore, *Causation and Responsibility*, p. 410 n. 44.
69 *Id.*, p. 354.
70 *Id.*, p. 355.
71 Toepel, "Causal Overdetermination," at p. 121.

(2a) It is not the case that, if S_1, then H; and
(2b) It is not the case that, if S_2, then H.

(1), (2a), and (2b) are indeed contradictory. But then, this is due to our symbolizing causal relations in terms of *sufficient* conditions; no literal contradiction arises if we otherwise conceive of causation, as Toepel-Mackie does for *singular* causal relations at least.

Still, there is a residual oddity here. Both exclusive and inclusive disjunctive facts are seemingly made true by either of the facts (of which they are composed), itself being true. "Either snow is white or it is raining in Tibet" is made true by either "snow is white" or "it is raining in Tibet" being true. Yet the Toepel-Mackie disjunctive proposition lacks this seemingly essential attribute for disjunctive facts. So Toepel-Mackie must reject the set $\{S_1, S_2\}$ being construed to be a disjunctive fact. But that means they lack the resources to distinguish two very different kinds of sets $\{S_1, S_2\}$, the ordinary garden variety (conjunctive) kind versus the overdetermining (disjunctive) kind.

Toepel's second move is to question whether there really are any overdetermining concurrent cause cases. Toepel flirts with the thought that perhaps if we look at the microphysics of these situations we would always find that either S_1 or S_2 pre-empted the other from having any effect on some suitably small swatch of the overall result. In which event concurrent overdetermination cases would really be combinations of pre-emptive overdetermination cases.

I am not sure I understand the motivation for this speculation by Toepel. It is easy to understand the reverse speculation of David Lewis late in his career, that all pre-emptive overdetermination cases are really concurrent overdetermination cases (because even the pre-empted cause has some impact on the effect).[72] For Lewis could then reconcile the pre-emptive cases with his counterfactual theory of causation as he sought to reconcile the concurrent cases (which is to say, via a sufficiently fine-grained individuation of the result so that in its exact manner of occurrence, each seemingly sufficient cause was really only necessary). But Toepel's reverse speculation offers him no such gain, because the counterfactual theory has as bad a problem with pre-emptive overdetermination cases as it does with concurrent overdetermination cases.

In any case, Toepel puts aside his speculations here. His third point is to join Lewis somewhat in Lewis' fine-grained individuation of effect events so that more factors will be *necessary* to such fine-grained (or "fragile") effects. Yet this familiar strategy has two disqualifying drawbacks: first, it doesn't eliminate

72 David Lewis, "Causation as Influence," *Journal of Philosophy*, Vol. 97 (2000), pp. 182–197.

counterexamples where there is no qualitative difference between the result caused by two overdetermining concurrent causes, and the result that would have been caused by one operating alone.[73] Second, the fine-graining-of-effect strategy has the well-known consequence of expanding what is a cause of what.[74] It is true that Toepel allows himself to go only part way down Lewis' line of march here. Toepel doesn't share the zealot's zeal to save the counterfactual theory no matter what the costs. This is of course commendable; but then, the theory isn't saved from these overdetermining concurrent cause counterexamples, either.

At the end of the day Toepel turns back on his own accurate sociology about common causal and moral intuitions in these kind of cases. These are, he cautions us, just intuitions, intuitions whose reliability can and should be questioned. Toepel ups the ante here by also questioning our common intuitions about pre-emptive overdetermination cases too; in cases of trumping pre-emption, where there is no difference in result caused by the pre-empting versus the pre-empted factor, Toepel would have us overthrow common intuition in favor of the "discerning scholar's" view (which Toepel thinks is that neither factor in such cases is the cause).

Toepel purports to question these intuitions because they "appeal to our emotional responses than to our intellects," because they are, "vague" and inadequate to resolve "fine distinctions," and because "they tend to be contradictory."[75] Yet Toepel makes out none of these charges about either moral or causal intuitions in the overdetermination cases. What seems to drive him is his own preferred theory of singular causation, the counterfactual theory. That theory demands that where one overdetermining factor "would foreseeably have produced the same result by itself without the ... help" of the other overdetermining factor, neither factor be deemed a cause of the result.[76] Toepel is thus simply overruling common moral and causal intuitions based on his preferred theory of causation.

Surely such overrulings of common intuition counts against a theory of causation. Because such intuitions are not veridical, one might hold to one's theory *despite* its need to issue such overrulings; but surely one would not hold one's theory *because* of such overrulings. In my book I outline thirteen common sense intuitions about causation enshrined in the law, several of which involve overdetermination cases of both kinds.[77] One of these, that of there being "inter-

---

73 Moore, *Causation and Responsibility*, p. 414.
74 *Id.*, pp. 412–413.
75 Toepel, "Causal Overdetermination," p. 122–125.
76 *Id.*, p. 124.
77 Moore, *Causation and Responsibility*, pp. 152–154.

vening causes," I myself abandon.[78] But abandoning causation by overdetermining factors of either the concurrent or pre-emptive kind would be like abandoning the direction of causation through time or the distinction between epiphenomenal and causal relations. All of these concessions are conceivable, and in that sense the intuitions are possible to give up; but any theory demanding that we make such radical alterations in how we think about causation would have to have a great deal to be said for it in other dimensions.

3 Birnbacher, Hommen, and Negative Causation

Professor Birnbacher and David Hommen pick up on the issue I earlier put aside in my discussion of Puppe and Wright, namely, whether omissions and other absences can enter into singular causal relations. Birnbacher and Hommen's paper is an apt opportunity to pursue an issue central to Puppe's and Wright's concerns, because Birnbacher and Hommen share with Wright and Puppe a view of the causal relation that allows (indeed, requires) that absences count as relata of that relation.

Birnbacher and Hommen adopt what they call "the condition view of causality."[79] This view is non-committal between the counterfactualist, nomic sufficiency, and interventionist theories of the causal relation. Nonetheless, the condition view, like the NESS theory of Wright and Puppe more specifically, embraces absences as causes and effects. On this implication of these theories, we are all five of us agreed. The issue between me, on the one hand, and the four of them, on the other, is whether it is a good or a bad thing for a theory to be committed to absence-causation. I argue in my book that is a bad thing, whereas they argue the opposite; so issue is here joined.

In my book I raise four arguments as to why omissions are not causes (and why more generally absences cannot serve as causes or effects), and thus why any theory that counts them as causes is a bad theory of causation.[80] Birnbacher and Hommen deal with three of these arguments of mine, and I shall organize my discussion by their responses to these three arguments. (The fourth argument, the argument from omissive overdetermination cases, is not discussed by them but has been discussed extensively above in my reply to Puppe and Wright.)

---

78 *Id.*, chaps. 12–13.

79 Dieter Birnbacher and David Hommen, "Omissions as Causes – Genuine, Quasi, or not at All?," this volume, p. 144.

80 Moore, *Causation and Responsibility*, pp. 444–451.

My first argument was one of ontology: absences are not particulars and thus cannot serve as the relata of singular causal relations. Birnbacher and Hommen deal at length with this issue. I think that the most favorable statement of the argument for their side of this issues goes as follows. For the generalist about the causal relation (such as Millians like Puppe and Wright), singular causal relations are constructions out of what is more basic, which are causal laws. As such, no real particulars are needed to serve as causal relata. On this general view all that is needed for absences to serve as causes is: (1) the showing that absences can serve as "conditions" within causal laws; and (2) the showing that such types of absences as figure in causal laws can be instantiated in space/time locations with no ontological commitments to absences as particulars.

In my book I actually concede to generalists both of these points. About (1): "At the level of laws, negative existential propositions are all that are needed, and these raise no ontological hackles."[81] About (2): "the truth-maker for negative conditions is the absence of any positive instances of some type. The law is 'instantiated' in this sense whenever its negative conditions are made true by the world [by such positive conditions being absent at a particular time and place]."[82]

Ultimately I find this reply by generalists to be inadequate. If the reply is not a way of being committed to facts (in the sense of true propositions) being the relata of the singular causal relation – as I say in my book that it might be[83] – then the reply is hostage to the view that singular causal relations are only constructions (out of causal laws). Any form of even moderate singularism will reject this demotion of singular causal relations. The strategy makes omissions singular causes only at the cost of saying "really, there are no singular causes as a matter of basic ontology."

In any event, Birnbacher and Hommen do not appear to take the route just sketched. For unlike Toepel, their threefold subdivision of the question of omissions does not distinguish negative *conditions* in causal laws from negative *causes* in singular causal relations. Rather, in their second and third questions about omissions they distinguish negative conditions that are parts of minimally sufficient sets from negative conditions only part of Mackie's background causal field. In both cases they appear to equate the question of whether negative ac-

81 *Id.*, p. 479.
82 *Id.*
83 *Id.*, p. 445 n. 42.

tions (and negative events more generally) can be the cause of some particular outcome, with the question of whether there can be negative conditions.

Birnbacher and Hommen pay me the compliment of finding me intellectually honest in my eschewal of any easy escape routes about omissions. Let me repay the compliment: they too are refreshingly honest and forthright in refusing to countenance these intellectual dodges. Thus, they recognize that most legal theorists adopt the "diplomatic solution" of saying that omissions cause harms in some secondary, derived, or lesser sense of "cause," whereas they refuse to be diplomatic,[84] as do I; the choice is a stark one: either omissions are really causal, or they are not at all or in any way causal.

I defend the latter answer, they, the former. Their defense begins by noting (like others such as Hart and Honoré[85] and Jonathan Schaffer[86]) that negative linguistic expressions can be used to refer to positive items that unproblematically exist. On this we are all agreed: such negative expressions *can* be so used.[87] But the question remains whether, in our typical omission talk, they *are* so used. Birnbacher and Hommen tell us that, "saying that B fails to water A's plants is specifying, by means of negation, the way B behaves or the way B is. It is picking out a particular and in the circumstance explanatorily relevant aspect of what B *does* or how he *is*."[88]

One would have expected Birnbacher's and Hommen's next sentence following the one just quoted would have been to tell us just what the particular is that is picked out by the phrase, "B's failure to water A's plants." But nowhere in their paper, and nowhere in the oral defense of their paper at Cologne University, did Birnbacher and Hommen give any answer whatsoever to this crucial question of reference. They criticize me by saying that it is their "conviction that negative actions are less of a 'nothing' than Moore supposes."[89] Perhaps – but then surely we are entitled to hear what sort of a thing these "not-nothings" are.

The puzzle is only heightened by what Birnbacher and Hommen do say about other theorists' attempts to specify the positive reference of negative language. They rightly eschew, as do I: (1) the idea that omissions refer to intentions

---

84 Birnbacher and Hommen, "Omissions as Causes," at p. 137.

85 Hart and Honore, *Causation in the Law*, p. 38.

86 Jonathan Schaffer's long held view. See Schaffer, "Contrastive Causation," *Philosophical Review*, Vol. 114 (2005), pp. 327–358, sec. 2; Schafffer, "Causes Need Not Be Physically Connected to Their Effects," p. 212; Schaffer, "Disconnection and Responsibility," p. 418. As noted earlier, Markus Stepanians critically reviews Schaffer on this point, in his "Why Schaffer's Solution to the Problem of Absence Causation Fails."

87 Moore, "Four Friendly Critics: A Response," p. 510.

88 Birnbacher and Hommen, "Omissions as Causes," p. 142.

89 *Id.*

to omit; (2) the thought that omissions refer to the positive acts people like B are doing when they omit to water plants; (3) the thought that omissions refer to the totality of events and states of affairs occurring at the time of omission, which totality fails to include a watering of the plants by B; (4) the reduction of omissions to a circumstance in which some positive acts of B are done; (5) the spooky idea that negative descriptions refer to "spooky entities that exist in some barely intelligible mode of existence...things that somehow exist even though they actually do not exist."[90] Just so! But then, what is the reference for omission talk like, "B failed to water A's plants?"

It is no good for Birnbacher and Hommer to take refuge in "best explanation" arguments, concluding as they do that "negative actions or events are real if they are explanatorily necessary."[91] For we won't know *what* is real or *what* is explanatorily necessary until we know what is being referred to. In one of their examples Birnbacher and Hommen explain why there is a commotion at a certain party, in terms of "Jones's failing to come to the party."[92] I would paraphrase this into fact language: "the fact that Jones did not come to the party best explains all the fuss." Facts do a lot of explaining, and they may easily be negative because they are nothing more than true propositions. Yet Birnbacher and Hommen explicitly put "fact-like conditions" aside; they assert that Jones's failure to attend is "a condition in the metaphysical sense," viz, it is "a real aspect" of Jones that "enters into explanatory relations."[93] Yet just what that condition – that "real aspect" of Jones – is, is still quite mysterious, at least to me.

So I literally do not know what Birnbacher and Hommen are talking about in their reply to my first argument. I shall thus leave it. My second and third arguments are about the metaphysical and moral differences, respectively, that we sense to exist between actions causing harm, on the one hand, and omissions failing to prevent harm, on the other.

The metaphysical intuition of difference I share with Phil Dowe.[94] We both sense – and think that virtually everyone else senses – that there is a real difference in terms of causality between my beating Jones to death with a club and you failing to stop me. We would explain this intuition of difference by a metaphysical difference: I caused Jones death, and you didn't. Birnbacher and Hommen would explain the intuition by a different metaphysical difference:

90 *Id.*
91 *Id.*
92 *Id.*, p. 143.
93 *Id.*.
94 Phil Dowe, *Physical Causation* (Cambridge: Cambridge University Press, 2000), pp. 217–218; Moore, *Causation and Responsibility*, pp. 445–447.

> there is a difference between positive and negative causes: negative causes are negative, whereas positive causes are positive. This difference seems perfectly sufficient to explain the 'intuition of difference.' No 'deeper' difference seems to be called for.[95]

While they recognize that many find "that this simple answer may be too simple,"[96] at the end of the day they nonetheless reaffirm that answer. Such reaffirmation is based, first, on their rejecting my answer because it can be no stronger than "the weaknesses of the ontological argument from nothingness," and second, on their rejecting a variety of others' answers on grounds they are not "coherent."[97]

I agree with Birnbacher and Hommen in rejecting the six overlays on the positive/negative distinction that others have suggested, items like causally relevant versus causally operative, triggering versus preparatory, dynamic versus static, background versus here and now, etc. I disagree with their attempt to add me as a proposer of a seventh overlay on the positive/negative distinction, that of enabling versus causing. For in truth I promote no such distinction. Most of the passages they quote from me on this distinction are from chapter 5 of my book, where I was detailing *Anglo-American criminal law's* concept of causation; I later devote an entire chapter, Chapter 13, to saying what I myself think, which is that enabling another to cause some harm is often just a way of causing that harm oneself. And in any case, all of the examples relied upon by Birnbacher and Hommen are *not* omission examples; they are examples of acts causing harms or of acts that remove a defense to nature causing harm (what I call, "double preventions"). So it is simply a misreading to stick me with yet another "ill-conceived" overlay on the positive/negative distinction.

That leaves only the two original competitors still standing, my cause/no-cause explanation for the intuition of difference between causings and failures to prevent, or Birnbacher and Hommen's positive/negative explanation. Yet in this competition, doesn't my explanation win hands down? After all, theirs is no more than a restatement of the distinction: present events causing is positive in the sense that such events are present and not absent, whereas absences of preventions is negative in the sense that such absences are not present. This "explains" the intuition of difference only in the Pickwickian sense that it restates it. Moreover, if Birnbacher and Hommen were correct in their ontological argument above, do they have any positive/negative distinction left to draw? If omissions are conceived as just negative ways of talking about positive events, as we have

95 Birnbacher and Hommen, "Omissions as Causes," p. 146.
96 *Id.*
97 *Id.*, p. 148.

seen that Birnbacher and Hommen at times suggest, then at the ontological level they have no positive/negative distinction with which to work in explaining the intuition of difference.

My third argument for why omissions are not causal builds on the moral difference between omissive versus causal liability. Our positive duties to prevent harm are both fewer and less stringent than our negative duties not to act so as to cause harm; moreover, our blameworthiness for failing to prevent harm is much less severe than for causing that same harm. I take these moral differences to be best explained by a metaphysical difference: the first responsibility is non-causal and only counterfactual, whereas the second responsibility is causal (and may or may not also be counterfactual).

I am frankly puzzled by Birnbacher's and Hommen's response here. They say that it takes some charitable interpretation (of what I said) on their part to save me from the "elementary mistake" of thinking that degrees of moral blameworthiness can effect causal metaphysics, that although I try "hard not to 'let the moral tail wag the metaphysical dog,'" I often do just that.[98] What I said is this: First on any plausibly naturalistic meta-ethics, all moral properties supervene on natural properties.[99] Second, since supervenience means asymmetrical co-variance, any difference in supervening moral properties must be accompanied by some difference in the natural base properties.[100] And third, the best distinction in natural properties with which to explain the moral differences above, is the distinction between causing and non-causally failing to prevent harm.[101] This was too clear to need much if any interpretation.

Birnbacher and Hommen do better when they deign to enter the lists of explanatory competition. As must be the case for any knights entering such a tournament, they both propose their own competing explanation of the moral facts, and also they seek to unseat my explanation by raising problems for it. One problem they raise for my explanation is that some positive duties (such as those of parent to child) can be quite stringent and their breach quite serious, even though these are omission-based duties. So, they urge, the metaphysical difference (between causing/failing to prevent) cannot always mark a moral difference. Yet notice, even in cases of special obligations (*Garantenpflichten*, in German law), there still are moral differences to be marked by the metaphysical

98 *Id.*, pp. 149–150.
99 Moore, *Causation and Responsibility*, p. vii. My extended defense of this kind of naturalist-realist meta-ethics is in Moore, *Objectivity in Ethics and Law* (Andershot, UK: Ashgate, 2004), essays 1, 2, and 6.
100 Moore, *Causation and Responsibility*, p. 448.
101 *Id.*

difference between causing and failing to prevent: the father who bludgeons his child to death is more blameworthy than the mother who fails to rescue the child from deadly peril.[102]

Birnbacher and Hommen also attempt to provide their own, competing, naturalistic explanations for the relevant moral differences. They note a series of nine "hidden parameters" and two pragmatic factors that to their mind better explain why we judge actions causing a given harm as more blameworthy than omissions failing to prevent that same harm.[103] Yet all eleven of these items do not even purport to explain the moral facts of the matter, which are that negative duties *are* more stringent than positive duties and that breaches of the former *are* more blameworthy than breaches of the latter. Their eleven items only purport to explain the sociological facts about people's blaming practices. To make these factors relevant to explaining the moral (rather than the sociological) facts, ask whether each such factor would matter to you in judging blameworthiness. Thus, imagine a pair-wise comparison between an act causing some harm H and an omission failing to prevent H, and now eliminate all eleven of Birnbacher's and Hommen's overlaid differences. Suppose, for example, H is equally intentional for the actor who intends to cause H by his action and for the omitter who intends to do nothing so that H will occur; etc. Then ask yourself: is there still not a moral difference (in degrees of blameworthiness) between the actor and the omitter? If you are like me, there is. In which case the factors are not marking the differences. My inference was and is that it is causation that makes the difference here.[104]

102 I use these kinds of examples to rebut a like criticism of my views by Larry Alexander and Kim Ferzan. See Moore, "Moore's Truths About Causation and Responsibility," pp. 451–453.
103 Birnbacher and Hommen, "Omissions as Causes," pp. 153–155.
104 Jonathan Schaffer too enters the explanatory competition with me on what best explains the moral differences between positive and negative moral duties. See his "Disconnection and Responsibility," pp. 429–431, 432–433. My response is in my "Four Friendly Critics," pp. 506–509.

4 Geert Keil, Philipp Huebl, Singular Necessity, and Events as Causal Relata

I am generally quite sympathetic to Professor Keil's project,[105] a project which Professor Huebl by-and-large shares with him.[106] Their insightful and sophisticated articulation of a singularist counterfactual theory of causation is one possible answer to the invitation my book issued to metaphysicians of causation, which was to see if one can articulate a singularist metaphysics of causation that answers to the legal, moral, and folk-psychological demands that we daily place on the concept. Still, that said, it would trouble me if the Keil/Huebl view were the one to fit the bill, that Lewis' counterfactual theory of causation could be amended in the ways Keil and Huebl propose so that it is this theory that fits the bill. There are a number of reasons for this.

To begin with, keeping counterfactual dependence as a desert base independent of causation is important, and this independence will be possible only if causation is neither identical to counterfactual dependence nor extensionally equivalent in yielding the same answer in all cases. A truly counterfactual theory of causation would elide important moral uses for the distinction between causal and counterfactual-based responsibility.

These uses include the following. First, there is the moral differences between acts that cause a harm, and omissions that fail to prevent that same harm. Those moral differences are two: there is the lesser blameworthiness for omissive liability that was at issue with Birnbacher and Hommen,[107] and there is a greater permissibility of consequentialist justification.[108] On the naturalist-realist meta-ethics to which I have long subscribed, all moral differences must be underlain by some differences in natural properties. If that difference in natural properties is not going to be found in the difference between causation and counterfactual dependence, some other natural difference will have to be found. Birnbacher and Hommen list a number of possibilities here,[109] and there are other suggestions in the literature.[110] However, none of these to my mind seem

---

105 Geert Keil, "Making Causal Counterfactuals More Singular, and More Appropriate for Use in Law," this volume. Professor Keil summarizes and builds on his own book on causation, *Handeln und Verursachen* (Frankfurt-am-Main: Vittorio Klostermann, 2000).

106 Philipp Huebl, "Events over Facts: Why Metaphysics Matters for Law," this volume.

107 Moore, *Causation and Responsibility*, pp. 447–449.

108 *Id.*, pp. 55–59.

109 Birnbacher and Hommen, "Omissions as Causes," pp. 153–155.

110 Schaffer, "Disconnection and Responsibility," pp. 429–433.

nearly as plausible (and as well fitting) as the causation/counterfactual dependence distinction.

An analogous use for the distinction is to be found in grounding the moral difference between allowings, other double preventions, and simple preventions, on the one hand, and causings, on the other.[111] The same two moral differences exist here as for omissions, and the most plausible natural basis for these moral differences lies in there being a cause/counterfactual distinction.

Yet another use for the distinction lies in what I call the "evil manipulator" cases.[112] Causation (as Keil, Huebl, and I agree) peters out over space and time, as the proverbial ripples in a pond peter out from a dropped stone. That feature of causation might seem to make non-responsible those evil manipulators who are clever enough to trace causally remote or physically minute connections and use them to further their own evil ends. E.g., the evil genius that flaps the butterfly's wings just the right way over the Sahara so that a hurricane hits Miami three months later; or the evil genius who destabilizes some precarious natural equilibrium, unleashing natural forces that cause the great harm that he intended them to cause. We want some non-causal (i.e., non-petering out) basis for holding such evil manipulators responsible for the harms that they intend. For me counterfactual dependency seems to fit the bill, so long as one does not think (as do Keil and Huebl) that counterfactual dependence must peter out since causation does so (and since for them, the two are one and the same thing).

Keil and Huebl might think that because they eschew *identifying* causation with counterfactual dependence, their theory can still deliver the moral goods just described. But it cannot. For their amended counterfactual theory is committed to a co-presence of counterfactual dependence (of a kind) with causation, and even without identity such a uniform co-presence will rule out the moral uses of a counterfactual/causation distinction described above.

So at bottom I am not sanguine about the possibility that the Keil/Huebl singularist theory of causation can be the kind of theory I invited in my book. I say this with some reluctance, because their general approach in building a theory of causation is very much in line with my own. They both believe, as do I, that such a theory should aim at articulating one unitary notion of causation serviceable in science, morals, law and common sense. This picture, although admittedly "quite optimistic," contrasts quite favorably to the balkanization of the concept favored in many quarters. They also join me in opposing those like Professor Toe-

111 Moore, *Causation and Responsibility*, pp. 61–65, 129–132.
112 *Id.*, pp. 468–469.

pel, who are willing to run roughshod over firm and settled causal intuitions in the name of furthering one's favored theory. As Keil puts it, "we expect philosophical theories to account for our intuitions, rather than the other way around."[113] Indeed, his list of seven deliverances of common sense intuitions about causation overlap substantially with my own list of thirteen.[114] Likewise, Huebl also sees that "the law...needs to presuppose a theory of causation that matches our pre-theoretic causal intuitions....[and that] a philosophical theory starts with our pre-theoretical intuitions as well."[115] So there is a broad agreement in both what we are looking for with a theory of causation, and how to proceed in developing one.

But, as the saying goes, the devil is in the details. Keil and Huebl begin by making life easy for the counterfactual theorist about causation. They do this by eschewing any reductionist ambitions for the theory: no identity between causation and counterfactual dependence is claimed. Indeed, Keil tells us that "neither Lewis nor any other serious proponent of the counterfactual theory endorses the identity claim."[116] The accusation, I take it, is that in my book's criticisms of the counterfactual theory I was torching a straw man.

Keil and Huebl here evidence a mood I sense to exist in many contemporary metaphysicians of causation, which is a mood of resigned tiredness. The theories of such metaphysicians start out full of ambition and promise, but then the counterexamples mount, the defensive epicycles in the theory proliferate, until such theorists stunt their ambitions in order to more easily defend their theory. They say that Factor X (irrespective of whether X is counterfactual dependence, increase in conditional probability, primitive chance-raisings, powers, manipulability, etc.) does not give the *nature* of causation – rather, Factor X is a mere *concomitant* of causation, or a *sort* of causation, or merely an *indicator* or criterion of causation, or merely good but not inevitably present *evidence* of causation, or a *heuristic* to seeing when causation is present, etc. Such truncated ambitions of course have their benefits. Keil articulates a big one: now you don't have to show that the bedrock features of causation in common sense all flow in some natural way from Factor X, because Factor X is no longer claimed to be the nature of causation. Yet such truncated ambitions equally obviously have their cost: causation either remains unexplicated or, what is a bit different, its only explication is the truncated explication of the metaphysical primitivist. Primitivists may indeed be able to give what Huebl attributes to Peter Strawson,

---

113 Keil, "Making Causal Counterfactuals More Singular," p. 167.
114 Compare *id.*, pp. 167–168, with Moore, *Causation and Responsibility*, pp. 152–154.
115 Huebl, "Events over Facts," p. 203.
116 Keil, "Making Causal Counterfactuals More Singular," p. 169.

a kind of "connective analysis" whereby one relates our use of one basic concept to another;[117] even so, one's concept of cause remains primitivist.

Primitivism may be the best we can do about causation, at the end of the day. And perhaps that is where Keil's and Huebl's theory ends up. But if so, it ill-suits them to pooh-pooh other primitivisms like that of David Armstrong with his primitive necessitation between universals.[118] As Armstrong himself wrote (about Hugh Mellor's primitive chance-raisings), "those who live in ontological glass houses should not throw stones at others."[119]

There are half-way houses for tired metaphysicians about causation. One such half-way house is where an identity is claimed, not between causation and some Factor X, but rather, between causation and some subset of things that possess Factor X. Keil sounds like this when he says that not all counterfactual dependencies are causal, only a kind of them is. Yet now the criticisms I make (and that Keil would put aside) get reinvigorated. Even if there is a differentium that differentiates the species (*causal* counterfactual dependencies) from the genus (counterfactual dependencies), one wants one of two things to be true of such differentium. Either it flows naturally from the genus (counterfactual dependency); or it is itself a plausible theory of (part of) the nature of causation. An example of the latter kind is the probabilistic counterfactual theory,[120] where the independently plausible chance-raising nature of causation is used to modify the counterfactual theory.

Some of what Keil says can be construed as an attempt to occupy this last version of a half-way house. If events are independently plausible as the relata of the singular causal relation, for example, restricting the counterfactual dependencies eligible to be considered causal to those that exist between distinct events, might be legitimate.

Yet Keil goes beyond this. He thinks it legitimate to take all the constraints on causation implicit in our common sense causal judgments, and "turn them into constraints for the class of counterfactuals that a counterfactual analysis of causation has to consider."[121] Just like that, with no showing of any unity to those constraints in terms of counterfactual dependence or in terms of any other plausible, unified nature to causation. An ad hoc theory of causation con-

117 Huebl, "Events over Facts," p. 205.
118 David Armstrong, *What Is a Law of Nature?* (Cambridge: Cambridge University Press, 1983).
119 David Armstrong, "The Open Door: Counterfactual versus Singular Theories of Causation," in H. Stanken, ed., *Causation and Laws of Nature* (London: Kluwer Academic Pub., 1999).
120 I discuss this theory briefly in Moore, *Causation and Responsibility*, pp. 312–314.
121 Keil, "Making Causal Counterfactuals More Singular," p. 170.

structed along these lines of Keil's would not be without value; but it is not an ambition worthy only of scarecrows to want more.

Indeed, Keil himself sometimes shows us he wants more too. He betrays this when he says, for example, that "a singularist counterfactual theory has a nice explanation for...[the intransitivity of causation]."[122] If counterfactual dependency of a certain kind is a mere concomitant of causation, and in no way constitutive of the nature of the causal relation, in what sense can features of counterfactual dependence (like intransitivity) *explain* features of causation?

I now turn to the question of whether Keil and Huebl succeed in taming the counterfactual theory so as to meet even their stated, modestly non-reductionist criteria of successful theory construction. Consider in this regard Keil's and Huebl's treatment of overdetermination cases. They both rightly see that a fixed judgment of common sense (that any theory of causation presumptively must accommodate) is that in the pre-emptive kind of overdetermination cases, the pre-empting factor is a cause and the pre-empted factor is not. They pick up on my two fires illustration: Fire one (F_1) is sufficient to burn down the victim's house, but so is fire two (F_2); F_1 reaches the house first and burns it down; F_2 arrives when there is no house to be burnt. F_1 pre-empted F_2 from burning down the house, and only F_1 causes the destruction.

Keil agrees with common sense here, but claims that his amended "counterfactual theory delivers the goods...had the first fire been absent, the effect would not have occurred."[123] Keil and Huebl get this result out of their theory by the familiar expedient of doing a fine-grained individuation of the effect: if F_1 had not existed, F_2 would have destroyed the house but it would have been a different destruction than the destruction that actually occurred; the destruction that actually occurred *was*, thus, counterfactually dependent upon F_1, contrary to what one would think if one asked the more coarse-grained question about destructions in general rather than about *this* destruction in all of its detail. If I understand them rightly, Keil and Huebl wish to distinguish their move here from the traditional fine-grained strategy. Thus, Huebl allows that he is "dubious" of the "strategy of fine-grained individuation that makes more and more details necessary for the event to occur."[124] Huebl is "dubious for metaphysical reasons, because the details are endless."[125] Yet it turns out Huebl's only reason for doubt here is that the traditional fine-grained strategy does not go far enough. His and

122 *Id.*, p. 181.
123 *Id.*, p. 177.
124 Huebl, "Events over Facts," p. 213.
125 *Id.*

Keil's idea is to refer to these events that are effects, "in all their detail," and sees that "there is no finer graininess available" than their revised strategy.[126]

What is new here is thus not the Keil/Huebl fine-grained solution. Rather, it is Keil's argument (seconded by Huebl) for why such fine-graining is a plausible thing to do, independently of its usefulness in getting rid of troublesome counterexamples of the overdetermination kind. Keil does this by arguing for Davidsonian whole events as causal relata; recognizing that such Davidsonian whole events (unlike Kimian events) will have innumerably many properties or "aspects";[127] recognizing that "no ever so slightly different event could have been numerically identical with the event that actually happened;"[128] and (most importantly in Keil's view) recognizing that singular counterfactual dependencies are between particular events and thus can exist even when certain general counterfactual dependencies (as are often described in terms of "necessary conditions") do not exist.[129]

Keil recognizes that this train of argument utilizes a not well-regarded theory of cross-world identification. For Keil takes the indisputable truth of Leibniz – no two particulars not sharing all of their properties at a time can be numerically identical – and transforms it into a criterion of cross-world identity. Yet the Leibnizian criterion so transformed is no more plausible than it would be if transformed into a criterion of identity over time.[130] Lewis at least came to recognize this by allowing that the *same* event in different possible worlds could have different properties, calling such changes in the properties of events, "alterations" in one and the same event.[131] But Keil makes no such accommodation to our normal views of cross-world identity of events.

Neither does Huebl. For Huebl argues that, on his and Keil's Davidsonian whole events view of causal relata, for events that occur at a particular time and place, "all their properties at this space-time position are essential."[132] Any destruction that differs in any respect from the destruction that actually occurred will thus be a different token of destruction, on this view. As Huebl puts

---

126 *Id.*, p. 213.
127 Keil, "Making Causal Counterfactuals More Singular," pp. 174–176.
128 *Id.*, p. 177.
129 *Id.*, pp. 178–180.
130 I so argue in Moore, *Causation and Responsibility*, pp. 413–414.
131 Lewis, "Causation as Influence," For a discussion, see Moore, *Causation and Responsibility*, p. 414 n. 48.
132 Huebl, "Events over Facts," p. 213.

it: "events cannot undergo changes and remain the same [event], because they *are* changes."[133]

This last bit surely is not true. Movement of a body through space during an interval of time is surely a change and thus an event on Huebl's understanding; yet that change in position can itself change – we call that change in a change, *acceleration*. More generally, it is highly implausible to think that events have all of their properties essentially. Other spatio-temporally located particulars such as persons and other objects, are not like this, as Huebl recognizes. Events have (typically) shorter temporal durations than do objects; yet I see no purchase given by that difference justifying the thought that spatio-temporal locations are more essential to event-token identity than to object-token identity.

But we can put this criticism aside, because Keil's and Huebl's argument, even if impeccable, does not do the work they want from it. Keil's is a sophisticated way of defending a non-ad hoc fine-graining of the effects in counterfactual dependencies. Yet the route only gets him to the fine-grained solution for overdetermination counterexamples; Keil's argumentative route in no way remedies the defects of the solution itself.

Those defects are two in number. One is that even the extreme fine-graining demanded by Keil's theory does not eliminate the overdetermination counterexamples.[134] In cases of *concurrent* overdetermination (which Keil does not discuss), such as where F_1 and F_2 join to burn down the house, there need be no qualitative difference whatsoever between the destruction that actually occurred and the destruction that would have occurred if F_1 had been absent. The same is true in cases of pre-emptive overdetermination (which Keil does discuss).[135] In a well-known example of trumping pre-emption, troops march in response to a major's order given at the same time as the order of a sergeant; the marching done as a result of the major's order need not differ in any way from the marching that would have been done as a result of the sergeant's order in cases where the major was silent.[136] So there is no singular counterfactual dependence in such cases. But (common sense firmly tells us), there is causation.

133 *Id.*

134 Moore, *Causation and Responsibility*, p. 414.

135 Ned Hall: "It is child's play to come up with counter-examples where the substitution of the pre-empted factor for the pre-empting cause makes absolutely no difference to the event caused." Hall, "Causation and the Price of Transitivity," *Journal of Philosophy*, Vol. 97 (2000), pp. 198–222, at p. 221.

136 Moore, *Causation and Responsibility*, p. 424.

Huebl disputes whether there can be such cases. He asserts: "quite frankly, I cannot imagine such a case."[137] Really? Two fires join before they reach the house in question; the joined fire ignites the fuse leading to the house, the same fuse that either fire would have ignited by itself. The house destruction is *exactly the same in every detail* as it would have been if either fire itself had ignited the fuse.

Or take Huebl's other example, that of two bullets.[138] Suppose the bullets collide just before the heart of the victim is hit; and suppose the collision halves off ½ of each bullet, so that the two halves remaining form a single bullet of mass, direction, and velocity equal to that of each original bullet by itself. There need be no difference whatsoever in the death suffered by the victim in such a case from the death he would have suffered if struck in the heart by only one of the bullets. (I realize that this scenario is about as likely as was Robin Hood's splitting the Sheriff of Nottingham's arrow in the archery contest of English legend; but Hollywood has its uses in inspiring possible worlds.)

Perhaps Keil and Huebl only have pre-emptive overdetermination cases in mind, not concurrent ones. Yet that would be a lacunae in their analysis that they could ill afford. Unrebutted, the concurrent overdetermination cases by themselves undermine any version of the counterfactual theory of causation. In any case, there also exist pre-emptive overdetermination cases where the harm caused by the pre-empting factor need differ not at all from the harm that would have been caused by the pre-empted factor. The trumping pre-emption cases are of this kind, such as the two orders case mentioned earlier.

Huebl pulls one last arrow from his quiver here. Even if, Huebl says, the effects in the counterfactual scenarios in these cases are qualitatively identical to the effect that occurred in the actual world, "this is not *numerical identity*."[139] For Huebl, a qualitatively identical house destruction or death in another possible world, cannot be the same destruction or death as in the actual world, just by virtue of there being two different possible worlds. This is just to say there are *no* cross-world identifications to be made for events.

Huebl here takes Keil's singularist counterfactual theory to the point of absurdity. For if events can never be identified as the same in any possible world save the one in which they actually occur, then all counterfactual statements are true, and necessarily true to boot. This, because all counterfactual statements suppose a world differing from the actual world at least by the changes descri-

137 Huebl, "Events over Facts," p. 213.
138 *Id.*
139 *Id.*, p. 214.

bed in the antecedent clauses of such counterfactuals; and no matter what (according to Huebl), the event described in the consequent clause will be absent in that possible world. So all events would be necessary for all events, on Huebl's view. This is a reductio that Keil and Huebl cannot possibly accept.

The second defect of the fine-grained solution is also well known. It is the extraordinary promiscuity introduced into the relation if it is construed in Keil's way. (Such promiscuity is a problem even without Huebl's extraordinary requirements for numerical identity of events across possible worlds.) Counterfactual dependencies will proliferate to an embarrassing extent for Keil and, by his theory of causation, so will causal relations.[140] Everything won't quite be the cause of everything else – as Keil recognizes in his only advertence to this problem, "events outside the light cones" of other events will not be causally related.[141] But that hardly cabins causation to an intuitive degree. A Davidsonian, whole-event house destruction (in all its glorious detail) will counterfactually depend on: the spring rains; the termite infestation; the potassium in the wiring insulation; the air temperature...etc., etc...as much as on F_1 or F_2.

To test further whether Keil's theory succeeds on its own terms, consider next the ability of the theory to account for causes petering out over time. Keil agrees with me (and the law) that "an adequate theory of causation should account for these judgments."[142] Keil finds that my own quantitative account "echoes rather than explains the intuition,"[143] and claims more for his amended counterfactual theory.

Keil devotes most of his analysis to showing why counterfactual dependence is an intransitive relation. As he notes, both Lewis and I have also so argued. But Keil gives his own reasons for this conclusion, couched in the language of his singular counterfactual relations. He then faults Lewis for not using this feature of counterfactual dependence to account for the intransitivity of the causal relation, if indeed the causal relation is intransitive. My criticism of Lewis at this point is a bit different than Keil's. Keil's intended advance over Lewis here is to claim that, because of its intransitivity, "the counterfactual analysis nicely explains non-transitivity" of relations like causation that depend on it.[144]

Yet this last I dispute. For the intransitivity of the counterfactual dependence relation does not match the intransitivity of the causal relationship. The intransitivity of counterfactual dependence does not prevent it from being true that a

140 Moore, *Causation and Responsibility*, pp. 396–399, 412–413.
141 Keil, "Making Causal Counterfactuals More Singular," p. 178.
142 *Id.*, p. 181.
143 *Id.*, p. 182.
144 *Id.*, p. 186.

hurricane in Miami counterfactually depends on a butterfly flapping its wings over the Sahara three months earlier. I say in my book, "counterfactual dependence...does not, as causation seems to, weaken or peter out."[145] And this is true despite the acknowledged intransitivity of the counterfactual dependency relation.[146] So, while both relations are intransitive, the intransitivity of counterfactual dependence does a poor job of explaining the intransitivity of the causal relation. Nothing in Keil's singularist theory of counterfactual dependence changes the intransitivity of that relation in any way that remedies this mismatch.

Huebl comes a little closer (to matching up the intransitivity of counterfactual dependence to the intransitivity of causation (with his "straightforward temporal interpretation" of petering out):

> The longer the time lapse between two events, the more that can happen in between. The larger the *funnel of possibilities*, the thinner is thus the basis of our intuitions about counterfactual dependencies.[147]

This comes closer to my "inverted causal cone" account of causal intransitivity that I discuss below in my discussion of Mumford and Anjum. Still, one suspects that the details of Huebl's "funnel of possibilities" will not match my "degrees of causal contribution in an inverted causal cone" account of causal intransitivity. After all, *possibilities* of intervention will not often turn out to be the same as the realities of actual causal contributions by other events.

5 Markus Stepanians, States of Affairs as Truth-makers and as Causal Relata

Markus Stepanians takes me to task on an issue of general ontology, namely, whether what are variously called facta, states of affairs, real situations, or spatio-temporal facts, really exist.[148] Professor Stepanians' argument consists of a rather lucid exposition of how the argument I gave for generally believing in the existence of such things – their role as truth-makers – could as easily and perhaps better be satisfied with facts in the sense of true propositions.

Yet in my book I had very limited ambitions for such issues of general ontology. My concern was with the nature of causal relata. In framing the debate

---

145 Moore, *Causation and Responsibility*, p. 399.
146 *Id.*, p. 397 n. 23.
147 Huebl, "Events over Facts," p. 210.
148 Markus Stepanians, "Moore on 'the true metaphysics of causation,'" this volume.

about what causal relata might be, I only demanded general ontological plausibility for the candidates for such relata:

> [T]he list that follows is limited to these entities in whose existence we have reasons to believe, reasons that are independent of any role such entities may or may not have as causal relata. I do not pretend to answer the ultimate questions on ontology raised in forming such a list....I only require that there be some *plausible* metaphysical basis for the existence of the entities in question, a basis uncontaminated by any alleged causal role for such entities.[149]

I thus focused my entire argument structure on arguments particular to the causal relata issue, not on those of general ontology.

It is true that on the one occasion that Stepanians cites[150] I do betray my sympathies on an issue of general ontology. But this was in response to two other theorists, Hugh Mellor and Doug Ehring, who had framed the facta/tropes debate in general ontological terms. As I said there: "this is not an issue we need to resolve here..."[151]

So Stepanians wishes me to enter a battle I pretty explicitly declined to fight. Still, he might say, I must fight this battle; for if my preferred causal relata, states of affairs, do not exist at all as a matter of general ontology, then they cannot be the relata of the causal relation (assuming that that relationship really exists.)

Yet Stepanians is not offering us an argument that states of affairs do not exist.[152] He is only rebutting my argument – what he calls, "the Ramsey Argument" – for thinking that states of affairs do exist. For all he has said here, perhaps we have perfectly good reasons to think that states of affairs exist, even if they are not the reasons I gave.

I thus decline Stepanians' invitation to debate the large issues of truth, correspondence, truth-making, etc., that he raises. It was enough for my purposes to find the existence of states of affairs plausible. And they are plausible enough

---

149 Moore, *Causation and Responsibility*, p. 332.

150 Stepanians, "Moore on 'the true metaphysics of causation,'" p. 192.

151 Moore, *Causation and Responsibility*, p. 366.

152 Compare Stepanians here to Fraser MacBride, "Lewis' Animadversions on the Truthmaker Principle," in Helen Beebee and Julian Dodds, eds., *Truthmakers: The Contemporary Debate* (New York: Oxford University Press, 2005); MacBride argues (incorrectly, to my mind) that states of affairs cannot exist because if they did they would offend against the Humean principle that there can be no necessary connections between distinct states of affairs.

constituents of our general ontology that we can get on to the main show,[153] which was: "Are they the best candidates to be causal relata?"

I was disappointed that Stepanians nowhere addresses my more specific, causal-relata-focused arguments, those based on omissions, disjunctions, transitivity, or feature-drivenness.[154] This is the more surprising in light of Stepanians' own rejection of facts (in the sense of true propositions) as causal relata. If he also rejects states of affairs, does that leave him defending (like Keil and Huebl) Davidsonian whole events as causal relata? And if so, the problems I raise for that view (based on transitivity and the feature-driver nature of causation)[155] would seemingly need to be addressed.

6 Stephen Mumford and Rani Anjum on Filling in the Metaphysics of Causation Needed by Law and Morality

Like Geert Keil and Phillipp Huebl, Stephen Mumford and Rani Anjum take seriously the need for our responsibility assessments in law and morals to be based on an accurate metaphysics of causation. Also like Keil, Mumford and Anjum share a large agreement with me as to what sorts of parameters such metaphysics of causation should meet if it is to do the work demanded of it by our responsibility assessments. Such agreements between Mumford, Anjum and me include the views that:

1. Omissions are absences and absences "are not real things in any way."[156]

153 That truth is correspondence, that truth bearers are propositions, and that truth-makers are states of affairs, are all *plausible* things to believe is evidenced by David Armstrong's centrality to the discussion of these issues in current metaphysics. See the essays collected in Beebee and Dodd, eds., *Truthmakers: the Contemporary Debate*. That this view is not only plausible, but *true*, see: David Armstrong, *Truths and Truthmakers* (Cambridge: Cambridge University Press, 2004); David Armstrong, *A World of States of Affairs* (New York: Cambridge University Press, 1997); Richard Fumerton, *Realism and the Correspondence Theory of Truth* (New York: Rowman and Littlefield, 2002); William Alston, *A Realist Conception of Truth* (Ithaca, N.Y.: Cornell University Press, 1997); Marion David, *Correspondence and Disquotation: An Essay on the Nature of Truth* (Oxford: Oxford University Press, 1994). I thank Richard Fumerton for directing me to some of these sources.

154 Moore, *Causation and Responsibility*, chap. 15.

155 *Id.*, pp. 356–365.

156 Stephen Mumford and Rani Lill Anjum, "With Great Power Comes Great Responsibility," this volume, p. 224.

2. An "omission has no causal powers." As they also put it: "omissions cannot be causes. Nothing comes from nothing: we reject causation *ex nihilo*."[157]
3. Yet "omissions are sometimes linked to responsibility."[158] That is, we are sometimes responsible for harms we fail to prevent, even if such failures do not cause such harms.
4. Counterfactual dependence is by itself (i.e., without identifying it as causation) a solid basis for responsibility.[159]
5. Responsibility for a harm one omitted to prevent requires (and is based on) the counterfactual dependence of that harm on that omission. Alternatively put: "the ability to prevent a harm...could suffice to ground...responsibility for the harm."[160]
6. Such responsibility for omissions is lesser when compared to a cause-based responsibility for the same harm.
7. The removing of a defense to nature and thus allowing nature to take its course, is doubly preventative: such acts prevent a preventer from preventing a harm. Such double preventions, like omission, thus involve absences.
8. Such allowings and double-preventions are not causal because they do involve absences. They may provide "the *occasion* for the causing of G without being one of the causes of G."[161]
9. Nonetheless there can be responsibility for harms thus not prevented.
10. Such responsibility for double preventions is, like omissions, based on counterfactual dependence (of the harm on the act preventing the preventer).
11. Such responsibility for double preventions is lesser when compared to a cause-based responsibility for the same harm.
12. Causation is scalar.[162]
13. Causation is "polygenic," i.e., there are usually multiple causes for any given effect.[163]
14. Causation between successive events comes not as a chain but as a backward causal cone.
15. Causation is not a (fully) transitive relation in that over time causation peters out.
16. Counterfactual dependence is also scalar.

---

157 *Id.*
158 *Id.*, p. 219.
159 *Id.*, p. 233.
160 *Id.*, p. 219.
161 *Id.*, p. 225.
162 *Id.*, p. 222–223.
163 *Id.*, p. 229.

17. With greater power comes greater responsibility,[164] that is:
    (a) The more an act causes some harm, the more the actor is blameworthy for that harm's occurrence.
    (b) The more an actor has the ability to prevent some harm that he omits to prevent, the more the actor is blameworthy for that harm's occurrence.
18. In cases of concurrent overdetermination (such as where two poisoners unbeknownst to each other each place a sufficient amount of poison in the victim's drink to kill him, and the victim drinks the drink and dies), each actor causes the harm.
19. Yet in such cases there is no counterfactual dependence of the harm on the act of each poisoner, considered individually.
20. Causation is not to be reduced (à la David Lewis) to counterfactual dependence; these are two distinct relations.
21. Causation is not to be reduced (à la David Hume) to uniformities in nature.
22. Causation is not to be reduced (à la John Stuart Mill) to nomic sufficiency.

This is a serious amount of agreement. Mumford and Anjum detail it as they do not so that the three of us can lock arms and sing Kum Bayah together or celebrate how "great minds think alike." Rather, what Mumford and Anjum wish to show is how the invitation issued in my book to develop singularist theories of causation can be met by their own preferred theory – a powers-based, primitivist singularism – in a way that yields (or at least is consistent with) the above twenty-two propositions.

Mumford and Anjum give but a slight sketch of the singularist theory of causation that they favor. They regard causation as a continuous process, one in which the irreducible powers of properties is central. The powers of properties lies in their disposing the future in some ways rather than others. Mumford supplements this sketch with another sketch in another commentary he has written about my book.[165] But the definitive statement of Mumford's and Anjum's theory is in their own book, *Getting Causes From Powers*.[166] This is thus not the place to assess Mumford's and Anjum's interesting and distinctive theory of causation. A review of their own book would be the proper venue for that, allowing as it would the taking into account the subtleties and nuances of their view.

What can be inventoried here is the cost of their theory of causation to the conclusions about responsibility that I care about in my book. And these, as

164 *Id.*, p. 235.
165 Stephen Mumford, "Causes for Laws," *Jurisprudence*, Vol. 4 (2013), pp. 109–114.
166 Stephen Mumford and Rani Lill Anjum, *Getting Causes From Powers* (Oxford: Oxford University Press, 2011).

Mumford and Anjum detail them here at least, seem minimal. Indeed, there seems to be only one or two significant lapses, by my lights. The main one lies in how we define and explain what we all agree is the intransitivity of the causal relation across extended chains of events. Let me describe my own account before addressing Mumford and Anjum's criticisms of it and the advantages they claim in this respect for their account.

In a recent article on my notion of causal scalarity, Helen Beebee accurately traces the development of the notion of causal scalarity. Beebee "begins by distinguishing two dimensions along which causation might (and according to Moore, does) come in degrees..."[167] The first, which Beebee calls "limited transitivity," is a limitation on tracing causal responsibility through long chains of causes. It corresponds to simple "remoteness" theories of proximate causation in the law. The second, which Beebee calls "degrees of influence," focuses on a given time-slice in a chain of causation, and conceives of each link in such chains to be but a contributor competing with other causes in the degree of their influence on the next link down the chain.

These distinctions are not explicitly cast in temporal terms by Beebee, and rightly so, but it is nonetheless a helpful heuristic (enabling us to more easily see the distinction) to superimpose a temporal distinction on it. Because most (if not all) causal relations are not simultaneous, chains of causes will exist over temporal durations and they can exist over long periods of time. The existence of a number of causes over time is thus some indication of a limited transitivity problem. By contrast, truly simultaneous events causing some common effect indicate a degrees of influence problem. The two dimensions do not perfectly track this temporal distinction, however. Events occurring *seriatim* through time will present a degrees of influence problem, not a limited transitivity problem, if such events are co-causes of some common effect. (Think of the Murder on the Orient Express, where 13 successive stab wounds are inflicted on the victim, who dies of loss of blood flowing from all of the wounds.) So long as each cause in a succession of causes does not operate *through* the cause that succeeds it, then we have a "degrees of influence" rather than a "limited transitivity" problem. Still, most temporally extended succession of causes do present a "limited transitivity" problem, just as most temporally compressed or simultaneously operative causes present a "degrees of influence" problem. So the temporal dimension can be a helpful heuristic to seeing the distinction.

---

167 Helen Beebee, "Legal Responsibility and Scalar Causation," *Jurisprudence*, Vol. 4 (2013), pp. 102–108, at p. 102. My own distinguishing of these two dimensions is in *Causation and Responsibility*, pp. 71–72, 118–123.

Having taken some pains to distinguish these two dimensions of causal scalarity, now see how they depend on each other. Consider by way of example an explosion of a beaker in a high school chemistry lab. Suppose the explosion occurs at t_5. At t_4, hydrogen and oxygen were introduced into the beaker and a lighted match also passed into the mixture of gases in the beaker. At t_3, each of the relevant events at t_4 was caused by, respectively: the connection of a hose from a hydrogen gas nozzle to the beaker, the turning on of the valve to the gas nozzle, the pressure in the tank of hydrogen to which the nozzle is attached; and [the same three features, for the oxygen tank, nozzle, and hose]; and the clumsy dropping of a lit match, the force of gravity operating upon it, the wind currents in the lab, the positioning of the match roughly over the beaker. At t_2, each of the events/states of affairs occurring at t_3 was caused by a number of factors. For example, the lighting (at t_2) of the match that was dropped at t_3, was itself due to: the dryness of the match, the roughness of the surface against which it was struck, the striking of that surface by the match.

The picture I advert to in my book is that of an inverted cone of causation:[168]

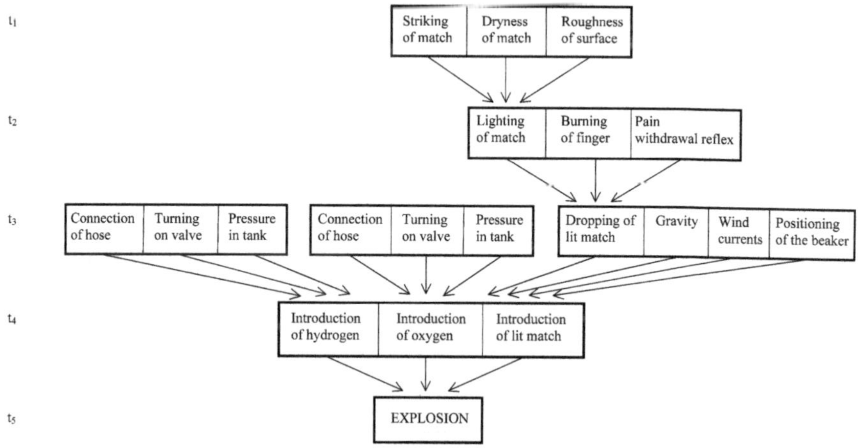

The degrees of influence question is to be asked within each time-slice. One might be assessing, for example, the relative causal contributions to the introduction of the lit match into the beaker at t_4 of: the force of gravity; the impact of minor wind currents; the positioning of the beaker, and the dropping of the match. The limited transitivity question is to be asked across time-slices, asking,

168 Moore, *Causation and Responsibility*, pp. 72, 276.

for example, after the relative causal contribution of the dryness of the match at t_1, to the explosion at t_5.

Of the two dimensions of causal scalarity, the degree of influence idea is most basic. Limited transitivity compares the causal contribution of one event to some other more remote event first, by asking the degrees of influence question about this event vis-à-vis the other causes in the set of events causing the next link in the chain; and then, comparing this degree of influence to that of all other causes (of causes of causes of causes) of the effect in question at that level. The intuition of petering out is rooted in this double comparison of causal contribution involved in limited transitivity questions.

I think my intransitivity metaphor of causation "tiring" through events misleads people. The actual metaphysics that underlies the metaphor is the inverted cone of causation. It is because every effect plausibly has numerous causes, and thus each such cause itself has multiple causes, that as we move backwards in time, the causes for any remote effect proliferate. And thus, compared to other causes at that time, the causal contribution of any single event is less the more one moves back in time. In my earlier example, the dryness of the match contributes more to the match's lighting at t_2 than to the explosion at t_5 because it has fewer other causes with which to be compared in the former case than in the latter.

The upshot is that we count numbers of intervening events in order to assess the degree of causal contribution of some remote cause only as a proxy for degree of causal contribution. We get at the latter by comparing the degree of influence of a cause vis-à-vis its co-causes of the next link in the chain, and then discount that by the degree of influence possessed by that next link vis-à-vis the set of its co-causes, and so on down the chain. If dryness were 20 % of the cause of the match lighting, which itself was 40 % of the cause of the match at t_1 being dropped, which was 40 % of the cause of the match entering the beaker, which was 50 % of the cause of the explosion, then the dryness of the match was only 1.6 % of the cause of the explosion.

Beebee worries that this account is hostage to solving mereological problems about events that (as the conventional wisdom at least has it) are insoluble. She thinks that if we "go small on" (i.e., individuate finely) events at levels $t_2 - t_4$, that will effect how much some event at t_1 will contribute to some event at t_5. Yet smaller causal intermediaries will also each make proportionately smaller causal contributions within the set of causes of which they are a member. So the "discount rate" for remote causes, based on the causal contribution of its causal intermediaries, should stay the same no matter how one slices the mereological pie. Of course, if one also subdivides the causes at t_1 into their many parts, and asks of some *part* of the match (such as the dryness of one-half of the tip that is rubbed) how much causal contribution that part has made, one will get a different answer. No surprise, because one will have asked a different question. So even if one accepts a mereology-based skepticism on the sizing of events, it doesn't have the devastating effect that Beebee imagines. It only seems to if one mistakes the proxy (number of intervening events) for the thing proxied (degree of causal influence vis-à-vis other remote causes).[169]

Mumford and Anjum have a different account of the intransitivity of causation. On their powers-based theory of causation, some event in the distant past like the Big Bang can be the cause of certain current events but not others. The Big Bang, for example, has caused the continuing expansion of the universe; it did not cause Jones to go speeding in his automobile yesterday. Whereas, by contrast, I am supposed to be committed to saying that remote events like the Big Bang have by now faded away as causes of *any* current events.

The Big Bang is a quite special example. For some of the things occurring now (such as the continued expansion of the universe), the Big Bang is intuitively regarded as a non-de minimus cause. But the foregoing analysis of inverted causal cones shows that this is as it should be. After all, the Big Bang had no co-causes that along with it caused the expansion of the universe from a singularity; its degree of causal influence was thus at 100 %, and there is no discount to be applied over time to this initial degree of contribution, because all more immediate causes of contemporary events were themselves caused by the Big Bang. So no "petering out" here, despite the temporal remove and the number of intervening events. The Big Bang *is* the cause of the current expanding of the universe.

More troublesome is the other causal conclusion that Mumford and Anjum also find intuitive, viz, that the Big Bang did *not* cause some man to speed on some occasion in 2012. By my analysis, it did. Mumford and Anjum urge that their dispositionalist account of causation can avoid that unwanted conclusion because the Big Bang did not dispose the man in question one way or the other in the speed of his driving in 2012. By contrast, my "substantiality of causal

169 In fairness to Beebee and others, I probably mislead her and other of my readers on this point. When discussing the law's supposition that causation peters out, I said that "causation diminishes over the number of events through which it is transmitted." (Moore, *Causation and Responsibility*, p, 153). Yet I was only speaking of the presuppositions about causation made by the law:

"[W]hat the law uses here is simply sheer numbers of events that intervene between the defendant's act and the harm...The particular scalarity the law presupposes causation to have is thus a diminishment in the strength of causation in proportion to the number of events through which it is transmitted." (*Id.*, pp. 122–123)

contribution" criterion of de minimus causation cannot be so discriminating. Rather, I must base my denial of the unwanted conclusion in pragmatics: while it is true that the Big Bang caused the 2012 speeding, it is odd in almost all contexts of utterance to mention it because of the omnipresence of the Big Bang in causing everything to exist.

I am not, if truth be told, very happy with this reliance on pragmatics by me.[170] But I am consoled by the specialness of the example. The Big Bang is the only *prima causa* modern physics allows as plausible; for it and it alone the cone of causation is *not* inverted. Thus it (alone amongst causes) does not peter out. For all causes that are part of an inverted cone of causation – which is to say, everything else – causation "tires through its links" in the sense indicated earlier, namely, each cause contributes less and less to ever more remote events because of the joint causes needed at every step of the way.

Leaving the Big Bang for more mundane examples, Mumford and Anjum also worry that my "petering out" idea is too rigid in its implications for what is and what is not a cause. They write:

> Moore's diagnosis would seem to imply that factors in e's backwards causal cone of equal temporal distance from e are either both causes of e or both not causes of e...[By contrast] We do not have...to say that distinct factors in a causal cone that are at equal temporal or causal distance from an effect are either both causes of that effect or both not causes.[171]

Yet by seeing that I explicate the sense of "petering out" over time or over causal links by reference to the cone of causation, Mumford and Anjum should also see that my account is not rigid in the way that they depict. How far one traces causation depends on the degrees of causation at each link of the various causal chains. For example, suppose in my explosion example, the lit match is 60 % the cause of the explosion, whereas the introduction of hydrogen and oxygen was 20 % apiece. Then, ceteris paribus, one would trace back three times as far when one traces causal links in the chain ending in the introduction of the lit match as one would trace the antecedents of the introduction of the hydrogen or of the oxygen. So some quite remote causal contributors might be non-de minimus, even while other, equally remote causal contributors are below the de minimus threshold. One would get parity (in degrees of causal contribution) across each level of the backwards cone of causation, only in the special examples like

170 For my unhappiness with David Lewis' more general use of this "pragmatics" escape route, see *id.*, p. 398.

171 Mumford and Anjum, "With Great Power," pp. 230 – 232.

the one Mumford elsewhere gives,[172] viz, where each of the four causes at each level of the cone are equal in their causal contributions to the next succeeding effect.

Even if one accepts everything I have said so far, this does not give Mumford and Anjum all the discriminating power they seek over what is properly regarded as causal in the remote past (even as it does blunt the objection that I am committed to there being some rigid proportionality between causal contribution and temporal distance or number of causal links). Yet some of the additional discriminating power they achieve with their dispositional theory of causation, I achieve by a non-petering out, counterfactual dependency basis for responsibility. Thus, in their examples of remote causation other than the Big Bang – the tipping cases where a very small and/or very remote causal contributor can tip the situation over some threshold – I can equally find responsibility, grounding it, however, in counterfactual dependence rather than causation.[173] If I give a slight tap to a precariously perched boulder, or train a butterfly to flap its wings in the Sahara in just the way needed to send a hurricane to Miami months later, my causal contribution is indeed tiny but my (counterfactual based) responsibility is great.

Mumford's and Anjum's other objection to my mode of conceptualizing and explaining causal intransitivity is that any line I might draw between de minimus and non-de minimus causation must be "arbitrary."[174] By this I take it they are making two criticisms: first, according to my analysis, the line "would not be something dictated by nature but only by our decisions."[175] And second, not only is it a decision by us, it is a decision attaching a bivalent characterization ("causal" or "non-causal") onto a smooth continuum in nature – which they think is arbitrary in the same way that stipulating that five stones (but not six) is a *heap*, is arbitrary.

Perhaps lawyers and ethicists are so familiar with these line-drawing situations that they regard them with more tolerance than others.[176] Whether there is a contract or not depends on a range of factors that all vary on a smooth continuum (such as definiteness and completeness of offers, degree of match between acceptances and offers, degree of consideration, etc.); yet there either is a contract, or there isn't. Mutatis mutandis for promissory obligations in ethics. I

---

172 Mumford, "Causes for Laws".
173 Moore, *Causation and Responsibility*, pp. 468–469.
174 Mumford and Anjum, "With Great Power," p. 230.
175 *Id.*
176 See Leo Katz, "Why Is the Law So Either Or," in his *Why the Law Is So Perverse* (Chicago: University of Chicago Press, 2011).

tend to think of the seeming arbitrariness of a precise line of de minimus causation, as like the seeming arbitrariness of lack of significance in mathematics. Rounding off numbers to some level of significance makes perfectly good sense in various contexts, giving us good reason to do so in those contexts. The same is true of the small degrees of causation that fade into nothingness.

Indeed it would seem that Mumford's and Anjum's theory of causation would suffer from the same problem, if it is a problem. Take a variation of one of their examples, that of the arsonist who starts a fire, the fire triggers the sprinkler system to start, the sprinkler system puts out the fire and leaves the building wet. The starting of fires in general, they say, does not dispose to wetness. Yet doesn't it so dispose to some degree, depending on the sprinkler or other system in place in what is being burnt? Granting a scalarity to *disposing* (that Mumford and Anjum rightly and explicitly affirm), doesn't starting a fire in something dispose towards wetness a little bit? They say that wetness comes from the intervention of another action, one that is "extrinsic to the arsonist's actions."[177] But what if the arsonist's actions starting the fire consist of pouring water onto very hot grease, which splatters and starts the fire? Presumably this disposing is ruled out, but on what grounds other than de minimus?

Having attempted to dampen down this first difference between my theory and that of Mumford and Anjum, I leave it. A second and more minor difference between what law and morality demands of causation, and what Mumford's and Anjum's theory can deliver, lies in the treatment of simple preventions. A simple (i.e., not double) prevention occurs when some actor prevents something from happening. E.g., Smith saves Jones from drowning. If preventions were causal, one might say that Smith caused a non-drowning of Jones. This would require causation of an absence.

Mumford and Anjum affirm causation *of* absences while they deny there can be causation *by* absences.[178] They do this because on their powers view of causation, two or more powers opposed to each other but in equilibrium, are nonetheless powers that are exercised. There is thus causation but, as they put it, "nothing happens."

Our law, and the morality on which it is built, by contrast, both suppose that preventions are distinct from causings.[179] Our law supposes this because one's moral responsibility is lesser for prevention of some benefit (to which we were entitled) than it is for causing some harm (to the absence of which we were

177 Mumford and Anjum, "With Great Power," p. 231.
178 Mumford and Anjum, *Getting Causes from Powers*, p. 144.
179 Moore, *Causation and Responsibility*, pp. 130–132.

also entitled).[180] Mumford's and Anjum's allowance of absences as effects would erase the metaphysical difference (between causation and the kind of counterfactual dependence that is preventative on my view) on which these legal and moral differences depend. That, by my lights, would count against Mumford's and Anjum's theory.

Three responses are possible for Mumford and Anjum here. One is that they could deny that there are the legal and moral differences (between causing and preventings) that I say there are. Two, they could think that the moral force of the prevent/cause distinction could be achieved by some other distinction, such as the distinction between two kinds of entitlements, entitlements to benefits versus entitlements not to be harmed. (I seek to cut off this escape route in my book.)[181] Three, they could re-examine whether their theory of causation need allow that absences can be effects. Their present thought is that causal powers can do their work when they produce an equilibrium, conceived by them as nothing happening, so that in such cases we cause an absence. Yet perhaps an equilibrium is not an absence but is rather, the presence of something, a positive state of affairs. After all, Douglas Ehring (whom Mumford cites approvingly) conceives of his "unchanges" as presences and not absences (on Ehring's metaphysics, such unchanges, like changes, are property tropes).[182] Only someone like Huebl, who requires changes of state (i. e., events) for causal relata, need regard equilibria states as absences, and I see nothing in Mumford and Anjum's theory that commits them to that.

So at the end of the day Mumford's and Anjum's metaphysics might not prove at all disturbing to the legal and moral uses of causation that I depict in my book. In which event their proposal is just the sort I should (and do) find welcome. Whether it in fact describes the true metaphysics of causation I leave for others to decide.

180 *Id.*, pp. 455–457.

181 *Id.*

182 Douglas Ehring, *Causation and Persistence* (Oxford: Oxford University Press, 1997). I discuss this aspect of Ehring's theory in Moore, *Causation and Responsibility*, p. 502.

7 Alex Broadbent's Attempted Resuscitation of "Causal Selection" in Serious Philosophical Discussions of Causation

Alex Broadbent has divided up his essay into four topics, and I shall follow suit. In section 1 he seeks to characterize the aims of my book in a way that he thinks will set up the main criticism of it he makes in sections 2 and 3, namely, that I have ignored "causal selection" when I cannot afford to do so, and that my theory lacks the resources to do such selection even if it tried to. Broadbent then offers his own "contrastive" theory of causal relata as a superior alternative in section 4.

I disagree with a number of Broadbent's theses pretty much down the line of his argument. Let me highlight the disagreements between us, for whatever light that might shine on the nature and the plausibility of each of our views on causation and responsibility. Broadbent rightly sees that in the early chapters of my book I seek to justify why there should be legal and moral interest in the metaphysics of causation. Broadbent focuses on the legal part of this thesis,[183] despite the fact that my book is as interested in the moral part as it is in the legal part. Thus I am interested in how causation impacts upon moral responsibility for its own sake,[184] and not only interested in that topic because of the intimate relation I see between moral responsibility and the legal liability we both do and ought to have in Anglo-American law.

Restricting our focus to the legal theses, because those are the only ones discussed by Broadbent, he secondly seeks to narrow my ambitions even there. Broadbent believes that my "analysis of the role causation does in fact play in determining legal liability is conducted with a view to assessing to what extent the law is right."[185] That is certainly part of my motivations in assessing how causation is a universal (if sometimes submerged) element in all criminal liability rules presently extent in Anglo-American legal systems;[186] and it is part of my motivations in the detailed explanation of the causal doctrines of Anglo-American tort and criminal law in nine more chapters of my book.[187] But what the law on causation is I find to be an interesting topic, independent of any desire to reform it. Indeed, the complexity of existing legal doctrines about causation makes

183 Alex Broadbent, "Explanation and Responsibility," this volume, p. 239.
184 Moore, *Causation and Responsibility*, chaps. 2–3.
185 Broadbent, "Explanation and Responsibility," p. 239.
186 Moore, *Causation and Responsibility*, chap. 1.
187 *Id.*, chaps. 1, 4–11.

it a worthwhile challenge simply to lay out in a coherent way what the law of causation is.

But I shall confine my focus here to what interests Broadbent in his essay, which is my normative thesis that legal liability should track causal metaphysics because moral responsibility does so. Broadbent is "tempted to criticize [me] for confusing law and morality";[188] in addition, if I am not so confused, I at least "must face the fact that most moral philosophers and legal theorists regard it as settled that the relation between law and morality is in fact much *less* intimate than we ordinarily suppose."[189]

As stated, this last is a fact of intellectual sociology (about what "most moral philosophers and legal theorists" think). As such, it is hard to get a handle on it without some clarification of who the "we" is that is the baseline of comparison. If "we" is to include Broadbent, we get little help because his views on this topic are not well developed, at least in print. If "we" is taken as ordinary folk – the proverbial "man on the Clapham omnibus" – one would need more data than I have to know whether this is true. In fact, my suspicion is that by "we" Broadbent really means to refer to me. My views on the relation(s) of law and morality, both generally and more specifically in criminal law, are well known.[190] Where the mistakes are in such views, however, Broadbent doesn't tell us.

This point actually matters for Broadbent's purposes in his essay because he wants to use this point (about the "less-than-we-think" intimacy between law and morality) to motivate his admitted "main interest" in his essay, which is my supposed need for a theory of "causal selection." Whatever mistakes I or others have supposedly made about the intimacy of the relation of law to morality, I don't get how from this Broadbent concludes that "the theory of causation that he [Moore] needs must be radical and unorthodox...", namely, a theory of "*causal selection.*"[191]

However peculiar the route by which he gets there, Broadbent plainly thinks my main mistake lies is dissing the enquiring into causal selection, and he devotes section 2 of his essay to arguing this. He begins by expressing surprise

188 Broadbent, "Explanation and Responsibility," p. 239.

189 *Id.*, p. 240.

190 See the articles collected in the symposium held at Bologna University in 2011, "International Symposium on Law and Morality in Contemporary Legal Philosophy: The Perspective of Michael Moore," collected in Ratio Juris, Vol. 25 (2012), My own keynote address in this collection, "The Various Relations Between Law and Morality in Contemporary Legal Philosophy," Ratio Juris, Vol. 25 (2012), pp. 435–471, cites and summarizes my 25 articles on this topic published over the last 30 years.

191 *Id.*, p. 240.

at "the strange fact...that Moore does not realize that he needs a theory of causal selection."[192] What is it that I don't realize that I need? Causal selection, as Broadbent defines it, consists "in our exceptionless habit of mentioning only some of the many events that are, in some loose sense, causally (or perhaps nomically) responsible for a given effect,"[193] and a theory of that is a set of principles for how such selection is to be done together with a grounding of such principles in one way or another.

We can exhume Broadbent's clearest examples of "theories of causal selection" from the history of philosophy. Causal selectionists were philosophers/theorists like R.G. Collingwood,[194] Morton White,[195] Douglas Gasking,[196] Joel Feinberg,[197] Herbert Hart, and Tony Honoré,[198] all of whom took on Mill's challenge to find grounds for honoring one amongst a number of conditions equally necessary for some event, as "the cause" of that event. The contemporary consensus about all such theorists is that expressed by Judith Thomson on the last two of them: the principles favoring selections of such items as abnormal natural events or deliberate human actions are not "ontological but only pragmatic."[199] Thomson, like Lewis, Mill, and myself, puts aside such interest-and-context relative principles when our thoughts about causation turn seriously ontological.

Broadbent would reverse this consensus (as he must if he is to make sense of his own contrastivist view of causation later on). If he could succeed, his theory would indeed be "radical and unorthodox," in his own words. But finding it surprising that I don't wish to join his decidedly un-contemporary causal metaphysics, is itself surprising.

Broadbent gives two arguments for why I must join him in his "radical and unorthodox" theory. The first, which he rightly calls less "substantive," aims to show that at times I inconsistently "endorse some kind of selective view of causation."[200] Unfortunately this charge involves some misunderstanding both of what I think and of what the law holds on causal matters, so let me clear up this "less substantive" bit first.

---

192 *Id.*
193 *Id.*
194 R.G. Collingwood, *The Idea of History* (Oxford: Oxford University Press, 1946).
195 Morton White, *Foundations of Historical Knowledge* (New York: Harper and Row, 1965).
196 Douglas Gasking, "Causation and Recipes," *Mind*, Vol. 64 (1955), pp. 479 – 487.
197 Joel Feinberg, "Action and Responsibility," in his *Doing and Deserving* (Princeton: Princeton University Press, 1970).
198 Hart and Honore, *Causation in the Law.*
199 Judith Jarvis Thomson, "Casuality and Rights: Some Preliminaries," *Chicago-Kent Law Review*, Vol. 63 (1987), pp. 471–496, at p. 473.
200 Broadbent, "Explanation and Responsibility," p. 242.

Broadbent poses a case where a driver (Richard) swerves off the road because he is fiddling with his radio. Jane is a pedestrian who is walking along the side of the road. Richard's car hits Jane and breaks her leg. Both Richard's swerving and Jane's walking were necessary conditions for Jane's leg to be broken. Broadbent is right to think that a case like that of Richard and Jane "is not rare but *typical*"[201] in that there are two or more necessary conditions for the harm. But Broadbent is simply wrong in his assertion that our law discriminates between Richard and Jane *on causal grounds*. Contributory and causal fault doctrines in Anglo-American tort law show this plainly. In order to eliminate or reduce Jane's recovery of damages for her broken leg, our tort law requires that any fault on her part be a cause of her injury (along with Richard's act, of course). If Jane were negligent in how she walked (walking with the traffic, for example), then her recovery would be barred or reduced because her walking was a cause of her injury. When tort lawyers talk about "causal fault," they mean cases just like Jane's.

Broadbent urges that I would be "ill-advised to insist that there is some other, non-causal reason for Jane's innocence... [for] this would be hard to reconcile with the general stance on the centrality of causation to moral responsibility...."[202] Ill-advised or not, I do so insist. Where Jane is not liable in torts (in the sense of having her recovery in tort eliminated or reduced), this will only be because she was not negligent (or otherwise at fault), or, if she were negligent in her actions, those acts were not necessary for her injury to occur. Jane will not be liable in criminal law because causing oneself injury is not typically made into a crime; and this, because there is no moral responsibility for self-injury. But contrary to what Broadbent thinks, Jane *will be* responsible for her injury in torts (in the sense that she will have to bear some or all of her loss uncompensated) because her walking was in law as much a cause of that injury as was Richard's poor driving.

Moreover, I can agree with the law here. And saying this is no way inconsistent with my "general stance" that causation matters to liability. I never have advocated that causation alone determines liability, for that would be an unfair strict liability. Causation indeed matters to liability, but so does intention, voluntary action, excuse, etc.

The upshot is that I really mean what I say in my book, which was that it is rare for the law to be causally selective in the sense of discriminating between

201 *Id.*, p. 244.
202 *Id.*

"temporally co-present equally necessary conditions."[203] As I further say in my book, the law on occasion does do this, but only in its rare, "sole cause" doctrines.[204] To the extent the law does this in those doctrines, the law is by my lights wrong. The law is wrong in the metaphysics presupposed by these sole cause doctrines because we should refuse "to grant semantic status to the discriminatory principles by which we select amongst the various causes...and thusly honoring one as 'the cause.'"[205]

I am at a loss to see how Broadbent sees any inconsistency or even hesitancy on my part here. The law correctly regards necessary conditions for a harm not to be a cause of that harm when those conditions are too de minimus or too remote; it only tries to discriminate between non-remote, non de minimus, necessary conditions in its "sole cause" doctrines, but these are both rare and, more importantly, incorrect because unfaithful to the nature of causation. For these sole cause doctrines, like the discarded causal selectionist theories of the philosophers earlier cited, wrongly attribute causal status to mere context-and-interest relative principles of pragmatically appropriate causal utterance.

Broadbent thinks he has a second argument against me here, one that will show that the "entire project" in my book forces me to be a causal selectionist like Broadbent himself.[206] What Broadbent really has, however, is a shift in what he means by "causal selection." Broadbent thinks that I am "confused about causal selection."[207] What I am actually confused about is what Broadbent means by, "causal selection."

The paradigm cases of causal selection theorists are those like Collingwood, White, Gasking, Feinberg, Hart, and Honoré, above cited, theorists who thought they were giving causal criteria in their criteria for selecting "the cause" from amongst a raft of necessary conditions. And I am in agreement with metaphysicians from Mill to Lewis: these older theorists were mistaken. All those older theorists' criteria of selection amounted to were conditions of appropriate utterance in certain contexts and relative to certain interests. So, contrary to Broadbent, it is not the case "that Moore does not agree with Lewis and Mill about causal selection even if he thinks he does."[208] I not only think that I agree with Mill and Lewis. I really do agree with them.

203 Moore, *Causation and Responsibility*, p. 114.
204 *Id.*, pp. 114, 152.
205 *Id.*, p. 397.
206 Broadbent, "Causation and Explanation," p. 244.
207 *Id.*, p. 241.
208 *Id.*, p. 244.

Now if one extends what one means by "causal selection" to include any notion of causation more discriminating in what it counts as causal than Mill's and Lewis' kinds of notion, then many theories are "causally selective" in this new and much broader sense. And in their greater discriminatory power, such theories do differ from the non-discriminating theories of Lewis and Mill. In this broader sense, for example, Keil's and Huebl's theories are "causally selectionist" in light of their refusal to countenance mere presences (like Jane's) as causes because not necessary (in their singularist sense of necessary); so is the powers theory of Stephen Mumford and Rani Anjum, with its discriminating notion of dispositions; so is Phil Dowe's physicalist theory;[209] so is the trope-persistence theory of Doug Ehring;[210] likewise David Fair's[211] and Wesley Salmon's[212] kinds of causal process theories. Indeed, almost all theories of causation are more discriminating in what they allow as a cause than the "promiscuous" theories of Lewis and Mill. If this is what we are now to mean by "causally selectionist," then the entire range of metaphysical theories I find plausible are "causally selectionist." Indeed, the singularist theories of Keil, Huebl, Anjum, Mumford, Dowe, Salmon, Fair and Ehring are all examples of singularist theories I find plausible, so in that harmless sense we are all causal selectionists.

So I see no inconsistency here by me; only an inconsistency in the way Broadbent uses "causal selection." If Broadbent's substantive point is that I need a theory of causation that is more discriminating in what it regards as causal than the necessary or NESS conditions of Lewis and Mill, he is correct. I do – although I would not call the needed discriminating power, "causal selection," because given the history of that phrase in causal metaphysics, it denotes a view that I reject.

But enough quibbling over labels. In section 3 of his article Broadbent queries whether "Moore's positive theory makes causation selective [i.e., discriminating] enough to ground moral responsibility?"[213] Broadbent has his work cut out for him if he is going to answer the question he poses, for I do not in my book defend a discrete theory of causation. Rather, I defend singularist *kinds* of metaphysical theories as being superior both to counterfactual theories like that of David Lewis, and generalist theories like that of John Stuart Mill and today's numerous Millians. And I lay out the parameters that any such singularist theory must satisfy if it is to do the work demanded of it by our moral and legal uses

209 Dowe, *Physical Causation.*

210 Ehring, *Causation and Resistence.*

211 David Fair, "Causation as the Flow of Energy," *Erkenntnis*, Vol. 14 (1979), pp. 219–250.

212 Wesley Salmon, *Causality and Explanation* (Oxford: Oxford University Press, 1998).

213 Broadbent, "Causation and Explanation," p. 244.

of causation. (These I adverted to earlier in my discussion of Mumford and Anjum.)

Any fair reading of my book has to recognize this stepping away by me from mounting a defense of any particular kind of singularist theory of causation. As Chris Hitchcock noted in his interesting review of my book, "Moore's goal...is not to advance an original theory of the nature of causation, but rather to explore the range of proposals that are on offer...The real pay off is not in the metaphysics *per se*, but in the intriguing discussions of the relationship between the metaphysics and moral and legal theory."[214] Despite this, Broadbent reads me as making a "tentative proposal"[215] that the causal relation is a metaphysical primitive; he later abandons the "tentative" qualification, talking about "the primitivist who is also a singularist, as Moore is..."[216] Moreover, Broadbent thinks that I celebrate the "vision of the happy primitivist"[217] who makes causation as discriminating a relation as he needs it to be. Broadbent then proceeds to dispatch the happy primitivist he imagines me to be, on the familiar grounds that primitivism doesn't allow one to say enough about the nature of causation to make it sufficiently discriminating.

There are two problems with this criticism of Broadbent's: it is not about me; and it is wrong. As to the first, no careful or fair reading of my book could think that I propose primitivism (tentatively or not) any more than I propose non-primitivist, reductionist theories of the causal relation. Not only was I studiously neutral about this in the Guest Editor's Introduction to *The Monist's* symposium issue on singularist causal theories that eventually became chapter 20 of my book; but I make plain is the Preface of the latter my agnosticism here:

> The view of the relation this book ultimately defends is singularist. Not necessarily a primitivist singularism...but perhaps instead a physically reductionist version of singularism.[218]

As to the second problem with Broadbent's criticism, he thinks that metaphysically primitivist causal theorists must be quiet in their primitivism. He thinks they cannot say enough about causation's nature to make plausible the features of it that give it discriminatory power. Yet this seems quite false of what we might call "talky primitivists" like Mumford and Anjum. Although they regard powers as "too close" to causation to provide a base for reduction and are thus self-con-

214 Hitchcock, "The Metaphysical Basis of Liability," p. 377–378.
215 Broadbent, "Causation and Explanation," p. 245.
216 *Id.*, p. 246.
217 *Id.*
218 Moore, *Causation and Responsibility*, p. xii.

fessed primitivists, their theory is very discriminating in what it allows as causes (because of the vector-like directions of dispositions in their theory). Indeed, recall that their criticism of me was that my quantitative approach could not match their primitivist approach in terms of providing causation with a large amount of discriminating power.

Like Anjum and Mumford, Broadbent also questions whether the scalar features of causation to which I advert and which admittedly eliminate causal responsibility for de minimus contributors, are adequate to account for causation's discriminating power. This is a question worth a great deal more exploration than we can give it here. It involves two subquestions. First, of the discriminations we make between who is and who is not morally responsible for some harm, which ones of these are made on causal grounds and which ones are made on non-causal grounds? For example, much of what lawyers regard as issues of "proximate causation" have to do with what might be called "mismatch cases." These are cases much discussed by Erasmus Mayr in his contribution to this volume and which I take up shortly. These are cases where there is a mismatch between the actual harm done and the type of harm intended, foreseen, or consciously risked by the agent who causes such harm. In contrast to the law, I take mismatch discriminations off the demands fairly placed on a concept of causation; these are culpability discrimiations having to do with whether the act done was intended, intentional, foreseen, or consciously risked.[219]

Our responsibility ascription "tool-kit," as I call it in my extended debate with Larry Alexander and Kim Ferzan on this issue,[220] includes much in it besides degrees of causal contribution. It includes: degrees of counterfactual dependence; the distinctions between causing, on the one hand, and preventing, failing to prevent, doubly preventing, and allowing, on the other; degrees of culpability between intending, foreseeing, and risking; degrees of mental capacity, coercion, ignorance, or other excuse; etc. These distinctions lessen the discriminatory power needed to be possessed by causation. About Broadbent's Richard and Jane example, as I said earlier, no causal discrimination is needed or used

219 *Id.*, pp. 158–159, 208–210.

220 Moore, "Causation Revisited," at pp. 456–459. That debate includes, besides my book just cited: Larry Alexander, "Michael Moore and the Mysteries of Causation in the Law," *Rutgers Law Journal* Vol. 42 (2011), pp. 301–314; Kimberly Ferzan, "The Unsolved Mysteries of Causation and Responsibility," *Rutgers Law Journal*, Vol. 42 (2011), pp. 347–376; Moore, "Causation Revisited," *Rutgers Law Journal*, Vol. 42 (2011), pp. 451–509; Larry Alexander and Kim Ferzan, "More or Less Causation and Responsibility," *Criminal Law and Philosophy*, Vol. 6 (2012), pp. 81–92; Moore, "Moore's Truths About Causation and Responsibility: A Reply to Alexander and Ferzan," *Criminal Law and Philosophy*, Vol. 6 (2012), pp. 445–462; Larry Alexander and Kimberly Ferzan, "Ferzander's Surrebuttal," *Criminal Law and Philosophy*, Vol. 6 (2012), pp. 463–465.

by our law to show why Richard is responsible for Jane's broken arm and Jane is not.

The second subquestion is just how discriminating my causal principles are. Mumford and Anjum urge that scalarity (in both of its uses) is not enough, but as I said earlier, that would depend on how scalarity is cashed out in its details (which itself depends on having and applying a discrete theory of the causal relation). If "petering out" were to be cashed out so as to be in line with the implications of Anjum and Mumford's own primitivist, singularist theory, it would be very discriminating indeed.

Broadbent ignores all of these interesting issues because he has, he thinks, some across-the-board, knock-down objections to scalarity giving rise to any discriminating power. Broadbent tells us that my scalarity suggestion "conflates the notion of a relation obtaining with a much less well-defined notion, something like *contribution*."[221] According to Broadbent:

> Whether a relation obtains is usually understood as a yes/no matter. Moore needs a logic of relations which supports his claim that relations can obtain in greater or lesser degrees.[222]

I don't think this thought of Broadbent's is very clear. Indeed, one might say that it is *less* clear than many other things that Broadbent says. In fact, it stands in (scalar) relations of various degrees of comparative clarity with various other utterances by Broadbent. Broadbent's bivalent vision of the world is unrecognizable to me, because the world is full of "relations [that] can obtain in greater or less degrees." For example: "A is clearer than B, which is clearer than C," "A is heavier than B, which is heavier than C;" "A is redder than B, which is redder than C;" etc.

Related in Broadbent's mind is his next point: "If several short causal links add up to one long one, we don't regard that long link as somehow 'weaker' than the constituents."[223] This is given as an explanation for why causation does not peter out. Well, yes – if causation is transitive – if, that is, links "add up" *without diminishment* – then causation does not peter out. That seems true by definition. Presumably in other work Broadbent has avoided the seeming triviality of this sense of "adds up," but he doesn't here tell us how he does so.

In section 4 of his article Broadbent plumps for his own, "contrastive" theory of causation. Like Jonathan Schaffer's well known contrastivism about causal

---

221 Broadbent, "Causation and Explanation," p. 247.
222 *Id.*
223 *Id.*

relata,[224] Broadbent's contrastivism would make for a highly discriminating relation. If he can defend such a view as part of a theory of causation – and not merely as part of a theory of appropriate explanatory utterance – it would indeed be to resuscitate the causal selectionist views of the moribund philosophers earlier mentioned.

Contrastivism in our *explanatory* practices is very intuitive. As we have seen with Geert Keil and Phillip Huebl (here echoing Donald Davidson), explanation looks on its face very different than causal relations. Explanations are context-sensitive and interest-relative in the various ways that Broadbent and Schaffer describe. The sticky wicket for their view is transitioning from explanation to casual relations. Prima facie the contrastivist agenda is one of describing the pragmatics of appropriate explanatory utterance. The trick is to show how the principles of appropriate utterance are not pragmatic but semantic, i.e., they have to do with the truth of causal ascriptions. As with Mumford's and Anjum's powers metaphysics of causation, the contrastivist view too is an interesting approach to causation, but one too detailed in its exposition to assess here.

8 Benedikt Kahmen and the Causal Theory of Action

Most of my philosophical colleagues are, like me, a defender of the causal theory of action ("CTA") in one form or another.[225] In modern form the CTA is most famously dated from the publication of Donald Davidson's "Actions, Reasons, and Causes" in 1962.[226] That article both criticized the non-causal theories of action of the ordinary language philosophers of action, such as Elizabeth Anscombe,[227] and laid out the rudiments of the CTA. The CTA essentially holds that, for those actions constituted at least in part by the bodily movements of the actor, those bodily movements must be caused "in the right way" by some propositional at-

224 Schaffer, "Contrastive Causation." Schaffer contrasts his contrastivism with that of Broadbent in Schaffer, "Contrastive Causation in the Law," *Legal Theory*, Vol. 16 (2010), pp. 359–297.

225 See the collection of views in J.H. Agular and A.A. Buckareff, eds., *Causing Human Action: New Perspectives on the Causal Theory of Action* (Cambridge, Mass.: MIT Press, a Bradford Book, 2010).

226 Donald Davidson, "Actions, Reasons, and Causes," *Journal of Philosophy*, Vol. 60 (1962), pp. 685–700, reprinted in Davidson, *Essays on Actions and Events* (Oxford: Oxford University Press, 1980).

227 G.E.M. Anscombe, *Intention* (2d edit., Ithaca, N.Y.: Cornell University Press, 1963).

titudes of belief, desire, and/or intention. Kahmen is correct that I have been a defender of a version of the CTA throughout my career.[228]

In the last decade or so the philosophical orthodoxy on the CTA has been challenged by a revival of the Anscombean view that the CTA doesn't square with the requirements of first person practical knowledge. Kahmen's paper is part and parcel of that challenge. Kahmen's challenge essentially is that intentional actions could not be practically known to the actors who did them if actions were as the CTA says they are, *viz*, bodily movements caused by propositional attitudes. Although the actor might know what he is doing, on the CTA's account of what action is he wouldn't know it *in the right way*. He would only know it by observation, including the internal observation of proprioceptive sensation; but he wouldn't know it non-observationally because he actively created it.

If intentional actions require the kind of knowledge Kahmen thinks they do, then I take his criticism of the CTA to be on the mark: I don't think that the causal relations: (1) between intention and bodily movements or (2) between bodily movements and further real world effects either foreseen or intended, can be known in the way that Anscombeans like Kahmen demand. For Kahmen, that means the CTA must go. For me, that means Kahmen's demand for knowledge of this kind should go. Let's see which it is.

Kahmen divides his presentation between his discussion of intended actions and a separate discussion of intentional actions. He is right to do so because these are two quite different things.[229] I shall follow him in his organization, beginning with the simpler and more basic notion, that of intended acts.

Even though the point is widely contested, I think Anscombe and Kahmen are largely correct in their description of how we must know our own intentions if they are truly intentions and if they are truly ours. As I put it many years ago:

---

228 Michael Moore, *Act and Crime: The Implications of the Philosophy of Action for the Criminal Law* (Oxford: Oxford University Press, 1993), second, paperback edit., 2010; Moore, "Moore on Act and Crime," *University of Pennsylvania Law Review*, Vol. 142 (1994), pp. 1749–1840, revised and reprinted in Moore, *Placing Blame: A General Theory of the Criminal Law* (Oxford: Oxford University Press, 1997), paperback edition, 2010, chap. 6; Moore "Renewed Questions About the Causal Theory of Action," in Agular and Buckareff, eds., *Causing Human Action: New Perspectives on the Causal Theory of Action* (Cambridge, Mass.: MIT Press, 2010).

229 As everyone from Elizabeth Anscombe on has noticed. See Anscombe's distinction between "intentional," "intentionally," on the one hand, and "intention," "intend," on the other, in her *Intention*. For an update, see Moore, "Intention as a Marker of Moral Responsibility and Legal Punishability," in Antony Duff and Stuart Green, eds., *The Philosophical Foundations of Criminal Law* (Oxford: Oxford University Press, 2011.), pp. 179–205, at pp. 185–187.

> On those occasions when we know what we desire, what we believe, or that we are in pain, do we come to such knowledge in a nonobservational or noninferential way? Rather plainly, it is usually the case that we do. Except to a well-conditional behaviorist, it is surprising to be asked how we know, for instance, that we want an ice-cream cone, that we believe going downtown will get us one, or that our left foot hurts.[230]

Kahmen would add that in the case of intentions, we come to such nonobservational knowledge through the process of forming the intention, that is, through deciding upon a course of action.[231] And that seems to me to be correct too.[232]

The first problem for Kahmen is that he makes more of these points than he should. As a contemporary of Anscombe's, John Wisdom, once rightly noted:

> It is a common mistake to identify the fact that a person has, necessarily has, a way of knowing what's in his own mind which no one else has, with the claim that he can't be mistaken about his own mind. That's a very different matter indeed.[233]

Kahmen makes this mistake insofar as he thinks intentions must be *transparent* to their holders: to intend p is to know (in the right way and at the right times) that one intends p. This rules out as "irrational" for Kahmen actions done in response to unconscious intentions.

This is a mistake because unconscious execution of unconscious intentions is a regular feature of everyone's daily life, and it is not "irrational" that this is so.[234] One of the main theses of my first book was that there is such a thing as

---

230 Michael Moore, "The Nature of Psychoanalytic Explanation," in Larry Laudan, ed., *Mind and Medicine: Problems of Explanation and Evaluation in Psychiatry and the Biomedical Sciences*, Vol. 8 of the *Pittsburgh Studies in the Philosophy and History of Science* (Berkeley: University of California Press, 1983), reprinted in Moore, *Law and Psychiatry: Rethinking the Relationship* (Cambridge: Cambridge University Press, 1984), p. 256.

231 Although Kahmen goes further in this direction than I believe is correct. He holds that knowledge of one's intention must be *directly* responsive to one's reasons for action so that one's "consciously held reasons for action constitute reasons for belief about one's intention." Benedikt Kahmen, "Intentions, Intentional Actions, and Practical Knowledge," this volume, pp. 258–259. I think the truth of the matter is rather: knowledge of one's intentions is *indirectly* responsive to one's reasons for action, even if one's intentions are *directly* responsive to one's reasons for action.

232 Moore, *Law and Psychiatry*, pp. 291–295, 311–322.

233 Quoted *id.*, p. 256.

234 Non-Freudian examples are those given by William James, *The Principle of Psychology* (Cambridge, Mass.: Harvard Universityi Press 1890), Vol. 2, p. 496; Freudian examples may be found in Moore, *Law and Psychiatry*, pp. 322–337. Non-Jameseon, non-Freudian examples may be found in John Bargh, "The Automaticity of Everyday Life," in R.S. Wyer, ed., *Advances in Social Cognition*, Vol. 10 (1997) pp. 1–61.

"deferred privileged access" to one's unconscious mental states;[235] this is where one comes to know such states in the same nonobservational, noninferential way that one knows one's own conscious mental states. While Kahmen recognizes the possibility of reflection by an actor leading to a belief by that actor that he had a certain intention at an earlier time and that he did what he did because of it, he nonetheless objects that the actor wouldn't have any way of knowing any better or different than would an outside observer of his behavior, and further, that such an "actor" would be "passive in his action." [236] I have argued at length that neither of these things is true – unconsciously cruel actor's, such as in Kahmen's husband example, can recover not only the content of their unconscious intention but also the "actish phenomenal feel" of having acted because of it.[237]

My suspicion is that Kahmen compounds this mistake by also thinking that we are *incorrigible* in our beliefs about our own intentions. Incorrigibility is the converse of transparency: now the claim is that if I believe that I intend p, necessarily I do intend p. I think Kahmen thinks intentions are incorrigibly known to us because of his view of how the content of intentions (and, indeed, of all Intentional states such as beliefs, desires, etc.) is fixed. On Kahmen's apparent view, I can't be wrong about having an intention, say, to "go downtown soon," because the description of the action that I intend is fixed by the description I have in mind as the content of my belief about my intention. On such a view, if I believe that I intend p, necessarily I do intend p.

Incorrigibility too, like transparency, is not a plausible attribute of our mental life.[238] We can be mistaken about our unconscious intentions and unconscious actions no less than we can be ignorant of their existence. Good novelists well appreciated this fact long before Freud, James, or the Bargean psychologists of today.

Eliminating these "privileged access overclaims" of incorrigibility and transparency leaves Kahmen with a truncated although still significant claim of privileged access to our intentions. We do have a special mode of knowing our own intentions not available to others, and we have this privileged access to our intentions because the forming of them – the making of a decision – is something we actively do. The significance of such "privileged access" lies in the fact that

---

235 Moore, *Law and Psychiatry*, pp. 256–257.
236 Kahmen, "Intentions, Intentional Actions," p. 258.
237 Moore, *Law and Psychiatry*, pp. 314–322.
238 *Id.*, pp. 261–265.

boundaries of self and personhood are most plausibly drawn, at least in part, by this kind of ability.[239]

So far so good, but what Kahmen needs to mount his attack on my causal theory of action is move his knowledge claim from intentions, to intended actions. He needs to claim, in other words, that we not only have privileged access to our intentions because we choose them, but that we also have the same privileged access to our intended actions because we do them. On its face, this claim seems false, and pretty obviously so. We have no privileged access to whether our bodies in fact move as we intend them to do, nor to whether such bodily movements as we do achieve in fact cause the more remote effects in the world that we intend them to cause. These are matters for observation and theoretical inference rather than "practical" knowledge, for actors no less than for observers. True, in the class of cases we are here considering, we intend certain bodily movements and we intend that those movements themselves have certain real world effects, and such intentions are accessible to those whose intentions they are in a privileged way. Yet such intentions cannot make it true that the effects intended actually occur. As Stanley Cavell said in a related context, no amount of intending can "produce horses for beggars, or home runs from pop flies, or successful poems out of unsuccessful poems."[240] A batter in baseball may intend to hit a home run every time he is at bat; whether he in fact performs that feat is something he and everyone else will have to observe to see.

Kahmen recognizes the counterintuitive nature of the conclusion he needs here. So while at the end of the day the obvious problem with his conclusion is indeed the killer problem for his project that it appears to be, it is worth following his train of thought. As I understand it, it goes like this.

Kahmen thinks that when an actor – say a batter in baseball – succeeds in doing what he intends to do – hit a home run, for example – there is a description of action problem we have to solve before we can conclude that his action was intended (and, because intended, intentional). Under the Anscombean view that Kahment accepts, actions are only intended or intentional "under a description." A home run will be intended only if "hit home run" is the description we fix on to ask, "was his act intended?" Since there are many descriptions of any-

---

239 Moore, "The Unity of the Self," in Michael Ruse, ed., *Nature Animated: Western Ontario Series in the Philosophy of Science* (Dordrecht: D. Reidel Publishing, 1983), reprinted in Moore, *Law and Psychiatry*, chap. 11; see also Moore, "Responsible Choices, Desert-Based Legal Institutions, and the Challenges of Contemporary Neuroscience," *Social Philosophy and Policy*, Vol. 29 (2012), pp. 233–279 at pp. 242, 254–258, 272–276.

240 Stanley Cavell, *Must We Mean What We Say?* (Cambridge, Mass.: Harvard University Press, 1969), pp. 38–39.

one's act (such as, "strike the ball," "please my fans," "win the game," etc.), we need a privileging of some descriptions over others. Kahmen's principle of privilege is the agent's own description of what action he intends, and this description is one to which he does and must have privileged access. As Kahmen summarizes Anscombe here: "practical knowledge is supposed to fix the descriptions under which an action is intentional."[241]

There are two rather glaring problems with Kahmen's accurate enough rendition of Anscombe's argument. One is the mystery of why *failure* to do what we intend can (and must) be a matter for observation and theoretical inference for the actor no less than everyone else; but *success* gives rise to a non-observational, privileged way of knowing that the action intended came about. Kahmen might respond that with failure there is no question to ask about intended home runs; no home run was hit so the question of whether it was intended does not arise. Whereas the question does arise with success, where a home run was hit; and the question of whether the home run hit was intended requires a solution to the description problem, a solution privileged access is supposed to provide.

Surely this is an inadequate response. If there is a description problem for the content of successfully executed intentions, surely there is the same description problem for the content of unsuccessfully executed intentions. But in any case, this entire analysis of what makes an action intended is mistaken, root and branch. There is no "description problem" here for which practical knowledge needs to be called in as the solution. Let me lay this out as quickly as I can.

Begin with Anscombe's coarse-grained theory of act-token individuation.[242] Anscombe believes that when an actor moves his arm on a pump handle, and by so doing moves the handle, and by so doing pumps water containing poison in it onto a house, and by so doing poisons the water in that house, he is doing but one action, not four. There are four descriptions of that action; but they all refer to one and the same act-token. On this, all but the Kimians about events are agreed.[243]

Anscombe also correctly observes that the hypothesized actor may have intended to move his hand, intended to move the pump handle, and intended to pump the water without intending to poison the water in the house. This leads Anscombe (and latter day Anscombeans like Kahmen) to conclude that actions are only intended "under a description." Moreover, the insight that if this is

241 Kahmen, "Intentions, Intentional Action," p. 262.

242 Anscombe, *Intention*, Section 26.

243 Moore, *Act and Crime*, pp. 380 – 292; Moore, *Causation and Responsibility*, pp. 334 – 338.

an action at all, *at least* the actor must intend to move his arm (a "basic act"), leads Anscombeans also to say: "all actions are intended under some description if they are actions at all."

It was my hope that we had gotten rid of this way of thinking a long time ago, with the death of ordinary language philosophy. For seemingly Anscombe blatently violates Leibriz's law (the indiscernability of identicals): If there is one action in this example of Anscombe's, and if "intended" names a property of that action, it cannot be the case that the action has or has not that property depending on how that action is described. The proper conclusion to draw here was Donald Davidson's: "intended" (and "intentional") are not true adjectives, despite their superficial grammatical form, nor is "intentionally" a true adverb.[244] "Intended" as used in the phrase "intended action," does not predicate a property of an action. Compare: "pumping the water was the first thing he did in the morning." Temporal location *is* a property of this act; the act either has or lacks that property no matter how we describe that action. This not being true of "intended" evidences that something else is going on when we describe an act as intended or intentional, other than ascribing a property to it and thusly showing it to be within some subclass of actions.

What is going on is this: "his poisoning of the water was intended (or intentional)" is an ellipsis for two separate statements: (1) he performed some act having the causal properties making the description, "poisoning the water," accurate; and (2) that act was the causal product of an intention having as its object a poisoning-of-water type of act.[245] What is elided is an ascription of action, and an ascription of an intention with Intentional content. Once these are separated, one can see (again) the implausibility of the Anscombean idea that we have privileged access to (1). The actor does have privileged access to the having of the intention mentioned in (2); but that cuts no ice with respect to there being such privileged access to (1).

One last gasp here might go like this: for an actor to have done his poisoning as an intended action, it is not enough that he, (1), in fact poisoned the water with his hand movement, and, (2), intended to poison the water. It is not even enough that the act in (1) was caused in the right way by the intention in (2). In addition, the act done must be an instance of the type of act intended, for the poisoning to be an intended action.

---

244 Donald Davidson, "On the Logical Form of Action Sentences," reprinted in his *Essays on Actions and Events* (Oxford: Oxford University Press, 1980), at p. 121.

245 See Moore, "Plain Meaning and Linguistics – A Case Study," *Washington University Law Quarterly*, Vol. 75 (1995), pp. 1253–1262, at pp.1254–1258; Moore, *Placing Blame*, p. 58 n. 103.

As I have urged elsewhere in greater detail,[246] all of this is exactly right. But on this account, there is no description-fixing problem on which the intended status of the action depends. We and the actor settle on the description of what was done by the causal properties of the act in (1), not by any belief or intention of the actor. We and the actor discern whether the act under any description (including this one) is an instance of the type of act intended by the same observational methods. That the actor has and needs non-observational knowledge of what he intended to begin this matching question, in no way justifies a conclusion that he has or needs such privileged access to make the match. An actor can no more make such a match true, than he can make the action be a success simply by intending that it be so. That would be truly "magical."

Things change very little for Kahmen if we move from intended actions, to intentional actions. In the case of such intentional but not intended actions, the relevant mental states are those of belief, not intention. (Kahmen's observation that such actions will be intended "under some other description" is true but irrelevant here.) But despite the shift in mental state, both Kahmen's analysis, and the problems for it, remain the same. We no more believe we are performing an action "under a description" than we intend an action "under a description." Our predictive beliefs are formed about types of actions, and the question of whether an act of poisoning was done intentionally turns on the question of whether that act-token is an instance of the type of action the actor foresaw himself doing at the time he acted. And again, that the actor has, and must have, privileged access to what he predictively believes, does not mean he has, or can have, such privileged access to what he does or whether what he does matches what he had predicted he would do.

For these reasons I conclude that Kahmen cannot make out his Anscombean thesis that actors must know their intended or intentional actions in a privileged way if these actions are truly intended or intentional. And without support for the "knowledge requirement," as Kahmen calls it, his argument against the CTA drops to the ground.

It is interesting to speculate where Kahmen would go for a positive theory of action if his criticism of the CTA could have been made out. From what he says in his paper, it looks like he would become yet another "mysterian" about agency and action, like Richard Taylor, Roderich Chisholm, Jennifer Hornsby, David Vellerman, and others.[247] The nature of human agency is shrouded in mystery for

246 Moore, "Intention as a Marker," pp. 196–205.
247 I discuss some of the mysterians in Moore, "Renewed Questions About the Causal Theory of Action," pp. 29–31.

such theorists because it cannot be reduced to any mental state causation of anything. And if this non-answer is the alternative to some version of the CTA, we all would do well to repair the CTA, not reject it.

9 Erasmus Mayr and the Understanding of Human Agency

The topic of Erasmus Mayr's paper nicely complements the topic of Benedikt Kahmen's paper. Kahmen deals with the practical knowledge an actor must have if an action of his can properly be considered intended or intentional. My response to Kahmen was to reject his requirement of practical knowledge of results "under a description" and to substitute an analysis I had developed elsewhere, an "act-token done instantiating an type of act intended" analysis. Mayr in his paper challenges my substituted analysis of when an action is intended or done intentionally.

On one fundamental issue here Mayr and I are in agreement. This is that "consequential waywardness" – where the act actually done in some way does not match the type of act intended – is "not a problem about causation."[248] Although German law treats it as a problem of "objective ascribability," and although American law treats it as a problem of "proximate causation," Mayr and I both regard the problem to be one of ascribing intentionality to actions. In my terminology, it is a problem of subjective culpability, not objective wrongdoing.

Despite the fact that Mayr is not dealing with a problem of causation, he is dealing with something that needs addressing in the context of my book on causation. For often enough counterexamples are thrown up to my book that are instances of consequential waywardness, as if my theory of causation should have an answer as to how such cases should be resolved.[249] That such cases can be dealt with by a good theory of culpability, relieves the pressure on my theory of causation. Indeed, this is exactly how I use my analysis of these cases in defense of my book against critics like Larry Alexander and Kimberly Ferzan.[250]

The theory of culpability that I have used in this way, and defended more generally in other contexts, is pretty much the theory criticized by Mayr both

---

248 Erasmus Mayr, "The Problem of Consequential Waywardness: Between Internalism and Externalism About Intentional Agency," this volume, p. 271.

249 See, e.g., Larry Alexander, "Michael Moore and the Mysteries of Causation," pp. 301–314.

250 Moore, "Causation Revisited," pp. 456–459.

in his book[251] and in his contribution to this volume. Mayr calls this "the standard picture of human agency," and he correctly ascribes the picture to me. The crucial aspects of the theory on which Mayr focuses his criticisms, are that the factors constituting human agency in general, and intentionality of actions in particular, are "'local,' psychological, physical and causal facts about the agent himself," and these factors can be analyzed in "purely factual, non-normative terms."[252] Since I believe both of these things to be true, I am an appropriate target for Mayr's criticisms.

Mayr raises four criticisms of my kind of view. All of these criticisms focus on the view's treatment of cases of consequential waywardness. Mayr illustrates the latter with Donald Davidson's old example: A would-be murderer, A, intends to kill his victim, V, by shooting V; A's shot misses V, but the sound of it stampedes a herd of wild pigs that trample V to death.[253] Any analysis of culpability that rates intentional wrongdoing as more culpable than reckless or merely negligent wrongdoing, has to have a means of classifying such cases of consequential waywardness as one or the other. Mayr thinks of this particular case, for example, that A did not intentionally kill V "because the causal route to the intended result was too far off from anything he had foreseen, for the result to be, from his point of view, anything but 'mere luck.'"[254] A is thus merely a reckless (or perhaps only negligent wrongdoer), not an intentional one.

My analysis of this kind of case, given elsewhere,[255] is what Mayr anticipates. It is the analysis I gave in answer to Kahmen. A had a hierarchy of intentions when he shot at V, the kind of organized hierarchy Bratman calls a *plan.*[256] The plan includes an intention about a desirable end state to bring about – here, V's death. If the plan was actually executed in action, as here, it also includes a variety of executory intentions. These executory intentions all include one or more very particular intentions having discrete, immediate bodily movements as their objects. I call these, "volitions," in my work.[257] Whether A's act amounts to a *killing* of V depends on: (1) whether his moving his finger on the trigger of his gun was caused by a volition having that bodily movement as its

---

251 Erasmus Mayr, *Understanding Human Agency* (Oxford: Oxford University Press, 2011).
252 Mayr, "The Problem of Consequential Waywardness," p. 273.
253 *Id.*, p. 276.
254 *Id.*
255 Moore, "Causation Revisited," pp. 456–459; Moore, "Moore's Truths About Causation and Responsibility," pp. 453–459.
256 Michael Bratman, *Intentions, Plans, and Practical Reason* (Cambridge, Mass.: Harvard University Press, 1987).
257 Moore, *Act and Crime*, chap. 6.

object; and (2) whether his finger movement was a cause of the death of V (recognizing that the trampling of V done by the pigs can also be a cause of V's death). If A did the *act* of killing V, there remains the question of whether A *intentionally* killed V. On my analysis, whether A intentionally killed V depends on: (1) whether the hierarchy of intentions in the plan that caused A to act, included intentions whose objects matched what in fact happened to V; or (2) whether the predictive beliefs A had accompanying his intentions had objects matching what in fact happened to V.

Mayr focuses his criticism on the ascription of intentionality part of this account, and he further restricts his attention to the first disjunct (having to do with actions intentional because intended) only. His first argument against my account here is initially presented as the objection that "it is not generally true that we can ascribe to agents who intend to perform a non-basic action a plan comprising all the basic actions to be performed, nor one comprising all the causal paths from their basic actions to the more distant result to be brought about."[258] This version of the objection is supplemented with the thought that the agent will lack even *awareness* (let alone intention) that he is performing all such basic actions. This objection, after anticipating a denial that such detail in intention or awareness needs to exist, then morphs into the objection that "there seems to be *no* general standard...for how specific the content of the action-plan has to be which is required for intentional action."[259] The latter idea is that some moral judgment needs to be made in setting a required degree of specificity, and such need for moral judgment defeats the idea that some non-normative matter of fact about intentionality of action determines moral responsibility.

Consider the first version of this objection first. Mayr is right to anticipate the response he does to it, for it is a response with a long history. Plans *are* necessarily incomplete in their specifications of how an end is to be achieved, and even hazy about what precisely is the end itself; and awareness of those means also recedes when not needed, as in habitual and skilled behaviors.[260] Even so, there is more content to the intentions constituting a plan than it may seem, because: (1) intentions and volitions (and beliefs too for that matter) need not be conscious to be the mental states that they are; (2) there is a "deferred privileged access" to such unconscious mental states, so lack of awareness of these mental states need be only temporary; (3) the brain itself, with or without

258 Mayr, "The Problem of Consequential Waywardness," p. 281.

259 *Id.*, p. 282.

260 William James, *Principles of Psychology* (Cambridge, Mass.: Harvard University Press, 1890), Vol. 2, p. 496.

the agent's privileged access, recognizes when an intention is fulfilled or frustrated, revealing the existence of such intentions irrespective of the agent's knowledge of them;[261] and (4) plans do not consist of but one intention – which would have to have an implausibly broad and inclusive content – but rather, of a series of intentions ordered by temporal position of the actions intended and by the abstractness with which those intentions' objects are characterized.

My own conclusion is that there is enough content to the series of intentions making up a plan to meaningfully ask and answer my match question, so long as one does not demand (as I do not) a perfect fit or a complete match of Intentional content to the actual train of events. But then there is Mayr's second version of the objection: he urges that there is no general standard governing when act done is close enough in its match to the type of act intended, that that act should be considered intentionally done.

Mayr's objection here is unrealistically demanding. I find a vague answer to the question of how tightly matching an act done must be to the intention causing it, to be no more troublesome than vague answers generally are. A lot of stones piled up make a heap, and no stones do not, even if precisely how many stones it takes cannot be non-arbitrarily fixed. And if this nonchalant acceptance of vagueness is still disquieting, then remember why we ask the match question: it is to grade culpability. We could grade culpability along a smooth continuum (rather than in two clumps, "negligent/reckless" versus "intentional"), lining up degrees of match to degrees of culpability.

Mayr's better objection here is his second one. Here he concedes that "we clearly don't always need perfect fit..."[262] His objection nonetheless is that "we cannot spell out the standard of similarity – or relevant differences – for the required fit...in non-normative terms."[263] Mayr seeks to support this conclusion by imagining pairs of cases where the degree of fit is the same yet for normative reasons we judge intentionality differently. Thus, the marksman trying to kill his victim ("V") with a long range, low probability shot, is judged to have killed V intentionally if his shot in fact kills V; whereas the darts-thrower who hits the bulls eye with an equally low probability throw is judged not to have hit the bulls eye intentionally. It is only that we are blaming in the first case, praising in the second, that we get such different conclusions of intentionality, according to Mayr.

Notice three things about such examples by Mayr. First, the equally low probability of success is irrelevant to the point at hand. What we should be in-

261 Stephen Taylor, Emily Stern, and William Gehring, "Neural Systems for Error Monitoring: Recent Findings and Theoretical Perspectives," *Neuroscientist*, Vol. 13 (2007), pp. 160–172.
262 Mayr, "The Problem of Consequential Warwardness," p. 283.
263 *Id.*, p. 284.

terested in are cases where the degree of fit (between consequence-with-route achieved, and consequence-with-route intended) is the same. But let us bypass this worry by stipulating that the degree of fit in each of such pairs of cases is the same in that each actor pretty much achieves exactly what he intended in the way he intended to achieve it. That allows me to get to my second point: I don't share Mayr's intuition. I think the hit of the bulls eye no less intentional than the death of the long range victim. That one can conduct experiments in social psychology whereby common folk will draw a distinction here, is neither here nor there. I should have thought that the point of philosophy was to correct such warping of judgment by the common folk, not to elevate such folk misperceptions into metaphysical "truths."

Thirdly, even if one shares Mayr's intuitions about such cases, that would only show that the "symmetry principle" about praise and blame is false, that is, that the conditions for ascribing blame do not mirror the conditions for ascribing praise. Such a large scale contextualism can easily be accommodated by non-normative views of intentionality such as my own.

Let me turn to Mayr's third objection. Mayr's third objection is actually just a rewording of his first objection. As he now puts the objection: the details of what does happen will always outstrip the representational capacities of the actor who intentionally causes it to happen. Therefore, there will always be some mismatch between action done and action intended. And therefore...what? Mayr: "even though the chain therefore fits precisely the ex ante specification, it will still be wayward."[264] No, it won't. Little mismatches count as "close enough for government work," even if big ones do not. Zero stones do not make a heap, even if a huge pile of them does. If we got over the worry about vagueness earlier, we should get over it here too, for it presents no new worries here.

Mayr's fourth objection imagines cases where the actor intends some action A to produce some prohibited harm H to another person; he does A, and H does indeed result. Yet he had no reason to believe that acts of type A can produce harms of type H. They do in this case, but he had no reason to believe that they do. Mayr urges that my analysis "would have to assess this as a case of intentional killing. But this result is clearly false..."[265]

But is it? Here the very low probability cases can do some work for us, for here they provide an apt analogy. If X shoots across a river where the odds of hitting victim V are 1000:1 against, yet he does hit V with the shot as he intended to do, I think the killing of V is intentional by X. True, it was a very lucky shot,

264 *Id.*, p. 288.
265 *Id.*, p. 288–289.

and true, he had no reason to think he could succeed in hitting V; yet he thought he could, and he did. X by my lights is an intentional hitter of V.

Reaching this conclusion avoids the "external standards of justification" with which Mayr would stick me. Whether X is an intentional hitter of V depends only on X's internal representations of what he was trying to do, and upon how well what happened matched those representations of X's.

I thus conclude that none of Mayr's four objections should convince us of the incorrectness of the non-normative, "internalist" account of intentionality that I have long defended. That is fortunate, because unlike Mayr I am not sanguine about his proposed alternative, an irreducibly normative account of intentional agency. I find that possibility no more attractive than an irreducibly normative account of causation. In both cases, moral properties like responsibility are treated as non-natural primitives, ungrounded as they would be in natural properties like intention or causation. As acceptable as that might be to those with a Wittgensteinian turn of mind, to my naturalist-realist meta-ethics, it is anathema.

10 Thomas Schmidt and Increased Blameworthiness for Causing a Result Intended, Foreseen, or Risked

Thomas Schmidt raises an issue I have long found to be an interesting one, namely, the relationship between the so-called moral luck debate and the older debate on free will. Professor Schmidt is correct in his interpretation of me as holding there to be an intimate relation between the two debates.

The badly-named moral luck debate has been about the question of whether causing the results one has either tried to cause or unreasonably risked causing, increases one's blameworthiness beyond the blameworthiness already accruing to one for the trying or the risking. The older free will debate has been about the question of whether causation of choice and action lessens or eliminates one's blameworthiness for one's choices or actions. Although both are concerned with the impact of causation upon responsibility, prima facie the two issues are distinct. The latter debate is about causation *of* choice, the former debate is about causation *by* choice.

Even so, as Schmidt accurately and carefully reproduces, I urge in my book that the issues are related.[266] More specifically the thought is that those who think that lack of *control* by an agent over the results of her chosen actions preclude those results from increasing her responsibility, are also committed to thinking that causation *of* choice by factors over which the chooser lacks *control* also renders such choices as not increasing responsibility. For one has no more control over the factors causing choice than one has of the factors caused by choice; if lack of control of the latter precludes responsibility, so should lack of control of the former.

As Schmidt recognizes, everything turns on what one means by *control.* Schmidt correctly notes that I by-and-large leave control undefined when I distinguish (in his words) complete from partial control. I do this because in the context of answering the argument from lack of control in the moral luck debate, I need do no more. That is, the sense of control often used by my opponents in that debate is "complete control," defined as, "ruling out all possible preventers of that of which one has such control." In this sense, I do not *control* your death when I put a gun to your head and blow your brains out, as I intended to do, because: a bird could have flown in the way; blanks could have been substituted for real bullets; the gun could have jammed; etc., etc. My point is not that this is a very peculiar notion of "control," although it is;[267] rather, the point is that in this sense of (complete) control, we don't control our choices, our characters, or any other possible desert base.[268] In this sense of control, we control nothing. There is no responsibility if this kind of control is required for it.

My opponents on the moral luck debate have only two routes of reply open to them here. One is to urge that actors have *more* complete control over their choices than they do over the results of those choices. This I deal with in my books as an unpromising strategy.[269] Or they can go in the direction in which Schmidt heads: don't leave "control" (of both the partial and complete kinds) primitive; rather, define "control" in such a way that we have *control* over our choices that we do not have over the results of those choices.

Schmidt recognizes that for this second reply to work, "a more worked-out conception of control is required."[270] Unfortunately he then eschews the task as one that "cannot be accomplished in this paper."[271] My own recent work

266 Moore, *Causation and Responsibility*, p. 25; Moore, *Placing Blame*, pp. 242–243.
267 See Moore, *Placing Blame*, pp. 211–218.
268 *Id.*, pp. 233–246.
269 *Id.*, pp. 239–243; Moore, *Causation and Responsibility*, pp. 26–29.
270 Thomas Schmidt, "How to Understand the Problem of Moral Luck," this volume, p. 307.
271 *Id.*, p. 308.

has been devoted to precisely this issue,[272] so let me fill in the lacunae in Schmidt's argument.

"Control" as I define it has to do with one's *ability* to have altered that over which one is said to have *control*. Control over the *results* of our choices is to have the ability to have avoided those results if one had chosen differently than one did; control over our *choices* themselves is to have the ability to have chosen differently if one had wanted to do so more than one in fact did.

Because *ability* – or synonymously, what we *can* do or choose, what we are *able* to do or choose, what we are *free* to do or choose, what it is *possible* for us to do or choose, what we have the *capacity* to do or choose what is within our *power* to do or choose – is itself counterfactual, so is control. Actor X controls the results R of some choice C if but only if:

(1) R would not have occurred if A had chosen other than C.

Likewise, actor X controls his choice C if but only if:

(2) C would not have occurred if A had wanted C not to occur more than he did.

One verifies counterfactuals (1) and (2) by seeing whether R or C occur in possible worlds very close to the actual world, save that in those possible worlds either C is different (for (1)) or X's want is different (for (2)).

The trick for counterfactuals, here as elsewhere, is to specify the dimensions that make a possible world close to the actual world.[273] That means for Schmidt, he needs to specify relevantly *close* possible worlds for (1) where the consequent comes out *false*, i.e., R would have occurred anyway, even if X's choice C had been other than it was. For then, X had no *control* over R. By contrast, Schmidt needs to specify relevantly close possible worlds for (2) where the consequent comes out *true*, i.e., X would have chosen other than C if he wanted to enough. For then, X had *control* over C. These two manipulations together would allow

---

272 See two overlapping papers, Moore, "The Can't/Won't Distinction and the Nature of Volitional Incapacity," in Rowan Cruft and Sandra Marshall, eds., *Crime, Punishment and Responsibility* (Oxford: Oxford University Press, 2013); Moore, "The Philosophy and the Neuroscience of Volitional Incapacity," in Dennis Patterson, ed., *Law and Neuroscience* (Oxford: Oxford University Press, 2013). In these papers I first collapse the "lack of opportunity" sense of "lack of control" into the "incapacity" sense of that phrase, and then, second, give six folk psychological models for when one is relevantly incapacitated in making causally efficacious choices, and then, thirdly, give a counterfactual translation of these six models, so that, fourth, one can assess the extent to which the pertinent counterfactuals can be verified or falsified by contemporary neuroscience.

273 *Id.*

Schmidt to say that we control our choices in a way we do not control the results of those choices in the real world.

Schmidt cites with approval the efforts in this direction of my long-time friend, colleague on two faculties, and opponent on the moral luck issue, Stephen Morse.[274] Morse urges that choices are "reasons-responsive" whereas results are not. Put in my language, Morse is urging that for counterfactual (2), if our reasons were different – i.e., if X wanted something incompatible with choice C a good deal more than in fact he did – then actors like X would choose other than C. So far so good. But then Morse must also be urging, with respect to counterfactual (1): if our choices were different – i.e., if X had chosen differently than in fact he did – then results like R would have come about anyway, despite actors like X choosing against them. And this is surely false. If I had chosen not to kill you by putting the gun next to your head, you would not have died, in my earlier hypothetical (I can tell you this with certainty because it is *my* hypothetical!)

So, while there is logical space for the Schmidt-Morse response, when we spell out what *control* should mean in these contexts, there is no argument for saying that we *control* our choices but we lack *control* over the results of those choices.

11 Alexander Aichele and (Re)Slicing the Pie of Responsibility Via "Imputation"

Alexander Aichele in the first sentence of his essay urges that my "theory of singular moral judgments, especially the ones reached in criminal law, goes without the time-honored concept of imputation."[275] That may be so insofar as I did not use the name, *imputation* (or "Zurechnung," or "imputatio"); whether the thing referred to by that name nonetheless figures in my theory of legal and moral blameworthiness, is another question.

---

274 Stephen Morse, "Culpability and Control," *University of Pennsylvania Law Review*, Vol. 142 (1994), pp. 1587–1660; Morse, "Uncontrollable Urges and Rational People," *Virginia Law Review*, Vol. 88 (2002), pp. 1025–1078; Morse, "Reasons, Results, and Criminal Responsibility," *University of Illinois Law Review*, Vol. [2004], pp. 363–444; Larry Alexander, Kimberly Ferzan, with Stephen Morse, *Crime and Culpability: A Theory of the Criminal Law* (Cambridge: Cambridge University Press, 2008).

275 Alexander Aichele, "Causation to Culpability: Why Imputation Matters," this volume, p. 311.

Aichele defines imputation as denoting "a moral judgment which ascribes to a person to have done wrong by violating a natural or positive law so that she has to be punished just for this reason."[276] The idea was introduced by Samuel Pufendorf,[277] as Aichele recognizes. Kant's restatement of Pufendorf was: "Imputation...is the judgment through which one is seen as the author (free cause) of an event, which is then called a deed and is subject to the law."[278] Joachim Hruschka's gloss on Kant, in turn, is that "imputed events are seen as deeds which thereby are traced to a person as their author, whose decisive characteristic consists of being the free cause thereof."[279]

Hruschka tells us that there is "a difference between the application of a law to an event and the imputation of this event..."[280] There is thus a distinction to be drawn between the rules that make up the substantive criminal law, and the rules of imputation.[281] The law is addressed to citizens; it "necessarily has a prospective character,"[282] it forbids or requires *types* of actions. Whereas rules of imputation are addressed to the one making a moral or legal judgment about such citizens; such rules "are employed *retro*spectively in order to determine whether the duty party who did not fulfill the relevant requirements;"[283] and judgments of imputation are about particular actions done on some particular occasion by some particular agent.

In my own language, I would describe the rules of imputation (in morality and in German criminal law theory) as the "conditions of fair fault ascription."[284] Such rules generalize about what must be true to connect a moral agent to some event in the natural world in a way that makes that agent responsible for that event. For centuries now Anglo-American criminal lawyers have dubbed such conditions of fair fault ascription, "the general part" of the criminal law. And, as I have sought to show in a recent article,[285] these same conditions constitute morality's "general part" as well. In both criminal law and morality, such con-

276 *Id.*

277 For the history, see Joachim Hruschka, "Imputation," *Brigham Young University Law Review*, Vol. [1986], pp. 669 – 710, at p. 673.

278 See *id.* (Hruschka's translated quote is from Kant's *Rechtslehre*).

279 *Id.*, p. 674.

280 *Id.*, p. 672.

281 *Id.*, pp. 680 – 682.

282 *Id.*, p. 680.

283 *Id.*, p. 681.

284 See Moore, *Law and Psychiatry*, pp. 53 – 90; Moore, *Placing Blame*, pp. 43 – 64.

285 Michael Moore, "The Specialness of the General Part of the Criminal Law," in Dennis Baker, ed., *The Sanctity of Life and the Criminal Law: Essays in Honour of Glanville Williams* (Cambridge: Cambridge University Press, 2012), pp. 69 – 105, at pp. 80 – 85.

ditions determine when responsibility for any particular event can be ascribed to some moral agent or legal actor.

So I fail to understand Aichele's charge that my theory of moral judgment goes without the concept of imputation. It does not, as a lifetime of my work on the criteria of fair fault ascription testifies.

This mistaken charge by Aichele is based on a second misinterpretation of me by him. He urges that "if causation is regarded as not a moral concept but only a theoretical one, applied to physical objects, causation can't accomplish that task...[the task of imputation]."[286] He further charges that "imputation, closely connected to causation as it is, cannot be reduced to causation, imputation does not just substitute causation..."[287] I think he thinks that I disagree with these last remarks; but in fact I do not. Indeed, I suspect that my view (of the relation of causation to imputation) is very similar to that of Aichele, Hruschka, and other German criminal law theoreticians. That can only be seen by taking a brief excursion into comparative criminal law theory.

In a recent article on the general part of Anglo-American criminal law (and of the morality on which it is built), I gave an overview of the conditions of fair fault ascription.[288] On my view of the general part, it consists of seven ways in which an agent can be so connected to a natural event that he can fairly be held responsible for that event: he can culpably cause that event; he can fail to prevent such an event; he can try to cause that event; he can unreasonably risk causing that event; he can aid another in causing that event; he can procure another to cause that event; or he can conspire with another that that other cause that event.[289]

The primary mode of being responsible for some natural event is what Anglo-American criminal lawyers call, "principal liability for a completed crime." Such mode of responsibility requires that one cause the event in question oneself, or that one fail to prevent such event when one had the ability to do so at little cost to oneself. The easiest way to depict the conditions of these two modes of responsibility is as a four square matrix:

286 Aichele, "Causaiton to Culpability," p. 311.

287 *Id.*, p. 312.

288 Moore, "The Specialness of the General Part."

289 *Id.* See also Moore, *Causation and Responsibility*, chap. 13.

	PRIMA FACIE	ALL OUT
WRONG-DOING	1. Voluntary act, consisting of: a. Volition b. Causing c. Bodily movements d. When those bodily movements are the object of that volition 2. That causes 3. In certain circumstances 4. A state of affairs that is harmful to the interests of others (or is in some other way bad) or 5. An omission to prevent that bad state of affairs when the actor had the ability and the duty to prevent it.	Without any of those circumstances being present that render a prima facie wrong not wrong on this occasion (i. e., without *justification*); such justifications may be: 1. Agent-neutral (consequentialist), or 2. Agent-relative (deontological)
And CULPABILITY	1. A culpable mental state, consisting of: a. An intention, or b. A belief to a practical certainty, or c. A belief of a substantial and unjustified risk 2. Having as its object the material elements of the type of wrong that is prohibited 3. When that mental state causes that wrong to be done by the agent whose mental state it is 4. And when the wrong done in fact instantiates the type of wrong that is the object of the actor's mental state.	When that culpable mental state was formed in circumstances affording a fair opportunity to one possessed of sufficient capacity not to do the wrong in question (i. e., when there is no *excuse*); such excuses may be: 1. Particular excuses a. Cognitive i. Mistake ii. Ignorance b. Volitional i. External (duress, necessity) ii. Internal (provocation, addiction, excessive self-defense) or 2. Status excuses a. Insanity b. Infancy c. Involuntary intoxication d. Diminished capacity

A word about this chart. Overall blameworthiness (or responsibility) as a principal for a completed wrong or crime requires both wrongdoing and culpability.[290]

290 Moore, *Placing Blame*, pp. 191–193, 403–404. Notice that "culpability" is here used in a narrow, stipulated sense that is *not* synonymous with overall blameworthiness. John Gardner

One is guilty of *prima facie* wrongdoing if one *either:* performed a voluntary act that caused a prohibited state of affairs; *or* omitted to prevent such state of affairs when one had both the ability and duty to do so. One is guilty of *all-out* (or actual) wrongdoing only if, in addition, one's voluntary act or omission was not done in justifying circumstances. One possesses *prima facie* culpability when one wants, intends, accepts, or is willing to risk bringing about a state of affairs that it is wrong to bring about. *Prima facie* culpability is in that sense wrongdoing in one's own mind.[291] One is *all-out* culpable only if one's prima facie culpable mental state was formed and acted upon in conditions (of adequate capacity and opportunity) that do not afford an excuse.

I mention all of this so that we can pinpoint the role of causation within it. But since I wish to pinpoint the role of causation within the German system of imputation as well, let me first draw the parallels between the Anglo-American general part and the German rules of imputation.

German criminal law theorists distinguish various "levels" of imputation. The traditional view, as I understand it, is to divide imputation into three such levels,[292] although historically some have made do with two,[293] and others require four or five to do the job.[294] Let me taxonomize imputation in the traditional three-fold way. Winefrid Hassemer describes the first level, that of "Tatbestand" or "imputatio facti," as consisting of two sub-levels: at the first of these, "all events which are not somehow controlled by a human being are eliminated from the system of penal attribution."[295] At the second sub-level here, one "excludes from attribution all harms which, although caused by human behavior, have no relevance to the criminal law."[296] Hruschka describes these two sub-levels together this way: "Imputation of the deed...being the judgment that an event, as a "deed," is the possible object of the application of a law."[297]

---

quibbles about my stipulated sense of culpability in his "Wrongdoing by Results: Moore's Experiential Argument," *Legal Theory*, Vol. 18 (2012), pp. 459–471, at pp. 462–463. For the corrective, see Moore, "Four Friendly Critics," p. 527.

291 In Moore, "Intention as a Marker of Moral Responsibility," at pp. 196–203, I give a detailed account of just what this means.

292 Friedrich Toepel, "The Fault Element in the History of German Criminal Theory: With Some General Conclusions for the Rules of Imputation in a Legal System," *Criminal Law and Philosophy*, Vol. 6 (2012), pp. 167–186, at pp. 169, 173.

293 Hruschka, "Imputation."

294 Winefred Hassemer, "Justification and Excuse in Criminal Law: Theses and Comments," *Brigham Young University Law Review*, Vol. [1986], pp. 573–609, p. 583.

295 *Id.*

296 *Id.*

297 Hurshka, "Imputation," p. 673.

At the second level, that of "Rechtfestigung," or "imputatio juris," one excludes some harms even though they are caused by human agents and are of the kind that is morally or legally prohibited; one "excludes some of these harms from the system of imputation where there was an objective and legitimate interest of greater importance in committing the harmful act."[298] Hruschka describes this second level as requiring a "judgment as to the merit of the deed."[299] Significantly, for Kant excuses like duress and heavy intoxication do not exclude liability for the deed,[300] but justifications certainly do.

Let us pause to make comparative notes before we come to the third level. The first two levels of imputation correspond very closely to prima facie and all-out wrongdoing in the Anglo-American scheme. Hassemer speaks of "control by a human being" of a natural event; we speak of two modes of such control, voluntary acts causing or omissions failing to prevent. The ideas are the same. Also, Hassemer rules out human-caused harms that "have no relevance to the criminal law;" we speak of results caused in certain circumstances that instantiate the types of actions prohibited by law or morality. Again, the idea is the same. German theory speaks of the merit or demerit of the act rather than the actor at its second level of imputation; we speak of justification of actions. The idea again is wholly the same, for an act merits no blame when it is justified (whereas the *act* still merits blame when the actor is excused).

The third level of imputation is where guilt, or "schuld," is attributed to the doer of the deed that is wrong.[301] Here one includes the culpable mental state, where intention is central but not necessary for blame; and one includes excuses like duress and intoxication.[302] This third level is, of course, nothing different than what the Anglo-American system calls culpability, both prima facie and all-out.

So the Anglo-American system of fair fault ascription, at least as I have described it in my work, is very strongly isomorphic to the German system of imputation, if not downright identical. And causation has a crucial role to play in both systems, even though it is far from being the whole of either.

Causation's role can be seen most clearly by attending to the Anglo-American version of imputation. Causation's principal role is to connect an offender's voluntary act to a harm. It is not necessary that there be some causal connection,

---

298 Hassemer, "Justification and Excuse," p. 583.
299 Hruschka, "Imputation," p. 679.
300 *Id.*
301 Toepel, "The Fault Element in the History," p. 169.
302 See *id.*, although Toepel seeks to argue with traditional inclusion of intent at level 3 rather than, in part, in level 1.

because counterfactual dependence of a harm on an offender's act or omission will also suffice;[303] but nonetheless causation is the central basis on which we ascribe responsibility for a harm to an actor. But not by itself, of course. In addition, one needs the kind of intention often called "volition"; one also needs culpable mens rea of intention, belief, or desire; one also needs absence of justification, and absence of excuse. In this way causation is an important element of imputation without constituting the whole of imputation.

So I find Aichele's second criticism of my views wide of the mark because my views are not actually the target of those criticisms. I do have considerable sympathy for his criticism of contemporary German criminal law (without knowing enough about German criminal law to know if those criticisms are warranted). As Aichele points out,[304] he and I are both apparently revolutionaries when it comes to the standard accounts given of causation in our respective countries, and it would not surprise me if German legal orthodoxy on causation were as confused as is the Anglo American legal orthodoxy.

I have less sympathy for Aichele's attempt to revive Kant's transcendental idealism about causation.[305] The philosophy of causation has rightly followed Hume rather than Kant here.[306] I do have considerable sympathy for the essentially Kantian notion of imputation that Aichele articulates. Although even here, I would strip imputation of the Kantian idea that for a person to cause a natural event (and thus to do a "deed"), the person must act freely, understood as, "free of sufficient causation of his will."[307] But this last is a long story, to be pursued elsewhere.[308]

* * *

303 Moore, *Causation and Responsibility*, chap. 18.
304 Aichele, "Causation to Culpability," pp. 316–318.
305 *Id.*, p. 321–328.
306 See, e.g., John Mackie's passing nod to Kant's transcendental idealism with respect to causation, in Mackie, *The Cement of the Universe*, chap. 4. Mackie is exceptional in that virtually all other contemporary philosophers of causation do not mention Kant at all.
307 See Hruschka, "Imputation," pp. 704–710.
308 See my "Causation and the Excuses," *California Law Review*, Vol. 73 (1985), pp. 1091–1149, now chapter 12 of my *Placing Blame*, which was initially written and delivered as the answering paper to Hruschka's "Imputation" at the 1984 German Anglo-American Workshop on Basic Problems in Criminal Theory," held at the Max Planek Institute for Comparative and International Criminal Law in Freiburg-im-Breisgau, Germany. For an update for why freedom in Hruschka's (and Kant's) sense is not required for imputation of responsibility, see Moore, "The Can't/Won't Distinction."

This last exchange with Aichele takes me back a long ways in my career, to the conference at which I was the commentator on Joachim Hruschka's paper on imputation, and he on my own paper, at the Max Planck Institute at Freiburg in 1984. At that conference, now almost thirty years ago, I was pleasantly surprised at the similarities (and similar level of sophistication) that German criminal law theory had to Anglo-American criminal law theory. At the conferences at Aachen, Bonn, and Cologne in 2010 and 2011, mentioned at the start of this essay, I was also pleased, although not this time surprised, at the similarities (and similar level of sophistication) that German philosophy bears to Anglo-American philosophy. The papers collected in this volume push the frontiers of our collective understanding of the topics in the theory of responsibility on which they touch. It is gratifying to see, once again, how crucial a part of what makes up that "collective," are philosophers and legal theorists working in the German tradition.

Notes on Contributors

Alexander Aichele teaches philosophy at the Martin-Luther-University Halle-Wittenberg, Germany. Beside his historical interest in ancient philosophy and philosophy of enlightenment his main fields of systematical research are metaphysics (and its relation to logic), aesthetics, general ethics and philosophy of law. He is presently working on an Aristotelian theory of action which dispenses with the need for singular efficient causation.

Rani Lill Anjum is Research Fellow of Philosophy and Principal Investigator of the interdisciplinary research project "Causation in Science" at the Norwegian University of Life Sciences. Her main research area is causation, dispositions and modality. She is the co-author of *Getting Causes from Powers* (Oxford University Press, 2011) with Stephen Mumford.

Dieter Birnbacher is Professor Emeritus of Practical Philosophy at Heinrich-Heine-University Düsseldorf, Germany. His main fields of interest are ethics, applied ethics and action theory. He is the author of *Tun und Unterlassen* (Reclam, 1995) and the co-author of *Negative Kausalität* (de Gruyter, 2012) with David Hommen.

Alex Broadbent is Associate Professor of Philosophy at the University of Johannesburg, South Africa, where he holds a President's Award from the National Research Foundation of South Africa. His research concerns causation, explanation, and prediction, with a special interest in these topics as they feature in scientific and legal contexts. He has a special philosophical interest in epidemiology and is author of *Philosophy of Epidemiology* (Palgrave Macmillan, 2013).

David Hommen is Post-Doctoral Research Fellow in the DFG Research Unit "Causation, Laws, Dispositions and Explanations at the Interface of Science and Metaphysics" at Heinrich-Heine-University Düsseldorf, Germany. His main research interests are special problems in causal theory, such as negative causation and mental causation. He is co-author of *Negative Kausalität* (de Gruyter, 2012) with Dieter Birnbacher.

Philipp Hübl is Associate Professor ("Juniorprofessor") at the University of Stuttgart, Germany. His main research area is the philosophy of mind, action theory and metaphysics. He has published on action theory and is author of an introduction to Philosophy (in German).

Benedikt Kahmen is Doctoral Research Fellow in the DFG Research Unit "Causation, Laws, Dispositions and Explanations at the Interface of Science and Metaphysics" at RWTH Aachen University. His current research focuses on action, intention and rationality. He has published on self-knowledge and action theory.

Geert Keil is Professor of Philosophy at Humboldt University, Berlin, Germany. His main areas of research are the philosophy of mind and action, philosophy of language, philosophy of science and metaphysics. He is the author of five books, including *Handeln und Verursachen* (Klostermann, 2000), *Quine* (Junius, 2011), and *Willensfreiheit* (de Gruyter, 2013), and the co-editor of nine anthologies, including *Naturalismus* (Suhrkamp, 2000), *Fifty Years of Quine's 'Two Dogmas'* (Rodopi, 2003), and *Unscharfe Grenzen im Technik- und Umweltrecht* (Nomos, 2012).

Erasmus Mayr is Junior Research Fellow in Philosophy at The Queen's College, Oxford. His main research areas are philosophy of action and moral philosophy. He is author of *Understanding Human Agency* (Oxford University Press 2011).

Michael S. Moore holds the Charles Walgreen Chair at the University of Illinois, United States, the only University-level Chaired Professorship within the University. In addition, he is a Professor of Law, Professor of Philosophy, and Professor in the Center for Advanced Sudies at the flagship campus of that University at Urbana-Champaign. Over the course of his career he has held faculty positions in law, philosophy, and medicine at numerous universities within the United States, including Penn, Berkeley, Southern California, Iowa, Virginia, Stanford, Northwestern, San Diego, and others; and he is a regular visitor on the faculties of the Australian National University in Canberra, Tel Aviv University, and Toceato di Tella University in Buenos Aires. His most recent book is *Causation and Responsibility* (Oxford University Press, 2009), the subject of the papers in this volume. Causation has long been one of his research interests, both by itself and as part of a larger interest in responsibility issues.

Stephen Mumford is Professor of Metaphysics in the Department of Philosophy and Dean of the Faculty of Arts at the University of Nottingham, United Kingdom. He is the author of *Dispositions* (Oxford University Press, 1998), *Russell on Metaphysics* (Routledge, 2003), *Laws in Nature* (Routledge, 2004), *David Armstrong* (Acumen, 2007), *Watching Sport: Aesthetics, Ethics and Emotion* (Routledge, 2011) and *Getting Causes from Powers* (Oxford, 2011 with Rani Lill Anjum). He was editor of George Molnar's posthumous *Powers: a Study in Metaphysics* (Oxford University Press, 2003). His PhD was from the University of Leeds in 1994 and he has been at Nottingham since 1995 having served as Head of the Department of Philosophy and Head of the School of Humanities.

Ingeborg Puppe is Professor Emeritus of Criminal Law, Criminal Procedure and Legal Theory at the University of Bonn, Germany. Her research focuses on theories of attribution, intent and error as well as forgery. Her most recent publication is her commentation on these matters in the forthcoming *Nomos* commentary.

Thomas Schmidt is Professor of Philosophy at the Institute of Philosophy, Humboldt University, Berlin, Germany. His current research focuses on issues in normative ethics (deontology, Rossian pluralism, the role of moral principles) and on moral epistemology.

Markus Stepanians is Professor of Philosophy at the University of Bern, Switzerland. He mainly works on the philosophy of law and political philosophy. He has authored, most recently, *Rights as Relational Properties* (de Gruyter, forthcoming).

Friedrich Toepel is Associate Professor of Criminal Law and Criminal Procedure at the University of Bonn, Germany. His main areas of research are the theoretical foundations of criminal law. His publications are characterised by the effort to clarify legal problems with the means of analytic philosophy. He has edited a book on *Free Will in Criminal Law and Procedure* (Steiner, 2010).

Richard W. Wright is Distinguished Professor of Law, Chicago-Kent College of Law, Illinois Institute of Technology, United States. Professor Wright's teaching and research focus on domestic and comparative tort law, jurisprudence, law and economics, and law and artificial intelligence. His published work appears in several international collections of leading scholarship on tort law and legal philosophy, including numerous writings on the nature, meaning and proof of causation and its role in assessing moral and legal responsibility – most recently two chapters in *Perspectives on Causation* (Hart Publishing, 2011)

Index